FILM IT WITH MUSIC

FILM IT WITH MUSIC

An Encyclopedic Guide to the American Movie Musical

Thomas Hischak

GREENWOOD PRESS
Westport, Connecticut • London

Library of Congress Cataloging-in-Publication Data

Hischak, Thomas S.
   Film it with music : an encyclopedic guide to the American movie musical / Thomas
Hischak.
      p.   cm.
   Includes bibliographical references and index.
   ISBN 0–313–31538–8 (alk. paper)
   1. Musical films—United States—Encyclopedias.   I. Title.
PN1995.9.M86H57   2001
791.43′6—dc21   00–061707

British Library Cataloguing in Publication Data is available.

Library of Congress Catalog Card Number: 00–061707
ISBN: 0–313–31538–8

First published in 2001

Greenwood Press, 88 Post Road West, Westport, CT 06881
An imprint of Greenwood Publishing Group, Inc.
www.greenwood.com

Printed in the United States of America

The paper used in this book complies with the
Permanent Paper Standard issued by the National
Information Standards Organization (Z39.48–1984).

10 9 8 7 6 5 4 3 2 1

To Steve and Jon . . . who waited the longest.

Contents

Preface

Had the world ever seen a more *realistic* medium than the movies when the first photographs began to move? The possibilities to recreate real life on the screen must have been mind boggling to the early filmmakers. Yet the moment sound came in, the movies started singing. Had the world ever seen a more *unrealistic* medium than the Hollywood film musical? Perhaps on the musical stage but movies were able to go places that Broadway could not. At first the studios simply tried to film song-and-dance shows, but before long the movie musical became its own genre with rules and conventions that were written (and broken) over the next seven decades. And now that the genre has all but disappeared, we can look back and admire and even stand in awe of that glorious dinosaur known as the Hollywood movie musical.

Until the 1960s, when the genre was quickly waning, few took film musicals seriously, including their creators. They were making magic, flagrantly unrealistic magic, and aside from technique and craftsmanship, there was little concern about the art of the artificial genre. But as scholars and students rediscovered Busby Berkeley extravaganzas, the Marx Brothers, Fred and Ginger flicks, and World War Two patriotic flag wavers, the not-so-new genre became a pop art form. In a way, this unrealistic form of entertainment was given its own reality. Plays, television shows, and even later movie musicals spoofed or paid homage to the old film musicals. More than plays that were long closed or books that were no longer read, Hollywood musicals were living evidence of a form of fantasy that amused and dazzled past decades. It was a display of Americana that burst out of the museum and onto the late late show, revival houses, and later, videocassettes.

The way movie musicals came about is as carefree as the form itself. How often we forget that no one—not the audiences nor the artists—was anxious for movies to talk. Even when the technology was in place, none of the major studios wanted to pursue it. There was little or no ambition on the audience's part to hear actors speak on the screen. But to hear them sing—that was a different matter. To put Al Jolson in a film and not have him sing was equivalent to making an Esther Williams movie in the 1940s and not have her swim. So Warner Brothers wisely included sound in *The Jazz Singer* only when Jolson broke into song. The few words that were included, from his famous "you ain't heard nothin' yet" to some ad-libbing to his mama in between verses of a song, were almost accidental. But they were enough to start a revolution, and talkies quickly took over. It is worth remembering that in a way, movies sang before they talked.

This book aims to explore that revolution and its aftermath by looking at the major artists and films in an encyclopedic format. Although there have been countless books about American movies and several specifically about musicals, there is a need for a one-volume encyclopedia that covers performers, songwriters, directors, choreographers, producers, studios, and designers who have participated in film musicals since 1927. Many books are lavishly illustrated or packed with lists and dates. What has not been available is a reference work that tries to explain the particular talents of a given artist besides just giving statistics. Film guides abound (though few on musicals), but it is hoped that in describing the 383 film musicals included here we have captured the essence of the picture and given the reader a taste of each movie's merits, rather than simply identifying and rating it. Choosing which films to include has been the least-rewarding aspect of the project. But an effort has been made to include samples of all major stars, filmmakers, studios, types, and eras. Animated musicals are included, as are movies from recent decades that may not exactly fit the old definition of a musical, such as films with plenty of dance but little song (and vice versa) and movies with their scores heard more than seen performed. These and other atypical films must be considered because that is what the movie musical evolved into in the late 1970s. The 383 selected films are far from a list of the best musicals made between 1927 and 2000 but, we hope, are accurately indicative of the genre. Names, titles, and subjects presented in UPPER-CASE TYPE have individual entries. (Names and titles in **BOLD** are not cross-references.) A chronological listing of all the movies described follows the entries. Also included in the appendices are lists of Academy Awards given to musicals in various fields. Finally, a selected bibliography and a complete index are attached.

I should like to acknowledge the continued assistance from the staff at the Cortland Free Library and the Cortland Memorial Library at the State University of New York College at Cortland. William Whiting was very helpful again in checking the text, the staff at Greenwood Press performed their usual and exacting talents on the manuscript, and, as always, my wife Cathy and children Mark and Karen must be publicly thanked for their love, patience, and support.

A

ABBOTT, BUD (1895–1974) and his comedy partner **LOU COSTELLO** (1906–1959) were one of the top box office draws of the World War Two years, rarely singing a note but headlining a series of such patriotic musicals as *BUCK PRIVATES* (1941), *In the Navy* (1941), and *Keep 'Em Flying* (1941), as well as *Hold That Ghost* (1941), *Ride 'Em Cowboy* (1942), *RIO RITA* (1942), *Pardon My Sarong* (1942) *Comin' Round the Mountain* (1851), and ten others. The slender straight-man Abbott was forever badgering the short, baby-faced Costello, whose catch phrase was "I'm a ba-a-ad boy!" The popular team, which started in burlesque and vaudeville, performed their most famous routine, "Who's on First?," in *ONE NIGHT IN THE TROPICS* (1940) and again in *The Naughty Nineties* (1945).

ABBOTT, GEORGE (1887–1995), the prolific Broadway director and playwright, helmed the screen versions of his stage hits *TOO MANY GIRLS* (1940), *THE PAJAMA GAME* (1957), and *DAMN YANKEES* (1958). Although not a very cinematic artist, Abbott's famous "touch" for speed, efficiency, and potency can be seen in his films, and they do preserve much of the original casts, dances, and staging of these theatre classics.

ACADEMY AWARDS, the film industry's most powerful and recognized set of prizes, have been given for achievement in various categories of movie making since 1927 by the American Academy of Motion Picture Arts and Sciences. Although the areas of expertise being honored have changed throughout its history, the Academy's actual award has always been a thirteen-and-a-half-inch-high gold-plated statuette known as an Oscar, the origin of the name having diverse anecdotes connected with it. The Academy strives to recognize excellence but throughout its long history has sometimes been a popularity contest or political ploy in disguise. At various points over the decades, Oscars have been given for score, song, choreography, background scoring, and other areas related to musicals. Only nine musicals over the years have won for Best Picture: *THE BROADWAY MELODY* (1929), *THE GREAT ZIEGFELD* (1936), *GOING MY WAY* (1944), *AN AMERICAN IN PARIS* (1951), *GIGI* (1958), *WEST SIDE STORY* (1961), *MY FAIR LADY* (1964), *THE SOUND OF MUSIC* (1965), and *OLIVER!* (1968). A list of all the Academy Award nominees and the winners in other categories can be found in the Appendices.

ADAMS, LEE (1924–), a Broadway lyricist, and his composer partner **CHARLES STROUSE** (1928–) saw their stage hit *BYE BYE BIRDIE* (1963) filmed, but none of their other Broadway efforts reached the screen. The team scored *The Night They Raided Minsky's* (1968), and Strouse's *ANNIE* (1982), written with lyricist Martin Charnin, was recreated on the movie and television screen.

ADAMSON, HAROLD (1906–1980) was a reliable Hollywood lyricist who partnered with many composers, turning out hit songs ("I Couldn't Sleep a Wink Last Night," "You," "It's a Most Unusual Day") over a busy career that ranged from *DANCING LADY* (1933) to *An Affair to Remember* (1957). With BURTON LANE he provided scores for *Bottoms Up* (1934), *Reckless* (1935), and *Jupiter's Darling* (1955); with WALTER DONALDSON, *Here Comes the Band* (1935) and *THE GREAT ZIEGFELD* (1936); and with HOAGY CARMICHAEL, some song interpolations for *GENTLEMEN PREFER BLONDES* (1953). But Adamson's most frequent collaborator was JIMMY McHUGH, the team scoring nineteen films together, including *Banjo on My Knee* (1936), *Mad About Music* (1938), *Higher and Higher* (1943), *Four Jills in a Jeep* (1944), *Nob Hill* (1945), *Hit Parade of 1947*, and *If You Knew Susie* (1948).

ADLER, LARRY (1914–), a harmonica virtuoso who was acclaimed in both concert halls and nightclubs, was a featured specialty in a handful of movie musicals in the 1930s and 1940s. Adler's most remembered screen appearance was performing "Night Over Shanghai" in *The Singing Marine* (1937). Other movie credits include *Many Happy Returns* (1934), *THE BIG BROADCAST OF 1937* (1936), and *Three Darling Daughters* (1948).

ADLER, RICHARD (1921–) and his partner **JERRY ROSS** (1926–1955) wrote both music and lyrics together for two Broadway smashes that were filmed—*THE PAJAMA GAME* (1957) and *DAMN YANKEES* (1958)—before Ross's premature death. Adler later scored some stage and television musicals, as well as ballet and concert pieces.

ADRIAN (1903–1959) was the moniker for costume designer Gilbert A. Adrian, who was responsible for the "look" sported by Norma Shearer, Greta Garbo, JOAN CRAWFORD and other stars at MGM. Adrian costumed both period pieces and contemporary stories, including several musicals such as *Smilin' Through* (1932), *BROADWAY MELODY OF 1936* (1935), *NAUGHTY MARIETTA* (1935), *SAN FRANCISCO* (1936), *ROSE MARIE* (1936), *THE GREAT ZIEGFELD* (1936), *MAYTIME* (1937), *THE WIZARD OF OZ* (1939), *ZIEGFELD GIRL* (1941), and *LOVELY TO LOOK AT* (1952). He was married to JANET GAYNOR.

ADRIAN, IRIS (1913–1994) specialized in playing dumb blondes and wisecracking chorines in over 100 films beginning with *PARAMOUNT ON PARADE* (1930). Her other musical credits include *GOLD DIGGERS OF 1937* (1936), *ROAD TO ZANZIBAR* (1941), *ORCHESTRA WIVES* (1942), *THE PALEFACE* (1948), and *BLUE HAWAII* (1961).

ADVENTURES OF ELMO IN GROUCHLAND, THE. See *Follow That Bird*

AFRICAN AMERICAN MUSICALS were rare in Hollywood until after the civil rights movement in the 1960s, and even then black musicals were far less prevalent in the movies than they were on Broadway and other media. Two early movie musicals that featured mostly African American casts were *Hearts in Dixie* (1929) and *HALLELUJAH* (1929), both containing black stereotypes but generally quite effective. "Race" musicals, both shorts and features, were made throughout the 1930s and 1940s to be shown in black neighborhood movie houses. These low-budget efforts sometimes had African American writers and directors as well as performers, but they were rarely given a wide release. Performers such as the NICHOLAS BROTHERS, BILL ROBINSON, LOUIS ARMSTRONG, CAB CALLOWAY, and LENA HORNE were often featured in mainstream Hollywood musicals but usually in specialty bits that could easily be edited out for showings in the South. Some pre–civil rights musicals that had substantial participation by black performers, musicians, or songwriters include *CABIN IN THE SKY* (1943), *STORMY WEATHER* (1943), *CARMEN JONES* (1954), *St. Louis Blues* (1958), and *PORGY AND BESS* (1959). Although many more films with African Americans in nonstereotypic roles were made in the late 1960s and thereafter, black musicals were still not so common, though ethnic performers were now cast in most movie musicals. Some of the more notable African American musicals include *LADY SINGS THE BLUES* (1972), *Lost in the Stars* (1974), *Leadbelly* (1976), *Scott Joplin* (1977), *The Wiz* (1978), and, to a degree, *THE COTTON CLUB* (1984). In the silent days, white actors wore blackface to play major African American roles. This practice was abandoned for the most part by the advent of the talkies, but up through the 1940s white performers such as AL

JOLSON, EDDIE CANTOR, JACK OAKIE, MICKEY ROONEY, JUDY GARLAND, BING CROSBY, and FRED ASTAIRE still "blacked up" for a specialty musical number on film. By the 1960s the idea of doing a song in blackface was anathema to most, although Neil Diamond made a cutting reference to the past when he performed a number in blackface for the third remake of *THE JAZZ SINGER* (1980).

AGER, MILTON (1983–1979) was a Tin Pan Alley composer who, with lyricist JACK YELLEN, scored some early film musicals such as *Honky Tonk* (1929) and *KING OF JAZZ* (1930). Their most popular song together was "Happy Days Are Here Again."

AKST, HARRY (1894–1963) was a composer most remembered for writing "Am I Blue?" the first hit song introduced by an African American on film. ETHEL WATERS sang it in *ON WITH THE SHOW* (1929), and GRANT CLARKE provided the lyric. Also with Clarke, Akst scored *Is Everybody Happy?* (1929) and *Song of the Flame* (1930). With lyricist SIDNEY CLARE, he wrote songs for a half dozen musicals, such as *Paddy O'Day* (1935) and *Rascals* (1938). A popular pianist in vaudeville and a band leader, Akst appeared as a musician in *THE SHOW OF SHOWS* (1929), *June Moon* (1931), *42ND STREET* (1933), and others.

ALADDIN (Disney 1992) was one of the funniest entries in the DISNEY animated catalog, a fast-paced "Arabian Nights" farce that only occasionally slowed down for romance, as in the Oscar-winning song "A Whole New World." Scott Weinger provided the voice of the hero (singing vocals by Brad Kane), and Linda Larkin (with Lea Salonga doing her vocals) was his spunky heroine Princess Jasmine. They were a sassy pair, but the broad comedy came from the supporting characters, such as the villainous Jafar (Jonathan Freeman), the wisecracking parrot Iago (Gilbert Gottfried), and especially Robin Williams' Genie, which was a visual and vocal explosion of lines and sounds. ALAN MENKEN provided the pseudo-exotic music and HOWARD ASHMAN completed half the lyrics before his untimely death. British lyricist TIM RICE finished the score, which included the satirical parade "Prince Ali," the jazzy "One Jump Ahead," and the vaudeville showstopper "Friend Like Me."

ALDA, ROBERT (1914–1986) was a nightclub singer who made his film debut playing GEORGE GERSHWIN in the musical bio *RHAPSODY IN BLUE* (1945) but failed to find success in the handful of minor 1940s films that followed, such as *Cinderella Jones* (1946), *The Man I Love* (1947), and *April Showers* (1948). Alda did have better luck on Broadway, originating the role of Sky Masterson in *Guys and Dolls* (1950). He was the father of popular actor Alan Alda.

ALEXANDER'S RAGTIME BAND (Fox 1938) was the first of a handful of nostalgic films utilizing the vast IRVING BERLIN song catalog, this one squeezing in twenty-one old favorites and two new numbers: "Now It Can Be Told" and "My Walking Stick." The plot, an on-and-off romantic triangle among bandleader Alexander (TYRONE POWER), singer ALICE FAYE, and composer-pianist DON AMECHE spread out from 1911 to 1938, was fairly routine, but the way the film captured the changing musical styles of the decades was rather accurate (even if the three principals didn't age one day over the years). FAYE was particularly effective, singing the title number as well as "Everybody's Doin' It," "All Alone," "Remember," and "What'll I Do?" ETHEL MERMAN was on hand to belt out "Pack Up Your Sins and Go to the Devil," "Say It With Music," and "Heat Wave," and JACK HALEY interpreted "Oh, How I Hate to Get Up in the Morning." Other Berlin standards included "Easter Parade," "A Pretty Girl Is Like a Melody," "Everybody Step," and "Blue Skies." The DARRYL F. ZANUCK production cost a staggering $2 million, but the box office was healthy so other Berlin anthologies followed.

ALICE IN WONDERLAND (Disney/RKO 1951) may have lost Lewis Carroll's sense of satire and the original look by illustrator Tenniel, but the animators' artistry was deliciously surreal and often overshone many of the film's characters and songs. Adding sections from Carroll's *Alice Through the Looking Glass*, the episodic tale bounced along without sweetness or pathos, climaxing in a madcap montage that tied the whole extravaganza together. For the first time, WALT DISNEY employed recognized performers (ED WYNN, JERRY COLONNA, and STERLING HOLLOWAY as the Mad Hatter, March Hare, and Cheshire Cat) for the voices, and his artists suggested the actors in their drawn characterizations. Bob Hilliard and SAMMY FAIN's score consisted mostly of short songs ("All in a Golden Afternoon," "I'm Late," and the dreamy title number) that rarely stopped the action or, as with "The Walrus and the Carpenter" and "The Caucus Race," musicalized the original Carroll text. Kathryn Beaumont supplied the voice of Alice, and Verna Felton, who was so warm as the Fairy Godmother in the previous year's *CINDERELLA*, did the bombastic vocals for the bloodthirsty Queen of Hearts.

ALL THAT JAZZ (Fox/Columbia 1979) was a gritty backstager that was, despite its title, more interested in the hard work and neurotic creators than the razzle dazzle of putting together a Broadway musical. Director-choreographer Joe Gideon (Roy Scheider) juggles both a stage musical and a film, popping pills, striving for perfection, cheating on his wife Leland Palmer with his mistress ANN REINKING, trying to hang onto his daughter Erzsebet Foldi, and eventually suffering a heart attack and dying. Anyone familiar with the film's author-director-choreographer BOB FOSSE knew that this was autobiography at its most abrasive, but the electric musical numbers did not disappoint. Using old and new standards ("Some of These Days," "Bye Bye Love,"

"After You've Gone," "Who's Sorry Now?"), Fosse found new and exciting ways to film dance. Particularly effective was the opening, a montage of the audition process set to "On Broadway." But Joe's open-heart surgery, graphically portrayed with a production number swirling around it, was a bit too self-indulgent even for Fosse fans. Ben Vereen, Cliff Gorman, and Jessica Lange (as Death) wandered in and out of the action, but it was clear there was only one star in this musical and he was in the director's chair.

ALLEN, FRED (1894–1956), the nasal-sounding radio comedian with a low-key delivery, was featured in *THANKS A MILLION* (1935), *Sally, Irene and Mary* (1938), and *LOVE THY NEIGHBOR* (1940), the last about the celebrated radio feud he had with JACK BENNY over the airwaves.

ALLEN, GRACIE (1902–1964) and her husband **GEORGE BURNS** (1896–1996) proved to be one of the most durable of all comedy teams, headlining in vaudeville and then conquering radio, film, and television. Allen was the high-pitched, scatterbrained foil to the quiet Burns, who fed her straight lines as he puffed on his cigar. They made their film debut playing themselves in *THE BIG BROADCAST* (1932) and continued their routines in *INTERNATIONAL HOUSE* (1933), *College Humor* (1933), *WE'RE NOT DRESSING* (1934), *Many Happy Returns* (1934), *Love in Bloom* (1935), *Here Comes Cookie* (1935), and *BIG BROADCAST OF 1936* (1935). Burns and Allen played characters in *BIG BROADCAST OF 1937* (1936), *A DAMSEL IN DISTRESS* (1937), *College Swing* (1938), and *Honolulu* (1939), although the basic stand-up conventions remained the same. Allen retired in 1958, but Burns was active in every show business medium, beginning a second busy film career with the nonmusical *The Sunshine Boys* (1975). He was still performing at the age of ninety-nine.

ALLYSON, JUNE (1917–   ), a favorite "girl next door" type in several films of the 1940s and 1950s, moved from the Broadway chorus to Hollywood when her featured role as the coed Minerva in *BEST FOOT FORWARD* (1943) was repeated on the screen. Other typical credits for the perky, husky-voiced actress included the canteen worker Patsy in *TWO GIRLS AND A SAILOR* (1944), turn-of-the-century socialite Martha in *TWO SISTERS FROM BOSTON* (1946), college student Connie in *GOOD NEWS* (1947), bandleader's wife Helen Goodman in *THE BENNY GOODMAN STORY* (1954), and Park Avenue housewife Kay in *The Opposite Sex* (1956). Allyson also did specialty bits in *Girl Crazy* (1943), *TILL THE CLOUDS ROLL BY* (1946), and *WORDS AND MUSIC* (1948). She was once married to DICK POWELL.

ALTER, LOUIS (1902–1980) was a vaudeville and Broadway revue composer who provided songs for *Trail of the Lonesome Pine* (1936), *Rainbow on the River* (1936), *Make a Wish* (1937), and *New Orleans* (1947), the last with lyricist EDDIE DeLANGE and introducing the jazz favorite "Do You Know What It Means to Miss New Orleans?" With FRANK LOESSER, Alter wrote "Dolores" which introduced FRANK SINATRA to filmgoers in *Las Vegas Nights* (1941).

ALTON, ROBERT (1897–1957) was a classically trained choreographer who maintained prodigious (and simultaneous) careers both on Broadway and in Hollywood. Alton staged the dazzling musical numbers for two dozen films, including *Strike Me Pink* (1936), *YOU'LL NEVER GET RICH* (1941), *Broadway Rhythm* (1944), *ZIEGFELD FOLLIES* (1946), *GOOD NEWS* (1947), *THE PIRATE* (1948), *EASTER PARADE* (1948), *THE BARK-LEYS OF BROADWAY* (1949), *SHOW BOAT* (1951), *THE BELLE OF NEW YORK* (1952), *WHITE CHRISTMAS* (1954), and *THERE'S NO BUSINESS LIKE SHOW BUSINESS* (1954). Perhaps his most memorable film sequence is the "On the Atchison, Topeka and the Santa Fe" train number in *THE HARVEY GIRLS* (1946). Alton understood the medium of film as well as the stage and found intriguing ways to allow the camera to capture dancing cinematically without excessive cutting or gimmicky angles.

AMECHE, DON (1908–1993) was a dapper, mustached leading man of over forty films, nearly half of them musicals at 20TH CENTURY–FOX. Leaving a lucrative radio career, Ameche made his film debut in 1935 and was often partnered with ALICE FAY, BETTY GRABLE, and SONJA HENIE. Among his most notable roles: impresario George McRae in *You Can't Have Everything* (1937), composer-pianist Charlie in *ALEXANDER'S RAGTIME BAND* (1938), swashbuckling D'Artagnan in *The Three Musketeers* (1939), songwriter Stephen Foster and put-upon husband Edward Solomon in the musical bios *Swanee River* (1939) and *LILLIAN RUSSELL* (1940), movie director Lloyd Lloyd in *Kiss the Boys Goodbye* (1941), and suave Latin lovers in *DOWN ARGENTINE WAY* (1940), *THAT NIGHT IN RIO* (1941), and *MOON OVER MIAMI* (1941). Frequently on the stage as well, Ameche saw his film career rejuvenated with his Oscar-winning performance in the nonmusical *Cocoon* (1985)

AMERICAN IN PARIS, AN (MGM 1951) is perhaps the most arty of all MGM musicals but is quite a lot of fun all the same and few films are more beautiful to look at. Ex-GI Jerry Mulligan (GENE KELLY) remains in Paris after the war to pursue his dream of becoming an artist, falling in love with perfume counter salesgirl LESLIE CARON, who is engaged to the older Georges Guetary, a music hall entertainer. Jerry, in turn, is pursued by art patroness Nina Foch, who wants to set him up in his own studio and promote his work. The quadrangle was hardly as riveting as director VINCENTE MINNELLI's romantic recreation of Paris (it was all done in a studio) and the marvelous GERSHWIN brothers' songs that screenwriter ALAN JAY LERNER worked into the plot. Kelly singing "I Got Rhythm" with a bunch of French kids or romancing Caron along the banks of the Seine with "Love Is Here to Stay" were only topped by the final "An American in Paris" dream ballet, an eighteen-minute sequence in which Kelly pursues Caron across Paris, each section portrayed in the style of Duffy, Renoir, Utrillo, Van Gogh, Toulouse-Lautrec, and other painters he has dreamt about. OSCAR LEVANT was on hand to play "Fascinating Rhythm" and the third movement of Gershwin's Concerto in F on the piano, and Guetary made a fine showcase of "I'll Build a Stairway to Paradise." Arty or not, the film was very popular, winning six Oscars including one for Best Picture.

AMES, PRESTON (1905–1983) was one of postwar Hollywood's busiest and most acclaimed art directors, winning ACADEMY AWARDS for *AN AMERICAN IN PARIS* (1951) and *GIGI* (1958). Other musicals he designed include *BRIGADOON* (1954), *KISMET* (1955), *BELLS ARE RINGING* (1960), *THE UNSINKABLE MOLLY BROWN* (1964), and *Lost Horizon* (1973).

ANASTASIA (Fox 1997) was an attempt to create a classy ANIMATED MUSICAL with the quality (and hopefully the box office) of the DISNEY renaissance products, and much of it was quite accomplished. Teenage orphan Anya (voice of Meg Ryan, singing by Liz Callaway) is discovered by the enterprising Dimitri (John Cusack, singing by Jonathan Dokuchitz), who brings her from St. Petersburg to Paris to present her to the Dowager Empress (ANGELA LANSBURY) as the lost Princess Anastasia of the Romanov family. Much of the tale was hardly children's fare (a sequence showing the Russian revolution and the capture of the Romanovs was powerful and frightening), but the studio put in some lovable Disney-like sidekicks and a back-from-the-dead Rasputin (Christopher Lloyd, singing by Jim Cummings) that recalled the most dastardly of animated villains. Lynn Ahrens and Stephen Flaherty wrote the atmospheric score that included the evocative ballad "Once Upon a December," the warm character song "Journey to the Past," and a rousing "Paris Holds the Key" sung by the worldly-wise Parisian Sophie (BERNADETTE PETERS).

ANCHORS AWEIGH (MGM 1945) was another "sailors on leave" musical (it was neither the first nor the last), but it afforded GENE KELLY and FRANK SINATRA one of their best vehicles to date. Sinatra, in his first starring role, played a shy sailor, whereas Kelly was a girl-chasing cad who tells aspiring singer KATHRYN GRAYSON that he can get her an audition with JOSÉ ITURBI. While he tries to make good on his promise, Sinatra falls for Pamela Britton, who hails from his hometown of Brooklyn. Sinatra got to sing the JULE STYNE–SAMMY CAHN ballad "I Fall in Love Too Easily," and Iturbi presented a few classical selections, but it was the dance sections, choreographed by Kelly and STANLEY DONEN, that were most memorable: a bombastic sequence in which Kelly wooed Grayson as he scaled battlements and parapets, a lively "Mexican Hat Dance" routine with Sharon McManus, and a brilliant *pas de deux* with the cartoon character Jerry the Mouse.

ANDERSON, EDDIE "ROCHESTER" (1905–1977), fondly remembered as JACK BENNY's comic sidekick on radio and television, was featured in fifteen film musicals, recreating his manservant Rochester in the Benny vehicles *Man About Town* (1939), *Buck Benny Rides Again* (1940), and *LOVE THY NEIGHBOR* (1940). Making his film debut as an extra in 1932, the raspy-voiced Anderson was glimpsed as a Negro youth in *SHOW BOAT* (1936), a groom in *Going Places* (1938), and other bit parts before being featured in *Honolulu* (1939), *BIRTH OF THE BLUES* (1941), *STAR SPANGLED RHYTHM* (1943), and others. His most memorable movie role was the luckless Little Joe Jackson in *CABIN IN THE SKY* (1943).

ANDERSON, MAXWELL (1888–1959), the distinguished author of poetic dramas on Broadway, penned the lyrics for two KURT WEILL Broadway musicals that were filmed: *Knickerbocker Holiday* (1944) and *Lost in the Stars* (1974). With composer ALLIE WRUBEL, Anderson provided the score for *Never Steal Anything Small* (1959). His most acclaimed ballad is "September Song."

ANDREWS, DAME JULIE (1935–   ), one of the few bankable female stars of the 1960s, made her film debut (and won an Oscar) as *MARY POPPINS* (1964) after conquering Broadway (*My Fair Lady*) and television (*Cinderella*). The British singer-actress was a CHILD STAR on the stage, her crystal-clear soprano voice and crisp persona in place at an early age. Her most popular film role was Maria Von Trapp in *THE SOUND OF MUSIC* (1965), but she was equally skillful as the flapper Millie in *THOROUGHLY MODERN MILLIE* (1967), British legend Gertrude Lawrence in *STAR!* (1968), music hall singer–spy Lili Smith in *DARLING LILI* (1969), and the cross-dressing *VICTOR/VICTORIA* (1982). She recreated this last role on Broadway in 1995. Andrews was first married to scenic designer Tony Walton and later to film producer BLAKE EDWARDS.

ANDREWS SISTERS, the phenomenally popular harmonizing trio who shot to fame with their recording of "Bei Mir Bist du Schon," played themselves in a series of 1940s films, rarely having many lines but providing the musical highlights of the movie. LaVerne (1915–1967), Maxine (1918–1995), and Patti (1920–   ) made their celluloid debut in *Argentine Nights* (1940) and continued to belt out war-time hits in *BUCK PRIVATES* (1941), *In the Navy* (1941), *Hold That Ghost* (1941), *Private Buckaroo* (1942), *Always a Bridesmaid* (1943), *Follow the Boys* (1944), *Moonlight and Cactus* (1944), *HOLLYWOOD CANTEEN* (1944), and others. They were also heard on the soundtracks of the DISNEY animated anthology films *Make Mine Music* (1946) and *Melody Time* (1948). "Boogie Woogie Bugle Boy" is probably the threesome's most famous number.

ANIMAL CRACKERS (Paramount 1930) lost most of its songs on the way from Broadway to the sound stage but this second MARX BROTHERS film established the zany brothers as box office gold. The plot revolved around the theft of a painting at the Long Island mansion of millionairess Mrs. Rittenhouse (MARGARET DUMONT), but Groucho as the African explorer Captain Jeffrey T. Spaulding, Chico as Emanuel Ravelli, and Harpo as the Professor were all that mattered. The only notable musical number was the BERT KALMAR–HARRY RUBY ditty "Hooray for Captain Spaulding," one of Groucho's theme songs throughout his long career.

ANIMATED MUSICALS that went beyond short subjects arrived a decade after the advent of sound with DISNEY's *SNOW WHITE AND THE SEVEN DWARFS* (1937), but music and songs had been used in cartoons made by several studios before then. Although WALT DISNEY was America's most recognized innovator with animated characters and made bold experiments with his "Silly Symphony" series and Mickey Mouse shorts, other studios offered a steady stream of cartoons to go with their feature films. MGM offered Tom and Jerry shorts, WARNER BROTHERS' series featured "Looney Tunes" with Bugs Bunny and friends, UNIVERSAL had Oswald the Rabbit, PARAMOUNT its Puppetoon flicks, COLUMBIA offered "Color Rhapsodies," and independent animators such as Max Fleischer created Popeye and Betty Boop, all of them utilizing music to some degree. When Disney broke new ground by giving his audience a full-length animated movie, few followed in his steps at first. Fleischer produced *GULLIVER'S TRAVELS* (1939) but most studios were content to stick to shorts. Disney, in contrast, plowed new ground with such classics in animation as *PINOCCHIO* (1940), *FANTASIA* (1940), *DUMBO* (1941), *THE THREE CABALLEROS* (1945), *SONG OF THE SOUTH* (1946), *CINDERELLA* (1950), *LADY AND THE TRAMP* (1955), and *SLEEPING BEAUTY* (1959). Music was integral to all the features, some films having extensive scores and providing songs that became hits. Among the few non-Disney ventures during the 1960s and 1970s were *Gay Purr-ee* (1962), *A Boy Named Charlie Brown* (1969), *Shinbone Alley* (1971), and *Charlotte's Web* (1973). The animation division at Disney declined in the late 1960s, and after Walt Disney's death many animators left the studio to work elsewhere. Feature-length cartoons by various studios started appearing regularly in the 1970s, but few were musicals, most being content to have one theme song and rely on action or spectacle to tell the story. Only in the 1990s, when the Disney studio was back in full force with *BEAUTY AND THE BEAST* (1991) and *THE LION KING* (1994), did other studios enter the market. The quality varied, but many of the features found success and helped open up the field of musical animation. Among the non-Disney entries were *Rock-a-Doodle* (1992), *The Swan Princess* (1994), *Thumbelina* (1994), *A Troll in Central Park* (1994), *The Pebble and the Penguin* (1995), *Cats Don't Dance* (1996), *ANASTASIA* (1997), *Quest for Camelot* (1998), *The Prince of Egypt* (1998), and *The Road to El Dorado* (2000). The recent interest in stop-action animation has yielded the Disney musicals *The Nightmare Before Christmas* (1993) and *James and the Giant Peach* (1996), and computer animation has quickly found an audience with *Toy Story* (1995), *A Bug's Life* (1998), *Antz* (1998), and *Toy Story 2* (1999), all utilizing songs but not traditional musicals.

ANNIE (Columbia 1982) went on record as one of the most expensive flops in the history of COLUMBIA and helped seal the lid on the big-budget musical coffin. Many changes and mistakes were made in transferring the 1977 Broadway hit to the screen (six songs were dropped, the plot was altered, esteemed veteran John Huston was hired to direct even though he had never done a musical), and the $52 million spent on the picture solved none of its many problems. Aileen Quinn as Little Orphan Annie found little favor, and Albert Finney's cartoonish Daddy Warbucks was more odd than entertaining. But some fun was to be found in Carol Burnett's brawling Miss Hannigan, ANN REINKING's elegant and dancing secretary Grace, and TIM CURRY and BERNADETTE PETERS' lowlife villains. The Martin Charnin–CHARLES STROUSE songs seemed less enjoyable on the screen than on the stage, even the hit ballad "Tomorrow" falling flat. A 1999 television version of the musical with Alicia Morton, Victor Garber, and Kathy Bates fared much better.

ANNIE GET YOUR GUN (MGM 1950) was, by the standards of its day, a faithful screen version of a Broadway hit, retaining most of IRVING BERLIN's dynamite 1946 score and sticking to the original story about backwoods hick Annie Oakley (BETTY HUTTON), who rises to sharpshooting fame in Buffalo Bill's Wild West Show and nabs shootist Frank Butler (HOWARD KEEL) along the way. ARTHUR FREED's production was plagued with difficulties: JUDY GARLAND was signed as Annie but her illness forced the studio to recast after months of filming, FRANK MORGAN died and LOUIS CALHERN was brought in to play Bill Cody, and director-choreographer BUSBY BERKELEY quit during production and GEORGE SIDNEY and ROBERT ALTON had to take over. But the result was still a colorful musical extravaganza that did well at the box office. Hutton, in the plum role of her career, got to sing such Berlin favorites as "You Can't Get a Man With a Gun," "I Got the Sun in the Morning," "They Say It's Wonderful," and "I'm an Indian Too," and Keel, in his first screen role, made the most of "My Defenses Are Down" and "The Girl That I Marry." Also in the score were the playful duet "Anything You Can Do" and the performers' anthem "There's No Business Like Show Business."

ANN-MARGARET (1941–   ) is the glittering, leggy star of nightclubs and television who has appeared in films since 1961, moving back and forth from musicals to comedies and even dramas. Her movie musical roles include nightclub singer Emily in the remake of *STATE FAIR* (1962), Ohio teenager Kim McAfee in *BYE BYE BIRDIE* (1963), swimming instructress Rusty Martin in *VIVA LAS VEGAS* (1964), boozing mother Norma in *TOMMY* (1975), and a vaudeville star in *Newsies* (1992). Ann-Margaret is married to television actor Roger Smith.

ANYTHING GOES (Paramount 1936) should have been as much fun as the 1934 Broadway smash, for the film kept ETHEL MERMAN and her acclaimed performance as the brazen nightclub-singer-turned-evangelist Reno Sweeney. But only four of the delectable COLE PORTER songs made it to the screen, and much of the cast was routine. BING CROSBY stows away on an ocean liner heading to Europe to be with his sweetheart IDA LUPINO but gets mixed up with Public Enemy No. 13, disguised as the Rev. Moon (CHARLIE RUGGLES). Reno falls for the British Sir Evelyn (ARTHUR TREACHER) who is engaged to Lupino but all is sorted out before they reach England. Although Merman got to sing Porter's "I Get a Kick Out of You" and the witty title song, her duet "You're the Top" with Crosby was laundered for the screen. Crosby did get to sing a pleasing new song, "Moonburn" by EDWARD HEYMAN and HOAGY CARMICHAEL. PARAMOUNT remade *Anything Goes* in 1956 with Crosby again on board an ocean liner, but the plot this time concerned two showmen (Crosby and DONALD O'CONNOR) on a world cruise looking for a star for their new show. They found MITZI GAYNOR and Jeanmarie, as well as some of the Porter score (Crosby got to sing "All Through the Night" this time) and a few new songs by SAMMY CAHN and JIMMY VAN HEUSEN, the best being "You Can Bounce Right Back" delivered by the rubber-boned O'Connor.

APPLAUSE (Paramount 1929) was an early and uncompromising musical melodrama about show business that boasted an unforgettable performance by HELEN MORGAN that has rarely been equaled in screen musicals. Kitty Darling is an aging burlesque queen who lives with the two-timing drunk Hitch (Fuller Melish, Jr.) and uses all her money to support her teenage daughter April (Joan Peers), who is away at a convent school. When April returns from school, Kitty marries Hitch to make the girl's home respectable. But Hitch treats her even worse and then leaves; in order not to be a burden on her daughter, Kitty takes poison and dies. This grim drama was raised to high art by ROUBEN MAMOULIAN's fluid direction (his first film) and Morgan's heartbreaking rendition of such torchy classics as "I've Got a Feelin' I'm Fallin' " and "What Wouldn't I Do for That Man," as well as the pathetically cheerful "Give Your Baby Lots of Lovin' " that was used throughout the film as an ironic leitmotif. Although primitive and dated, *Applause* remains a potent work and a landmark in the development of the genre.

ARDEN, EVE (1912–1990), a favorite wisecracking character actress of the stage, film, and television (*Our Miss Brooks*), appeared in over sixty films, rarely in a leading role but always memorably featured. After bit parts in the musicals *DANCING LADY* (1933) and *Cocoanut Grove* (1938), Arden started playing the droll, efficient friend of the heroine or the caustic secretary in *Having Wonderful Time* (1938), *No No Nanette* (1940), *ZIEGFELD GIRL* (1940), *COVER GIRL* (1944), *One Touch of Venus* (1949), *Tea for Two* (1950), and others. After many years on television, Arden returned to the musical film, playing Principal McGee in *GREASE* (1978) and *Grease II* (1982)

ARISTOCATS, THE (Disney 1970) was a stylish animated tale of a family of pampered Parisian cats who are kidnapped by a greedy butler so that his wealthy mistress won't leave all her money to the felines. Although not as popular as most DISNEY products, the beautifully-drawn feature had a distinct charm of its own, and the score, by various tunesmiths, was memorable. Jive cats PHIL HARRIS and Scatman Crothers led the riproaring "Everybody Wants to Be a Cat," momma cat EVA GABOR sang a playful "Scales and Arpeggios" with her kittens, and MAURICE CHEVALIER crooned (in English and French) the title song, the last time he lent his voice to a movie musical.

ARLEN, HAROLD (1905–1986) was the masterful composer of blues and jazz songs for Broadway and Hollywood, mostly recognized for his atypical score for *THE WIZARD OF OZ* (1939) with lyricist E.Y. HARBURG. As a fledgling composer, Arlen wrote for the Cotton Club and other Harlem haunts, capturing a rich and melodic ethnic sound that was unequaled by any other white composer. He scored a handful of Broadway shows and revues (often with Harburg) before going to Hollywood in 1934, where he wrote such popular hits as "The Man That Got Away," "That Old Black Magic," "Ac-cent-tchu-ate the Positive," "My Shining Hour," "Lydia, the Tattooed Lady," and "Blues in the Night." With Harbach he scored *The Singing Kid* (1936), *GOLD DIGGERS OF 1937* (1936), *AT THE CIRCUS* (1939), *CABIN IN THE SKY* (1943), and the animated *Gay Purr-ee* (1962). With his other frequent collaborator, JOHNNY MERCER, Arlen wrote for *BLUES IN THE NIGHT* (1941), *STAR SPANGLED RHYTHM* (1942), *The Sky's the Limit* (1943), *HERE COME THE WAVES* (1944), and others. Teaming up with lyricist IRA GERSHWIN, he provided scores for *A STAR IS BORN* (1954) and *THE COUNTRY GIRL* (1954). Other movie credits with various partners include *UP IN ARMS* (1944), *CASBAH* (1948), *My Blue Heaven* (1950), and *THE FARMER TAKES A WIFE* (1953).

ARMSTRONG, LOUIS (1900–1971), the dean of jazz trumpet players who was affectionately nicknamed "Satchmo," sang and played with his band in over twenty films during his long career. The raspy-voiced African American usually played himself on the screen, appearing as a specialty but often stealing the show. His film musical debut was in *PENNIES FROM HEAVEN* (1936), followed by featured spots in *ARTISTS AND MODELS* (1937), *Every Day's a Holiday* (1937), *Doctor Rhythm* (1938), *Going Places* (1939), *CABIN IN THE SKY* (1943), *Jam Session* (1944), *HOLLYWOOD CANTEEN* (1944), *New Orleans* (1947), *A Song Is Born* (1948), *HERE COMES THE GROOM* (1951), *THE GLENN MILLER STORY* (1954), *HIGH SOCIETY* (1956), *THE FIVE PENNIES* (1959), *When the Boys Meet the Girls* (1965), and others. His final screen appearance, as the bandleader sassing out the title tune with BARBRA STREISAND in *HELLO, DOLLY!* (1969), is perhaps his most fondly remembered.

ARNAZ, DESI (1917–1986), the dashing Cuban singer and bandleader, found only limited success on stage and screen but became one of television's most popular personalities and shrewdest producers, presenting *I Love Lucy* with his then-wife LUCILLE BALL. Arnaz was brought to Hollywood to recreate his Broadway role of Latin exchange student Manuelito in *TOO MANY GIRLS* (1940). His subsequent appearances in *Four Jacks and a Jill* (1941), *Cuban Pete* (1946), and *Holiday in Havana* (1949) never caught on, so he concentrated on nightclubs and television. He was the father of actors Lucie Arnaz and Desi Arnaz, Jr.

ARTISTS AND MODELS (Paramount 1937) had as thin a plot as any musical of the era—ad agency president JACK BENNY must see that the top model is crowned at the "Artists and Models Ball"—but the snappy dialogue, charming cast, tuneful songs, and superb specialty acts made it seem like a real gem. IDA LUPINO and Richard Arlen costarred with BENNY but the real fun came from specialties by MARTHA RAYE, LOUIS ARMSTRONG, CONNEE BOSWELL, the Yacht Club Boys, and the puppeteering Personettes. The score, by several different teams, included the jazzy "Public Melody No. 1," the alluring ballads "I Have Eyes" and "Whispers in the Dark," and the swinging duet "Stop, You're Breaking My Heart," to which BEN BLUE and JUDY CANOVA sang and danced. PARAMOUNT's 1938 SEQUEL *ARTISTS AND MODELS ABROAD* also featured Benny, this time guiding a stranded acting troupe around Paris and romancing Texas heiress JOAN BENNETT. It was much less satisfying than the original, although it did boast the lively torch song "What Have You Got That Gets Me?" and the catchy "You're Broke, You Dope," both sung by the Yacht Club Boys. Paramount used the title *Artists and Models* again in 1955 for a JERRY LEWIS–DEAN MARTIN musical about two struggling artists in Greenwich Village. It was one of the team's best vehicles with SHIRLEY MacLAINE and Dorothy

Malone as the pair's love interests and an amiable JACK BROOKS–HARRY WARREN score that included the Italian ballad "Innamorata."

ARTISTS AND MODELS ABROAD. See *Artists and Models*

ASHMAN, HOWARD (1950–1991) was a theatre lyricist who found success in Hollywood before his premature death from AIDS. Ashman and his composer partner ALAN MENKEN scored a handful of Off-Broadway shows, their most popular being *LITTLE SHOP OF HORRORS*, which was filmed in 1986. Hired by DISNEY to write the songs for *THE LITTLE MERMAID* (1989), the team helped in turning the studio around and launching an era of superb ANIMATED MUSICALS. Ashman and Menken won Oscars for "Under the Sea" in *The Little Mermaid* and for the title song in their next film project, *BEAUTY AND THE BEAST* (1991). Before his death, Ashman wrote half the songs for *ALADDIN* (1992).

ASTAIRE, FRED (1899–1987), the most graceful, original, and sophisticated of Hollywood song-and-dance men, excelled in all manners of dance (tap, soft shoe, ballet, jazz, modern) while maintaining a distinctive persona of wit and romance that has never been equaled. Coming from vaudeville and Broadway, where he was teamed with his sister Adele, Astaire felt his career was finished after she retired to get married, and so he turned to Hollywood where he debuted playing himself in a featured spot in *DANCING LADY* (1933). It was his teaming with GINGER ROGERS as the secondary couple in *FLYING DOWN TO RIO* (1933) that launched both their careers, and they were paired in nine subsequent musicals: *THE GAY DIVORCEE* (1934), *ROBERTA* (1935), *TOP HAT* (1935), *FOLLOW THE FLEET* (1936), *SWING TIME* (1936), *SHALL WE DANCE* (1937), *CAREFREE* (1938), *THE STORY OF VERNON AND IRENE CASTLE* (1939), and *THE BARKLEYS OF BROADWAY* (1949). Other memorable credits with other leading ladies include *A DAMSEL IN DISTRESS* (1937), *BROADWAY MELODY OF 1940*, *YOU'LL NEVER GET RICH* (1941), *The Sky's the Limit* (1943), *Yolanda and the Thief* (1945), *ZIEGFELD FOLLIES* (1946), *DADDY LONG LEGS* (1955), *FUNNY FACE* (1957), and *SILK STOCKINGS* (1957). Astaire was equally enchanting when his co-star was a male, such as his teaming with BING CROSBY in *HOLIDAY INN* (1942) and *BLUE SKIES* (1946). His final screen musical credit was the Irishman Finian in *FINIAN'S RAINBOW* (1968). Astaire usually played dancers in his films, the show business setting giving him plenty of opportunity for hoofing. But there was no limit to Astaire's inventiveness in finding unusual locations for dance or creating steps using unlikely props, even going so far as a *pas de deux* with a hat stand or dancing on the ceiling. Although not a crooner or a full-voiced singer, Astaire had a nimble way with a lyric and introduced dozens of hit songs during his long career.

AT THE CIRCUS (MGM 1939) may not have been a top-drawer MARX BROTHERS film, but it still had its fair share of laughs as lawyer J. Cheever Loophole (Groucho) tried to dig up $10,000 to help KENNY BAKER save his circus troupe. The comedy had three exceptional musical numbers: Baker and Florence Rice singing the warm E.Y. HARBURG–HAROLD ARLEN ballad "Two Blind Loves" at a lunch counter, Harpo plucking out RODGERS and HART's "Blue Moon" on the harp, and Groucho singing and prancing to "Lydia, the Tattooed Lady" on a train, the last also by Harburg and Arlen and arguably the best song ever written for a Marx brothers movie.

AUER, MISCHA (1905–1967) was a sad-looking, heavily accented character actor who livened up over sixty Hollywood movies, including the musicals *PARAMOUNT ON PARADE* (1930), *ONE HUNDRED MEN AND A GIRL* (1937), *SWEETHEARTS* (1938), and *JOY OF LIVING* (1938). Although he began his film career playing villains, Auer later excelled at eccentric comic types.

AUTRY, GENE (1907–1998), the singing cowboy who wrote hundreds of western songs and whose recording propelled "Rudolph the Red-Nosed Reindeer" to the top of the charts, was a hit on radio before he was featured in western serials with his sidekick Smiley Burnett and his horse Champion. Although Autry sang in most of his feature films, only a handful of his films could be classified as musicals: *Tumbling Tumbleweeds* (1935), *Manhattan Merry-Go-Round* (1937), *Melody Ranch* (1940), and a few others.

AVALON, FRANKIE (1939–   ), a teenage singing idol of the 1960s, played the youthful hero in a series of "beach" musicals, often with ANNETTE FUNICELLO. After a specialty spot in *Jamboree* (1957), he appeared as an amorous teen (usually named Frankie) in *Beach Party* (1963), *Muscle Beach Party* (1964), *Bikini Beach* (1964), *Beach Blanket Bingo* (1965), *I'll Take Sweden* (1965), *How to Stuff a Wild Bikini* (1967), and others. He returned to mock his own screen image when he played the crooning Teen Angel in *GREASE* (1978) and then reteamed with Funicello for the nostalgic *Back to the Beach* (1987).

B

BABES IN ARMS (MGM 1939) is perhaps the quintessential "let's put on a show" backstager, the first teaming of MICKEY ROONEY and JUDY GARLAND (fresh off the set from *THE WIZARD OF OZ*) and producer ARTHUR FREED's first of many musicals at MGM. Only two RODGERS and HART songs ("Where or When" and the title number) were retained from the 1937 Broadway hit, but the plot, about a group of youngsters keeping their vaudevillian parents out of the poor house by putting on a show to raise money, was not radically different from the original and from the many others that would follow. The Rooney-Garland romance was threatened by a SHIRLEY TEMPLE–like movie star (JUNE PREISSER) but ended happily with the big show. The score included the NACIO HERB BROWN–Freed songs "Good Morning," "You Are My Lucky Star," and "Broadway Rhythm," the last two sung contrapuntally by Garland and Betty Jaynes. A handful of old standards were also included, such as "Moonlight Bay," "Oh, Susannah," "Ida, Sweet as Apple Cider," "I'm Just Wild About Harry," and even a choral version of Sousa's "Stars and Stripes Forever." BUSBY BERKELEY directed, his first full assignment at MGM and the beginning of the second part of his remarkable career.

BABES IN TOYLAND, VICTOR HERBERT's perennial OPERETTA favorite first seen on Broadway in 1903, has been filmed three times since sound came in. The most satisfying version is the 1934 MGM offering that in only seventy-nine minutes captured the charm and mystery of the tale of Toyland invaded by Bogeymen but saved by the bumbling efforts of two toymakers, STAN LAUREL and OLIVER HARDY. Added to the Herbert favorites "Toyland," "I Can't Do the Sum," "Don't Cry, Bo-Peep," and "March of the Toys" was the recent hit tune "Who's Afraid of the Big Bad Wolf?" by Ann Ronell and FRANK CHURCHILL. DISNEY's 1961 version of *Babes in*

Toyland was the company's first live action musical. Henry Calvin and Gene Sheldon were the comic toymakers, but more emphasis was put on their boss ED WYNN, RAY BOLGER (miscast as the villain), and Disney stars ANNETTE FUNICELLO and TOMMY SANDS as the persecuted young lovers. Elaborate and colorful, it had some inventive numbers (choreographer Tommy Maloney staged "Castle in Spain" with dancing fountains) but was too overproduced to genuinely please. More dismal was a 1986 made-for-television version that jettisoned most of the Herbert score and left Drew Barrymore, Keanu Reeves, Richard Mulligan, Eileen Brennan, and Pat Morita with some forgettable LESLIE BRICUSSE songs to sing.

BABES ON BROADWAY (MGM 1942) was a follow-up to the MICKEY ROONEY–JUDY GARLAND vehicles *BABES IN ARMS* (1939) and *STRIKE UP THE BAND* (1940) with the youthful cast once again putting on a big show, this time to raise money to send settlement-house kids to the country. The formula was already running thin, but the musical numbers were exceptional, including three E.Y. HARBURG–BURTON LANE gems: the standard "(I Like New York in June) How About You," the wry "Anything Can Happen in New York," and the patriotic "Chin Up, Cheerio, Carry On" that encouraged the British to stand up to Hitler. Rooney, at the peak of his popularity, got to pull out all the stops, leading both a minstrel show and a hoe down, impersonating Sir Harry Lauder, Walter Hampton, and GEORGE M. COHAN in a dream sequence, and spoofing CARMEN MIRANDA in a hilarious drag routine. BUSBY BERKELEY directed as well as choreographed the frolic, which was filled with more-than-usual musical numbers, including Americana favorites such as "Yankee Doodle Boy," "By the Light of the Silvery Moon," "Swanee River," and "Waiting for the Robert E. Lee."

BACHARACH, BURT (1928–   ), one of Hollywood's most successful composers of soundtracks in the 1960s and 1970s, wrote a series of hit songs for the movies with lyricist **HAL DAVID** (1921–   ), including "Alfie" and "Raindrops Keep Fallin' on My Head." David also co-wrote the musical score for *Two Gals and a Guy* (1951) with Marty Nevins, and with Bacharach the ill-fated *Lost Horizon* (1972).

BACON, IRVING (1893–1965) was a busy character actor in Hollywood, playing simple-minded comic types in over 200 movies from the early 1920s until the late 1950s. Bacon's sorrowful look of confusion was seen in such musicals as *BIG BROADCAST OF 1937* (1936), *SING YOU SINNERS* (1938), *Hollywood Cavalcade* (1939), *HOLIDAY INN* (1942), *Footlight Serenade* (1942), *WABASH AVENUE* (1950), *THE GLENN MILLER STORY* (1954), and *A STAR IS BORN* (1954).

BACON, LLOYD (1890–1955) was a durable and prolific film director who staged a score of early WARNER BROTHERS musicals, often with choreographer BUSBY BERKELEY, such as *THE SINGING FOOL* (1928), *Honky Tonk* (1929), *42ND STREET* (1933), *WONDER BAR* (1934), and *GOLD DIGGERS OF 1937* (1936). In the 1940s and 1950s Bacon moved to 20TH CENTURY–FOX and directed *Wake Up and Dream* (1946), *You Were Meant for Me* (1948), *Call Me Mister* (1951), *The French Line* (1954), and other musicals. Originally an actor in Charles Chaplin silents, Bacon was known for his fast-paced direction and crackling comic style.

BAILEY, PEARL (1918–1990), the distinctive jazz singer whose breezy and slurred singing style made her a favorite on Broadway, records, nightclubs, and television, appeared in a handful of films, including *Variety Girl* (1947), *Isn't It Romantic?* (1948), and *St. Louis Blues* (1958). The African American singer's most challenging film roles were the worldly-wise Frankie in *CARMEN JONES* (1954) and the Charleston "Catfish Row" resident Maria in *PORGY AND BESS* (1959).

BAKER, KENNY (1912–1985), a youthful-looking tenor with an innocent and naive persona, gained recognition on JACK BENNY's radio show and was featured in some dozen musical films in the 1930s and 1940s. After doing specialty bits in *KING OF BURLESQUE* (1935), *Mr. Dodd Takes the Air* (1937), and others, Baker played juvenile leads in *THE GOLDWYN FOLLIES* (1938), *AT THE CIRCUS* (1939), *The Mikado* (1939), and *The Hit Parade of 1941* (1940). He was later seen in featured roles in such musicals as *STAGE DOOR CANTEEN* (1943) and *THE HARVEY GIRLS* (1947). Despite his melodic high range and affable looks, Baker was a lightweight actor who rarely commanded attention unless he was singing.

BALALAIKA (MGM 1939) was based on a 1936 London OPERETTA that never made it to Broadway, but Hollywood (and audiences) was eager for more costume dramas set to music, and so the studio threw out the original score save one number ("At the Balalaika") and had HERBERT STOTHART compose flowing Russian melodies to which GEORGE FORREST and ROBERT WRIGHT wrote stirring lyrics. The plot, resembling a Ruritanian romance more than a Russian revolution, concerned NELSON EDDY as Prince Peter Karagin, who disguises himself as a lowly music student in order to woo the revolutionary peasant ILONA MASSEY. The score included the rousing "Ride, Cossack, Ride" as well as classical snippets by Bizet, Lehar, Rimsky-Korsakov, Glinka, and Chopin and some traditional Russian hymns and drinking songs. Eddy's popularity and the renewed interest in all things Russian (as war escalated in Europe, it was beginning to look like Russia was to be America's new ally) helped the film do well at the box office, though it doesn't stand up so well today.

BALL, LUCILLE (1910–1989), the undisputed queen of early television, appeared in over seventy films before the advent of *I Love Lucy* in 1951, playing everything from glamour girls to innocent ingenues to smart aleck sidekicks. She made her film debut in *Broadway Through a Keyhole* (1933) and appeared as a model, chorine, or Goldwyn Girl in such musicals as *ROMAN SCANDALS* (1933), *MURDER AT THE VANITIES* (1934), *KID MILLIONS* (1934), *ROBERTA* (1935), and *TOP HAT* (1935). Ball was featured in supporting roles in *I DREAM TOO MUCH* (1935), *FOLLOW THE FLEET* (1936), *Dance, Girl, Dance* (1940), and others, then finally in leading roles, such as the rich coed Consuelo in *TOO MANY GIRLS* (1940) and nightclub songstress May Daly in *DuBarry Was a Lady* (1943). After playing the *nouveau riche* Agatha in *Fancy Pants* (1950), she went into television, returning to the film musical decades later for her last screen role, the title auntie in *Mame* (1974). Although the red-headed comedienne was often a bright and sassy presence on the screen, her farcical genius was best displayed on television.

BAND WAGON, THE (MGM 1953) poked fun at pretentious musical theatre, backstage movie musicals, detective thrillers, and "let's put on a show" formula films. No wonder it is still so enjoyable. Aging and bankrupt Hollywood hoofer FRED ASTAIRE returns to Broadway in a new musical written by songwriters Nanette Fabray and OSCAR LEVANT but faces disaster when the arty director JACK BUCHANAN wants to turn the musical comedy into a ponderous theatre piece based on *Faust*. But everyone realizes at the last minute the value of "entertainment" and the show is saved by throwing out pretension and putting in a handful of HOWARD DIETZ–ARTHUR SCHWARTZ songs. BETTY COMDEN and ADOLPH GREEN wrote the satiric screenplay (the two songwriters were thinly disguised versions of themselves just as Buchanan's character was partially based on the film's director VINCENTE MINNELLI) and producer ARTHUR FREED hired Dietz and Schwartz to write "That's Entertainment," the movie's only new song. (All the other numbers came from the team's REVUE songs of the 1930s.) The sparkling score included "Dancing in the Dark" with Astaire and CYD CHARISSE gliding through a moonlit Central Park, "I Guess I'll Have to Change My Plan" turned into a debonair soft-shoe by Astaire and Buchanan, "A Shine on Your Shoes" with Astaire and LeRoy Daniels tapping through a Times Square penny arcade, the hilarious "Triplets" sung and screamed by Buchanan, Fabray, and Astaire, and the mock modern ballet "The Girl Hunt" (sly narration written by ALAN JAY LERNER in the style of then-popular Mickey Spillane) in which private eye Astaire meets up with a "bad, dangerous" floozy (Charisse) in a crime-ridden dive. In many ways *The Band Wagon* was a climax and summation of both Astaire's remarkable career and the series of Freed musicals at MGM.

BARBIER, GEORGE (1865–1945) was a busy character actor in films from the 1920s until his death, often playing older men who blustered and fretted but with a harmless air. Barbier appeared in hundreds of features, including the musicals *THE SMILING LIEUTENANT* (1931), *ONE HOUR WITH YOU* (1932), *THE BIG BROADCAST* (1932), *THE PHANTOM PRESIDENT* (1932), *THE MERRY WIDOW* (1934), *ON THE AVENUE* (1937), *Little Miss Broadway* (1938), *SWEETHEARTS* (1938), *WEEK-END IN HAVANA* (1941), *Song of the Islands* (1942), *HELLO, FRISCO, HELLO* (1942), *YANKEE DOODLE DANDY* (1942), and many others.

BARI, LYNN (1913–1989), publicized as "The Girl With the Million-Dollar Figure," was second only to BETTY GRABLE when it came to pin-up popularity in the 1940s. The dark-haired beauty was first seen on screen as a chorine in *DANCING LADY* (1933), *George White's Scandals* (1935), *ON THE AVENUE* (1937), and several other 20TH CENTURY–FOX musicals. Bari later graduated to supporting roles, often playing the "other woman" in comedies, dramas, and musicals such as *Pack Up Your Troubles* (1939), *LILLIAN RUSSELL* (1940), *SUN VALLEY SERENADE* (1941), *ORCHESTRA WIVES* (1942), *HELLO, FRISCO, HELLO* (1943), *On the Sunny Side of the Street* (1951), and *Has Anybody Seen My Gal?* (1952).

BARKLEYS OF BROADWAY, THE (MGM 1949) reteamed FRED ASTAIRE and GINGER ROGERS after nine years of partnering with other stars. When Astaire crooned "You'd Be Hard to Replace" to Rogers, America wholeheartedly agreed, confirming the notion that this was the greatest dance team of all filmdom. The plot, by BETTY COMDEN and ADOLPH GREEN, involved a pair of married dance stars whose career and marriage are threatened by her wish to abandon hoofing and pursue serious acting roles. There were few surprises in the story, but the musical sequences (new songs by IRA GERSHWIN and HARRY WARREN in their sole collaboration) were all winners, including the couple's "Bouncin' the Blues" at rehearsal, spoofing Scottish dourness in "My One and Only Highland Fling," and reprising "They Can't Take That Away From Me," which they had sung on screen twelve years earlier. Astaire also got to perform an inventive "Shoes With Wings On," dancing with dozens of pairs of disembodied white shoes. OSCAR LEVANT was on hand as the married couple's songwriter friend, joined them in the wry comedy number "A Weekend in the Country," and played Tchaikovsky's "Concerto in B-flat Minor" on the piano. *The Barkleys of Broadway* was the tenth and final Astaire-Rogers picture and a merry conclusion to a magical collaboration.

BARTON, JAMES (1890–1962) was a crusty character actor and song-and-dance man of vaudeville, Broadway, and four movie musicals: *The Daughter of Rosie O'Grady* (1950), *WABASH AVENUE* (1950), *HERE*

COMES THE GROOM (1951), and *Golden Girl* (1951). Barton usually played fathers or derelicts, his drunk routine being his specialty.

BARTY, BILLY (1924–   ), Hollywood and television's most recognized and accomplished "midget" actor, was on screen from the age of three, playing children for several years (he was MICKEY ROONEY's little brother in a series of comedy shorts in the 1920s) and then a smiling imp who enlivened such musical films as *GOLD DIGGERS OF 1933* (1933), *FOOTLIGHT PARADE* (1933), *ROMAN SCANDALS* (1933), and *JUMBO* (1962). The three-foot nine-inch actor championed the cause of short performers, founding the Little People of America in 1957 and the Billy Barty Foundation in 1975.

BASIE, COUNT (1904–1984), the popular pianist and bandleader whose long career stretched from 1936 into the 1970s, was featured with his band in eight movie musicals, always playing himself. Basie's film credits include *Hit Parade of 1943*, *Crazy House* (1943), *STAGE DOOR CANTEEN* (1943), *Jamboree* (1957), *Cinderfella* (1960), and *Blazing Saddles* (1974).

BAXTER, WARNER (1889–1951) was a dashing leading man in silent films who made the transition to talkies, usually playing the distinguished "man about town" in such musicals as *Stand Up and Cheer* (1934), *KING OF BURLESQUE* (1935), *Vogues of 1938* (1937), and *Lady in the Dark* (1944). Baxter's most notable role was Broadway producer Julian Marsh in *42ND STREET* (1933).

BEATLES, THE, the most influential rock group to come out of England in the 1960s and the trendsetters in music, fashion, and lifestyle, wrote and performed songs for three film musicals: *A HARD DAY'S NIGHT* (1964), *HELP!* (1965), and the animated *YELLOW SUBMARINE* (1968). The quartet consisted of John Lennon (1940–1980), Ringo Starr (1940–   ), Paul McCartney (1942–   ), and George Harrison (1943–   ), and though McCartney and Lennon were the primary songwriters, all four contributed to the scores. Although the group disbanded in 1970, their songs were used in *Sgt. Pepper's Lonely Hearts Club Band* (1978), *I Wanna Hold Your Hand* (1978), and others. The foursome can be seen together in the documentary *Let It Be* (1970) and individually in other ROCUMENTARIES and nonmusicals.

BEATON, SIR CECIL (1904–1980), the celebrated photographer and designer, contributed to only a few movie musicals but the result was always distinctive. He designed sets and costumes for *GIGI* (1958) and *MY FAIR LADY* (1964) and the costumes for *ON A CLEAR DAY YOU CAN SEE FOREVER* (1970).

BEAUMONT, HARRY (1888–1966) was a prolific film director who started as an actor in silents and later helmed several talkies for MGM, including the studio's first musical, *THE BROADWAY MELODY* (1929). Other movie musicals in his extensive credits include *Lord Byron of Broadway* (1930), *Children of Pleasure* (1930), and *The Floradora Girl* (1930).

BEAUTY AND THE BEAST (Disney 1991), the only animated film ever nominated for the Best Picture Oscar, was one of the DISNEY company's finest accomplishments, a magical mixture of fantasy, romance, and comedy. Linda Woolverton adapted the famous French fairy tale into a moving drama that still allowed for farcical business and comic characters to fill out the story. Directors Gary Tousdale and Kirk Wise gave the film a soft and romantic rendering, and the HOWARD ASHMAN–ALAN MENKEN score had a French flavor with more than a touch of Broadway: "Belle," "Gaston," "Something There," "Be Our Guest," and the Oscar-winning title ballad. The voices included Paige O'Hara (Belle), Robby Benson (the beast), ANGELA LANSBURY (Mrs. Potts), Jerry Orbach (Lumiere), Richard White (Gaston) and David Ogden Stiers (Cogsworth). The climactic scene when the beast is transformed back into a human because of Belle's love may be one of the most affecting in all the Disney canon. The film was very popular and represented a highpoint for the new Disney era of animation in the 1990s.

BEAVERS, LOUISE (1902–1962), the frequently seen African–American character actress who played maids or cooks in dozens of films, livened up such musicals as *42ND STREET* (1933), *SHE DONE HIM WRONG* (1933), *Rainbow on the River* (1936) *HOLIDAY INN* (1942), and *DuBarry Was a Lady* (1943). Although rarely given complex characters to play, Beavers was a gifted dramatic actress, as proved by her performance in the nonmusical *Imitation of Life* (1934). She was also one of the first black performers to be starred in a television series, the popular *Beulah* in the early 1950s.

BEDKNOBS AND BROOMSTICKS (Disney 1971) was one of the DISNEY company's several efforts to recapture the magic (and success) of *MARY POPPINS* (1964), but despite some marvelous sequences, the movie was never that popular until it came out on video decades later. Based on a book by Mary Norton, the story concerned three London children (Cindy O'Callaghan, Roy Snart, and Ian Weighill) who are evacuated to the countryside to escape the Blitz and are taken in by the eccentric ANGELA LANSBURY, who is studying to become a witch through a correspondence course offered by David Tomlinson. The foursome's misadventures included traveling through the air in a magical bed and routing some German invaders with the help of a museum full of medieval armor. The score by RICHARD M. and ROBERT B. SHERMAN was not their best, though there was the lovely ballad "Age of Not Believing" and a catchy tune, "The Beautiful Briny," in which the humans joined a selection of fish for an underwater dance contest, the animated live-action sequence being the musical highlight of the film. The supporting cast of colorful character actors included Tessie O'Shea, Roddy McDowell, Sam Jaffe, Bruce Forsythe, and REGINALD OWEN.

BELLE OF NEW YORK, THE (MGM 1952) was based on a forgotten 1897 Broadway flop (but a success in London) about Manhattan playboy FRED ASTAIRE who has left five brides standing at the altar as he goes about his carefree ways. But Astaire meets his match in VERA-ELLEN (singing dubbed by Anita Ellis), a conservative worker for a Salvation Army–like organization who sets him straight. The original stage score was tossed out by producer ARTHUR FREED, and the new one by JOHNNY MERCER and HARRY WARREN included the hit song "Baby Doll." ROBERT ALTON staged the musical numbers, letting Astaire dance on the clouds for "Seeing's Believing" and putting Vera-Ellen into various Currier and Ives lithographs as she imagines season after season in "Thank You, Mr. Currier, Thank You, Mr. Ives." MARJORIE MAIN, KEENAN WYNN, and ALICE PEARCE headed the supporting cast, and CHARLES WALTERS directed the turn-of-the-century piece with a warm and nostalgic feel to it.

BELLS ARE RINGING (MGM 1960) came to the screen with its Broadway star JUDY HOLLIDAY recreating her vibrant performance as telephone answering service worker Ella Peterson who falls for one of her customers, a playwright (DEAN MARTIN) suffering from writer's block. Also from the 1956 stage production came Jean Stapleton, Dort Clark, Bernie West, some of JEROME ROBBINS' staging, and most of the BETTY COMDEN–ADOLPH GREEN–JULE STYNE score, including the two hits "Just in Time" and "The Party's Over." VINCENTE MINNELLI directed but it was a pretty lifeless affair except when Holliday took over, singing the winsome "It's a Perfect Relationship," the sassy "Mu-cha-cha," or the brassy "I'm Going Back (To the Bonjour Tristesse Brassierre Company)." Another highpoint: EDDIE FOY, JR., singing "It's a Simple Little System" about his gambling racket that uses classical composers as code names.

BELLS OF ST. MARY'S, THE (Rainbow/RKO 1945) was a tame sequel to *GOING MY WAY* (1944) with BING CROSBY reprising his role of Father Chuck O'Malley and JOHNNY BURKE and JAMES VAN HEUSEN again providing Crosby with a hit song, "Aren't You Glad You're You?," which he sang to the dejected youth Joan Carroll. The understanding priest is transferred to a poor parish where the school is run by the not-so-understanding Sister Superior Ingrid Bergman, and the two clash before sentimentality conquers all. LEO McCAREY directed the melodrama (it had only four songs and one of them was a hymn) and it was nearly as popular as *Going My Way*.

BENCHLEY, ROBERT (1889–1945), the noted American humorist and theatre critic, dabbled in film from the early talkies, writing and appearing in a series of comic shorts and later playing supporting roles in feature films. Benchley usually was the dapper, witty friend to the hero, as seen in such musicals as *DANCING LADY* (1933), *YOU'LL NEVER GET RICH* (1941), *The Sky's the Limit* (1943), *Pan-American* (1945), *The Stork Club* (1945), and others. He can be heard doing the droll narration in *ROAD TO UTOPIA* (1945).

BENNETT, JOAN (1910–1990) was a delicate leading lady in films for over thirty years, playing a variety of roles and starring in eight musicals even though she rarely sang. On screen from 1928, Bennett's first musical was *PUTTIN' ON THE RITZ* (1930), followed by *Maybe It's Love* (1930), *Careless Lady* (1932), *MISSISSIPPI* (1935), *Two for Tonight* (1935), *Vogues of 1938* (1937), *ARTISTS AND MODELS ABROAD* (1938), and *Nob Hill* (1957).

BENNY, JACK (1894–1974), the quiet yet commanding comic genius who conquered radio and later television, had an on-and-off movie career beginning with a brief appearance as himself in *HOLLYWOOD REVUE OF 1929*. Sometimes playing a leading role, other times as a featured guest, Benny was seen in the musicals *Chasing Rainbows* (1930), *Transatlantic Merry-Go-Round* (1934), *BROADWAY MELODY OF 1936* (1935), *THE BIG BROADCAST OF 1937* (1936), *ARTISTS AND MODELS* (1937), *ARTISTS AND MODELS ABROAD* (1938), *Man About Town* (1940), *Buck Benny Rides Again* (1940), and *LOVE THY NEIGHBOR* (1940). He also made cameo appearances in *HOLLYWOOD CANTEEN* (1944), *Somebody Loves Me* (1952), *Beau James* (1957), and *GYPSY* (1962). Benny's on-stage persona, the violin-playing miser who was eternally thirty-nine years old, carried over into many of his films, and he often brought his radio co-stars EDDIE ANDERSON, KENNY BAKER, and DENNIS DAY with him to the screen.

BERGEN, EDGAR (1903–1978), the premiere ventriloquist of his era, and his nemesis, the wooden dummy Charlie McCarthy, were favorites on the radio, and the arguing duo appeared as themselves in a handful of movie musicals: *THE GOLDWYN FOLLIES* (1938), *Here We Go Again* (1942), *STAGE DOOR CANTEEN* (1943), *Fun and Fancy Free* (1946), and others. The pair was last seen on film in a cameo in *THE MUPPET MOVIE* (1979), which creator Jim Henson dedicated to Bergen. He was the father of actress Candice Bergen.

BERGMAN, ALAN (1925–   ) and his wife and co-lyricist **MARILYN** (1929–   ) provided the words for a handful of song hits first heard in nonmusicals: "The Windmills of Your Mind," "The Way We Were," "What Are You Doing for the Rest of Your Life?," and others. They contributed songs to the musical remake *A STAR IS BORN* (1976) and, with long-time collaborator MICHEL LEGRAND, wrote the score for *YENTL* (1983).

BERKELEY, BUSBY (1895–1976) was one of Hollywood's most distinctive choreographers, creating new methods to film dance and inventing ways to make the camera dance as well. Berkeley was known for his spectacular musical numbers using a large chorus (often all-female) and filming it from odd angles, such as through dancer's legs or from above, letting human bodies form moving kaleidoscopic patterns. A veteran Broadway choreographer, Berkeley was brought to Hollywood by SAMUEL GOLDWYN in 1930 to stage the musical numbers in a series of EDDIE CANTOR vehicles. After gaining notice in *WHOOPEE* (1930), *Palmy Days* (1931), and *The Kid From Spain* (1932), he went to WARNER BROTHERS, where he revitalized the movie musical with his dances for *42ND STREET* (1933), *GOLD DIGGERS OF 1933*, *FOOTLIGHT PARADE* (1933), *ROMAN SCANDALS* (1933), *DAMES* (1934), and others. With *GOLD DIGGERS OF 1935*, Berkeley sometimes directed as well as choreographed his films. But it was still his lavish, sometimes vulgar, but always stupendous dance numbers that shone. Other outstanding musicals from the nearly fifty he worked on include *GO INTO YOUR DANCE* (1935), *GOLD DIGGERS OF 1937* (1936), *BABES IN ARMS* (1939), *STRIKE UP THE BAND* (1940), *ZIEGFELD GIRL* (1941), *BABES ON BROADWAY* (1940), *FOR ME AND MY GAL* (1942), *CABIN IN THE SKY* (1943), *THE GANG'S ALL HERE* (1943), *TAKE ME OUT TO THE BALL GAME* (1949), *Call Me Mister* (1951), *Easy to Love* (1953), *ROSE MARIE* (1954), and *JUMBO* (1962).

BERLE, MILTON (1908–), the broad comic who sold millions of television sets in the 1950s because of his popular television show, had appeared in silent movies, toured vaudeville, appeared on Broadway, and then returned to the movies in the late 1930s, playing sidekicks in a handful of musicals such as *New Faces of 1937*, *SUN VALLEY SERENADE* (1941), *Rise and Shine* (1941), and *Always Leave Them Laughing* (1949). Berle played himself in *Let's Make Love* (1960) and made cameo appearances in the musicals *Can Heironymus Merkin Ever Forget Mercy Humppe and Find True Happiness?* (1969) and *THE MUPPET MOVIE* (1979).

BERLIN, IRVING (1888–1989), America's most popular songwriter, maintained phenomenally successful careers on Broadway and Tin Pan Ally while scoring twenty film musicals. Some of these included Berlin standards already popular but the prolific composer-lyricist also wrote dozens of song hits directly for the movies. Berlin's first screen assignment was *HALLELUJAH* (1929), followed by the early musicals *PUTTIN' ON THE RITZ* (1930), *Mammy* (1930), and *Reaching for the Moon* (1931). With *TOP HAT* (1935), Berlin scored a series of unforgettable screen classics including *FOLLOW THE*

FLEET (1936), *ON THE AVENUE* (1937), *ALEXANDER'S RAGTIME BAND* (1938), *CAREFREE* (1938), *HOLIDAY INN* (1942), *BLUE SKIES* (1946), *EASTER PARADE* (1948), *WHITE CHRISTMAS* (1954), and *THERE'S NO BUSINESS LIKE SHOW BUSINESS* (1954). Of his many Broadway shows, the only ones brought to the screen were *Louisiana Purchase* (1941), *THIS IS THE ARMY* (1943), *ANNIE GET YOUR GUN* (1950), and *CALL ME MADAM* (1953). Berlin's songs were sometimes unsophisticated and direct but often heartfelt and endearing, whether about love, patriotism, or national holidays.

BERMAN, PANDRO S. (1905–1996) was a proficient producer at RKO in the 1930s and at MGM thereafter, presenting a wide range of musicals from seven FRED ASTAIRE–GINGER ROGERS films to the ELVIS PRESLEY vehicle *JAILHOUSE ROCK* (1957). Berman's movies were known for their quality production standards as well as their high entertainment value. His twenty musicals include *Hips Hips Hooray* (1934), *THE GAY DIVORCEE* (1934), *ROBERTA* (1935), *TOP HAT* (1935), *FOLLOW THE FLEET* (1936), *SWING TIME* (1936), *SHALL WE DANCE* (1937), *A DAMSEL IN DISTRESS* (1937), *Having Wonderful Time* (1938), *CAREFREE* (1938), *ZIEGFELD GIRL* (1941), *RIO RITA* (1942), and *LOVELY TO LOOK AT* (1952).

BERNIE, BEN (1891–1943) was a popular bandleader who usually played himself in a handful of musicals in the 1930s. The nasal-sounding Bernie had a celebrated feud with columnist Walter Winchell, which was the subject of *WAKE UP AND LIVE* (1937) and *Love and Hisses* (1937).

BERNSTEIN, LEONARD (1918–1990), the celebrated composer and internationally acclaimed conductor, found time in his busy career to score five Broadway musicals, two of which were filmed: *ON THE TOWN* (1949) and *WEST SIDE STORY* (1961). He also composed the soundtrack for the nonmusical *On the Waterfront* (1954).

BEST FOOT FORWARD (MGM 1943) retained much of the zest of the 1941 Broadway hit, including the rousing fight song "Buckle Down, Winsocki" by HUGH MARTIN and RALPH BLANE. With the country now at war, producer ARTHUR FREED changed Winsocki Prep to Winsocki Military Academy, where student Tommy Dix has invited a movie star to a school dance and complications follow when she accepts. LUCILLE BALL played the glamorous celebrity and (with dubbing by Gloria Grafton) sang "You're Lucky" to the cadets. NANCY WALKER and JUNE ALLYSON, both from the Broadway production, made their film debuts as two of the coeds and they were joined by GLORIA DeHAVEN, WILLIAM GAXTON, VIRGINIA WEIDLER, Kenny Bowers, CHILL WILLS, and HARRY JAMES and his

Music Makers. Also in the Martin-Blane score was "Alive and Kicking," "The Three B's," and the new "Wish I May, Wish I Might."

BIG BROADCAST, THE (Paramount 1932) capitalized on the popularity of radio during the Depression and allowed fans to see what some of their favorite radio stars looked like. The result was so successful that the film spawned three sequels and encouraged other studios to make broadcast-based movies. The thin plot by George Marion, Jr., centered on the rivalry between airwaves singer BING CROSBY and Texas millionaire STUART ERWIN over the affections of Leila Hyams, but the story was happily interrupted by a dozen performing radio stars. KATE SMITH sang "It Was So Beautiful" and her theme song "When the Moon Comes Over the Mountain," CAB CALLOWAY delivered "Minnie the Moocher" and "Kickin' the Gong Around" with his orchestra, the MILLS BROTHERS harmonized through "Tiger Rag" and "Goodbye Blues," Vincent Lopez and his Orchestra played their trademark "Nola," and Crosby got to sing his theme song "Where the Blue of the Night Meets the Gold of the Day" as well as "Please," "Dinah," and "Here Lies Love." ***THE BIG BROADCAST OF 1936*** (1935) dealt with both radio and the newfangled invention of the "radio eye" (an early form of television). Broadcast singer JACK OAKIE goes by the moniker Lochinvar on the airwaves, but his singing is actually dubbed by Henry Wadsworth (whose actual singing was dubbed by KENNY BAKER). When the rich countess LYDA ROBERTI comes to woo Lochinvar, complications involve GEORGE BURNS and GRACIE ALLEN. Crosby was on hand again to sing "I Wished on the Moon" and he was joined by the NICHOLAS BROTHERS, BILL ROBINSON, ETHEL MERMAN, Amos 'n' Andy, and even the Vienna Boys Choir. The merry score, by various tunesmiths, also included "Double Trouble," "It's the Animal in Me," "Why Dream?," and "Miss Brown to You." ***THE BIG BROADCAST OF 1937*** (1936) continued the series, this time pitting small-town radio announcer SHIRLEY ROSS against tenor star Frank Forrest while radio network owner JACK BENNY had to deal with Burns and Allen, sponsors of the station's "Platt Golf Ball Hour." BENNY GOODMAN provided the swing music, LEOPOLD STOKOWSKI represented the classics, and LEO ROBIN and RALPH RAINGER supplied such delightful songs as "Vote for Mr. Rhythm" (wailed by MARTHA RAYE), "I'm Talking Through My Heart," "Here's Love in Your Eye," and "You Came to My Rescue." Perhaps the best entry in the series was the last: ***THE BIG BROADCAST OF 1938***. A transatlantic race between two ocean liners provided the plot and W. C. FIELDS played both shipping tycoon J. Frothingale Bellows and his twin brother, but it was the broadcasts from the ships that provided the musical fun. Radio emcee BOB HOPE (in his film debut) introduced such stars as DOROTHY LAMOUR singing "You Took the Words Right Out of My Mouth," opera diva Kirsten Flagstad bellowing Brunnhilde's "War Cry" from *Die Walkuere,* and Raye clowning around with "Mama, That Moon Is

Here Again." But the highlight of the film was Hope and ex-wife Ross singing the Oscar-winning "Thanks for the Memory" by Rainger and Robin, one of the decade's most touching musical sequences.

BILLY ROSE'S JUMBO. See *Jumbo*

BING, HERMAN (1889–1947) was a thick-accented, easily excitable German character actor who spiced up many a film operetta or musical, including *FOOTLIGHT PARADE* (1933), *THE MERRY WIDOW* (1934), *In Caliente* (1935), *ROSE MARIE* (1936), *THE GREAT ZIEGFELD* (1936), *MAYTIME* (1937), *SWEETHEARTS* (1938), *BITTERSWEET* (1940), and *NIGHT AND DAY* (1946).

BIOGRAPHICAL MUSICALS have provided Hollywood with some of its most lucrative products, especially when a tunesmith's catalog of songs was available and guest stars could be plugged into specialty spots for an all-star bonanza. It seemed to be an unwritten rule that the facts be greatly distorted, even more so than the typical Hollywood biography. Sometimes the real story was too dull, other times too sensational. Usually the biographical musicals aimed to please audiences looking for a rags-to-riches story interrupted by familiar songs and glittering productions numbers. *NIGHT AND DAY* (1946), about COLE PORTER, and *WORDS AND MUSIC* (1948), about RODGERS and HART, were among the least accurate examples but both were extremely popular. The musical bio that started the gold rush was *THE GREAT ZIEGFELD* (1936), which told a laundered history of the Broadway impresario Florenz Ziegfeld (played by WILLIAM POWELL) but filled the screen with eye-popping spectacle and a thrilling collection of songs from the past. The film won the Best Picture Oscar, and all the studios jumped on the biographical band wagon. The lives and careers of songwriters Paul Dresser, Stephen Foster, Chauncey Olcott, VICTOR HERBERT, Scott Joplin, John Philip Sousa, GUS KAHN, KALMAR and RUBY, SIGMUND ROMBERG, GEORGE GERSHWIN, De SYLVA, (LEW) BROWN, and HENDERSON, and JEROME KERN have all been filmed. Entertainers and musicians AL JOLSON, the Dolly Sisters, Anna Held, Jenny Lind, Billie Holiday, Eddie Foy, Eva Tanguay, Pearl White, GEORGE RAFT, Nora Bayes, FANNY BRICE, LILLIAN ROTH, Ruth Etting, EDDIE CANTOR, GLENN MILLER, the DORSEY brothers, Vernon and Irene Castle, Jane Froman, HELEN MORGAN, MARILYN MILLER, BENNY GOODMAN, EDDY DUCHIN, GYPSY ROSE LEE, Gertrude Lawrence, GENE KRUPA, GRACE MOORE, Bix Beiderbecke, Red Nichols, Joe E. Lewis, Enrico Caruso, Woody Guthrie, Charlie "Bird" Parker, Buddy Holly, Loretta Lynn, ELVIS PRESLEY, Ritchie Valens, and many others have all received the musical bio treatment, sometimes with actors who barely resembled them in the roles. Arguably the most entertaining of all biographical musicals was *YANKEE DOODLE DANDY*

(1942), in which the truth was stretched but JAMES CAGNEY captured the charisma and talent of showman GEORGE M. COHAN. The musical bio noticeably missing is one for IRVING BERLIN, who strongly guarded his privacy and would not let the studios film his life or career. (Also see CLASSICAL COMPOSERS for films based on their lives.)

BIRD (Warner 1988) was an appropriately somber biography of Charlie "Bird" Parker, the brilliant alto saxophonist who died at the age of thirty-four after an influential but self-destructive career in jazz. Forest Whitaker portrayed Parker, but what came out of his sax were authentic recordings that Parker had made in the early 1950s. Charles McPherson and other jazz musicians supplied the stunning soundtrack, which included Parker standards "All of Me," "Laura," "This Time the Dream's on Me," "Cool Blues," and "April in Paris." Clint Eastwood directed a cast that also included Diana Venora, Keith David, Michael Zelniker, and Samuel E. Wright as Parker's friend Dizzy Gillespie.

BIRTH OF THE BLUES (Paramount 1941) was the first Hollywood musical to deal with the history of jazz and the blues, yet the BING CROSBY vehicle seemed more like a traditional backstager than a chronicle of a musical movement. Clarinetist Crosby puts together a Dixieland jazz band in New Orleans, incorporating trumpeter Brian Donlevy, trombonist Jack Teagarden (who did his own playing), and band singer MARY MARTIN, and fights for recognition in a town content with the waltz. Eventually the musicians find popularity and head up river to Chicago and fame and fortune. Martin gave what is arguably her finest movie performance, singing "Cuddle Up a Little Closer," joining Crosby on "Wait Till the Sun Shines, Nellie," and letting loose with Teagarden and Crosby on the sly number "The Waiter, and the Porter and the Upstairs Maid" by JOHNNY MERCER. Other highlights include Ruby Elzy's impassioned rendition of "St. Louis Blues," Crosby's singing of "My Melancholy Baby," and the title song by B.G. DE SYLVA, LEW BROWN, and RAY HENDERSON.

BLACK MUSICALS. See African American Musicals

BLAINE, VIVIAN (1921–1995), a former band singer, was usually featured as such in several 1940s musicals, including *Jitterbugs* (1943), *Something for the Boys* (1944), *STATE FAIR* (1945), *Doll Face* (1945), and *THREE LITTLE GIRLS IN BLUE* (1946). Her greatest role was that of the ditzy showgirl Miss Adelaide in *GUYS AND DOLLS* (1955), which she had created on Broadway in 1950.

BLAIR, JANET (1921–   ) often played the wholesome girl-next-door in a handful of 1940s musicals such as *Broadway* (1942), *Something to Shout About*

(1943), *Tonight and Every Night* (1944), *Tars and Spars* (1946), and *The Fabulous Dorseys* (1947). Originally a singer with Hal Kemp's orchestra, Blair returned to nightclub singing in the 1950s with a few scattered credits thereafter, such as Mama Bower in *The One and Only Genuine Original Family Band* (1968).

BLANE, RALPH (1914–1995) and his long-time collaborator **HUGH MARTIN** (1914–   ) went to Hollywood when their Broadway hit *BEST FOOT FORWARD* (1943) was filmed and stayed to score such musicals as *MEET ME IN ST. LOUIS* (1944), *Abbott and Costello in Hollywood* (1945), *Athena* (1954), *The Girl Rush* (1955), and *The Girl Most Likely* (1957). Although both men wrote music and lyrics, Blane served as lyricist only for composers HAROLD ARLEN, HARRY WARREN, and others, providing songs for *SUMMER HOLIDAY* (1948), *My Dream Is Yours* (1949), *My Blue Heaven* (1950), *Skirts Ahoy* (1952), and *The French Line* (1954). Also, Blane worked solo on the score for *One Sunday Afternoon* (1948).

BLONDELL, JOAN (1909–1979), the perennial wisecracking blonde in over eighty movies, was a regular in WARNER BROTHERS musicals in the 1930s, appearing in *GOLD DIGGERS OF 1933, FOOTLIGHT PARADE* (1933), *DAMES* (1934), *Broadway Gondolier* (1935), and *Colleen* (1936). For various studios she was featured in *Stage Struck* (1936), *GOLD DIGGERS OF 1937* (1936), *East Side of Heaven* (1939), *TWO GIRLS ON BROADWAY* (1940), *The Opposite Sex* (1956), *This Could Be the Night* (1957), and others. The wide-eyed comedienne returned to the film musical with the small part of Vi in *GREASE* (1978). Blondell was once married to DICK POWELL and later to producer Mike Todd.

BLORE, ERIC (1887–1959) was one of Hollywood's favorite character actors, a short rotund man with fussy mannerisms and forever playing frustrated butlers, hotel managers, and valets. He delighted audiences in five FRED ASTAIRE–GINGER ROGERS musicals, from *FLYING DOWN TO RIO* (1933) to *SHALL WE DANCE* (1937), as well as *FOLIES BERGÈRE DE PARIS* (1935), *I DREAM TOO MUCH* (1935), *JOY OF LIVING* (1938), *The Boys From Syracuse* (1940), *ROAD TO ZANZIBAR* (1940), *The Sky's the Limit* (1943), *HAPPY GO LUCKY* (1943), *ROMANCE ON THE HIGH SEAS* (1948), *Love Happy* (1949), and *Fancy Pants* (1950). Blore also provided the voice of Mr. Toad in the animated *Ichabod and Mr. Toad* (1949).

BLUE, BEN (1901–1975) brought his comedy, mime, and hoofing talents from vaudeville to the screen, usually appearing in specialty spots that capitalized on his sad-faced, deadpan delivery, and agile dancing. After appearing in a series of silents, Blue lit up such musicals as *Follow Your Heart* (1936), *HIGH, WIDE AND HANDSOME* (1937), *ARTISTS AND MODELS* (1937), *BIG*

BROADCAST OF 1938, FOR ME AND MY GAL (1942), *Broadway Rhythm* (1943), *TWO GIRLS AND A SAILOR* (1944), *Two Sisters From Boston* (1946), and *My Wild Irish Rose* (1947).

BLUE HAWAII (Paramount 1961) spent equal time showing off its star EL-VIS PRESLEY and the beautiful scenery in the new state. The plot had return-ing GI Presley forsaking his mother ANGELA LANSBURY and the family pineapple business in order to work for a travel agency showing pretty girls the sights of Honolulu. There were no less than fifteen songs along the way, in-cluding the title standard by LEO ROBIN and RALPH RAINGER and the new ballad "Can't Help Falling in Love" by Hugo Peretti, George David Weiss, and Luigi Creatore that was actually a sentimental waltz for the hip-swinging star to sing. NORMAN TAUROG directed a cast that also in-cluded Joan Blackman, Roland Winters, and Iris Adrian.

BLUE SKIES (Paramount 1946) was one of the most successful musicals of the decade, reuniting FRED ASTAIRE and BING CROSBY as a couple of song-and-dance men fighting over the same girl (Joan Caulfield) as they sang new and old IRVING BERLIN songs. It was rather too similar to their earlier *HOLIDAY INN* (1942) but no one seemed to mind, especially with twenty musical numbers ranging from the old "A Pretty Girl Is Like a Melody" to the new "You Keep Coming Back Like a Song." The most ingenious sequence in the film was Astaire dancing to "Puttin' on the Ritz" while eight miniature Astaires danced behind him on a split screen, all choreographed with rapid-fire precision by HERMES PAN. Since the plot followed the team's career from 1919 to 1946, each era had its own Berlin standards: "How Deep Is the Ocean," "Heat Wave," "All By Myself," "Always," and the title number. For the vaudeville section, Berlin wrote "A Couple of Song and Dance Men" for the movie, and the two stars were at their comic best performing it. Also very funny was BILLY DeWOLFE wandering in and out of the proceedings doing his signature comedy bits.

BLUTH, DON (1938–) was an animator for the DISNEY studios, work-ing on such musicals as *Robin Hood* (1973), *The Rescuers* (1977), and *Pete's Dragon* (1977), before setting out on his own and directing/animating *An American Tail* (1986), *Rock-a-Doodle* (1991), *An American Tale: Fievel Goes West* (1991), *Thumbelina* (1994), *A Troll in Central Park* (1994), *The Pebble and the Penguin* (1995), *ANASTASIA* (1997), and other animated musicals.

BLYTH, ANN (1928–), a multitalented dramatic actress and operatic singer, was a CHILD STAR on stage and screen before appearing in musicals as a teenager and later a leading lady. The dark-haired beauty was featured in minor musicals such as *The Merry Monahans* (1944) and *Bowery to Broadway* (1944) before playing Dorothy Caruso in *THE GREAT CARUSO* (1951), the waitress Kathie in *THE STUDENT PRINCE* (1954), the title role in *ROSE MARIE* (1954), the poet's daughter Marsinah in *KISMET* (1955), and the title torch singer in *The Helen Morgan Story* (1957).

BOCK, JERRY (1928–), the Broadway composer, and his lyricist partner **SHELDON HARNICK** (1924–) scored six stage musicals but only their long-running hit *FIDDLER ON THE ROOF* (1971) was filmed. "Sunrise, Sunset" is perhaps their most famous song, often used for wedding ceremonies.

BOLAND, MARY (1880–1965) excelled at playing madcap housewives or society matrons in dozens of films, starting with silent features in 1915 and later appearing in a handful of 1930s musicals. Boland can be seen in *Melody in Spring* (1934), *BIG BROADCAST OF 1936* (1935), *ARTISTS AND MODELS ABROAD* (1938), *New Moon* (1940), *ONE NIGHT IN THE TROPICS* (1940), and others.

BOLES, JOHN (1895–1969) was a handsome, if somewhat stiff, leading man who started in silents but saw his career soar when sound revealed his rich baritone singing voice. Boles was featured in such OPERETTA movies as *THE DESERT SONG* (1929), *RIO RITA* (1929), *MUSIC IN THE AIR* (1934), and *Rose of the Rancho* (1936), but he was also seen in Broadway-style musicals such as *KING OF JAZZ* (1930), *Careless Lady* (1932), *Stand Up and Cheer* (1934), *CURLY TOP* (1935), and *The Littlest Rebel* (1935), the last three with SHIRLEY TEMPLE.

BOLGER, RAY (1904–1987) will always be remembered as the Scarecrow in *THE WIZARD OF OZ* (1939), but the rubber-limbed dancer and comic also starred in a handful of Broadway shows and was featured in a dozen film musicals. Bolger made his screen debut doing a specialty in *THE GREAT ZIEGFELD* (1936) and was the comic relief in *ROSALIE* (1937) and *SWEETHEARTS* (1938) before achieving renown as the Scarecrow wishing for a brain. Subsequent musicals roles included hoofer Bunny Billings in *Sunny* (1940), struggling musician "Jack" in *Four Jacks and a Jill* (1941), frontier hoofer Chris Maule in *THE HARVEY GIRLS* (1945), celebrated Broadway dancer Jack Donahue in *Look for the Silver Lining* (1949), State Department official S. Winthrop Putnam in *April in Paris* (1952), and the villain Barnaby in *BABES IN TOYLAND* (1961), as well as a specialty spot in *STAGE DOOR CANTEEN* (1943). Bolger got to recreate his best stage role, the cross-dressing Charley Wykeham, on the screen in *Where's Charley?* (1952).

BOLTON, GUY (1885–1979), the author of many plays and musicals, saw several of his stage works transferred to the screen, and he wrote new material (or adapted his own) for silents and early talkies. As the librettist for the innovative team of Bolton-Wodehouse-KERN, he was one of the first writers to try to integrate story and songs. After seeing his stage hits *Sally* (1925), *Oh, Kay!* (1928), and *Lady, Be Good* (1928) filmed before the advent of talkies, Bolton worked on the sound versions of *Sally* (1929), *RIO RITA* (1929), *THE LOVE PARADE* (1930), *The Cuckoos* (1930), *DELICIOUS* (1931), *Girl Crazy* (1932), *ANYTHING GOES* (1936 and1956), *ROSALIE* (1937), *TILL THE CLOUDS ROLL BY* (1946), *WORDS AND MUSIC* (1948), and others.

BOONE, PAT (1934–   ), the squeaky-clean pop singer who rose to fame in the late 1950s, was featured in a half dozen film musicals, his gentle singing voice often compensating for his stiff acting. Boone made his screen debut in *Bernadine* (1957) and crooned though such subsequent movies as *April Love* (1957), *Mardi Gras* (1958), *All Hands on Deck* (1961), and *STATE FAIR* (1962). He is the father of pop singer Debbie Boone.

BORN TO DANCE (MGM 1936) was COLE PORTER's first screen assignment (though his Broadway songs had appeared in earlier films) and he did not disappoint, providing a rich and varied collection of songs like "I've Got You Under My Skin," "Rap Tap on Wood," and "Easy to Love." The plot contained the familiar backstage device of the star (VIRGINIA BRUCE) unable to go on and the newcomer (ELEANOR POWELL) taking her place at the last minute. There were also three sailors on leave (JAMES STEWART, SID SILVERS, and BUDDY EBSEN), which would become another cliché in time. But the most memorable number in the film, and one satirized for years after, was the finale, "Swinging the Jinx Away," set on a sleek, art deco battleship with FRANCES LANGFORD singing with white uniformed officers and Powell swinging down from the crow's nest to tap in rapid rhythm all over the shiny deck. Also on hand were UNA MERKEL, Raymond Walburn, REGINALD GARDNER, Alan Dinehart, and Georges and Jalna, under the direction of ROY DEL RUTH.

BORZAGE, FRANK (1893–1962) was known mainly as the director of heart-tugging "women's pictures" and soft-focused romances, but his prodigious career, spanning from silent comedies to 1950s melodramas, included eight musicals as well. Among his credits are *Song o' My Heart* (1930), *Flirtation Walk* (1934), *Shipmates Forever* (1935), *Smilin' Through* (1941), and *STAGE DOOR CANTEEN* (1943).

BOSWELL, CONNEE (1907–1976) was one of America's most popular recording stars of the 1940s and 1950s, singing with Big Bands and touring the States and Europe. She began her career (as Connie) on radio with her sisters Martha and Vet, the Boswell Sisters introducing hit songs and appearing together on screen in *THE BIG BROADCAST* (1932), *Moulin Rouge* (1934), and *Transatlantic Merry-Go-Round* (1934). The sister act broke up in 1935, but Connee went solo and was seen in *ARTISTS AND MODELS* (1937), *Kiss the Boys Goodbye* (1941), *Syncopation* (1942), *Swing Parade of 1946,* and *Senior Prom* (1959). A victim of polio as a child, Boswell always performed in an upright wheelchair, which she disguised under her long dresses.

BOX OFFICE CHAMPS for movie musicals are dominated by animated features that have, over the years since the first one in 1937, played to more patrons and brought in more dollars than live-action musicals. *THE LION KING* (1994) currently holds the record, having grossed $313 million since its initial release. Four other DISNEY musicals are near the top of the list: *Toy Story 2* (1999), *ALADDIN* (1992), *Toy Story* (1995), and *Tarzan* (1999), with the live-action *GREASE* (1978) coming close with $182 million in receipts. But these figures are deceiving and reflect box office prices paid in the 1990s. A more accurate and revealing way to look at box office champs is to adjust the grosses in terms of inflation of prices and see how older movies compare. The chart below shows which movie musicals are in the list of the one hundred best-selling films based on domestic sales and with the figures adjusted for inflation. Disney animated films still prevail, but the chart indicates that a variety of movies have been box office hits over the years.

Ranking	Musical/Year	Studio
3	*THE SOUND OF MUSIC* (1965)	20TH CENTURY–FOX
9	*THE JUNGLE BOOK* (1967)	DISNEY
10	*SNOW WHITE AND THE SEVEN DWARFS* (1937)	DISNEY/RKO
12	*101 Dalmations* (1961)	DISNEY
21	*FANTASIA* (1940)	DISNEY/RKO
24	*MARY POPPINS* (1964)	DISNEY
25	*THE LION KING* (1994)	DISNEY
27	*SLEEPING BEAUTY* (1959)	DISNEY
28	*GREASE* (1978)	PARAMOUNT
30	*Bambi* (1942)	DISNEY
34	*PINOCCHIO* (1940)	DISNEY/RKO
44	*BELLS OF ST. MARY'S* (1945)	Rainbow/RKO
48	*MY FAIR LADY* (1964)	WARNER BROTHERS
55	*WEST SIDE STORY* (1961)	Mirisch/ UNITED ARTISTS
56	*LADY AND THE TRAMP* (1955)	DISNEY
70	*ALADDIN* (1992)	DISNEY
85	*Peter Pan* (1953)	DISNEY
87	*FUNNY GIRL* (1968)	Rastar/COLUMBIA
91	*Toy Story* (1995)	Pixar/DISNEY

BOY FRIEND, THE (MGM-EMI 1971) was a spoof of a spoof about a play within a play and operated on so many levels that it started to resemble a psychedelic trip. But there was much to enjoy in the musical and it still holds up as a unique film experience. Producer-director KEN RUSSELL took Sandy Wilson's pastiche stage musical and used it as the vehicle that a down-and-out theatre company is performing on a poorly attended week-day matinee. A Hollywood producer (Vladek Sheybal) comes to the perfor-mance and, watching the ragtag production from a theatre box, imagines how he will film it in the BUSBY BERKELEY style. To complicate matters, leading lady Glenda Jackson has broken her leg and errand girl Twiggy has to go on for her while the company's manager Max Adrian vainly tries to impress the film mogul enough for him to take them all to Hollywood. Much of the charming Wilson score was retained, including the insipid "I Could Be Happy," the comic "It's Never Too Late to Fall in Love," and the delightful "A Room in Bloomsbury," and old standards "All I Do Is Dream of You" and "You Are My Lucky Star" were added with satisfying effect. Christopher Gable was Twiggy's leading man and lanky TOMMY TUNE (in his film debut) was certainly noticeable as an anxious hoofer. Also of interest were Tony Walton's stylized sets for both the stage and the fantasy sequences.

BRACKEN, EDDIE (1920–), a boyish-looking, bubbling comic who be-fuddled his way through several comedies, came to Hollywood to recreate his stage role of the inept chaperone JoJo Jordan in *TOO MANY GIRLS* (1940). In addition to many comic roles in nonmusicals, Bracken was seen as hapless characters in such musicals as *THE FLEET'S IN* (1942), *Sweater Girl* (1942), *STAR SPANGLED RHYTHM* (1942), *HAPPY GO LUCKY* (1943), *Out of This World* (1945), *Duffy's Tavern* (1945), *SUMMER STOCK* (1950), and *Two Tickets to Broadway* (1951), as well as the voice of the cockroach "archy" in the animated *Shinbone Alley* (1971).

BRADLEY, GRACE (1913–) was a pert redhead who played the attrac-tive "second girl" in several PARAMOUNT musicals, showing off her singing and dancing talents in *The Way to Love* (1933), *Stolen Harmony* (1935), *Rose of the Rancho* (1936), *ANYTHING GOES* (1936), *WAKE UP AND LIVE* (1937), *BIG BROADCAST OF 1938*, and others.

BRADY, ALICE (1892–1939), a distinguished actress on the stage and in si-lent films, became a favorite character player on screen in the 1930s portraying both comic and dramatic roles. Among her musical credits are *THE GAY DI-VORCEE* (1934), *GOLD DIGGERS OF 1935*, *ONE HUNDRED MEN AND A GIRL* (1937), *IN OLD CHICAGO* (1938), and *JOY OF LIVING* (1938).

BREAUX, MARC and his wife **DEEDEE WOOD** (1927–   ) created the choreography for a series of family films including *MARY POPPINS* (1964), *THE SOUND OF MUSIC* (1965), *The Happiest Millionaire* (1967), *CHITTY CHITTY BANG BANG* (1968), and *Huckleberry Finn* (1974). Wood also staged the dances for *LI'L ABNER* (1959) and Breaux did the choreography for *The Slipper and the Rose* (1976). Breaux has managed to keep his birth date a secret for decades.

BRECHER, IRVING S. (1914–   ), a comedy writer for notable vaudeville stars such as MILTON BERLE and AL JOLSON, contributed to the screenplays for the movie musicals *AT THE CIRCUS* (1939), *Go West* (1940), *BROADWAY MELODY OF 1940, DuBarry Was a Lady* (1943), *BEST FOOT FORWARD* (1943), *MEET ME IN ST. LOUIS* (1944), *Yolanda and the Thief* (1945), *SUMMER HOLIDAY* (1948), *BYE BYE BIRDIE* (1963), and others.

BREEN, BOBBY (1927–   ), the singing moppet who was the male equivalent to SHIRLEY TEMPLE, was featured in eight RKO musicals before retiring from the screen to become a nightclub singer. Breen was known for his unabashed sentimentality in acting and high-pitched trilling in singing. The boy soprano made his debut with *LET'S SING AGAIN* (1936) and continued to warble through *Rainbow on the River* (1936), *Make a Wish* (1937), *Hawaii Calls* (1938), *Fisherman's Wharf* (1939), and others.

BREMER, LUCILLE (1923–1996), a comely redheaded dancer who came from ballet, Broadway, and Radio City Music Hall, had a brief but notable career in some 1940s MGM musicals. Bremer played JUDY GARLAND's sister Rose in *MEET ME IN ST. LOUIS* (1944), the title role in *Yolanda and the Thief* (1945), and specialty spots in *ZIEGFELD FOLLIES* (1946) and *TILL THE CLOUDS ROLL BY* (1946). When the studio dropped her contract in 1947, she retired from the screen.

BRENDEL, EL (1890–1964) was a Scandinavian-accented character actor who specialized in gentle, innocent comedy in several 20TH CENTURY–FOX films. Brendel's musical credits, usually playing someone named Swenson, include *SUNNY SIDE UP* (1929), *Happy Days* (1930), *Just Imagine* (1930), *DELICIOUS* (1931), *Little Miss Broadway* (1938), *If I Had My Way* (1940), and *The Beautiful Blonde From Bashful Bend* (1949).

BRENNAN, WALTER (1894–1974), a veteran character actor of over 100 films and a three-time Oscar-winner, was a favorite on the movie and television screen playing everything from crusty rural types to slick villains. Brennan was featured in the musicals *KING OF JAZZ* (1930), *THE STORY OF VERNON AND IRENE CASTLE* (1939), *CENTENNIAL SUMMER* (1946), *The One and Only Genuine Original Family Band* (1968), and others.

BRESSART, FELIX (1890–1949) was an amiable German character actor who fled Nazi Germany and found a home playing sweetly comforting types in Hollywood films. The gentle Bressart was featured in such musicals as *Swanee River* (1940), *Bitter Sweet* (1940), *ZIEGFELD GIRL* (1941), *A Song Is Born* (1948), and others.

BRICE, FANNY (1891–1951), the Yiddish queen of comedy on stage and on the radio, never conquered the screen, but her few film appearances are treasured records of her considerable talents. After a specialty bit in *Night Club* (1928), she was featured in *MY MAN* (1928), *Be Yourself* (1930), and *Everybody Sing* (1938). Brice played herself in *THE GREAT ZIEGFELD* (1936) and did one of her famous comic routines in *ZIEGFELD FOLLIES* (1946). Her life inspired the movie musicals *FUNNY GIRL* (1968), *FUNNY LADY* (1975), and, more loosely, *Broadway Through a Keyhole* (1933) and *ROSE OF WASHINGTON SQUARE* (1939). Brice was once married to producer Mike Todd.

BRICUSSE, LESLIE (1931–   ), the successful composer-lyricist from the London and Broadway stage, provided the scores for *DOCTOR DOOLITTLE* (1967), *GOODBYE, MR. CHIPS* (1969), *SCROOGE* (1970), and *WILLY WONKA AND THE CHOCOLATE FACTORY* (1971), as well as several film soundtracks. Bricusse wrote the lyrics for *VICTOR/VICTORIA* (1982), and his stage musical *Stop the World—I Want to Get Off*, co-written with ANTHONY NEWLEY, was filmed in 1966 with Newley and in 1978 with SAMMY DAVIS, JR.

BRIGADOON (MGM 1954), the celebrated romantic fantasy by ALAN JAY LERNER and FREDERICK LOEWE, came to the screen as a ponderous dance piece plagued by bad judgment, the biggest being producer ARTHUR FREED's decision to film the pastoral tale in a studio with artificial flora and fauna. Whereas Lerner's plot, about a magical Scottish town that appears every 100 years, remained, half of the glorious score was dropped and replaced with distinctly un-Scottish dance. GENE KELLY and VAN JOHNSON played the vacationing Americans who stumble onto the village and CYD CHARISSE (singing by Carole Richards) and Virginia Bosler were their love interests. Salvaged from the 1947 Broadway score was "It's Almost Like Being in Love," "The Heather on the Hill," and "I'll Go Home With Bonnie Jean." VINCENTE MINNELLI directed, Kelly did the choreography, and CEDRIC GIBBONS designed the phony settings; it was not their finest hour.

BRISSON, CARL (1895–1958), a dapper, smiling leading man who found success on the London stage, made a few Hollywood films in the 1930s but never caught on. The charming Continental type was seen in *MURDER AT*

THE VANITIES (1934), *All the King's Horses* (1935), *Ship Café* (1935), and a few British film musicals.

BROADWAY MELODY, THE (MGM 1929) boasts a series of firsts in film history: the first all-talking musical film (*The Jazz Singer* had only a few lines of dialogue heard), the first use of Technicolor (for the vibrant "The Wedding of the Painted Doll" sequence), the first score (by ARTHUR FREED and NACIO HERB BROWN) written specifically for a film, the first original screenplay written for a musical, the first production shot in a large sound stage with some of the music prerecorded, and the first musical to win the Best Picture ACADEMY AWARD. In addition, it had a cunning backstage story and flashy production numbers that still hold up. Vaudeville performing sisters BESSIE LOVE and Anita Page see their act (and their hearts) broken up when a man (CHARLES KING) gets engaged to one of them but then falls in love with the other. All three were involved in a Broadway production of the title, so there was plenty of opportunity for song and dance. The score included "Harmony Babies," "You Were Meant for Me," "The Boy Friend," and the title song. HARRY BEAUMONT directed it, Irving Thalberg produced it, and MGM had a giant hit that spurred on the film musical genre. It also introduced a typical kind of backstage musical that would receive dozens of imitations. The original was most closely repeated with **TWO GIRLS ON BROADWAY** (MGM 1940), in which LANA TURNER and JOAN BLONDELL played the sisters and GEORGE MURPHY was the hoofer who came between them. None of the original songs were used but Freed, Brown, and ROGER EDENS provided "My Wonderful One, Let's Dance," which Turner and Murphy delivered with zest.

BROADWAY MELODY OF 1936 (MGM 1935) had little in common with *THE BROADWAY MELODY* (1929) except for another marvelous score by ARTHUR FREED and NACIO HERB BROWN and another backstage story, this one about Broadway producer ROBERT TAYLOR, who is being bribed by a vicious gossip columnist (JACK BENNY) but is saved by newcomer ELEANOR POWELL, who goes on stage in the leading lady's part at the last minute. The musical made Powell a star and added some new songs to the growing list of standards to come out of Hollywood: "Broadway Rhythm," "I've Got a Feeling You're Fooling," and "You Are My Lucky Star." Vilma and BUDDY EBSEN, UNA MERKEL, June Knight, FRANCES LANGFORD, and SID SILVERS filled out the supporting cast, and DAVE GOULD and ALBERTINA RASCH staged the glittering production numbers. The picture was a box office smash, so the inevitable **BROADWAY MELODY OF 1938** (MGM 1937) again featured Powell and Taylor putting on a Broadway show. Producer Taylor has trouble raising the money, but when Powell's race horse wins the grand prize, she saves the show once again and takes on the star role herself. SOPHIE TUCKER ran a boarding house for actors (and got to sing her signature song "Some of These Days") and her daughter, newcomer JUDY GARLAND, stopped the show by quietly singing the favorite standard "You Made Me Love You" to a picture of CLARK GA-BLE, thereby launching her film career. Among the other songs featured were "Your Broadway and My Broadway" sung by Tucker and Charles Igor Gorin, "Follow in My Footsteps" delivered by Powell, Ebsen, and GEORGE MURPHY, and "Everybody Sing" led by Garland and Tucker. The final film in the series, *BROADWAY MELODY OF 1940* (MGM 1940), paired Powell with FRED ASTAIRE (surprisingly, their only movie together) and the two created magic together dancing to "Begin the Beguine" on a shiny black floor and surrounded by stars. The song was by COLE PORTER, who also provided "I Concentrate on You," "I've Got My Eyes on You," and "Please Don't Monkey With Broadway." The last was sung by dance partners Astaire and Murphy, whose act is broken up when one gets a contract to dance with Powell on Broadway. In a way, the silly plot was a reversal of that for the original *The Broadway Melody* so the series had come around full circle.

BROADWAY MELODY OF 1938/1940. See *Broadway Melody of 1936*

BROADWAY MUSICALS have proved to be a primary source for films since before the advent of talkies. Broadway OPERETTA and musical comedy hits were often filmed, title cards even quoting from the famous songs that the new medium could not provide save a live orchestra in the pit. The first talkie, *THE JAZZ SINGER* (1927), was based closely on a 1925 Broadway success though the film chose its own songs, only one of which was original for the project. The first Broadway musical to arrive on the screen resembling its original production was the operetta *THE DESERT SONG* (1929), but *THE COCOA-NUTS* (1929) was the first to capture a wide audience, mostly because of the presence of the MARX BROTHERS. Over the years most Broadway musicals found their way to the screen even if sometimes the transfer bore little in common with the stage work. For example, COLE PORTER's 1928 Broadway musical *ROSALIE* was filmed in 1937 with none of the stage score remaining, though Porter provided a whole new one for the screen. When his *ANYTHING GOES* was filmed in 1956, some of the songs remained but the plot had little to do with the stage libretto. *Irma la Douce*, a popular 1960 Broadway musical from France and England, was brought to the screen in 1963 with all the stage songs deleted and no new ones replacing them. Despite Hollywood's seemingly cavalier approach to stage musicals, the industry always felt a movie musical based on a Broadway show had more class. Of the nine musical films to win the Best Picture ACADEMY AWARD, five were screen versions of Broadway hits. The most often filmed musicals over the decades have been *SHOW BOAT* and *THE DESERT SONG* (each made into a talkie three times). Among the many Broadway musicals filmed twice were *Girl Crazy, GOOD NEWS, HIT THE DECK, THE MERRY*

WIDOW, New Moon, No No Nanette, RIO RITA, ROBERTA, ROSE MARIE, Sunny, and *The Vagabond King.*

BRODERICK, HELEN (1891–1959) was a deadpan comic who left the stage to play worldly-wise dames or tell-it-like-it-is aunts in such movie musicals as *TOP HAT* (1935), *To Beat the Band* (1935), *SWING TIME* (1936), *Life of the Party* (1937), *Naughty But Nice* (1939), *No No Nanette* (1940), *STAGE DOOR CANTEEN* (1943), and *Chip Off the Old Block* (1944). She was the mother of actor Broderick Crawford.

BRODSZKY, NICHOLAS (1905–1958) was an operetta-flavored composer who provided challenging music for MARIO LANZA, JANE POWELL, KATHRYN GRAYSON, and others to sing in movie musicals. With lyricist SAMMY CAHN he scored *The Toast of New Orleans* (1950), *Rich, Young and Pretty* (1951), *Meet Me in Las Vegas* (1956), *The Opposite Sex* (1956), and *Ten Thousand Bedrooms* (1957); with LEO ROBIN, *Small Town Girl* (1953) and *Latin Lovers* (1953); and with PAUL FRANCIS WEBSTER, interpolations for *THE STUDENT PRINCE* (1954).

BROOKS, JACK (1912–1971) wrote lyrics for a variety of Hollywood composers at several studios, even putting words to Rimsky-Korsakoff's music for *Song of Scheherezade* (1947). Other musical credits include *Melody Lane* (1941), *The Countess of Monte Cristo* (1948), *SON OF PALEFACE* (1952), *ARTISTS AND MODELS* (1956), and *Cinderfella* (1960). Brooks' most popular song was "That's Amore," which he wrote with composer HARRY WARREN for *The Caddy* (1953).

BROWN, JOE E. (1892–1973) was the wide-mouthed comic from vaudeville who was featured in a series of low-budget comedies after the advent of sound. Brown also appeared in a dozen musicals, usually displaying his acrobatic and farcical talents, such as *ON WITH THE SHOW* (1929), *Hold Everything* (1930), *Bright Lights* (1935), *Sons o' Guns* (1936), *Pin-Up Girl* (1944), and *HOLLYWOOD CANTEEN* (1944), and as Cap'n Andy in the remake of *SHOW BOAT* (1951). His most remembered role was that of millionaire Osgood Fielding III in the semimusical *Some Like It Hot* (1959).

BROWN, LEW (1893–1958), of the Broadway songwriting team of DE SYLVA, Brown, and HENDERSON, saw his stage musicals *GOOD NEWS* (1930 and 1947), *Follow the Leader* (1930) based on their play *Manhattan Mary,* and *Follow Thru* (1930) brought to the screen, and he contributed lyrics to original film musicals such as *THE SINGING FOOL* (1928), *SUNNY SIDE UP* (1929), *Just Imagine* (1930), *Stand Up and Cheer* (1934), *Strike Me Pink* (1936), *Yokel Boy* (1942), and *Swing Fever* (1947). Ernest Borgnine portrayed Brown in the musical bio *The Best Things in Life Are Free* (1956).

BROWN, NACIO HERB (1896–1964) was one of the first composers to concentrate on scores for the early talkies, providing hit tunes with lyricist ARTHUR FREED for *THE BROADWAY MELODY* (1929), *HOLLYWOOD REVUE of 1929, Lord Byron of Broadway* (1930), *GOOD NEWS* (1930), *BROADWAY MELODY OF 1936* (1935), *BROADWAY MELODY OF 1938* (1937), and others. With other lyricists, Brown scored such films as *Take a Chance* (1933), *Wintertime* (1943), *Greenwich Village* (1944), and *The Kissing Bandit* (1948). "Singin' in the Rain" is perhaps his best-known song, but other hits include "You Were Meant for Me," "All I Do Is Dream of You," "You Are My Lucky Star," "Pagan Love Song," and "You Stepped Out of a Dream." The Brown-Freed catalog of songs supplied the score for *SINGIN' IN THE RAIN* (1952).

BRUCE, VIRGINIA (1910–1982) was a classic blonde beauty who was featured in Hollywood films of the 1930s and 1940s, though she never became a top-ranked star. Fondly remembered for introducing "I've Got You Under My Skin" in *BORN TO DANCE* (1936), Bruce was also seen in such musicals as *THE LOVE PARADE* (1929), *PARAMOUNT ON PARADE* (1930), *Safety in Numbers* (1930), *WHOOPEE* (1930), *Metropolitan* (1935), *THE GREAT ZIEGFELD* (1936), *When Love Is Young* (1937), *Pardon My Sarong* (1942), and *Brazil* (1944). She was once married to silent film star John Gilbert.

BUCHANAN, JACK (1890–1957), a popular debonair song-and-dance man of the London stage, had a sporadic film career. After conquering Broadway in the 1920s, he was featured in the Hollywood movies *Paris* (1929) and *MONTE CARLO* (1930) but then returned to England, where he appeared in British stage and film musicals for years. Buchanan reappeared on the American screen as the dapper *artiste* Jeff Cordova in *THE BAND WAGON* (1952).

BUCK PRIVATES (Universal 1941) was the war effort musical that made *bona fide* movie stars out of BUD ABBOTT and LOU COSTELLO and helped propel the career of the ANDREWS SISTERS as well. The two comics played necktie salesmen who, running away from the police, accidentally enter an Army induction center (they think it's a movie house) and soon find themselves fumbling through boot camp and military life. The top-billed Lee Bowman and Alan Curtis played fellow inductees, and the plot was supposed to deal with their adjustment to Army ways (Bowman was a rich socialite and Curtis was his bodyguard), but Abbott and Costello stole the show. The Sisters delivered their trademark number "Boogie Woogie Bugle Boy From Company B" and a swinging "Bounce Me Brother With a Solid Four" (both songs by DON RAYE and Hughie Prince), as well as the old favorite "I'll Be With You in Apple Blossom Time," which got a new lease on life. *Buck Privates* was the studio's top-grossing film of the year, and Abbott and Costello became box office gold for the rest of the war years.

BUDDY HOLLY STORY, THE (Columbia 1978) followed the formula rags-to-riches plot of BIOGRAPHICAL MUSICALS of the past, but Gary Busey's performance as the early rock-and-roll star was more authentic than most such efforts. The gangly, buck-toothed Busey captured the singer's stage persona (Busey did his own vocals) as well has his shy, awkward personality. The story followed the young Texan Holly as he struggled for recognition and eventually became the first white performer to sing at Harlem's Apollo Theatre. (His tragic death in a plane crash at the age of twenty-two was, oddly, not included in the film.) Holly's hit songs were all represented, including "That'll Be the Day," "Chantilly Lace," "Peggy Sue," "Rock Around With Ollie Vee," and "You Send Me."

BUGSY MALONE (Rank/Paramount 1976) was a novelty of a movie, a gangster spoof performed completely by preteens, but it had an odd charm, an accurate ear for pastiche, and an exceptional score by PAUL WILLIAMS. Scott Baio played the small-time hood of the title, Florrie Dugger was the aspiring chorine he befriends, and Jodi Foster lit up the screen as the saucy vamp who headlines at Fat Sam's speakeasy. The miniature sets and half-pint vintage autos of the 1920s were clever, and the playful tone was maintained by having whipped cream come out of the tommy guns that the gangsters sported. The score included the wistful ballad "Tomorrow," the rousing sing-along "You Give a Little Love," the tender torch song "Ordinary Fool," and the zesty title song that Williams himself sang over the credits. In England, where the film was much more popular than in the States, the musical has been done as a stage work on a few occasions.

BULLOCK, WALTER (1907–1953) was a journeyman lyricist who collaborated with composers Harold Spina, VICTOR SCHERTZINGER, JULE STYNE, and others on such musicals as *Follow Your Heart* (1936), *Nobody's Baby* (1937), *Little Miss Broadway* (1938), *Just Around the Corner* (1938), *The Blue Bird* (1940), and *Hit Parade of 1941* (1940). Among Bullock's most-known songs are "I Love to Walk in the Rain" and "When Did You Leave Heaven?"

BURKE, BILLIE (1885–1970), immortalized as the good witch Glinda in *THE WIZARD OF OZ* (1939), had a long and colorful life and career in show business. On the London stage as a youth, Burke became one of the most glamourous stars on Broadway in the 1910s, marrying producer Florenz Ziegfeld, who featured her in some of his shows. By 1916 Burke was wooed by Hollywood, where she appeared in many silent films before maturing into the fluttery character actress that delighted movies audiences for decades. Burke's other musical film credits include *Glorifying the American Girl* (1929), *Everybody Sing* (1938), *Irene* (1940), *What's Cookin'?* (1943), *Swing Out, Sister* (1945), *THE BARKLEYS OF BROADWAY* (1950), *Small Town Girl* (1953), and *Pepe* (1960). MYRNA LOY played Burke in the musical bio *THE GREAT ZIEGFELD* (1936).

BURKE, JOE (1884–1950) composed songs, often with lyricist AL DUBIN, for a handful of early musicals, including *GOLD DIGGERS OF BROADWAY* (1929), *Sally* (1929), *Hold Everything* (1930), *Top Speed* (1930), *Life of the Party* (1930), and others. His most remembered song is the Burke-Dubin standard "Tiptoe Through the Tulips."

BURKE, JOHNNY (1908–1964) was one of Hollywood's most reliable and successful lyricists, writing several hit songs over a three-decade career. With composer ARTHUR JOHNSTON, Burke scored *Go West, Young Man* (1936), *PENNIES FROM HEAVEN* (1936), and *DOUBLE OR NOTHING* (1937); with JAMES V. MONACO, *Doctor Rhythm* (1938), *SING YOU SINNERS* (1938), *East Side of Heaven* (139), *RHYTHM ON THE RIVER* (1940), and others. His most important collaborator was composer JAMES VAN HEUSEN, with whom he first worked with on *LOVE THY NEIGHBOR* (1940). They went on to score *Playmates* (1941), *Dixie* (1943), *GOING MY WAY* (1944), *And the Angels Sing* (1944), *Belle of the Yukon* (1944), *Cross My Heart* (1946), *A CONNECTICUT YANKEE IN KING ARTHUR'S COURT* (1949), *Ridin' High* (1950), and others, including five "Road" movies for BOB HOPE and BING CROSBY. In fact, Burke wrote more song hits for Crosby than did any other songwriter. Burke was an agile writer who could turn an everyday phrase into an intoxicating lyric. Among his most notable songs are "Pennies From Heaven," "Only Forever," "Moonlight Becomes You," "Personality," and "It Could Happen to You." The Burke–Van Heusen song catalog was celebrated in the 1995 Broadway musical revue *Swinging on a Star*.

BURNS, BOB (1896–1956) was a hillbilly comic on radio and film who was nicknamed the "Arkansas Philosopher" and "Bazooka" (after the odd wind instrument he invented and played). Burns usually portrayed rural characters with crusty common sense and was teamed up with MARTHA RAYE on several occasions. His musical credits include *The Singing Vagabond* (1935), *Rhythm on the Range* (1936), *THE BIG BROADCAST OF 1937* (1936), *Waikiki Wedding* (1937), *Tropic Holiday* (1938), and *Belle of the Yukon* (1944).

BURNS, GEORGE. See Allen, Gracie

BURNS, RALPH (1922–   ), the much-respected Broadway orchestrater and musical director, performed similar tasks for such movie musicals as *CAB-*

ARET (1972), *Mame* (1974), *NEW YORK, NEW YORK* (1977), *MOVIE MOVIE* (1978), *ANNIE* (1982), *The Muppets Take Manhattan* (1984), and others.

BUTLER, DAVID (1895–1979) was a reliable director of comedies and musicals who was highly valued by the studios during his long career for his efficient work methods and profitable results. Butler's thirty-odd movie musicals include *Fox Movietone Follies* (1929), *SUNNY SIDE UP* (1929), *High Society Blues* (1930), *Just Imagine* (1930), *DELICIOUS* (1931), *CAPTAIN JANUARY* (1936), *East Side of Heaven* (1939), *ROAD TO MOROCCO* (1942), *Shine On Harvest Moon* (1944), *My Wild Irish Rose* (1947), *Look for the Silver Lining* (1949), *Tea for Two* (1950), *Lullaby of Broadway* (1951), *April in Paris* (1952), and *CALAMITY JANE* (1953).

BUTLER, FRANK (1890–1967) started as a character actor in silent films but turned to scriptwriting with the advent of sound, collaborating on dozens of comedies, dramas, and musicals. Among Butler's most notable musicals are *BABES IN TOYLAND* (1934), *Waikiki Wedding* (1937), *ROAD TO SINGAPORE* (1940), *ROAD TO ZANZIBAR* (1941), *ROAD TO MOROCCO* (1942), *GOING MY WAY* (1944), *The Kid From Brooklyn* (1946), and *ROAD TO BALI* (1953).

BUTTERWORTH, CHARLES (1896–1946) specialized in innocent millionaires, academics, and other uppity types in many films from the early talkies to his untimely death in a car crash. Originally on the musical stage, the thin and sniffling comedian played supporting roles in the movie musicals *Life of the Party* (1930), *LOVE ME TONIGHT* (1932), *THE CAT AND THE FIDDLE* (1934), *Every Day's a Holiday* (1937), *The Boys From Syracuse* (1940), *Sis Hopkins* (1941), *THIS IS THE ARMY* (1943), *Follow the Boys* (1944), and many others.

BUZZELL, EDWARD (1895–1985) directed comedies and musicals at various studios after an acting career on stage and in early talkies. Buzzell's musical credits include *The Girl Friend* (1935), *Honolulu* (1939), *AT THE CIRCUS* (1939), *Go West* (1940), *Ship Ahoy* (1942), *BEST FOOT FORWARD* (1943), and *NEPTUNE'S DAUGHTER* (1949).

BYE BYE BIRDIE (Columbia 1963) boasted the star (DICK VAN DYKE in his screen debut), most of the songs (by LEE ADAMS and CHARLES STROUSE), and the basic plot of the 1960 Broadway hit, but the film turned into a showcase for the blossoming talents of ANN-MARGARET, who was supposed to be a perky high school girl but came off more like a star in ascendance. ELVIS PRESLEY–like rock star Conrad Birdie (Jesse Pearson) is drafted by the Army, so songwriter Van Dyke and his long-term fiancée

JANET LEIGH plan to have a teenager sing "One Last Kiss" to the departing singer on Ed Sullivan's television show. Complications involved Ann-Margaret's boyfriend Bobby Rydall and father Paul Lynde (from the stage production) as well as Van Dyke's interfering mother, Maureen Stapleton. The breezy spoof of rock-and-roll hysteria was ably directed by GEORGE SIDNEY, with ONNA WHITE providing the spirited dancing, particularly in the gossip number "The Telephone Hour" and Leigh's dance with a bunch of Shriners. Other songs carried over from the play were "Put on a Happy Face," "How Lovely to Be a Woman," "Kids," and "One Boy," as well as a title number that Adams and Strouse wrote for Ann-Margaret to sing over the credits because the studio insisted on a title song.

BYINGTON, SPRING (1886–1971), a beloved character actress on Broadway, film, and television (*December Bride*), excelled at playing ditzy matrons and animated relatives. Although she did not sing, Byington was featured in a handful of musicals such as *The Blue Bird* (1940), *Presenting Lily Mars* (1943), *IN THE GOOD OLD SUMMERTIME* (1949), and *Because You're Mine* (1952).

C

CABARET (ABC/Allied Artists 1972) was an uncompromising reworking of the 1966 Broadway hit, rethought in cinema terms and utilizing material from the play's source (Christopher Isherwood's short stories about Berlin in the late 1920s). Jay Presson Allen and Hugh Wheeler wrote the screenplay, dropping characters and plot lines from the stage version and adding new ones, and BOB FOSSE directed and choreographed, putting all the musical numbers save one in the small, smoky, tawdry Kit Kat Club. LIZA MINNELLI, in her first screen musical (unless you count her brief appearance as a toddler in *IN THE GOOD OLD SUMMERTIME*), lit up the screen as the eager, decadent nightclub singer Sally Bowles (changed from a Brit to an American for the film), and she was balanced by a calmly amused performance by Michael York as her bisexual lover. Joel Grey recreated his sleazy Emcee role from Broadway and was an icy and disturbing presence throughout the movie. Also in the cast were Helmut Griem as a millionaire that beds both the leads and Fritz Wepper and Marisa Berenson as a young Jewish couple whose dreams are thwarted by the growing Nazi party. Only six songs from the FRED EBB–JOHN KANDER score made it to the movie but the team wrote three news ones for the screen and all were gems: "Mein Herr," "Maybe This Time," and "Money Money." Grey and Minnelli handled most of the singing, belting out "Wilkommen," "If You Could See Her," and the title song, but the most chilling number was "Tomorrow Belongs to Me," a seemingly innocent anthem sung by young Nazi Oliver Collignon (dubbed by Mark Lambert) at an outdoor beer garden. Fosse's hypnotic choreography was remarkably effective on screen, and his movie career soared, though he never topped *Cabaret*.

CABIN IN THE SKY (MGM 1943) may have been filled with Negro folklore stereotypes, but this musical, one of the few with an all-black cast, still holds a lot of charm and boasts some of the finest screen performances by African Americans in the history of Hollywood. Small-time gambler Little Joe (EDDIE ANDERSON) often strays from the path of right, but his faithful wife Petunia (ETHEL WATERS) pulls him through with prayers and understanding. Joe dreams that he is killed in a night spot brawl and that the devil (Rex Ingram) and an angel (Kenneth Spencer) fight over his soul, even sending down the seductive Georgia Brown (LENA HORNE) to test his resistance. The characters were types but were handled with sincere dignity, especially when they sang the marvelous songs. From the 1940 stage score by John LaTouche, Ted Fetter, and VERNON DUKE came "Taking a Chance on Love," "Honey in the Honeycomb," and the title song; for the screen, E.Y. HARBURG and HAROLD ARLEN wrote "Happiness Is a Thing Called Joe," "Li'l Black Sheep," and "Life's Full of Consequence." Waters and Anderson gave the musical performances of their careers, and they were supported by LOUIS ARMSTRONG, John W. "Bubbles" Sublett, Willie Best, Butterfly McQueen, DUKE ELLINGTON and his Orchestra, and the Hall Johnson Choir. VINCENTE MINNELLI made an auspicious directorial debut, keeping the fantasy and folklore elements firmly in place.

CAESAR, IRVING (1895–1996), the Broadway and Tin Pan Alley lyricist, saw his stage hit *No No Nanette* filmed in 1930, 1940, and in 1950 as *Tea for Two*, after his most famous song. Caesar also contributed musical numbers to *George White's Scandals* (1934) and *CURLY TOP* (1935) in which SHIRLEY TEMPLE sang his "Animal Crackers in My Soup."

CAGNEY, JAMES (1899–1986), the hyperactive, fast-talking star of melodramas, comedies, and musicals, was able to play a variety of characters while maintaining his own distinct persona. After gaining attention for his gangster roles, Cagney went on to conquer the movie musical as well, playing the ambitious producer Chester Kent in *FOOTLIGHT PARADE* (1933), conniving bandleader Terry Rooney in *Something to Sing About* (1937), song-and-dance man GEORGE M. COHEN in the biopics *YANKEE DOODLE DANDY* (1942) and *The Seven Little Foys* (1955), producer-turned-cadet Elwin Bixby in *West Point Story* (1950), jealous husband Marty "Gimp" Snyder in *LOVE ME OR LEAVE ME* (1955), and ruthless union boss Jake MacIllaney in *Never Steal Anything Small* (1959).

CAHN, SAMMY (1913–1993), a prolific Tin Pan Alley and Hollywood lyricist, was nominated for Oscars thirty times and won four ACADEMY AWARDS during his long career working with a variety of composers. Although he often wrote theme songs for nonmusicals, Cahn also scored the musicals *Youth on Parade* (1942), *Thumbs Up* (1943), *Step Lively* (1944), *Tonight and Every Night* (1945), *ANCHORS AWEIGH* (1945), *IT HAPPENED IN BROOKLYN* (1947), *ROMANCE ON THE HIGH SEAS* (1948), *It's a Great Feeling* (1949), and others with composer JULE STYNE. With composer NICHOLAS BRODZSKY he wrote the songs for *The Toast of New Orleans* (1950), *Rich, Young and Pretty* (1951), *Meet Me in Las Vegas* (1956), and others. In the late 1950s, Cahn teamed up with composer JAMES VAN HEUSEN and contributed songs to such musicals as *Let's Make Love* (1960), *High Time* (1960), *THE ROAD TO HONG KONG* (1962), *ROBIN AND THE SEVEN HOODS* (1964) and *THOROUGHLY MODERN MILLIE* (1967). Other Cahn musicals include *Time Out for Rhythm* (1941), *She's Working Her Way Through College* (1952), *April in Paris* (1952), *Peter Pan* (1953), *Three Sailors and a Girl* (1953), *THE COURT JESTER* (1956), *Rock-a-Bye Baby* (1958), and *STAR!* (1968). Cahn wrote more songs for FRANK SINATRA than did any other songwriter (it is estimated the singer recorded over eighty Cahn songs) and provided lyrics for such hits as "I've Heard That Song Before," "High Hopes," "My Kind of Town," "Call Me Irresponsible," "The Tender Trap," "Be My Love," "I Fall in Love Too Easily," "It's Magic," "All the Way," and many others.

CALAMITY JANE (Warner 1953) may have been an attempt to cash in on the popularity of *ANNIE GET YOUR GUN* (1950), but this FRONTIER MUSICAL about another gun-slinging spitfire had plenty of its own to be proud of. DORIS DAY cut loose as the title character as she protected the Dakota stagecoach line, fetched a Chicago singing star (Allyn McLerie) for the local saloon, and chased after Wild Bill Hickock (HOWARD KEEL). It was beautifully filmed in Technicolor, had some spirited dances by JACK DONOHUE, and contained a tuneful score by PAUL FRANCIS WEBSTER and SAMMY FAIN that included "The Black Hills of Dakota," "Just Blew in From the Windy City," and the hit ballad "Secret Love." Dick Wesson, Philip Carey, Gale Robbins, and Paul Harvey were also in the cast, all under the firm direction of DAVID BUTLER.

CALHERN, LOUIS (1895–1956), a leading man in silents, became a favorite character actor in the 1930s and added a touch of class to any film in which he appeared. His handful of musicals include *ROAD TO SINGAPORE* (1931), *DUCK SOUP* (1933), *UP IN ARMS* (1944), *ANNIE GET YOUR GUN* (1950), *THE STUDENT PRINCE* (1954), and *HIGH SOCIETY* (1956).

CALL ME MADAM (Fox 1953) was one of the rare opportunities when ETHEL MERMAN got to recreate her stage role on film and the result was a blockbuster for the star and the 1950 IRVING BERLIN show. Washington socialite Sally Adams (Merman) is named ambassador to the small country of Lichtenberg, where she throws around American money like confetti, has a romance with a general, George Sanders, and matches up her secretary DONALD O'CONNOR with VERA-ELLEN. Almost all the Berlin songs made it to the screen version, including "The Hostess With the Mostes' (on the Ball),"

"It's a Lovely Day Today," "Marrying for Love," "Something to Dance About," "Can You Use Any Money Today?," and the hit contrapuntal duet "You're Just in Love." WALTER LANG directed the likable cast, which also included Walter Slezak, BILLY DEWOLF, Helmut Dantine, and Walter Woolf King.

CALLOWAY, CAB (1907–1994) was the energetic scat-singing bandleader who flourished for decades in nightclubs and theatres, on television and records, and in a few films scattered throughout his long career. Calloway and his band was featured in *THE BIG BROADCAST* (1932), *INTERNATIONAL HOUSE* (1933), *The Singing Kid* (1936), *Manhattan Merry-Go-Round* (1937), and *STORMY WEATHER* (1943). He also made solo appearances in *St. Louis Blues* (1958) and *The Blues Brothers* (1980).

CAMELOT (Warner 1967) took a while to come to the screen because the 1960 musical had such an unwieldy book, but ALAN JAY LERNER rewrote his libretto and the studio spent $15 million to create an opulent fairy tale world for the story of King Arthur (Richard Harris), his queen Guenevere (Vanessa Redgrave), and the knight Lancelot (Franco Nero, dubbed by Gene Merlino) who comes between them. JOSHUA LOGAN, somewhat past his prime, directed with a heavy hand, and despite all the castles (it was filmed in Spain) and glittering costumes, the movie rarely took off. Harris was an agreeable king, but the major surprise was Redgrave, seemingly miscast but presenting a witty, enchanting queen (and doing her own singing). Also in the cast were David Hemmings as the evil Mordred, Lionel Jeffries as the blustering King Pellinore, and Laurence Naismith as the wizard Merlin. Most of the Lerner and FREDERICK LOEWE Broadway score was used (such as "If Ever I Could Leave You," "The Lusty Month of May," "How to Handle a Woman," and the title song), but little of it was as effective on the screen. The picture lost millions at the box office and led the way for other overproduced Broadway adaptations that would help destroy the Hollywood musical.

CAN-CAN (Fox 1960) boasted SHIRLEY MACLAINE, FRANK SINATRA, MAURICE CHEVALIER, and a score by COLE PORTER, so the result should have been more delectable than this tired tale about café owner MacLaine, who gets in trouble with the law by allowing the scandalous can-can dance to be performed in her club. It was set in Paris in the 1890s, but much of it seemed like a 1950s product with lawyer Sinatra defending and falling in love with MacLaine, much to the chagrin of her lover Louis Jourdan, who confides in his friend, the easygoing judge Chevalier, just as he had in *GIGI* (1958). Juliet Prowse, in a supporting role, handled the dancing chores and was one of the livelier aspects of the film. Half of the 1953 Broadway score was dropped and the rest was misused (the beautiful ballad "I Love Paris" was sung only over the credits), while some Porter standards from other shows ("Let's Do

It," "Just One of Those Things," and "You Do Something to Me") were awkwardly added to give the stars plenty of hits to sing. Regardless, the picture was very popular and certainly helped MacLaine's career.

CANOVA, JUDY (1916–1983) was a loud-mouthed hillbilly comedienne known for her broad facial expressions and cackling yodel, which was heard in vaudeville, on Broadway, and on the radio. Republic Pictures featured her in a series of low-budget musical comedies and she made a few appearances in top-class features. Often playing someone named Judy, Canova was seen in *Going Highbrow* (1935), *In Caliente* (1935), *ARTISTS AND MODELS* (1937), *Sis Hopkins* (1941), *True to the Army* (1942), *Louisiana Hayride* (1944), *The WAC From Walla Walla* (1952), *The Adventures of Huckleberry Finn* (1960), and several others.

CAN'T HELP SINGING (Universal 1944) gave more than just a passing nod to the hit musical *Oklahoma!*, which opened on Broadway the year before. The FRONTIER MUSICAL captured the enthusiasm for land (there was even a rousing song celebrating "Californ-i-ay") and the pioneer spirit of *Oklahoma!*, yet the movie also had a charm all its own. Senator's daughter DEANNA DURBIN set off in 1847 for the West to wed an Army officer, but on the wagon train heading to California she fell in love with outdoorsman ROBERT PAIGE. E. Y. HARBURG and JEROME KERN provided the best original score of Durbin's career, mixing OPERETTA and Broadway in such songs as "Any Moment Now," "Swing Your Partner," "More and More," and the lilting title number. Ray Collins played the disapproving senator, and AKIM TAMIROFF and Leonid Kinskey supplied the humor as a pair of European fortune hunters bumbling across the prairie.

CANTOR, EDDIE (1892–1964) rolled his "banjo eyes" and sang in his thin yodeling voice for nearly five decades starting in burlesque, then in vaudeville and on Broadway. SAMUEL GOLDWYN brought him out to Hollywood to film Cantor's stage hit *WHOOPEE* (1930), and he soon became one of the top box office draws of the 1930s. Usually playing meek and mousy types who manage to outwit the villain and get the girl, Cantor starred in *Palmy Days* (1931), *The Kid From Spain* (1932), *ROMAN SCANDALS* (1933), *KID MILLIONS* (1934), *Strike Me Pink* (1936), *Ali Baba Goes to Town* (1937), *Forty Little Mothers* (1940), and *THANK YOUR LUCKY STARS* (1943). He made subsequent appearances in *HOLLYWOOD CANTEEN* (1944), *Show Business* (1944), and *If You Knew Susie* (1948). He played himself in *The Story of Will Rogers* (1952) and provided the singing voice for Keefe Brasselle in the bio musical *The Eddie Cantor Story* (1953). Cantor's radio show in the 1930s was very popular, and during his long career he popularized several hit songs, including "Dinah," "If You Knew Susie," "Ida, Sweet as Apple Cider,"

"Makin' Whoopee," "My Baby Just Cares for Me," and his theme song "One Hour With You."

CAPTAIN JANUARY (Fox 1936) was the first of four SHIRLEY TEMPLE films released that year, the busy moppet keeping the studio afloat and demonstrating her surprising vocal range (she even sang a section's of Donizetti's *Lucia di Lammermoor*) and heart-tugging theatrics. The shipwrecked Temple is rescued and raised by kindly old Captain January (GUY KIBBEE), but the purveyors of the law want to separate the two and put the child in an institution. Among all the melodramatics were some lively songs by SIDNEY MITCHELL, LEW POLLACK, and JACK YELLEN: the optimistic "Early Bird," the affectionate "The Right Somebody to Love," and the merry "At the Codfish Ball." BUDDY EBSEN joined Temple for a memorable dance routine, and Slim Summerville provided some rustic comedy as the captain's cribbage-playing friend.

CAREFREE (RKO 1938) gave FRED ASTAIRE a chance to play someone besides a song-and-dance man, but his portrayal of a psychiatrist, who is treating GINGER ROGERS because she can't decide whether or not to marry Ralph Bellamy, took some imagination on the audience's part. Astaire got to do a lot of hoofing all the same (including a tap routine on a golf course that HERMES PAN choreographed) and Rogers, falling in love with her doctor, got to pursue Astaire for once instead of the other way around. IRVING BERLIN wrote three new songs, and they were radiant: "Change Partners," "I Used to Be Color Blind," and the latest Berlin dance song "The Yam." JACK CARSON, Luella Gear, FRANKLIN PANGBORN, and HATTIE McDANIEL filled out the cast, and MARK SANDRICH directed zestfully.

CARLISLE, KITTY (1914–   ), the classy lady with an operatic voice and astute sense of fashion, was featured in a handful of musicals, usually playing the attractive ingenue: *MURDER AT THE VANITIES* (1934), *She Loves Me Not* (1934), *Here Is My Heart* (1934), *A NIGHT AT THE OPERA* (1935), *Larceny with Music* (1943), and *HOLLYWOOD CANTEEN* (1945). Carlisle later was a regular on television and a proponent of arts organizations. She was married to playwright Moss Hart.

CARLISLE, MARY (1912–   ) had a brief film career playing blonde coed types in such musicals as *College Humor* (1933), *Sweetheart of Sigma Chi* (1933), *Million Dollar Ransom* (1934), *DOUBLE OR NOTHING* (1937), *Doctor Rhythm* (1938), and others. Carlisle retired from the screen in 1942 and later ran the Elizabeth Arden beauty salon in Hollywood.

CARMEN JONES (Fox 1954) was OSCAR HAMMERSTEIN's adaptation of Bizet's opera *Carmen*, reset in the American South with Carmen (DORO-

THY DANDRIDGE, dubbed by Marilyn Horne) as a worker in a parachute factory and José as Joe (Harry Belafonte, dubbed by LeVern Hutcherson), an Army corporal who falls for the seductive lady. Filling out the all-black cast were Olga James as Cindy Lou, the girl who loves Joe, Joe Adams (dubbed by Marvin Hayes) as Husky Miller the prize fighter (instead of a matador as in the original opera), Diahann Carroll (dubbed by Bernice Peterson), PEARL BAILEY, and BROCK PETERS. Hammerstein supplied new lyrics for Bizet's music and the conceit worked better on Broadway, where the show was a hit in 1943. But many of the film's performances are riveting, and there is still that glorious Bizet music to enjoy. OTTO PREMINGER directed, perhaps too literally for the melodic piece.

CARMICHAEL, HOAGY (1899–1981), the distinctive songwriter, singer, pianist, and sometime actor, appeared in nine movie musicals, usually with a cigarette dangling from his mouth and playing the piano as he sang in his characteristic nasal twang. Carmichael could be seen in *Road Show* (1941), *True to Life* (1943), *Night Song* (1947), *The Las Vegas Story* (1952), *GENTLEMEN PREFER BLONDES* (1953), and other musicals, although his most famous role was as the piano player Cricket in the nonmusical *To Have and Have Not* (1944). Writing music and lyrics solo or with collaborators, Carmichael contributed to the scores of the above films as well as *ANYTHING GOES* (1936), *Every Day's a Holiday* (1938), *College Swing* (1938), *SING YOU SINNERS* (1938), *The Stork Club* (1945), *HERE COMES THE GROOM* (1951), *Three for the Show* (1955), and others. Although Carmichael had his greatest success with the Tin Pan Ally hit "Star Dust," his film scores produced such song favorites as "Two Sleepy People," "Heart and Soul," "My Resistance Is Low," and "In the Cool Cool Cool of the Evening."

CARMINATI, TULLIO (1894–1971) was a dashing continental leading man who moved back and forth from stage to screen and from Europe to Hollywood throughout his considerable career. Carminati made four movie musicals in America in the 1930s, playing romantic leads in *Moulin Rouge* (1934), *One Night of Love* (1934), *Let's Live Tonight* (1935), and *Paris in Spring* (1935).

CARON, LESLIE (1931–), a former French ballet dancer, was discovered by GENE KELLY, who cast her as his dancing partner Lise Bourvier in *AN AMERICAN IN PARIS* (1951). The slight, dark-haired beauty stayed in Hollywood, where she starred in a handful of musicals: as boxing fan Angela in *Glory Alley* (1952), the orphaned waif *LILI* (1953), the orphaned Ella in *The Glass Slipper* (1955), the orphaned French girl Julie André in *DADDY LONG LEGS* (1955), and the tomboy Parisian *GIGI* (1958). Caron usually had her singing dubbed, but her dancing talents and gamine charm made her a unique leading lady on film. She later moved on to dramatic roles in films and on stage.

CAROUSEL (Fox 1956) reunited SHIRLEY JONES and GORDON MacRAE, the romantic leads of the earlier RODGERS and HAMMER-STEIN movie musical *OKLAHOMA!* (1955), but this 1945 stage musical was a much more problematic piece and the film only intermittently came to life. The story of a boastful carousel barker (MacRae) who weds a cotton mill worker (Jones) but abuses her and dies in a payroll robbery was tricky melo-drama, with fantasy added when Billy returns from heaven to see his grown-up daughter (Susan Luckey). HENRY KING directed on location in Maine, yet much of the film looked artificial and was not enhanced by the wide-screen color treatment it received. But the score was glorious and just about all of it made it to the screen: "If I Loved You," "Soliloquy," "June Is Bustin' Out All Over," "Mr. Snow," "Blow High, Blow Low," "A Real Nice Clambake," " You'll Never Walk Alone," "What's the Use of Wonderin'?," and the intoxicat-ing "Carousel Waltz." Although the result was less than perfect, it might have been even less satisfying had FRANK SINATRA had not walked off the set but remained to play Billy as originally planned.

CARPENTER, CARLETON (1926–   ), a gangly, youthful hoofer and nightclub singer, played the juvenile lead in a handful of 1950s movies, includ-ing the musicals *THREE LITTLE WORDS* (1950), *SUMMER STOCK* (1950), and *Two Weeks With Love* (1950), in which he introduced "Aba Daba Honeymoon" with DEBBIE REYNOLDS. At the end of the decade he re-turned to nightclubs and later became a mystery writer.

CARR, ALLAN (1941–1999), a former artists' manager, turned to produc-ing (and sometimes scriptwriting) films in the 1970s, presenting the musicals *SATURDAY NIGHT FEVER* (1977), *GREASE* (1978), *Can't Stop the Music* (1980), and *Grease 2* (1982).

CARRILLO, LEO (1880–1961), a character actor in dozens of films begin-ning with the early talkies, specialized in playing amiable Hispanic characters and later found fame as the agreeable Pancho on *The Cisco Kid* television series. Carrillo's movie musicals include *In Caliente* (1935), *Manhattan Merry-Go-Round* (1937), *LILLIAN RUSSELL* (1940), and *Bowery to Broadway* (1944).

CARROLL, JOHN (1905–1979) was a mustached, Latin-looking leading man in Hollywood who often played dashing lovers in such musicals as *MONTE CARLO* (1930), *Rose of the Rio Grande* (1938), *Go West* (1940), *Sunny* (1941), *Lady, Be Good* (1941), *RIO RITA* (1942), *Hit Parade of 1943*, *Hit Parade of 1951* (1950), and *THE FARMER TAKES A WIFE* (1953).

CARROLL, NANCY (1905–1965) was one of the first stars of the talkies, a wide-eyed beauty who excelled at comedy and singing and captured the hearts of moviegoers in the 1930s as few others did. Often teamed with CHARLES

"BUDDY" ROGERS, Carroll starred in the musicals *The Shopworn Angel* (1929), *Close Harmony* (1929), *Sweetie* (1929), and *Honey* (1930). She was also featured in *PARAMOUNT ON PARADE* (1930), *Follow Thru* (1930), *Transatlantic Merry-Go-Round* (1934), *After the Dance* (1935), and *That Certain Age* (1938) before retiring from the screen in 1939.

CARSON, JACK (1910–1963), the stocky character actor who came from vaudeville, often played second leads ranging from heavies in westerns to buffoonish sidekicks in musicals. In the 1940s he appeared in a series of DORIS DAY musicals, such as *ROMANCE ON THE HIGH SEAS* (1948), *It's a Great Feeling* (1949), and *My Dream Is Yours* (1949). Other musical credits include *Having Wonderful Time* (1938), *CAREFREE* (1938), *Destry Rides Again* (1939), *Blues in the Night* (1941), *Shine On Harvest Moon* (1944), *April Showers* (1948), *Two Guys From Texas* (1948), *Dangerous When Wet* (1953), *Red Garters* (1954), and *A STAR IS BORN* (1954).

CASBAH (Marston/Universal 1948) was a musical remake of the Charles Boyer-Hedy Lamarr romantic intrigue *Algiers* (1938) with TONY MARTIN playing the French jewel thief Pepe Le Moko, Marta Toren as his love interest, and YVONNE DeCARLO as the tobacco shop owner who comes between them. But the finest performance came from Peter Lorre as Inspector Slimane, who hunts Pepe down. Although the story was not an improvement over the original, LEO ROBIN and HAROLD ARLEN wrote a rich and romantic score that included "It Was Written in the Stars," "Hooray for Love," "What's Good About Goodbye?," and "For Every Man There's a Woman."

CASTLE, NICK (1910–1968) was a much-in-demand choreographer who staged musical numbers for some fifty films at various studios from *Love and Hisses* (1937) to *STATE FAIR* (1962). Working with such stars as SHIRLEY TEMPLE, FRED ASTAIRE, JUDY GARLAND, BETTY GRABLE, and CARMEN MIRANDA, Castle provided dances for such musicals as *REBECCA OF SUNNYBROOK FARM* (1938), *Swanee River* (1939), *DOWN ARGENTINE WAY* (1940), *BUCK PRIVATES* (1941), *ORCHESTRA WIVES* (1942), *THIS IS THE ARMY* (1943), *SUMMER STOCK* (1950), *ROYAL WEDDING* (1951), *Red Garters* (1954), *ANYTHING GOES* (1956), *Rock-a-Bye Baby* (1958), and many others. He is the father of contemporary director Nick Castle.

CAT AND THE FIDDLE, THE (MGM 1934) came to the screen with all of its 1931 Broadway score by OTTO HARBACH and JEROME KERN intact, a rare feat for even the best of stage musicals. The plot, however, was greatly altered, though it still concerned an American songwriter (JEANETTE MacDONALD) and a Rumanian composer (Ramon Novarro) who meet at a music conservatory in Brussels, fall in love, move to Paris, and are troubled by her success and his lack of recognition. The movie's ending, in which prima dona Vivienne Segal walks out on Novarro's operetta and MacDonald fills in at the last moment, was fairly ridiculous, but the opening night performance was filmed in a new three-color Technicolor process that enthralled audiences. The lovely OPERETTA score included "Try to Forget," "The Breeze Kissed Your Hair," "The Night Was Made for Love," and "She Didn't Say Yes." Novarro's career was fading, but MacDonald, in her first MGM film, was gaining in popularity. Also in the cast were FRANK MORGAN, CHARLES BUTTERWORTH, Jean Hersholt, HERMAN BING, STERLING HOLLOWAY, and Frank Conroy.

CATLETT, WALTER (1889–1960), the comic character actor who specialized in scatterbrained sidekicks and frustrated officials, appeared in such musicals as *ON THE AVENUE* (1937), *WAKE UP AND LIVE* (1937), *My Gal Sal* (1942), *YANKEE DOODLE DANDY* (1942), *UP IN ARMS* (1944), *Dancing in the Dark* (1950), *HERE COMES THE GROOM* (1951), and others. Catlett also provided the voice of the fox J. Worthington Foulfellow in the animated classic *PINOCCHIO* (1940).

CENTENNIAL SUMMER (Fox 1946) was, without question, trying to copy *MEET ME IN ST. LOUIS* (1944) and rarely did it measure up, but the musical boasted JEROME KERN's last score, and the songs were as resplendent as the story and characters were mediocre. A Philadelphia family, parented by Dorothy Gish and WALTER BRENNAN, is caught up in the excitement of the 1876 Exposition in their home town, especially daughters Linda Darnell and JEANNE CRAIN (dubbed by Louanne Hogan), who both fall for Frenchman Cornel Wilde when he comes to visit the fair. The cast also included William Eythe, Barbara Whiting, Buddy Swan, Kathleen Howard, Avon Long, and Larry Stevens. Working with lyricists OSCAR HAMMERSTEIN, LEO ROBIN, and E.Y. HARBURG, Kern came up with the soulful ballad "All Through the Day," the rustic "Cinderella Sue," the cheerful "Up With the Lark," and the torchy "In Love in Vain." Despite such songs, very little of the film was involving, and director OTTO PREMINGER failed to capture the nostalgia or sense of Americana it so desperately needed.

CHAKIRIS, GEORGE (1933–   ) was a dark, dashing dancer of Greek origin who is most remembered for his tense portrayal of the Puerto Rican gang leader Bernardo in *WEST SIDE STORY* (1961). Under the name George Kerris, he appeared as a dancer in *Song of Love* (1947), *GENTLEMEN PREFER BLONDES* (1953), *BRIGADOON* (1954), *WHITE CHRISTMAS* (1954), *THERE'S NO BUSINESS LIKE SHOW BUSINESS* (1954), *The Girl Rush* (1955), and *Meet Me in Las Vegas* (1956). After his acclaim in *West Side Story*, Chakiris did only one other musical, *The Young Girls of Rochefort* (1967), before concentrating on dramatic roles on film and television.

CHAMPION, GOWER (1920–1980) and his wife and **MARGE CHAM-PION** (1921–   ) were featured as a dance team in a handful of 1950s musicals, sometimes choreographing as well. Gower moved from nightclubs and the Broadway stage to Hollywood at the end of World War Two and after marrying Marge Belcher in 1947 partnered with her in *WORDS AND MUSIC* (1948), *Mr. Music* (1950), *SHOW BOAT* (1951), *LOVELY TO LOOK AT* (1952), *Everything I Have Is Yours* (1952), *GIVE A GIRL A BREAK* (1955), *Jupiter's Darling* (1955), and *Three for the Show* (1955). After choreographing *The Girl Most Likely* (1957), Gower returned to Broadway and became one of the most successful director-choreographers of the 1960s and 1970s. The couple divorced in 1973, and Marge also turned to choreographing for television programs and nonmusical films. Before her dancing career took off, Marge Belcher was the model for the heroine of DISNEY's *SNOW WHITE AND THE SEVEN DWARFS* (1937) and the Blue Fairy in *PINOCCHIO* (1940).

CHAMPION, MARGE. See Champion, Gower

CHANDLER, CHICK (1905–1988) was a character actor who played a wide range of roles in melodramas, comedies, and musicals. Among his musical credits are *ALEXANDER'S RAGTIME BAND* (1938), *Swanee River* (1940), *SPRINGTIME IN THE ROCKIES* (1942), *Irish Eyes Are Smiling* (1944), *MOTHER WORE TIGHTS* (1947), *SHOW BOAT* (1951), *A STAR IS BORN* (1954), and *THERE'S NO BUSINESS LIKE SHOW BUSINESS* (1954).

CHAPLIN, SAUL (1912–1997) had notable careers as a Tin Pan Alley songwriter, Hollywood composer and musical arranger, and a film producer. Working with a variety of lyricists, Chaplin provided songs for *Rookies on Parade* (1941), *Redhead From Manhattan* (1943), *Meet Me on Broadway* (1946), *Merry Andrew* (1959), and others. But he was even more successful as an arranger of musical scores, working on such musicals as *ON THE TOWN* (1949), *SUMMER STOCK* (1950), *LOVELY TO LOOK AT* (1952), *KISS ME, KATE* (1953), *HIGH SOCIETY* (1956), and many more, winning Oscars for *AN AMERICAN IN PARIS* (1951), *SEVEN BRIDES FOR SEVEN BROTHERS* (1954), and *WEST SIDE STORY* (1961). As a producer, Chaplin presented *LES GIRLS* (1957), *CAN-CAN* (1960), *THE SOUND OF MUSIC* (1965), *STAR!* (1968), and others.

CHARISSE, CYD (1921–   ), the leggy, dark-haired beauty and one of the screen's finest dancing stars, was a member of the Ballet Russe as a teenager and soon found herself playing featured parts in such movie musicals as *Something to Shout About* (1944), *THE HARVEY GIRLS* (1946), *ZIEGFELD FOLLIES* (1946), *TILL THE CLOUDS ROLL BY* (1946), *Fiesta* (1947), *On an Island With You* (1948), *WORDS AND MUSIC* (1948), and *SINGIN' IN THE RAIN* (1952). Charisse graduated to such leading lady roles as prima

ballerina Gabrielle Gerard in *THE BAND WAGON* (1953), Scottish lass
Fiona Campbell in *BRIGADOON* (1955), boxing enthusiast Jackie Leighton
in *IT'S ALWAYS FAIR WEATHER* (1955), and Russian government official
Ninotchka Yoshenko in *SILK STOCKINGS* (1956). Her other musical credits
include *The Kissing Bandit* (1948), *Easy to Love* (1953), *DEEP IN MY
HEART* (1954), *Meet Me in Las Vegas* (1956), and *Black Tights* (1962). Although Charisse's singing was usually dubbed, her dancing talents were im-
peccable, partnering with FRED ASTAIRE and GENE KELLY in some of
their finest routines. Her second husband is singer TONY MARTIN.

CHARLOTTE'S WEB (Paramount 1973) animated and musicalized the
E.B. White children's classic without vulgarizing it, and the result was charming and entertaining. The spider Charlotte (voice of DEBBIE REYNOLDS)
sets out to save the pig Wilbur (Henry Gibson) from the slaughterhouse by
making him famous. The supporting cast of animal characters was voiced by
Paul Lynde, AGNES MOOREHEAD, Martha Scott, Rex Allen, and Dave
Madden. RICHARD M. and ROBERT B. SHERMAN supplied the tuneful
songs, including the gentle ballad "Mother Earth and Father Time," the
comic number "A Veritable Smorgasbord," and the haunting title song.

CHEVALIER, MAURICE (1888–1972), perhaps the greatest of all French
entertainers, was a star of stage and the cabaret before making his Hollywood
film debut in *INNOCENTS OF PARIS* (1929). Rarely straying far from his
bow tie/straw hat persona of a roguish *bon vivant*, Chevalier played variations
of the same amorous boulevardier for decades. After finding fame as the lusty
Count Alfred Renard in *THE LOVE PARADE* (1929), he starred in a series of
musical romances throughout the 1930s: *The Big Pond* (1930), *Playboy of
Paris* (1930), *THE SMILING LIEUTENANT* (1931), *ONE HOUR WITH
YOU* (1932), *LOVE ME TONIGHT* (1932), *A Bedtime Story* (1933), *The
Way to Love* (1933), *THE MERRY WIDOW* (1934), and *FOLIES BERGÈRE
DE PARIS* (1935), as well as memorable specialty numbers in *PARAMOUNT
ON PARADE* (1930). After several films made in Europe, Chevalier returned
to the American screen as the lovable old playboy Honoré Lachaille in *GIGI*
(1958). Subsequent appearances in film musicals include *CAN-CAN* (1960),
Pepe (1960), *Jessica* (1962), and *I'd Rather Be Rich* (1964). Chevalier's final
screen credit was singing the title song on the soundtrack for the animated
THE ARISTOCATS (1970).

CHILD STARS on film go back to the earliest shorts when moviemakers re-
alized the potency of children on screen for both pathos and comedy. Mary
Pickford, Jackie Coogan, and the *Our Gang* kids were probably the most popular child stars of the silent era. Little Davey Lee brought audiences to tears
when he died in the early musical *THE SINGING FOOL* (1928), and talkies
were more than anxious to have tots who could sing and dance as well as break

hearts. They found it all in SHIRLEY TEMPLE, the most famous of all child stars, who made her first feature in 1933 at the age of five and was the most beloved movie figure (adult or child) for most of the decade. JANE WITHERS was of a different type than Temple, and BOBBY BREEN was a male counterpart of the curly blonde moppet; both made several musicals in the 1930s. MICKEY ROONEY had been performing on the screen since he was a toddler but became a box office headliner as a teenager. Like DONALD O'CONNOR, who also started in musicals as a child, Rooney would be able to brave a career as an adult performer, a rarity for kid performers then and now. Other teenage favorites who appeared in musicals were JUDY GARLAND, DEANNA DURBIN, VIRGINIA WEIDLER, ANN BLYTH, BOBBY DRISCOLL, Tommy Rettig, NATALIE WOOD, Tommy Kirk, ANNETTE FUNICELLO, and FRANKIE AVALON.

CHITTY CHITTY BANG BANG (Warfield/United Artists 1968) sought to capture the magic of *MARY POPPINS* (1964), and producer Albert Broccoli even hired DICK VAN DYKE for the lead and RICHARD M. and ROBERT B. SHERMAN to write the songs. But this musical fantasy, based on an Ian Fleming story, was only intermittently successful and there were long stretches between the scenes that worked. Crackpot inventor Caractacus Potts (Van Dyke) is always developing new gizmos to entertain his young children Adrian Hill and Heather Ripley and his sweetheart Truly Scrumptious (Sally Ann Howes). His most useful invention is a flying/floating automobile, Chitty Chitty Bang Bang (named for the odd noise pattern it makes), which helps the foursome escape the evil kingdom of Vulgaria. Some of the special effects were delightful, and the score was very tuneful, as in the silly "Toot Sweets" (about a whistle made out of candy), the lullaby "Hushabye Mountain," and the catchy title song.

CHORUS LINE, A (Universal 1984), the beloved Broadway musical about a group of "gypsies" auditioning for the chorus line of a new show, was a unique concept musical on stage and it was probably impossible to please its millions of fans with any film version; yet they deserved better than the lackluster treatment screenwriter Arnold Schulman and director Richard Attenborough came up with. The 1975 Edward Kleban–MARVIN HAMLISCH score was altered, and one plotline, involving moody director Michael Douglas and ex-lover Alyson Reed, was built up into the semblance of a story. But the musical was about the need and love to dance, and Jeffrey Hornaday's choreography rarely expressed that. Chorus line hopefuls Terrence Mann, Gregg Burge, Pam Klinger, Justin Reed, Vicki Frederick, Matt West, Michelle Johnston, and others did their best, but they hoofed in vain. Among the songs retained from the original score were "I Can Do That," "At the Ballet," "Dance: Ten, Looks: Three," "What I Did for Love," and "One."

CHURCHILL, FRANK (1901–1942) was a composer who provided songs for a handful of DISNEY animated features, most memorably *SNOW WHITE AND THE SEVEN DWARFS* (1937) with lyricist LARRY MOREY. Churchill contributed to *Breaking the Ice* (1938), *DUMBO* (1941), *The Reluctant Dragon* (1941), and *Bambi* (1942), as well as writing "Who's Afraid of the Big Bad Wolf?" for the Disney short *The Three Little Pigs* (1933).

CINDERELLA (Disney 1950) mixed the right amount of romance with humor, adding DISNEY touches such as friendly mice and a villainous cat to the familiar Charles Perrault tale. As with the earlier *SNOW WHITE AND THE SEVEN DWARFS* (1937), the heroine (voice of Ilene Woods) was much more memorable than her prince (William Phipps), and over the years audiences of all ages have identified with Cinderella perhaps more than with any other Disney character. Eleanor Audley was the voice of the cold-hearted stepmother, Rhoda Williams and Lucille Bliss were the grotesque stepsisters, and Verna Felton was the warm Fairy Godmother. MACK DAVID, JERRY LIVINGSTON, and AL HOFFMAN wrote the magical score than ranged from the heartfelt "A Dream Is a Wish Your Heart Makes" to the nonsense delight "Bibbidi Bobbidi Boo." The musical fantasy seems to be timeless and unforgettable, from the mice making Cinderella's ball gown to the gleaming castle that inspired the centerpiece of the Disney World theme park in Florida.

CLARE, SIDNEY (1892–1972) was a former vaudvillian who found success in Hollywood as a lyricist, collaborating with composer-actor OSCAR LEVANT and others. Clare wrote songs for a dozen musicals in the 1930s, including *Love Comes Along* (1930), *Transatlantic Merry-Go-Round* (1934), *Bright Eyes* (1934), *Song and Dance Man* (1936), *Sing and Be Happy* (1937), and *Rascals* (1938). His most notable song is the SHIRLEY TEMPLE signature number "On the Good Ship Lollipop" with composer RICHARD A. WHITING.

CLARK, PETULA (1932–   ), the British pop singer of the 1960s, began as a child performer singing in concert halls in the 1940s, including the musical *London Town* (1946), and appearing in ingenue roles in British films in the 1950s. After her success with the song "Downtown" in America, Clark was starred as the Irish immigrant Sharon McLonergan in *FINIAN'S RAINBOW* (1968) and music-hall-singer-turned-schoolmaster's-wife Katherine Chipping in *GOODBYE MR. CHIPS* (1969). She more recently returned to the musical stage on Broadway and in London's West End.

CLARKE, GRANT (1891–1931) was a Broadway and Tin Pan Alley lyricist who, with his composer-partner HARRY AKST, provided songs for the films *ON WITH THE SHOW* (1929), *Is Everybody Happy?* (1929), *So Long, Letty* (1930), and *Song of the Flame* (1930). Clarke's most remembered songs are "Second Hand Rose" and "Am I Blue?" but his most important number was

"Mother of Mine, I Still Have You," which he wrote with Louis Silvers for *THE JAZZ SINGER* (1927), the first song ever written directly for a movie musical.

CLARKE, MAE (1907–1992), forever remembered for JAMES CAGNEY's pushing a grapefruit into her face in *The Public Enemy* (1931), fell from leading lady status to character actress in the late 1930s. Her musical appearances include *HERE COME THE WAVES* (1944), *ANNIE GET YOUR GUN* (1950), *THE GREAT CARUSO* (1951), *SINGIN' IN THE RAIN* (1952), and *THOROUGHLY MODERN MILLIE* (1967).

CLASSICAL COMPOSERS have often been the subject of film biographies over the years, and though they may not strike one as traditional movie musicals, they celebrate music and parallel the popular songwriters' MUSICAL BIOGRAPHIES in showmanship and historical inaccuracy. Mozart's tragic life has been filmed no less than six times by various countries with Schubert, Beethoven, Chopin, and Tchaikovsky nearly as often. Other composers whose lives and works have been turned into feature films include Berlioz, Brahms, Donizetti, Gilbert and Sullivan, Grieg, Handel, Liszt, Mahler, Offenbach, Paganini, Rimsky-Korsakov, Rossini, Verdi, and Wagner. The most-filmed composer is waltz king Johann Strauss, Jr., who has been the subject of ten musicals over the years. Among the most popular film bios of classical composers were *Blossom Time* (1934) and *The Great Waltz* (1938) about Strauss, *A Song to Remember* (1944) about Chopin, *Song of My Heart* (1948) about Tchaikovsky, *The Story of Gilbert and Sullivan* (1953), *Amadeus* (1984) about Mozart and Salieri, and *Topsy Turvy* (1999) about Gilbert and Sullivan. Director KEN RUSSELL made a series of bizarre films about classical composers in the 1970s that pretty much wore out the genre, but every once in a while a hit movie on the subject surfaces and classical composers are on the screen again.

CLOONEY, ROSEMARY (1928–), the renowned Big Band singer and jazz stylist, made only a few film appearances in the 1950s but was usually quite memorable with her mellow and smooth singing voice. Clooney was featured in *The Stars Are Singing* (1953), *Here Come the Girls* (1953), *Red Garters* (1954), and *DEEP IN MY HEART* (1954) and most notably as band singer Betty Haynes in *WHITE CHRISTMAS* (1954). Her stormy life and bouts with insanity were recounted in the television bio-pic *Rosie: The Rosemary Clooney Story* (1982), in which she was portrayed by Sandra Locke. Clooney was married to actor José Ferrer and is the aunt of actor George Clooney.

COAL MINER'S DAUGHTER (Universal 1980) was the BIOGRAPHICAL MUSICAL about country music star Loretta Lynn as portrayed by Sissy Spacek, whose dynamic performance (she did her own singing) raised the film far above the usual celebrity rags-to-riches tale. Fourteen-year-old Loretta from the hills of Kentucky marries war veteran Mooney Lynn (Tommy Lee Jones), who discovers her talent for writing and singing songs and promotes her. Her rise to fame in Nashville was handled with unromantic realism, as were Lynn's bout with depression and a nervous breakdown right on stage. Beverly D'Angelo shone as her friend Patsy Cline who died in a plane crash, which contributed to Lynn's downfall. The songs by Lynn and others heard in the film included "Honky-Tonk Girl," "You're Lookin' at Country," "Sweet Dreams of You," and the title number.

COCOANUTS, THE (Paramount 1929) was the MARX BROTHERS' first film, a stagy version of their 1925 Broadway hit that was technically primitive but enjoyable all the same. Groucho runs the Hotel de Cocoanut in speculator-crazy Florida and his guests include brothers Chico, Harpo, and Zeppo, as well as MARGARET DUMONT. There are also a pair of static lovers, Mary Eaton and Oscar Shaw, who sing "When My Dreams Come True," which IRVING BERLIN added to his stage score for the film. Most of the highlights in the movie were not musical, such as the hilarious auction led by Groucho and the famous "viaduct" routine, but "The Tale of the Shirt" was a daffy spoof of the "Toreador Song" from Bizet's *Carmen*.

COHAN, GEORGE M. (1878–1942), the perennial song-and-dance man and pioneer in American musical comedy, made only one movie musical appearance: the dual roles of Theodore Blair and Doc Varney in *THE PHANTOM PRESIDENT* (1932). But Cohan's music and lyrics were featured in *Little Johnny Jones* (1930), *Little Nellie Kelly* (1940), and *YANKEE DOODLE DANDY* (1942), the musical story of his life with JAMES CAGNEY as the famous hoofer. Cagney also played Cohan in *The Seven Little Foys* (1955).

COLE, JACK (1914–1974), the distinctive Broadway choreographer who was instrumental in bringing jazz and modern dance to musicals, staged the dances in many films in the 1940s and 1950s. His first assignment was *COVER GIRL* (1944), followed by *Eadie Was a Lady* (1945), *Tonight and Every Night* (1945), *Tars and Spars* (1946), *THE JOLSON STORY* (1946), *ON THE RIVIERA* (1951), *THE MERRY WIDOW* (1952), *THE FARMER TAKES A WIFE* (1953), *GENTLEMEN PREFER BLONDES* (1953), *THERE'S NO BUSINESS LIKE SHOW BUSINESS* (1954), *KISMET* (1955), *LES GIRLS* (1957), *Let's Make Love* (1960), and others.

COLE, NAT "KING" (1919–1965), the velvet-voiced singer and pianist, appeared in some twenty musical and nonmusical films before his untimely death, usually playing himself or in a specialty bit. The African American singer's movie musicals include *Here Comes Elmer* (1943), *Pin-Up Girl* (1944), *Stars on Parade* (1944), *Breakfast in Hollywood* (1946), *Small Town Girl* (1953), and *Cat Ballou* (1965). Cole's only major film role was as W.C. Handy in the musical bio *St. Louis Blues* (1958). He was the father of singer-song-writer Natalie Cole.

COLLEGE RHYTHM (Paramount 1934) had an impossible premise for a musical (two department stores go collegiate and compete via a climactic football game), but the film had a breezy pace, a splendid cast, and a vivacious score by MACK GORDON and HARRY REVEL. Comic JOE PENNER and his pet duck provided the broad humor, LYDA ROBERTI and LANNY ROSS supplied the melodic voices, and JACK CARSON, GEORGE BARBIER, and FRANKLIN PANGBORN contributed strong comic characters. The score featured "Stay As Sweet As You Are," "Take a Number From One to Ten," "Let's Give Three Cheers for Love," and the pulsating title number.

COLONNA, JERRY (1904–1986) rolled his eyes, bristled his bushy mustache, and bellowed through clenched teeth during a long career that included nightclubs, radio, film, and television. Often BOB HOPE's sidekick on live and radio shows, Colonna popped up in the Hope movie musicals *College Swing* (1938), *ROAD TO SINGAPORE* (1940), *ROAD TO RIO* (1947), and *THE ROAD TO HONG KONG* (1962). Colonna's other film credits include *ROSALIE* (1937), *Sis Hopkins* (1941), *True to the Army* (1942), *STAR SPANGLED RHYTHM* (1942), and *Meet Me in Las Vegas* (1957). His distinctive voice can be heard telling and singing the tale of "Casey at the Bat" in the animated *Make Mine Music* (1946) and as the March Hare in *ALICE IN WONDERLAND* (1951).

COLUMBIA PICTURES grew from a minor operation founded in 1924 on "Poverty Row" in Hollywood to one of the major studios in the 1930s through the astute leadership of the ruthless Harry Cohn (a former salesman who founded the company in 1924), the artistry of directors like Frank Capra, and stars like RITA HAYWORTH. In the 1930s, Columbia prospered by producing economic second features and occasional box office hits, though rarely in the musical genre. In the 1940s, Hayworth kept the musical end of the studio afloat with such vehicles as *YOU'LL NEVER GET RICH* (1941), *YOU WERE NEVER LOVELIER* (1942), and *COVER GIRL* (1944), and the popular bios *THE JOLSON STORY* (1946) and *JOLSON SINGS AGAIN* (1949) certainly helped. By the 1950s, Columbia dealt with the threat of television by investing in the new media and establishing the subsidiary Screen Gems. But the musical offerings of the decade were scarce, ranging from the star-driven *PAL JOEY* (1957) to the prestige opera *PORGY AND BESS* (1959). The studio's musicals fared better in the 1960s, finding box office success with *BYE BYE BIRDIE* (1963), *FUNNY GIRL* (1968), and *OLIVER!* (1969). But Columbia was not spared the glut of musicals in the 1970s, and financial fiascos like *ANNIE* (1982) sealed the fate of the movie musical. The company was taken over by conglomerates in the 1980s, first by Coca-Cola and then by SONY Corporation.

COLUMBO, RUSS (1908–1934) was a mellow singing star of Big Bands and radio whose career was cut short by a freak shotgun accident at the age of twenty-six. Columbo's crooning style was intimate and caressing, much in the manner of BING CROSBY or the later FRANK SINATRA. He formed his own band, wrote a handful of his own songs, and was featured in the films *Street Girl* (1929), *Dynamite* (1929), and *Broadway Through a Keyhole* (1933). Columbo played himself in *Moulin Rouge* (1934) and vaudvillian Paul Scott in *Wake Up and Dream* (1934).

COMDEN, BETTY (1917–) and her partner **ADOLPH GREEN** (1915–) have the longest-running collaboration in Broadway history as well as a twenty-year career writing scripts and/or lyrics for films. After breaking onto Broadway with *On the Town* in 1944, the team went to Hollywood and worked on *GOOD NEWS* (1947), *TAKE ME OUT TO THE BALL GAME* (1949), *THE BARKLEYS OF BROADWAY* (1949), *THE BAND WAGON* (1953), *IT'S ALWAYS FAIR WEATHER* (1955), and *What a Way to Go* (1964). Two of their many stage hits were filmed—*ON THE TOWN* (1949) and *BELLS ARE RINGING* (1960)—but their greatest film success was the screenplay for *SINGIN' IN THE RAIN* (1952). Comden appeared in a bit part in *Greenwich Village* (1944) and a few nonmusicals as well.

COMO, PERRY (1912–), the durable singing star noted for his relaxed performance style and cozy, unexciting persona, started as a vocalist with Ted Weems' orchestra but by the 1940s went solo and was popular on records, radio, and television for decades. Far from charismatic on the screen, Como nevertheless made warm appearances in *Something for the Boys* (1944), *Doll Face* (1945), *If I'm Lucky* (1946), and *WORDS AND MUSIC* (1948).

CONEY ISLAND (Fox 1943) was a period musical that showcased BETTY GRABLE, then at the peak of her popularity with movie audiences at home and with GIs overseas. Grable played a saloon singer at the turn-of-the-century amusement park of the title who is fought over by two business rivals, GEORGE MONTGOMERY and CESAR ROMERO, both of whom love her and want to further her career. Several old standards from the period were dusted off for the score, such as "Cuddle Up a Little Closer," "The Darktown Strutters' Ball," "Pretty Baby," and "Put Your Arms Around Me, Honey," and LEO ROBIN and RALPH RAINGER supplied such new ditties as "Take It From There," "Lulu From Louisville," and the elaborate finale "There's Danger in a Dance," which HERMES PAN choreographed with dozens of chorus couples illustrating through the ages the perils of passionate dancing. Grable starred in a thinly disguised remake seven years later called *WABASH AVE-*

NUE (1950), which told the same story in Chicago during the 1892 World's Fair. As a shimmy dancer in a Windy City dive, she got to sing "I Wish I Could Shimmy Like My Sister Kate" as PHIL HARRIS and VICTOR MATURE fought over her attentions and career. MACK GORDON and JOSEF MYROW wrote a new score that included "Walking Along With Billy," "Wilhelmina," and "Baby, Won't You Say You Love Me?" The war was over, but Grable was still required to flash her famous legs, even in a period picture like this.

CONNECTICUT YANKEE IN KING ARTHUR'S COURT, A (Paramount 1949) was one of BING CROSBY's few costume movies, and he looked more comfortable in playful medieval garb than he did in some of his other period efforts. The Mark Twain story was given a lush Technicolor rendering as New England blacksmith Crosby gets bumped on the head and dreams he is at Camelot, where he meets the redheaded beauty Lady Alesande (Rhonda Fleming), the bumbling Sir Sagrimore (William Bendix), and King Arthur himself (Cedric Hardwicke). Crosby's favorite songwriting team, JOHNNY BURKE and JAMES VAN HEUSEN, wrote the agreeable score that featured the optimistic ballad "If You Stub Your Toe on the Moon," the genial "Busy Doing Nothing," and the love duet "Once and For Always."

CONNOLLY, BOBBY (1890–1944) was one of the top choreographers during Hollywood's golden age of musicals, working at WARNER BROTHERS in the early 1930s and at MGM from 1939 to his premature death. A Broadway choreographer in the 1920s and 1930s, Connolly's first screen assignment was *Moonlight and Pretzels* (1933), followed by *Take a Chance* (1933), *Flirtation Walk* (1935), *SWEET ADELINE* (1935), *GO INTO YOUR DANCE* (1935), *The Singing Kid* (1936), *Ready, Willing and Able* (1937), *Fools for Scandal* (1938), and others. Among his MGM musicals credits are *THE WIZARD OF OZ* (1939), *AT THE CIRCUS* (1939), *BROADWAY MELODY OF 1940*, *TWO GIRLS ON BROADWAY* (1940), *FOR ME AND MY GAL* (1942), and *I Dood It* (1943).

CONRAD, CON (1891–1938), a Tin Pan Alley composer who was among the first to go West and write songs for the talkies, won the first ACADEMY AWARD for Best Song when he and lyricist HERB MAGIDSON wrote "The Continental" for *THE GAY DIVORCEE* (1934). Conrad's other musical films include *Fox Movietone Follies* (1929), *Broadway* (1929), *The Cockeyed World* (1929), *Let's Go Places* (1930), *Movietone Follies of 1930*, and *The Gift of Gab* (1934).

CONREID, HANS (1917–1982) was a versatile character actor who played a variety of foreign types, from snarling Nazis to finicky Brits. His most memorable musical role was the villainous piano teacher Terwilliger in *THE 5,000 FINGERS OF DR. T* (1953) but he made notable appearances in *ON THE*

TOWN (1949), *THE BARKLEYS OF BROADWAY* (1949), *SUMMER STOCK* (1950), *Rock-a-Bye Baby* (1958), *ROBIN AND THE SEVEN HOODS* (1964), and others.

COSLOW, SAM (1902–1982) wrote lyrics (and sometimes music as well) for some two dozen film musicals, as well as a handful of Tin Pan Alley hits, with such composers as ARTHUR JOHNSTON, RICHARD A. WHITING, BURTON LANE, and others. The first Coslow songs were heard on screen in *Dance of Life* (1929), followed by *The Vagabond King* (1930), *Honey* (1930), *This Is the Night* (1932), *Hello, Everybody* (1933), *College Humor* (1933), *Too Much Harmony* (1933), *MURDER AT THE VANITIES* (1934), *Many Happy Returns* (1934), *Belle of the Nineties* (1934), *Coronado* (1935), *Every Day's a Holiday* (1937), *Out of This World* (1945), *Copacabana* (1947), and others. Among Coslow's many hit songs were "Thanks," "Cocktails for Two," "Sing You Sinners," "Learn to Croon," and "My Old Flame."

COSTELLO, LOU. See Abbott, Bud

COTTON CLUB, THE (Orion 1984) was one of the most talked about movies in production that year (mainly about how the cost escalated to $47 million), so the resulting musical melodrama was a disappointment and a financial disaster. The bumpy plot concerned the rivalry between gangsters Dutch Schultz (James Remar) and Owney Madden (Bob Hoskins) while cornet player Richard Gere tried to break into the all-black entertainment at Harlem's famed nightclub of the title. Gregory Hines played an African American hoofer trying to make it on Broadway, and he also choreographed the nightclub numbers with Henry LeTang and Michael Shuin, all of which were dazzling if rarely seen in their entirety. Director Francis Ford Coppola, who co-wrote the convoluted screenplay, managed to capture the Roaring Twenties and the Harlem milieu beautifully, and the use of old standards like "Crazy Rhythm," "Am I Blue?," "Doin' the New Low-Down," and "Minnie the Moocher" certainly helped. Diane Lane and Lonette McKee were the love interests for Gere and Hines, and the supporting cast was one of the most impressive of the decade with appearances by Nicholas Cage, Fred Gwynne, GWEN VERDON, Maurice Hines, Julian Beck, Diane Venora, Woody Strode, Larry Fishburne, Jennifer Grey, Giancarlo Esposito, and Charles "Honi" Coles.

COUNTRY GIRL, THE (Paramount 1954) was another melodrama masquerading as a musical (or vice versa) as four songs by IRA GERSHWIN and HAROLD ARLEN were added to Clifford Odets' 1950 drama about an ex-alcoholic actor (BING CROSBY) who tries for a comeback on stage with the help of his put-upon wife (Grace Kelly) and the director (William Holden) who is attracted to her. In the musical film, the actor was turned into a has-been singer who is cast in a Broadway musical, but much of the dynamics remained the same. Crosby gave what is arguably the best dramatic performance of his career, and his singing of "It's Mine, It's Yours," "The Search Is Through," and "Dissertation on the State of Bliss" (aka "Love and Learn"), though far from necessary to the narrative, appeased his many fans expecting songs.

COURT JESTER, THE (Paramount 1956) was one of DANNY KAYE's best vehicles, allowing him to clown around as a medieval potboy who disguises himself as a jester to break into the court ruled by the villainous Basil Rathbone. The plot was a merry chase with Kaye helping the mysterious Black Fox regain the throne as he dallied with court ladies ANGELA LANSBURY and Glynis Johns. The songs by SAMMY CAHN and Sylvia Fine (Kaye's wife) ranged from the silly "Maladjusted Jester" to the lovely ballad "I'll Take You Dreaming," all showing off Kaye's considerable talents. Yet the most remembered sequence in the film was not a song but the hysterical comic exchange between Kaye and Mildred Natwick as she explained to him that "the pellet with the poison is in the vessel with the pestle."

COVER GIRL (Columbia 1944) was intended as another showcase for RITA HAYWORTH, but it was up-and-coming GENE KELLY who dominated the picture, proving to be a better actor and more versatile dancer than previously seen. The trite plot dwelt on small-time Brooklyn nightclub singer Hayworth, who abandons her lover Kelly and sidekick PHIL SILVERS when she is signed on as a cover girl model for a publishing empire. Hayworth got to run down a long-winding ramp during the title song (a scene ripe for parody over the years) and played her own grandmother singing "Sure Thing" (vocals by Martha Mears) in a flashback. The most outstanding number was Kelly's *pas de deux* with his own alter ego as he scampered down a lonely Brooklyn street. The IRA GERSHWIN–JEROME KERN score also included "Put Me to the Test," "Make Way for Tomorrow" (lyric by E.Y. HARBURG), and the hit ballad "Long Ago and Far Away."

COWARD, Sir NOEL (1899–1973), the dapper British songwriter, playwright, and actor who wrote for the stage and screen, saw his operetta *Bitter Sweet* filmed twice: in England in 1933 and in Hollywood in 1941. Coward's revue *Tonight at 8:30* was filmed as *Meet Me Tonight* (1952) in Great Britain. He made many screen appearances, but oddly, his song-and-dance talents were never put on film and only recordings and television tapes attest to his unique showmanship.

CRAIN, JEANNE (1925–   ), a former model who appeared in many films in the 1940s and 1950s, usually played wholesome girls in light comedies and musicals. She made her debut in a bit part in *THE GANG'S ALL HERE*

(1943) before she was cast in her two most notable musical roles: Iowa farm girl Margy Frake going to the fair in *STATE FAIR* (1945) and Philadelphian Julia Rogers going to the 1876 Exposition in *CENTENNIAL SUMMER* (1946). Although her singing was usually dubbed, Crain brought a homespun charm to such musicals as *Margie* (1946), *You Were Meant for Me* (1948), *I'll Get By* (1950), *Gentlemen Marry Brunettes* (1955), *The Second Greatest Sex* (1955), and *THE JOKER IS WILD* (1957).

CRAWFORD, JOAN (1904–1977), the glamourous star of romances, melodramas, and later horror films, started as a Charleston dancer and appeared in a handful of film musicals early in her career. After a specialty bit in *HOLLYWOOD REVUE OF 1929*, Crawford was teamed with FRED ASTAIRE for his screen debut in *DANCING LADY* (1933) and played leading roles in *Sadie McKee* (1934), *Ice Follies of 1939*, and *Torch Song* (1953). She also made guest appearances in the musicals *HOLLYWOOD CANTEEN* (1944) and *It's a Great Feeling* (1949). Crawford's four husbands included actors FRANCHOT TONE and Douglas Fairbanks, Jr.

CROSBY, BING (1903–1977) recorded more songs than any other singer and introduced more hits than any other American entertainer, remaining popular during five decades of vaudeville, film, radio, concerts, and television. Crosby started out in silent comedies before making his screen musical debut as one of the Rhythm Boys singing with PAUL WHITEMAN's orchestra in *KING OF JAZZ* (1930). After bit parts in *Reaching for the Moon* (1931) and *Confessions of a Co-Ed* (1931) and playing himself in *THE BIG BROADCAST* (1932), he graduated to leading roles in *College Humor* (1933), *Too Much Harmony* (1933), *GOING HOLLYWOOD* (1933), *WE'RE NOT DRESSING* (1934), *MISSISSIPPI* (1935), *ANYTHING GOES* (1936), *PENNIES FROM HEAVEN* (1936), *Waikiki Wedding* (1937), *DOUBLE OR NOTHING* (1937), *SING YOU SINNERS* (1938), *East Side of Heaven* (1939), and others. By this time Crosby was the top recording star in the nation and his weekly radio show made him America's favorite crooner. With *THE ROAD TO SINGAPORE* (1940), he began a series of seven "Road" pictures with BOB HOPE. In the 1940s he graduated to more serious roles, though rarely drifting far from his easygoing, likable persona. Father Chuck O'Malley in both *GOING MY WAY* (1944) and *THE BELLS OF ST. MARY'S* (1945) and the ex-alcoholic actor Elgin in *THE COUNTRY GIRL* (1954) were his most challenging roles, though usually he played an affable nonconformist as in *RHYTHM ON THE RIVER* (1940), *BIRTH OF THE BLUES* (1941), *BLUE SKIES* (1946), and others. His few costume pictures include *Dixie* (1943), *The Emperor Waltz* (1948), and *A CONNECTICUT YANKEE IN KING ARTHUR'S COURT* (1949). *HOLIDAY INN* (1942) and its follow-up *WHITE CHRISTMAS* (1954) gave Crosby the chance to sing several IRVING BERLIN standards, but his most frequent suppliers of songs were

JAMES VAN HEUSEN and JOHNNY BURKE, who scored most of the "Road" pictures and other Crosby vehicles. Even as he gracefully aged and mellowed in the 1950s and 1960s, Crosby still found notable roles and songs in *HERE COMES THE GROOM* (1951), *HIGH SOCIETY* (1956), a second *ANYTHING GOES* (1956), and *High Time* (1960). His last musical role was the fussy reformer Alan A. Dale in *ROBIN AND THE SEVEN HOODS* (1964). Crosby's second wife was actress Kathryn Grant, his brother was bandleader BOB CROSBY, and actor Gary Crosby was one of his sons.

CROSBY, BOB (1913–1993), the younger brother of BING CROSBY, enjoyed a long career as an actor, singer, and popular bandleader. After singing with the DORSEY brothers' orchestras in the 1930s, Crosby formed his own Dixieland band and was heard on radio and featured in a dozen films in the 1940s. He later went solo and was a frequent celebrity on 1950s radio and television. Crosby's film credits include *Let's Make Music* (1940), *Sis Hopkins* (1941), *Presenting Lily Mars* (1943), *Thousands Cheer* (1943), *Kansas City Kitty* (1944), *Pardon My Rhythm* (1944), *Two Tickets to Broadway* (1951), and *THE FIVE PENNIES* (1959).

CUGAT, XAVIER (1900–1990), the Cuban bandleader who was crowned the "Rhumba King" and popularized Spanish rhythms in America, appeared in fifteen film musicals in the 1940s. His orchestra, which was considered the finest Latin-American dance band in the country, was featured with Cugat in *Go West, Young Man* (1936), *YOU WERE NEVER LOVELIER* (1942), *STAGE DOOR CANTEEN* (1943), *TWO GIRLS AND A SAILOR* (1944), *Weekend at the Waldorf* (1945), *A Date With Judy* (1948), *NEPTUNE'S DAUGHTER* (1949), and others. Singers Abbe Lane and Charo were among his four wives.

CUKOR, GEORGE (1899–1983), the skillful Hollywood director who was known for getting vibrant performances from his leading ladies, directed classy romantic comedies, atmospheric period pieces, and a half dozen musicals, including *A STAR IS BORN* (1954), *LES GIRLS* (1957), *Let's Make Love* (1960), and *MY FAIR LADY* (1964).

CUMMINGS, IRVING (1888–1959) was a Hollywood director who guided SHIRLEY TEMPLE, BETTY GRABLE, and CARMEN MIRANDA through some of their finest vehicles. After appearing as an actor in silents, Cummings started directing action films when talkies came in. By the mid-1930s he was a favorite at 20TH CENTURY–FOX, directing musicals up through the war years. His sixteen musicals include *Cameo Kirby* (1930), *CURLY TOP* (1935), *POOR LITTLE RICH GIRL* (1936), *Vogues of 1938* (1937), *Little Miss Broadway* (1938), *LILLIAN RUSSELL* (1940), *DOWN ARGENTINE WAY* (1940), *THAT NIGHT IN RIO* (1941), *Louisiana Purchase* (1941), *My Gal Sal* (1942), *SPRINGTIME IN THE ROCKIES* (1942), and *THE DOLLY SISTERS* (1945). Cummings produced *Double Dynamite* (1951), which was directed by his son, Irving Cummings, Jr.

CUMMINGS, JACK (1905–1989) produced some two dozen musical films at MGM between 1936 and 1955. Working his way up from office boy to producer (aided by the fact that his uncle was MGM mogul Louis B. Mayer), Cummings' first musical was *BORN TO DANCE* (1936), followed by *BROADWAY MELODY OF 1938* (1937), *Honolulu* (1939), *BROADWAY MELODY OF 1940*, *TWO GIRLS ON BROADWAY* (1940), *Go West* (1940), *I Dood It* (1943), *Broadway Rhythm* (1944), *IT HAPPENED IN BROOKLYN* (1947), *NEPTUNE'S DAUGHTER* (1949), *THREE LITTLE WORDS* (1950), *LOVELY TO LOOK AT* (1952), *KISS ME, KATE* (1953), *SEVEN BRIDES FOR SEVEN BROTHERS* (1954), and *Interrupted Melody* (1955). His last feature was the ELVIS PRESLEY vehicle *VIVA LAS VEGAS* (1964).

CUMMINGS, ROBERT (1918–1990) went to Hollywood in 1933 and appeared in over sixty films before starring in his own television show in the 1950s, maintaining his youthful looks and boyish charm for decades. Cummings usually played rich Ivy League playboys or the amiable boy next door in his fifteen musicals, most notably in *Three Smart Girls Grow Up* (1939), *ONE NIGHT IN THE TROPICS* (1940), and *MOON OVER MIAMI* (1941). His other musical films include *Millions in the Air* (1935), *Three Cheers for Love* (1936), *College Swing* (1938), *Spring Parade* (1940), *It Started With Eve* (1941), *Lucky Me* (1954), and *Beach Party* (1963).

CURLY TOP (Fox 1935) let SHIRLEY TEMPLE introduce one of her most popular ditties, "Animal Crackers in My Soup," as well as tug on the heart strings of Depression America as she played matchmaker for her elder sister Rochelle Hudson and dashing millionaire JOHN BOLES. TED KOEHLER, RAY HENDERSON, IRVING CAESAR, and EDWARD HEYMAN all contributed to the score, which included "The Simple Things in Life," "When I Grow Up," and the title number, which Boles sang while the beloved moppet tap danced atop his white grand piano. The same general plot served for the later *DADDY LONG LEGS* (1955), though LESLIE CARON and FRED ASTAIRE played the roles as much older characters.

CURRY, TIM (1946–   ), the tall British actor who appeared in everything from social drama to light comedy, made his film debut recreating his stage performance as Dr. Frank-N-Furter in *THE ROCKY HORROR PICTURE SHOW* (1975). Curry's subsequent musical roles were con man Rooster in *ANNIE* (1982), Captain Long John Silver in *Muppets' Treasure Island* (1996), and a voice-over for the animated *The Pebble and the Penguin* (1995).

CURTIZ, MICHAEL (1888–1962), the prolific Hollywood director who filmed everything and anything, from *The Adventures of Robin Hood* (1938) to *The Adventures of Huckleberry Finn* (1960), with everyone from AL JOLSON to ELVIS PRESLEY, managed to fit in sixteen musicals among his over 100 films in Hungary, Austria, Germany, and Hollywood. Curtiz directed the early musicals *Mammy* (1930) and *Bright Lights* (1930) but found more success with the later musical bios *YANKEE DOODLE DANDY* (1942), *NIGHT AND DAY* (1946), *YOUNG MAN WITH A HORN* (1950), *I'll See You in My Dreams* (1951), *THE JAZZ SINGER* (1953), *The Best Things in Life Are Free* (1956), and *The Helen Morgan Story* (1957). His other musical credits include *THIS IS THE ARMY* (1943), *ROMANCE ON THE HIGH SEAS* (1948), *My Dream Is Yours* (1949), *WHITE CHRISTMAS* (1954), *The Vagabond King* (1956), and *KING CREOLE* (1958).

D

DADDY LONG LEGS (Fox 1955) gave the maturing FRED ASTAIRE a chance to romance a much younger woman, LESLIE CARON, by becoming her guardian when she is a child and letting her fall in love with him later. The plot was an old one (under the same title the tale had been filmed as nonmusicals in 1919 and 1931), but with Caron as an orphan in France who is educated in America, the possibilities for song and dance were opened up. Without knowing that State Department diplomat Astaire is her mysterious guardian, Caron fantasized about her unknown "papa faucheux" in a dream ballet before the two get together in the end. JOHNNY MERCER wrote both music and lyrics this time and came up with the entrancing ballad "Something's Gotta Give" and the college dance number "Sluefoot," which proved that the agile Astaire was not too old for his young charge after all. Also in the cast, under Jean Negulesco's direction, were Thelma Ritter, Fred Clark, Terry Moore, Ralph Dumke, Larry Keating, and Ray Anthony's orchestra.

DAILEY, DAN (1914–1978), the light-haired leading man of several musicals and nonmusicals, was a hoofer in vaudeville and on Broadway before a bit part in the film *Stars in Your Eyes* (1939) brought him to the attention of the studios. Thereafter he played confident romantic leads in MGM and FOX musicals starting with *Hullabaloo* (1940). Dailey is mostly remembered for the four films in which he partnered with BETTY GRABLE: *MOTHER WORE TIGHTS* (1947), *When My Baby Smiles at Me* (1948), *My Blue Heaven* (1950), and *Call Me Mister* (1951). But he also gave capable performances in *ZIEGFELD GIRL* (1941), *You Were Meant for Me* (1948), *Give My Regards to Broadway* (1948), *You're My Everything* (1949), *Meet Me at the Fair* (1952), *THERE'S NO BUSINESS LIKE SHOW BUSINESS* (1954), *IT'S ALWAYS FAIR WEATHER* (1955), and *Meet Me in Las Vegas* (1956) and as songwriter RAY HENDERSON in the musical bio *The Best Things in Life Are Free*

(1956). Soon after his last film musical, *Pepe* (1960), he returned to the stage and nightclubs, and then later television.

DALE, VIRGINIA (1917–1994) was a blonde leading lady in 1940s films whose only memorable performance was as FRED ASTAIRE's dancing partner in *HOLIDAY INN* (1942). Her other musical credits include *Start Cheering* (1938), *Buck Benny Rides Again* (1940), *LOVE THY NEIGHBOR* (1940), *Dancing on a Dime* (1941), *Las Vegas Nights* (1941), and *Kiss the Boys Goodbye* (1941).

DALEY, CASS (1915–1975), a former band singer who discovered she had a talent for broad comedy, was featured in several musicals during the war years and early 1950s. The gangly, buck-toothed comedienne excelled in physical humor, outlandish singing, and contortion-like dancing. Her first film was *THE FLEET'S IN* (1942), followed by *STAR SPANGLED RHYTHM* (1942), *Riding High* (1943), *Out of This World* (1945), *Duffy's Tavern* (1945), *Ladies' Man* (1947), *Variety Girl* (1947), *HERE COMES THE GROOM* (1952), *Red Garters* (1954), and others.

DAMES (Warner-Vitaphone 1934) had a weaker plot than most of the WARNER BROTHERS' golden age musicals, but AL DUBIN and HARRY WARREN wrote three superior songs, and BUSBY BERKELEY gave each one an inventive staging. In order to raise money for a floundering Broadway musical scored by DICK POWELL, chorine JOAN BLONDELL fleeces millionaire GUY KIBBEE of his money and RUBY KEELER gets to star in the hit show. Powell introduced the lyrical title number, explaining to the producers what the audiences want to see, and his argument was supported by a lavish production number that included Berkeley's geometric patterns of girls. "I Only Have Eyes for You" became a salute to Keeler as her face appears everywhere in Powell's imagination. Most ingenious of all was "The Girl at the Ironing Board," in which Blondell is pressing men's garments and they spring to life and start dancing around her. Zazu Pitts, PHIL REGAN, and HUGH HERBERT filled out the cast, and composer SAMMY FAIN had a cameo bit as a songwriter.

DAMN YANKEES (Warner 1958) came to the screen with most of the same cast and creative staff as the 1955 Broadway hit, including BOB FOSSE's choreography, GEORGE ABBOTT's fluid script and (with STANLEY DONEN) direction, and the sparkling score by RICHARD ADLER and JERRY ROSS. RAY WALSTON again played the devilish Mr. Applegate, who makes a deal with middle-aged baseball fan Robert Shafer to become youthful Tab Hunter and lead his beloved Washington Senators to the World Series. GWEN VERDON repeated her sexy, funny role of temptress Lola, the only time she got to film one of her stage triumphs, and she was effervescent performing "A

Little Brains, a Little Talent," "Whatever Lola Wants," and (with Hunter) "Two Lost Souls." Other songs retained from the stage score included "Who's Got the Pain?," "Shoeless Joe from Hannibal, Mo," and "(You've Gotta Have) Heart."

DAMONE, VIC (1928–   ), a popular singer on records, radio, television, and nightclubs, was featured in a handful of movie musicals in the 1950s. The slight, dark, and handsome performer had his best roles as the romancing Johnny Nyle in *Athena* (1954) and the young Caliph in *KISMET* (1955), but he was also seen in *Rich, Young and Pretty* (1951), as himself in *The Strip* (1951), *DEEP IN MY HEART* (1954), *HIT THE DECK* (1955), and *Meet Me in Las Vegas* (1956), and on the soundtrack of *An Affair to Remember* (1957). He was married to actress Diahann Carroll.

DAMSEL IN DISTRESS, A (RKO 1937) was FRED ASTAIRE's first film without GINGER ROGERS after partnering with her seven times. Audiences were disappointed, but it was a wondrous musical in many ways, the GEORGE and IRA GERSHWIN score alone worth the price of admission. American dancer Astaire is in London doing a show and is smitten by the aristocratic Lady Alyce (Joan Fontaine), so he pursues her to the countryside and eventually rescues the lady from her stuffy life in Totleigh Castle. GEORGE BURNS and GRACIE ALLEN were on hand as Astaire's press agents, and there were comic turns as well by REGINALD GARDINER and RAY NOBLE as British stereotypes. The exceptional score included the hypnotic "A Foggy Day (In London Town)," a jazzy version of "I Can't Be Bothered Now," the harmonizing madrigal "Nice Work If You Can Get It," the breezy "Things Are Looking Up," and the satirical "Stiff Upper Lip," which Astaire, Burns, and Allen performed in an amusement park fun house complete with turning barrels and distorted mirrors. HERMES PAN came up with the ingenious choreography and George Stevens directed with a felicitous touch.

DANCE MUSICALS, those movies that emphasize dance and use extended dance sequences to help tell the story, were not as common as one would think. Movie studios were usually wary of losing their audiences with an artsy dance piece or dream ballet like the kind frequently used on Broadway. Yet there are shining examples of dance musicals that proved the producers wrong, such as *AN AMERICAN IN PARIS* (1951) and *SINGIN' IN THE RAIN* (1952), both choreographed by GENE KELLY and STANLEY DONEN. Yet when Kelly offered his choreographic film *INVITATION TO THE DANCE* (1956), critics balked and audiences stayed away. Other movie musicals over the years that offered an extended dance scene or ballet include *42ND STREET* (1933), *GOLD DIGGERS OF 1935, On Your Toes* (1939), *ZIEGFELD FOLLIES* (1946), *WORDS AND MUSIC* (1948), *ON THE TOWN* (1949), *HANS CHRISTIAN ANDERSEN* (1952), *THE BAND WAGON*

(1953), *SEVEN BRIDES FOR SEVEN BROTHERS* (1954), *A STAR IS BORN* (1954), *BRIGADOON* (1954), *OKLAHOMA!* (1955), *CAROUSEL* (1956), *WEST SIDE STORY* (1961), *HELLO, DOLLY!* (1969), and *A CHORUS LINE* (1984).

DANCING LADY (MGM 1933), MGM's answer to WARNER BROTHERS' popular *42ND STREET* (1933), told the familiar backstage story of a Broadway musical in trouble. Chorus girl JOAN CRAWFORD hopes to make it big in show business but her rich boyfriend FRANCHOT TONE bribes the backers to pull out. So director CLARK GABLE has to put up his own money, and Crawford takes over for the leading lady, all ending happily if not surprisingly. What makes the movie memorable are the songs (by various tunesmiths) and the production numbers in the musical-within-the-musical, especially "Heigh-Ho, the Gang's All Here" and "Let's Go Bavarian," in which Crawford was partnered by FRED ASTAIRE in his film debut. NELSON EDDY sang the big finale number, "The Rhythm of the Day" by RODGERS and HART, and Art Jarrett delivered the hit song "Everything I Have Is Yours" by HAROLD ADAMSON and BURTON LANE. The supporting cast included May Robson, ROBERT BENCHLEY, Ted Healy, and the Three Stooges. As directed by ROBERT Z. LEONARD and choreographed by SAMMY LEE and Eddie Prinz, the musical is a mishmash of styles but an agreeable experience all the same.

DANDRIDGE, DOROTHY (1923–1965), one of Hollywood's first African American leading ladies, was a child performer in vaudeville and had a bit part in *A DAY AT THE RACES* (1937) before gaining attention as the teenager who helped introduced "Chattanooga Choo-Choo" in *SUN VALLEY SERENADE* (1941). After specialty bits in *Hit Parade of 1943* and *Atlantic City* (1944), Dandridge was given the two most demanding black roles yet seen on the musical screen: the seductive *CARMEN JONES* (1954) and the abused Bess in *PORGY AND BESS* (1959). Although she was a recognized singer, Dandridge was dubbed in both pictures because of their operatic scores, but her powerful performances in both films were landmarks for African Americans on film. She appeared on television and in nightclubs before her premature death in 1965. Dancer-singer HAROLD NICHOLAS was her first husband.

DANIELS, BEBE (1901–1971), a veteran of hundreds of silent shorts and features, appeared in some early movie musicals, often playing a dark-haired beauty with lots of spirit. After portraying the heroine in *RIO RITA* (1929), Daniels was featured as the title character in *Along Comes Peggy* (1930) and *Dixiana* (1930), as well as in *Reaching for the Moon* (1931), *Music Is Magic* (1935), and others. Her most remembered role is that of temperamental star Dorothy Brock in *42ND STREET* (1933). By the late 1930s Daniels moved to

England, where she and her husband BEN LYON starred in British plays, films, radio shows, and nightclubs.

DARE, DANNY (1905–1996) had an unusual career in that he gained fame as a choreographer and then later worked as a film producer. Dare started staging musical numbers on film with *Three Cheers for Love* (1936) but hit his stride with *HOLIDAY INN* (1942), *STAR SPANGLED RHYTHM* (1942), *HERE COME THE WAVES* (1944), *Incendiary Blonde* (1945), and *ROAD TO UTOPIA* (1945). He moved into producing with *Duffy's Tavern* (1945) and performed both chores for *Variety Girl* (1947) as well. Among the musicals he later produced were *ROAD TO RIO* (1947) and *Isn't It Romantic?* (1948).

DARIN, BOBBY (1936–1973), the pop singer and songwriter whose recording of "Mack the Knife" sold over two million copies, appeared in three movie musicals—*Pepe* (1960), *Too Late Blues* (1962), and *STATE FAIR* (1962)—and wrote the score for *The Lively Set* (1964). Darin also was featured in dramatic film roles until his untimely death by heart disease.

DARLING LILI (Paramount 1970) may have been a bit of a mess as it tried to decide whether it was a farce, an adventure, or a romance film, but star JULIE ANDREWS conquered the material and got to sing the haunting "Whistling Away the Dark," JOHNNY MERCER's last great song in his last movie score. BLAKE EDWARDS produced, directed, and (with William Peter Blatty) wrote the World War One–era tale about a Mata Hari–like music hall star (Andrews) who is passing information on to the Germans. American flying ace Rock Hudson is on to her game but is charmed by her all the same, the two engaging in some romantic banter reminiscent of his tangles with DORIS DAY in their many 1960s comedies. HENRY MANCINI composed the music for Mercer's lyrics and some war-time standards like "It's a Long Way to Tipperary" and "Pack Up Your Troubles in Your Old Kit Bag" were added for period flavor. Although Andrews got to do a mock striptease (choreographed by HERMES PAN in the final days of his career) and play a bad girl, it was her familiar crisp and wholesome persona that carried the film. The musical was a box office failure but over the years has acquired some kind of cult status.

DARWELL, JANE (1879–1967), a versatile character actress in silents, on stage, and later in talkies, is remembered for her piercing performance as Ma Joad in the nonmusical *The Grapes of Wrath* (1940) but can be seen in such musicals as *ROMAN SCANDALS* (1933), *WONDER BAR* (1934), *CURLY TOP* (1935), *CAPTAIN JANUARY* (1936), *Little Miss Broadway* (1938), *The Lemon Drop Kid* (1951), and others. Her final screen appearance was as the Bird Lady sitting on the steps of St. Paul's Cathedral in *MARY POPPINS* (1964).

DAVENPORT, HARRY (1866–1949), an actor-director descended from an old and illustrious stage family, appeared in and directed many silent movies before becoming a reliable character actor after the advent of sound. His dozens of film credits include the musicals *MAYTIME* (1937), *MEET ME IN ST. LOUIS* (1944), *Music for Millions* (1944), *Three Darling Daughters* (1948), and *That Lady in Ermine* (1948).

DAVES, DELMER (1904–1977) was a director, screenwriter, and sometime-producer who excelled at westerns but contributed to several notable musicals as well. Daves' meticulous touch and eye for detail can be seen in his scripts and/or direction of *DAMES* (1934), *Flirtation Walk* (1935), *YOU WERE NEVER LOVELIER* (1942), *HOLLYWOOD CANTEEN* (1944), and others.

DAVID, HAL. See Bacharach, Burt

DAVID, MACK (1912–1993), the prolific Tin Pan Alley lyricist who also wrote the theme songs for dozens of Hollywood nonmusicals, only scored four musicals. With AL HOFFMAN and JERRY LIVINGSTON, he wrote the memorable songs for the animated *CINDERELLA* (1949) as well as the JERRY LEWIS–DEAN MARTIN service comedies *At War With the Army* (1950), *Sailor Beware* (1951), and *Jumping Jacks* (1952). He is the elder brother of lyricist HAL DAVID.

DAVIES, MARION (1897–1961), who had a notable career on the New York stage, in silent films, and later in musicals, is more famous for her long-term liaison with newspaper king William Randolph Hearst, but she was a perky and gifted comedienne who lit up nine movie musicals. Davies was featured as a specialty in the early revue *HOLLYWOOD REVUE OF 1929* and then played the title role in *Marianne* (1929). Her other musical credits include *The Floradora Girl* (1930), *Blondie of the Follies* (1932), *GOING HOLLYWOOD* (1933), *Cain and Mabel* (1936), and her final screen appearance in *Ever Since Eve* (1937).

DAVIS, JOAN (1907–1961), a popular comedienne with a forever-forlorn expression of despair, displayed her slapstick talents in several comedy shorts and musical features from 1935 to 1948. Davis' antics can be seen in *ON THE AVENUE* (1937), *WAKE UP AND LIVE* (1937), *Love and Hisses* (1937), *Sally, Irene and Mary* as Irene (1938), *Just Around the Corner* (1938), *SUN VALLEY SERENADE* (1941), *Yokel Boy* (1932), *Kansas City Kitty* (1944), *George White's Scandals* (1945), *If You Knew Susie* (1948), and others.

DAVIS, JOHNNY "SCAT" (1910–1983) got his nickname from the scat-singing he did with the Big Bands and in movies. Davis played trumpet and vocalized with Fred Waring's orchestra before performing on screen in *Varsity Show* (1937), followed by *Cowboy From Brooklyn* (1938), *You Can't Ration Love* (1944), *Knickerbocker Holiday* (1944), and others. He is most remembered for introducing "Hooray for Hollywood" in *HOLLYWOOD HOTEL* (1937) and for the many popular recording he made over the years.

DAVIS, SAMMY, JR. (1925–1990), the dynamic African American entertainer who was a star of nightclubs, records, and television, rarely saw his talents handled well on the screen. A child performer in a family vaudeville act, Davis was first heard on film on the soundtrack of *Meet Me in Las Vegas* (1956). His finest film role was that of the slick Sportin' Life in *PORGY AND BESS* (1959), followed by supporting performances in *Pepe* (1960), *ROBIN AND THE SEVEN HOODS* (1964), *The Threepenny Opera* (1964), and *SWEET CHARITY* (1969). His stage version of *Stop the World—I Want to Get Off,* called *Sammy Stops the World,* was filmed in 1978.

DAY AT THE RACES, A (MGM 1937) had more musical numbers than the usual MARX BROTHERS vehicle, but once again the highlights were comic sequences rather than songs. Wealthy philanthropist MARGARET DUMONT brings in horse doctor Hugo Hackenbush (Groucho) to save her sanitarium, but he only manages to bring ALLAN JONES and Maureen O'Sullivan together while Harpo saves the day by winning a race horse in the farcical climax. The most notable musical number was "All God's Chillun Got Rhythm" by GUS KAHN, Walter Jurmann, and BRONISLAW KAPER, in which Pied Piper Harpo led a gang of African American kids (including a young DOROTHY DANDRIDGE) in a jubilant celebration of gospel, jazz, and swing.

DAY, DENNIS (1921–1988) and his high tenor voice were heard on JACK BENNY's radio and television shows for years, but he was also featured in eight film musicals in the 1940s and 1950s. Day usually played innocent or lame-brained sidekicks, and his high pitch singing also seemed like caricature. His first film was the Benny vehicle *Buck Benny Rides Again* (1940), followed by *Sleepy Lagoon* (1943), *Music in Manhattan* (1944), *I'll Get By* (1950), *The Girl Next Door* (1953), and others. He played himself in *The Powers Girl* (1943) and was heard on the soundtrack of the animated *Melody Time* (1948).

DAY, DORIS (1924–   ) was one of Hollywood's most popular stars in the 1950s for her musicals and in the 1960s for her coy sex comedies. A band singer during the war years, Day was gaining fame for her recordings when she made her film debut as a last-minute replacement in *ROMANCE ON THE HIGH SEAS* (1948). Her subsequent roles were lightweight leading ladies in tuneful musicals: *It's a Great Feeling* (1949), *My Dream Is Yours* (1949), *Tea for Two* (1950), *Lullaby of Broadway* (1951), *On Moonlight Bay* (1951), *I'll See*

You in My Dreams (1951), *April in Paris* (1952), *By the Light of the Silvery Moon* (1953), *CALAMITY JANE* (1953), and others. Day got to play more complex characters with band singer Jo Jordan in *YOUNG MAN WITH A HORN* (1950), unhappy wife Laurie in *Young at Heart* (1954), and abused singer RUTH ETTING in *LOVE ME OR LEAVE ME* (1955). Her last film musicals were screen adaptations of the Broadway hits *THE PAJAMA GAME* (1957) and *JUMBO* (1962). Also, Day sang the Oscar-winning "Que Sera, Sera" in the nonmusical *The Man Who Knew Too Much* (1956), and it became her signature song. Because of her later comedies and television show, Day was typecast as the wholesome, ever-virginal heroine, but behind it all lay a very troubled life and a talent that went much deeper.

DAY, RICHARD (1896–1972) was one of Hollywood's most accomplished art directors and designers, winning five ACADEMY AWARDS and raising the level of screen design during the final years of the silents. Although Day was acclaimed for his realistic sets, he provided fanciful designs for such musicals as *WHOOPEE* (1930), *HALLELUJAH, I'M A BUM* (1933), *ROMAN SCANDALS* (1933), *THE GOLDWYN FOLLIES* (1938), *LILLIAN RUSSELL* (1940), *My Gal Sal* (1942), *HANS CHRISTIAN ANDERSEN* (1952), and many others.

DE LUISE, DOM (1933–   ), a rotund comic actor who usually played the hero's sidekick in film comedies, appeared in the musicals *THE MUPPET MOVIE* (1979) and *The Best Little Whorehouse in Texas* (1982) and lent his cartoon-like voice to the animated musicals *An American Tail* (1986), *OLIVER AND COMPANY* (1988), *An American Tail: Fievel Goes West* (1991), *A Troll in Central Park* (1994), and *All Dogs Go to Heaven* (1996).

DE PAUL, GENE (1919–   ), a Broadway and Hollywood composer, is mainly remembered for his two collaborations with lyricist JOHNNY MERCER: *SEVEN BRIDES FOR SEVEN BROTHERS* (1954) and *LI'L ABNER* (on Broadway in 1956, filmed in 1959). De Paul also scored *You Can't Run Away From It* (1959) with Mercer, but all of his other movie scores were with DON RAYE, beginning with *In the Navy* (1941) and followed by *Keep 'Em Flying* (1941), *Behind the Eight Ball* (1941), *Hellzapoppin* (1941), *Ride 'Em Cowboy* (1942), *Pardon My Sarong* (1942), *Broadway Rhythm* (1944), *A Song Is Born* (1948), and others.

DE SYLVA, B.G. (1895–1950), a successful lyricist and producer, was a member of the illustrious team of De Sylva, (LEW) BROWN, and HENDERSON, who scored several Broadway hits in the 1920s, some of which were filmed, such as *GOOD NEWS* (1930 and 1947), *Follow the Leader* (1930) based on their play *Manhattan Mary*, and *Follow Thru* (1930). The trio also wrote directly for the screen, as with *THE SINGING FOOL* (1928), *Say It With Songs*

(1929), *SUNNY SIDE UP* (1929), *Just Imagine* (1930), and *Indiscreet* (1931). With RICHARD A. WHITING, NACIO HERB BROWN, and VINCENT YOUMANS, De Sylva scored *Take a Chance* (1933) based on their 1932 Broadway hit, and *My Weakness* (1933). In 1930 De Sylva began a second career as a film producer, first at 20TH CENTURY–FOX and then at PARAMOUNT, where he presented the musicals *Under the Pampas Moon* (1035), *The Littlest Rebel* (1935), *CAPTAIN JANUARY* (1935), *Sing, Baby, Sing* (1936), *POOR LITTLE RICH GIRL* (1936), *Merry-Go-Round of 1938* (1937), *You're a Sweetheart* (1937), *BIRTH OF THE BLUES* (1941), *Lady in the Dark* (1943), and *The Stork Club* (1946). In the musical bio *The Best Things in Life Are Free* (1956), GORDON MacRAE played De Sylva.

DeCAMP, ROSEMARY (1913–   ) usually played the friend, sister, or mother to the hero or heroine in a series of 1940s films, including the musicals *YANKEE DOODLE DANDY* (1942), *THIS IS THE ARMY* (1943), *RHAPSODY IN BLUE* (1945), *Look for the Silver Lining* (1949), *On Moonlight Bay* (1951), and *By the Light of the Silvery Moon* (1953).

DeCARLO, YVONNE (1922–   ) was often cast as sexy femme fatales or seductive slave girls because of her dark and exotic looks, but she started out as a dancer and was occasionally featured in musicals throughout her long career: *ROAD TO MOROCCO* (1942), *Youth on Parade* (1942), *Rhythm Parade* (1943), *Let's Face It* (1943) *HERE COME THE WAVES* (1944), *CASBAH* (1948), and others. DeCarlo was popular on television in the 1960s (*The Munsters*) and returned to the stage in 1971 with the Broadway musical *Follies*.

DEEP IN MY HEART (MGM 1954), the BIOGRAPHICAL MUSICAL about composer SIGMUND ROMBERG, boasted a superb performance by José Ferrer as the title character and included enough stars and songs that few minded the trite rags-to-riches plot. Because OPERETTA was a risky item in the 1950s, many of Romberg's musical comedy numbers were featured and provided the most fun: GENE KELLY and his brother Fred (their only film appearance together) showing off their pectorals with "I Like to Go Swimmin' With Wimmen," Ferrer and opera singer Helen Traubel cutting loose in "The Leg of Mutton Rag," ANN MILLER turning "It" into a seductive showcase for herself, and Ferrer and ROSEMARY CLOONEY singing the sly "Mr. and Mrs." Some of the operetta selections included JANE POWELL and VIC DAMOME in the duet "Will You Remember?," TONY MARTIN and Joan Weldon in "Lover, Come Back to Me," William Ovis singing "Serenade," and HOWARD KEEL giving full force to "Your Land and My Land." David Burns, Doe Avedon, CYD CHARISSE, James Mitchell, WALTER PIDGEON, Merle Oberon, and Jim Backus filled out the cast of singing and nonsinging, fictional and factual characters.

DeHAVEN, GLORIA (1925–   ) played glamorous leading ladies or secondary leads in several film musicals at MGM, but her career waned as the Hollywood musical declined in the late 1950s. DeHaven started as a child performer in a family act in vaudeville before making her musical film debut as the student Ethel in *BEST FOOT FORWARD* (1943). Her best role was that of innocent New Englander Muriel McComber in *SUMMER HOLIDAY* (1946) and she got to play her own mother, Mrs. Carter DeHaven, in the bio *THREE LITTLE WORDS* (1950). DeHaven's other musical credits include *Broadway Rhythm* (1944), *TWO GIRLS AND A SAILOR* (1944), *Step Lively* (1944), *SUMMER STOCK* (1950), *Two Tickets to Broadway* (1951), *So This Is Paris* (1954). and *The Girl Rush* (1955).

DEL RIO, DOLORES (1905–1983), the exotic Latin beauty of silent and sound films, made only a handful of musicals but her appearance in each was memorable: *FLYING DOWN TO RIO* (1933), *WONDER BAR* (1934), *I Live for Love* (1935), and *In Caliente* (1935). The Mexican-born actress was limited in her roles because of her accent, so she left Hollywood in the 1940s to make films in Mexico, returning to American movies in character roles on occasion. She was married to Hollywood art director CEDRIC GIBBONS.

DEL RUTH, ROY (1895–1961) was a reliable director at several studios from the early talkies to 1960, staging some two dozen lavish musicals beginning with *THE DESERT SONG* (1929). Other early musicals include *GOLD DIGGERS OF BROADWAY* (1929), *Hold Everything* (1930), *Life of the Party* (1930), *KID MILLIONS* (1934), *FOLIES BERGÈRE DE PARIS* (1935), *BROADWAY MELODY OF 1936* (1935), *BORN TO DANCE* (1936), *ON THE AVENUE* (1937), and *BROADWAY MELODY OF 1938* (1937). Del Ruth's subsequent films were not as impressive, but there was still some quality work in *Happy Landing* (1938), *My Lucky Star* (1938), *The Star Maker* (1939), *The Chocolate Soldier* (1941), *DuBarry Was a Lady* (1943), *Broadway Rhythm* (1944), *The West Point Story* (1950), *On Moonlight Bay* (1951), *Starlift* (1951), *Three Sailors and a Girl* (1953), and others.

DeLANGE, EDDIE (1904–1949) was a Tin Pan Alley lyricist ("Moonglow") who, with various composers, contributed to a few Hollywood musicals in the 1940s. With JOSEF MYROW he scored *If I'm Lucky* (1946), with SAUL CHAPLIN *Meet Me on Broadway* (1946), and with LOUIS ALTER *New Orleans* (1947), which introduced the jazz hit "Do You Know What It Means to Miss New Orleans?"

DELICIOUS (Fox 1931) showcased the popular romantic team of JANET GAYNOR and CHARLES FARRELL, who captured the hearts of America in silent and then talking films. Gaynor was a Swedish immigrant who, escaping the clutches of Ellis Island official Lawrence O'Sullivan, soon finds herself having to choose between the affections of Russian composer Raul Roulien and American playboy Farrell. There was no question where the audience's sympathies lay, but there were some wonderful GEORGE and IRA GERSHWIN songs to make the contest interesting: the delicate lullaby "Somebody From Somewhere," a satirical number about lyricwriting called "Blah Blah Blah," and the Gershwinesque "Delishious," the first hit song the brothers had written for the screen. The comedy was provided by MISCHA AUER and Swedish comic EL BRENDEL, who massacred the English language every time he opened his mouth.

DEMAREST, WILLIAM (1892–1983) was one of Hollywood's most distinctive character actors, often stealing the show in a series of Preston Sturges films and in over 100 movies between 1926 and 1975. The paunchy-faced comic with a crude wisecracking manner made appearances in the musicals *THE JAZZ SINGER* (1927), *THE BROADWAY MELODY* (1929), *THE GREAT ZIEGFELD* (1936), *ROSALIE* (1937), *REBECCA OF SUNNY-BROOK FARM* (1938), *THE JOLSON STORY* (1946), *JOLSON SINGS AGAIN* (1949), *VIVA LAS VEGAS* (1964), and many others. Demarest found a whole new career on television (*My Three Sons*) in the 1960s.

DESERT SONG, THE (Warner 1929) was the first OPERETTA filmed with sound, and after previous silents in which thin operetta plots were told with titles, it must have been exhilarating to hear OSCAR HAMMERSTEIN and SIGMUND ROMBERG's 1926 score coming from the mouths of the characters. "One Alone," " The Riff Song," "Then You Will Know," "The Sabre Song," "Romance," and the romantic title number were among the songs that enlivened the improbable tale about a French beauty (Carlotta King) who falls for the dashing JOHN BOLES in North Africa, not knowing he is the Red Shadow, leader of the revolutionary Riffs. ROY DEL RUTH directed the mostly sung story but had trouble keeping it visually interesting. The musical was neither a critical nor a popular hit, but WARNER BROTHERS dusted off the property in 1943 and filmed it again, this time with an altered screenplay in which the Riffs were fighting against the Nazis in French Morocco. DENNIS MORGAN was an American soldier from the Spanish Civil War who disguised himself to help the Riffs, and Irene Manning was his sweetheart. As contemporary as it tried to be, the music was what counted and the voices were more thrilling than the lavish Technicolor production directed by Robert Florey. The studio presented yet a third version in 1953 and cast the latest singing favorites GORDON MacRAE and KATHRYN GRAYSON as the two lovers. This time any reference to the Red Shadow had to be dropped because of Cold War jitters, and the plot seemed more antique than its twenty-eight years. H. BRUCE HUMBERSTONE directed and could not hide the tale's shortcomings. The melodic score was trimmed to allow more intrigues (Raymond

Massey was the wicked sheik who was after Grayson), and the result was the least satisfying version of the three.

DEUTSCH, ADOLPH (1897–1980) was an award-winning conductor, composer, and music arranger who scored many Hollywood dramas and did the musical direction for such films as *TAKE ME OUT TO THE BALL GAME* (1949), *ANNIE GET YOUR GUN* (1950), *THE BAND WAGON* (1953), *SEVEN BRIDES FOR SEVEN BROTHERS* (1954), *OKLAHOMA!* (1955), *FUNNY FACE* (1957), and *LES GIRLS* (1957).

DeWOLF, BILLY (1907–1974), a delightful lisping comic with a pencil-thin mustache and a very proper persona, was famous for his quiet but hilarious routines in vaudeville and nightclubs, some of which he recreated in his nine movie musicals. DeWolfe's most remembered films are *Dixie* (1946), *BLUE SKIES* (1946), *Tea for Two* (1950), *Lullaby of Broadway* (1951), and *CALL ME MADAM* (1953).

DICK TRACY (Touchstone/Disney 1990) was such a dazzling display of stylized settings, use of color, cartoonish makeup, and high-flying performances that it was difficult to detect a superb score by STEPHEN SONDHEIM hidden or edited out of recognition. Director Warren Beatty played the Chester Gould comic strip hero, Glenne Headley was his love interest, and Charlie Korsmo portrayed the waif they befriended. But it was the villains and cops that provided all the fun: Charles Durning, Dustin Hoffman, James Caan, Michael J. Pollard, DICK VAN DYKE, Paul Sorvino and, best of all, Al Pacino in an over-the-top comic performance as the hood Big Boy Caprice. The musical numbers were limited to Big Boy's nightclub, where sexy songstress Bubbles Mahoney (MADONNA) and piano player MANDY PATINKIN delivered four dynamite songs, none seen in its entirety as the camera usually cut away to the action elsewhere. "Sooner or Later (I Always Get My Man)" must have stuck with some audience members because it won the ACADEMY AWARD for Best Song, but just as proficient were "Back in Business," "What Can You Lose," and the jazzy "More," which Pacino tried to teach the chorus girls to sing at a comical rehearsal.

DIETERLE, WILLIAM (1893–1972), the busy German-born director who specialized in costume dramas and biographical films, directed only a handful of musicals in Hollywood, including *Her Majesty Love* (1931), *Adorable* (1933), *Fashions of 1934,* and *Syncopation* (1942).

DIETRICH, MARLENE (1901–1992) was one of Hollywood's most mysterious and exotic leading ladies, a European beauty who epitomizes foreign glamour and sex appeal. Although none of her American films were traditional musicals, Dietrich often played performers in her melodramas and usually sang a few songs in her husky, world-weary singing voice. Later in her career she also sang in nightclubs and on television. Among the films that allowed Dietrich to display her musical talents were *The Blue Angel* (1930), *Morocco* (1930), *Blonde Venus* (1932), *Song of Songs* (1933), *Destry Rides Again* (1939), *Follow the Boys* (1944), and *A Foreign Affair* (1948).

DIETZ, HOWARD (1896–1983), a Broadway lyricist who, with composer ARTHUR SCHWARTZ, scored some of the best musical REVUES in Broadway history, had a second career as an executive at MGM (he developed the Leo the lion trademark). Although Dietz provided songs for *Hollywood Party* (1934), *Under Your Spell* (1936), and a few other musical films, he is most remembered for *Dancing in the Dark* (1949) and *THE BAND WAGON* (1953), both of which used the Dietz-Schwartz song catalog for their musical numbers. For the latter he and Schwartz wrote the piquant number "That's Entertainment," an anthem of sorts for movie musicals.

DIRTY DANCING (Vestron 1987) had so much dancing and such an unrelenting score that it seemed like a full-fledged musical even though the characters hardly sang a note. In the 1960s, reclusive teen Jennifer Grey visits a Catskills resort with her family and discovers the joys of sex and dancing, both with Patrick Swayze. The film even ended with a Big Show, this time a dance piece featuring Grey that endeared her to her family (and to audiences). The soundtrack included new songs by various writers that became hits, such as the Oscar-winning "(I've Had) The Time of My Life," and older favorites like "You Don't Own Me" and "Be My Baby." Both the movie and the soundtrack were very popular and defined what was meant by a musical film in the 1980s.

DISNEY COMPANY. See Walt Disney Company, The

DISNEY, WALT (1901–1966), the one-man dynamo behind cartoon shorts, animated features, live action adventure films, television, documentaries, big-budget movie musicals, and theme parks pioneered the use of music on film by animating popular and classical pieces of music first in shorts and then, beginning with *SNOW WHITE AND THE SEVEN DWARFS* (1937), in feature films. Of the nineteen animated features Disney supervised and produced during his lifetime, all used songs. His early masterworks include *PINOCCHIO* (1940), *FANTASIA* (1940), *DUMBO* (1941), and *Bambi* (1942). During the war years he created *Saludos Amigos* (1943) and *THE THREE CABALLEROS* (1945) to support the country's "Good Neighbor" policy with South America. Disney's animated anthology features included *Make Mine Music* (1946), *Fun and Fancy Free* (1947), and *Melody Time* (1948), followed by a series of popular fairy tale musicals such as *CINDERELLA* (1950), *ALICE IN WONDERLAND* (1951), *Peter Pan* (1953), *LADY AND THE TRAMP* (1955), and *Sleeping Beauty* (1959). In the 1960s the animation department of Disney's studio produced fewer features, although *101 Dalmations* (1961) and *THE JUNGLE BOOK* (1967) were still first-class productions. Live-action musicals such as *BABES IN TOYLAND* (1961) and *MARY POPPINS* (1964) continued the Disney tradition with songs on film. The last film Disney oversaw before his death was *The Happiest Millionaire* (1967).

DIXON, LEE (1914–1953) was a tall, leggy dancer-singer who appeared in a few 1930s musicals, such as *GOLD DIGGERS OF 1937* (1936), *Ready, Willing and Able* (1937), *The Singing Marine* (1937), and *VARSITY SHOW* (1937). Dixon returned to the stage in the 1940s and originated the role of Will Parker in *Oklahoma!* on Broadway in 1943.

DIXON, MORT (1892–1956), a lyricist who often worked with composer ALLIE WRUBEL, supplied the songs for *Flirtation Walk* (1934), *Happiness Ahead* (1934), *Broadway Hostess* (1935), *I Live for Love* (1935), and *In Caliente* (1935). The Tin Pan Alley songwriter, who wrote "Bye Bye Blackbird," "I'm Looking Over a Four-Leaf Clover," and other standards, had his greatest screen hit with "The Lady in Red."

DOCTOR DOLITTLE (APJAC/Fox 1967) may have been overlong and overproduced (it just about bankrupted 20TH CENTURY–FOX), but there was a cockeyed kind of charm in the musical fantasy as it lumbered from sequence to sequence revealing new and unusual creatures and special effects along the way. Based on a series of stories by Hugh Lofting, the film centers on veterinarian REX HARRISON, who is taught hundreds of animal languages by his pet parakeet Polynesia and then sets off with Samantha Eggar, ANTHONY NEWLEY, and Richard Attenborough to use them. On their journey they encounter the Giant Lunar Moth, a double llama called a Pushmi-Pullyu, the Great Pink Sea Snail, and a homesick seal named Sophie to whom Harrison sang the mellifluous "When I Look Into Your Eyes." LESLIE BRICUSSE wrote the script and songs, which also included "Beautiful Things," "Something in Your Smile," and the Oscar-winning "Talk to the Animals."

DOLAN, ROBERT EMMETT (1908–1972) was a respected composer, musical arranger, and conductor and even a producer of musical films, most memorably *WHITE CHRISTMAS* (1954), *The Girl Rush* (1955), and *ANYTHING GOES* (1956). Dolan made his name on Broadway but started in Hollywood with *BIRTH OF THE BLUES* (1941) and went on to arrange and/or conduct the music in *HOLIDAY INN* (1942), *STAR SPANGLED RHYTHM* (1942), *Dixie* (1943), *Lady in the Dark* (1944), *THE BELLS OF ST. MARY'S* (1945), *BLUE SKIES* (1946), *ROAD TO UTOPIA* (1946), and others.

DOLLY SISTERS, THE (Fox 1945) made little attempt at historical accuracy when telling the story of Hungarian beauties Jennie and Rosie Dolly, who starred in vaudeville and on Broadway. The two dark-haired Europeans were played by blonde all-Americans BETTY GRABLE and JUNE HAVER, and the settings, costumes, makeup, and even the new songs seemed more 1940s than turn-of-the-century since the film's entertainment values were strictly contemporary. JOHN PAYNE and Frank Latimore were the sisters' love interests, and the two couples were joined by Frank Middlemass as their discoverer Oscar Hammerstein I, S.K. SAKALL as their cuddly uncle Latsie, SIG RUMMAN, Gene Sheldon, REGINALD GARDINER, and Collette Lyons. "I Can't Begin to Tell You" by MACK GORDON and JAMES V. MONACO was the best of the original numbers, which were augmented by old favorites such as "I'm Always Chasing Rainbows," "Smiles," and "The Sidewalks of New York." GEORGE JESSEL, who knew about the period firsthand, was the producer. The whole production seems garish by modern sentiments, but, mainly because of Grable's popularity, the movie was a box office hit.

DONALDSON, WALTER (1893–1947), a busy Tin Pan Alley and Broadway composer, went to Hollywood when his stage hit *WHOOPEE* (1930) was filmed and stayed long enough to score *KID MILLIONS* (1934), *Operator 13* (1934), and *THE GREAT ZIEGFELD* (1936). Among Donaldson's many hit songs were "Carolina in the Morning," "Love Me or Leave Me," "Yes, Sir, That's My Baby," and "Makin' Whoopee."

DONEN, STANLEY (1924–   ), one of the most accomplished movie choreographers and directors in postwar Hollywood, began as a chorus line dancer on Broadway, where he first worked with GENE KELLY. When Kelly went to California, Donan accompanied him and assisted on the choreography for *BEST FOOT FORWARD* (1943), *COVER GIRL* (1944), *ANCHORS AWEIGH* (1945), and *TAKE ME OUT TO THE BALL GAME* (1949). He also staged the musical numbers for *Jam Session* (1944), *No Leave, No Love* (1946), *A Date With Judy* (1948), *The Kissing Bandit* (1948), and others. Donan's directing career began with *ON THE TOWN* (1949), which he co-directed with Kelly, as he would with *SINGIN' IN THE RAIN* (1952) and *IT'S ALWAYS FAIR WEATHER* (1955). Leaving the choreography to others, Donan also directed *ROYAL WEDDING* (1951), *SEVEN BRIDES FOR SEVEN BROTHERS* (1954), *DEEP IN MY HEART* (1954), and *FUNNY FACE* (1957). He also directed the movie versions of the Broadway hits *THE PAJAMA GAME* (1957) and *DAMN YANKEES* (1958) and the original screen musicals *The Little Prince* (1973) and *MOVIE MOVIE* (1978), all four of which he also co-produced. Donan was an innovative artist who explored new ways to portray dance on film. He was instrumental in developing such famous film sequences as Kelly's "Singin' in the Rain" dance, FRED ASTAIRE's tap dancing on the ceiling, Kelly's dancing with the animated Jerry the Mouse, and the unique montage scenes in *On the Town* and *Funny Face*.

DONOHUE, JACK (1908–1984) rose from Broadway chorus boy to one of the busiest choreographers of film musicals in the 1930s and 1940s, staging the numbers in four SHIRLEY TEMPLE films and working at four different studios. Donohue's first screen assignment was *George White's Scandals* (1934), and he refined his craft choreographing *MUSIC IN THE AIR* (1934), *Under Pressure* (1935), and *Lottery Lover* (1935) before gaining recognition for *The Little Colonel* (1935), *CURLY TOP* (1935), *THANKS A MILLION* (1935), *CAPTAIN JANUARY* (1936), and others. In the 1940s he prospered at MGM doing the dances for *Louisiana Purchase* (1941), *THE FLEET'S IN* (1942), *Girl Crazy* (1943), *Broadway Rhythm* (1944), *Two Sisters From Boston* (1946), *IT HAPPENED IN BROOKLYN* (1947), *CALAMITY JANE* (1953), and many others. Donohue turned to directing in the 1950s and staged some light comedies and the musicals *Lucky Me* (1954) and *BABES IN TOYLAND* (1961).

DORSEY, JIMMY (1904–1957), one of the giants of the Big Band era, was a saxophone player in his brother TOMMY DORSEY's orchestra before breaking away and forming his own popular band. He and his orchestra were featured in nine movie musicals in the 1940s and introduced such hits as "I Remember You" and "Tangerine." Dorsey's most memorable films were *Lady, Be Good* (1941), *THE FLEET'S IN* (1942), *Four Jills in a Jeep* (1944), *HOLLYWOOD CANTEEN* (1944), and *Make Believe Ballroom* (1949). He played himself in *The Fabulous Dorseys* (1947) and *Music Man* (1949).

DORSEY, TOMMY (1905–1956) and his orchestra introduced several hits during the 1940s and were given specialty spots in a dozen film musicals. The trombone player and his band made their screen debut with *Las Vegas Nights* (1941) and were featured in *Ship Ahoy* (1942), *Presenting Lily Mars* (1943), *DuBarry Was a Lady* (1843), *Girl Crazy* (1943), *Swing Fever* (1943), *Broadway Rhythm* (1944), *The Thrill of a Romance* (1945), and *Disc Jockey* (1951). He played himself in *The Fabulous Dorseys* (1947) and *A Song Is Born* (1948).

DOUBLE OR NOTHING (Paramount 1937) was an odd and unique little musical that was filled with surprises along the way, many of them in the unusual way the musical numbers were handled. A millionaire, believing that people are basically honest, states in his will that wallets containing $500 each be left in various spots in Manhattan to see who is honest enough to return them. BING CROSBY, WILLIAM FRAWLEY, MARTHA RAYE, and Andy Devine pass the test and have the chance for $5,000 if they can double the money in a month's time. Crosby wins by investing the cash in a nightclub. The songs, by various tunesmiths, were memorable in themselves but benefited by their distinctive staging by Theodore Reed: Crosby makes shadow puppets on the wall while singing "It's the Natural Thing to Do," the music for the sidewalk dance number "All You Want to Do Is Dance" comes from a car radio, Raye satirizes stripteasers with "It's On, It's Off," and a nightspot orchestra creates their sounds vocally while accompanying "The Moon Got in My Eyes."

DOWN ARGENTINE WAY (Fox 1940) created two new stars: BETTY GRABLE, who got the leading role when illness forced ALICE FAYE out, and CARMEN MIRANDA, who reached a wide American audience for the first time and swept them off their feet. The nearly invisible plot concerned American heiress Grable, who goes to Argentina to buy a horse from wealthy DON AMECHE and falls into a romance with him despite the disapproval of his rich father, Henry Stephenson. Miranda did not fit into the story or characters at all (in fact, her specialty numbers were filmed in New York), but she stopped the show cold with "South American Way" and "Mama Yo Quiero." Grable got to sing the ballad "Two Dreams Met" and show off her gams dancing to "Down Argentina Way." Leggy CHARLOTTE GREENWOOD, who managed to dance and get laughs at the same time, and the NICHOLAS BROTHERS were also showcased. The movie was so successful that a series of Latin-flavored musicals (usually featuring Miranda, Ameche, and Grable or Faye) were launched by 20TH CENTURY–FOX.

DOWNS, JOHNNY (1913–1994) was an agile singer-dancer who usually played clean-cut college types in film musicals of the 1930s and 1940s, though more often than not in B movies with mediocre scores and few opportunities for his talents. A veteran of the *Our Gang* comedies, Downs got his experience in vaudeville and on Broadway before going to Hollywood and acting in silents. His first screen musical was *BABES IN TOYLAND* (1934), followed by *Coronado* (1935), *Pigskin Parade* (1936), *College Holiday* (1936), *Hold That Coed* (1937), *Melody and Moonlight* (1940), *All-American Coed* (1941), *Campus Rhythm* (1943), *The Kid From Brooklyn* (1946), *CALL ME MADAM* (1953), *Here Come the Girls* (1953), and many others.

DRAKE, DONA (1920–1989), a fiery little dynamo of a singer and dancer who billed herself as "Rio Rita" in nightclubs in the 1930s, was usually featured as the second lead or comic friend in such musicals as *Strike Me Pink* (1936), *Louisiana Purchase* (1941), *ROAD TO MOROCCO* (1942), *STAR SPANGLED RHYTHM* (1942), *Let's Face It* (1943), *Salute for Three* (1043), and *Hot Rhythm* (1944).

DRISCOLL, BOBBY (1937–1968), an agreeable child star in the late 1940s and early 1950s, appeared in the musicals *SONG OF THE SOUTH* (1946), *If You Knew Susie* (1948), *Melody Time* (1949), and *So Dear to My Heart* (1949), as well as in nonmusicals before he reached his teens and fell out of favor with audiences. Driscoll collapsed when his career did, becoming a drug addict and dying of a heart attack at the age of thirty. He is best remembered for playing

Jim Hawkins in the nonmusical *Treasure Island* (1950) and for providing the voice of the title boy-hero in the animated *Peter Pan* (1953).

DUBIN, AL (1891–1945) was one of the most important of Hollywood lyricists, centering his career on films as opposed to the stage or Tin Pan Alley and scoring some landmark movie musicals in the 1930s. Dubin's first collaborator was composer JOE BURKE, with whom he scored seven early talkies, including *GOLD DIGGERS OF BROADWAY* (1929), *She Couldn't Say No* (1930), *Hold Everything* (1930), *Life of the Party* (1930), and *Oh, Sailor Behave* (1930). It was with composer HARRY WARREN that Dubin wrote his greatest scores, beginning with *42ND STREET* (1933), followed by *GOLD DIGGERS OF 1933, FOOTLIGHT PARADE* (1933), *ROMAN SCANDALS* (1933), *Moulin Rouge* (1934), *WONDER BAR* (1934), *Twenty Million Sweethearts* (1934), *DAMES* (1934), *GOLD DIGGERS OF 1935, GO INTO YOUR DANCE* (1935), *Broadway Gondolier* (1935), *Shipmates Forever* (1935), *Stars Over Broadway* (1935), *Cain and Mabel* (1936), *GOLD DIGGERS OF 1937* (1936), *Mr. Dodd Takes the Air* (1937), *The Singing Marine* (1937), *GOLD DIGGERS IN PARIS* (1938), *Garden of the Moon* (1938), and others. Dubin was the first lyricist to create a catalog of hit songs written for the screen, leaving behind such standards as "Shuffle Off to Buffalo," "I Only Have Eyes for You," "We're in the Money," "Lullaby of Broadway," "Tip Toe Through the Tulips," and many others.

DUCHIN, EDDY (1909–1951), a renowned pianist and band leader, appeared with his famous orchestra in *Coronado* (1935) and *Hit Parade of 1937* and was the subject of the BIOGRAPHICAL MUSICAL *The Eddy Duchin Story* (1956) in which the high society musician was played by TYRONE POWER with Carmen Cavallero dubbing his piano work.

DUCK SOUP (Paramount 1933) is arguably the MARX BROTHERS' funniest film, perhaps because the few songs in it are comic and none stops the comedic flow of the surreal farce. Rufus T. Firefly (Groucho) is made dictator of the little kingdom of Freedonia by the wealthy MARGARET DUMONT, but before you know it the tiny country is at war. HARRY RUBY and BERT KALMAR wrote the script and the songs, which satirized everything from GEORGE M. COHAN to Gilbert and Sullivan: the mocking anthem "Freedonia Hymn," the foot-stomping spiritual "The Country's Going to War," and the patter song "The Laws of My Administration." LEO McCAREY directed with free abandon, allowing the story to stop for such classic bits as Harpo and Chico dressed identically as Groucho and simulating a mirror between them. Today considered a classic, the movie was not very popular and did such poor box office that PARAMOUNT dropped the brothers, and they went to MGM.

DUKE, VERNON (1903–1969), the Russian-born composer with classical training who also wrote popular music for Broadway, saw his stage piece *CABIN IN THE SKY* (1943) filmed and contributed to such movie musicals as *She's Working Her Way Through College* (1952) and *April in Paris* (1952), both with lyricist SAMMY CAHN. Duke completed the score for *THE GOLD-WYN FOLLIES* (1938) when his friend GEORGE GERSHWIN died halfway through production. Duke's concert music was written and performed under his birth-given name, Vladimir Dukelsky.

DUMBO (Disney/RKO 1941) was one of the shortest of all DISNEY animated features (only sixty-four minutes), but every moment counted in this tender-hearted tale of a misfit elephant named Dumbo whose oversized ears, the subject of much scorn by other animals, eventually made him famous by allowing him to fly and become the circus's top attraction. The animation was expert throughout, but the dream sequence "Pink Elephants on Parade" contained the most innovative use of color and line yet seen on film. Oliver Wallace, NED WASHINGTON, and FRANK CHURCHILL penned the songs, which included the catchy "When I See an Elephant Fly" and the lilting lullaby "Baby Mine." The title character never uttered a word, but his friends were voiced by Edward Brophy, Verna Felton, STERLING HOLLOWAY, HERMAN BING, and CLIFF EDWARDS. The musical was one of the top-grossing movies of the year and has remained a favorite over the decades.

DUMONT, MARGARET (1889–1965), the stately, very proper character actress who is mainly known for playing the foil in seven MARX BROTHERS films, began as a singer on Broadway but later played upper-class matrons on the screen beginning with *THE COCOANUTS* (1929). In addition to the Marx Brothers vehicles, Dumont appeared in the musicals *Born to Sing* (1942), *Sing Your Worries Away* (1942), *UP IN ARMS* (1944), and *Bathing Beauty* (1944).

DUNA, STEFFI (1913–1992), a ballet dancer from Budapest, was cast as Latin types in a handful of shorts and musical features. Duna's credits include *Hi, Gaucho* (1936), *The Dancing Pirate* (1936), *Rascals* (1938), *Way Down South* (1939), and *The Girl From Havana* (1940). Since none of her musicals were grade-A products, she moved on to dramatic roles.

DUNBAR, DIXIE (1915–1991), a perky dancing treat in several Broadway musicals, appeared in a dozen 20TH CENTURY–FOX musicals before retiring at the age of nineteen. Among Dunbar's film credits are *George White's Scandals* (1934), *KING OF BURLESQUE* (1935), *Pigskin Parade* (1936), *Sing and Be Happy* (1937), *REBECCA OF SUNNYBROOK FARM* (1938), and *ALEXANDER'S RAGTIME BAND* (1938).

DUNN, JAMES (1905–1967) was a singer from Broadway who never made star status in film musicals but later gained a reputation for his dramatic roles. The round-faced leading man was featured in *Dance Team* (1932), *Jimmy and Sally* (1933), *Take a Chance* (1933), *Stand Up and Cheer* (1934), *Baby, Take a Bow* (1934), *Bright Eyes* (1934), *George White's Scandals* (1935), and others.

DUNNE, IRENE (1901–1990) was a film favorite for over twenty years playing a variety of roles in musicals, screwball comedies, and dramas. Trained as an opera singer, Dunne was discovered by RKO when she was touring in *Show Boat* and signed to play the cabaret singer Addie in *SWEET ADELINE* (1935), the Russian princess Stephanie in *ROBERTA* (1935), leading lady Magnolia Hawks in *SHOW BOAT* (1936), backwoods singer Sally in *HIGH, WIDE AND HANDSOME* (1937), and Broadway star Maggie Garret in *JOY OF LIVING* (1938). After several memorable roles in nonmusicals, Dunne returned to the musical screen to play songwriter Kay Kingsley in *Never a Dull Moment* (1950) before retiring from the movies.

DURANTE, JIMMY (1893–1980), with his gravel voice, large "schnozzola" of a nose, and raspy sense of comic delivery, was one of the most unique personalities in show business. A headliner in vaudeville, on Broadway, in nightclubs, and on television, Durante also appeared in twenty-seven film musicals beginning with *Roadhouse Nights* (1930) and concluding as circus owner Pop Wonder in *JUMBO* (1966). He often played the piano as he sang in his musicals, and his stiff-kneed strut was as characteristic as his bulbous profile. Among his other musical credits are *The Cuban Love Song* (1931), *THE PHANTOM PRESIDENT* (1932), *Palooka* (1934), *Strictly Dynamite* (1934), *Sally, Irene and Mary* (1938), *Little Miss Broadway* (1938) in which he played his former stage partner Lou Clayton, *TWO GIRLS AND A SAILOR* (1944), *IT HAPPENED IN BROOKLYN* (1947), *On an Island With You* (1948), *Beau James* (1957), and *Pepe* (1960).

DURBIN, DEANNA (1921–   ), a classically trained singer who excelled at playing wholesome youths with a bubbly personality, was one of the top box office attractions in the late 1930s and 1940s and, coupled with her popularity on the radio, perhaps the most-heard female singer of her era. Producer JOE PASTERNAK discovered Durbin, and she was an instant star when her first feature *Three Smart Girls* (1936) was released. Her subsequent musicals were built around Durbin's clear, chirping soprano voice and spirited persona: *ONE HUNDRED MEN AND A GIRL* (1937), *Mad About Music* (1938), *That Certain Age* (1938), *Three Smart Girls Grow Up* (1939), *First Love* (1939), *It's a Date* (1940), *Spring Parade* (1940), and others. Durbin matured into an attractive adult leading lady and still managed to please audiences with *CAN'T HELP SINGING* (1944), *Because of Him* (1946), *I'll Be Yours* (1946), *Some-*

thing in the Wind (1947), *Up in Central Park* (1948), and others. Though still a box office draw, Durbin retired from the screen at the age of twenty-seven.

DVORAK, ANN (1911–1979), though mainly remembered for her dramatic performances opposite Spencer Tracy and Paul Muni, started as a dancer and a silent screen CHILD STAR before talkies came in. Dvorak appeared in the early musicals *HOLLYWOOD REVUE OF 1929*, *Lord Byron of Broadway* (1930), and others before getting better roles in such musicals as *Bright Lights* (1935), *THANKS A MILLION* (1935), *Manhattan Merry-Go-Round* (1937), *Masquerade in Mexico* (1945), and *The Bachelor's Daughters* (1946).

DWAN, ALLAN (1885–1981) was a pioneering director who, working with D.W. Griffith in silents, helped develop the dolly shot and elevator crane cinematography. Dwan directed dozens of features before sound came in, but his career in talkies was never as innovative and notable as his earlier work. Nonetheless, he directed some dozen musicals (and produced half of them himself) and brought his craftsmanship to such films as *Hollywood Party* (1934), *Song and Dance Man* (1936), *REBECCA OF SUNNYBROOK FARM* (1938), *Rise and Shine* (1941), *Calendar Girl* (1947), *I Dream of Jeanie* (1952), and *Sweethearts on Parade* (1953).

E

EASTER PARADE (MGM 1948) brought FRED ASTAIRE out of a brief retirement and launched a new phase in his remarkable career. The forty-eight-year-old hoofer was paired with JUDY GARLAND, who was practically half his age and not known for her dancing abilities, but the team set off sparks all the same and the movie was a giant hit. Vaudevillian Astaire loses his dancing partner ANN MILLER to the *Ziegfeld Follies*, so he picks up untalented little Hannah Brown (Garland) and in one year turns her into a star, falls out of love with Miller and in love with Garland, and the two go strutting down Fifth Avenue on Easter Sunday. Both old and new IRVING BERLIN songs were used, all of them top drawer. "A Fella With an Umbrella" (sung by Garland's admirer PETER LAWFORD), "Better Luck Next Time," and "It Only Happens When I Dance With You" were the quieter numbers while Miller tapped her way through "Shaking the Blues Away," Astaire danced in distorted time with images of himself in "Stepping Out With My Baby," and Garland and Astaire cut loose as a duo of happy hoboes in "A Couple of Swells." All in all, there were seventeen Berlin songs (seven of them new), and the title number, first heard on Broadway fifteen years before, became more popular than ever.

EBB, FRED (1931–), the Broadway lyricist, and his composer partner **JOHN KANDER** (1927–), wrote some of the most challenging theatre scores of the last decades of the century, but only *CABARET* (1972) was filmed. The team did contribute new songs to that musical film as well as for *FUNNY LADY* (1975), *A Matter of Time* (1977), and *NEW YORK, NEW YORK* (1977).

EBSEN, BUDDY (1908–), one of Hollywood and television's busiest actors, started as part of a dance team with his sister Vilma Ebsen in vaudeville and on Broadway before making their screen debut in *BROADWAY MEL-ODY OF 1936* (1935). The tall and lanky dancer then struck out on his own and played sidekicks and comic bumpkins. Ebsen's musical films include *CAPTAIN JANUARY* (1936), *BORN TO DANCE* (1936) with Vilma, *Banjo on My Knee* (1936), *BROADWAY MELODY OF 1938* (1937), *My Lucky Star* (1938), *They Met in Argentina* (1941), *Sing Your Worries Away* (1942), *Red Garters* (1954), and *The One and Only Genuine Family Band* (1968).

EDDY, NELSON (1901–1967), America's favorite screen tenor in the 1930s, reached the peak of his popularity when he was teamed with JEANETTE MacDONALD for a series of OPERETTAS. The blond-haired, baby-faced singer was a stiff actor and had little charisma on screen, but when he burst into song with MacDonald the effect was mesmerizing for audiences still clinging to the innocence of prewar Americana. Eddy began singing in nightclubs and concert halls before making his screen debut in the musical *Broadway to Hollywood* (1933), followed by *DANCING LADY* (1933) and *Student Tour* (1934). The Eddy-MacDonald collaboration began with *NAUGHTY MARIETTA* (1935) and continued with *ROSE MARIE* (1936), *MAYTIME* (1937), *The Girl of the Golden West* (1938), *SWEETHEARTS* (1938), *New Moon* (1940), *Bitter Sweet* (1940), and *I Married an Angel* (1942). In between, Eddy starred in similarly operatic films without MacDonald: *ROSALIE* (1937), *BALALAIKA* (1939), *The Chocolate Soldier* (1941), *Phantom of the Opera* (1943), and *Northwest Outpost* (1947). But Eddy without MacDonald rarely caught fire, and after a solo appearance in *Knickerbocker Holiday* (1944) and doing the vocals for the animated *Make Mine Music* (1946), he retired from the screen and returned to clubs and concert halls. Although the soaring duets by Eddy and MacDonald are the stuff of parody today, their partnership made for the most successful singing team in the history of the movies and represented a romanticized entertainment never seen again.

EDENS, ROGER (1905–1970) wore many hats in Hollywood—composer, music arranger, producer, lyricist—and although never a household name, he was responsible for some of the screen's favorite musical moments. Starting as a piano accompanist for ETHEL MERMAN when she went to California, Edens was soon doing the musical arrangements and supervising the songs for *BABES IN ARMS* (1939), *Little Nellie Kelly* (1940), *Lady, Be Good* (1941), and *BABES ON BROADWAY* (1941). In these and subsequent musicals, Edens composed song interpolations with lyricst-producer ARTHUR FREED or sometimes wrote his own lyrics. His other collaborators included RALPH FREED, BETTY COMDEN, and ADOLPH GREEN. Whereas a musical scored totally by Edens was rare, he contributed numbers to over a dozen movies including *ZIEGFELD GIRL* (1941), *ZIEGFELD FOLLIES* (1946), *GOOD NEWS* (1947), *TAKE ME OUT TO THE BALL GAME* (1949), *ON THE TOWN* (1949), *SINGIN' IN THE RAIN* (1952), *FUNNY*

FACE (1957), and *JUMBO* (1962). Among the memorable films in which Edens did the scoring and acted as associate producer were *Yolanda and the Thief* (1945), *THE HARVEY GIRLS* (1946), *THE PIRATE* (1948), *EASTER PARADE* (1948), *WORDS AND MUSIC* (1948), *THE BARKLEYS OF BROADWAY* (1949), *ANNIE GET YOUR GUN* (1950), *ROYAL WEDDING* (1951), *SHOW BOAT* (1951), *AN AMERICAN IN PARIS* (1951), *THE BELLE OF NEW YORK* (1952), *THE BAND WAGON* (1953), *BRIGADOON* (1954), *DEEP IN MY HEART* (1954), *THE UN-SINKABLE MOLLY BROWN* (1964), and *HELLO, DOLLY!* (1969).

EDWARDS, BLAKE (1922–) acted as producer, director, and sometimes screenwriter for several comedies, dramas, and musicals in the 1950s and 1960s, some of them featuring his wife JULIE ANDREWS. Edwards' musical credits include *All Ashore* (1953), *He Laughed Last* (1956), *High Time* (1960), *DARLING LILI* (1969), and *VICTOR/VICTORIA* (1982).

EDWARDS, CLIFF (1895–1971) was a high-pitched singer from vaudeville and Broadway who was nicknamed "Ukelele Ike" because he accompanied himself on a tinny little ukelele. Edwards made his film debut crooning "Singin' in the Rain" in *HOLLYWOOD REVUE OF 1929* and then was featured in specialty numbers in *So This Is College* (1929), *Lord Byron of Broadway* (1930), *GOOD NEWS* (1930), *Take a Chance* (1933), and two editions of *George White's Scandals* (1934 and 1935). He is most remembered for providing the voice of Jiminy Cricket and singing "When You Wish Upon a Star" in *PINOCCHIO* (1940), as well as other numbers in the animated musicals *DUMBO* (1941) and *Fun and Fancy Free* (1946). Edwards was seen in some 100 films and heard in nightclubs, on radio, and later on television.

ELISCU, EDWARD (1902–1998), a Broadway and Tin Pan Alley lyricist, collaborated with GUS KAHN and VINCENT YOUMANS on the score for the landmark musical *FLYING DOWN TO RIO* (1933). His only other screen scores were *The Heat's On* (1943) and *Hey, Rookie* (1944) with Henry Myers and JAY GORNEY. Among Eliscu's popular songs were "Great Day," "The Carioca," and "More Than You Know."

ELLINGTON, DUKE (1899–1974), the world-renowned jazz composer, arranger, pianist, and conductor, started his first band at the age of nineteen and wrote and performed for the next fifty years. Ellington's film appearances were limited to specialty numbers in such musicals as *Check and Double Check* (1930), *MURDER AT THE VANITIES* (1934), *Belle of the Nineties* (1934), *Hit Parade of 1937, CABIN IN THE SKY* (1942), and *Reveille with Beverly* (1943), but he also composed songs for the musical *Paris Blues* (1961) and some nonmusical films. "Sophisticated Lady," "Don't Get Around Much Anymore," "I Got It Bad (And That Ain't Good)," "It Don't Mean a Thing

(If It Ain't Got That Swing)," and "Satin Doll" are among Ellington's many popular compositions. His work was celebrated in the Broadway revue *Sophisticated Ladies* (1981).

ENRIGHT, RAY (1896–1965), the prolific Hollywood director who often staged westerns for various studios, also directed a dozen musicals in the 1930s, six of them starring DICK POWELL. *Song of the West* (1930) was Enright's first film musical, followed by *Golden Dawn* (1930), *Twenty Million Sweethearts* (1934), *DAMES* (1934), *Sing Me a Love Song* (1936), *Ready, Willing and Able* (1937), *The Singing Marine* (1937), *GOLD DIGGERS IN PARIS* (1938), *Going Places* (1938), and others.

ERROL, LEON (1881–1951) was a rubber-legged comedian who endeared himself to audiences in vaudeville and on Broadway by his physical antics and put-upon comic style. Mostly known for his comedy shorts in silent and sound pictures, Errol was also featured in some two dozen musicals in the 1930s and 1940s. Making his sound debut in a specialty act in *PARAMOUNT ON PARADE* (1930), he went on to deliver his routines in *WE'RE NOT DRESSING* (1934), *Coronado* (1935), *Make a Wish* (1937), *The Girl From Mexico* (1939), *Moonlight in Hawaii* (1941), *Follow the Band* (1941), *Higher and Higher* (1943), *Riverboat Rhythm* (1946), and several others.

ERWIN, STUART (1902–1967) had a long and successful career playing bumbling but likable guys in comedies and musicals, later finding a new audience on television. A veteran of over 100 films, Erwin's musical credits include *Sweetie* (1929), *PARAMOUNT ON PARADE* (1930), *THE BIG BROADCAST* (1932), *INTERNATIONAL HOUSE* (1933), *GOING HOLLYWOOD* (1933), *Pigskin Parade* (1936), *Dance, Charlie, Dance* (1937), and many others.

ETTING, RUTH (1896–1978), one of the most distinctive torch singers in show business, was primarily known as a nightclub and recording star but did appear in a handful of Broadway musicals and was seen on screen in *ROMAN SCANDALS* (1933), *Hips Hips Hooray* (1934), and *Gift of Gab* (1934). Her difficult life was made into the bio musical *LOVE ME OR LEAVE ME* (1955), in which DORIS DAY played Etting and sang her signature song of the title. Etting also popularized "Ten Cents a Dance" and "Get Happy" and revived interest in "Shine On Harvest Moon."

EVANS, DALE (1912–) was a nightclub vocalist who appeared in such musicals as *ORCHESTRA WIVES* (1942) and westerns such as *Don't Fence Me In* (1945) before marrying **ROY ROGERS** (1911–1998) in 1947 and co-starring with him on film and, more successfully, on television. As a member of the Sons of the Pioneers, Rogers made his film debut in *Tumbling Tumbleweeds*

(1935) and soon became the most famous singing cowboy after GENE AUTRY. Rogers sang in most of his westerns and was featured in a few traditional musicals, such as *SON OF PALEFACE* (1952). He also provided vocals for the animated anthology *Melody Time* (1948).

EVANS, RAY (1915–   ) wrote the lyrics and his collaborator **JAY LIVING-STON** (1915–   ) composed the music for twenty Hollywood musicals, producing such hits as "Buttons and Bows" and "Silver Bells." The team's first movie assignment was *Footlight Glamour* (1943), but their best scores were written for *THE PALEFACE* (1948), *Fancy Pants* (1950), *The Lemon Drop Kid* (1951), *HERE COMES THE GROOM* (1951), *SON OF PALEFACE* (1952), *Those Redheads From Seattle* (1953), *Red Garters* (1954), and *All Hands on Deck* (1961). Livingston and Evans also wrote award-winning songs for nonmusical films, including the hits "Mona Lisa," "To Each His Own," "Que Sera Sera," and "Tammy."

EVERGREEN (Gaumont 1934) is arguably the finest British film musical of the 1930s and is considered here because its songwriters were American and the movie was popular in the States. Based on a 1930 London stage hit with a score by RODGERS and HART, the film interpolated some new songs by American Harry M. Woods in telling the tale of an Edwardian music hall performer, Harriet Green, who disappears and is impersonated on stage by her daughter. British musical favorite JESSIE MATTHEWS played both roles and scored the triumph of her film career. (She had played the double role on stage as well.) Rodgers and Hart's "Dancing on the Ceiling" was the standout song, but there was much to enjoy in "Daddy Wouldn't Buy Me a Bow-Wow," "When You've Got a Little Springtime in Your Heart," and "Over My Shoulder."

EVERY NIGHT AT EIGHT (Paramount 1935) was a routine backstage saga spiced up by engaging performances and a superior score by DOROTHY FIELDS, JIMMY McHUGH, and others. When struggling singers ALICE FAYE, FRANCES LANGFORD, and PATSY KELLY are fired from their jobs at a mint-julep factory, bandleader GEORGE RAFT takes over their management, makes them stars, and ends up (surprisingly) in Langford's rather than Faye's arms. The three ladies were pure gold, and the songs they were given to sing nonetheless precious: the mellow "I'm in the Mood for Love," the sprightly "I Feel a Song Comin' On," the swinging "Take It Easy," and the breezy ballad "Speaking Confidentially." Action film director RAOUL WALSH helmed the musical, which also featured Harry Barris, HERMAN BING, Jimmie Hollywood, Henry Taylor, and WALTER CATLETT in the cast.

EVERYONE SAYS I LOVE YOU (Miramax 1997) celebrated the musicals of old while it also satirized them, a pleasing mixture of contemporary comedy and nostalgic romance. Woody Allen wrote and directed this comedy of manners about rich New Yorkers looking for love and had the characters, very few of them experienced singers, express themselves by breaking into old song standards. Goldie Hawn, Alan Alda, Edward Norton, and others sounded fine, whereas Allen, Julia Roberts, Tim Roth, and others struggled vocally. Yet the effect was deliciously unpretentious, and Graciela Daniele's choreography was contagiously fun. Hawn floated through the air as she and Allen sang "I'm Through With Love," doctors and patients in a hospital romped around singing "Makin' Whoopee," various New Yorkers joined Norton in singing "Just You, Just Me," and a party of Parisians dressed like GROUCHO MARX and pranced through the Ritz Hotel and sang "Hooray for Captain Spaulding" in French. An unusual and one-of-a-kind film, it either charmed or annoyed audiences and critics yet was another unique contribution by America's most successful *auteur* film director.

EVITA (Hollywood Pictures 1997), the only big-budget film musical made in the 1990s, was an ambitious and epic version of the acclaimed London and Broadway hit filmed on location in Argentina (and elsewhere) and matching the oversized characters and score with spectacular scenes and lavish splendor. MADONNA played the heroine Eva Perón, who rose from poverty to an international figure, Jonathan Pryce was her husband Juan Perón, and Antonio Banderas kept popping up in various guises to comment on the action. As on the stage, the film was completely sung, songwriters TIM RICE and Andrew Lloyd-Webber adding one new number to their film score for Madonna to sing, "You Must Love Me," which won the ACADEMY AWARD for Best Song. ALAN PARKER adapted (with Oliver Stone) and directed the mammoth production, which was very satisfying and proved that the big movie musical was not dead and gone forever.

F

FAIN, SAMMY (1902–1989) was a Broadway composer who, working with various lyricists, scored two dozen movie musicals and wrote hit theme songs for nonmusicals, such as "Love Is a Many Splendored Thing." Fain began his film career with the early talkie *Young Man of Manhattan* (1930) but came to recognition with his tuneful score for *FOOTLIGHT PARADE* (1933) with lyricist IRVING KAHAL. The same team scored *College Coach* (1933), *Harold Teen* (1934), portions of *DAMES* (1934), and *Sweet Music* (1934). With lyricists RALPH FREED, JACK YELLEN, SAM COSLOW, SAMMY CAHN, Bob Hilliard, and others, Fain contributed songs to *Goin' to Town* (1935), *George White's Scandals* (1945), *Two Sisters From Boston* (1946), *No Leave, No Love* (1946), *Call Me Mister* (1951), *ALICE IN WONDERLAND* (1951), *THE JAZZ SINGER* (1953), *Peter Pan* (1953), *Three Sailors and a Girl* (1953), and others. Fain's last collaborator was lyricist PAUL FRANCIS WEBSTER, with whom he scored *CALAMITY JANE* (1953), *Lucky Me* (1954), *Hollywood or Bust* (1956), *April Love* (1957), *Mardi Gras* (1958), and *The Big Circus* (1959). Fain's final musical was the animated *The Rescuers* (1977). "Secret Love," "I'll Be Seeing You," and "Let a Smile Be Your Umbrella" are among Fain's many hit songs.

FAME (MGM 1980) wavered between a gritty, realistic look at show business and a romanticized "let's put on a show" musical, all set in Manhattan's High School of Performing Arts over a four-year period. As young hopefuls struggle through auditions, classes, rehearsals, setbacks, family troubles, and sexual anxiety, they burst into song and dance everywhere from the street to the cafeteria. The film was highly charged, noisy, and very popular, inspiring a television series and later a stage version. ALAN PARKER directed Irene Cara, Lee Curreri, Barry Miller, Antonia Franceschi, Gene Anthony Ray, and other young cast members, with Anne Meara, Albert Hague, and Debbie Allen on hand to play faculty members. Most of the songs were by Dean Pitchford and Michael Gore, the most memorable being "I Sing the Body Electric," "Red Light," and the explosive title number.

FANTASIA (Disney/RKO 1940) was a surprisingly unique musical experience, even by the innovative standards of WALT DISNEY and his artists. Eight classic concert pieces were illustrated and animated in various ways to bring the music to life rather than just serve as background: Bach's "Toccata and Fugue in D Minor" became an abstract expression of lines and music; Dukas' "The Sorcerer's Apprentice" told a story with Mickey Mouse as an overeager wizard-in-training who loses control of his magic; Tchaikovsky's "The Nutcracker Suite" came to life as a nature ballet with fairies, flowers, fish, and even dancing mushrooms; Beethoven's "Pastoral Symphony" served for mythological characters; Ponchielli's "La Gioconda" was turned into a comic ballet featuring ostriches, crocodiles, and hippos; Stravinsky's "Rite of Spring" showed the creation of the planet and primeval life; Mussorgsky's "Night on Bald Mountain" illustrated the battle between good and evil with devils, ghosts, and skeletons; and Schubert's "Ave Maria" presented a dawn of tranquility and hope. Each section had a distinct visual style, all under the supervision of Ben Sharpsteen, and the music was performed by the Philadelphia Orchestra conducted by LEOPOLD STOKOWSKI. In 1982 the old print was refurbished and a new soundtrack conducted by Irwin Kostal replaced the original. A SEQUEL, *FANTASIA 2000*, released sixty years later, retained the Dukas sequence and added seven new concert pieces: Beethoven's Fifth Symphony was interpreted abstractly; Respighi's "Pines of Rome" became a water ballet for whales; GEORGE GERSHWIN's "Rhapsody in Blue" captured frantic New Yorkers in busy Hirschfeld-like line drawings; Shostakovich's Piano Concerto No. 2 served to illustrate a Hans Christian Andersen tale, "The Steadfast Tin Soldier"; Saint-Saens' "Carnival of the Animals" was used for a playful sequence with bouncing pink flamingos and a yo-yo; Elgar's "Pomp and Circumstance" provided the music for all the animals marching onto Noah's Ark with Donald Duck as Noah's helper; and Stravinsky's "Firebird Suite" dramatized a mythic parable about a sprite and an elk restoring life to a ravaged forest. James Levine conducted the Chicago Symphony and various guests, from ANGELA LANSBURY to STEVE MARTIN, introduced each section.

FARMER TAKES A WIFE, THE (Fox 1953), a musical version of the 1935 JANET GAYNOR–Henry Fonda film of the same name, was still set on the Erie Canal in 1850, but BETTY GRABLE and Dale Robertson seemed more like Broadway hopefuls than the canal cook and driver they were supposed to be. A rivalry between Robertson and canal boat owner John Carroll provided the less-than-gripping plot, but the dances by JACK COLE (with a young GWEN VERDON seen kicking up her heels) and a pleasing score by DOROTHY FIELDS and HAROLD ARLEN certainly helped. The exuberant "Today I Love Everybody," the lazy ballad "With the Sun Warm Upon Me," and the chipper "We're in Business" were the standout numbers. The comedy was supplied by Thelma Ritter and EDDIE FOY, JR., both of whom also looked less comfortable on the Erie than in a sassy backstager.

FARRELL, CHARLES (1901–1990) became a star with the silent film classic *Seventh Heaven* (1927) and together with his co-star JANET GAYNOR, went on to make twelve films (four of them musicals), becoming the era's favorite romantic screen couple. The stiff but dashing leading man made his musical debut as a rich Long Island playboy in *SUNNY SIDE UP* (1929), where he sang "If I Had a Talking Picture of You" with Gaynor. He also appeared in the musicals *Happy Days* (1930), *High Society Blues* (1930), *DELICIOUS* (1931), *Girl Without a Room* (1933), and *Just Around the Corner* (1938) before retiring. Farrell later had a second career in television.

FARRELL, GLENDA (1904–1971) specialized in playing wisecracking blondes in 1930s melodramas and musicals, later maturing into a popular character actress on television and on Broadway. Farrell first gained attention in the crime dramas *Little Caesar* (1931) and *I Am a Fugitive From a Chain Gang* (1932) but was appearing in musicals a few years later with *GOLD DIGGERS OF 1935*, *GO INTO YOUR DANCE* (1935), *In Caliente* (1935), *GOLD DIGGERS OF 1937* (1936), *HOLLYWOOD HOTEL* (1938), and others. She retuned to the film musical with a supporting role in the ELVIS PRESLEY vehicle *Kissin' Cousins* (1964).

FAYE, ALICE (1915–1998) was the queen of 20TH CENTURY–FOX musicals in the late 1930s and early 1940s, her husky speaking voice and deep contralto singing voice a welcome change from chirping sopranos. The blonde actress was discovered by RUDY VALLEE, who brought her to Hollywood when he made *George White's Scandals* (1934). When the leading lady Lilian Harvey walked off the set, Faye was given her part and was an immediate hit. *She Learned About Sailors* (1934), *365 Nights in Hollywood* (1934), *EVERY NIGHT AT EIGHT* (1935), *KING OF BURLESQUE* (1936), *POOR LITTLE RICH GIRL* (1936), and others followed, but she really hit her stride with *ON THE AVENUE* (1937), *WAKE UP AND LIVE* (1937), *You Can't Have Everything* (1937), *IN OLD CHICAGO* (1938), *ALEXANDER'S RAGTIME BAND* (1938), the bio musicals *ROSE OF WASHINGTON SQUARE* (1939) and *LILLIAN RUSSELL* (1940), *TIN PAN ALLEY* (1940), and other prewar musicals. In the 1940s, Faye starred in such Latin-flavored movies as *THAT NIGHT IN RIO* (1941), *WEEK-END IN HAVANA* (1941), and *THE GANG'S ALL HERE* (1943), as well as the popular period piece *HELLO, FRISCO, HELLO* (1943). After doing a specialty bit in *Four Jills in a Jeep* (1944), Faye retired from films, only to return decades later as the mother Mrs. Frack in *STATE FAIR* (1962) and a guest spot in *The Magic of Lassie*

(1978). She was married to TONY MARTIN and then later to PHIL HARRIS, with whom she had a popular radio show.

FELIX, SEYMOUR (1892–1961) was a Broadway choreographer who arrived in Hollywood with the early talkies and staged dance numbers for some thirty musicals over the next twenty-five years. After his first assignment with *SUNNY SIDE UP* (1929), Felix was kept busy choreographing *Just Imagine* (1930), *THE CAT AND THE FIDDLE* (1934), *KID MILLIONS* (1934), *THE GREAT ZIEGFELD* (1936), *ON THE AVENUE* (1937), *ALEXANDER'S RAGTIME BAND* (1938), *TIN PAN ALLEY* (1940), *YANKEE DOODLE DANDY* (1942), *COVER GIRL* (1944), *THE DOLLY SISTERS* (1945), *THREE LITTLE GIRLS IN BLUE* (1946), *Down Among the Sheltering Palms* (1952), and others.

FIDDLER ON THE ROOF (Mirisch/United Artists 1971) was brought to the screen faithfully, with all but two of the stage songs intact and Joseph Stein adapting his Broadway libretto. JEROME ROBBINS' famous choreography was recreated by his assistant Tom Abbott, and director Norman Jewison treated the material with respect and integrity. Yet the result was an overlong (180 minutes) movie that often failed to capture the spirit and exuberance of the stage work. Topol was more than capable as the dairyman Tevye, Norma Crane underplayed his wife Golde to the point of disappearing on the screen, and even the crusty old comic Molly Picon seemed subdued as the matchmaker Yenta. But there were definite pluses as well: Rosalind Harris, Michele Marsh, and Neva Small were engaging as Teyve's three marriageable daughters, the locations were picturesque and poetic, the surreal "Tevye's Dream" was spirited and funny, and the wonderful SHELDON HARNICK and JERRY BOCK songs still pleased: "Sunrise, Sunset," "If I Were a Rich Man." "Matchmaker, Matchmaker," "To Life," "Far From the Home I Love," and others. A bonus treat the play could not provide was Isaac Stern's brilliant violin playing during the opening credits. In 1979 the film was re-released in Dolby stereo with thirty-two minutes cut out, resulting in an improved movie.

FIELDS, DOROTHY (1904–1974) had a long and productive career as one of America's finest lyricists, writing songs for Broadway and Hollywood for nearly fifty years. She was also the first woman to win an ACADEMY AWARD for Best Song: "The Way You Look Tonight" with composer JEROME KERN. Fields' first collaborator was composer JIMMY McHUGH, with whom she wrote her early stage musicals as well as her first films: *Love in the Rough* (1930), *The Cuban Love Song* (1931), *Hooray for Love* (1935), and *EVERY NIGHT AT EIGHT* (1935). She first teamed up with Kern when she wrote additional songs for *ROBERTA* (1935), and the two of them continued working together, providing classic film scores for *I DREAM TOO MUCH* (1935), *SWING TIME* (1936), *JOY OF LIVING* (1938), *ONE NIGHT IN*

THE TROPICS (1940), and *LOVELY TO LOOK AT* (1952). With various other composers, Fields also scored *In Person* (1935), *The King Steps Out* (1936), *Mr. Imperium* (1951), *Excuse My Dust* (1951), *Texas Carnival* (1951), and *THE FARMER TAKES A WIFE* (1953). Of her eleven Broadway shows, only *Up in Central Park* (1948) and *SWEET CHARITY* (1968) were filmed. Fields came from a theatrical family that included her father, comic and producer Lew Fields, and her brothers, playwrights JOSEPH and HERBERT FIELDS.

FIELDS, Dame GRACIE (1898–1979) was the most popular singing-dancing star in Great Britain in the 1930s and 1940s and reputedly the highest paid entertainer in the world. The British public adored "Our Gracie" with her thick dialect and down-to-earth ways (she was once called the English Will Rogers), but her films never caught on in America. Fields appeared as a specialty in the Hollywood musical *STAGE DOOR CANTEEN* (1943), but only years later would some Americans appreciate her dazzling performances in such British film musicals as *Sally in Our Alley* (1931), *This Week of Grace* (1933), *Look Up and Laugh* (1935), *Keep Smiling* (1938), *Shipyard Sally* (1939), and *Holy Matrimony* (1943).

FIELDS, HERBERT (1897–1958) wrote the librettos for a series of RODGERS and HART Broadway musicals in the 1920s and started contributing to movie scripts in the 1930s. Among the film musicals that he wrote or were based on his stage works were *Leathernecking* (1930), *The Hot Heiress* (1931), *MISSISSIPPI* (1935), *JOY OF LIVING* (1938), *Honolulu* (1939), *DuBarry Was a Lady* (1942), *Up in Central Park* (1948), *ANNIE GET YOUR GUN* (1950), and *HIT THE DECK* (1955). Fields' theatrical family included his sister, lyricist DOROTHY FIELDS, and brother, playwright JOSEPH FIELDS.

FIELDS, JOSEPH (1895–1966), the eldest of the three Fields siblings, wrote several successful comedies and a few musical librettos for Broadway, most of which were filmed. Fields' musical film credits include *TWO GIRLS ON BROADWAY* (1940), *Louisiana Purchase* (1942), *THE FARMER TAKES A WIFE* (1953), *GENTLEMEN PREFER BLONDES* (1953), and *FLOWER DRUM SONG* (1961).

FIELDS, W.C. (1879–1946), the legendary large-nosed comic whose cynical drawl made him a favorite on Broadway and in films, was featured in only eight movie musicals, but each appearance was hilarious and memorable. Usually playing con men with a dislike for wholesome things like children and nonalcoholic beverages, Fields was the barmaid's father Torrek in *Her Majesty Love* (1931), Professor Quail in *INTERNATIONAL HOUSE* (1933), Commodore Jackson in *MISSISSIPPI* (1935), Professor Eustace McGargle in

Poppy (1936), and twin brothers T. Frothingale Bellows and S.B. Bellows in *BIG BROADCAST OF 1938*. Fields played himself in specialty bits in *Follow the Boys* (1944), *Song of the Open Road* (1944), and *Sensations of 1945* (1944).

FINIAN'S RAINBOW (Warner-Seven Arts 1968) took twenty-one years to transfer from the Broadway stage to the screen, and it was easy to see why in this Francis Ford Coppola–directed production. The musical's plot by E.Y. HARBURG and Fred Saidy (who also wrote the screenplay) was filled with uncomfortable satire (a bigoted southern senator is changed into an African American to teach him a lesson) and tricky fantasy (a leprechaun looking for his stolen pot of gold starts to turn human) that were difficult to capture on the screen. FRED ASTAIRE, in his last musical film role, played an Irish immigrant in "Missitucky" hoping to bury his gold near Fort Knox so it would grow, PETULA CLARK was his daughter, Don Francks played the co-op manager who loves her, and TOMMY STEELE was the agonizing leprechaun. Filmed outdoors on location, the film never quite had the look of whimsy it required, but the remarkable Harburg–BURTON LANE score survived the transition, all but one of the stage songs heard in the film: "How Are Things in Glocca Morra?," "Old Devil Moon," "When I'm Not Near the Girl I Love," "If This Isn't Love," "Something Sort of Grandish," "The Begat," "Look to the Rainbow," and others, every one as fresh and sassy as the day they were first heard on Broadway.

FIREFLY, THE (MGM 1937) bore little resemblance to the 1912 OPERETTA hit, only five of the songs being retained and the libretto thrown out for a completely new one. But JEANETTE MacDONALD, as a Spanish spy saving Spain's King Ferdinand VII from the Napoleonic invasion, and ALLAN JONES, as a counterspy for the French, were paired for some melodious duets, and audiences thought it the next best thing to the MacDonald and NELSON EDDY combination. RUDOLF FRIML's music (with lyrics by OTTO HARBACH) soared in songs such as "Sympathy," "Giannina Mia," and "Love Is Like a Firefly," and ROBERT WRIGHT and GEORGE FORREST put some new lyrics to a piano piece by Friml and came up with the hit song "Donkey Serenade," which Jones would sing throughout his career.

FISHER, DORIS (1915–   ) and her partner ALAN ROBERTS wrote songs for a dozen B movie musicals in the 1940s and contributed theme songs for some nonmusicals as well. Both wrote music and lyrics together, their most famous song being "Put the Blame on Mame." The team's film credits include *Gilda* (1946), *The Thrill of Brazil* (1946), *Talk About a Lady* (1946), *Cigarette Girl* (1947), and *Down to Earth* (1947).

FITZGERALD, ELLA (1918–1996), the foremost jazz singer and song interpreter for several decades, was so popular in concert, in nightclubs, and on records that she made film appearances in the musicals *Ride 'Em Cowboy* (1941), *PETE KELLY'S BLUES* (1955), and *St. Louis Blues* (1958).

FIVE PENNIES, THE (Dena/Paramount 1959) was a BIOGRAPHICAL MUSICAL that relied more on sentiment than on historical accuracy in telling the story of cornet player Red Nichols, but the music was true to its period (the 1920s and 1930s) and the new songs by Sylvia Fine were engaging. DANNY KAYE played Nichols and, for the most part, forsook his clowning for pathos. Barbara Bel Geddes (singing dubbed by Eileen Wilson) was his noble and suffering wife, and Susan Gordon was their polio-stricken young daughter, who survived to grow up to be Tuesday Weld. Also on hand were BOB CROSBY, Ray Anthony (as JIMMY DORSEY), Harry Guardino, Nichols himself to provide the cornet playing on the soundtrack, and, most important, LOUIS ARMSTRONG, whose duet of "When the Saints Go Marching In" with Kaye was the highlight of the movie. Other old favorites heard in the musical included "After You've Gone," "Out of Nowhere" and "Runnin' Wild," with "Lullaby in Ragtime," "Good Night, Sleep Tight," and the touching title song as the new entries.

5,000 FINGERS OF DR. T, THE (Columbia 1953) looked and felt like no other musical, being a fantasy created by Theodore Geisel, otherwise known as Dr. Seuss. Young Tommy Rettig is forced to practice his piano lessons when he would rather be outside playing baseball, so when the youth dozes off he dreams that his piano teacher Mr. Terwilliker (HANS CONREID) becomes the diabolical Dr. T, who imprisons 500 young boys in his dungeon and forces them to play on long curling pianos that only Dr. Seuss could dream up. Also in the prison are non-piano musicians who have grown green and moldy and finally break out in song and dance. Rettig, with the help of his widowed mother MARY HEALY and kindly plumber Peter Lind Hayes, outwits Dr. T, and the boy awakes to find the plumber and his mother in love. Much of the film doesn't quite work, but Rudolph Sternad's optical illusion sets, Conreid's spirited performance, and the pleasant songs by Geisel and FREDERICK HOLLANDER help get one through the dead spots.

FLASHDANCE (Paramount 1983) was a Cinderella story for the 1980s set in Pittsburgh, where Jennifer Beals worked as a steel welder by day and danced in a go-go club at night, all the time dreaming of becoming a prima ballerina with the Pittsburgh Ballet. Her fairy godmother is her boss, Michael Nouri, who gets her an audition and then at the end becomes her Prince Charming as well. The ridiculous premise was given a rock video staging with dances that elicited more laughs than intended, but audiences somehow bought into it and the film was a major hit. The pounding score by Giorgio Moroder, Irene Cara, and Keith Forsey made for a popular soundtrack, with the song "Flashdance . . . What a Feeling" even winning an Oscar.

FLEET'S IN, THE (Paramount 1942) was a wartime frolic that told an old story (it served for two previous nonmusicals) about a shy sailor (William Holden) who everyone mistakenly thinks is a real ladies' man. His fellow gobs made a bet with him that he couldn't kiss the beautiful but aloof nightclub singer DOROTHY LAMOUR in public, but the audience knew better. As Lamour's brazen roommate, BETTY HUTTON made a sensational film debut singing "Build a Better Mousetrap" and, with her love interest EDDIE BRACKEN, "Arthur Murray Taught Me Dancing in a Hurry." JOHNNY MERCER and VICTOR SCHERTZINGER wrote the bouncy score that also included "I Remember You" and "Tangerine," both performed by TOMMY DORSEY and his orchestra (vocals by Bob Eberle and Helen O'Connell) and identified forever after with the bandleader. Schertzinger also directed, but it was his last film; he died before it was released. The musical was remade in 1951 as the JERRY LEWIS–DEAN MARTIN vehicle *Sailor Beware*.

FLOWER DRUM SONG (Universal-International 1961) did not solve the Broadway show's book problems, but the RODGERS and HAMMERSTEIN musical had superior songs and the performers, some from the 1958 stage production, made this, Hollywood's only Asian-cast musical, memorable. Picture bride Miyoshi Umeki from Hong Kong arrives in San Francisco's Chinatown to wed playboy Jack Soo, who is more interested in fully Americanized Nancy Kwan, who sings and dances in his nightclub. But handsome James Shigeta rebels against his conservative relatives and ends up with Umeki. JUANITA HALL, who was African American rather than Asian, repeated her performance as the crafty aunt who sings "Chop Suey" and bemoaned what has become of "The Younger Generation." Other songs included the bubbly "I Enjoy Being a Girl" boasted by Kwan (singing dubbed by B.J. Baker), Soo's comic "Don't Marry Me," Umeki's plaintive "A Hundred Million Miracles," and the lovely ballads "Love Look Away" and "You Are Beautiful."

FLYING DOWN TO RIO (RKO 1933) introduced the dance team of FRED ASTAIRE and GINGER ROGERS and also initiated a nationwide interest in Latin-flavored music. On top of that, it is still an amusing and romantic film. Brazilian DOLORES DEL RIO cannot choose between her fiancé, countryman Raul Roulien, or the American bandleader-aviator GENE RAYMOND. While she was deciding, Astaire and Rogers climbed atop seven white pianos in a nightclub and danced "The Carioca," thereby changing the history of movie dancing. EDWARD ELISCU, GUS KAHN, and VINCENT YOUMANS wrote the powerhouse score that also included the rhythm number "Music Makes Me," the warm ballad "Orchids in the Moonlight," and the title number, sung by Astaire on the ground as the chorus girls also sang while strapped to the wings of airplanes flying above the hotel. It is a scene often parodied but unforgettably delightful all the same. As for "The Carioca," it started a rage for the samba and other south-of-the-border dances and music.

FOLIES BERGÈRE DE PARIS (20th Century/United Artists 1935) had such a reliable bedroom farce plot that it served for three popular movie musicals. The first starred MAURICE CHEVALIER as a wealthy French businessman who is married to Merle Oberon but has ANN SOTHERN as a mistress. When he has to be in two places at once (a grand ball and a business meeting), Chevalier employs a *Follies* entertainer (also Chevalier) who looks like him and even impersonates the rich man in his nightclub act. Complications arise when Oberon spots the impostor, and when she is sleeping with her husband that night, no one else is sure if she knows the true identify of the man. The score, by various tunesmiths, featured "I'm Lucky," "You Took the Words Right Out of My Mouth," and "Rhythm of the Rain," which served for a lavish Follies production number with Chevalier, Sothern, and the chorus singing and dancing away with twirling umbrellas in a manufactured downpour. Without too many plot changes, the studio moved the locale to Brazil and remade it as ***THAT NIGHT IN RIO*** (Fox 1941) with DON AMECHE in the double leading role. ALICE FAYE was his worldly-wise wife, and CARMEN MIRANDA as the girlfriend who is also getting the two look-alikes confused. MACK GORDON and HARRY WARREN penned the Latin-flavored score and gave Miranda two of her biggest hits, "Chica Chica Boom Chic" and "I Yi Yi Yi Yi (I Like You Very Much)." Also heard were "Cae Cae," "They Met in Rio," and the lullaby "Boa Noite (Good Night)." Ten years later the tale resurfaced as ***ON THE RIVIERA*** (Fox 1951) with DANNY KAYE as both businessman and entertainer. Gene Tierney was the wife, and Corrine Calvet the girlfriend. Kaye's wife Sylvia Fine wrote some songs particularly suited to his style: "Popo the Puppet," "Rhythm of a New Romance," and the Gallic title song, which Kaye sang in a broad Chevalier impersonation as an inside joke. The most memorable song in the film, and one Kaye would return to throughout his career, was "Ballin' the Jack" by Jim Burris and Chris Smith.

FOLLOW THAT BIRD (Warner 1985) was a feature film put out by the Children's Television Workshop and the creators of *Sesame Street* and, like the television program, was aimed at young children, but there was plenty for adults as well, from the various guest stars in cameo performances to the spirited musical numbers. When Big Bird (voice of Carroll Spinney) is sent to a foster family of birds, he misses his friends back on Sesame Street and journeys to be reunited with them even as they set off to find him. Oscar the Grouch (also Spinney) opened the film with a satire on *Patton* (1970) by addressing the viewers in front of a huge American flag and urging everyone to sing "The Grouch Anthem." Other musical treats included Waylon Jennings and Big Bird singing the country tune "Ain't No Road Too Long" as they rode along in a truck full of turkeys, and the whole cast of characters, human and cloth, joining in singing the tender lullaby "One Little Star." (The film is sometimes listed as *Sesame Street Presents Follow That Bird*.) Some of the same team reunited fifteen years later for ***THE ADVENTURES OF ELMO IN GROUCHLAND*** (Columbia

1999), which had fun paralleling *THE WIZARD OF OZ* (1939). The red and furry Elmo (voice of Kevin Clash) enters Grouchland looking for his blanket and runs across a city of grouches, the Queen of Trash (Vanessa Williams), and the evil collector Huxley, MANDY PATINKIN in a vibrant and and cunning performance. Again the songs were tuneful, Williams celebrating with "I See a Kingdom," Patinkin gloating with "Make It Mine," and everybody singing the optimistic "Together Forever."

FOLLOW THE FLEET (RKO 1936) showcased FRED ASTAIRE, GINGER ROGERS, and seven new IRVING BERLIN songs; all nine elements were in top form. Ex-hoofer Astaire is on leave in San Francisco with his sailor buddy RANDOLPH SCOTT when they come across Rogers and HARRIET HILLIARD at the Paradise Ballroom. Hilliard falls for Scott and makes plans to refurbish an old schooner for him, necessitating a benefit performance highlighted by Astaire and Rogers performing "Let's Face the Music and Dance," perhaps Berlin's most seductive and magical song. Other numbers included Astaire and the sailors chanting "We Saw the Sea" and breaking into "I'd Rather Lead a Band" on deck, Hilliard's solo renditions of the ballads "But Where Are You?" and "Get Thee Behind Me, Satan," and Rogers and Astaire cutting loose on the dance floor with "Let Yourself Go" and rehearsing "I'm Putting All My Eggs in One Basket" as a competitive dance on board the schooner. HERMES PAN and Astaire did the choreography and a yet-undiscovered LUCILLE BALL, BETTY GRABLE, and TONY MARTIN can be spotted in some of the numbers. MARK SANDRICH directed for producer PANDRO S. BERMAN, and the result was movie musical gold at the box office and in the archives of the genre.

FOOTLIGHT PARADE (Warner 1933) is notable for its fantastical BUSBY BERKELEY staging, a dynamite score by AL DUBIN, HARRY WARREN, and others, and another corny but enticing DICK POWELL and RUBY KEELER pairing. But what raises the movie to silly heights is JAMES CAGNEY (in his first film musical) playing a hyperactive, demanding producer who puts on a series of "Prologues" (lavish minimusicals that no real theatre could contain) to be presented before features in Manhattan movie palaces. Its plot was more far-fetched than even the thinnest backstager, but Cagney's energy propelled the movie like a time bomb that exploded in three famous production numbers at the end: dozens of girls diving and swimming about for fifteen minutes in "By a Waterfall" (by IRVING KAHAL and SAMMY FAIN), a group of newlyweds checking into the "Honeymoon Hotel" in Jersey City with a lot of singing and smirking about the activities to follow, and the saga of "Shanghai Lil" with sailor Cagney searching through a Chinese saloon and an opium den looking for (and finding) his long-lost Lil (Keeler) before they both set out for sea. JOAN BLONDELL, HUGH HERBERT, GUY KIBBEE,

FRANK McHUGH, HERMAN BING, and BILLY BARTY filled out the usual WARNERS roster, under the zippy direction of LLOYD BACON.

FOOTLOOSE (IndieProd/Paramount 1984) had a plot that would make the corniest 1930s musical blush, but audiences were so busy buying the soundtrack album that they went *into* the film singing the songs. Although the small midwestern town of Beaumont has outlawed dancing, newcomer Kevin Bacon routs the restless teens and battles local minister John Lithgow to allow everyone to cut the rug. Former choreographer HERBERT ROSS directed, letting Lynne Taylor-Corbett handle the dances, and the movie kept moving even though it had nowhere to go. Except for the title song by Kenny Loggins, the rest of the score was written and tacked onto the soundtrack after filming was complete. The result was another 1980s musical in which no one in the cast sang, but some of the songs became hits: "Let's Hear It for the Boy," "Almost Paradise," and "Holding Out for a Hero." The far-fetched tale became a Broadway musical in 1999.

FOR ME AND MY GAL (MGM 1942) introduced GENE KELLY to film audiences and gave JUDY GARLAND her first screen partner other than MICKEY ROONEY. The cocky Kelly and the hesitant Garland made an electric duo, especially when they delivered the title song together. The story was a bit heavier than usual but still rather contrived. World War One–era vaudeville trio Kelly, Garland, and GEORGE MURPHY struggle from a hick burg in Iowa to the Palace Theatre in New York, but there are complications. Murphy loves Garland, Garland loves Kelly, and Kelly only loves success. Just as the trio is about to make the big time, Kelly gets his draft notice. So he purposely smashes his hand in a trunk and is rejected by the Army (and by Garland). Only after seeing the error of his ways and entertaining troops in Europe does Kelly reunite with Garland for a triumph at the Palace. All the songs came from the period and were delivered with gusto by the cast: "Oh, You Beautiful Doll," "After You've Gone," "When You Wore a Tulip," "Till We Meet Again," "Where Do We Go From Here?," and many others.

FORAN, DICK (1910–1979) was a rugged leading man who made well over 100 feature films during his long career, mostly westerns but also a dozen musicals. The redheaded Foran (who went by the name Nick Foran earlier in his career) did a specialty in *Stand Up and Cheer* (1934), then played leading men or second leads in *Lottery Lover* (1935), *Shipmates Forever* (1935), *Cowboy From Brooklyn* (1938), *Keep 'Em Flying* (1941), *Behind the Eight Ball* (1941), *Ride 'Em Cowboy* (1942), *Private Buckaroo* (1942), and others.

FORREST, GEORGE (1915–1999) and his longtime partner **ROBERT WRIGHT** (1914–   ) collaborated on both music and lyrics together, writing Broadway and film scores over a period of fifty years. They also adapted classical music works into popular stage scores, two of which were filmed: *KISMET* (1955), using Borodin themes, and *Song of Norway* (1970), with Grieg melodies. The team made their film debut writing song interpolations for the operettas *THE FIREFLY* (1937) and *SWEETHEARTS* (1938). Forrest and Wright also contributed to the scores for *BALALAIKA* (1939), *Music in My Heart* (1940), *Dance, Girl, Dance* (1940), *Blondie Goes Latin* (1941), *Fiesta* (1942), and *I Married an Angel* (1942).

FORREST, SALLY (1928–   ) was featured in dance roles in a handful of 1940s musicals beginning with *TILL THE CLOUDS ROLL BY* (1947), working her way up from the chorus to leading roles and then on to dramatic parts in nonmusicals. The petite blonde appeared in *Are You With It?* (1948), *THE PIRATE* (1948), *TAKE ME OUT TO THE BALL GAME* (1949), *Excuse My Dust* (1951), and *The Strip* (1951).

42ND STREET (Warner-Vitaphone 1933) was a pivotal movie in the history of the musical film because it revitalized the genre after two years of declining interest. It is the quintessential backstager with almost every aspect of it later becoming a cliché from overuse. Producer Julian Marsh (WARNER BAXTER) has been stung by the Depression but is still fighting to put on a big Broadway show featuring star Dorothy Brock (BEBE DANIELS). When the star gets drunk and breaks her ankle, backer GUY KIBBEE wants his favorite chorus girl "Anytime Annie" (GINGER ROGERS) to go on for her. But juvenile lead Tommy (DICK POWELL) and Annie herself suggest that Peggy Sawyer (RUBY KEELER), a newcomer to the cast, has the right stuff. So Marsh convinces Peggy ("Sawyer, you're going out a youngster but you've got to come back a star!"); she takes over at the Philadelphia tryout and indeed does become a star. So did Keeler; it was her first character role on film. The script, by James Seymour and Rian James (based on a book by Bradford Ropes), crackled with sarcasm, oversized emotions, and energy, and LLOYD BACON directed it in a slam-bang manner that made most previous musicals seem dull. In addition to the players, the star of the production was BUSBY BERKELEY, who staged the musical numbers by AL DUBIN and HARRY WARREN with a splash of genius and insanity. The two highlights were a train that opened up to reveal pajama-clad honeymooners for "Shuffle Off to Buffalo" and the elaborate production number for the title song showing hundreds of jaded and hedonistic New Yorkers going through a night of revelry. Also in the score were the jaunty "You're Getting to Be a Habit With Me" and the spirited "Young and Healthy." Depression audiences loved both the gritty texture to the film as well as its escapism, and once again the movie musical was a popular art form. *42nd Street* was made into a long-running Broadway musical in 1980, the score augmented by Dubin-Warren songs from other 1930s movies.

FOSSE, BOB (1927–1987), one of the most dynamic director-choreographers on Broadway and film from the mid-1950s until his untimely death, created a distinctive form of dance that mixed modern jazz with old-time vaudeville. A child performer, Fosse went from burlesque to the Broadway stage as a dancer and was choreographing stage musicals at the same time he made occasional appearances in Hollywood movies. He played supporting characters in the film musicals *The Affairs of Dobie Gillis* (1953), *KISS ME, KATE* (1953), *GIVE A GIRL A BREAK* (1953), and *My Sister Eileen* (1955) before his choreography was seen in *THE PAJAMA GAME* (1957) and *DAMN YANKEES* (1958). Fosse directed as well as choreographed *SWEET CHARITY* (1968), *CABARET* (1972), and *ALL THAT JAZZ* (1979), the last an autobiographical musical that he also wrote. He also appeared as the Snake in *The Little Prince* (1975) and directed some gritty nonmusical films. Fosse was once married to Broadway dancer-actress GWEN VERDON and choreographed her in many of her stage triumphs.

FOSTER, SUSANNA (1924–   ) was trained as an opera singer as a child and by the time she was a teenager she was performing in films as PARAMOUNT's version of DEANNA DURBIN. Foster's remarkable range (she was able to sing F above high C) made her ideal for her most famous role, opera singer Christine DuBois in *The Phantom of the Opera* (1943). Her other musical credits include *The Great Victor Herbert* (1939), *There's Magic in Music* (1941), *Glamour Boy* (1941), *Top Man* (1943), *Follow the Boys* (1944), *This Is the Life* (1944), *Bowery to Broadway* (1944), and *Frisco Sal* (1945). When her film career declined, Foster returned to the stage and then disappeared from record in the 1970s.

FOY, EDDIE, JR. (1905–1983), son of the famous vaudvillian Eddie Foy, was on Broadway by the late 1920s and appeared in film musicals almost from their beginning, debuting in *Queen of the Night Clubs* (1929). The small, wiry song-and-dance man usually played chipper sidekicks and impersonated his own father in *LILLIAN RUSSELL* (1940), *YANKEE DOODLE DANDY* (1942), and the nonmusicals *Frontier Marshall* (1939) and *Wilson* (1944). The most memorable of Foy's twenty movie musicals were *Broadway Thru a Keyhole* (1933), *Four Jacks and a Jill* (1941), *Yokel Boy* (1942), *Dixie* (1943), *And the Angels Sing* (1944), *THE FARMER TAKES A WIFE* (1953), *Lucky Me* (1954), *THE PAJAMA GAME* (1957), and *BELLS ARE RINGING* (1960). The story of his family was told in the BIOGRAPHICAL MUSICAL *The Seven Little Foys* (1955), which he narrated. One of his brothers was Hollywood producer-director Bryan Foy.

FRANCIS, CONNIE (1938–   ), a popular recording artist of the 1960s, was discovered on a television talent show and started making hit records as a teenager. The dark-haired singer, who often seemed to cry her songs, was first heard on film when she dubbed Tuesday Weld's singing voice in *Rock Rock Rock* (1956). After a specialty bit in *Jamboree* (1957), she started appearing on screen as a plucky teenager or a wild college girl: *Where the Boys Are* (1960), *Follow the Boys* (1963), *Looking for Love* (1964), and *When the Boys Meet the Girls* (1965). When her career collapsed in the 1970s and Francis suffered a brutal rape, she lost her voice. She slowly recuperated and made a comeback in nightclubs and concerts in the 1990s.

FRANK, MELVIN (1913–1988) was a successful screenwriter, director, and producer, often working with his partner Norman Panama. Frank scripted such musical films as *HAPPY GO LUCKY* (1943), *THANK YOUR LUCKY STARS* (1943), *And the Angels Sing* (1944), *Duffy's Tavern* (1945), *ROAD TO UTOPIA* (1946), and *WHITE CHRISTMAS* (1954). He added director and sometimes producer credits to his musicals *THE COURT JESTER* (1956), *LI'L ABNER* (1959), *THE ROAD TO HONG KONG* (1962), and *A Funny Thing Happened on the Way to the Forum* (1966).

FRAWLEY, WILLIAM (1887–1966), a beloved character actor who often played gruff but warm-hearted types, made over 150 films before starting a lucrative television career (*I Love Lucy*). Frawley appeared in all genres of film, including the musicals *Moonlight and Pretzels* (1933), *HIGH, WIDE AND HANDSOME* (1937), *ROSE OF WASHINGTON SQUARE* (1939), *RHYTHM ON THE RIVER* (1940), *GOING MY WAY* (1944), *ZIEGFELD FOLLIES* (1946), *MOTHER WORE TIGHTS* (1947), and *The Lemon Drop Kid* (1951).

FRAZEE, JANE (1918–1985) rose from child performer singing in nightclubs and on the radio to leading lady in 1940s movie musicals, but her nearly thirty films were usually grade B, and she retired from the screen to act on television in the 1950s. Frazee made her screen debut with *Melody and Moonlight* (1940), followed by *BUCK PRIVATES* (1941), *Hellzapoppin* (1941), *Moonlight in Havana* (1942), *Rosie the Riveter* (1944), *Springtime in the Sierras* (1947), *The Gay Ranchero* (1948), and many others.

FREED, ARTHUR (1894–1973) was one of the most influential figures in the history of the Hollywood musical, first as a songwriter and then later as a producer whose famous "Freed Unit" represented the best in movie musicals. Freed started as a song plugger in Tin Pan Alley and a vaudeville performer but was soon writing his own song lyrics and collaborating with composer NACIO HERB BROWN on the early film musicals *THE BROADWAY MELODY* (1929), *HOLLYWOOD REVUE OF 1929*, *Lord Byron of Broadway* (1930), *GOOD NEWS* (1930), and *GOING HOLLYWOOD* (1933). Freed would also contribute songs lyrics to *Sadie McKee* (1934), *BROADWAY MELODY OF 1936* (1935), *BROADWAY MELODY OF 1938* (1937), *Yolanda and the*

Thief (1945), *Pagan Love Song* (1950), and others, but his interests lay in producing, and after serving as associate producer on *THE WIZARD OF OZ* (1939), Freed formed his own production team at MGM and presented a string of beloved movie musicals: *BABES IN ARMS* (1939), *STRIKE UP THE BAND* (1940), *Little Nelly Kelly* (1940), *Lady, Be Good* (1941), *BABES ON BROADWAY* (1941), *Panama Hattie* (1942), *FOR ME AND MY GAL* (1942), *CABIN IN THE SKY* (1943), *DuBarry Was a Lady* (1943), *BEST FOOT FORWARD* (1943), *Girl Crazy* (1943), *MEET ME IN ST. LOUIS* (1944), *THE HARVEY GIRLS* (1946), *ZIEGFELD FOLLIES* (1946), *TILL THE CLOUDS ROLL BY* (1947), *GOOD NEWS* (1947), *SUMMER HOLIDAY* (1948), *THE PIRATE* (1948), *EASTER PARADE* (1948), *WORDS AND MUSIC* (1948), *TAKE ME OUT TO THE BALL GAME* (1949), *THE BARKLEYS OF BROADWAY* (1949), *ON THE TOWN* (1949), *ANNIE GET YOUR GUN* (1950), *ROYAL WEDDING* (1951), *SHOW BOAT* (1951), *AN AMERICAN IN PARIS* (1951), *THE BELLE OF NEW YORK* (1952), *SINGIN' IN THE RAIN* (1952), which used the Freed-Brown song catalog, *THE BAND WAGON* (1953), *BRIGADOON* (1954), *IT'S ALWAYS FAIR WEATHER* (1955), *KISMET* (1955), *INVITATION TO THE DANCE* (1957), *SILK STOCKINGS* (1957), *GIGI* (1958), and *BELLS ARE RINGING* (1960). Freed gathered together the best directors, designers, songwriters, and stars for his musicals and oversaw all the elements of the movie, so there was a definite look and feel to a Freed film. His career faded as the movie musical declined, but the legacy he left behind has not diminished over the years.

FREED, RALPH (1907–1973), the younger brother of ARTHUR FREED, was also a lyricist and, working with composer BURTON LANE, provided the scores for *She Married a Cop* (1939), *BABES ON BROADWAY* (1941), and *This Time for Keeps* (1947). With other composers Freed wrote songs for *First Love* (1939), *TWO GIRLS AND A SAILOR* (1944), *No Leave, No Love* (1945), *Holiday in Mexico* (1946), and *Two Sisters From Boston* (1946). His most remembered song is "(I Love New York in June) How About You?"

FREELAND, THORNTON (1898–1987) worked his way up from assistant cameraman in silents to director of sound comedies and musicals. After helming the early musicals *Be Yourself* (1930), *FLYING DOWN TO RIO* (1933), and *George White's Scandals* (1934), Freeland went to England to direct films. He returned to Hollywood in the 1940s and directed a handful of comedies and the musical *Too Many Blondes* (1941).

FRIML, RUDOLF (1879–1972), one of Broadway's finest composers of OPERETTA, saw three of his popular stage works filmed: *The Vagabond King* (1930 and 1956), *ROSE MARIE* (1936 and 1954), and *THE FIREFLY*

(1937). With various lyricists, Friml also provided scores for the films *The Lottery Bride* (1930), *Music for Madame* (1937), and *Northwest Outpost* (1947).

FRONTIER MUSICALS have been popular from the early talkies, probably for two reasons: America's fascination with movie westerns and the way the film medium could outdo the most lavish Broadway production when it came to scenic vistas. At first movie producers were wary of having actors sing outdoors, feeling more comfortable with musical numbers done on a stage, in a radio studio, or in a nightclub, where the orchestra is logically present. From the hills of Pennsylvania to the Wild West to New Orleans to the Canadian Rockies, audiences immediately accepted music seemingly coming from nature and had no trouble with such early musicals set in the great outdoors as *RIO RITA* (1929), *WHOOPEE* (1930), *NAUGHTY MARIETTA* (1935), *MISSISSIPPI* (1935), *ROSE MARIE* (1936), *SHOW BOAT* (1936), and *HIGH, WIDE AND HANDSOME* (1937). The genre was even more effective when color was perfected, and many a frontier musical was improved upon by being visually thrilling. Among the many outdoor musicals over the decades were *New Moon* (1940), *Girl Crazy* (1943), *Riding High* (1943), *CAN'T HELP SINGING* (1944), *Belle of the Yukon* (1945), *THE HARVEY GIRLS* (1946), *The Kissing Bandit* (1948), *THE PALEFACE* (1948), *The Beautiful Blonde From Bashful Bend* (1949), *ANNIE GET YOUR GUN* (1950), *SON OF PALEFACE* (1952), *CALAMITY JANE* (1953), *THE FARMER TAKES A WIFE* (1953), *SEVEN BRIDES FOR SEVEN BROTHERS* (1954), *OKLAHOMA!* (1955), *THE UNSINKABLE MOLLY BROWN* (1964), and *PAINT YOUR WAGON* (1969).

FUNICELLO, ANNETTE (1942–   ) was the most famous of television's *Mickey Mouse Club* members and as a teenager she made a handful of DISNEY films, including the musical *BABES IN TOYLAND* (1961). Funicello then graduated to a series of "beach" movie musicals such as *Beach Party* (1963), *Muscle Beach Party* (1964), *Bikini Beach* (1964), *Beach Blanket Bingo* (1965), *How to Stuff a Wild Bikini* (1967), and others. She was reunited with her frequent co-star FRANKIE AVALON for the nostalgia musical *Back to the Beach* (1987).

FUNNY FACE (Paramount 1957) was one of the most stunning-looking musicals of the 1950s, being about fashion photography and having celebrated photographer Richard Avedon as a consultant. The on-site locations in New York and Paris certainly helped too, as director STANLEY DONAN turned each sequence into a dazzling magazine display. The film's title, its title song, and some other musical numbers came from a 1927 Broadway hit by GEORGE and IRA GERSHWIN that starred FRED ASTAIRE and his sister Adele. Thirty years later Astaire again played the leading role for the film, though little of the original plot or character survived the transition. Fashion photographer Astaire discovers the brainy intellectual AUDREY HEPBURN (doing her own singing) working in a Greenwich Village bookstore and is determined to make a star model out of her. With the help of magazine editor KAY THOMPSON (who wants the women of the world to "Think Pink"), Astaire whisks Hepburn off to Paris for a shoot, and succumbing to the charms of the man and the city, she falls in love while becoming a celebrated cover girl. EUGENE LORING and Astaire did the choreography, the most memorable moments being Astaire's solo "Let's Kiss and Make Up," in which a raincoat and umbrella become his partner, and a lyrical *pas de deux* with Hepburn and Astaire dancing to "He Loves and She Loves" through a morning mist rising from a pond. The other Gershwin songs included "Clap Yo' Hands," "How Long Has This Been Going On?," and " 'S Wonderful," while Leonard Gershe (who also wrote the script) and ROGER EDENS added "Bonjour, Paris!," "On How to Be Lovely," and others.

FUNNY GIRL (Rastar/Columbia 1968) on stage had made a Broadway star out of BARBRA STREISAND, and the film version made her a movie star. And since the story was about the making of another star, FANNY BRICE, life seemed to imitate art in a most convenient and entertaining way. Like the 1964 stage production, the plot told of the rise of Brice from a gawky ugly duckling trying to break into vaudeville to the comic star of the *Ziegfeld Follies*, paralleled by her courtship, wedding, see-saw marriage, and divorce from gambler Nick Arnstein (Omar Sharif). Only half of the stage songs by BOB MERRILL and JULE STYNE stayed, with the team writing three new ones (including the touching title song) and three old Brice standards ("I'd Rather Be Blue Over You," "Second Hand Rose" and "My Man") added for period authenticity. The score's big hit was "People" (popular even before the play opened), but there was quality to be found in "I'm the Greatest Star," "You Are Woman," and "Sadie, Sadie." WILLIAM WYLER directed with HERBERT ROSS staging the musical numbers, most effectively with a farcical spoof on "Swan Lake," a satiric *Follies* number in which a pregnant bride extols "His Love Makes Me Beautiful," and an energetic "Don't Rain on My Parade," in which Streisand pursues Sharif by train, auto, and finally atop a barge heading out of New York harbor.

FUNNY LADY (Rastar/Columbia 1975), a SEQUEL to *FUNNY GIRL* (1968) that used some of the same creative team, did not enjoy the success of the original, but it did boast another high-powered performance by BARBRA STREISAND, a surprisingly agreeable one by James Caan, and a wealth of old song favorites mixed in with a handful of new numbers by FRED EBB and JOHN KANDER. The story picked up where *Funny Girl* left off, Streisand as *Follies* star FANNY BRICE still in love with gambler Nick Arnstein (Omar Sharif). When Nick asks for a divorce, Brice marries songwriter-producer Billy Rose (Caan) on the rebound, but his infidelities destroy the marriage and

Brice is alone once again. The plot was mercifully broken up by no less than eighteen songs, directed and choreographed by HERBERT ROSS. Few production numbers had the impact of those in *Funny Girl*, but the opportunity to hear "I Found a Million Dollar Baby in a Five-and-Ten Cent Store," "It's Only a Paper Moon," "Am I Blue?," "I Caught a Code in My Dose," "Great Day," "More Than You Know," and others was nothing to sneer at. The new Kander and Ebb numbers included the breezy "How Lucky Can You Get?," the plaintive "Isn't This Better?," and the affirming "Let's Hear It for Me."

G

GABLE, CLARK (1901–1960), named the King of Hollywood by his many fans, was known for his rugged, masculine roles in comedies and dramas but also appeared in three musicals: as Broadway choreographer Patch Gallagher in *DANC-ING LADY* (1933), saloon owner Blackie Norton in *SAN FRANCISCO* (1936), and boxer Larry Cain in *Cain and Mabel* (1936). Gable's most-remembered musical bit was not in a musical at all, but as an ex-hoffer singing and dancing to "Puttin' on the Ritz" in the dark comedy *Idiot's Delight* (1939).

GABOR, EVA (1921–1995), the youngest of the three glamourous Gabor sisters from Hungary, was the first to come to America and found steady work on Broadway, in the movies, and later on in television (*Green Acres*). Her musical films include *ARTISTS AND MODELS* (1955), *GIGI* (1958), and voices for *THE ARISTOCRATS* (1970) and *The Rescuers* (1977). Her sister, the oft-married **ZSA ZSA GABOR** (1918–   ), was seen in *LOVELY TO LOOK AT* (1952), *LILI* (1953), and *Pepe* (1960).

GABOR, ZSA ZSA. See Gabor, Eva

GALLAGHER, RICHARD "SKEETS" (1891–1955) was a busy song-and-dance man from vaudeville and Broadway who appeared in lightweight roles in many silent shorts and over fifty feature films, including a handful of musicals. The blonde hoofer appeared in *Close Harmony* (1929), *Pointed Heels* (1929), *Honey* (1930), *PARAMOUNT ON PARADE* (1930), *Let's Go Native* (1930), *Love Among the Millionaires* (1930), *Too Much Harmony* (1933), *Hats Off* (1936), and *Zis Boom Bah* (1942).

GANG'S ALL HERE, THE (Fox 1943) was one of 20TH CENTURY–FOX's most expensive musicals of the war years and, looking at BUSBY BERKE-LEY's lavish production numbers, it's easy to see where the money went. "The

Lady in the Tutti-Frutti Hat" number featured CARMEN MIRANDA, wagon-loads of colorfully dressed peasants on a plantation, and thousands of bananas (including some large phallic ones making risque waving patterns) all combined to form geometric patterns. For the finale, "The Polka Dot Polka," ALICE FAYE (in her last film before her first retirement), a gang of children from different periods, and a nightclub chorus all performed in front of revolving mirrors that made dizzying kaleidoscopic images. It was Berkeley's first film in Technicolor and the effect was practically psychedelic. The plot centered on a showgirl (Faye) at a Manhattan nightclub who romances soldier James Ellison and makes him forget his fiancée Sheila Ryan. CHARLOTTE GREENWOOD, EDWARD EVERETT HORTON, Phil Baker, and EUGENE PALLETTE wandered in and out to grab the laughs when Miranda was occupied elsewhere and BENNY GOODMAN provided the requisite band needed to fill out the nightclub numbers. LEO ROBIN and HARRY WARREN wrote most of the score, which also included the hit ballads "No Love, No Nothin' " and "A Journey to a Star" (both sung by Faye).

GARDINER, REGINALD (1903–1980), a dapper Englishman who delighted theatre audiences on both sides of the Atlantic, made his Hollywood debut as a policeman with a yearning to conduct a symphony in *BORN TO DANCE* (1936) and went on to play aristocrats, butlers, and silly but genteel types. With his characteristic clipped accent and mustache, Gardiner appeared in a dozen other musicals, including *A DAMSEL IN DISTRESS* (1936), *SWEETHEARTS* (1938), *Sweet Rosie O'Grady* (1943), *THE DOLLY SISTERS* (1945), *That Lady in Ermine* (1948), *WABASH AVENUE* (1950), *Ain't Misbehavin'* (1955), and *Rock-a-Bye Baby* (1958).

GARDNER, AVA (1922–1990), the dark and beautiful star who excelled at sultry and dramatic roles for three decades, made several appearances in movie musicals, usually in bit parts, before playing leading roles in *One Touch of Venus* (1948), *SHOW BOAT* (1951), and *The Blue Bird* (1976). Gardner can be seen briefly in *BABES ON BROADWAY* (1941), *DuBarry Was a Lady* (1943), *Swing Fever* (1943), *TWO GIRLS AND A SAILOR* (1944), *Music for Millions* (1944), and *THE BAND WAGON* (1953). She was married to and divorced from MICKEY ROONEY, Artie Shaw, and FRANK SINATRA.

GARLAND, JUDY (1922–1969) bonded with her audiences with a greater emotional grip than any other movie musical star, appealing to them with her innocence in her early films, a sense of eager romance in her adult musicals, and the struggle for survival in her later movies. Small but memorable roles in *Pigskin Parade* (1936), *BROADWAY MELODY OF 1938* (1937), *Everybody Sing* (1939), *Listen, Darling* (1938), and *Love Finds Andy Hardy* (1938) were only a preview to Garland's watershed role of Dorothy in *THE WIZARD OF OZ* (1939). She strengthened her audience appeal as an ever-hopeful teen in

BABES IN ARMS (1939), *Andy Hardy Meets Debutante* (1940), *STRIKE UP THE BAND* (1940), and *Little Nellie Kelly* (1940) before edging into adulthood in *ZIEGFELD GIRL* (1941), *BABES ON BROADWAY* (1941), *FOR ME AND MY GAL* (1942), *Presenting Lily Mars* (1943), *Girl Crazy* (1943), *MEET ME IN ST. LOUIS* (1944), and *THE HARVEY GIRLS* (1946). Because of physical and emotional problems, Garland aged quicker than normal and the blush of innocence was missing when she valiantly played ingenues in *THE PIRATE* (1948), *EASTER PARADE* (1948), *IN THE GOOD OLD SUMMERTIME* (1949), and *SUMMER STOCK* (1950). She also spiced up many a film by doing specialty bits, as in *Thousands Cheer* (1943), *ZIEGFELD FOLLIES* (1946), *TILL THE CLOUDS ROLL BY* (1946), and *WORDS AND MUSIC* (1948). After several setbacks, Garland made a triumphant return to the movie musical playing the bittersweet role of Esther Blodgett Maine in *A STAR IS BORN* (1954), arguably her finest performance. The rest of her career was occupied with concerts, nightclub acts, and television shows, only lending her voice to the musical *Pepe* (1960) and the animated *Gay Purr-ee* (1962). Her last film appearance was in *I Could Go on Singing* (1963), six years before the fatal overdose that ended her tragic life. Although Garland was primarily a singer with the ability to interpret a song in a personal and sometimes even desperate way, her acting and dancing talents were considerable and her persona on screen was never less than magnetic. Garland was married to composer David Rose, director VINCENTE MINNELLI, and producer Sid Luft, and her daughters are entertainers LIZA MINNELLI and Lorna Luft.

GARRETT, BETTY (1919–   ), a sharp comic actress and singer who appeared in several Broadway shows, had a short but notable film career playing second leads and smart sidekicks in musicals. Garrett was seen as saloon singer Shoo-Shoo Grady in *Big City* (1948), Broadway performer Peggy McNeil in *WORDS AND MUSIC* (1948), predatory baseball fan Shirley Delwyn in *TAKE ME OUT TO THE BALL GAME* (1949), gold digger Betty Barrett in *NEPTUNE'S DAUGHTER* (1949), man-hungry cab driver Hildy in *ON THE TOWN* (1949), and sarcastic authoress Ruth Sherwood in *My Sister Eileen* (1955). Her film career was damaged when her husband LARRY PARKS was blacklisted as a Communist, so she returned to clubs and the stage, making a second career in the 1970s on television.

GAXTON, WILLIAM (1893–1963), the perennial leading man in Broadway musicals in the 1930s, was limited to stock character types (usually beefy press agents) in films. Gaxton was featured in *STAGE DOOR CANTEEN* (1943), *BEST FOOT FORWARD* (1943), *Something to Shout About* (1943), *The Heat's On* (1943), and *Diamond Horseshoe* (1945).

GAY DIVORCEE, THE (RKO 1934) reached the screen with little of the original 1932 Broadway show *The Gay Divorce* intact. (The title was changed because the film censors thought something as unseemly as a divorce could never be happy.) Producer PANDRO S. BERMAN tossed out COLE PORTER's stage songs except for "Night and Day," and the plot was softened so that FRED ASTAIRE was only mistakenly thought to be the correspondent in a divorce case. The real correspondent was prissy ERIK RHODES, so any chance of eroticism was eliminated. What resulted was a totally new animal that was different from the play, but a sublime beast indeed. The new story had GINGER ROGERS, anxious to get a divorce, going to a resort where she thinks dancer Astaire is the man she is to be caught spending the night with. Astaire and Rogers played principal characters for the first time and secured their careers dancing across a ballroom floor together to "Night and Day" and cutting loose with "The Continental," the first number to win the ACADEMY AWARD in the new Best Song category. CON CONRAD and HERB MAGIDSON wrote the tango number, and MACK GORDON and HARRY REVEL penned "Don't Let It Bother You" and "Let's K-nock K-nees," which BETTY GRABLE and EDWARD EVERETT HORTON sang as they strummed ukeleles. ERIC BLORE, Lillian Miles, and ALICE BRADY were also in the cast, which was directed by MARK SANDRICH and choreographed by DAVE GOULD, HERMES PAN, and Astaire uncredited. The musical was a huge hit, and never again could Rogers and Astaire be anything but the feature attraction in their movies.

GAYNOR, JANET (1906–1984) was a small, dimpled all-American sweetheart who rose to fame in silents and maintained her stardom through the 1930s. Often paired with CHARLES FARRELL, the duo were America's favorite screen couple and Gaynor herself was the most popular film actress in Hollywood in 1934. Although her singing voice was thin, Gaynor starred in four early musicals: as the Yorkville "Cinderella" Molly Carr in *SUNNY SIDE UP* (1929), the *nouveau riche* "Juliet" Eleanor Divine in *High Society Blues* (1930), Scottish immigrant Heather Gordon in *DELICIOUS* (1931), and Princess Marie Christine disguised as a manicurist in *Adorable* (1933). She also did a specialty bit in *Happy Days* (1930). Gaynor's second husband was costume designer GILBERT ADRIAN.

GAYNOR, MITZI (1930–   ) grew up in a family of dancers and was performing on stage as a child. Although she made several film appearances as a dancer, recognition did not come until much later. Gaynor's most notable musical roles were entertainer Gloria Adams in *My Blue Heaven* (1950), nineteenth-century child stage star Lotta Crabtree in *Golden Girl* (1951), hillbilly Emily Ann Stackerlee in *Bloodhounds of Broadway* (1952), sassy Broadway singer Eva Tanguay in *The I-Don't-Care Girl* (1953), Katy Donahue of a family act in *THERE'S NO BUSINESS LIKE SHOW BUSINESS* (1954), shipboard actress Patsy Blair in *ANYTHING GOES* (1956), nightclub cutie Martha Stewart in *THE JOKER IS WILD* (1957), Parisian café singer Joy

Henderson in *LES GIRLS* (1957), and Navy nurse Nellie Forbush in *SOUTH PACIFIC* (1958). Gaynor retired from films in 1963 but remained active on stage, on television, and in nightclubs.

GENTLEMEN PREFER BLONDES (Fox 1953) was a jewel box of a musical that showcased MARILYN MONROE and JANE RUSSELL, each giving her finest musical performance. The movie version dropped most of the 1949 Broadway musical's plot and all but three of the songs by LEO ROBIN and JULE STYNE, but what remained was still delicious. The two stars performed the coy "Bye Bye Baby" and the cynical "A Little Girl From Little Rock" as a duet, and choreographer JACK COLE turned "Diamonds Are a Girl's Best Friend" into a sexy production number for Monroe. HAROLD ADAMSON and HOAGY CARMICHAEL added "When Love Goes Wrong" for the two to sing at a Paris café and "Ain't There Anyone Here for Love?" for Russell to ask in a gymnasium full of body builders. The simplified plot had to do with gold digger Monroe and man-hunter Russell on an ocean liner sailing to Paris, a stolen diamond tiara belonging to wealthy Charles Coburn, a millionaire (Taylor Holmes) who hires a detective (Elliott Reid) to keep Monroe away from his son (Tommy Noonan), and a double wedding where each girl gets her man. What was once a satire on the Roaring Twenties (based on Anita Loos' famous novel) was now a contemporary and glamourous vehicle for two stars and, as such, was a diamond mine all its own, earning over $5 million at the box office.

GERSHWIN, GEORGE (1898–1937) was one of America's most experimental and gifted composers, making landmark contributions to Broadway, Hollywood, and the concert hall. Gershwin made his name with the Tin Pan Alley hit "Swanee River" and then was on Broadway, scoring twenty-three Broadway musicals in the 1920s and 1930s, most of which were filmed but usually with the scores edited or added to by others. From the mid-1920s he usually worked with his older brother, the lyricist IRA GERSHWIN, and their stage shows to make it to Hollywood included *Girl Crazy* (1932 and 1943), *Lady, Be Good* (1941), and *FUNNY FACE* (1957), as well as *DELICIOUS* (1931), which they wrote directly for the screen. After making his mark in the concert world with "Rhapsody in Blue" and in the opera world with *PORGY AND BESS* (1935 but not filmed until 1959), Gershwin went to California with his brother and scored *SHALL WE DANCE* (1937), *A DAMSEL IN DISTRESS* (1937), and *THE GOLDWYN FOLLIES* (1938) before his premature death from a brain tumor. George Gershwin's life was the subject of the bio musical *RHAPSODY IN BLUE* (1945), in which he was portrayed by ROBERT ALDA, and the Gershwin catalog of songs was used for *THE SHOCKING MISS PILGRIM* (1947), *AN AMERICAN IN PARIS* (1951), *Kiss Me, Stupid* (1964), and *When the Boys Meet the Girls* (1965). Although primarily thought of as a jazz composer, Gershwin excelled in all forms of music, from comic operetta to musical comedy to folk opera.

GERSHWIN, IRA (1896–1983), one of America's finest lyricists, was often in the shadow of his illustrious brother, the composer GEORGE GERSHWIN, but he had a remarkable career writing for the stage and for Hollywood with his brother and several others as well. The Gershwins' first score for film was *DELICIOUS* (1931), and except for the screen versions of their Broadway hits like *Girl Crazy* (1932 and 1943) and *Lady, Be Good* (1941), they did not return to Hollywood until they scored *SHALL WE DANCE* (1937), *A DAMSEL IN DISTRESS* (1937), and *THE GOLDWYN FOLLIES* (1938). After his brother's untimely death, Ira Gershwin started working with such composers as KURT WEILL, JEROME KERN, HARRY WARREN, BURTON LANE, and HAROLD ARLEN and scored such movie musicals as *Lady in the Dark* (1944), based on his stage score, *COVER GIRL* (1944), *Where Do We Go From Here?* (1945), *THE BARKLEYS OF BROADWAY* (1949), *GIVE A GIRL A BREAK* (1953), *A STAR IS BORN* (1954), and *THE COUNTRY GIRL* (1954). Songs written with his brother were used in the musical bio *RHAPSODY IN BLUE* (1945), in which Ira was played by Herbert Rudley, *THE SHOCKING MISS PILGRIM* (1947), *AN AMERICAN IN PARIS* (1951), *FUNNY FACE* (1957), *PORGY AND BESS* (1959), *Kiss Me, Stupid* (1964), and *When the Boys Meet the Girls* (1965). Gershwin's lyrics are characterized by their zesty use of slang, creative wordplay, and casual but highly romantic sentiments.

GIBBONS, CEDRIC (1893–1960) was arguably Hollywood's most prolific, influential, and awarded scenic designer. Educated as an architect, Gibbons started doing sets for silent movies and trained a staff of co-designers who together did the art direction for over 1,000 films. Gibbons designed everything from period epics to modern comedies and dramas (many of his film designs were copied by architects and interior decorators across the country) to the Oscar statuette itself, which he won eleven times. Among the many musicals Gibbons designed were *HALLELUJAH* (1929), *THE MERRY WIDOW* (1934), *A NIGHT AT THE OPERA* (1935), *SAN FRANCISCO* (1936), *The Great Waltz* (1938), *CABIN IN THE SKY* (1943), *Yolanda and the Thief* (1945), *ZIEGFELD FOLLIES* (1946), *THE PIRATE* (1948), *ON THE TOWN* (1949), *AN AMERICAN IN PARIS* (1951), and *KISMET* (1955).

GIBSON, VIRGINIA (1928–   ), a Broadway singer-dancer, played second leads or featured roles in eight musicals in the 1950s. Gibson's most notable films were *Tea for Two* (1950), *Painting the Clouds With Sunshine* (1951), *SEVEN BRIDES FOR SEVEN BROTHERS* (1954), *Athena* (1954), and *FUNNY FACE* (1957).

GIGI (MGM 1958) was the last great musical film of the 1950s and, in many ways, the last of the classic studio musicals that Hollywood had done so efficiently for decades. ALAN JAY LERNER wrote the screenplay from a Colette novella and turned the unlikely story of a young French girl being groomed as a courtesan into a perfectly charming period musical. In *fin de siécle* Paris, tomboy teenager Gigi (LESLIE CARON with singing dubbed by Betty Wand) is being raised by her Aunt Alicia (Isabel Jeans) and ex-courtesan grandmother Mme. Alvarez (HERMIONE GINGOLD) to behave like a refined lady, avoid marriage, and live off the favors of wealthy gentlemen. Young and aristocratic Gaston (Louis Jourdan) has known Gigi since she was a child and, after being dumped by his latest flame (EVA GABOR), shocks his grandfather, the aging rogue MAURICE CHEVALIER, and Gigi's family by proposing marriage to Gigi. VINCENTE MINNELLI directed on location in Paris, CECIL BEATON designed the elegant period costumes, and Lerner and FREDERICK LOEWE wrote the scintillating score: the bubbly "The Night They Invented Champagne," the pouting character number "(I Don't Understand) The Parisians," the sly "Thank Heaven for Little Girls," the piquant "I'm Glad I'm Not Young Anymore," the tender "Say a Prayer for Me Tonight," the waltzing "She Is Not Thinking of Me," the wistful comic duet "I Remember It Well" for Gingold and Chevalier, and the expansive title song in which Gaston realizes he loves Gigi. The film won an armful of Oscars, and an era never to be seen again went out in a stylish blaze of glory. The musical was turned into a Broadway show in 1973 with additional songs by Lerner and Loewe, but it was a failure.

GILBERT, BILLY (1893–1971), a huge character actor who specialized in small but noticeable roles, appeared in over 200 feature films from the silents to the 1960s. The rotund giant came from vaudeville, where his comic sneezing routine was his trademark. Gilbert repeated the bit in some of his films and supplied the voice (and sneezes) for the dwarf Sneezy in *SNOW WHITE AND THE SEVEN DWARFS* (1938). Among Gilbert's musical credits were *ON THE AVENUE* (1937), *THE FIREFLY* (1937), *BROADWAY MELODY OF 1938* (1937), *ONE HUNDRED MEN AND A GIRL* (1937), *ROSALIE* (1937), *JOY OF LIVING* (1938), *My Lucky Star* (1938), *TIN PAN ALLEY* (1940), *No No Nanette* (1940), *WEEK-END IN HAVANA* (1941), *Song of the Islands* (1942), *ANCHORS AWEIGH* (1945), and *Down Among the Sheltering Palms* (1953).

GINGOLD, HERMIONE (1897–1987) was an audience favorite in musical revues in London and New York, playing eccentric characters with her raspy voice and acidic delivery. Gingold's movie musical credits were few but each one was memorable: the worldly Mme. Alvarez in *GIGI* (1958), the voice of Mme. Rubens-Chatte in the animated *Gay Purr-ee* (1962), the mayor's wife Eulalie Shinn in *THE MUSIC MAN* (1962), the no-nonsense Miss Grimshaw in *I'd Rather Be Rich* (1964), and the aging courtesan Mme. Armfeldt in *A Little Night Music* (1978).

GIVE A GIRL A BREAK (MGM 1953) was intended to be a B picture with a small budget and a lot of newcomers in the cast and on the staff. But this unpretentious backstager is filled with pleasing scenes, songs, and performers and holds up better than many more polished products. When the star walks out of a Broadway show in rehearsal, director GOWER CHAMPION decides to replace her with an unknown. The choice comes down to three chorines: the director's former dancing partner MARGE CHAMPION, composer KURT KASZNAR's favorite Helen Wood, and assistant director BOB FOSSE's protégé DEBBIE REYNOLDS. The competition keeps the plot crackling until Wood finds out she's pregnant, Marge Champion falls for the director and doesn't care about a career, and Reynolds gets the plum part. STANLEY DONAN directed and choreographed, with Gower Champion assisting in the dances and starting his remarkable career as a choreographer. The score by IRA GERSHWIN and BURTON LANE had few hits but a handful of commendable songs, including the patriotic love proposal "In Our United State," the upbeat "It Happens Every Time," and the tongue-in-cheek rouser "Applause, Applause."

GLEASON, JACKIE (1916–1987), the portly comedian who turned bumbling exasperation into a comic art form, struggled in burlesque, vaudeville, Broadway, films, and nightclubs before finding stardom on television (*The Honeymooners*). Gleason appeared in some two dozen films but rarely had the chance to fully display his comic talents. His musicals, in which he usually played the hero's sidekick, include *Navy Blues* (1941), *ORCHESTRA WIVES* (1942), and *SPRINGTIME IN THE ROCKIES* (1942). Gleason also played dramatic parts on film and managed a tender pathos not seen in his television shows, such as singing "Call Me Irresponsible" in the nonmusical *Papa's Delicate Condition* (1963).

GLENN MILLER STORY, THE (Universal 1954) was probably the best of the many BIOGRAPHICAL MUSICALS of Big Band conductors, if not one of the better musical bios to come out of Hollywood. It followed the usual rags-to-riches format, and because Miller had died in a plane crash going to entertain troops in World War Two, it could not help but be sentimental. But JAMES STEWART played Miller as a dedicated, very human artist searching for the distinctive sound that would make his band special, JUNE ALLYSON was his overly understanding wife, and LOUIS ARMSTRONG, GENE KRUPA, FRANCES LANGFORD, and others from the 1940s played themselves. All of the Miller song favorites were heard, from "Basin Street Blues" to "In the Mood" to "Pennsylvania 6–5000" to "Chattanooga Choo-Choo," and audiences nostalgic for the previous decade were in bliss.

GO INTO YOUR DANCE (Warner 1935) was another cliché-filled back-stager—it was based on a novel by Bradford Ropes, whose earlier book was the source for *42ND STREET* (1933)—but the movie boasted AL JOLSON and RUBY KEELER (Mrs. Jolson at the time) in their only feature together, and it had a superior score by AL DUBIN and HARRY WARREN. Egotistical entertainer Jolson is soon on the outs because no one will work with him. But humble dancer Keeler believes in him and manages to open a nightclub in New York for Jolson to star in. Some gangsters and a bum murder rap slowed down her plans, but the night spot opened with a splash and the twosome were seen dancing atop a globe to "A Latin From Manhattan." Other songs in the score included the rhythmic "About a Quarter to Nine" and the snappy title song. A touching but sad moment in the musical was HELEN MORGAN, in a supporting role as a gangster's mistress, sitting on a piano and delivering the morose torch song "The Little Things You Used to Do." Alcoholism had pretty much destroyed Morgan's career by this time, but Jolson insisted that she be given the cameo part and she was indelibly poignant.

GODDARD, PAULETTE (1905–1990), the Hollywood beauty known for her comedies and roles in Charles Chaplin features, was a *Follies* girl on Broadway before getting bit parts in such early musicals as *The Kid From Spain* (1932), *KID MILLIONS* (1934), *The Bohemian Girl* (1936), *Second Chorus* (1940), and *Pot o' Gold* (1941). Once she achieved stardom, Goddard returned to musicals in guest bits only: *STAR SPANGLED RHYTHM* (1942), *Duffy's Tavern* (1945), and *Variety Girl* (947). Among her husbands were Chaplin, actor Burgess Meredith, and author Erich Maria Remarque.

GODSPELL (Columbia 1973) was certainly opened up from its small Off-Broadway roots, the biblical musical now taking place all over New York City and celebrating its many locations like no other movie since *ON THE TOWN* (1949). The retelling of St. Matthew's Gospel featured Jesus (Victor Garber) as an androgynous flower child and a hobo hoofer (David Haskell) playing both John the Baptist and Judas, both surrounded by a merry band of urchins who were the early disciples. The parables became vaudeville bits, and the songs by STEPHEN SCHWARTZ utilized everything from rock to soft-shoe to actual gospel. It was an inventive theatre piece, and a lot of its originality and playfulness made it to the screen, helped by having the original creator-director John-Michael Tebelak write the screenplay with film director David Greene. Jesus and his child-like followers dashed all over the cityscape, from tap dancing on top of the World Trade Center towers to high kicking it in front of a twinkling sign in Times Square, singing such joyous songs as "O Bless the Lord My Soul," "All for the Best," "Light of the World," and the hit hymn "Day by Day." Schwartz even wrote a new number for the film, "Beautiful City," that capsulized the musical celebration of Manhattan as a city of love.

GOING HOLLYWOOD (Cosmopolitan/MGM 1933) used Tinsel Town as *42ND STREET* (1931) had used Broadway, both conveniently wounding the star so the newcomer could go on. The newcomer in this case was MARION DAVIES, a French teacher in a girls school, who follows true love BING CROSBY to Hollywood and rescues him from drink and the arms of Fifi D'Orsay, then goes on to the sound stage and makes a stellar debut in a feature film musical. *Cosmopolitan*'s mogul William Randolph Hearst built the movie around his mistress Davies, and she gave one of the most radiant performances of her mismanaged career. A lovesick Crosby sang the fervent "Temptation" in a Tijuana saloon as he hallucinated and saw the unfaithful D'Orsay's face appear in his liquor glass; the bizarre scene made Crosby a film star. The other songs by ARTHUR FREED and NACIO HERB BROWN included "We'll Make Hay While the Sun Shines," "After Sundown," "Our Big Love Scene," and the jaunty title song. The musical was one of the first to use Hollywood and the movie business as its setting, but it would be far from the last.

GOING MY WAY (Paramount 1944) was one of the studio's biggest hits of the decade and helped keep BING CROSBY the top box office attraction for several years running. In many ways it was a breakout film for the crooner, playing the gentle priest Father Chuck O'Malley who is sent to a rundown urban parish where aging, conservative Barry Fitzgerald is pastor. Crosby got to organize a boys choir out of the riffraff on the street, bring a young couple together, raise money for the poor parish, and even bring Fitzgerald's ninety-year-old mother from Ireland for Christmas. It was sentimental stuff all around, but director LEO McCAREY handled it expertly. The supporting cast featured Gene Lockhart, FRANK McHUGH, Jean Heather, and opera singer RISE STEVENS helping Bing get the choir heard by record producer WILLIAM FRAWLEY. What he heard was the gentle title ballad and the hit novelty number "Swinging on a Star," both by JOHNNY BURKE and JAMES VAN HEUSEN. The film collected a choir loft of Oscars and was soon followed by a SEQUEL, *THE BELLS OF ST. MARY'S* (1945).

GOLD DIGGERS IN PARIS. See *Gold Diggers of Broadway*

GOLD DIGGERS OF BROADWAY (Warner 1929) was an agreeable backstage musical that inspired a SERIES of five "Gold Digger" films, some of them much better than this original. The plot was an old one, coming from a 1919 play and a 1923 silent film. Three chorus girls (WINNIE LIGHTNER, Nancy Welford, and Ann Pennington) are after wealthy husbands and help fool a Boston snob (Conway Tearle) who comes to New York into paying off the gold digger who is after his nephew. After a night on the town with the stuffy uncle put in a compromising position, all ends happily as each girl gets the chump of her choice. AL DUBIN and JOE BURKE's songs, both in the plot and in the show the girls are appearing in, gave the film a lift, especially when they were as catchy as "Tiptoe Through the Tulips" and "Painting the

Clouds With Sunshine." ROY DEL RUTH directed with a folksy kind of familiarity with backstage life, and the sections filmed in the new Technicolor format certainly impressed audiences. The next installment, *GOLD DIGGERS OF 1933* (Warner 1933), was the best of the series, dealing with a backstage milieu again but now it was Broadway in the depths of the Depression. The musical, in fact, is one of the few to deal with the economic condition that had so affected audiences watching the film. Some of the plot remained from the 1929 film, with GINGER ROGERS, JOAN BLONDELL, RUBY KEELER, and Aline McMahon as chorus girls whose show is closed down in rehearsal because the producer runs out of money. The nephew this time was songwriter DICK POWELL, who loved Keeler but whose family was out to break up the relationship. More emphasis was put on the production numbers, and choreographer BUSBY BERKELEY turned each one of the songs by Dubin and HARRY WARREN into a visual as well as a musical feat. Rogers and the girls were dressed in outfits made of coins for the optimistic "We're in the Money," lovers cuddled and kissed in "Pettin' in the Park" until a sudden thunder shower sends the girls scurrying for cover and we see them change out of their wet clothes in silhouette, and violin-playing chorines form patterns and even glow in the dark for "The Shadow Waltz." The finale was a tribute to veterans out of a job during the Depression, with Etta Moten and Blondell singing "Remember My Forgotten Man" as flashbacks of soldiers marching off to war dissolved into the same men now in bread lines. It was musical comedy at its most socially conscious and yet was still enormously entertaining. *GOLD DIGGERS OF 1935* (Warner 1935) abandoned the Broadway backstage setting for a New Hampshire summer resort but the gold digging continued with Russian ADOLPHE MENJOU trying to fleece society matron ALICE BRADY, secretary GLENDA FARRELL blackmailing snuff box collector HUGH HERBERT, and struggling med student Powell falling for heiress GLORIA STUART. For the first time, Berkeley directed as well as choreographed, and while the integrated number "Going Shopping With You" had its charm, it was the big productions once again that made the film special. The score was again by Dubin and Warren, who came up with "The Words Are in My Heart," which was staged with fifty-six pianos being played by fifty-six girls, the pianos moving about to created designs and patterns. The "Lullaby of Broadway" sequence was the most ambitious, a narrative ballet that showed twenty-four hours in the hedonistic life of a New York chorus girl. A long shot of WINIFRED SHAW's face grew from a distant speck of light into a closeup that dissolved into the Manhattan skyline. Then a montage of the city's nightlife climaxed in hundreds of couples dancing in an expansive nightclub and ending with the chorine being pushed out a window to her death. It was Berkeley's most dramatic film sequence and relied on precision dancing and dynamic camera work rather than gimmicks. Blondell got to play the leading lady in *GOLD DIGGERS OF 1937* (Warner 1936), which concerned insurance salesman Powell trying to sell producer VICTOR MOORE a huge policy so that his cronies could have enough money to produce a Broadway show after he dies. But Moore lives and the show goes on anyway, featuring a military finale, "All's Fair in Love and War" by Dubin and Warren, in which Blondell led dozens of goose-stepping chorus girls in a battle of the sexes. The same songwriters also came up with the catchy "With Plenty of Money and You," whereas E.Y. HARBURG and HAROLD ARLEN penned "Let's Put Our Heads Together," which fifty couples sang as they rocked to the rhythm of the music in giant rocking chairs. The series ended with *GOLD DIGGERS IN PARIS* (Warner 1938), a frail musical in which RUDY VALLEE and his nightclub dancing girls are invited to a Paris festival with the misunderstanding that they are a ballet troupe. Berkeley again staged the musical numbers, though on a much less lavish scale than earlier in the series. Dubin and Warren's "The Latin Quarter" was a breezy song about the Left Bank that Berkeley choreographed with grace, and Warren and JOHNNY MERCER penned the ballad "Day Dreaming (All Night Long)," which Vallee and ROSEMARY LANE sang together. Years later the series returned somewhat with *Painting the Clouds With Sunshine* (Warner 1951), a remake of the original *Gold Diggers of Broadway* with VIRGINIA MAYO, Lucille Norman, and VIRGINIA GIBSON as the three showgirls and some old standards (including two from the 1929 film) were dusted off and used again.

GOLD DIGGERS OF 1933/1935/1937. See *Gold Diggers of Hollywood*

GOLDWYN FOLLIES (Goldwyn/United Artists 1938) was not a true *Follies* in that it had a plot rather than a series of production numbers, but the story, about short-order cook KENNY BAKER trying to make it in Hollywood with the help of girlfriend Andrea Leeds, was so thin and the *Follies* numbers so lavish that it may as well have been a REVUE. Producer SAMUEL GOLDWYN planned to do an annual *Follies* on screen as Florenz Ziegfeld had once done on Broadway, but this first entry took so long to make (seven years from conception to release) and cost so much that subsequent *Follies* never materialized. Goldwyn assembled an impressive array of talent: veteran playwright Ben Hecht for the screenplay, the GERSHWIN brothers for the songs, classical choreographer George Balanchine and Broadway ballerina VERA ZORINA for the ballets, EDGAR BERGEN with his dummy Charlie McCarthy, Bobby Clark, and the RITZ BROTHERS for the comedy, opera diva Helen Jepson to sing two opera arias, and Baker and Ella Logan to sing the ballads. It was all filmed in the new three-color Technicolor process so the film had a new look even if the whole was far less than the sum of its parts. It was the Gershwins' last score (George Gershwin died before all the songs were finished and VERNON DUKE had to come in and finish them) and was filled with marvelous songs, even if they were not always shown to their best advantage. "Love Walked In," "I Was Doing All Right," "I Love to Rhyme," and "(Our) Love Is Here to Stay" each deserved a better film. It was a sad anticlimax for George Gershwin's too-brief movie career.

GOLDWYN, SAMUEL (1882–1974), one of Hollywood's most colorful and tireless executives, was an independent producer for much of his career and championed stars and feature films of personal interest. He brought Broadway musical stars, such as EDDIE CANTOR and DANNY KAYE, to the movies and produced film versions of such stage works as *WHOOPEE* (1930), *GUYS AND DOLLS* (1955), and *PORGY AND BESS* (1959). Of the sixty-two features Goldwyn presented, the musicals included *Palmy Days* (1931), *The Kid From Spain* (1932), *ROMAN SCANDALS* (1932), *KID MILLIONS* (1934), *THE GOLDWYN FOLLIES* (1938), *UP IN ARMS* (1934), *Wonder Man* (1945), *The Kid From Brooklyn* (1946), *A Song Is Born* (1948), and *HANS CHRISTIAN ANDERSEN* (1959).

GOOD NEWS (MGM 1930) did not begin to capture the vitality and playfulness of the 1927 Broadway hit, and the studio, nervous about the public's growing disenchantment with movie musicals, cut two of the best DE SYLVA–BROWN–HENDERSON songs ("The Best Things in Life Are Free" and "Lucky in Love") in order to shorten the picture. The plot, about a football player (Stanley Smith) at Tait College who will let the team down if he flunks out and so is helped by bookish coed Mary Lawlor, was getting stale already, and campus frivolity did not look as appealing in the early days of the Depression as it had in the Roaring Twenties. But the "Varsity Drag" still packed a wallop and the title tune was as catchy as ever. MGM polished off the old chestnut in 1947 and had much better luck. BETTY COMDEN and ADOLPH GREEN (in their first screen assignment) tightened up the script, and PETER LAWFORD played the footballer, with JUNE ALLYSON helping him pass French class. The supporting cast included Joan McCracken, MEL TORMÉ, Patricia Marshall, and RAY McDONALD, all of them in youthful high spirits and choreographed by ROBERT ALTON and CHARLES WALTERS (who also directed) with such sparkle that everybody thought college life was just grand. Much of the original stage score was revived, and there were two new numbers that stood up to them: the conversational duet "The French Lesson" by Comden, Green, and ROGER EDENS that Lawford and Allyson sang and the contagious "Pass That Peace Pipe" by Edens, HUGH MARTIN, and RALPH BLANE that McCracken and McDonald led in a campus ice cream parlor.

GOODBYE, MR. CHIPS (APJAC/MGM 1969) was a big-budget musical hoping to be an intimate character piece based on James Hilton's beloved story of a reclusive teacher looking back on his years of teaching at a boys school in England. Peter O'Toole was quite effective as the reticent "Mr. Chips," singing his songs as such an introvert would, and PETULA CLARK paired with him nicely as his wife, a former music hall singer. But too rarely did LESLIE BRICUSSE's songs add much to the sentimental tale. In fact, they were often sung by the characters on the soundtrack only as background for montage sequences. There was an authentic ring about the school anthem

"Fill the World With Love" and the love song "Walk Through the World" was charming. The movie was well acted all around, with Michael Redgrave as the headmaster and Sian Phillips as a flamboyant old chum of Mrs. Chips. British playwright Terence Rattigan wrote the screenplay and HERBERT ROSS directed on location in England. The film had its quiet merits, but the public would have none of it and it ranked as another big-budget musical disaster for Hollywood.

GOODMAN, BENNY (1909–1986), famed clarinetist and bandleader, was proclaimed the "King of Swing" by Americans in the late 1930s and 1940s, his orchestra being the most popular in the country at the time. Goodman and his band made personal appearances, ruled the airwaves, sold millions of records, and usually played themselves in a handful of movie musicals: *THE BIG BROADCAST OF 1937* (1938), *HOLLYWOOD HOTEL* (1937), *The Powers Girl* (1942), *Syncopation* (1942), *THE GANG'S ALL HERE* (1943), *STAGE DOOR CANTEEN* (1943), *Sweet and Lowdown* (1944), and *A Song Is Born* (1948). His clarinet playing was heard in the animated anthology *Make Mine Music* (1946) and for Steve Allen who played Goodman in the musical bio *The Benny Goodman Story* (1955).

GOODRICH, FRANCES (1891–1984) and her husband **ALBERT HACKETT** (1900–1995) wrote many plays together and collaborated on several screenplays, often adapting material from the stage or other sources. The team's movie musical scripts include *NAUGHTY MARIETTA* (1935), *ROSE MARIE* (1936), *THE FIREFLY* (1937), *Lady in the Dark* (1944), *THE PIRATE* (1948), *SUMMER HOLIDAY* (1948), *EASTER PARADE* (1948), *IN THE GOOD OLD SUMMERTIME* (1949), *GIVE A GIRL A BREAK* (1954), and *SEVEN BRIDES FOR SEVEN BROTHERS* (1954).

GORDON, MACK (1904–1959) was one of Hollywood's busiest lyricists, writing hundreds of songs with composers HARRY REVEL, HARRY WARREN, and others. Gordon scored such early musicals as *Pointed Heels* (1929), *Swing High* (1930), *Broadway Thru a Keyhole* (1933), and *Sitting Pretty* (1933), the last two with Revel, with whom he would write two dozen other scores. Other notable Gordon-Revel films include *WE'RE NOT DRESSING* (1934), *COLLEGE RHYTHM* (1934), *Love in Bloom* (1935), *POOR LITTLE RICH GIRL* (1936), *WAKE UP AND LIVE* (1937), and *Love Finds Andy Hardy* (1938). Gordon worked with Warren for the first time with *Young People* (1940), and their dozen subsequent collaborations included *DOWN ARGENTINE WAY* (1940), *THAT NIGHT IN RIO* (1941), *SUN VALLEY SERENADE* (1941), *WEEK-END IN HAVANA* (1941), *ORCHESTRA WIVES* (1942), *SPRINGTIME IN THE ROCKIES* (1942), and *SUMMER STOCK* (1950). Other Gordon films with various composers include *Song of the Islands* (1942), *Pin-Up Girl* (1944), *THE DOLLY SISTERS* (1945), *THREE LITTLE*

GIRLS IN BLUE (1946), *MOTHER WORE TIGHTS* (1947), *WABASH AV-ENUE* (1950), *Call Me Mister* (1951), and *Bundle of Joy* (1956). Among Gordon's many hit songs were "Did You Ever See a Dream Walking?," "Chattanooga Choo-Choo," "You'll Never Know," "I Can't Begin to Tell You," and "You Make Me Feel So Young."

GORNEY, JAY (1896–1990), a Broadway composer who went to Hollywood in the early 1930s, worked with a variety of lyricists on eight films, most of them B movies that had little impact on his career: *Jimmy and Sally* (1933), *Moonlight and Pretzels* (1933), *Stand Up and Cheer* (1934), *Redheads on Parade* (1935), *Hey, Rookie* (1944), and others. Gorney's most famous song, "Brother, Can You Spare a Dime?" written with E.Y. HARBURG for the stage in 1932, became a theme song for the Depression.

GOULD, DAVE (1905–1969), a clever choreographer who staged musical numbers in some twenty musicals in the 1930s and 1940s, is mostly remembered for his spectacular finales, such as the airplane sequence in *FLYING DOWN TO RIO* (1933) and the battleship climax in *BORN TO DANCE* (1936). Gould also choreographed *Melody Cruise* (1933), *THE GAY DIVORCEE* (1934), *FOLIES BERGÈRE DE PARIS* (1935), *BROADWAY MELODY OF 1936* (1935), *A DAY AT THE RACES* (1937), *BROADWAY MELODY OF 1938* (1937), *The Boys From Syracuse* (1940), *Rosie the Riveter* (1944), and others.

GRABLE, BETTY (1916–1973), the queen of Technicolor musicals in the 1940s and American GIs' favorite pin-up girl during the war, came from the Broadway stage and appeared in bit or overlooked roles in thirty-one films before becoming a star when she replaced ALICE FAYE and played the lead in *DOWN ARGENTINE WAY* (1940). Her popularity lasted into the 1950s, helped by such winning films as *TIN PAN ALLEY* (1940), *MOON OVER MIAMI* (1941), *SPRINGTIME IN THE ROCKIES* (1942), *CONEY ISLAND* (1943), *Pin-Up Girl* (1944), *THE DOLLY SISTERS* (1945), *MOTHER WORE TIGHTS* (1947), *WABASH AVENUE* (1950), *My Blue Heaven* (1950), and *Call Me Mister* (1951). The shapely blonde was known for her feisty persona, chipper singing voice, and gorgeous legs, which 20TH CENTURY–FOX insured for $1 million in a crafty publicity stunt. Grable showed off her gams in many of her over forty film musicals but was also effective in period musicals such as *THE SHOCKING MISS PILGRIM* (1947) and *THE FARMER TAKES A WIFE* (1953), where she hardly showed an ankle. With the decline of the Hollywood musical in the 1950s, Grable returned to the stage and nightclubs before her premature death at the age of fifty-six. She was married to actor Jackie Coogan and later to bandleader HARRY JAMES.

GRANT, CARY (1904–1986) was a box office champ for decades, playing comic leads, engaging dramatic heroes, and sophisticated lovers in dozens of films between 1932 and 1966. Although he rarely sang, Grant was featured in eight musicals opposite such seductive leading ladies as MAE WEST and MARLENE DIETRICH: *This Is the Night* (1932), *Blonde Venus* (1932), *SHE DONE HIM WRONG* (1933), *I'm No Angel* (1933), *Kiss and Make-Up* (1934), *When You're in Love* (1937), and *An Affair to Remember* (1957). Grant played COLE PORTER in the musical bio *NIGHT AND DAY* (1946) and sang "Did I Remember?" in the nonmusical *Suzy* (1936). He was married to heiress Barbara Hutton and actresses Virginia Cherrill, Betsy Drake, and Dyan Cannon.

GRAVET, FERNAND (1904–1970), a charming continental type from Belgium, made many films in France (where he was known as Gravey) and England (where he was billed Graavey) and a few Hollywood musicals, most notably *The Great Waltz* (1938), in which he played Johann Strauss, Jr. He can also be seen in the American musicals *The King and the Chorus Girl* (1937) and *Fools for Scandal* (1938).

GRAY, ALEXANDER (1902–1975) was a vaudeville singer who appeared in such early movie musicals as *THE SHOW OF SHOWS* (1929), *Sally* (1929), *No No Nanette* (1930), *Song of the Flame* (1930), *Spring Is Here* (1930), *Viennese Nights* (1930), and *Moonlight and Pretzels* (1933). Gray often co-starred on film and stage with Bernice Claire.

GRAY, DOLORES (1924–), a brassy Broadway belter who also found fame on the London stage, only appeared in three Hollywood musicals but was memorable in each role: television hostess Madeline Bradbille in *IT'S AL-WAYS FAIR WEATHER* (1955), in which she got to sing "Thanks a Lot but No Thanks," the Wazir's sexy wife Lalume in *KISMET* (1955), and the conniving Park Avenue gossip Sylvia in *The Opposite Sex* (1956). The blonde singer-actress was also popular in nightclubs and on television.

GRAY, LAWRENCE (1898–1970) was a dashing leading man in silents who possessed a full singing voice and so was featured in eight early musicals, including *Marianne* (1929), *It's a Great Life* (1929), *The Floradora Girl* (1930), *Spring Is Here* (1930), *Sunny* (1930), and *Dizzy Dames* (1936). Lawrence retired from performing in the mid-1930s and spent the next three decades as an international film executive.

GRAYSON, KATHRYN (1922–) possessed one of the clearest coloratura soprano voices in Hollywood and, combined with her buxom figure and heart-shaped face, was a favorite in musicals and OPERETTAS in the 1940s and 1950s. Discovered on a radio show, Grayson was whisked to California, where her first musical assignment was the title role in *RIO RITA* (1942). She played ingenues in *Thousands Cheer* (1943), *ANCHORS AWEIGH* (1945), *Two Sisters From Boston* (1946), *IT HAPPENED IN BROOKLYN* (1947), *The Kissing Bandit* (1948), *The Toast of New Orleans* (1950) in which she sang "Be My Love" with MARIO LANZA, *SHOW BOAT* (1951), *LOVELY TO LOOK AT* (1952), and *THE DESERT SONG* (1953). Her more mature roles included opera singer GRACE MOORE in *So This Is Love* (1953), temperamental actress Lilli Vanessi in *KISS ME, KATE* (1953), and the aristocrat Catherine de Vaucelles in *The Vagabond King* (1956). Grayson was married to actor John Shelton and later to singer JOHNNY JOHNSTON.

GREASE (Paramount 1978) was so popular at the box office ($100 million by its tenth anniversary and a hit all over again when it was re-released in theatres in 1998) that the movie studios were convinced a musical could make money only if it was a youth product. So there were many imitations to follow, but few were as much fun as *Grease*. Leather-jacketed high schooler JOHN TRAVOLTA has a summer romance with Australian exchange student OLIVIA NEWTON-JOHN, but trouble brews when the fall comes and they find themselves at the same school, where he is popular and she is not. But by the finale, Newton-John learns how to dress tacky and act crude and everybody celebrates. The stars' charisma helped make the story palatable, and there was strong support from Stockard Channing, Jeff Conaway, and Didi Conn and, for nostalgia's sake, appearances by EVE ARDEN, Sid Caesar, JOAN BLONDELL, FRANKIE AVALON, and other luminaries from the past. Most of the songs by Warren Casey and Jim Jacobs from the long-running 1972 Broadway show were still in place ("Freddie, My Love," "Greased Lightning," "Summer Nights," "Beauty School Dropout," "We Go Together"), and songwriters Barry Gibb and John Farrar added a few new ones ("Hopelessly Devoted to You," "You're the One That I Want") plus a title song that Frankie Valli sang over the playful cartoon credits. The inevitable SEQUEL, *Grease 2* (Paramount 1982), was virtually ignored by the public since neither Travolta nor Newton-John were in it and it was as poorly plotted as the original. But it had its own merits, mainly some creative choreography by Patricia Birch (who also directed) and a few tuneful numbers written by various pop songsters. A female high schooler (Michelle Pfeiffer) was the cool one this time, and British exchange student (Maxwell Caulfield) had to become a biker to win her in time for the finale, a rock-and-roll luau with hula hoops.

GREAT CARUSO, THE (MGM 1951) was MARIO LANZA's best and most successful movie, so popular that many Americans became interested in opera and Hollywood jumped in with a half dozen other opera singer bios during the decade. The story was as trite as it was inaccurate, but watching the great Italian tenor Enrico Caruso struggle from cafés in Naples to singing at the Met was another variation of the Cinderella tale and Lanza played it beautifully. ANN BLYTH was Caruso's high society wife who got to sing the film's biggest hit, "The Loveliest Night of the Year," which Irving Aaronson and PAUL FRANCIS WEBSTER adapted from an old Mexican waltz tune. Lanza sang opera selections from Verdi, Puccini, and Leocavallo, and he was joined by opera singers Dorothy Kirsten, Blanche Thebom, Teresa Celli, Nicola Moscona, and Giuseppe Vandengo. The forty-eight-year-old Caruso's collapsing and dying on stage while singing *Martha* was the film's tearful climax. Sadly, Lanza himself would die of a heart attack at the age of thirty-eight after bouts with obesity, drugs, and alcoholism.

GREAT ZIEGFELD, THE (MGM 1936) was an early and opulent BIOGRAPHICAL MUSICAL about Florenz Ziegfeld that so dazzled audiences that it has rarely been topped for pure showmanship and glamour. WILLIAM POWELL played the moody, inspired showman, LUISE RAINER played his first wife Anna Held, and MYRNA LOY his second wife BILLIE BURKE. Not only were all three excellent (Rainer won an Oscar), but for once in a musical bio, the story (screenplay by William Anthony McGuire) was as intriguing as the production numbers. SEYMOUR FELIX staged the songs with a lavish and even reverent tone, the whole movie taking the form of a tribute to Ziegfeld as much as a biography would do. The most famous musical sequence was IRVING BERLIN's "A Pretty Girl Is Like a Melody," staged on a spiral tower filled with dozens of singers and dancers on the 170 steps and topped by VIRGINIA BRUCE as the spirit of the *Follies*. As the camera climbed the staircase and the tower turned, sections of the chorus broke out in classical selections by Puccini, Strauss, Liszt, and others (even GEORGE GERSHWIN's "Rhapsody in Blue" was heard for a while), then a giant curtain descended and surrounded the entire menagerie. It was a scene often copied (and parodied) in future films but was never surpassed. Other memorable moments included FANNY BRICE (one of the few actual *Follies* stars in the film) singing "Yiddle on Your Fiddle," "Queen of the Jungle," and (briefly) "My Man," Buddy Doyle as EDDIE CANTOR performing "If You Knew Suzie," Rainer delivering Held's signature songs "Won't You Come and Play With Me?" and "It's Delightful to Be Married," A.A. Trimble impersonating Will Rogers, and a medley of "You," "You Never Looked So Beautiful (Before)," "You Gotta Pull Strings," and "She's a (Ziegfeld) Follies Girl" that was pure cinema as Ziegfeld himself would have liked it. The large cast of factual and fictional characters also included RAY BOLGER, FRANK MORGAN, Nat Pendleton, REGINALD OWEN, HERMAN BING, Harriet Hoctor, WILLIAM DEMAREST, DENNIS MORGAN, and many others.

GREEN, ADOLPH. See Comden, Betty

GREEN, ALFRED E. (1889–1960) was a reliable if not distinctive director who turned out dozens of silent and sound films over a fifty-year career. Green tackled any genre and usually came in on time and under budget. Yet few of his products were beyond B movie grade. His best work was *THE JOLSON STORY* (1946), and he directed other musicals such as *Sweet Music* (1935), *Colleen* (1936), *Mr. Dodd Takes the Air* (1937), *Tars and Spars* (1946), *The Fabulous Dorseys* (1947), *Copacabana* (1947), *The Eddie Cantor Story* (1953), and *Top Banana* (1954).

GREEN, JOHNNY (1908–1989) rose from rehearsal pianist to composer to studio arranger to the head of music at MGM in the 1950s. Green won five Oscars for his music scoring of musicals, such as *IT HAPPENED IN BROOKLYN* (1947), *EASTER PARADE* (1948), *SUMMER STOCK* (1950), *AN AMERICAN IN PARIS* (1951), *BRIGADOON* (1954), *HIGH SOCIETY* (1956), *WEST SIDE STORY* (1961), *OLIVER!* (1968), and others. He also wrote songs with various lyricists for *The Sap From Syracuse* (1930), *Start Cheering* (1938), *Bathing Beauty* (1944), *Easy to Wed* (1946), and *Something in the Wind* (1947). But Green's greatest hits, such as "Body and Soul," were written for the stage or Tin Pan Alley. He also had a famous orchestra and made many hit recordings, several with FRED ASTAIRE.

GREEN, MITZI (1920–1969) was a CHILD STAR in silents, in talkies, and on Broadway who could belt out a song and mimic famous celebrities. She appeared in *Our Gang* shorts and then in the feature musicals *Honey* (1930), *PARAMOUNT ON PARADE* (1930), *Love Among the Millionaires* (1930), *Girl Crazy* (1932), and *Transatlantic Merry-Go-Round* (1934) before starring on Broadway in *Babes in Arms* in 1937. Green returned to films in the 1950s but with little success, appearing in the musicals *Lost in Alaska* (1952) and *Bloodhounds of Broadway* (1952).

GREENWOOD, CHARLOTTE (1890–1978), the tall, leggy comedienne whose high-kicking act made her a favorite in vaudeville, in nightclubs, and on Broadway, starred in a series of grade B movie musicals but was better known for spicing up many 20TH CENTURY–FOX musicals playing a wisecracking friend, a sarcastic aunt, or an eccentric mother. Greenwood's fifteen musical films include *So Long, Letty* (1930), *Palmy Days* (1931), *Flying High* (1931), *Star Dust* (1940), *DOWN ARGENTINE WAY* (1940), *MOON OVER MIAMI* (1941), *SPRINGTIME IN THE ROCKIES* (1942), *THE GANG'S ALL HERE* (1943), *Wake Up and Dream* (1946), *Dangerous When Wet* (1953), *OKLAHOMA!* (1955), and *The Opposite Sex* (1956).

GREY, CLIFFORD (1887–1941) was an English-born lyricist who scored musicals on Broadway and in London, his hits *Sally* (1929) with JEROME KERN and *Hit the Deck* (1930 and 1955) with LEO ROBIN and VINCENT YOUMANS being filmed. Grey also worked with various Hollywood composers and wrote songs for the movie musicals *THE LOVE PARADE* (1929),

Devil May Care (1929), *The Rogue Song* (1930), and *THE SMILING LIEU-TENANT* (1931).

GROT, ANTON (1884–1974), a Polish designer and artist who immigrated to the States and started working in silent films beginning in 1913, was the art director at WARNER BROTHERS for twenty years and was responsible for the distinctive look of the studio's gangster films, period pieces, and musicals. Among the many musicals Grot designed were *No No Nanette* (1930), *FOOTLIGHT PARADE* (1933), *GOLD DIGGERS OF 1933, RHAPSODY IN BLUE* (1945), and *ROMANCE ON THE HIGH SEAS* (1948).

GUIZAR, TITO (1909–1999), a major singing star in Mexico, strummed his guitar and sang in such Hollywood musicals as *Under the Pampas Moon* (1935), *BIG BROADCAST OF 1938, Tropic Holiday* (1938), *St. Louis Blues* (1939), *Blondie Goes Latin* (1941), *Brazil* (1944), *The Thrill of Brazil* (1946), and *The Gay Ranchero* (1948).

GULLIVER'S TRAVELS (Paramount 1939) was one of the very few feature-length animated musicals not from the DISNEY studio, and although it could not complete in the craftsmanship of the Disney artists, it was often very entertaining. Based on the Lilliput section of Jonathan Swift's satire, the plot concerned two rival kingdoms who are brought together by the giant Gulliver. Animator Max Fleischer kept the comic characters broad and the lovers dull but the songs, mostly by LEO ROBIN and RALPH RAINGER, were expert, ranging from fervent love ballads like "Faithful/Forever," sung on the soundtrack by Jessica Dragonette and LANNY ROSS, to zippy rhythm numbers such as "It's a Hap-Hap-Happy Day" and "Bluebirds in the Moonlight."

GUYS AND DOLLS (Goldwyn/MGM 1955), one of the great Broadway musicals of the 1950s, was purchased by producer SAMUEL GOLDWYN for a record $1 million and then filmed with several miscalculations working against it: nonsinger Marlon Brando was cast as gambler Sky Masterson; FRANK SINATRA was cast in the nonsinging comic role of Nathan Detroit; nonmusical director Joseph L. Mankiewicz was slated to helm the $5 million project; and two of the show's hit songs by FRANK LOESSER ("Bushel and a Peck" and "I've Never Been in Love Before") were dropped and replaced with lesser Loesser efforts. But Goldwyn did some things right: VIVIAN BLAINE got to recreate her unforgettable stage performance as Miss Adelaide; Broadway choreographer MICHAEL KIDD was retained to stage the musical numbers; lovely Jean Simmons was found to have an agreeable singing voice and was hired to play Sky's love interest, Sarah Brown; and Broadway designer Oliver Smith was brought out to Hollywood to create a cartoonish Runyonland that captured the spirit of the musical beautifully. The result was a film far better than anyone expected. Brando did his own singing and found a sincere charm in the con man Sky. The dances, particularly the opening "Runyonland" ballet and the energetic "Luck Be a Lady Tonight," rivaled the Broadway version. And there were wonderful supporting performances by STUBBY KAYE, Johnny Silver, B.S. Pully (all three from the stage production), Sheldon Leonard, Regis Toomey, Robert Keith, and Dan Dayton, all having a great time with the Runyonese dialogue by Abe Burrows. Other songs included "Fugue for Tinhorns," "Adelaide's Lament," "I'll Know," "The Oldest Established," "If I Were a Bell," and "Sit Down, You're Rockin' the Boat." Goldwyn's gamble paid off; the movie was one the top-grossing pictures of the year.

GYPSY (Warner 1962) came to the screen with its libretto and score (except for one song) intact, was given a handsome production directed by MERVYN LEROY that captured the vaudeville era and the sleazy burlesque milieu, and was well acted and sung. But the heart of the project was missing when the studio decided not to let ETHEL MERMAN recreate her dynamic portrayal of Mama Rose, easily one of the great musical theatre performances of the century. ROSALIND RUSSELL was far more than adequate in the role and certainly captured the humor, if not the terror, in the ambitious stage mother who pushes her two daughters into show business at all costs. NATALIE WOOD (singing dubbed by MARNI NIXON) made the transition from wall flower to stripper GYPSY ROSE LEE believable and touching, and Karl Malden, as Rose's manager-lover Herbie, was an effective foil for Russell's theatrics. "Together, Wherever We Go" was dropped, but the rest of the sterling STEPHEN SONDHEIM–JULE STYNE score survived, including "Everything's Coming Up Roses," "Little Lamb," "All I Need Now Is the Girl," "You Gotta Have a Gimmick," "Some People," " Small World," "Let Me Entertain You," and the climatic solo "Rose's Turn," in which Lisa Kirk helped fill out some of Russell's vocals on the soundtrack.

H

HACKETT, ALBERT. See Goodrich, Frances

HACKETT, BUDDY (1924–), a short, rotund comic who honed his craft in Borscht Belt nightclubs, found fame as a stand-up comedian and intermittently appeared in films, including the musicals *Walking My Baby Back Home* (1953), *The Wonderful World of the Brothers Grimm* (1962), *THE MUSIC MAN* (1962), and *Muscle Beach Party* (1964). Hackett also provided the voice of the seagull Scuttle in the animated *THE LITTLE MERMAID* (1989).

HAIR (United Artists 1979) came to the screen nearly a decade after the peak of the antiwar protests and the Age of Aquarius movement, so there was almost a touch of nostalgia in Milos Forman's movie version. Michael Weller took the plotless "tribal love rock musical" of 1968 and fashioned a thin story about an Oklahoma boy (John Savage) who travels to New York City before being inducted into the Army and falls in with a group of hippies in Central Park. Not only does the youth adopt their lifestyle of drugs, sex, and nonconformity, his place at the induction center is taken by "tribe" leader Treat Williams, who goes off to Vietnam and dies for him. Most of the songs by Gerome Ragni, James Rado, and Galt MacDermot were used in the films, in particular the hits "Aquarius," "Let the Sunshine In," "Where Do I Go?," "Easy to Be Hard," "Good Morning, Starshine," and the mocking title song. Beverly D'Angelo was a Manhattan deb who joined the tribe, which included Melba Moore, Ronnie Dyson (both from the stage version), Annie Golden, Dorsey Wright, Don Dacus, Cheryl Barnes, and Twyla Twarp, who also choreographed the energetic dances.

HALE, ALAN (1892–1950) was one of Hollywood's most recognized character actors, playing Errol Flynn's sidekick in several movies and appearing as big but gentlehearted character types in hundreds of films. Hale's movie musicals include *HIGH, WIDE AND HANDSOME* (1937), *On Your Toes* (1939), *THIS IS THE ARMY* (1943), *THANK YOUR LUCKY STARS* (1943), *NIGHT AND DAY* (1946), *The Time, the Place and the Girl* (1946), and *My Wild Irish Rose* (1947). His look-alike son was Alan Hale, Jr., who appeared for many years on television (*Gilligan's Island*).

HALEY, JACK (1899–1979) will always be remembered for playing the Tin Man in *THE WIZARD OF OZ* (1939), but he also appeared in twenty other film musicals in the 1930s and 1940s. Haley performed in vaudeville and on Broadway before going to Hollywood to recreate his character of shy millionaire Jack Martin in *Follow Thru* (1930). The wide-eyed innocent type stayed and played featured roles in *Sitting Pretty* (1933), *Redheads on Parade* (1935), *Pigskin Parade* (1936), *POOR LITTLE RICH GIRL* (1936), *WAKE UP AND LIVE* (1937), *REBECCA OF SUNNYBROOK FARM* (1938), *ALEXANDER'S RAGTIME BAND* (1938), *Navy Blues* (1941), *MOON OVER MIAMI* (1941), *Higher and Higher* (1943), *George White's Scandals* (1945), and others. He is the father of film producer Jack Haley, Jr., who compiled *THAT'S ENTERTAINMENT* (1974).

HALL, ALEXANDER (1894–1968) worked his way from silent screen actor to film editor to director, handling various genres during his twenty-five-year career. Hall's musical credits include mostly secondary products, such as *Torch Singer* (1933), *Little Miss Marker* (1934), *Give Us This Night* (1936), *Down to Earth* (1947), and *Because You're Mine* (1952).

HALL, JUANITA (1901–1968) was a light-skinned, heavy-set African American actress who played a variety of ethnic types in Broadway musicals. She got to recreate two of her finest stage portrayals on film: the crafty Polynesian Bloody Mary in *SOUTH PACIFIC* (1958) and the meddling Chinese Madame Liang in *FLOWER DRUM SONG* (1961).

HALLELUJAH (MGM 1929) was the first all-black talking feature film and an impressive achievement by any standards as a result of director-producer KING VIDOR's demand for authenticity and avoidance of stereotyping. Cotton farm worker Daniel L. Haynes loves the honest Victoria Spivey, but the temptress Nina Mae McKinney lures him into a crooked crap game, where he is cheated out of all his money and, in anger, accidentally shoots his younger brother Everett McHarrity. It was highly melodramatic and the many Negro spirituals used throughout the movie practically turned the whole tale into an opera (six years before GEORGE GERSHWIN did just that with *Porgy and Bess*). Two IRVING BERLIN songs were added to the traditional numbers and both were very effective: "Waiting at the End of the Road," sung by Haynes and the other plantation workers (dubbed by the Dixie Jubilee Singers) as they waited in line to sell their bales of cotton, comparing it to waiting to get into heaven, and "Swanee Shuffle," the seductive number McKinney sang to tempt Haynes. The film was shot on location (dialogue and music were added in the studio later), so it has a documentary look to it that is still potent. Though rarely seen today, the early musical is a landmark of sorts and explores African American culture more effectively than do most movies that followed it.

HALLELUJAH, I'M A BUM (United Artists 1933) gave AL JOLSON his most demanding screen role and he rose to the occasion by giving a heartbreaking performance with none of the gushing he used when crying "Mammy!" on stage. The film, scripted by Broadway playwrights Ben Hecht and S.N. Behrman, is the antithesis of the *Gold Diggers* movies of the decade, this bittersweet tale being about the many homeless in the Depression who lived in Central Park as opposed to the chorines who were struggling on Broadway. When mayor FRANK MORGAN has a quarrel with his fiancée Madge Evans, she tries to commit suicide but is rescued by Bumper (Jolson), a tramp in the park who rules as mayor of the homeless ones. Evans suffers from amnesia and cannot recall her past, but she and Bumper fall in love, only for her to leave him for the real mayor when she regains her memory. It was far from escapism, yet the songs by RICHARD RODGERS and LORENZ HART had extended sections of rhythmic dialogue and so the film often sounded like a cockeyed romantic operetta. Jolson got to sing "You Are Too Beautiful" to Evans, a restrained ballad that he delivered with perfection. Other numbers included the sly "What Do You Want With Money?," "I've Got to Get Back to New York," and the philosophical title song that had to be recorded twice, the word "tramp" substituted for the England release because "bum" refers to buttocks in British slang. (The musical was released as *Hallelujah, I'm a Tramp* in Great Britain.) The movie was a box-office failure but a milestone in inventive musical filmmaking.

HAMILTON, MARGARET (1902–1985) was always recognized as the actress who played the Wicked Witch of the West in *THE WIZARD OF OZ* (1939) but she made several other films where she portrayed spinsters, housekeepers, and even kindly ladies. *BABES IN ARMS* (1939), *George White's Scandals* (1945), and *WABASH AVENUE* (1950) were among Hamilton's musical credits.

HAMLISCH, MARVIN (1944–   ), the Broadway composer mostly known for his long-running *A CHORUS LINE*, which was filmed in 1985, has had a more lucrative career in Hollywood scoring and writing theme songs for many nonmusicals since 1968. Hamlisch also did the musical arrangements for the old standards used in *PENNIES FROM HEAVEN* (1981).

HAMMERSTEIN, OSCAR, II (1895–1960), America's most influential and accomplished lyricist and librettist, had a lengthy career on Broadway writing scores for dozens of musicals between 1920 and 1959. Throughout his life, Hammerstein contributed original songs to Hollywood, collaborated on the film versions of his stage works, and had his catalog of songs used in musical and nonmusical movies. Hammerstein's first film credit was when his landmark musical *SHOW BOAT* (music by JEROME KERN) was filmed in 1929; subsequent versions were made in 1936 and 1951. Many of his operettas and musicals written with composers SIGMUND ROMBERG, RUDOLPH FRIML, Kern, and others were also filmed: *THE DESERT SONG* (1929, 1943, and 1953), *Song of the Flame* (1930), *Golden Dawn* (1930), *New Moon* (1930 and 1940), *Sunny* (1930 and 1941), *MUSIC IN THE AIR* (1934), *SWEET ADELINE* (1935), *ROSE MARIE* (1936 and 1954), *Very Warm for May*, which became *Broadway Rhythm* (1944), *CARMEN JONES* (1954), and others. With OTTO HARBACH, Kern, and others, Hammerstein wrote original scores for the films *Viennese Nights* (1930), *The Night Is Young* (1935), *HIGH, WIDE AND HANDSOME* (1937), *The Great Waltz* (1938), *The Lady Objects* (1938), *THE STORY OF VERNON AND IRENE CASTLE* (1939), and others. Hammerstein's career took on a new phase when he teamed up with composer RICHARD RODGERS and produced a series of hit stage musicals in the 1940s and 1950s. Most of them were filmed, including *OKLAHOMA!* (1955), *CAROUSEL* (1956), *THE KING AND I* (1956), *SOUTH PACIFIC* (1958), *FLOWER DRUM SONG* (1961), and *THE SOUND OF MUSIC* (1965). The team also scored *STATE FAIR* (1945) directly for the screen; after Hammerstein's death, Rodgers wrote additional songs for the 1962 remake. Hammerstein's lyrics are known for their beautiful imagery, simple and sincere emotion, and superior craftsmanship.

HANEY, CAROL (1924–1964), a Broadway-dancer-turned-choreographer, appeared as a featured hoofer in such musical films as *ON THE TOWN* (1949), *SUMMER STOCK* (1950), *KISS ME, KATE* (1953), and *INVITATION TO THE DANCE* (1956), but she was most known for recreating from the stage her funny, sexy Gladys in *THE PAJAMA GAME* (1957). Haney became a recognized Broadway choreographer before her untimely death.

HANS CHRISTIAN ANDERSEN (Goldwyn/RKO 1952) contains FRANK LOESSER's best film score, a lovely mixture of ballads, rousing chorus numbers, and playful children's ditties. Moss Hart's screenplay about the life of the Danish storyteller was so inaccurate that the government of Denmark insisted on a disclaimer at the beginning of the film saying that this was a fairy tale version of the fairy tale author's life. Story-telling cobbler Andersen (DANNY KAYE in a surprisingly restrained performance) leaves his little village with his apprentice Joey Walsh and travels to Copenhagen, where he makes shoes for the famous ballerina Jeanmarie and is smitten with her. But the affection is not at all returned, and after providing the plot for her "Little Mermaid" ballet, Andersen returns home and becomes an author. The plot was far from gripping, but the musical interruptions were wonderful and included a handful of colorful ballets choreographed by Roland Petit. The Loesser songs included the rousing "Wonderful Copenhagen," the dreamy "Anywhere I Wander," the tuneful duet "No Two People," and the children's numbers based on Andersen stories: "The Ugly Ducking," "Inch Worm," "Thumbelina," and "The King's New Clothes." Producer SAMUEL GOLDWYN gambled $4 million on the elaborate production (he boasted that $14,000 was spent on shoes alone), but the audiences loved it and the musical grossed $6 million within a year.

HAPPY GO LUCKY (Republic 1943) was a good example of a small-scale, unpretentious 1940s musical in which all the elements were delightfully in place. Nightclub cigarette-girl MARY MARTIN disguises herself as an heiress and goes down to the Caribbean Islands to land a rich husband, finicky RUDY VALLEE in particular. She is aided by beachcomber DICK POWELL, whom she falls in love with just as his pal EDDIE BRACKEN is landed by the robust BETTY HUTTON. FRANK LOESSER and JIMMY McHUGH provided a tuneful score that included the pseudo-calypso "Sing a Tropical Song," the seductive "Let's Get Lost," the breezy title song, and two comic specialty numbers for Hutton's siren voice: "The Fuddy Duddy Watchmaker" and "Murder, He Says."

HARBACH, OTTO (1873–1963) was a Broadway librettist and lyricist who pioneered a higher level of craftsmanship for the musical theatre and trained OSCAR HAMMERSTEIN in a more serious approach to writing for the musical stage. Harbach rarely wrote songs directly for the screen but many of his stage works, with various composers, were filmed: *THE DESERT SONG* (1929, 1943, and 1953), *Song of the Flame* (1930), *No No Nanette* (1930 and 1940), *Golden Dawn* (1930), *Sunny* (1930 and 1941), *THE CAT AND THE FIDDLE* (1934), *ROBERTA* (1935), *ROSE MARIE* (1936 and 1954), *THE FIREFLY* (1937), and *LOVELY TO LOOK AT* (1952). Harbach's most famous song is "Smoke Gets in Your Eyes."

HARBURG, E.Y. (1896–1981), the sly Broadway lyricist and librettist who used fantasy and satire to write about weighty issues, made his most important mark in Hollywood with his songs for *THE WIZARD OF OZ* (1939) with composer HAROLD ARLEN. Harburg found the stage more receptive to his socially conscious ideas, but his wit and cutting sense of humor can be heard in his film scores on occasion. Working with composers Arlen, JOHNNY GREEN, BURTON LANE, JEROME KERN, SAMMY FAIN, and others, Harburg contributed songs and/or scripts to many films, including *RIO RITA* (1929 and 1942), *APPLAUSE* (1929), *Glorifying the American Girl* (1929), *The Sap From Syracuse* (1930), *Moonlight and Pretzels* (1933), *Take a Chance* (1933), *Broadway Gondolier* (1935), *The Singing Kid* (1936), *THE GOLD DIGGERS OF 1937* (1936), *AT THE CIRCUS* (1939), *BABES IN*

ARMS (1939), *Ship Ahoy* (1942), *BABES ON BROADWAY* (1942), *Cairo* (1942), *Presenting Lily Mars* (1943), *CABIN IN THE SKY* (1943), *Thousands Cheer* (1943), *DuBarry Was a Lady* (1943), *CAN'T HELP SINGING* (1944), *Meet the People* (1944), *Gay Purr-ee* (1962), *I Could Go on Singing* (1963), and *FINIAN'S RAINBOW* (1968), based on his Broadway hit with Lane.

HARD DAY'S NIGHT, A (United Artists 1964) was a low-budget feature made to cash in on the international popularity of THE BEATLES (John Lennon, Paul McCartney, Ringo Starr and George Harrison) and gain the rights to the soundtrack album. But director RICHARD LESTER took the opportunity to make a frenetic mock-documentary about a typical day in the life of the "Fab Four" and the result was an original: a freewheeling celebration of rock that might even be called a forerunner to the later MTV videos. The movie, filmed in black and white to save money, had a *cinema vérité* quality that was very tongue-in-cheek as the foursome ran from hoards of females, took McCartney's grandfather (Wilfred Brambell) on a train ride to a rehearsal, and ended the day performing in a theatre full of screaming fans. All the songs were written and/or sung by the group, some written for the film ("And I Love Her," "Can't Buy Me Love," "I Should Have Known Better," and the title number), others already famous ("All My Loving," "If I Fell," and "She Loves You"). The musical was a critical as well as a financial hit. The group's second film, **HELP!** (United Artists 1965) was just as popular but it was less accomplished. Again Lester directed the foursome, but this time the production was in color and the big budget showed. Spoofing the current James Bond films, the farce had the boys caught up in a plot to blow up the world and a religious cult with a high priest (Leo McKern) chasing them about for a missing sacrificial ring. The frolicing this time took place on ski slopes, a beach in the Bahamas, and on Salisbury Plain with tanks coming to the rescue. It all looked a bit forced but the music was still classic rock-and-roll: "Ticket to Ride," "You're Gonna Lose That Girl," "You've Got to Hide Your Love Away," and the title song. Before they broke up in 1970, the Beatles made some ROCKUMENTARY films and supplied the voices and songs for the animated **YELLOW SUBMARINE** (United Artists 1968), a surreal fantasy that told a good-versus-evil tale with plenty of psycheledic and pop-art design. When Pepperland is overrun by the Blue Meanies, the foursome get in a yellow submarine and travel to exotic places and meet up against some fantastical creatures before defeating the Meanies and restoring music to Pepperland. Most of the ten songs were already hits from the group's albums, so it was probably the finest collection of Beatles songs ever heard in one film, including "Sgt. Pepper's Lonely Hearts Club Band," "When I'm Sixty-Four," "Nowhere Man," "Lucy in the Sky With Diamonds," "All You Need Is Love," "Eleanor Rigby," "All Together Now," and the title song.

HARDY, OLIVER. See Laurel, Stan

HARLINE, LEIGH (1907–1969) was a music arranger, conductor, and composer at WALT DISNEY's studio, where he wrote the songs for *PINOCCHIO* (1940) with lyricist NED WASHINGTON. Harline worked on the music for several musicals and nonmusicals at various studios over a thirty-year career. Among his credits were *SNOW WHITE AND THE SEVEN DWARFS* (1937), *George White's Scandals* (1945), *ROAD TO UTOPIA* (1946), *Beat the Band* (1947), and *The Wonderful World of the Brothers Grimm* (1962). Harline's most famous song is the ACADEMY AWARD–winning "When You Wish Upon a Star."

HARLING, W. FRANKE (1887–1958), a busy composer on Tin Pan Alley, on Broadway, and in opera houses, wrote background music for several nonmusical films and penned memorable scores for *Honey* (1930) with lyricist SAM COSLOW and *MONTE CARLO* (1930) with RICHARD A. WHITING and LEO ROBIN. "Beyond the Blue Horizon" from the latter is perhaps Harling's most well known song.

HARNICK, SHELDON. See Bock, Jerry

HARRIS, PHIL (1904–1995) started his career as a drummer, then founded his own band, and eventually started performing characters in films. Harris often played overconfident Romeos and shady businessmen in such musicals as *Melody Cruise* (1933), *Man About Town* (1939), *Dreaming Out Loud* (1940), *I Love a Bandleader* (1946), *WABASH AVENUE* (1950), and *ANYTHING GOES* (1956). But just as often he played himself, as in *Turn Off the Moon* (1937), *Buck Benny Rides Again* (1940), *Starlift* (1951), and *HERE COMES THE GROOM* (1951). Harris' distinctive raspy singing voice was heard in three DISNEY animated musicals—as Baloo the bear singing "The Bare Necessities" in *THE JUNGLE BOOK* (1967), the jazz cat J. Thomas O'Malley in *THE ARISTOCATS* (1970), and Little John in *Robin Hood* (1973)—as well as in the non-Disney *Rock-a-Doodle* (1990). With his wife ALICE FAYE Harris made many recordings and personal appearances, and they had their own radio show for a while.

HARRISON, SIR REX (1908–1990), the sophisticated British actor known for urbane roles in light comedies, Shavian characters, and period dramas, was equally adept on stage and in film. His two movie musical roles were characteristic of his career: the temperamental linguistics professor Henry Higgins in *MY FAIR LADY* (1964) and the inquiring veterinarian John Dolittle in *DOCTOR DOLITTLE* (1967).

HART, LORENZ (1895–1943) was one of America's most clever and playful lyricists, writing over two dozen Broadway shows with composer RICHARD RODGERS and experimenting with the movie musical by employing extended musical sequences rather than individual songs. Many of the Rodgers and Hart stage works were filmed, though several suffered script and score changes that rendered them barely recognizable. Among the movies made from their plays were *Spring Is Here* (1930), *Heads Up* (1930), *EVERGREEN* (1934), based on a London hit, *BABES IN ARMS* (1939), *The Boys From Syracuse* (1940), *TOO MANY GIRLS* (1940), *I Married an Angel* (1942), *PAL JOEY* (1957), and *JUMBO* (1962). The team had little or no control over these films but managed to show their creative hand in the movies they scored directly for the screen: *The Hot Heiress* (1931), *LOVE ME TO-NIGHT* (1932), *THE PHANTOM PRESIDENT* (1932), *HALLELUJAH, I'M A BUM* (1933), *Hollywood Party* (1934), *MISSISSIPPI* (1935), *The Dancing Pirate* (1936), *Fools for Scandal* (1938), and *They Met in Argentina* (1941). Hart also provided new lyrics for Lehar's *THE MERRY WIDOW* (1934). A highly inaccurate but very entertaining BIOGRAPHICAL MUSICAL about the team called *WORDS AND MUSIC* (1948) featured MICKEY ROONEY as Hart and Tom Drake as Rodgers. Hart's lyrics ranged from the cynical to the romantic with the wordplay in each case extremely potent and the rhyming delectable.

HART, MOSS (1904–1961), one of Broadway's finest authors of comedies and musical comedies, contributed to the scripts for the film musicals *BROADWAY MELODY OF 1936* (1935), *Frankie and Johnny* (1936), *Lady in the Dark* (1944), based on his Broadway hit, *HANS CHRISTIAN AN-DERSEN* (1952), *A STAR IS BORN* (1954), and others. He was married to KITTY CARLISLE.

HARTMAN, DON (1900–1958) was a Hollywood director, producer, and songwriter, but he is mostly remembered for the many screenplays he wrote in the 1930s and 1940s. His musical credits include *Coronado* (1935), *Waikiki Wedding* (1937), for which he also wrote the songs, *Tropic Holiday* (1938), *Paris Honeymoon* (1939), *The Star Maker* (1939), *ROAD TO SINGAPORE* (1940), *ROAD TO ZANZIBAR* (1941), *ROAD TO MOROCCO* (1942), *UP IN ARMS* (1944), *Wonder Man* (1945), *The Kid From Brooklyn* (1946), *Mr. Imperium* (1951), and others.

HARVEY GIRLS, THE (MGM 1946) was perhaps the best of the FRONTIER MUSICALS that were inspired by the success of *Oklahoma!* on Broadway in 1943. This one was set in Sandrock, New Mexico, in 1880, where easterner JUDY GARLAND comes to work as a waitress in Frank Harvey's restaurant chain that promises good food and a genteel eating atmosphere in the rugged West. The Harvey girls are pitted against the less wholesome gals in town, particularly the ladies at the Alhambra Saloon run by Preston Foster and John Hodiak and presided over by the worldly-wise ANGELA LANSBURY. The rivalry gets nasty, but Garland ends up with Hodiak and the audience ended up with sparkling MGM entertainment filled with terrific songs by JOHNNY MERCER and HARRY WARREN. Garland sang the yearning ballad "In the Valley (Where the Evening Sun Goes Down)" and joined the crowd in the Oscar-winning "On the Atchison, Topeka and the Santa Fe," choreographed by ROBERT ALTON and arguably the best train number in movie musicals. Lansbury (dubbed by Virginia Reese) led her girls in the sly "Oh, You Kid," but Garland, MARJORIE MAIN, and RAY BOLGER joined the Harvey girls in the contagious waltz "Swing Your Partner Round and Round." Garland and fellow waitresses VIRGINIA O'BRIEN and CYD CHARISSE (dubbed by Marion Doenges) lamented that "It's a Great Big World," and O'Brien sarcastically sang about "The Wild Wild West." Also in the cast were KENNY BAKER singing the ballad "Wait and See," CHILL WILLS, Stephen McNally, and Selena Royale. ARTHUR FREED produced the movie, GEORGE SIDNEY directed with the right amount of suspense and playfulness, and it brought in a whopping $5 million in its first release.

HARVEY, LILIAN (1906–1968) was truly an international musical comedy star, making films in Germany, France, Hollywood, and her native land Great Britain. The lively blonde performer made only a few American musicals in the 1930s, few of them as popular as her work overseas. Harvey's Hollywood musicals include *My Weakness* (1933), *My Lips Betray* (1933), *I Am Suzanne* (1934), and *Let's Live Tonight* (1935). She retired from acting during World War Two and became a nurse in Los Angeles, later going back to Europe to return to the stage.

HAVER, JUNE (1926–   ), a blonde singer-dancer that 20TH CENTURY–FOX groomed to be another BETTY GRABLE, was featured in a dozen musical films but never approached a similar kind of popularity. Haver appeared in *THE GANG'S ALL HERE* (1943), *Irish Eyes Are Smiling* (1944), and *Where Do We Go From Here?* (1945) before co-starring with Grable in *THE DOLLY SISTERS* (1945). She gave memorable performances in *THREE LITTLE GIRLS IN BLUE* (1946) and *Wake Up and Dream* (1946) but soon found herself in second-class features such as *I Wonder Who's Kissing Her Now* (1947), *Oh, You Beautiful Doll* (1949), *Look for the Silver Lining* (1949), as MARILYN MILLER, *The Daughter of Rosie O'Grady* (1950), *I'll Get By* (1950), and *The Girl Next Door* (1953). Haver retired in 1953 to become a nun, then left the convent and married FRED MacMURRAY.

HAVOC, JUNE (1916–   ) was a CHILD STAR in vaudeville who worked her way into Broadway shows before being brought out to Hollywood in 1940 to perform in musicals. The petite blonde usually played acid sidekicks or the "other woman" in such films as *Four Jacks and a Jill* (1941), *Sing Your Worries Away* (1942), *HELLO, FRISCO, HELLO* (1943), and *Red, Hot and Blue* (1949). Havoc went back to the stage in the late 1950s and performed for another four decades. She made a return to film musicals with a role in the campy *Can't Stop the Music* (1980). Havoc is the sister of GYPSY ROSE LEE, and the story of their childhood in vaudeville was told in *GYPSY* (1962).

HAYMES, DICK (1916–1980) gained popularity as a singing star on radio and with bands before he was signed to play leading roles in Hollywood musicals. The attractive, smooth-voiced baritone proved to be a rather stiff actor but audiences enjoyed him in some dozen films. After playing a band singer in *DuBarry Was a Lady* (1943), Haymes was usually seen as innocent juveniles or even-handed professionals in *Four Jills in a Jeep* (1944), *Irish Eyes Are Smiling* (1944), *Diamond Horseshoe* (1945), *STATE FAIR* (1945), *THE SHOCKING MISS PILGRIM* (1947), *Carnival in Costa Rica* (1947), *Up in Central Park* (1948), *One Touch of Venus* (1948), *Cruisin' Down the River* (1953), and others. Among his seven wives were singer Fran Jeffries and actresses Joanne Dru and RITA HAYWORTH.

HAYWARD, SUSAN (1918–1975), the ravishing, redheaded actress known for her gripping dramatic roles, portrayed two famous singers with tortured lives in BIOGRAPHICAL MUSICALS: Jane Froman in *WITH A SONG IN MY HEART* (1952) and LILLIAN ROTH in *I'LL CRY TOMORROW* (1955). Hayward can also be seen in the musicals *HOLLYWOOD HOTEL* (1937), *Sis Hopkins* (1941), *STAR SPANGLED RHYTHM* (1942), *Hit Parade of 1943*, and *Smash-Up* (1947).

HAYWORTH, RITA (1918–1987) was COLUMBIA's reigning star in the 1940s, a sensual beauty who, at the same time, projected the all-American girl image. Hayworth's singing was usually dubbed, but her dancing talents were considerable and she held her own partnered with FRED ASTAIRE, GENE KELLY, and others. A professional dancer since childhood, Hayworth was featured in several forgettable films in the 1930s, including the musicals *Under the Pampas Moon* (1935), *Paddy O'Day* (1935), and *Music in My Heart* (1940), until she gained recognition and stardom in *YOU'LL NEVER GET RICH* (1941). She retained her popularity for two decades, starring in such musicals as *My Gal Sal* (1942), *YOU WERE NEVER LOVELIER* (1942), *COVER GIRL* (1944), *Tonight and Every Night* (1945), *Gilda* (1946), *Affair in Trinidad* (1952), and *PAL JOEY* (1957). Hayworth's career and personal life collapsed in the late 1950s, and she later only made intermittent screen appearances in nonmusicals in Europe and Hollywood. Among her husbands were singer DICK HAYMES, actor-director Orson Welles, and millionaire Aly Kahn.

HEAD, EDITH (1907–1981), Hollywood's most prolific and trend-setting costume designer, was responsible for the glamourous look of many stars over her fifty-year career. Among the musicals Head designed were *LOVE ME TO-*

NIGHT (1932), *SHE DONE HIM WRONG* (1933), *BIRTH OF THE BLUES* (1941), *ROAD TO ZANZIBAR* (1941), *GOING MY WAY* (1944), *Lady in the Dark* (1944), *BLUE SKIES* (1946), *The Emperor Waltz* (1948), *WHITE CHRISTMAS* (1953), *THE COUNTRY GIRL* (1953), *HIGH SO-CIETY* (1956), *FUNNY FACE* (1957), *Pepe* (1960), and *SWEET CHARITY* (1969).

HEALY, MARY (1918–   ) came to Hollywood from Broadway in 1938 to make *SECOND FIDDLE* (1939), but her screen career never took off and by the mid-1940s she was back in nightclubs and on stage. The dark-haired singer can also be seen in *Star Dust* (1940), *Zis Boom Bah* (1941), *The Yanks Are Coming* (1942), *Strictly in the Groove* (1943), and *THE 5,000 FINGERS OF DR. T* (1953).

HEINDORF, RAY (1908–1980), a respected musical arranger and conductor who headed the music department at WARNER BROTHERS, wrote original scores for nonmusicals, and supervised the music for such notable films as *GOLD DIGGERS OF 1937* (1936), *YANKEE DOODLE DANDY* (1942), *THIS IS THE ARMY* (1943), *THE DESERT SONG* (1943), *UP IN ARMS* (1944), *Wonder Man* (1945), *RHAPSODY IN BLUE* (1945), *NIGHT AND DAY* (1946), *YOUNG MAN WITH A HORN* (1950), *Tea for Two* (1950), *THE JAZZ SINGER* (1953), *A STAR IS BORN* (1954), *THE PAJAMA GAME* (1957), *DAMN YANKEES* (1958), *THE MUSIC MAN* (1962), *FINIAN'S RAINBOW* (1968), *1776* (1972), and others.

HELLO, DOLLY! (Fox 1969) reunited, for the last time, several artists from the famous "Freed Unit" of the glory days of MGM: ROGER EDENS as associate producer, GENE KELLY as director, MICHAEL KIDD as choreographer, costumer IRENE SHARAFF, and even cinematographer Harry Stradling and set designer Jack Martin Smith. The musical did resemble the old days in its colorful period spectacle and celebratory dancing, but the movie seemed almost out of place in the 1960s and was poorly received by the press. Much of the fuss was over the twenty-seven-year-old BARBRA STREISAND playing the middle-aged matchmaker Dolly Levi. Ironically, she was the over-produced film's saving grace and proved that a superstar can hold her own in a mammoth production. There were other joys as well. Much of the JERRY HERMAN score remained from the 1964 Broadway hit, and the songs were often given top-notch staging, as in a bucolic rendering of "Dancing" in a park, the contagious "Put on Your Sunday Clothes" climaxing in a train setting off from Yonkers for Manhattan, Streisand cutting loose and mocking her own exuberance with "So Long, Dearie," and the rousing title number in which LOUIS ARMSTRONG joined Streisand at the Harmonia Gardens Restaurant and the two created sparks that could rival the best moments from Hollywood's golden age. Also in the huge cast were Walter Matthau as Dolly's grumpy employer-turned-husband, Michael Crawford and Danny Lockin as two clerks out to paint the town red, Marianne McAndrew and E.J. Peaker as the two ladies they discover there, and TOMMY TUNE standing tall (and standing out) in the small role of an artist-turned-dancer. Although the film did very well box office, it still lost money because of its record $24 million cost.

HELLO, FRISCO, HELLO. See *King of Burlesque*

HELP! See *A Hard Day's Night*

HENDERSON, RAY (1896–1970) was the composer member of the team of DE SYLVA, (LEW) BROWN, and Henderson that provided songs for many Broadway musicals and revues in the 1920s. Their only shows brought to the screen were *GOOD NEWS* (1930 and 1947), *Follow the Leader* (1930), based on their play *Manhattan Mary*, and *Follow Thru* (1930). The trio wrote scores for the early musical films *THE SINGING FOOL* (1928), *Say It With Songs* (1929), *SUNNY SIDE UP* (1929), *Just Imagine* (1930), and *Indiscreet* (1931). Henderson also scored *George White's Scandals* (1934) and *CURLY TOP* (1935) with JACK YELLEN, TED KOEHLER, and IRVING CAESAR. "Animal Crackers in My Soup," "If I Had a Talking Picture of You," and "Sonny Boy" are among Henderson's most famous movie songs. DAN DAILY played Henderson in the BIOGRAPHICAL MUSICAL about the team called *The Best Things in Life Are Free* (1956).

HENIE, SONJA (1910–1969), an Olympic Gold Medal figure-skating star from Norway, was turned into a leading lady in 20TH CENTURY–FOX musicals with *ONE IN A MILLION* (1936). Nine films followed, each one allowing the petite blonde to show off her agile skating talents while downplaying her lack of singing skills. The perky star played optimistic Scandinavian characters in *Thin Ice* (1937), *Happy Landing* (1938), *My Lucky Star* (1938), *SECOND FIDDLE* (1939), *SUN VALLEY SERENADE* (1941), *ICELAND* (1942), *Wintertime* (1943), *It's a Pleasure* (19345), and *The Countess of Monte Cristo* (1948). Henie retired from films when her popularity waned and starred in ice shows around the world until 1960.

HEPBURN, AUDREY (1929–1993), the delicate and graceful star of American and British comedies and dramas, appeared in only two movie musicals but gave unforgettable performances in each: the bookstore-worker-turned-model Jo Stockton in *FUNNY FACE* (1957) and the Cockney flower-seller-turned-lady Eliza Doolittle in *MY FAIR LADY* (1964). Hepburn possessed a lightweight but engaging singing voice and had ballet experience, both of which were used charmingly in the first movie; she was dubbed by MARNI NIXON for the second.

HERBERT, HUGH (1887–1952), a vaudeville and Broadway comic and writer, became one of Hollywood's most identifiable character actors, appearing in over 100 films from the beginning of talkies to 1951. The fidgety, blundering Herbert usually played absent-minded professors or naive millionaires who would break into a "woo woo" as he clapped or rubbed his hands together. He appeared in over two dozen musicals, including *FOOTLIGHT PARADE* (1933), *Wonder Bar* (1934), *DAMES* (1934), *SWEET ADELINE* (1935), *GOLD DIGGERS OF 1935*, *To Beat the Band* (1935), *Colleen* (1936), *The Singing Marine* (1937), *HOLLYWOOD HOTEL* (1937), *GOLD DIGGERS IN PARIS* (1938), *The Great Waltz* (1938), *HIT PARADE OF 1941* (1940), *Hellzapoppin* (1941), *STAGE DOOR CANTEEN* (1943), *Music for Millions* (1944), *One Touch of Venus* (1948), *A Song Is Born* (1948), and *The Beautiful Blonde from Bashful Bend* (1949). Herbert's most interesting musical credit was *La Conga Nights* (1940), in which he played all the members of the Dibble family, including the sisters and mother.

HERBERT, VICTOR (1859–1924), America's first Broadway composer of note and one of the masters of OPERETTA, never lived to see the advent of talking pictures, but some of his stage works have been filmed: *Kiss Me Again* (1931), based on his *Mlle. Modiste*, *BABES IN TOYLAND* (1934 and 1961), *NAUGHTY MARIETTA* (1935), and *SWEETHEARTS* (1938). Herbert's songs were used in *The Great Victor Herbert* (1939), in which Walter Connolly played the Irish-born composer.

HERCULES (Disney 1997) took a lot of liberties with Greek mythology but had so much fun doing so that it resulted in one of the funniest of DISNEY's ANIMATED MUSICALS. Zeus' son Hercules is kidnapped by the god Hades' evil henchmen to be destroyed, but the baby is raised by humans and grows up to become a superhero who helps save Mt. Olympus from invading Titans. Despite such derring-do, the film never took itself at all seriously and was filled with sly anachronisms in the dialogue and songs by David Zippell and ALAN MENKEN. Teenage Hercules (voice of Roger Bart) sang the stirring "Go the Distance," but the rest of the score was more sassy, from the ribald "Gospel Truth" and "Zero to Hero," both sung by the Muses, to the self-aware ballad "I Won't Say I'm in Love," sung by Herc's temptress Meg (voice of Susan Egan). The film reached its comic highpoints in the characterizations of Hades (James Woods) and the satyr Phil (Danny DeVito), both bringing a modern slyness to the classical material.

HERE COME THE WAVES (Paramount 1944) stands out from the many World War Two–era musicals by way of its superior score by JOHNNY MERCER and HAROLD ARLEN and the way BING CROSBY made fun of the current fad of bobbysoxers swooning over singers like himself and FRANK SINATRA. (Crosby even satirized Sinatra by crooning "That Old Black

Magic" in the newcomer's style.) Crosby plays a singing idol who, with his pal SONNY TUFTS, meets a sister act, falling for one girl but being mocked by the other. (You don't have to guess which one he ended up with.) The fact that BETTY HUTTON played the twin sisters and behaved with reserve as one of them was just part of the movie's unusual sparkle. When Crosby joins the Navy, he is assigned to putting on a benefit show with the W.A.V.E.S. (including the sisters), and the resulting show is a humdinger. Crosby and Tufts (in blackface) introduced the movie's big hit song, "Ac-cent-tchu-ate the Positive," Crosby and Hutton sang the romantic duets "I Promise You" and "Let's Take the Long Way Home," and Hutton was at her comic best bragging "There's a Fellow Waiting in Poughkeepsie."

HERE COMES THE GROOM (Paramount 1951) may have had a convoluted plot (reporter BING CROSBY adopts two French orphans and has only five days to find a wife or he will lose them) but also had enough stars and felicitous musical numbers to brighten up even the dreariest story. Crosby and possible wife-candidate JANE WYMAN sang the Oscar-winning "In the Cool Cool Cool of the Evening" by JOHNNY MERCER and HOAGY CARMICHAEL, Crosby and CASS DALEY jumped and jived to "Misto Cristofo Colombo" by RAY EVANS and JAY LIVINGSTON, and Crosby put the two orphans to bed singing the English and French lullaby "Bonne Nuit— Good Night" by the same team. Also on hand for musical and comic fun were LOUIS ARMSTRONG, DOROTHY LAMOUR, WALTER CATLETT, ALEXIS SMITH, JAMES BARTON, PHIL HARRIS, Anna Maria Alberghetti (who sang an aria from *Rigoletto*), and FRANCHOT TONE as the millionaire that Wyman almost marries until she meets Crosby and the kids.

HERMAN, JERRY (1932–   ), the Broadway composer-lyricist of several tuneful hit shows and other intriguing near-misses, has had two of his 1960s blockbusters filmed: *HELLO, DOLLY!* (1969) and *Mame* (1974). Herman has not written any film scores but did contribute new songs to the former film.

HEYMAN, EDWARD (1907–1981), a Hollywood and Tin Pan Alley lyricist, worked with various composers during his career, including ARTHUR SCHWARTZ, RUDOLF FRIML, NACIO HERB BROWN, and Morton Gould. His film musicals include *Sweet Surrender* (1935), *That Girl From Paris* (1936), *Delightfully Dangerous* (1945), *Northwest Outpost* (1947), *On an Island With You* (1948), and *The Kissing Bandit* (1948). Among his hit songs are "I Cover the Waterfront" and "Love Letters."

HIGH SOCIETY (Siegel/MGM 1956) is one of those rare instances when a musical is so enjoyable that you are able to (temporarily) forget the matchless source material, in this case Philip Barry's 1939 Broadway comedy *The Philadelphia Story*, which had been filmed with perfection in 1940. John Patrick's screenplay reset the tale in Newport, where socialite songwriter BING CROSBY runs a jazz festival while wooing his ex-wife Grace Kelly on the eve of her wedding to stuffy John Lund. Cynical magazine reporter FRANK SINATRA and his equally cynical sidekick CELESTE HOLM come to cover the wedding, and a romance develops between Kelly and Sinatra. But Bing gets Grace Kelly back in the end and Holm has a better shot at Sinatra. COLE PORTER's score is arguably his finest screen work, from the lyrical ballads "True Love" and "You're Sensational" to the tongue-in-cheek character songs "Who Wants to Be a Millionaire?" and "Well, Did You Evah?" (the last from a Porter stage score). Perhaps the highlight of this musical feast was Crosby and LOUIS ARMSTRONG bringing down the house with "Now You Has Jazz." Also in the cast were LOUIS CALHERN, Sidney Blackmer, Margalo Gilmore, and Lydia Reed, all under the zippy direction of CHARLES WALTERS.

HIGH, WIDE AND HANDSOME (Paramount 1937) was a transitional piece that OSCAR HAMMERSTEIN wrote between the Broadway classics *Show Boat* (1929) and *Oklahoma!* (1943), and the movie has a little bit of each in it. In the wilds of western Pennsylvania in 1859, struggling oil prospectors are battling greedy railroad tycoons to hold onto their land and lay a pipeline, the former winning the fight when a circus troupe joins them to chase off the villainous businessmen. In the middle of it all, singer IRENE DUNNE finds romance with farmer RANDOLPH SCOTT while the sultry DOROTHY LAMOUR tries to cause trouble of her own. For a FRONTIER MUSICAL, it was unusually accurate and atmospheric, and the songs by Hammerstein and JEROME KERN were often integrated into the story. The domestic ballad "The Folks Who Live on the Hill," the farewell song "Can I Forget You?," the frolicking "Allegheny Al," the bluesy "The Things I Want," and the rollicking title number revealed two master songwriters at their best. ALAN HALE and AKIM TAMIROFF were the villains with Raymond Walburn, Charles Bickford, ELIZABETH PATTERSON, BEN BLUE, and WILLIAM FRAWLEY to round out the folksy cast. But the star was director ROUBEN MAMOULIAN, who recreated social gatherings, a medicine show, a square dance, music halls, saloons, riverboats, and a circus, all with striking visual imagery and experimental use of music on film.

HILLIARD, HARRIET (1909–1994), a band singer whose tiny voice held a lot of expression, married bandleader OZZIE NELSON in 1935 but used her maiden name when she appeared in *FOLLOW THE FLEET* (1936), *New Faces of 1937*, *Life of the Party* (1937), *Cocoanut Grove* (1938), *Jukebox Jennie* (1942), *Gals, Incorporated* (1943), *Swingtime Johnny* (1944), and others. Hilliard also appeared in four films with Nelson: *Sweetheart of the Campus* (1941), *Honeymoon Lodge* (1943), *Hi, Good Lookin'* (1944), and *Take It Big* (1944). In the mid-1940s she changed her name to Harriet Nelson and embarked on a new career with her husband (and later her sons) on radio and television (*The Adventures of Ozzie and Harriet*).

HIT THE DECK (RKO 1930) failed to transfer from a stage hit to a screen hit even though it remained fairly true to the 1927 Broadway musical. Polly Walker played the saucy Looloo, the owner of a dockside café, who falls for the sailor Bilge (JACK OAKIE). When Bilge goes back to sea, Looloo waits for him until she inherits some money and then chases him all the way to China. The stage score by LEO ROBIN, CLIFFORD GREY, and VINCENT YOUMANS had its share of hits ("Hallelujah" and "Sometimes I'm Happy," in particular) that were used, and added for the film was the new ditty by SIDNEY CLARE and Youmans called "Keeping Myself for You" and the recent standard "More Than You Know" that Youmans wrote for a Broadway flop the year before. Much of the same plot was used in *FOLLOW THE FLEET* (1936), but it had a score by IRVING BERLIN. A whole new plot was attached to the old title when MGM remade *Hit the Deck* in 1955 with TONY MARTIN, RUSS TAMBLYN, and VIC DAMONE as three sailors on leave who fall for ANN MILLER, DEBBIE REYNOLDS, and JANE POWELL, respectively. The story was hardly a nailbiter, but the youthful, energetic cast, the spiffy choreography by HERMES PAN, and eleven Youmans numbers from various sources turned into nonstop entertainment. In addition to the songs used in the earlier version, there was Miller slinking her way through "The Lady From the Bayou" and Tamblyn and Reynolds dancing though an amusement park funhouse. Also in the cast were WALTER PIDGEON, J. CARROLL NAISH, GENE RAYMOND, Kay Armen, and JANE DARWELL, under the direction of Roy Rowland.

HOFFMAN, AL (1902–1960) was an American composer who wrote scores for several British film musicals in the 1930s, such as *Jack of All Trades* (1935), *First a Girl* (1936), *This'll Make You Whistle* (1936), and *Gangway* (1937). But he is most remembered in the States for the score he wrote with JERRY LIVINGSTON and MACK DAVID for the DISNEY animated *CINDERELLA* (1949).

HOLIDAY INN (Paramount 1942) will always be remembered as the film in which BING CROSBY sat at the piano in his Connecticut inn on a snowy evening and sang "White Christmas" for the first time, but the film is filled with other treasures as well: Crosby attempting to dance like FRED ASTAIRE while Astaire tries to croon like Crosby in "I'll Capture Your Heart Singing," Astaire proving to VIRGINIA DALE that "You're Easy to Dance With," Crosby and MARJORIE REYNOLDS (dubbed by Martha Mears) as two blackfaced minstrels celebrating Lincoln's Birthday with "Abraham," and Astaire tapping to "Let's Say It With Firecrackers" as dozens of tiny explosions erupted at his feet. The plot was neatly serviceable: Nightclub partners Astaire and Crosby break up over a girl, so Crosby moves to the country, tries farming for a while, then turns his homestead into an inn open only on the holidays. When he falls for aspiring singer Reynolds, Crosby tries to keep her identity from Astaire so as not to lose her too. Each holiday brings a new show to the inn and another opportunity to keep the wolf-like Astaire at bay. But Astaire does discover Reynolds and whisks her off to Hollywood. She is eventually joined by Crosby, and Astaire, for the first time in his career, does not get the girl. Berlin recycled "Easter Parade" and wrote new songs to celebrate Christmas, New Year's Eve, Lincoln's Birthday, Valentine's Day, Washington's Birthday, the Fourth of July, and Thanksgiving. In addition to the numbers already mentioned, the score included "Let's Start the New Year Right," "Happy Holiday," "Be Careful, It's My Heart," "Song of Freedom," and others. DANNY DARE (and Astaire) devised the dances, and MARK SANDRICH produced and directed. It was a huge hit and continues to be so every December.

HOLLANDER, FREDERICK (1896–1976) was a German composer who wrote songs for Bertolt Brecht's stage productions and for some films, most notably "Falling in Love Again," which MARLENE DIETRICH sang in *The Blue Angel* (1930). PARAMOUNT brought him to Hollywood, where Hollander collaborated with various lyricists (and sometimes supplied his own lyrics) for *I Am Suzanne* (1934), *The Thrill of a Lifetime* (1937), *Zaza* (1938), *Man About Town* (1939), *Destry Rides Again* (1939), in which Dietrich sang "The Boys in the Back Room," *Seven Sinners* (1940), *A Foreign Affair* (1948), *That Lady in Ermine* (1948), *THE 5,000 FINGERS OF DR. T* (1953), and others. Hollander also composed soundtrack scores for several nonmusicals.

HOLLIDAY, JUDY (1921–1965), the not-so-dumb blonde star of stage and film comedies, started as a singer-comedienne in nightclubs and played bit parts in the film musicals *Greenwich Village* (1944) and *Something for the Boys* (1944) before achieving celebrity. She returned to the musical form playing the answering service operator Ella Peterson in *BELLS ARE RINGING* on Broadway in 1956 and on film in 1960.

HOLLOWAY, STANLEY(1890–1982) was one of England's favorite music hall comics, usually playing crusty, working-class characters in British stage and film musicals. Holloway made his film debut in 1921 and was featured in such English musicals as *The Co-Optimists* (1929), *Lily of Killarney* (1934), *Champagne Charlie* (1944), and others. He is most known to American audiences for playing the jailer Lockitt in *The Beggar's Opera* (1952) and the convivial dustman Alfred Doolittle in *MY FAIR LADY* (1964), which he had originated on Broadway.

HOLLOWAY, STERLING (1905–1992) probably did more voice-overs for DISNEY characters than any one actor, supplying the voice for Winnie the

Pooh, the Cheshire Cat, and many others. Holloway had one of the most distinctive voices heard on stage and in film, a nasal, raspy twang that was easily recognized over the six decades of his career. After appearing on stage in musicals and revues, Holloway went to Hollywood at the birth of the talkies and was featured as harebrained delivery boys, country hicks, naive soda jerks, and other types in over 100 films, including such musicals as *GOLD DIGGERS OF 1933, DANCING LADY* (1933), *THE MERRY WIDOW* (1934), *VARSITY SHOW* (1937), *Doctor Rhythm* (1938), *ICELAND* (1942), *The Beautiful Blonde From Bashful Bend* (1949), and others. But his fame rests on the many characters he voiced in Disney shorts and in the feature musicals *DUMBO* (1941), *THE THREE CABALLEROS* (1945), *Make Mine Music* (1946), *ALICE IN WONDERLAND* (1951), *THE JUNGLE BOOK* (1967), and *THE ARISTOCATS* (1978).

HOLLYWOOD CANTEEN. See *Stage Door Canteen*

HOLLYWOOD HOTEL (Warner 1937) started out with a bang and then rarely let go. JOHNNY "SCAT" DAVIS, FRANCES LANGFORD, and others, accompanied by BENNY GOODMAN's orchestra, ride to the St. Louis Airport and bid DICK POWELL farewell by singing "Hooray for Hollywood," a tongue-in-cheek salute to Tinsel Town that became the unofficial anthem of the place. Once he arrives, Powell is reduced to providing the singing voice for ham actor ALAN MOWBRAY, but he gets to meet aspiring actress ROSEMARY LANE, who is reduced to playing a double for the temperamental star LOLA LANE. The two fall in love and, in the finale, get to go on and show the world their stuff. JOHNNY MERCER and RICHARD A. WHITING wrote the scintillating score that also included the romantic ballad "Silhouetted in the Moonlight," the frolicsome "I'm Like a Fish Out of Water" (which Lane and Powell sang as they splashed in a fountain), the dreamy "I've Hitched My Wagon to a Star," and "Let That Be a Lesson to You," which BUSBY BERKELEY staged at a drive-in diner with carhops whizzing by and dancers prancing on top of parked cars. HUGH HERBERT, Ted Healy, GLENDA FARRELL, EDGAR KENNEDY, Allyn Joslyn, Mabel Todd, RONALD REAGAN, and Jerry Cooper filled out a cast that ribbed the cinema capital (even gossip columnist Louella Parsons was on hand to play herself) and provided vivacious entertainment at the expense of the studios.

HOLLYWOOD REVUE OF 1929 (MGM 1929) was the first of the all-star REVUES that the studios put out in the early days of the talkies to show off their roster of talent. Like most of the others, this one was a lavish, if mixed-bag, of an entertainment with everything from ballet to comedy turns to Shakespeare to song-and-dance numbers, all emceed by JACK BENNY and Conrad Nagel. John Gilbert and Norma Shearer did the balcony scene from *Romeo and Juliet*, Buster Keaton and LAUREL and HARDY provided the comedy, JOAN CRAWFORD danced as a flapper to "Got a Feelin' For You," Nagel (dubbed by CHARLES KING) sang "You Were Meant for Me," MARION DAVIES let loose with "Tommy Atkins on Parade," King sang "Orange Blossom Time" while the ALBERTINA RASCH Ballet fluttered around him, and much of the cast joined CLIFF EDWARDS in "While Strolling Through the Park One Day." Edwards was also featured in the film's most memorable number: ARTHUR FREED and NACIO HERB BROWN's "Singin' in the Rain" with Edwards strumming his ukelele while a chorus in slickers danced through the pounding rain.

HOLM, CELESTE (1919–) went to Hollywood after her sensational performance as Ado Annie in Broadway's *Oklahoma!* in 1943, but she usually played dramatic roles or wise and sarcastic women in comedies. The blonde actress-singer was featured in the musicals *THREE LITTLE GIRLS IN BLUE* (1946), *Carnival in Costa Rica* (1947), *Road House* (1948), *HIGH SOCIETY* (1956), and *Tom Sawyer* (1973).

HOPE, BOB (1903–) ranks as one of the most successful and beloved entertainers of the twentieth century, having conquered vaudeville, Broadway, films, radio, nightclubs, and television, as well as making personal appearances around the world entertaining everyone from royalty to GIs. The British-born comic went to Hollywood to play a featured role in *THE BIG BROADCAST OF 1938* and immediately tickled funny bones and tugged on emotions when he sang "Thanks for the Memory" with SHIRLEY ROSS. Hope appeared in the musicals *College Swing* (1938) and *Thanks for the Memory* (1938), as well as some comedies, before teaming up with BING CROSBY for *ROAD TO SINGAPORE* (1940), the first of the seven "Road" features they made together. It was followed by *ROAD TO ZANZIBAR* (1941), *ROAD TO MOROCCO* (1942), *ROAD TO UTOPIA* (1945), *ROAD TO RIO* (1947), *ROAD TO BALI* (1952), and *THE ROAD TO HONG KONG* (1962). In between these tuneful journeys, Hope also made the musicals *Louisiana Purchase* (1941), *STAR SPANGLED RHYTHM* (1942), *Let's Face It* (1943), *Duffy's Tavern* (1945), *Variety Girl* (1947), *THE PALEFACE* (1948), *Fancy Pants* (1950), *The Lemon Drop Kid* (1951), *SON OF PALEFACE* (1952), *Here Come the Girls* (1953), *The Seven Little Foys* (1955), *Beau James* (1957), and *THE FIVE PENNIES* (1959), as well as many comedies. Hope concentrated on television and concerts after the mid-1960s, although he made the movie musical *I'll Take Sweden* (1967) and appeared in a cameo spot in *THE MUPPET MOVIE* (1979). Throughout his long career Hope usually maintained his stage persona of the bumbling, wisecracking coward who rarely gets the girl but continues on with naive optimism.

HORNBLOW, ARTHUR, JR. (1893–1976) was a producer who was brought to Hollywood by SAMUEL GOLDWYN but later worked for PARAMOUNT and MGM, and then as an independent agent. Hornblow's musical credits include *MISSISSIPPI* (1935), *Swing High, Swing Low* (1937), *HIGH, WIDE AND HANDSOME* (1937), *Waikiki Wedding* (1937), *ARTISTS AND MODELS ABROAD* (1938), *Tropic Holiday* (1938), *Man About Town* (1939), *Million Dollar Mermaid* (1952), and *OKLAHOMA!* (1955).

HORNE, LENA (1917–   ) was the first African American performer to sign a long-term contract with a major studio, but Hollywood rarely used the stunning singer-actress to her full potential, and her film appearances were infrequent, short, and easily edited out for showings in the South. Horne came to prominence singing at the Cotton Club in New York, started appearing in films with *The Duke Is Tops* (1938), and got to play character roles in *CABIN IN THE SKY* (1943), *STORMY WEATHER* (1943), and *Broadway Rhythm* (1944). But more often she did specialty bits in movies, as in *Panama Hattie* (1942), *I Dood It* (1943), *Swing Fever* (1943), *Thousands Cheer* (1943), *TWO GIRLS AND A SAILOR* (1944), *ZIEGFELD FOLLIES* (1946), *TILL THE CLOUDS ROLL BY* (1946), *WORDS AND MUSIC* (1948), *The Duchess of Idaho* (1950), and *Meet Me in Las Vegas* (1956). By the 1960s Horne concentrated on recordings, nightclub and television appearances, and social causes. She returned to the film musical playing the good witch Glinda in *The Wiz* (1978). Horne's sultry, smooth singing voice and breezy interpretations of songs never dated, and she enjoyed a renaissance of interest in the 1980s on Broadway and on tour.

HORTON, EDWARD EVERETT (1886–1970) was a favorite character actor on stage and in over 150 films, usually playing fussy managers or easily frustrated sidekicks who often broke into double takes uttering "Oh, dear!" Horton appeared in some silents in the 1920s and then became a regular in talkies, including thirty-four musicals beginning with *Reaching for the Moon* (1931). Other memorable films include *A Bedtime Story* (1933), *THE GAY DIVORCEE* (1934), *THE MERRY WIDOW* (1934), *TOP HAT* (1935), *The Singing Kid* (1936), *SHALL WE DANCE* (1937), *College Swing* (1938), *ZIEGFELD GIRL* (1941), *Sunny* (1941), *I Married an Angel* (1942), *SPRINGTIME IN THE ROCKIES* (1942), *THE GANG'S ALL HERE* (1943), *Brazil* (1944), *Cinderella Jones* (1946), and others. He worked consistently in films for two decades before returning to the stage and doing television in between movie assignments. Horton was particularly effective at voices used in television cartoons and was acting until his death—a remarkable career of sixty years.

HOW TO SUCCEED IN BUSINESS WITHOUT REALLY TRYING (Mirisch/United Artists 1966) may have cut five songs from the 1961 Broadway hit, but just about everything and everyone else made the transfer from stage to screen. The satirical fable was about window washer Robert Morse who rises to the head of the World Wide Wickets Company by following the instructions of a little manual with the show's lengthy title. Among those he had to maneuver around were the company's president (RUDY VALLEE), an obnoxious nephew (Anthony Teague), and a sexy time bomb called Hedy LaRue (Maureen Arthur). But secretary Michele Lee loves the eager-beaver Morse for himself, and the hero gets both power and love in the end. FRANK LOESSER's songs were mostly in a cynical vein, even the show's hit ballad "I Believe in You," which was turned into a love song in the film. Other numbers included the mock school anthem "Grand Old Ivy," the cautionary "A Secretary Is Not a Toy," the frantic "Coffee Break," and the revival-like "Brotherhood of Man." Dale Moreda recreated BOB FOSSE's Broadway choreography, which was the next best thing under the circumstances.

HUGHES, HOWARD (1905–1976), the famous billionaire who dabbled in everything from aviation to real estate to films, produced four movie musicals at RKO (which he bought in 1948), three of them starring his sponsored favorite JANE RUSSELL: *Two Tickets to Broadway* (1951), *Double Dynamite* (1951), *The Las Vegas Story* (1952), and *The French Line* (1954).

HUMBERSTONE, H. BRUCE (1903–1984) was a proficient director in films and television who excelled at crime melodramas, light comedies, and musicals. The former script boy who worked his way up to director made most of his first musicals at 20TH CENTURY–FOX. Humberstone is most remembered for *SUN VALLEY SERENADE* (1941), *ICELAND* (1942), *HELLO, FRISCO, HELLO* (1943), *Pin-Up Girl* (1944), *Wonder Man* (1945), *THREE LITTLE GIRLS IN BLUE* (1946), *She's Working Her Way Through College* (1952), and *THE DESERT SONG* (1953).

HUNCHBACK OF NOTRE DAME, THE (Disney 1996) managed to be a very dark and sensual ANIMATED MUSICAL while still pleasing different age groups in the DISNEY manner. The Victor Hugo novel took a bit of tweaking in this screen adaptation (comic gargoyles, a singing hunchback, a satirical hero who mocks his macho image), yet the hypnotic pull of the story and the characters was still there and the exciting visuals, concise storytelling, and vibrant score made it one of the studio's finer achievements. STEPHEN SCHWARTZ and ALAN MENKEN wrote the songs, some of which, such as the opening "The Bells of Notre Dame," combined narrative and character beautifully. Quasimodo (voice of Tim Hulce) yearned for a life "Out There," Esmerelda (Demi Moore, singing voice of Heidi Mollenbauer) prayed "God Help the Outcasts," the three gargoyles (Jason Alexander, Charles Kimbrough, and MARY WICKES, singing dubbed by Mary Stout) hammed it up with "A Guy Like You," and the crowd celebrated a festival where everything turned dangerously "Topsy Turvy." The most potent number was the contrasting songs "Heaven's Light," sung by Quasimodo as he basks in the warmth of Esmerelda's smile, and "Hellfire," in which the villainous priest Frollo (Tony Jay) sung of both his hatred and his lust for the gypsy girl as the flames in his fireplace conjure up erotic images of passion and punishment. Americans did not flock to the film as they had with most Disney entries in the 1990s, yet it was extremely popular in Europe, so the company's stage version was produced in Germany first.

HUNTER, ROSS (1921–1996), a producer of a handful of musicals in the 1960s, had a very unusual career. The former school teacher went to Hollywood in the 1940s and played leading men in comedies and mostly B musicals such as *Louisiana Purchase* (1944), *She's a Sweetheart* (1944), *Hit the Hay* (1945), and *Sweetheart of Sigma Chi* (1946). Hunter then returned to teaching, only to reappear in show business as a producer in the 1950s. His movie musicals include *FLOWER DRUM SONG* (1964), *I'd Rather Be Rich* (1964), *THOROUGHLY MODERN MILLIE* (1967), and *Lost Horizon* (1973). Hunter later moved on to television production.

HUTTON, BETTY (1921–   ) was billed as the "Blonde Bombshell" because of her high-powered singing and comic·bombast. A child actress and then a comic singer with bands, Hutton made her film debut in a featured bit part in *THE FLEET'S IN* (1942), going on to play the comic lead in such PARAMOUNT musicals as *STAR SPANGLED RHYTHM* (1942), *HAPPY GO LUCKY* (1943), *Let's Face It* (1943), *And the Angels Sing* (1944), *HERE COME THE WAVES* (1944), *Duffy's Tavern* (1945), *The Stork Club* (1945), and others. She graduated to leading roles in *Incendiary Blonde* (1945), *The Perils of Pauline* (1947), *Dream Girl* (1948), and *Red, Hot and Blue* (1949), before landing the choice role of Annie Oakley in *ANNIE GET YOUR GUN* (1950) when she replaced JUDY GARLAND. Hutton's last musicals were *Let's Dance* (1950), *Sailor Beware* (1951), and *Somebody Loves Me* (1952). Despite her unforgettable presence in musicals and comedies, such as the classic farce *The Miracle at Morgan's Creek* (1944), the oft-married Hutton soon fell out of favor and years later was rediscovered living on charity and battling mental illness. No one put a song over like Hutton, blasting out the words with her full-throated voice and explosive expressions and turning her comic numbers, such as "Poppa, Preach to Me" and "Murder, He Says," into animated delights. Her sister was singer MARION HUTTON.

HUTTON, MARION (1919–1986) was a vocalist with GLENN MILLER's orchestra for many years and made a half dozen film musicals, mostly with Miller and usually as a band singer. She can be seen in *SUN VALLEY SERENADE* (1941), *ORCHESTRA WIVES* (1942), *Crazy House* (1943), *In Society* (1944) in which she got to introduce "My Dreams Are Getting Better All the Time," *Babes on Swing Street* (1944), and *Love Happy* (1949). She is the older sister of BETTY HUTTON.

I

I DREAM TOO MUCH (RKO 1935) was LILY PONS' first and most successful movie, a musical melodrama that proved the diminutive Metropolitan Opera diva could act as well as sing. She played a simple girl from the provinces who was discovered by impresario Osgood Perkins and taken to Paris, where her voiced was trained and her heart was lost to idealistic opera composer Henry Fonda. They married but Pons became famous and he didn't, so she decided to devote her energies to his career. But the studio came up with what it thought was a happy ending: Fonda's opera is turned into a musical comedy that becomes a hit with Pons as the leading lady. In addition to the expected opera arias, the score included some marvelous new numbers by DOROTHY FIELDS and JEROME KERN: the swinging "I Got Love," the lullaby "The Jockey on the Carousel," and the entrancing title song. The film was a hit, but Pons' three subsequent efforts were not as popular and so she gave up on the movies.

ICELAND (Fox 1942) was a showcase for Hollywood's one and only ice skating star, SONJA HENIE, and it came to life only when she was on the ice or others were singing the MACK GORDON and HARRY WARREN songs. The story revolved around an uninteresting love triangle between Reykjavik girl Henie, her local boyfriend STERLING HOLLOWAY, and American Marine corporal JOHN PAYNE. While the threesome straightened out their differences, Joan Merrill got to sing the hit song "There Will Never Be Another You" with SAMMY KAYE's orchestra. She also performed the sly "You Can't Say No to a Soldier," and JACK OAKIE joined Henie and Payne in the chummy "It's a Lovers' Knot." James Gonzales staged Henie's skating numbers, and they proved engaging even if her two patriotic numbers, "I Like a Military Tune" and "Let's Bring New Glory to Old Glory," were a bit tiresome even for loyal wartime Americans.

I'LL CRY TOMORROW (MGM 1955) was a hard-hitting BIOGRAPHI-
CAL MUSICAL about singer LILLIAN ROTH that gave SUSAN HAY-
WARD one of the best roles of her career. Based on Roth's autobiography, the
story pulled no punches in revealing the seamier side of show business and
marriage as the oft-wed Roth battled alcoholism, wife beating, and loss of
fame. Hayward did her own singing and recreated such Roth favorites as
"Happiness Is a Thing Called Joe," "Sing, You Sinners," and "When the Red
Red Robin Comes Bob Bob Bobbin' Along." Jo Van Fleet turned in a powerful performance as Roth's pushy mother, Eddie Albert, Don Taylor, and Richard Conte played Roth's husbands, and Daniel Mann directed them all with a
gritty kind of honesty.

IN OLD CHICAGO (Fox 1938) was one of that rare breed in Hollywood:
the musical disaster movie. The Great Chicago Fire of 1871 provided the disaster and ALICE FAYE provided the music. As a saloon singer who can't
decide between good-hearted DON AMECHE or his dark-hearted brother
TYRONE POWER, Faye and company sang some old favorites like "How
Many Miles Back to Dublin Town?" and some new songs such as the waltzing
"I've Taken a Fancy to You" by SIDNEY CLARE and LEW POLLOCK and
the vivacious title number by MACK GORDON and HARRY REVEL. The
romantic triangle was sorted out just about the time the fire broke out, and the
movie turned into catastrophic spectacle. ALICE BRADY was a standout in
the supporting cast that also featured Andy Devine, Brian Donlevy, and Burton Churchill.

IN THE GOOD OLD SUMMERTIME (MGM 1949) couldn't hold a can-
dle to the classic comedy *The Shop Around the Corner* (1940), on which it was
based, but was a cheerful diversion all the same and gave both JUDY GAR-
LAND and VAN JOHNSON a chance to show off their comic skills. Two
workers in a Chicago music store are always quarreling, neither knowing that
the secret pen pal each has been writing to is the other. The complications were
pleasant enough and the supporting cast was as charming as the two stars: S.Z.
SAKALL, in what is arguably his most full-blooded performance, as the owner
of the shop, SPRING BYINGTON as the secretary he has secretly loved for
years, Buster Keaton as a hapless clerk, Lillian Bronson, Clinton Sundberg,
Marcia Van Dyke, and LIZA MINNELLI as the toddler that Garland and
Johnson produce in the film's finale. Most of the songs came from the story's
turn-of-the-century setting, and directed by ROBERT Z. LEONARD and
choreographed by ROBERT ALTON, they seemed fresh as new: "I Don't
Care," "Meet Me Tonight in Dreamland," "Play That Barbershop Cord,"
"Put Your Arms Around Me, Honey," and the bucolic title number.

INNOCENTS OF PARIS (Paramount 1929) is the early talkie that made
MAURICE CHEVALIER a star in America. In his first feature-length movie

in English, the young Chevalier stumbled through the melodramatic plot battling weak dialogue and a new language, but when the musical numbers came along he soared and audiences were enamored with the funny, sexy little Frenchman. Chevalier, a Parisian junk collector who wants to be an entertainer, rescues a child from drowning in the Seine and then falls in love with the tot's aunt, Sylvia Beecher. Should he marry the aunt and become a family man or go into show business? He chose true love, but fortunately he sang and danced a few numbers before he did. LEO ROBIN and RICHARD A. WHITING wrote the new songs, including the Chevalier signature song "Louise," the suggestive "Wait 'Til You See Ma Cherie," and the torchy "On Top of the World Alone." Chevalier also included two favorites from his nightclub act in Paris, "Valentine" and "Dites-Moi Ma Mere," sporting his straw hat and cane and displaying the confidence of a veteran hoofer.

INTERNATIONAL HOUSE (Paramount 1933) had a more cockeyed and contrived plot than most 1930s musicals, but once W.C. FIELDS arrived in his "autogiro" the audience stopped worrying about it. Chinese scientist Edmund Breeze has invented a new communications device called a radioscope, an early sort of television set, and invites delegates from around the world to come to the International House Hotel in China and bid on it. STUART ERWIN comes from America but comes down with the measles so he has to be quarantined. (Luckily for the audience, GEORGE BURNS and GRACIE ALLEN were the hotel doctor and nurse who tended to him.) Then Fields arrives on the roof and proceeds to take over the film with his one-liners and sight gags, causing havoc driving throughout the hotel in a miniature car. The musical numbers came from the specialty acts that were demonstrated on the radioscope. LEO ROBIN and RALPH RAINGER provided the songs, the best being the mock kiddie song "My Bluebird's Singing the Blues" delivered tongue-in-cheek by Baby Rose Marie, "Thank Heaven for You" crooned by RUDY VALLEE while Fields made wisecracks at every musical rest, and the daffy "She Was a China Teacup and He Was Just a Mug," which STERLING HOLLOWAY sang as chorus girls dressed as cups danced around him. Also on hand were Bela Lugosi (as a Russian delegate), Peggy Hopkins Joyce, FRANKLIN PANGBORN, Lumsden Hare, and CAB CALLOWAY, whose rendition of "Reefer Man" is not easily forgotten.

INVITATION TO THE DANCE (MGM 1956) was clearly a labor of love on the part of GENE KELLY, who directed, choreographed, and danced in it. But the studio was less in love with the artsy film and delayed releasing it for four years. The movie had no dialogue or songs but premiered three ballets meant to expose the public to classical and modern dance. The resulting product has moments of both brilliance and pretentiousness but is rarely dull. In "Circus," with music by Jacques Ibert, Kelly played a tight-rope-walking Pierrot who falls to his death when his beloved (Claire Sombert) forsakes him for another. "Ring Around the Rosie" was the most satisfying ballet, with ANDRÉ PREVIN providing the music for a tale of a bracelet that a husband gives to his wife, who passes it to an artist, and it travels from person to person until a whore completes the circle by giving it to the husband. The final sequence, "Sinbad the Sailor," was set to Rimsky-Korsakov's *Scheherazade* and utilized live action and animation in telling a tale about sailor Kelly, his genie David Kasday, and storyteller Scheherazade (CAROL HANEY). The movie is a one-of-a-kind experience, though few could argue the experience ought to be repeated.

IRENE (1901–1962) was the professional moniker for Irene Lentz, a California dressmaker who was eventually hired by the Hollywood studios to design gowns for their stars. In the 1940s Irene headed the costume department at MGM, but by the end of the decade she founded her own fashion business and left films. She returned to movie design briefly in 1960. Among the many musicals Irene worked on were *FLYING DOWN TO RIO* (1933), *SHALL WE DANCE* (1937), *YOU WERE NEVER LOVELIER* (1942), *CABIN IN THE SKY* (1943), *DuBarry Was a Lady* (1943), *Thousands Cheer* (1943), *ANCHORS AWEIGH* (1945), *ZIEGFELD FOLLIES* (1945), *THE HARVEY GIRLS* (1946), *TILL THE CLOUDS ROLL BY* (1946), *EASTER PARADE* (1948), *THE BARKLEYS OF BROADWAY* (1949), and *NEPTUNE'S DAUGHTER* (1949).

IT HAPPENED IN BROOKLYN (MGM 1947) was a low-budget attempt to cash in on the continuing popularity of FRANK SINATRA, yet the modest film has some bountiful pleasures. GI Sinatra returns home to Brooklyn after the war to fall hopelessly in love with music teacher KATHRYN GRAYSON, but he loses her to composer PETER LAWFORD. It didn't seem fair, but Sinatra got to sing the beguiling SAMMY CAHN–JULE STYNE ballad "Time After Time" and it became one of his biggest hits, so everything worked out fine. Sinatra also got to join school janitor JIMMY DURANTE in "The Song's Gotta Come From the Heart" and "I Believe," paid tribute to his home with "Brooklyn Bridge," and pleased the customers in a music store by swinging to "It's the Same Old Dream." Perhaps Sinatra went one song too many when he and Grayson performed a duet from Mozart's *Don Giovanni*, but his many fans were very forgiving and the picture was a hit.

IT'S ALWAYS FAIR WEATHER (MGM 1955) may have resembled a sequel to *ON THE TOWN* (1949), but this cynical and even bitter musical had nothing to do with the earlier film's wartime optimism. Three soldiers and close friends (GENE KELLY, MICHAEL KIDD, and DAN DAILEY) agree at the end of the war to meet in ten years' time to see how they are getting on. Their reunion reveals that they no longer feel any comradeship and are even annoyed with each other. Their animosity is heightened when television coordinator CYD CHARISSE puts the three men on a local interview program, hosted by the phony DOLORES GRAY. But when Kelly is hunted down by a crooked boxing promoter, the old friends gang together once more. BETTY COMDEN and ADOLPH GREEN wrote the screenplay and the songs with ANDRÉ PREVIN, very few of which seemed to fit into the story but were wonderful all the same. The male trio danced down the street with trash can lids on their feet and were seen in split screen singing "Once Upon a Time," Charisse sang "Baby, You Knock Me Out" to a gym full of pugilists, Gray stopped the show with the satiric "Thanks a Lot but No Thanks" and noted "Music Is Better Than Words," and Kelly roller-skated down Broadway proclaiming "I Like Myself." STANLEY DONAN and Kelly directed and choreographed together, their last teaming before going separate ways.

ITURBI, JOSÉ (1895–1980), the classical conductor and pianist, added a touch of class to seven movie musicals, always playing himself either in a guest spot or as part of the plot. The Spanish-born Iturbi performed as a child and, after coming to America in 1929, became a respected symphony conductor. His film appearances were in *Thousands Cheer* (1943), *TWO GIRLS AND A SAILOR* (1944), *Music for Millions* (1944), *ANCHORS AWEIGH* (1945), *Holiday in Mexico* (1946), *Three Darling Daughters* (1948), and *That Midnight Kiss* (1949). It is believed that Iturbi's musical sequences in these movies helped popularize classical music in America. When he did the piano dubbing for the Chopin film bio *A Song to Remember* (1945), Iturbi's recording of the "Polonaise in A Flat" sold over a million copies.

J

JAILHOUSE ROCK (MGM 1957) was ELVIS PRESLEY's third film and one of his better efforts as he played an ex-con who rises to the top of the rock-and-roll industry with the help (and love) of Judy Tyler. As rags-to-riches tales go, it wasn't very unique but Presley got to play a more complex character (fame starts to destroy the young star) than he was usually handed. MIKE STOLLER and JERRY LEIBER wrote the songs, the best three being the confessional love song "(You're So Square), Baby, I Don't Care," the pleading "Treat Me Nice," and the propulsive title number that went to the top of the charts.

JAMES, HARRY (1916–1983), perhaps the finest trumpeter of the Big Band era, played in BENNY GOODMAN's orchestra and appeared with them in the musical *HOLLYWOOD HOTEL* (1937). In 1939 James formed his own band and it quickly became one of the hottest groups in the country, selling millions of records. He usually played his trumpet in his dozen film musicals, often with his band, and occasionally as a character. James' film credits include *Private Buckaroo* (1942), *SPRINGTIME IN THE ROCKIES* (1942), *Syncopation* (1942), *BEST FOOT FORWARD* (1943), *TWO GIRLS AND A SAILOR* (1944), *Carnegie Hall* (1950), *The Opposite Sex* (1956), and *The Ladies' Man* (1961). He dubbed the trumpet playing for Kirk Douglas in *YOUNG MAN WITH A HORN* (1950) and played himself in *The Benny Goodman Story* (1955). James was married to BETTY GRABLE.

JAZZ SINGER, THE (Warner-Vitaphone 1927) is commonly known as the first talking feature film, but in truth, it is a silent movie with sound added for the songs only. AL JOLSON does tell the patrons in a San Francisco night spot "Wait a minute! Wait a minute! You ain't heard nothin yet!" before he breaks into "Toot, Toot, Tootsie," and there is a lovely section when Jolson ad-libs some words of affection to his mother (Eugenie Besserer) while he sits at the piano and sings "Blue Skies." The nearly bankrupt WARNER BROTHERS gambled a lot on making the movie, but they hedged their bets by keeping it a silent weeper. Movie audiences had little interest in hearing actors talk in films, but the novelty of hearing them sing was something different. The feature was an immediate hit, changed the course of film history, and introduced the movie musical. The story stuck fairly closely to the 1925 Broadway play by SAMSON RAPHAELSON: Young Jakie Rabinowitz (Bobby Gordon), the son of a cantor (Warner Oland) in Manhattan's Lower East Side, loves jazz and upsets his parents by running off to become a professional singer. Grown up and on the verge of success (helped by the loving attention of May McAvoy), Jack Robin (Jolson), as he now bills himself, is about to premiere on Broadway but, hearing that his father is dying, returns to the local synagogue and sings the Yom Kippur service in the old man's place. Unlike the play, the scene then jumps to the future when Jack is a star and is singing "My Mammy" to his mother in the audience. Although much of the film is dated, there are still marvelous things to enjoy: director Alan Crosland's location footage of New York to set up the world Jakie comes from, the backstage milieu handled with tawdry realism, and Jolson's magnetic performance. The songs used were already familiar ("My Gal Sal," "Dirty Hands, Dirty Face," and those already mentioned), but GRANT CLARKE, Louis Silvers, and Jolson wrote the southern-style ballad "Mother of Mine, I Still Have You," which Jolson (in blackface) sang at a rehearsal while his mother watched tearfully from the wings. It has the distinction of being the first song ever written for a film musical. Warner remade *The Jazz Singer* in 1953 with DANNY THOMAS as the son of cantor Eduard Franz, who returns home from the Korean War and decides to go into show business. This time it was PEGGY LEE who provided the love and support, and again Jerry Golding (as he was called this time) went to the synagogue at the last moment. The songs were mostly recognized standards ("Birth of the Blues," "Just One of Those Things," "Lover," "I'll String Along With You"), which LeROY PRINZ staged in a very contemporary way. But the material was as sentimental as before and seemed less palatable in the 1950s, so the film did only marginal business. A third version of *The Jazz Singer* (EMI 1980) updated the story once again with Jess Rabinovitch (Neil Diamond) forsaking his cantor father LAURENCE OLIVIER for show business, but this time the old man finally accepts his son's calling and is seen at a rock concert cheering the boy on. Much of it was embarrassing (Olivier's hammy performance was the laugh of the industry), but Diamond had natural charisma and some of the songs, by Diamond and associates, were enjoyed by audiences. ("Love on the Rocks" and "America" were both on the charts.) As a tribute to the film's legacy, the screenwriters had Diamond don blackface in one number. The young audiences that the film attracted could hardly understand the connection.

JEAN, GLORIA (1926–), a singer in vaudeville and on radio as a child, was signed up by UNIVERSAL to play the teenage roles that DEANNA DURBIN was outgrowing. The cheery, wholesome Jean enjoyed some popularity in 1940s musicals but was dropped by audiences and the studios when she reached adulthood. Among her twenty films were *The Underpup* (1939), *If I Had My Way* (1940), *What's Cookin'?* (1942), *Moonlight in Vermont* (1943), *Follow the Boys* (1944), *Ghost Catchers* (1944), *I Remember April* (1945), *Copacabana* (1947), and *Manhattan Angel* (1949).

JESSEL, GEORGE (1898–1981), labeled America's "Toastmaster General" for his many benefit speaking engagements, appeared in vaudeville, in silent movies, on Broadway, in talkies and nightclubs, and on the radio and television, usually chomping on a cigar and telling stories. Jessel starred in *The Jazz Singer* on Broadway in 1925 but opted not to do the film version two years later. But when talkies looked as if they were here to stay, he went to Hollywood and was featured in the musicals *Lucky Boy* (1929), *Love, Live and Laugh* (1929), *STAGE DOOR CANTEEN* (1943), *Four Jills and a Jeep* (1944), *Beau James* (1957), and *Juke Box Rhythm* (1959). Jessel was also a songwriter on occasion and in the 1940s a successful film producer, presenting mostly period musicals such as *THE DOLLY SISTERS* (1945), *I Wonder Who's Kissing Her Now* (1947), *When My Baby Smiles at Me* (1948), *Oh, You Beautiful Doll* (1949), *Dancing in the Dark* (1949), *The Golden Girl* (1951), *The I-Don't-Care Girl* (1953), and others.

JESUS CHRIST SUPERSTAR (Universal 1973) approached the filming of a rock opera (that had started as an album and then a concert piece) with a play-within-a-play premise, the actors disembarking from a bus in the desert and telling the story of Jesus' last days as a kind of outdoor pageant. Filming on location in Israel, director Norman Jewison and choreographer Robert Iscove found clever ways to keep the visuals lively. Ted Neeley played Jesus, Carl Anderson his nemesis Judas, Yvonne Elliman the heartbroken Mary Magdalene, Barry Dennen the affected Pontius Pilate, and Josh Mostel the screaming King Herod. TIM RICE and Andrew Lloyd Webber's sung-through score was pretty much intact, the highlights being "What's the Buzz?," "Hosanna," "I Don't Know How to Love Him," "Everything's Alright," and "Superstar."

JOHNSON, CHIC. See Olsen and Johnson

JOHNSON, VAN (1916–), a heartthrob of the bobbysoxers in the 1940s, was so enamored for his boyish good looks that he was dubbed the "Voiceless Sinatra." Johnson was rarely given challenging acting roles and his singing talents were minor, but he projected a warm boy-next-door persona and handled light comedy well. After his film debut as a student in *TOO MANY GIRLS*

(1944), Johnson was featured in *TWO GIRLS AND A SAILOR* (1944), *Thrill of a Romance* (1945), *No Leave, No Love* (1946), *TILL THE CLOUDS ROLL BY* (1946), *IN THE GOOD OLD SUMMERTIME* (1949), *Easy to Love* (1953), *BRIGADOON* (1955), and others. In the 1960s Johnson returned to the stage and television and was rarely in films after 1970.

JOHNSTON, ARTHUR (1898–1954) was a Tin Pan Alley and film composer who, working with various lyricists, wrote such hits as "Pennies From Heaven," "Cocktails for Two," and "My Old Flame." Most of Johnston's movie scores were written with lyricist SAM COSLOW, including *Hello, Everybody* (1933), *College Humor* (1933), *Too Much Harmony* (1933), *MURDER AT THE VANITIES* (1934), and *Belle of the Nineties* (1934). With GUS KAHN he wrote songs for *The Girl Friend* (1935) and *THANKS A MILLION* (1935), and with JOHNNY BURKE, *Go West Young Man* (1936), *PENNIES FROM HEAVEN* (1936), and *DOUBLE OR NOTHING* (1937).

JOHNSTON, JOHNNY (1915–1996), a band singer from radio who appeared in a half dozen Hollywood musicals, is mostly remembered for introducing "That Old Black Magic" in *STAR SPANGLED RHYTHM* (1942). His other film credits were *Sweater Girl* (1942), *Priorities on Parade* (1942), *You Can't Ration Love* (1944), *This Time for Keeps* (1946), and *Rock Around the Clock* (1956). Johnston returned to nightclubs and the Broadway stage in the 1950s.

JOKER IS WILD, THE (AMBL/Paramount 1957) was a downbeat BIOGRAPHICAL MUSICAL about singer-turned-comic Joe E. Lewis that afforded FRANK SINATRA one of the best roles of his career. During Prohibition, crooner Lewis decides to leave one mobster's nightclub to work for a rival hood. But one night he is attacked by the mob and his vocal cords are so damaged that he cannot sing again. So he becomes a stand-up comic, making jokes about his alcohol and gambling addiction. Sinatra, who knew Lewis personally, found a harsh and gritty reality in the character that, as unlikable as he was, was fascinating. Eddie Albert was Lewis' longtime friend and accompanist, JEANNE CRAIN played a Chicago socialite, and MITZI GAYNOR a showgirl, both of whom Lewis weds and divorces, never willing to give either his love. Ironically, the hit song from the film, SAMMY CAHN and JAMES VAN HEUSEN's "All the Way," was about the kind of affection Lewis was not capable of. The film was not a success at the box office, but the song was one of Sinatra's biggest sellers; when the movie was later reissued, it was called *All the Way*.

JOLSON, AL (1886–1950) was already one of Broadway's biggest stars when he made motion picture history starring as the cantor's son Jakie Rabinowitz in *THE JAZZ SINGER* (1927) and introducing audiences to the glory of musical film. The Russian-born Jolson worked in circuses and vaudeville before becoming a Broadway sensation, captivating audiences with his vigorous singing, bubbling personality, and no-holds-barred emotions. Although he filmed two of his stage hits, *Big Boy* (1930) and *WONDER BAR* (1934), his best film roles were those written directly for the screen: *THE SINGING FOOL* (1928), *Say It With Songs* (1929), *Mammy* (1930), *HALLELUJAH, I'M A BUM* (1933), *GO INTO YOUR DANCE* (1935), *The Singing Kid* (1936), *ROSE OF WASHINGTON SQUARE* (1939), and *Swanee River* (1939). Jolson's popularity on the screen waned during the early 1940s, though he was a favorite entertaining American troops overseas, and he played himself in a cameo in the GEORGE GERSHWIN musical bio *RHAPSODY IN BLUE* (1945). But the release of the BIOGRAPHICAL MUSICAL of his life, *THE JOLSON STORY* (1946), in which he dubbed the singing for LARRY PARKS, endeared Jolson to a new generation. He also did the singing for the sequel *JOLSON SINGS AGAIN* (1949), which was released after his death. Jolson's performing style was so big and overwhelming that many felt his film roles could not match his stage performances. But the vibrancy of one who many felt was the entertainer of the century is captured on film, and it was that charisma that helped launch the movie musical. Jolson was married to RUBY KEELER.

JOLSON SINGS AGAIN. See *The Jolson Story*

JOLSON STORY, THE (Columbia 1946) was one of the most popular BIO-GRAPHICAL MUSICALS ever made, and even though it was filled with clichés and untruths, it was a solid piece of entertainment. LARRY PARKS played the great entertainer (the sixty-year-old Jolson supplied the singing on the soundtrack), WILLIAM DEMAREST was the man who discovered him in vaudeville and stuck with him, and Evelyn Keyes was his showgirl wife RUBY KEELER (though she was called Julie Benson in the movie to keep Keeler from suing). The plot was closer to *THE JAZZ SINGER* (1927) than Jolson's real story, but that's the way audiences wanted it. Young Asa Yoelson (Scotty Beckett) runs away from his cantor father Ludwig Donath, changes his name to Jolson, and becomes a star when he dons blackface and learns to go down on one knee. He weds Julie but she yearns for a home life and convinces him to retire. But the urge to perform is too great within him and his audience comes first; the marriage breaks up and Jolson becomes a bigger star than ever. The real Jolson's egotism came across as enthusiasm and love for his public in the screenplay, and the fading entertainer found a whole new audience to love him back. Jolson's catalog of song favorites was used unsparingly, including "Toot Toot Tootsie," "You Made Me Love You," "Rock-a-Bye Your Baby With a Dixie Melody," "I'm Sitting on Top of the World," and, of course, "Swanee." There was only one new number in the score, "Anniversary Song" by Jolson and SAUL CHAPLIN based on an old waltz tune, which Jolson/Parks sang to his parents; the Jolson recording sold over a million disks. With the film making $8 million at the box office, COLUMBIA released a sequel, *JOLSON SINGS AGAIN*, in 1949 and, though not as accomplished, it also was a hit. Parks again played Jolson (with the real Jolson again providing the singing) as he goes off to entertain the troops in World War Two, suffers a physical collapse, is cared for and brought back to health by nurse Barbara Hale (whom he later marries), and makes a big comeback at a Hollywood benefit show. It was no more truthful than the first film, but neither was it as engaging. The musical numbers remained the highlights, repeating some favorites from the original and adding plenty more. The most bizarre scene in the movie is when Jolson hears of the film they are making of his life and he goes to meet the actor who will portray him, with Parks playing both roles thanks to double exposure.

JONES, ALLAN (1907–1992) worked in the coal mines of Pennsylvania to earn money to study voice and found some success on the stage before going to Hollywood in the mid-1930s and becoming a tenor favorite in OPERETTAS and musicals. After his debut in *Reckless* (1935), Jones played the romantic leading man in *A NIGHT AT THE OPERA* (1935), *ROSE MARIE* (1936), *SHOW BOAT* (1936), *A DAY AT THE RACES* (1937), and *THE FIREFLY* (1937), where he sang "The Donkey Serenade," which became his signature song throughout his long career. Jones remained a staple in musicals at MGM and UNIVERSAL throughout the war years, featured in *Everybody Sing* (1938), *The Great Victor Herbert* (1939), *The Boys From Syracuse* (1940), *ONE NIGHT IN THE TROPICS* (1940), *True to the Army* (1942), *Moonlight in Havana* (1942), *Rhythm of the Islands* (1943), *Sing a Jingle* (1944), and *Honeymoon Ahead* (1945). With his movie vehicles decreasing in quality and popularity, Jones returned to the stage and nightclubs and performed for another thirty years, only returning to the musical film for *A Swingin' Summer* (1965). He was the father of singer Jack Jones.

JONES, SHIRLEY (1934–   ) made her film debut in the much-coveted role of Laurey in *OKLAHOMA!* (1955), followed immediately by another RODGERS and HAMMERSTEIN heroine, Julie Jordan in *CAROUSEL* (1956). After playing Liz, the girl next door, in *April Love* (1957), the good wife Linda battling JAMES CAGNEY in *Never Steal Anything Small* (1959), and dancer Suzie Murphy in *Pepe* (1960), Jones found her best musical role as Marian Paroo, the small-town librarian in *THE MUSIC MAN* (1962). Thereafter she concentrated on dramatic roles, stage musicals, nightclubs, and television (*The Partridge Family*). Jones possesses a rich soprano voice bordering on the Broadway belter but was able to successfully modify her performances for the screen. She was married to stage actor Jack Cassidy and is the mother of actor Shaun Cassidy and the stepmother of singer David Cassidy.

JOY OF LIVING (RKO 1938) was a screwball comedy with music in which the songs turned out better than the comic plot. Broadway star IRENE

DUNNE is too uptight to enjoy life, though her wacky relatives and other parasites are sure having a great time. It takes Boston banking heir Douglas Fairbanks, Jr., to teach the star to live by doing Donald Duck impressions, taking her to a beer hall and a skating ring, and whisking her off to a South Seas island. DOROTHY FIELDS and JEROME KERN wrote the songs, the best three being the swinging lullaby "You Couldn't Be Cuter," the farewell ballad "What's Good About Goodnight?," and the flowing "Just Let Me Look at You," which was used throughout the film as a leitmotif. The supporting cast read like a who's who of favorite character actors: GUY KIBBEE, LUCILLE BALL, ALICE BRADY, ERIC BLORE, BILLY GILBERT, FRANKLIN PANGBORN, MISCHA AUER, FUZZY KNIGHT, Jean Dixon, and Warren Hymer. They all deserved a better script.

JUMBO (MGM 1962) was made twenty-seven years after the Broadway original, and it lost much of its plot and some of its RODGERS and HART songs over the years. JIMMY DURANTE owns a nearly bankrupt circus whose only attraction is the elephant Jumbo. Rival circus owner Dean Jagger sends his son Stephen Boyd (singing dubbed by James Joyce) to infiltrate and sabotage Durante's circle, but instead he falls in love with the owner's daughter DORIS DAY. After some circus acts and great tunes like "The Most Beautiful Girl in the World" and "My Romance" (as well as some numbers borrowed from other Rodgers and Hart shows), Boyd gets Day, MARTHA RAYE snags Durante after years of trying, and they all imagine a sparkling new circus as they sing "Sawdust, Spangles and Dreams" by ROGER EDENS. Durante was never funnier, and BUSBY BERKELEY staged some of the musical numbers with panache; it was the last movie musical for both of them.

JUNGLE BOOK, THE (Disney 1967) was the last animated film that WALT DISNEY produced, and it was one of the most musical of all his features, the songs by Terry Gilkyson and RICHARD M. and ROBERT B. SHERMAN becoming the movie's highlights instead of pleasing diversions along the way. Loosely based on Rudyard Kipling's *Mowgli* stories, the simple story tells about the "man-cub" Mowgli (voice of Bruce Reitherman) who is orphaned in the jungle and raised by the panther Bagheera (Sebastian Cabot). But when the deadly tiger Shere Khan (George Sanders) returns to the jungle, Bagheera must convince Baloo the Bear (PHIL HARRIS) to escort the boy back to the "man-village." The journey is pleasantly interrupted by wonderful vaudeville turns, such as Harris cutting loose with "The Bare Necessities" and King Louis of the Apes (Louis Prima) going wild with "I Wanna Be Like You." J. Pat O'Malley, STERLING HOLLOWAY, Verna Felton, Chad Stuart, Lord Tim Abbott, and Ben Wright also loaned their voices for the brusque "Colonel Hati's March," the slithering "Trust in Me, " and the harmonizing "That's What Friends Are For." Directed by Wolfgang Reitherman, it was also one of the most painterly of Disney's later efforts, richly illustrated and beautifully animated.

K

KAHAL, IRVING (1903–1942) was a Tin Pan Alley lyricist who contributed songs to five movie musicals, all with composer SAMMY FAIN: *Young Man of Manhattan* (1930), *FOOTLIGHT PARADE* (1933), *College Coach* (1933), *Harold Teen* (1934), and *Sweet Music* (1935). Among Kahal's many hit songs were "Wedding Bells Are Breaking Up That Old Gang of Mine," "I'll Be Seeing You," and "Let a Smile Be Your Umbrella."

KAHN, GUS (1886–1941), a popular lyricist on Broadway and Tin Pan Alley, wrote songs for eighteen movie musicals with such composers as WALTER DONALDSON, VINCENT YOUMANS, ARTHUR JOHNSTON, WALTER JURMANN, and others. Kahn's only Broadway show to be filmed was *WHOOPEE* (1930), but he made his name in Hollywood contributing songs to such films as *FLYING DOWN TO RIO* (1933), *KID MILLIONS* (1934), *NAUGHTY MARIETTA* (1935), *THANKS A MILLION* (1935), *Three Smart Girls* (1937), *A DAY AT THE RACES* (1937), *Everybody Sing* (1938), *Honolulu* (1939), *Broadway Serenade* (1939), *Go West* (1940), and *ZIEGFELD GIRL* (1941). DANNY THOMAS played Kahn in the BIOGRAPHICAL MUSICAL of his life *I'll See You in My Dreams* (1951), titled after one of his many hit songs. Other standards by Kahn include "Love Me or Leave Me," "Ain't We Got Fun?," "Pretty Baby," "It Had to Be You," and "Yes Sir, That's My Baby."

KALMAR, BERT (1884–1947) was one of Broadway and Hollywood's most reliable lyricists for comedy songs and scripts, usually writing with composer HARRY RUBY. Of their nine Broadway shows, *The Cuckoos* (1930), which was called *The Ramblers* on stage, *ANIMAL CRACKERS* (1930), and *Top Speed* (1930) were filmed. Kalmar and Ruby stayed in Hollywood for most of the 1930s and contributed songs and often screenplays for *Check and Double Check* (1930), *HORSE FEATHERS* (1932), *The Kid From Spain* (1932),

DUCK SOUP (1933), *Hips Hips Hooray* (1934), *Walking on Air* (1936), *Everybody Sing* (1938), and others. FRED ASTAIRE played Kalmar in the musical bio of his career called *THREE LITTLE WORDS* (1950).

KANDER, JOHN. See Ebb, Fred

KANE, HELEN (1904–1966), the squealing "boop-boop-a-doop" girl who was featured in vaudeville and on Broadway, made a few early talkies but never caught on as she had on stage. The animated little pixie can be seen in *Sweetie* (1929), *Pointed Heels* (1929), *PARAMOUNT ON PARADE* (1930), *Heads Up* (1930), and *Dangerous Nan McGrew* (1930). DEBBIE REYNOLDS played Kane in the musical bio *THREE LITTLE WORDS* (1950), but Kane herself provided the vocals when Reynolds sang her signature song "I Wanna Be Loved By You."

KAPER, BRONISLAW (1902–1983) had already found success writing concert music and scoring films in Germany before he immigrated to America in the 1930s. Working with various lyricists, Kaper contributed songs to *A NIGHT AT THE OPERA* (1935), *SAN FRANCISCO* (1936), *Three Smart Girls* (1937), *A DAY AT THE RACES* (1937), *Everybody Sing* (1938), *LILLIAN RUSSELL* (1940), *LILI* (1953), and *The Glass Slipper* (1955). Kaper, whose first name is sometimes spelled Bronislau, also scored many nonmusical movies.

KASZNAR, KURT (1913–1979) was a child performer in his native Vienna and had many stage credits when he was brought to America in 1937 with Max Reinhardt's acting company. Kasznar soon developed into a favorite character actor on stage and screen, often playing eccentric and colorful European types. Among his movie musical appearances were *LOVELY TO LOOK AT* (1952), *LILI* (1953), *KISS ME, KATE* (1953), *GIVE A GIRL A BREAK* (1953), *My Sister Eileen* (1955), *ANYTHING GOES* (1956), and *For the First Time* (1959).

KAYE, DANNY (1913–1987), the beloved comic who made his name on Broadway and then conquered films, radio, nightclubs, and television, was a favorite with American and British audiences for forty years. The thin, physical actor-singer could light up like a cartoon character, squeeze pathos out of a situation, and rattle off words in a Gilbert and Sullivan-like patter. After becoming a star overnight in the Broadway musical *Lady in the Dark* (1940), Kaye was brought to Hollywood by SAMUEL GOLDWYN who starred the comic in a series of tailor-made musicals. He usually played the meek everyman who rises to the occasion and often gets the girl. *UP IN ARMS* (1944) was his film debut, followed by *Wonder Man* (1945), *The Kid From Brooklyn* (1946), *The Secret Life of Walter Mitty* (1947), *A Song Is Born* (1948), *It's a Great Feeling*

(1949), *The Inspector General* (1949), *ON THE RIVIERA* (1951), *HANS CHRISTIAN ANDERSEN* (1952), *Knock on Wood* (1954), *WHITE CHRIST- MAS* (1954), *THE COURT JESTER* (1956), *Merry Andrew* (1958), *THE FIVE PENNIES* (1959), and *On the Double* (1961). In the 1960s Kay concentrated on charitable causes and personal appearances in concert and on television. He was married to songwriter Sylvia Fine.

KAYE, STUBBY (1918–1997), a rotund character actor who performed on Broadway in several musical and comedy hits, is best remembered on film for recreating two of his stage roles: the bookie Nicely-Nicely Johnson in *GUYS AND DOLLS* (1955) and the preacher Marryin' Sam in *LI'L ABNER* (1959). Kaye appeared in a handful of Hollywood comedies and was also featured in the musical *SWEET CHARITY* (1969).

KEEL, HOWARD (1917–), one of Hollywood's favorite leading men in 1950s musicals, excelled at playing robust, full-voiced heroes, often with a roguish twinkle in his eye. Keel made his film debut playing sharpshooter Frank Butler in *ANNIE GET YOUR GUN* (1950) and would later portray other leads in film versions of Broadway hits: gambler Gaylord Ravenal in *SHOW BOAT* (1951), egotistical actor Fred Graham in *KISS ME, KATE* (1953), dashing Sgt. Mike Malone in *ROSE MARIE* (1954), and the wily poet Hajj in *KISMET* (1955). The masculine baritone was also seen as Tahiti plantation owner Hazard Endicott in *Pagan Love Song* (1950), Texan rancher Slim Shelby in *Texas Carnival* (1951), would-be producer Tony Naylor in *LOVELY TO LOOK AT* (1952), outdoorsman Bill Hickock in *CALAMITY JANE* (1953), backwoodsman Adam Pontipee in *SEVEN BRIDES FOR SEVEN BROTHERS* (1954), and the conqueror Hannibal in *Jupiter's Darling* (1955), as well as specialties in *I Love Melvin* (1952) and *DEEP IN MY HEART* (1954). Keel returned to the stage and nightclubs in the 1960s and was a regular on television in the 1980s.

KEELER, RUBY (1909–1993) was the reigning ingenue in 1930s WARNER BROTHERS' musicals, often paired with DICK POWELL and usually going on stage at the last minute for an ailing actress and becoming a star. Keeler's innocent face, sweet but thin singing voice, and heavy-handed tap dancing techniques thrilled Depression audiences whether she was teamed with Powell, JAMES CAGNEY, or AL JOLSON. Working her way up from the Broadway chorus to featured player, Keeler went to Hollywood with Jolson (then her husband) and made her film debut in a bit part in *Show Girl* (1930). But her next role, the starry-eyed Peggy Sawyer in *42ND STREET* (1933), endeared her to the public, and she did slight variations of the same character in *GOLD DIGGERS OF 1933*, *FOOTLIGHT PARADE* (1933), *DAMES* (1934), *Flirtation Walk* (1934), *GO INTO YOUR DANCE* (1935), *Shipmates Forever* (1935), *Colleen* (1936), *Ready, Willing and Able* (1937), and *Sweetheart of the Campus* (1941). Keeler retired in 1941 and faded from the public eye, but a revival of interest in the old Warner musicals in the 1960s encouraged her to make guest appearances and return to Broadway in a revival of *No No Nanette* (1970).

KELLY, GENE (1912–1996), one of the giants of the musical film and perhaps its most experimental dancer, choreographer, and director, revitalized the genre in the 1940s by finding new ways to portray dance on the screen. Kelly worked his way up from Broadway chorus jobs to the leading role in *Pal Joey* (1940) and choreographer for *Best Foot Forward* (1941). His first film role, the over-ambitious hoofer Harry Palmer in *FOR ME AND MY GAL* (1942), revealed a bold and athletic approach to performing that contrasted nicely with the more debonair style popularized by FRED ASTAIRE. Kelly assisted in the choreography of all his films, and by 1949 he was often the co-director, usually with STANLEY DONEN. The two men's innovative experiments with montage, animation, split screen, extended ballet sequences, and use of location shooting gave their musicals a unique look and feel. Kelly was also interested in ballet and modern dance, using them in his films with varying success. His other musical credits in the 1940s were *DuBarry Was a Lady* (1943), *Thousands Cheer* (1943), *COVER GIRL* (1944), *ANCHORS AWEIGH* (1945), *Living in a Big Way* (1947), *THE PIRATE* (1948), *TAKE ME OUT TO THE BALL GAME* (1949), and *ON THE TOWN* (1949). Co-directing and/or choreographing as well, Kelly appeared in *SUMMER STOCK* (1950), *AN AMERICAN IN PARIS* (1951), *SINGIN' IN THE RAIN* (1952), *BRIGADOON* (1954), *IT'S ALWAYS FAIR WEATHER* (1955), and *INVITATION TO THE DANCE* (1956). He also made specialty appearances in *ZIEGFELD FOLLIES* (1946), *WORDS AND MUSIC* (1948), and *DEEP IN MY HEART* (1954). By the mid-1950s Kelly made fewer films and usually only performed, as in *LES GIRLS* (1957), *Let's Make Love* (1960), *What a Way to Go* (1964), and *The Young Girls of Rochefort* (1967). He did return to directing with *HELLO, DOLLY!* (1969) and made many television appearances in his later career. Kelly's last singing-dancing role on screen was the aging hoofer Danny McGuire in the disco musical *Xanadu* (1980).

KELLY, PATSY (1910–1981) was a favorite comedienne on Broadway and the screen, usually playing wisecracking servants, secretaries, and best friends of the heroine. After being featured in several Broadway musicals, Kelly made her film debut in *GOING HOLLYWOOD* (1933), followed by *GO INTO YOUR DANCE* (1935), *EVERY NIGHT AT EIGHT* (1935), *THANKS A MILLION* (1935), *Sing, Baby, Sing* (1936), *Pigskin Parade* (1936), *WAKE UP AND LIVE* (1937), *Hit Parade of 1941* (1940), *Road Show* (1941), *Playmates* (1941), and others. After retiring from films in the 1940s, Kelly returned to Hollywood in the 1960s and played character roles in comedies. She made a triumphant return to Broadway in the 1970s playing supporting roles in the revivals of *No No Nanette* (1970) and *Irene* (1973).

KENNEDY, EDGAR (1890–1948) was one of Hollywood's busiest character actors, perfecting his "slow burn" reaction to others before exploding in frustration. Kennedy started in the silents, appearing in Keystone Kops and LAUREL and HARDY comedies before sound came in, and then moved into features. His thirty-year film career included such musicals as *DUCK SOUP* (1933), *KID MILLIONS* (1934), *SAN FRANCISCO* (1936), *HOLLYWOOD HOTEL* (1937), *ANCHORS AWEIGH* (1945), and *My Dream Is Yours* (1939).

KERN, JEROME (1885–1945), the pioneering American composer who brought a sophisticated sense of melody and harmony to the Broadway musical, saw nine of his many stage works filmed: *Sally* (1929), *SHOW BOAT* (1929, 1936, and 1951), *SWEET ADELINE* (1935), *THE CAT AND THE FIDDLE* (1934), *MUSIC IN THE AIR* (1934), *ROBERTA* (1935), which was remade as *LOVELY TO LOOK AT* (1952), *Sunny* (1941), and *Broadway Rhythm* (1944), based on his Broadway show *Very Warm for May* (1939). Kern often contributed revised or new songs for the film versions of his plays and then later settled in Hollywood, where he wrote original scores for movie musicals, working with various lyricists. With DOROTHY FIELDS he wrote *I DREAM TOO MUCH* (1935), *SWING TIME* (1936), *JOY OF LIVING* (1938), and *ONE NIGHT IN THE TROPICS* (1940), as well as additions to *LOVELY TO LOOK AT* (1952). With OSCAR HAMMERSTEIN, IRA GERSHWIN, JOHNNY MERCER, and others Kern penned songs for *HIGH, WIDE AND HANDSOME* (1937), *YOU WERE NEVER LOVELIER* (1942), *COVER GIRL* (1944), *CAN'T HELP SINGING* (1944), and *CENTENNIAL SUMMER* (1946), which was released after his death. Robert Walker played Kern in the BIOGRAPHICAL MUSICAL of his career called *TILL THE CLOUDS ROLL BY* (1946).

KIBBEE, GUY (1882–1956) was a paunchy character actor who specialized in cheerful millionaires and crafty civic leaders. After a career on the stage, he went to Hollywood in 1930 and appeared in dozens of comedies, action pictures, and musicals. Kibbee's movie musicals include *42ND STREET* (1933), *GOLD DIGGERS OF 1933, FOOTLIGHT PARADE* (1933), *WONDER BAR* (1934), *DAMES* (1934), *CAPTAIN JANUARY* (1936), *JOY OF LIVING* (1938), *BABES IN ARMS* (1939), and *Girl Crazy* (1943).

KID MILLIONS (Goldwyn/United Artists 1934) was one of EDDIE CANTOR's best vehicles, a frolic about an archeologist's son (Cantor) who inherits $77 million and is chased all the way to Egypt by con men out to fleece him of his dough. The plot may have resembled a two-reeler comedy, but no expense was spared, and the musical numbers, as directed by ROY DEL RUTH and choreographed by SEYMOUR FELIX, were lavish and playful. Cantor got to sing IRVING BERLIN's "Mandy" in blackface as part of a minstrel show on board ship, the NICHOLAS BROTHERS cut loose with "I Want to Be a Minstrel Man" by HAROLD ADAMSON and BURTON LANE, who also wrote the hit ballad "Your Head on My Shoulder" sung by the young lovers ANN SOTHERN and GEORGE MURPHY (in his screen debut). ETHEL MERMAN played Cantor's mother (even though she was seventeen years his junior) and belted out Berlin's "An Earful of Music." She was also featured in the Technicolor finale, "Ice Cream Fantasy" by GUS KAHN and WALTER DONALDSON, set in a Brooklyn ice cream factory.

KIDD, MICHAEL (1919–   ) choreographed several notable films near the end of the golden age of Hollywood musicals, most memorably *THE BAND WAGON* (1953) and *SEVEN BRIDES FOR SEVEN BROTHERS* (1954). Kidd was a ballet dancer before getting a name as a Broadway choreographer in the late 1940s. His first film assignment was *Where's Charley?* (1952), followed by *The Girl Next Door* (1953), *Knock on Wood* (1954), *IT'S ALWAYS FAIR WEATHER* (1955), in which he played one of the major characters, *GUYS AND DOLLS* (1955), which he had choreographed on Broadway, *Merry Andrew* (1958), which he also directed, *STAR!* (1968), *HELLO, DOLLY!* (1969), and *MOVIE MOVIE* (1978). Kidd's choreography was known for its robust and athletic character, usually favoring vigorous male dancers.

KING AND I, THE (Fox 1956) is arguably the best film made from a RODGERS and HAMMERSTEIN stage musical. Not only was the plot and score kept intact, but the opening up of the scenes by screenwriter ERNEST LEHMAN and director WALTER LANG enhanced the exotic tale. YUL BRYNNER got to repeat his towering performance as the King of Siam, who wrestles with his monarchy in an age of change, and Deborah Kerr (singing dubbed by MARNI NIXON) was both distant and warm as the governess who comes to tutor his many children. RITA MORENO played the concubine who tragically falls for the young Carlos Rivas (singing dubbed by Reuben Fuentes), though their soaring duet "I Have Dreamed" was cut. But what remained were some of Rodgers and Hammerstein's richest and most entrancing songs: "Hello, Young Lovers," "Getting to Know You," "Shall We Dance?," "Something Wonderful," and others. JEROME ROBBINS recreated his Broadway choreography, including the endearing "March of the Siamese Children" and the inventive "Small House of Uncle Thomas" ballet. IRENE SHARAFF was also brought from Broadway to recreate her glittering costumes, with sets by Walter M. Scott and Paul S. Fox that were lavish yet human in scale. The film is a vivid record of a great Broadway musical and a stunning movie in its own right.

KING, CHARLES (1889–1944), a light-footed song-and-dance man from vaudeville and Broadway, played leading roles in three early talkies: song-writer-hoofer Eddie Kerns in *THE BROADWAY MELODY* (1929), touring actor Terry in *Chasing Rainbows* (1930), and American tourist Charlie Carroll in Naples in *Oh, Sailor Behave* (1930). He also did specialty bits in *HOLLY-WOOD REVUE OF 1929* and *MISSISSIPPI* (1935). In his brief film career, King got to introduce two movie musical standards, "You Were Meant for Me" and "Happy Days Are Here Again."

KING CREOLE (Paramount 1958) was an ELVIS PRESLEY vehicle that didn't look or sound like the usual glossy features the star was stuck wit, and he gave his finest performances as a street-smart bus boy in New Orleans who, despite the meddling of some local thugs and suffocating family members, gets to be a singer in a Bourbon Street nightclub. MICHAEL CURTIZ's direction captured the gritty, tawdry milieu (the movie was filmed in black and white) of the French quarter at dawn and behind the scenes of the party hot spots. It probably helped that Presley was surrounded by solid nonmusical actors such as Walter Matthau, Vic Morrow, Dean Jagger, Dolores Hart, and Jan Shepard, who gave tough and honest performances. Carolyn Jones, in one of her best roles, was memorable as the mobster's girlfriend, who falls for Presley even as she belittles him. Even the score was a cut above the usual Presley vehicle. Pushcart peddler Kitty White moaned out the bluesy "Crawfish" (by Fred Wise and Ben Wiseman) at the top of the film, and audiences knew this was not a Las Vegas concert. The same team wrote the torchy rock ballad "Don't Ask Me Why," and JERRY LEIBER and MIKE STOLLER penned the title song, both sung by Presley and both bestsellers. But most satisfying was Claude De Metrius' "Hard Headed Woman" (also a hit), which was heard only briefly off camera.

KING, HENRY (1888–1982), a much-demanded Hollywood director from the silent days, helmed over fifty movies of all genres, from musicals to westerns. King's movie musicals include *I Love You Wednesday* (1933), *Marie Galante* (1934), *Ramona* (1936), *IN OLD CHICAGO* (1938), *ALEXANDER'S RAGTIME BAND* (1938), *Margie* (1946), *Wait Till the Sun Shines, Nellie* (1952), and *CAROUSEL* (1956).

KING OF BURLESQUE (Fox 1935) was a low-budget backstager that concentrated on the characters rather than spectacle and it worked nicely, thanks to a strong cast and superior score. Burlesque entrepreneur WARNER BAXTER wants to get class so he persuades his sweetheart ALICE FAYE and cohort JACK OAKIE to move uptown and try Broadway. In the process he falls for and marries society dame Mona Barrie, so Faye flees to London, where she becomes a star in the West End. When Baxter's big Broadway revue flops, Barrie ditches him and the producer turns to drink. But Faye returns, bankrolls his new nightclub, and all ends happily with a swell show that includes KENNY

BAKER, THOMAS "FATS" WALLER, DIXIE DUNBAR, and others. TED KOEHLER and JIMMY McHUGH wrote most of the score, which included the vibrant "Spreading Rhythm Around," the optimistic "I'm Shooting High," the waltzing "Lovely Lady," and the rhythmic "I've Got My Fingers Crossed." The same plot returned with Faye and Oakie for *HELLO, FRISCO, HELLO* (Fox 1943), a period musical that went to the trunk for song favorites to fill the score. This time JOHN PAYNE, Faye, Oakie, and JUNE HAVOC are entertainers on San Francisco's Barbary Coast with different fates in store. Although Payne loves Faye, he marries the Nob Hill socialite LYNN BARI to get money to open his nightclub, but the marriage is a fiasco and he loses everything. Faye goes to Broadway and the West End again, becomes a star, and then returns to bail out the divorced Payne. The many period songs (including "By the Light of the Silvery Moon," "Has Anyone Here Seen Kelly?," and the title number) and a memorable new one ("You'll Never Know" by MACK GORDON and HARRY WARREN) were beautifully presented by director H. BRUCE HUMBERSTONE and choreographer Val Raset.

KING OF JAZZ (Universal 1930) was an early film REVUE but spectacular by any standards, many of the visuals copied in subsequent movie musicals. The focal point of the jam-packed revue (there were seventy numbers performed in 101 minutes) was PAUL WHITEMAN and his orchestra, the most popular band in America and the custodians of jazz in nightclubs and on records. In one of John Murray Anderson's many inventive staging ideas, Whiteman and his boys performed GEORGE GERSHWIN's "Rhapsody in Blue" atop of a mammoth piano. For "The Melting Pot of Music" sequence, music and performers from eight different countries gathered, all the music coming out of one giant cauldron in the form of jazz. BING CROSBY made his film debut as one of the Rhythm Boys singing "So the Blackbirds and the Blue Birds Got Together" and joined with the Brox Sisters and others for "A Bench in the Park" with couples snuggling on various layers of turf. Other songs by various tunesmiths included "Happy Feet," "It Happened in Monterey," "Mississippi Mud," and "Ragamuffin Romeo."

KINGSLEY, DOROTHY (1909–1997) wrote several screenplays for musicals and light comedies in the 1940s and 1950s, turning to television writing in the 1960s. Among Kingsley's musicals were *Girl Crazy* (1943), *Broadway Rhythm* (1944), *Bathing Beauty* (1944), *A Date With Judy* (1948), *NEPTUNE'S DAUGHTER* (1949), *Texas Carnival* (1951), *Dangerous When Wet* (1953), *KISS ME, KATE* (1953), *SEVEN BRIDES FOR SEVEN BROTHERS* (1954), *Jupiter's Darling* (1955), *PAL JOEY* (1957), *CAN-CAN* (1960), and *Pepe* (1960).

KINSKEY, LEONID (1903–1998), a Russian-born character actor in films from 1932, played eccentric foreign types in such musicals as *DUCK SOUP*

(1933), *Rhythm on the Range* (1936), *Make a Wish* (1937), *The Great Waltz* (1938), *THE STORY OF VERNON AND IRENE CASTLE* (1939), *On Your Toes* (1939), *DOWN ARGENTINE WAY* (1940), *THAT NIGHT IN RIO* (1941), *WEEK-END IN HAVANA* (1941), *I Married an Angel* (1942), *Presenting Lily Mars* (1943), and *CAN'T HELP SINGING* (1944).

KISMET (MGM 1955) was filmed by VINCENTE MINNELLI with a luscious decor that matched its luscious music, but the result lacked the excitement of the 1953 Broadway "Arabian Nights" musical that ROBERT WRIGHT and GEORGE FORREST fashioned using musical themes by Alexander Borodin. HOWARD KEEL played the poet Hajj, who disguises himself as a beggar and enters Baghdad for adventure and romance. He outwits the Wazir (Sebastian Cabot), woos and wins his wife Lalume (DOLORES GRAY), and matches the Wazir's son VIC DAMONE with Hajj's daughter ANN BLYTH. It was all very lush but dull at times, and the sparkling score did not grab audiences as it had in the theatre. The two hits were "Stranger in Paradise" and "Baubles, Bangles and Beads," both choreographed rather routinely by JACK COLE.

KISS ME, KATE (MGM 1953) was COLE PORTER's best Broadway show, and the film version received the best screen treatment his stage works ever got. Samuel and Bella Spewack adapted their stage libretto for the film, keeping the backstage story and the onstage production of *The Taming of the Shrew* distinct and equally entertaining. HOWARD KEEL played the egotistical star (who also plays Petruchio), KATHRYN GRAYSON was his temperamental ex-wife (and his Kate), ANN MILLER was the starlet who performed the sexy Bianca, and TOMMY RALL was her gambling boyfriend. The other stars were choreographer HERMES PAN and dancer BOB FOSSE, who got to stage the "From This Moment On" number, the only one not from the play. The other dance highlights were Miller's rat-tat-tat "Too Darn Hot" and an inspired "Tom, Dick and Harry" with Fosse, Rall, Miller, and BOBBY VAN. Every one of Porter's songs was a gem, and most of them made it to the screen: "Where Is the Life That Late I Led?," "Wunderbar," "Why Can't You Behave?," "So in Love," "Always True to You in My Fashion," and "Brush Up Your Shakespeare." The supporting cast included KURT KASZNAR, CAROL HANEY, KEENAN WYNN, and James Whitmore under the confident direction of GEORGE SIDNEY.

KNIGHT, FUZZY (1901–1976), a character actor who played comic sidekicks in over 200 westerns, began his career as a singer and bandleader in nightclubs and vaudeville, and then appeared in a handful of musicals in the 1930s. Knight's musical credits include *SHE DONE HIM WRONG* (1933), *MUSIC IN THE AIR* (1934), *JOY OF LIVING* (1938), and *SHOW BOAT* (1951).

KOEHLER, TED (1894–1973) was a Tin Pan Alley lyricist who, with composer HAROLD ARLEN, wrote songs for editions of the Cotton Club revues in Manhattan. Koehler moved to Hollywood in the 1930s and, with a variety of composers, scored such musicals as *Let's Fall in Love* (1934), *CURLY TOP* (1935), *KING OF BURLESQUE* (1935), *Dimples* (1936), *ARTISTS AND MODELS* (1937), *STORMY WEATHER* (1943), *UP IN ARMS* (1944), *Rainbow Island* (1944), and *My Wild Irish Rose* (1947). Among Koehler's many song hits were "Animal Crackers in My Soup," "Get Happy," "I Gotta Right to Sing the Blues," and "Stormy Weather."

KOHLMAR, FRED (1905–1969), a Hollywood producer who had started with SAMUEL GOLDWYN, supervised musicals and comedies for different studios during his thirty-year film career. Among Kohlmar's musicals were *Riding High* (1943), *THAT NIGHT IN RIO* (1945), *You Were Meant for Me* (1948), *Call Me Mister* (1951), *Down Among the Sheltering Palms* (1953), *My Sister Eileen* (1955), *PAL JOEY* (1957), and *BYE BYE BIRDIE* (1963).

KOSTER, HENRY (1905–1988), a German filmmaker who immigrated to America in 1933, directed many comedies and musicals, often under producer JOE PASTERNAK, who discovered him. Koster's Hollywood musicals include *Three Smart Girls* (1937), *ONE HUNDRED MEN AND A GIRL* (1937), *Three Smart Girls Grow Up* (1939), *First Love* (1939), *Music for Millions* (1944), *Two Sisters From Boston* (1946), *The Inspector General* (1949), *WABASH AVENUE* (1950), *My Blue Heaven* (1950), *The Stars and Stripes Forever* (1952), *FLOWER DRUM SONG* (1961), and *The Singing Nun* (1966).

KRUPA, GENE (1909–1973), the gum-chewing drummer in BENNY GOODMAN's orchestra who formed his own band in 1938, made specialty appearances as himself in eleven Hollywood musicals, beginning with *THE BIG BROADCAST OF 1937* (1936). Krupa's subsequent films include *Syncopation* (1942), *George White's Scandals* (1945), *Glamour Girl* (1948), *THE GLENN MILLER STORY* (1954), and *The Benny Goodman Story* (1955). Sal Mineo played Krupa in the musical bio *The Gene Krupa Story* (1960), and Krupa himself provided the drum playing on the soundtrack.

KYSER, KAY (1897–1985), a bandleader who became famous on the radio with his program "Kay Kyser's Kollage of Musical Knowledge," was featured with his band in a handful of Hollywood musicals, often playing himself but usually worked into the comic plot instead of just performing specialty numbers. Kyser's films include *That's Right, You're Wrong* (1939), *You'll Find Out* (1940), *Playmates* (1941), *STAGE DOOR CANTEEN* (1943), *Thousands Cheer* (1943), *Swing Fever* (1943), *Carolina Blues* (1944), and others.

L

LA BAMBA (Columbia 1987) was one of the few studio films ever shot in both English and Spanish so as to reach a wide Hispanic audience as well as traditional moviegoers. It was an appropriate move, for the subject of the BIO-GRAPHICAL MUSICAL was young Chicano singer Richie Valens, portrayed by Lou Diamond Phillips, with David Hidalgo dubbing the singing for him. Luis Valdez wrote and directed the film and, as bio pics go, it was one of Hollywood's better efforts. California teenager Valens is discovered while still a student in high school, and he soars to stardom via three hit songs. The conflicts revolved around Valens' difficult relationship with his volatile brother (Esai Morales), and all ends tragically when Valens dies at the age of seventeen in the same plane crash that killed Buddy Holly. The group Los Lobos provided the musical accompaniment for the Valens' favorites: "All My Love, All My Kisses," "Baby, Baby," "Come On, Let's Go," "Little Darlin'," "Saturday Night," and others.

LADY AND THE TRAMP (Disney 1955), though not based on a classic children's tale, immediately became a DISNEY favorite with audiences and has remained so over the decades because of the sharp, truthful characterizations of the title canines and the very human feelings of rejection and love that the film explored. Pampered cocker spaniel Lady (voice of Barbara Luddy) feels on the outs when a new baby in the household usurps her position of spoiled pet. But the outside world is even less accepting of Lady, and only through the wily machinations of the street mutt Tramp (Larry Roberts) does Lady regain her place in the home and find a mate as well. The supporting characters were a colorful crew: the aging bloodhound Trusty (Bill Baucon), the wiry Scottish terrier Jock (Bill Thompson), the sassy, sexy Peg, and two stuck-up Siamese cats (all three voiced by PEGGY LEE). Lee wrote the songs with Sonny Burke, including the sly parody "Siamese Cat Song," the torchy "He's a Tramp," and the romantic ballad "Bella Notte" sung by Italian restauranteer Tony (George Givot) while Lady and the Tramp engage in the most famous spaghetti dinner in filmdom.

LADY SINGS THE BLUES (Paramount 1972) may have distorted more facts than it used, and purist fans of Billie Holiday might be discontented with DIANA ROSS when they could listen to the original Holiday on records, but as BIOGRAPHICAL MUSICALS go it was intriguing as well as entertaining. Following the usual rags-to-riches format that had been working since the 1930s, the film followed young Billie from the streets of Harlem to her triumph at Carnegie Hall, all the time showing her drug addiction, battles with racism while touring the country, and tempestuous relationship with her husband Billy Dee Williams. Holiday's death by a heroin overdose was alluded to in a film montage, another old device that still worked. Richard Pryor was outstanding as Billie's co-addict and friend, and the supporting cast included Sid Melton, James Callahan, Virginia Capers, Paul Hampton, and Scatman Crothers. Ross delivered the Holiday song hits in a smooth, velvety style that sounded more contemporary than the raw, aching voice of Holiday herself, but the old standards were interpreted well, including "Strange Fruit," "Good Morning, Heartache," "The Man I Love," " 'Tain't Nobody's Bizness If I Do," "Lover Man," "God Bless the Child," and the title number.

LAHR, BERT (1895–1967), one of the most inspired clowns in show business, started out in burlesque and never lost his low comedy genius in his subsequent careers on Broadway and in films. Lahr went to Hollywood to recreate his hysterical stage performance as klutzy mechanic Rusty Krause in *Flying High* (1931) and returned often, playing featured roles in *Merry-Go-Round* (1937), *Love and Hisses* (1937), *Josette* (1938), *Just Around the Corner* (1938), and *Zaza* (1939). Lahr's most remembered film role was the Cowardly Lion in *THE WIZARD OF OZ* (1939), followed by vivid performances in *Ship Ahoy* (1942), *Meet the People* (1944), *Always Leave Them Laughing* (1949), *ROSE MARIE* (1954), and *The Second Greatest Sex* (1955). His film career ended the same way his stage career had started, playing a burlesque comic in *The Night They Raided Minsky's* (1968). Except for his Cowardly Lion, Lahr's musical comedy gifts were not fully utilized on screen.

LAINE, FRANKIE (1913–   ), one of America's most popular singers on records and in nightclubs in the late 1940s and 1950s, made a half dozen film musicals. But he never really conquered the screen medium, so he later concentrated on television and personal appearances, lending his smooth singing voice to nonmusicals in which he sang the title song over the credits. Laine's musicals included *Make Believe Ballroom* (1949), *When You're Smiling* (1950), *On the Sunny Side of the Street* (1951), *Rainbow 'Round My Shoulder* (1952), *Meet Me in Las Vegas* (1955), and others.

LAKE, VERONICA (1919–1973) had a brief but popular career in 1940s films, her low purring voice and long blonde hair dangling over one eye (the "peek-a-boo" look) making her one of the glamour idols of the decade. Lake appeared in a half dozen musicals, usually playing guest bits or specialties, before falling into obscurity in the 1950s. Her musical credits were *STAR SPAN-GLED RHYTHM* (1942), *Bring on the Girls* (1945), *Out of This World* (1945), *Duffy's Tavern* (1945), *Variety Girl* (1947), and *Isn't It Romantic?* (1948).

LAMAS, FERNANDO (1915–1982) made several films in his native Argentina before going to Hollywood in 1949 and finding a career usually playing dashing Latin lovers. Lamas displayed his agreeable baritone voice in such musicals as *Rich, Young and Pretty* (1951), *THE MERRY WIDOW* (1952), *Dangerous When Wet* (1953), *ROSE MARIE* (1954), and *The Girl Rush* (1955). He was married to actress Arlene Dahl before he wed ESTHER WILLIAMS and was the father of actor Lorenzo Lamas.

LAMB, GIL (1906–1995), with his long sad face and erratic dancing style, was featured in a handful of PARAMOUNT musicals in the 1940s. His credits include *THE FLEET'S IN* (1942), *STAR SPANGLED RHYTHM* (1942), *Riding High* (1943), and *Hit Parade of 1947* (1946). Lamb returned to the screen as one of the dancing Shriners in *BYE BYE BIRDIE* (1963)

LAMOUR, DOROTHY (1914–1996) created her image as an exotic, primitive jungle princess when she donned a sarong in nonmusical films, then had fun poking fun at the image in the "Road" movies with BING CROSBY and BOB HOPE and in other musicals. The dark-haired beauty played bit parts in *FOOTLIGHT PARADE* (1933) and *College Holiday* (1936) before getting supporting roles in *Swing High, Swing Low* (1937), *HIGH, WIDE AND HANDSOME* (1937), *BIG BROADCAST OF 1938*, and *Her Jungle Love* (1938). With *Tropic Holiday* (1938) she moved into leading roles, followed by the musicals *St. Louis Blues* (1939), *Man About Town* (1939), *Johnny Apollo* (1940), *Moon Over Burma* (1940), *THE FLEET'S IN* (1942), *Beyond the Blue Horizon* (1942), *Dixie* (1943), *Riding High* (1943), *And the Angels Sing* (1944), *Rainbow Island* (1944), *Masquerade in Mexico* (1945), *Lulu Belle* (1948), and *Slightly French* (1949). Lamour also made specialty appearances in *Thrill of a Lifetime* (1937), *STAR SPANGLED RHYTHM* (1942), *Duffy's Tavern* (1945), *Variety Girl* (1947), and *HERE COMES THE GROOM* (1951). But her fame in movies still rests on her "Road" pictures: *ROAD TO SINGAPORE* (1940), *ROAD TO ZANZIBAR* (1941), *ROAD TO MOROCCO* (1942), *ROAD TO UTOPIA* (1945), *ROAD TO RIO* (1947), *ROAD TO BALI* (1952), and in a guest spot in *THE ROAD TO HONG KONG* (1962).

LANDIS, CAROLE (1919–1948) was a shapely blonde actress who appeared in a dozen Hollywood musicals before her untimely death by suicide. Landis possessed one of the finest pair of legs in Tinsel Town in the 1940s and was a favorite of GIs overseas during the war. After bit parts in *A DAY AT THE RACES* (1937), *BROADWAY MELODY OF 1938* (1937), *VARSITY SHOW* (1937), *HOLLYWOOD HOTEL* (1937), and *GOLD DIGGERS IN PARIS* (1938), she graduated to second leads in *Road Show* (1941), *MOON OVER MIAMI* (1941), *Cadet Girl* (1941), *My Gal Sal* (1942), *ORCHESTRA WIVES* (1942), *The Powers Girl* (1942), *Wintertime* (1943), and *Four Jills in a Jeep* (1944), which was based on Landis' excursion to Europe to entertain troops during the war.

LANE, BURTON (1912–1996), a Broadway and Hollywood composer who worked with many of the top lyricists during his career, broke into show business at a young age, his songs heard on Broadway when he was nineteen and working on his first movie score at the age of twenty-one. Lane saw two of his Broadway shows filmed, *FINIAN'S RAINBOW* (1968) and *ON A CLEAR DAY YOU CAN SEE FOREVER* (1969), and he wrote original scores for a dozen movies. With lyricist HAROLD ADAMSON, he contributed songs to *DANCING LADY* (1933), *Bottoms Up* (1934), and *Jupiter's Darling* (1955). With FRANK LOESSER, Burton scored *College Swing* (1938), *Cocoanut Grove* (1938), *St. Louis Blues* (1939), and *Dancing on a Dime* (1941); with E.Y. HARBURG and RALPH FREED, *She Married a Cop* (1939), *BABES ON BROADWAY* (1941), and *Ship Ahoy* (1942); *Rainbow Island* (1944) with TED KOEHLER; and *ROYAL WEDDING* (1951) with ALAN JAY LERNER. Lane was an estimable artist who never became a household name but is now ranked with the best composers of the 1940s and 1950s.

LANE, LOLA (1909–1981) and her younger sisters **PRISCILLA LANE** (1917–1995) and **ROSEMARY LANE** (1914–1974) hailed from rural Iowa and made their way to New York City, where each found modest success in nightclubs or in bit parts in Broadway musicals. Lola went out to Hollywood in 1928 and got featured roles in *Fox Movietown Follies* (1929), *Let's Go Places* (1930), and *GOOD NEWS* (1930). Priscilla and Rosemary went West later and the two were cast in *VARSITY SHOW* (1937). The three sisters made only one film together, the popular nonmusical *Four Daughters* (1938); then they went their separate ways: Lola appeared in *HOLLYWOOD HOTEL* (1937), Priscilla in *Cowboy From Brooklyn* (1938), *The Roaring Twenties* (1939), and *BLUES IN THE NIGHT* (1941), and Rosemary in *HOLLYWOOD HOTEL* (1937), *GOLD DIGGERS IN PARIS* (1937), *The Boys From Syracuse* (1940), *Time Out for Rhythm* (1941), *Chatterbox* (1943), *Harvest Melody* (1943), and *Trocadero* (1944).

LANE, LUPINO (1892–1959), a favorite British music hall comic, made some silent shorts and feature talkies in Hollywood, leaving evidence of his inspired comic acrobatics and nimble song-and-dance talents. Lane's four American musicals were *THE LOVE PARADE* (1929), *THE SHOW OF SHOWS* (1930), *Golden Dawn* (1930), and *Bride of the Regiment* (1930). His most famous stage role, the low-bred duke Bill Snibson in *Me and My Girl*, was recreated in the British film musical *Lambeth Walk* (1939).

LANE, PRISCILLA. See Lane, Lola

LANE, ROSEMARY. See Lane, Lola

LANFIELD, SIDNEY (1899–1972) had two long and successful directing careers, first with light comedies and musicals in Hollywood and then in television from its early days until his death. Lanfield's movie musicals include *Cheer Up and Smile* (1930), *Moulin Rouge* (1934), *KING OF BURLESQUE* (1935), *Sing, Baby, Sing* (1936), *ONE IN A MILLION* (1936), *WAKE UP AND LIVE* (1937), *Thin Ice* (1937), *Love and Hisses* (1937), *SECOND FIDDLE* (1939), *Swanee River* (1939), *YOU'LL NEVER GET RICH* (1941), *Let's Face It* (1943), *Bring on the Girls* (1945), *The Lemon Drop Kid* (1951), and *Skirts Ahoy* (1952).

LANG, WALTER (1896–1972), a prolific film director from the silent days, specialized in glossy musicals and comedies at 20TH CENTURY–FOX and directed successful film versions of Broadway hits by IRVING BERLIN and RODGERS and HAMMERSTEIN. Lang's first musical was *Hooray for Love* (1935), but he didn't return to the genre until *The Blue Bird* (1940), followed by *Star Dust* (1940), *TIN PAN ALLEY* (1940), *MOON OVER MIAMI* (1941), *WEEK-END IN HAVANA* (1941), *Song of the Islands* (1942), *CONEY ISLAND* (1943), *Greenwich Village* (1944), *STATE FAIR* (1945), *MOTHER WORE TIGHTS* (1947), *When My Baby Smiles at Me* (1948), *You're My Everything* (1949), *ON THE RIVIERA* (1951), *WITH A SONG IN MY HEART* (1952), *CALL ME MADAM* (1953), *THERE'S NO BUSINESS LIKE SHOW BUSINESS* (1954), *THE KING AND I* (1956), *CAN-CAN* (1960), and *Snow White and the Three Stooges* (1961).

LANGFORD, FRANCES (1914–   ), a radio singer with a smooth and creamy voice, appeared in twenty-seven Hollywood musicals, usually in supporting roles in grade A movies and leads in inferior products. Langford made her film debut with *EVERY NIGHT AT EIGHT* (1935), followed by roles in *BROADWAY MELODY OF 1936* (1935), *BORN TO DANCE* (1936), *HOLLYWOOD HOTEL* (1937), *TOO MANY GIRLS* (1940), *All American Coed* (1941), *Never a Dull Moment* (1943), *The Girl Rush* (1944), *Beat the Band* (1947), and *Purple Heart Diary* (1951). She did specialty bits in *YANKEE DOODLE DANDY* (1942), *Follow the Band* (1943), *THIS IS THE*

ARMY (1943), *People Are Funny* (1946), and *THE GLENN MILLER STORY* (1954), as well as providing one of the singing voices for the animated *Melody Time* (1948).

LANSBURY, ANGELA (1925–   ), one of the giants of the Broadway musical theatre, had an unusual career, often playing women much older than herself in movies, having her singing dubbed in musicals although she had started as a singer on the stage, finding her niche in Broadway musical comedy later in life, and becoming a television star when most actors are retiring. The British-born actress came to America during World War Two and appeared in supporting roles in nonmusical films, getting attention immediately for playing bad but beautiful women. Lansbury often returned to the British and Broadway stage, playing classical and contemporary roles. Her few movie musicals rarely revealed her singing talents, being dubbed in *THE HARVEY GIRLS* (1946), given only a specialty in *TILL THE CLOUDS ROLL BY* (1946), and playing nonsinging beauties in *THE COURT JESTER* (1956) and *BLUE HAWAII* (1961). New doors opened for her when Lansbury played *Mame* (1966) on Broadway, followed by a series of brilliant performances in challenging musicals, such as *Sweeney Todd, the Demon Barber of Fleet Street* (1979). Her only leading role in a film musical was the delightful witch Eglantine in *BEDKNOBS AND BROOMSTICKS* (1971), though she supplied the voices of Mrs. Potts in the animated *BEAUTY AND THE BEAST* (1991) and the Dowager Empress Marie in *ANASTASIA* (1997). Lansbury concentrated on television (*Murder, She Wrote*) after 1984.

LANZA, MARIO (1921–1959) was a popular operatic tenor who rose to fame quickly but because of problems with his weight, alcoholism, and emotional insecurity burned himself out quickly and died of a heart attack at the age of thirty-eight. The rugged and robust Lanza found fame in the concert hall before MGM starred him in a series of tailor-made vehicles to show off his powerful voice. With such movies as *That Midnight Kiss* (1949), *The Toast of New Orleans* (1950), *THE GREAT CARUSO* (1951), and *Because You're Mine* (1952), Lanza played dashing young men who sang classical and new pieces and did more to promote opera in America than any other screen singer. By the mid-1950s he was getting too stout for romantic leads and provided the singing voice of Edmund Purdom in *THE STUDENT PRINCE* (1954). He appeared on screen again in *Serenade* (1956), *The Seven Hills of Rome* (1958), and *For the First Time* (1959) before his untimely death.

LAUREL, STAN (1890–1965) and his partner **OLIVER HARDY** (1892–1957), the most successful comedy team in the history of movies with hundreds of shorts and features from the silent era to 1951, rarely sang or danced but were featured in eight movie musicals during their long career. The thin, weepy Laurel and the large, bullying Hardy were seen in *HOLLYWOOD REVUE OF 1929*, *The Rogue Song* (1930), *The Devil's Brother* (1933), *Hollywood*

Party (1934), *BABES IN TOYLAND* (1934), *The Bohemian Girl* (1936), *Swiss Miss* (1938), and *Jitterbugs* (1943). Hardy also appeared alone in the musical *Ridin' High* (1950).

LAWFORD, PETER (1923–1984), the British-born leading man who played debonair men of wealth in many nonmusicals, was also a favorite in movie musicals despite his thin singing voice and limited dancing talents. Sometimes Lawford got the girl, but often he was the gentleman who gave her up to the American star. His musical credits include *Two Sisters From Boston* (1945), *IT HAPPENED IN BROOKLYN* (1945), *GOOD NEWS* (1947), *EASTER PARADE* (1948), *ROYAL WEDDING* (1951), and *Pepe* (1960).

LeBARON, WILLIAM (1883–1958) left Broadway, where he had found some success as a playwright and lyricist, and became a Hollywood producer who supervised dozens of movies for various studios. Among LeBaron's projects were thirty-two musicals, most memorably *RIO RITA* (1929), *SHE DONE HIM WRONG* (1933), *College Humor* (1933), *I'm No Angel* (1933), *All the King's Horses* (1935), *Here Comes Cookie* (1935), *Rose of the Rancho* (1936), *RHYTHM ON THE RIVER* (1940), *WEEK-END IN HAVANA* (1941), *Song of the Islands* (1942), *ORCHESTRA WIVES* (1942), *SPRINGTIME IN THE ROCKIES* (1942), *ICELAND* (1942), *Footlight Serenade* (1942), *STORMY WEATHER* (1943), *THE GANG'S ALL HERE* (1943), *Pin-Up Girl* (1944), *THREE LITTLE GIRLS IN BLUE* (1946), and *Carnegie Hall* (1947).

LEE, GYPSY ROSE (1914–1970), America's most famous burlesque queen, started in vaudeville in a kiddie act with her sister JUNE HAVOC but eventually found fame as a stripper at Minsky's in New York. As Louise Hovick, she appeared in the movie musicals *Sally, Irene and Mary* (1937), *Ali Baba Goes to Town* (1937), *You Can't Have Everything* (1937), and *My Lucky Star* (1938). As the wisecracking Gypsy Rose Lee, she was featured in *STAGE DOOR CANTEEN* (1943) and *Belle of the Yukon* (1944). Lee wrote novels, plays, and an autobiography that was the basis for the Broadway and film musical *GYPSY* (1963).

LEE, PEGGY (1920–   ), whose smoky and precise way with a song made her one of America's top recording stars and a favorite in nightclubs, started as a vocalist with BENNY GOODMAN's orchestra and then went on her own, sometimes writing the songs she made hits. Lee appeared in five movie musicals, portraying a band singer in *The Powers Girl* (1942), *STAGE DOOR CANTEEN* (1943), and *Mr. Music* (1950), but she got to play challenging roles in *THE JAZZ SINGER* (1953) and *PETE KELLY'S BLUES* (1955). She and Sonny Burke wrote the songs for the animated feature *LADY AND THE TRAMP* (1955), and Lee provided the voices for the wife Darling, the Siamese cats, and the sultry canine Peg in the film.

LEE, SAMMY (1890–1968) was a veteran choreographer of Broadway shows in the 1920s before he went to Hollywood and staged the musical numbers for twenty films. Lee's choreography was seen in the early talkies *It's a Great Life* (1929) and *HOLLYWOOD REVUE OF 1929*, followed by *Adorable* (1933), *DANCING LADY* (1933), *365 Nights in Hollywood* (1934), *KING OF BUR-LESQUE* (1935), *Life of the Party* (1937), *Honolulu* (1939), *Meet the People* (1944), *TWO GIRLS AND A SAILOR* (1944), *Earl Carroll Vanities* (1945), and others.

LEGRAND, MICHEL (1931–   ) is one of the most prolific and awarded composers of music for nonmusicals in France, England, and America since 1955. His unique opera film *Les Parapluies de Cherbourg/The Umbrellas of Cherbourg* (1964) was very popular in America, as were several of the theme songs he wrote for Hollywood features. With lyricists ALAN and MARILYN BERGMAN, Legrand wrote the score for the movie musical *YENTL* (1983).

LEHMAN, ERNEST (1920–   ), a screenplay author and sometime film producer, wrote prize-winning scripts for nonmusicals and the screen adaptations of the Broadway musicals *THE KING AND I* (1955), *WEST SIDE STORY* (1961), *THE SOUND OF MUSIC* (1965), and *HELLO, DOLLY!* (1969).

LEIBER, JERRY (1933–   ) and his collaborator **MIKE STOLLER** (1933–   ) wrote many pop song hits in the 1950s and 1960s, from "On Broadway" to "Yakety Yak." The team also contributed to the scores for the ELVIS PRESLEY vehicles *JAILHOUSE ROCK* (1957), *Loving You* (1957), *KING CREOLE* (1958), *Girls! Girls! Girls!* (1962), *Fun in Acapulco* (1964), *Roustabout* (1964), and *Tickle Me* (1965). The collaborators' songs were celebrated in the long-running Broadway revue *Smokey Joe's Cafe* (1995).

LEIGH, JANET (1927–   ), a top Hollywood star in the 1950s and 1960s, played many dramatic roles but also had a charming presence in movie musicals. Leigh went to Hollywood in 1947 and played the wife of RICHARD RODGERS in her first musical, the film bio *WORDS AND MUSIC* (1948). She was subsequently seen in *Two Tickets to Broadway* (1951), *Walking My Baby Back Home* (1953), *Living It Up* (1954), *PETE KELLY'S BLUES* (1955), *My Sister Eileen* (1955), *Pepe* (1960), and *BYE BYE BIRDIE* (1963). Leigh was married to actor Tony Curtis and her daughter is film star Jamie Lee Curtis.

LEISEN, MITCHELL (1897–1972) moved from career to career in a life filled with variety and success. Trained as an architect, Leisen worked in graphic design before going to Hollywood in the days of the silents and designing first costumes and then sets for Cecil B. DeMille and other directors. He started directing films in the 1930s and specialized in "women's pictures," though he also helmed a dozen musicals. When he fell out of favor in the 1950s, Leisen moved on to television and directed numerous shows there before retiring from show business and going back to interior design and sculpture for a living. Leisen's movies were known for their striking visuals and the painterly way he created effects. His musicals include *MURDER AT THE VANITIES* (1934), *BIG BROADCAST OF 1937* (1936), *Swing High, Swing Low* (1937), *BIG BROADCAST OF 1938, ARTISTS AND MODELS ABROAD* (1938), *Lady in the Dark* (1944), *Dream Girl* (1948), and *The Girl Most Likely* (1957).

LeMAIRE, CHARLES (1897–1985) was a costume designer on Broadway for the *Ziegfeld Follies* and other lavish revues before going to Hollywood in the mid-1920s. LeMaire costumed hundreds of films over the next fifty years, winning many awards and creating a distinctive look for several female stars, most notably MARILYN MONROE. His movie musical credits include *George White's Scandals* (1934), *Sitting Pretty* (1948), *My Blue Heaven* (1950), *ON THE RIVIERA* (1951), *WITH A SONG IN MY HEART* (1952), *GENTLEMEN PREFER BLONDES* (1953), *THERE'S NO BUSINESS LIKE SHOW BUSINESS* (1954), and *The Girl Can't Help It* (1956).

LEMMON, JACK (1925–   ), the versatile actor who can play everything from farce to tragedy, appeared in four movie musicals early in his career: as fighter pilot Marty Stewart in *Three for the Show* (1955), as magazine publisher Robert Baker in *My Sister Eileen* (55), as newspaper reporter Peter Warner in *You Can't Run Away From It* (1956), and in drag in *Pepe* (1960), as he had appeared in the semimusical classic *Some Like It Hot* (1959) the year before.

LENNART, ISOBEL (1915–1971) was a reliable Hollywood screenwriter who penned light comedies, adventure dramas, and musicals such as *ANCHORS AWEIGH* (1945), *Holiday in Mexico* (1946), *IT HAPPENED IN BROOKLYN* (1947), *The Kissing Bandit* (1948), *Skirts Ahoy!* (1952), *LOVE ME OR LEAVE ME* (1955), *Meet Me in Las Vegas* (1956), *Merry Andrew* (1958), and *FUNNY GIRL* (1968).

LEONARD, ROBERT Z. (1889–1968), a Hollywood director known more for his expert craftsmanship than his creativity, started as an actor in silents and began directing in 1914. His most notable films were lavish musicals and lush melodramas in the 1930s and 1940s featuring the industry's most glamourous stars. Among Leonard's musicals were *Marianne* (1929), *DANCING LADY* (1933), *THE GREAT ZIEGFELD* (1936), *MAYTIME* (1937), *THE FIREFLY* (1937), *Broadway Serenade* (1939), *New Moon* (1940), *ZIEGFELD GIRL* (1941), *IN THE GOOD OLD SUMMERTIME* (1949), *Nancy Goes to Rio* (1950), *Everything I Have Is Yours* (1952), and *Kelly and Me* (1957).

LERNER, ALAN JAY (1918–1986), one of Broadway's most respected and gifted lyricists, saw most of his stage musicals written with composer FREDERICK LOEWE filmed, including *BRIGADOON* (1954), *MY FAIR LADY* (1964), *CAMELOT* (1967), and *PAINT YOUR WAGON* (1969). Also, Lerner's Broadway musical *ON A CLEAR DAY YOU CAN SEE FOREVER* with composer BURTON LANE was filmed in 1970. Lerner contributed scores for two movie musicals as well: *ROYAL WEDDING* (1951), written with Lane, and *GIGI* (1958), written with Loewe. Lerner, who usually wrote his own stage librettos, wrote the screenplay for *AN AMERICAN IN PARIS* (1951). His last film credit was the score with Loewe for *The Little Prince* (1974). Lerner's lyrics are recognized for their intelligent wit and evocative romanticism.

LeROY, MERVYN (1900–1987) worked his way up from vaudeville performer to cameraman to film actor to director, becoming one of Hollywood's most distinguished craftsmen and helming taut social dramas, escapist musicals, and romantic melodramas. LeRoy's early musicals *Broadway Babies* (1929), *Little Johnny Jones* (1930), and *Show Girl in Hollywood* (1930) got little attention, but his production of *GOLD DIGGERS OF 1933* was a hit. Subsequent films included *Happiness Ahead* (1934), *SWEET ADELINE* (1935), *LOVELY TO LOOK AT* (1952), *Million Dollar Mermaid* (1952), *ROSE MARIE* (1954), and *GYPSY* (1962), as well as producing the last two. LeRoy also produced *Mr. Dodd Takes the Air* (1937), *Fools for Scandal* (1938), *AT THE CIRCUS* (1939), and *THE WIZARD OF OZ* (1939).

LES GIRLS (MGM 1957) is notable for KAY KENDALL's inspired performance that hints at what the beloved English comedienne could have done had she made more American film musicals. John Patrick's screenplay was clever, allowing three different women (Kendall, Taina Elg, and MITZI GAYNOR) to each tell her version of what happened a decade earlier when they were billed as Les Girls and worked with song-and-dance man GENE KELLY in a Paris nightclub. Of course each version varies widely from the other, but the film gave Kelly a chance to give three slightly different performances. COLE PORTER was so ill at the time that he barely managed to complete the score (it was his last film assignment), but it had its moments: Kelly and Kendall (dubbed by Betty Wand) breaking into "You're Just Too Too," Kelly singing "Why Am I So Gone?" and then going into a ballet with Gaynor that spoofed Marlon Brando and the leather-jacketed motorcycle gangs currently in the movies, and the lovely ballad "Ca C'est L'Amour." Yet the musical highlight of the film wasn't a Porter number at all but Kendall trying to sing Bizet's "Habañera" from *Carmen* when she was pleasantly drunk.

LESLIE, JOAN (1925–   ) was the sweet and wholesome leading lady in several 1940s films and appeared in eleven musicals (though her singing was sometimes dubbed). As a child performer, Leslie appeared under the name Joan Brodel in a handful of 1930s movies. She changed her name when she played more mature roles in *Star Dust* (1940), *YANKEE DOODLE DANDY* (1942), *The Hard Way* (1942), *The Sky's the Limit* (1943), *THIS IS THE ARMY* (1943), *THANK YOUR LUCKY STARS* (1943), *HOLLYWOOD CANTEEN* (1944), *Where Do We Go From Here?* (1945), *RHAPSODY IN BLUE* (1945), *Cinderella Jones* (1946), and *Two Guys From Milwaukee* (1946). When Leslie's popularity waned in the 1950s she retired from films.

LESTER, RICHARD (1932–), the American director of many British television shows and films, usually looks for the offbeat and zany in his projects. Lester brought just such a sensibility to his three movie musicals: *A HARD DAY'S NIGHT* (1964), *HELP!* (1965), and *A Funny Thing Happened on the Way to the Forum* (1966).

LET'S SING AGAIN (RKO 1936) introduced youngster BOBBY BREEN to Depression audiences, and though no SHIRLEY TEMPLE, he endeared himself enough to make seven more tearful melodramas in which he sang his heart out in that high, bird-like chirp he possessed. EDDIE CANTOR discovered the boy on his radio show, and producer Sol Lesser built the film around him. As a youth abandoned on the streets by his Neapolitan mother, Breen is put in an orphanage, escapes to join a touring circus, is adopted by the kindly Henry Armetta, and then comes across his real father while hitchhiking to New York. Breen got to sing a handful of songs, the best being GUS KAHN and JIMMY McHUGH's Depression-chasing title number, which became a hit when Breen and others recorded it. To really show off their singing moppet, the studio had Breen sing "La Donna e Mobile" from Verdi's *Rigoletto* as some kind of freak show attraction.

LEVANT, OSCAR (1906–1972), the cynical piano-playing hypochondriac who was also a first-rate songwriter, appeared in several films, usually playing the wry friend of the hero. Levant was poised for a career as a concert pianist, but his dour comments and dark humor made him a radio talk show favorite. He was seen in the musicals *The Dance of Life* (1929), *RHYTHM ON THE RIVER* (1940), *Kiss the Boys Goodbye* (1941), *You Were Meant for Me* (1948), *ROMANCE ON THE HIGH SEAS* (1948), *THE BARKLEYS OF BROADWAY* (1949), *AN AMERICAN IN PARIS* (1951), *The I-Don't-Care Girl* (1953), and *THE BAND WAGON* (1953). As a songwriter, Levant collaborated with lyricist SIDNEY CLARE on the scores for *Street Girl* (1929), *Tanned Legs* (1929), *Love Comes Along* (1930), and *Music Is Magic* (1935), as well as *In Person* (1935) with lyricist DOROTHY FIELDS. Levant was a close associate of GEORGE GERSHWIN, became known as one of the finest interpreters of Gershwin's piano works, and played himself in the Gershwin musical bio *RHAPSODY IN BLUE* (1945).

LEVEN, BORIS (1900–1986) was one of Hollywood's top scenic designers for over a half-century career with various studios. The former architect did the art direction for all genres of film, including the musicals *ALEXANDER'S RAGTIME BAND* (1938), *Doll Face* (1945), *WEST SIDE STORY* (1961), *THE SOUND OF MUSIC* (1965), *STAR!* (1968), and *NEW YORK, NEW YORK* (1977).

LEVIEN, SONYA (1895–1960) was a Russian-born short story writer who, after adapting some of her works for the movies, became a Hollywood screenwriter. Levien's first of many scripts were written for silent films, but she later penned such musicals as *DELICIOUS* (1931), *REBECCA OF SUNNYBROOK FARM* (1932), *IN OLD CHICAGO* (1938), *ZIEGFELD GIRL* (1941), *RHAPSODY IN BLUE* (1945), *STATE FAIR* (1945), *THE GREAT CARUSO* (1951), *THE MERRY WIDOW* (1952), *THE STUDENT PRINCE* (1954), *HIT THE DECK* (1955), *Interrupted Melody* (1955), *OKLAHOMA!* (1955), and *Pepe* (1960).

LEVIN, HENRY (1909–1980) was a Broadway director who went to Hollywood in the mid-1940s and stayed to helm over fifty films for various studios. Known as a practical, on-budget director, Levin specialized in adventure yarns and musicals, such as *JOLSON SINGS AGAIN* (1949), *The Petty Girl* (1950), *THE FARMER TAKES A WIFE* (1953), *Bernadine* (1957), *April Love* (1957), *Where the Boys Are* (1960), and *The Wonderful World of the Brothers Grimm* (1962).

LEWIS, JERRY (1926–   ) had two film careers, one with his partner DEAN MARTIN with whom he made seventeen movies, and then as a solo artist often writing, producing, and directing his own vehicles. Martin and Lewis appeared first as secondary characters in *My Friend Irma* (1949), and the audience reaction was so great PARAMOUNT starred them in a series of musical comedies with the forever-juvenile Lewis as the erratic clown and Martin as the straightman providing the songs and romance. The most notable of their collaborations were *At War With the Army* (1950), *Sailor Beware* (1951), *Jumping Jacks* (1952), *The Stooge* (1952), *Scared Stiff* (1953), *The Caddy* (1953), *Living It Up* (1954), *ARTISTS AND MODELS* (1955), and *Pardners* (1956), as well as a cameo appearance in *ROAD TO BALI* (1952). After the team split up, Lewis made several solo features in which he matured somewhat but still played the naive clown. His musical credits included *Rock-a-Bye Baby* (1958), *Cinderfella* (1960), *The Ladies' Man* (1961), and *The Nutty Professor* (1963). Lewis was also very active in nightclubs and on television, and he even made a late Broadway debut in a revival of *Damn Yankees* in 1995.

LEWIS, TED (1891–1971), a clarinet-playing bandleader from vaudeville and nightclubs who typically wore a tattered top hat and kept asking the audience, "Is everybody happy?," made seven screen appearances, sometimes as a specialty act and other times in character roles. Lewis' musical credits were *Is Everybody Happy?* (1929 and again in 1943), *THE SHOW OF SHOWS* (1929), *Manhattan Merry-Go-Round* (1935), *Hold That Ghost* (1941), and *Follow the Boys* (1944).

LIBERACE (1919–1987) was the most popular pianist in show business, making hundreds of television (he had his own show in the 1950s), nightclub, and concert appearances over a four-decade career. Known for his flashy wardrobe as much as for his pianist skills, Liberace was the leading man in *Sincerely Yours* (1955) and made featured guest spots in the musicals *South Sea Sinner* (1950), *Footlight Varieties* (1951), and *When the Boys Meet the Girls* (1966).

LIGHTNER, WINNIE (1899–1971), a popular singing-dancing comedienne in vaudeville and in Broadway revues, was a highly animated blonde who made only a few films before marrying director ROY DEL RUTH and retiring in the mid-1930s. Lightner's musicals were *GOLD DIGGERS OF BROADWAY* (1929), *THE SHOW OF SHOWS* (1929), *Hold Everything* (1930), *Life of the Party* (1930), *She Couldn't Say No* (1930), and *DANCING LADY* (1933).

LI'L ABNER (Paramount 1959) was about as faithful a movie could be to the original Broadway source with most of the cast, score, libretto, and choreography repeated on the screen. Also, the stylized settings and cartoonish costumes (it was based on Al Capp's comic strip) made the whole thing seem more theatrical than cinematic. But it was such a hoot that no one seemed to mind the staginess of MELVIN FRANK and Norman Panama's direction. Peter Palmer was the naive, muscular Abner, Leslie Parrish his doting Daisy Mae, STUBBY KAYE as Marryin' Sam, and Joe E. Marks and Billie Hayes as Pappy and Mammy Yokum. The plot was a trifling affair about the U.S. government wanting to use Dogpatch as a testing ground for the A-bomb because it was such a worthless place, and much of Capp's satire was diluted into just plain silliness. The JOHNNY MERCER and GENE DE PAUL songs were tuneful, and MICHAEL KIDD and DEEDEE WOOD's choreography just as cleverly raucous as on the stage. The standout numbers were the celebratory "Jubilation T. Cornpone," the foot-stomping "(Don't That Take the) Rag Off'n the Bush," and the "Sadie Hawkins Day Ballet."

LILI (MGM 1953) hardly qualified as a musical with its lone hit song "Hi-Lili, Hi-Lo" (aka "Love Makes the World Go Round") by BRONISLAW KAPER and Helen Deutsch, but the circus setting was filled with background music and there was a lovely dream ballet choreographed by CHARLES WALTERS and Dorothy Jarnac that made the enchanting tale seemed like a musical. Orphan LESLIE CARON worked for a traveling carnival show and fell for the dashing magician Jean-Pierre Aumont while she was loved by the crippled

José Ferrer, who spoke (and wooed) Caron through his puppets. Walters directed, and ZSA ZSA GABOR, Amanda Blake, KURT KASZNAR, and Ralph Dumke moved in and out of the action like figures in a carousel. The whole venture was so fragile and bittersweet it might have been a French art house film, yet it was popular at the box office. In a reversal of the usual order of things, the film was turned into the Broadway musical *Carnival* (1961) with a whole new score by BOB MERRILL and it also was a hit.

LILLIAN RUSSELL (Fox 1940) recreated the costumes and interiors of the 1890s so well that audiences were led to believe that this fabricated BIOGRAPHICAL MUSICAL was close to the truth. Not only was it inaccurate but, more difficult, it was dull when the subject matter was so lively. The raucous hour-glass-figured Russell, who starred in vaudeville, on Broadway, and most memorably in a series of Joe Weber and Lew Fields revues, became just another showgirl as written for ALICE FAYE. Russell's four notorious marriages were reduced to two (with songwriter DON AMECHE and news reporter Henry Fonda) for the film, but her flamboyant association with Diamond Jim Brady (Edward Arnold) survived. Luckily, the songs were accurate for the time, and Faye did nicely with "Come Down, Ma Evenin' Star," "Ma Blushin' Rosie," "After the Ball," and other period numbers. There was another touch of authenticity: Weber and Fields came out of retirement and performed one of their comic routines in the film.

LILLIE, BEATRICE (1894–1989) was once dubbed "the funniest woman in the world" for her inspired comic performances in London and Broadway musical revues. Unfortunately the tall, madcap Lillie was rarely used well in the movies and little of her sly clowning is recorded on film. She played supporting roles or did specialty bits in *THE SHOW OF SHOWS* (1929), *Are You There?* (1930), *Doctor Rhythm* (1938), and *THOROUGHLY MODERN MILLIE* (1967).

LION KING, THE (Disney 1994) eschewed the DISNEY tradition of starting with a classic fairy tale or well-known story and came up with an original screenplay by Irene Mecchi, Jonathan Roberts, and Linda Woolverton that may have borrowed from *Hamlet* and the studio's own *Bambi* but was genuine gold, the top-grossing animated film of all time. The young lion cub Simba (voice of Jonathan Taylor Thomas) is tricked by his evil uncle Scar (Jeremy Irons) into thinking the cub was responsible for the death of his father, King Mufasa (James Earl Jones), when it was Scar himself who murdered his brother in order to take over the pride. Simba runs away, grows up under the "no worries" philosophy of meercat Timon (Nathan Lane) and warthog Pumbaa (Ernie Sabella), and as an adult (now voiced by Matthew Broderick) is encouraged by the wise old baboon Rafiki (Robert Guillaume) to return home and avenge his father's death. No animated film had taken on so many heavy issues, met them head on, and succeeded like *The Lion King*. The stampede in which Mufasa died was as powerful as any live-action adventure, yet the comedy of Timon and Pumba had the heart and soul of vaudeville. TIM RICE and ELTON JOHN wrote the pop songs, which sometimes bordered on the fervent, especially in the opening number, "The Circle of Life," which combined music, animation, and ritual in a way never captured on film before. Also, the superb musical background score by Hans Zimmer gave the movie an authentic African rhythm. Other songs included the freewheeling "Hakuna Matata," the Fascist "Be Prepared," and the Oscar-winning ballad "Can You Feel the Love Tonight?" The movie became a mammoth Broadway musical hit in 1997.

LITTLE MERMAID, THE (Disney 1989) is the movie that began the DISNEY renaissance of the 1990s by offering a classic tale, superb animation, vibrant characters, and a Broadway-like score of hit songs. Loosely based on a Hans Christian Andersen tale, the John Musker and Ron Clemens screenplay told of the mermaid Ariel (voice of Jodi Benson) who yearns to be human, especially after she meets and falls in love with Prince Eric (Christopher Daniel Barnes). Defying her father, King Triton (Kenneth Mars), Ariel makes a pact with the sea witch Ursula (Pat Carroll) to exchange her beautiful voice for a pair of human legs. The deal involves Ariel getting the Prince to kiss her or else she becomes the slave of Ursula. Andersen's tragic story was given a happy ending for the film, but not until a lot of plot twists and a thrilling sequence in which the gigantic Ursula is destroyed by Eric. In the Disney tradition, the heroine was surrounded by lively companions, such as the crab Sebastian (Samuel E. Wright), the fearful Flounder (Jason Marin), and the cockeyed seagull Scuttle (BUDDY HACKETT). Composer ALAN MENKEN began his string of award-winning movie scores with *The Little Mermaid*, and the songs (written with lyricist HOWARD ASHMAN) reminded audiences of what a top-notch Broadway score used to sound like: "Kiss the Girl," "Part of Your World," "Poor Unfortunate Souls," and the Oscar-winning "Under the Sea."

LITTLE SHOP OF HORRORS (Geffen/Warner 1986) followed the 1982 Off-Broadway hit fairly closely (both scripts were written by HOWARD ASHMAN) until the end, but it was a conclusion not out of place in this musical spoof of sci-fi movies of the late 1950s and early 1960s. Nerdy botanist Seymour (Rick Moranis) discovers a rare Venus flytrap–like plant that feeds on blood and has magical powers. The plant makes Seymour famous and even allows the blonde bimbo Audrey (Ellen Greene) to fall in love with him, but the price is high: The plant wants to take over the world. In the play it did, but in the film Seymour kills it, only to have little sprouts popping up out of the ground and winking at the audience. Vincent Gardenia played the flower shop owner who suspects the plant's carnivorous appetite, and Steve Martin gave a daffy performance as Greene's sadomasochistic dentist boyfriend. Ashman and ALAN MENKEN wrote the pastiche score that was funny and, inexplicably, touching at times. "Somewhere That's Green," "Dentist," "Suddenly Seymour," and "Mean Green Mother From Outer Space" (added for the film) were the standout numbers.

LIVINGSTON, JAY. See Evans, Ray

LIVINGSTON, JERRY (1909–1987), a former bandleader turned composer, collaborated with MACK DAVID and other lyricists on a handful of movie musicals, most memorably the score for the animated *CINDERELLA* (1949). Livingston's other musicals were the JERRY LEWIS–DEAN MARTIN vehicles *At War With the Army* (1950), *Sailor Beware* (1951), and *Jumping Jacks* (1952).

LOCATIONS FOR MUSICALS have ranged from *MONTE CARLO* (1930) to *New Orleans* (1947) to *Honolulu* (1939) and back again along the *ROAD TO ZANZIBAR* (1941), but *NEW YORK, NEW YORK* (1977) has remained the location of choice in Hollywood. More movie musicals are set on Broadway or in Manhattan nightclubs, radio studios, hotels, beer halls, tenements, even movie theatres, than anywhere else. As much as the studios wanted to outdo the theatre, they often put the big show, the opening night, the making of a star, and the tearful comeback all on a Broadway stage. Other musicals celebrated Manhattan itself and such favorite locales as *Carnegie Hall* (1947), *TIN PAN ALLEY* (1940), *The Stork Club* (1945), *42ND STREET* (1933), *CONEY ISLAND* (1943), *STAGE DOOR CANTEEN* (1943), *THE COTTON CLUB* (1984), *A NIGHT AT THE OPERA* (1935), *Up in Central Park* (1948), *PUTTIN' ON THE RITZ* (1930), *ON THE AVENUE* (1937), and all around the town. *THE JAZZ SINGER* (1927) contained some vivid location shooting on the Lower East Side and *ON THE TOWN* (194) was the first musical to film a good portion of its scenes at Manhattan landmarks, but Hollywood had been recreating New York City in studios and backlots for decades. Other musicals that seemed to be *about* as well as set in Gotham include *THE BROADWAY MELODY* (1929), *The Floradora Girl* (1930), *FOOTLIGHT PARADE* (1933), *HALLELUJAH, I'M A BUM* (1933), *Broadway Gondolier* (1935), *SHALL WE DANCE* (1937), *My Sister Eileen* (1942), *Broadway* (1942), *Sweet Rosie O'Grady* (1943), *GOING MY WAY* (1944), *IT HAPPENED IN BROOKLYN* (1947), *EASTER PARADE* (1948), *BABES ON BROADWAY* (1949), *THE BELLE OF NEW YORK* (1952), *THE BAND WAGON* (1953), *Top Banana* (1954), *GUYS AND DOLLS* (1955), *BELLS ARE RINGING* (1960), *WEST SIDE STORY* (1961), *FUNNY GIRL* (1968), *The Night They Raided Minsky's* (1968), *HELLO, DOLLY!* (1969), *SWEET CHARITY* (1969), *SATURDAY NIGHT FEVER* (1977), *HAIR* (1978), *The Wiz* (1978), *ALL THAT JAZZ* (1979), *FAME* (1980), *ANNIE* (1982), *LITTLE SHOP OF HORRORS* (1986), *OLIVER AND COMPANY* (1988), and many others. Hollywood,

California, is the second most popular location for movie musicals. Backstage musicals about the film business rarely showed much of the community except for the sound stages, but glimpses of Hollywood can be experienced in *GOING HOLLYWOOD* (1933), *Hollywood Party* (1934), *Kiss the Boys Good-bye* (1941), *Hellzapoppin* (1941), *HOLLYWOOD HOTEL* (1937), *THE GOLDWYN FOLLIES* (1938), *HOLLYWOOD CANTEEN* (1944), *ANCHORS AWEIGH* (1945), *SINGIN' IN THE RAIN* (1952), *A STAR IS BORN* (1954 and 1976), and others. Paris is another popular location for musicals, probably because of its romantic nature, nightclubs and cafés, and plenty of photographic locales. *Paris* (1929), *The Vagabond King* (1930 and 1956), *Playboy of Paris* (1930), *LOVE ME TONIGHT* (1932), *WONDER BAR* (1934), *Paris in Spring* (1935) *ROBERTA* (1935), *FOLIES BERGÈRE DE PARIS* (1935), *GOLD DIGGERS IN PARIS* (1938), *ARTISTS AND MODELS ABROAD* (1938), *The Phantom of the Opera* (1943), *AN AMERICAN IN PARIS* (1951), *GENTLEMEN PREFER BLONDES* (1953), *So This Is Paris* (1954), *FUNNY FACE* (1957), *SILK STOCKINGS* (1957), *LES GIRLS* (1957), *GIGI* (1958), *CAN-CAN* (1960), *THE ARISTOCATS* (1970), *VICTOR/VICTORIA* (1982), *THE HUNCHBACK OF NOTRE DAME* (1996), and *EVERYBODY SAYS I LOVE YOU* (1997) are among the musicals set in the City of Light. London is not far behind, providing the setting for such films as *EVERGREEN* (1934), *TOP HAT* (1935), *A DAMSEL IN DISTRESS* (1937), *ROYAL WEDDING* (1951), *A HARD DAY'S NIGHT* (1964), *MARY POPPINS* (1964), *MY FAIR LADY* (1964), *OLIVER!* (1968), *SCROOGE* (1970), and others. *SAN FRANCISCO* (1936) shared its setting with such films as *FOLLOW THE FLEET* (1936), *THE FLEET'S IN* (1942), *HELLO, FRISCO, HELLO* (1943), *Nob Hill* (1945), *HIT THE DECK* (1955), and *FLOWER DRUM SONG* (1961), whereas the Windy City was the locale for *IN OLD CHICAGO* (1938), *WABASH AVENUE* (1950), *PAL JOEY* (1957), *ROBIN AND THE SEVEN HOODS* (1964), and others. Most major American cities have been home to a movie musical or two, from *NASHVILLE* (1975) to *MEET ME IN ST. LOUIS* (1944) to *MOON OVER MIAMI* (1941), just as most states have, from *OKLAHOMA!* (1955) to *Carolina Blues* (1944) to *Paradise Hawaiian Style* (1966). Also, a series of FRONTIER MUSICALS brought music to various out-of-the-way places across the United States and Canada. *WEEK-END IN HAVANA* (1941), *ROAD TO RIO* (1947), *DOWN ARGENTINE WAY* (1940), and *THE THREE CABALLEROS* (1945) were among the many films set in Latin America, particularly during World War Two. Other locales from around the world include Berlin for *CABARET* (1972), Bangkok for *THE KING AND I* (1956), Brussels for *THE CAT AND THE FIDDLE* (1934), Baghdad for *KISMET* (1955), Scotland for *BRIGADOON* (1954), Russia for *FIDDLER ON THE ROOF* (1971), Johannesburg for *Lost in the Stars* (1974), Copenhagen for *HANS CHRISTIAN ANDERSEN* (1952), China for *Mulan* (1998), Buenos Aires for *EVITA* (1997), Eastern Europe for

YENTL (1983), Reykjavik for *ICELAND* (1942), and on and on. Of all the fantastical places not found on any globe, Munchkinland in *THE WIZARD OF OZ* (1939) has to be the most memorable.

LOESSER, FRANK (1910–1969), a songwriter who reversed the usual pattern by having a successful movie career before he struck gold on Broadway, started as a lyricist but in his later films and stage works wrote both music and lyrics. Loesser's first movie assignment was *College Swing* (1938), in which he collaborated with composer BURTON LANE. The two also scored *St. Louis Blues* (1939), *Dancing on a Dime* (1941), and *Las Vegas Nights* (1941). With songwriters JULE STYNE, FREDERICK HOLLANDER, JIMMY MCHUGH, and others, he contributed songs to *Zaza* (1939), *Man About Town* (1939), *Destry Rides Again* (1939), *Buck Benny Rides Again* (1940), *Sis Hopkins* (1941), *Kiss the Boys Goodbye* (1941), *Sweater Girl* (1942), *HAPPY GO LUCKY* (1943), *THANK YOUR LUCKY STARS* (1943), and others. When his solo effort "Praise the Lord and Pass the Ammunition" became one of the most popular songs of the war years, Loesser decided to write his own music for the rest of his career. His movie musicals scored alone include *The Perils of Pauline* (1947), *Variety Girl* (1947), *NEPTUNE'S DAUGHTER* (1949), *Red, Hot and Blue* (1949), *Let's Dance* (1950), and *HANS CHRISTIAN ANDERSEN* (1952). Loesser went to Broadway in 1948 and scored a series of musical hits, three of them later filmed: *Where's Charley?* (1952), *GUYS AND DOLLS* (1955), and *HOW TO SUCCEED IN BUSINESS WITHOUT REALLY TRYING* (1966).

LOEWE, FREDERICK (1904–1988), unlike his partner ALAN JAY LERNER, wrote songs directly for the screen only on two occasions: *GIGI* (1958) and *The Little Prince* (1974), both with Lerner. But the German-born composer did see four of his Broadway hits filmed: *BRIGADOON* (1954), *MY FAIR LADY* (1964), *CAMELOT* (1967), and *PAINT YOUR WAGON* (1969).

LOGAN, JOSHUA (1908–1988) was a prolific Broadway director of plays and musicals who helmed a handful of films as well. Logan's only movie musicals were *SOUTH PACIFIC* (1958), which he had coauthored and directed on Broadway, *CAMELOT* (1967), and *PAINT YOUR WAGON* (1969).

LOMBARD, CAROLE (1908–1942), one of the few Hollywood stars who could be glamourous, sexy, and funny at the same time, is mostly remembered for her classic screwball comedies in the 1930s. Lombard rarely sang but was featured in seven movie musicals: *Safety in Numbers* (1930), *WE'RE NOT DRESSING* (1934), *Bolero* (1934), *Rhumba* (1935), *The Princess Comes Across* (1936), *Swing High, Swing Low* (1937), and *Fools for Scandal* (1938).

She was married to WILLIAM POWELL and then CLARK GABLE before her death in a plane crash.

LOMBARDO, GUY (1902–1977), a popular bandleader who remained in the spotlight for five decades, was known for the mellow and romantic sound of his orchestra. Lombardo was also identified with New Year's Eve celebrations for most of his career. He and the band can be seen in specialty spots in the musicals *Many Happy Returns* (1934), *STAGE DOOR CANTEEN* (1943), and *No Leave, No Love* (1946).

LORING, EUGENE (1914–1982), a choreographer from the world of classical ballet, intermittently staged dance sequences in films between 1945 and 1960. Loring's film credits include *Yolanda and the Thief* (1945), *ZIEGFELD FOLLIES* (1946), *Mexican Hayride* (1948), *The Inspector General* (1949), *The Toast of New Orleans* (1950), *THE 5,000 FINGERS OF DR. T* (1953), *DEEP IN MY HEART* (1954), *Meet Me in Las Vegas* (1956), *FUNNY FACE* (1957), *SILK STOCKINGS* (1957), and *Pepe* (1960). He was also a dancer at the Ballet Theatre and sometimes performed in the films he choreographed, as in *Something in the Wind* (1947) and *Torch Song* (1953).

LOUIS, JEAN (1907–1997), a Paris-born fashion designer who went to Hollywood in 1943, designed costumes at various studios for thirty years, and was responsible for giving RITA HAYWORTH, LANA TURNER, and other stars their glamourous look. Louis' musical credits include *Tonight and Every Night* (1945), *THE JOLSON STORY* (1946), *JOLSON SINGS AGAIN* (1949), *A STAR IS BORN* (1954), *The Eddy Duchin Story* (1956), *PAL JOEY* (1957), *THOROUGHLY MODERN MILLIE* (1967), and *Lost Horizon* (1973).

LOVE, BESSIE (1989–1986) was a leading lady in silents whose career was on the descendant until sound came in and she gave a memorable performance as showgirl Hank Mahoney in *THE BROADWAY MELODY* (1929). Love was also featured in the musicals *HOLLYWOOD REVUE OF 1929, They Learned About Women* (1930), *Chasing Rainbows* (1930), and *GOOD NEWS* (1930) before leaving Hollywood and settling in London, where she made infrequent film appearances over the next fifty years. Love was a petite blonde who had an innocent and even helpless persona, but her singing and dancing were vivacious and spirited.

LOVE ME OR LEAVE ME (MGM 1955) gave DORIS DAY her first acting challenge, and she rose to it effectively, playing torch singer RUTH ETTING in this unsentimental BIOGRAPHICAL MUSICAL directed by CHARLES VIDOR. Dance hall hostess Etting is discovered by small-time mobster "Gimp" Snyder (JAMES CAGNEY), who is not above using unethical means to further her career. But Synder's jealousy, even after Etting marries him, is notorious, and when she falls in love with pianist Johnny Alderman (Cameron Mitchell), Snyder shoots him. Alderman survives, Snyder goes to jail, and in the film's only Hollywood concession, all three are reunited years later as Snyder, now out of prison, opens his new club. Cagney was as charismatic as ever, but Day held her own and got to sing Etting's title signature song as well as "Ten Cents a Dance," "Shaking the Blues Away," "You Made Me Love You," and others from her repertoire. There were also two new numbers, both torch songs for Day: "Never Look Back" by Chilton Price and "I'll Never Stop Loving You" by SAMMY CAHN and NICHOLAS BRODSZKY, which became a bestselling record for Day.

LOVE ME TONIGHT (Paramount 1932) blended song, background music, character, plot, camerawork, and editing in a miraculous way never seen before and only rarely accomplished since. ROUBEN MAMOULIAN produced and directed the charming musical with just the right balance of reality and romantic illusion. He was assisted by a witty screenplay by Samuel Hoffenstein, Waldemar Young, and George Marion, Jr., and a superlative score by RICHARD RODGERS and LORENZ HART. The comic OPERETTA plot follows Parisian tailor MAURICE CHEVALIER, who follows vicomte CHARLES RUGGLES to his provincial chateau to collect an unpaid debt, only to be mistaken for a baron and to fall in love with the haughty princess JEANETTE MacDONALD. Add an aristocratic uncle (C. Aubrey Smith), the princess's man-hungry friend, the Countess Valentine (MYRNA LOY), and others and the movie had all the makings for a bubbling boudoir comedy. But Mamoulian went far beyond that, using music and quick cutting to tell his story as a musical soufflé. MacDonald sings the mock-operatic "Lover" as she bounces along in a carriage, the music rising and falling with her movements. A deer hunt in the woods becomes a slow-motion ballet of people, horses, and stags. Chevalier and MacDonald are in different parts of the chateau as each sings the title song alone, but the split screen turns it into an intimate duet. When the household realizes that "The Son of a Gun Is Nothing but a Tailor," the camera cuts to various locations in time to the music. Best of all is the use of "Isn't It Romantic?" to tie the characters and plots together. Chevalier sings it with Bert Roach on a Paris street, and a taxi driver picks up the tune and sings it as a composer in the back seat writes it down. Soon a trainload of passengers are singing it, then a passing regiment of soldiers, then a gypsy woman whose repeating of the tune is picked up by MacDonald at her estate. Other songs in the score included the suggestive "Mimi" and the rhythmic "That's the Song of Paree" that utilized city noises in its accompaniment.

LOVE PARADE, THE (Paramount 1929) is filled with firsts: director-producer ERNST LUBITSCH's first talkie, JEANETTE MacDONALD's first film, the first of four MAURICE CHEVALIER–MacDonald movies, and the first attempt to integrate songs and music into the whole picture rather than settling for tacked-on numbers. (In fact, Chevalier's talk-singing of "Nobody's Using It Now" is the screen's first musical soliloquy.) Queen Louise (MacDonald) of Sylvania has heard so much about the amorous goings-on of Count Alfred (Chevalier), her emissary in Paris, that she summons him home out of anger and curiosity. The two are infatuated with each other and wed, but Alfred soon tires of the idle life in court and the marriage is saved only by Louise making him king. It was a tale fitting an antiquated European OPERETTA, but the famous "Lubitsch" touch made all the difference, resulting in a breezy, witty movie in which each song became an opportunity for fluid camera work and an intimate peek into character. CLIFFORD GREY and VICTOR SCHERTZINGER penned the scintillating score that included the wistful "Paris, Stay the Same," the trilling "Dream Lover" (the song that introduced MacDonald to film audiences), the pounding "March of the Grenadiers," the sly "Let's Be Common," and the airy serenade "My Love Parade." The delightful supporting cast included LUPINO LANE, LILLIAN ROTH, Edgar Norton, and EUGENE PALLETTE.

LOVE THY NEIGHBOR (Paramount 1940) utilized the famous radio feud between JACK BENNY and FRED ALLEN as its plot, a thin excuse for seeing the two radio stars on screen but an enjoyable diversion all the same. Allen's niece MARY MARTIN gets cast in the show Benny is producing, and she tries to get the two men to call a truce. EDDIE "ROCHESTER" ANDERSON was on hand as Benny's wily valet, as were VIRGINIA DALE, Theresa Harris, and the Merry Macs. The JOHNNY BURKE and JAMES VAN HEUSEN score offered Anderson the comic love song "Dearest, Dare I?," and Martin got three numbers: "Do You Know Why?," "Isn't That Just Like Love?," and COLE PORTER's "My Heart Belongs to Daddy," which she had sung on the stage two years earlier, when it had launched her career.

LOVELY TO LOOK AT. See *Roberta*

LOY, MYRNA (1905–1993), a Hollywood leading lady who played lusty vamps in the silents, smart comic heroines in the 1930s, and sophisticated ladies or mothers thereafter, appeared in seven musicals in the first decade of the talkies. Loy can be spotted as one of the chorus girls in *THE JAZZ SINGER* (1927), then in supporting roles in *The Desert Song* (1929), *THE SHOW OF SHOWS* (1929), *Cameo Kirby* (1930), and *Bride of the Regiment* (1930). Her best musical roles were the madcap Countess Valentine in *LOVE ME TONIGHT* (1932) and Ziegfeld's wife BILLIE BURKE in *THE GREAT ZIEGFELD* (1936).

LUBITSCH, ERNST (1892–1947) directed silents and talkies, comedies and musicals, all with the distinctive "Lubitsch touch" that turned them into romanticized satires and unforgettable comedies of manners. Lubitsch directed many films in his native Germany before coming to America in the early 1920s and embarking on a sensational career as a Hollywood director and producer. He performed both tasks for his half dozen musicals, including *THE LOVE PARADE* (1929), *MONTE CARLO* (1930), *THE SMILING LIEUTENANT* (1931), *ONE HOUR WITH YOU* (1932), and *THE MERRY WIDOW* (1934). He was working on the musical *That Lady in Ermine* (1947) when he died of a heart attack.

LUDWIG, WILLIAM (1912–1999), a screenwriter who penned many of the "Andy Hardy" films, collaborated with SONYA LEVIEN and other writers on such movie musicals as *THE GREAT CARUSO* (1951), *THE MERRY WIDOW* (1952), *THE STUDENT PRINCE* (1954), *HIT THE DECK* (1955), *Interrupted Melody* (1955), and *OKLAHOMA!* (1955).

LUPINO, IDA (1914–1995), the English-born leading lady who later typified the strong-willed American woman in her many dramatic films, made eight musicals during her career even though her singing had to be dubbed. Lupino's musical credits include *Paris in Spring* (1935), *ANYTHING GOES* (1936), *ARTISTS AND MODELS* (1937), *The Hard Way* (1942), *THANK YOUR LUCKY STARS* (1943), *HOLLYWOOD CANTEEN* (1944), *The Man I Love* (1946), and *Road House* (1948). She was the niece of British entertainer LUPINO LANE and one of the very few women in 1950s Hollywood to direct films.

LYNN, DIANA (1926–1971), a child prodigy at the piano, was featured as the piano-playing kid sister in several 1940s movies but failed to catch on in adult roles. Lynn appeared in ten musicals, among them *There's Magic in Music* (1941), *STAR SPANGLED RHYTHM* (1942), *And the Angels Sing* (1944), *Out of This World* (1945), *Duffy's Tavern* (1945), *My Friend Irma* (1949), *Meet Me at the Fair* (1952), and *You're Never Too Young* (1955). She left Hollywood in the mid-1950s and had a busy career on the stage and in television.

LYON, BEN (1901–1979) was a leading man in dramatic films but sang and danced in some musicals in the 1930s, including *The Hot Heiress* (1931), *Indiscreet* (1931), *Her Majesty Love* (1931), and *Dancing Feet* (1936). Lyon left Hollywood in the mid-1930s and lived in England, with his wife BEBE DANIELS where they became popular on the stage, in British films, and on the radio.

M

MacDONALD, JEANETTE (1903–1965) was Hollywood's reigning queen of OPERETTA and costume musicals in the 1930s, her classical features and high trilling voice making her a screen idol during the Depression. Having worked her way from the chorus to leads on Broadway, she was brought to Hollywood by ERNST LUBITSCH for the operatic lead in his *THE LOVE PARADE* (1929) opposite MAURICE CHEVALIER. MacDonald would be successfully paired with the Frenchman three more times: *ONE HOUR WITH YOU* (1932), *LOVE ME TONIGHT* (1932), and *THE MERRY WIDOW* (1934). After engaging performances in *The Vagabond King* (1930), *MONTE CARLO* (1930), *Let's Go Native* (1930), *Oh, for a Man!* (1930), and *THE CAT AND THE FIDDLE* (1934), she was paired with NELSON EDDY for *NAUGHTY MARIETTA* (1934), and the greatest singing team in the history of the movies was born. The two appeared together in *ROSE MARIE* (1936), *MAYTIME* (1937), *The Girl of the Golden West* (1938), *SWEETHEARTS* (1938), *New Moon* (1940), *Bitter Sweet* (1940), and *I Married an Angel* (1942). With other leading men, MacDonald made *SAN FRANCISCO* (1936), *Broadway Serenade* (1939), *Smilin' Through* (1941), and *Cairo* (1942). When audiences lost interest in operetta in the 1940s, MacDonald's career waned. After doing a specialty bit in *Follow the Boys* (1944) and roles in *Three Darling Daughters* (1948) and *The Sun Comes Up* (1949), she retired from the screen and returned to the stage and concert hall. MacDonald was married to GENE RAYMOND.

MacLAINE, SHIRLEY (1934–   ) became a star in the most cliché-ridden way: Working in the chorus of the Broadway musical *The Pajama Game* in 1954, featured player CAROL HANEY broke her leg and understudy MacLaine went on in her place, wowing audiences and getting a movie contract from producer HAL WALLIS, who was in the audience. Ironically,

MacLaine did few musicals after she went to Hollywood but, instead, played kookie ingenues in comedies at first, then in dramas, and later as a hard-boiled character actress in various film genres. But her four film musicals allowed her ample opportunity to display her singing and dancing talents: as Greenwich Village resident Bessie Sparrowbush in *ARTISTS AND MODELS* (1956), Parisian dance hall proprietor Simone Pistache in *CAN-CAN* (1960), lucky widow Louisa May Benson in *What a Way to Go* (1964), and taxi dancer Charity Hope Valentine in *SWEET CHARITY* (1968). MacLaine occasionally returned to musical performing in concerts and nightclubs. Her brother is actor Warren Beatty.

MACMURRAY, FRED (1907–1991), one of Hollywood and television's most personable leading men, started his career as a saxophone player and vocalist with bands and early in his film career often appeared in musicals playing musicians. MacMurray can be spotted as one of the band members in *To Beat the Band* (1935), followed by character roles in the musicals *The Princess Comes Across* (1936), *Champagne Waltz* (1937), *Swing High, Swing Low* (1937), *Cocoanut Grove* (1938), *Sing You Sinners* (1938), *Café Society* (1939), *STAR SPANGLED RHYTHM* (1942), *And the Angels Sing* (1944), *Where Do We Go From Here?* (1945), and *Never a Dull Moment* (1950). By the mid-1940s MacMurray was appearing in dramas and comedies as well and did fewer musicals. In the 1960s he was busy in television (*My Three Sons*) and making a series of nonmusical comedies for DISNEY. He returned to the film musical playing the eccentric Philadelphian Anthony J. Drexel Biddle in *The Happiest Millionaire* (1967). MacMurray was married to JUNE HAVER.

MACRAE, GORDON (1921–1986) and HOWARD KEEL pretty much had a monopoly on the robust leading men roles in movie musicals in the 1950s. MacRae sang on the radio, in clubs, and briefly on Broadway before going to Hollywood to play leading men in *Look for the Silver Lining* (1949), *The Daughter of Rosie O'Grady* (1950), *Tea for Two* (1950), *The West Point Story* (1950), *On Moonlight Bay* (1951), *About Face* (1952), *By the Light of the Silvery Moon* (1953), *THE DESERT SONG* (1953), and *Three Sailors and a Girl* (1953). MacRae did a specialty in *Starlift* (1951), played songwriter B.G. DE SYLVA in the musical bio *The Best Things in Life Are Free* (1956), but is mostly remember for his two RODGERS and HAMMERSTEIN heroes: cowboy Curly McLain in *OKLAHOMA!* (1955) and barker Billy Bigelow in *CAROUSEL* (1956). With the decline of movie musicals, MacRae kept busy doing stage work and television. His wife is Sheila MacRae, and his daughters are actresses Heather and Meredith MacRae.

MADONNA (1958–   ) is the stage name for Louise Veronica Ciccone, the international rock singer who manufactured and maintained a notorious persona that thrived on controversy. After making a name for herself in concert, on records, and on music videos, Madonna started playing supporting roles in movies in the late 1970s. In addition to filmed concerts, she performed in two movie musicals: as the sexy man-hunter Breathless Mahoney in *DICK TRACY* (1990) and the Argentine politico Eva Peron in *EVITA* (1996).

MAGIDSON, HERB (1906–1986) wrote lyrics for some dozen Hollywood musicals with a variety of composers, most frequently ALLIE WRUBEL. Magidson's film credits include *The Forward Pass* (1929), *Little Johnny Jones* (1930), *THE GAY DIVORCEE* (1934), *George White's Scandals* (1935), *Life of the Party* (1937), *Priorities on Parade* (1942), *Sleepytime Gal* (1942), and *Sing Your Way Home* (1945). His most famous song, written with composer CON CONRAD, is "The Continental," the first song to win an ACADEMY AWARD.

MAIN, MARJORIE (1890–1975), one of Hollywood's favorite character actresses, appeared in vaudeville and on Broadway before going West in 1932 and for a time being typecast as tragic mothers. But Main's forte was comedy, and she played crusty, no-nonsense women in dozens of films, including the "Ma and Pa Kettle" series of comedies. Her musical credits include *MUSIC IN THE AIR* (1934), *NAUGHTY MARIETTA* (1935), *MEET ME IN ST. LOUIS* (1944), *THE HARVEY GIRLS* (1946), *SUMMER STOCK* (1950), *THE BELLE OF NEW YORK* (1952), and *ROSE MARIE* (1954).

MAMOULIAN, ROUBEN (1898–1987), a Russian-born director who staged some of Broadway's most innovative and challenging musicals, brought his inspired sense of storytelling to a half dozen Hollywood musicals: *APPLAUSE* (1929), *LOVE ME TONIGHT* (1932), *The Gay Desperado* (1936), *HIGH, WIDE AND HANDSOME* (1937), *SUMMER HOLIDAY* (1947), and *SILK STOCKINGS* (1957). Mamoulian was famous for the way he moved the camera in his films, opening up the scene and finding new ways to create subjective point of view and set up the appropriate atmosphere, and his films, both musicals and dramas, were known for their lyrical impressionism.

MANCINI, HENRY (1924–1994) was one of Hollywood's most prolific (and most awarded) composers of soundtrack scores and songs for nonmusicals. He wrote only two musical scores for film, *DARLING LILI* (1969) with JOHNNY MERCER and *VICTOR/VICTORIA* (1982) with LESLIE BRICUSSE, but he arranged and/or conducted the music for such musicals as *THE GLENN MILLER STORY* (1954), *The Benny Goodman Story* (1956), *High Time* (1960), and the animated *The Great Mouse Detective* (1986). Of his dozens of hits, "Moon River" is perhaps his most famous song.

MARSHALL, GEORGE (1891–1975) had one of Hollywood's longest directing careers, helming films from 1917 to 1969. The former screen actor and scriptwriter was most known for his comedies, and he worked with the greatest comics of several generations, from LAUREL and HARDY to MARTIN and LEWIS. Among Marshall's two dozen film musicals were *She Learned About Sailors* (1934), *365 Nights in Hollywood* (1934), *THE GOLDWYN FOLLIES* (1938), *Destry Rides Again* (1939), *STAR SPANGLED RHYTHM* (1942), *Riding High* (1943), *And the Angels Sing* (1944), *Variety Girl* (1947), *My Friend Irma* (1949), *Fancy Pants* (1950), *Scared Stiff* (1953), and *Red Garters* (1954).

MARTIN, DEAN (1917–1996) was a handsome Italian singer who was straightman for JERRY LEWIS in sixteen films and in nightclubs before setting off on his own and playing laid-back playboys in nonmusicals. Martin's film debut was *My Friend Irma* (1949) with Lewis, and the comic chemistry between the two was so appealing that PARAMOUNT teamed them again in *My Friend Irma Goes West* (1950), *At War With the Army* (1950), *Sailor Beware* (1951), *The Stooge* (1952), *Scared Stiff* (1953), *The Caddy* (1953), *Living It Up* (1954), *ARTISTS AND MODELS* (1955), and many others. Martin provided the singing in these movies while Lewis supplied the frantic comedy, the two often joining in a character song or two. The team split up in 1956, and Martin made a few musicals on his own, including *Ten Thousand Bedrooms* (1957), *BELLS ARE RINGING* (1960), *ROBIN AND THE SEVEN HOODS* (1964), and *Kiss Me, Stupid* (1965). He also appeared in a series of thrillers on screen as part of the famous "Rat Pack" with FRANK SINATRA, PETER LAWFORD, and SAMMY DAVIS, JR., and had a popular variety show on television.

MARTIN, HUGH. See Blane, Ralph

MARTIN, MARY (1914–1990), one of the legends of the Broadway musical theatre, made only a dozen movies in her career, and although she shines in all of them, she never caught on with the movie public as she did on stage. Martin's first screen role was OPERETTA singer Louise Hall in *The Great Victor Herbert* (1939), and she followed it playing songwriter Cherry Lane in *RHYTHM ON THE RIVER* (1940), FRED ALLEN's niece Mary Allen in *LOVE THY NEIGHBOR* (1940), Southern chorine Cindy Lou Bethany in *Kiss the Boys Goodbye* (1941), New Orleans singer Betty Lou Cobb in *BIRTH OF THE BLUES* (1941), and gold digger Marjorie Stuart in *HAPPY GO LUCKY* (1943). She did a specialty bit in *STAR SPANGLED RHYTHM* (1942) and played herself in both *NIGHT AND DAY* (1946) and *Main Street to Broadway* (1953). Martin was active on the stage into the 1980s. Actor Larry Hagman is her son.

MARTIN, STEVE (1945–   ), the stand-up comic turned screen actor and screenwriter, has experimented with many forms of storytelling (he is also an accomplished playwright) and appeared in such unusual film musicals as *Sgt. Pepper's Lonely Hearts Club Band* (1978), *THE MUPPET MOVIE* (1979), *The Kids Are Alright* (1979), *PENNIES FROM HEAVEN* (1981), and *LITTLE SHOP OF HORRORS* (1986).

MARTIN, TONY (1912–   ), a nightclub and film crooner whose romantic way with a song was captured on millions of records, played leading men in some twenty movie musicals over three decades. Under the name Anthony Martin he was seen briefly in *FOLLOW THE FLEET* (1936), *POOR LITTLE RICH GIRL* (1936), *Pigskin Parade* (1936), and others. He graduated to better roles in *Sing and Be Happy* (1937), *You Can't Have Everything* (1937), *Sally, Irene and Mary* (1938), *Music in My Heart* (1940), and *ZIEGFELD GIRL* (1941). Martin was the dashing Pepe LeMoko in *CASBAH* (1948) and then returned to more traditional leads in *Two Tickets to Broadway* (1951), *Easy to Love* (1953), and *HIT THE DECK* (1955). He also made specialty appearances in *TILL THE CLOUDS ROLL BY* (1946), *DEEP IN MY HEART* (1954), and *Meet Me in Las Vegas* (1956). Martin was married first to ALICE FAYE and then to CYD CHARISSE, with whom he performed in nightclubs for several years.

MARTINI, NINO (1904–1976) was an Italian opera singer from the Metropolitan whose flowing tenor voice was heard in four Hollywood musicals: *PARAMOUNT ON PARADE* (1930), *Here's to Romance* (1935), *The Gay Desperado* (1936), and *Music for Madame* (1937).

MARX BROTHERS, THE, the farcical, surreal comedy family who were known for their comic anarchy, started in vaudeville but were soon starring in three Broadway musicals, two of which they filmed on Long Island: *THE COCOANUTS* (1929) and *ANIMAL CRACKERS* (1930). Chico (1886–1961) was the Italian-accented brother who played the piano, Harpo (1888–1964) the silent clown with an improbable blonde wig and mischievous leer, Groucho (1890–1977) the wisecracking con-man with a painted mustache and oversized cigar, and Zeppo (1901–1979) the juvenile straightman. The team's first film in Hollywood was *HORSE FEATHERS* (1932), followed by *DUCK SOUP* (1933), *A NIGHT AT THE OPERA* (1935), *A DAY AT THE RACES* (1937), *AT THE CIRCUS* (1939), *Go West* (1940), *The Big Store* (1941), and *Love Happy* (1949), as well as the nonmusical *A Night in Casablanca* (1946). The brothers went different ways after 1949. Groucho, who had appeared without his siblings in *Copacabana* (1947), was in the musicals *Mr. Music* (1950) and *Double Dynamite* (1951) and later found a second career in television (*You Bet Your Life*). The other brothers made appearances on television and radio but were dead by the time the Marx Brothers were rediscovered by a new generation in the 1960s. Although many of their films seem more like comedies than musicals, the brothers used music as another way to flaunt tradition and celebrate the absurdity of life.

MARY POPPINS (Disney 1964) was WALT DISNEY's finest musical film and the best musical fantasy since *THE WIZARD OF OZ* (1939). Among its many charms was a top-notch screenplay by Bill Walsh and Donald Da Gradi (based on P. L. Travers' children's book), the best score ever written by RICHARD M. and ROBERT B. SHERMAN, and a "practically perfect" film debut by JULIE ANDREWS as the "practically perfect in every way" nanny of the title. Set in 1910 London, the Banks family, headed by stuffy banker DAVID TOMLINSON and his suffragette wife GLYNIS JOHNS, has trouble keeping a nanny very long to supervise young Karen Dotrice and Matthew Garber. But Mary Poppins is no ordinary nanny as she flies through the air with an open umbrella, uses magic to straighten up the children's nursery, and takes her charges into a sidewalk chalk drawing for an afternoon's outing. Chimney sweep DICK VAN DYKE accompanies them on this excursion, which became the fantastical highlight of the film as live action and animation blend miraculously for a ride on a carousel, a dance with penguins, a horse race, and a sing-along of "Supercalifragilisticexpialidocious" with some street buskers. In another episode the foursome visit Van Dyke's daffy uncle ED WYNN and the quintet have tea floating in the air and singing "I Love to Laugh." But the father does not approve of Poppins' unorthodox ways and, seeking to instill practicality in his children, brings them downtown to his bank to invest their meager savings, only to have the kids panic and accidentally cause a run on the bank. Although he is fired by the crotchety old president (also played by Van Dyke), the father realizes that he has been missing all the joys of life and, in particular, his family and they all go to the park to fly kites as Poppins flies off on another assignment. ROBERT STEVENSON directed with a playful tone that allowed reality and fantasy to coexist, MARC BREAUX and DEEDEE WOOD choreographed the musical numbers (the raucous "Step in Time" on the London rooftops was another of the film's highpoints), and the special effects by Peter Ellenshaw were as wondrous as they were fun. Other songs in the score included "A Spoonful of Sugar," "Stay Awake," "Jolly Holiday," "Feed the Birds," "Let's Go Fly a Kite," "and the Oscar-winning "Chim Chim Cher-ee." All the principals were in top form (it was Van Dyke's finest screen performance and Andrews won an ACADEMY AWARD), supported by Elsa Lanchester, Hermione Baddeley, Reta Shaw, ARTHUR TREACHER, REGINALD OWEN, and JANE DARWELL. Not only was the movie a big hit, but DISNEY and other studios tried desperately to copy the formula and repeat its success for years afterward.

MASSEY, ILONA (1912–1974), a Hungarian opera singer who was featured in five Hollywood musicals, was a classic blonde beauty with an impenetrable aura. She was paired with NELSON EDDY in the operettas *ROSALIE*

(1937), *BALALAIKA* (1939), and *Northwest Outpost* (1947) and was also seen in *New Wine* (1942) and *Holiday in Mexico* (1945).

MATTHEWS, JESSIE (1907–1981) was Britain's most popular musical comedy star on the stage and, in the 1930s, in British movies. Her graceful dancing, innocent demeanor, and tremulous singing voice made her a star on both sides of the Atlantic even though she made only one Hollywood musical, *Tom Thumb* (1958), years after the peak of her career. Matthews' most-known film to Americans was *EVERGREEN* (1934), but she also triumphed in the British musicals *Out of the Blue* (1931), *The Good Companions* (1933), *Waltzes From Vienna* (1934), *Head Over Heels* (1937), *Sailing Along* (1937), and others.

MATURE, VICTOR (1915–1994), a muscular American actor with European good looks, was known mostly for his rugged action pictures in the 1940s and 1950s, but he revealed a lighter side in his seven musicals: *Song of the Islands* (1942), *My Gal Sal* (1942), *Footlight Serenade* (1942), *Seven Days' Leave* (1942), *Red, Hot and Blue* (1949), *The Las Vegas Story* (1952), and *Million Dollar Mermaid* (1952). Mature also made a guest appearance in the cult ROCK MUSICAL *Head* (1968).

MAXWELL, MARILYN (1921–1972) was a blonde beauty who rose from band vocalist on the radio to featured player in a handful of movie musicals. Maxwell played bit parts in *Presenting Lily Mars* (1943), *DuBarry Was a Lady* (1943), *BEST FOOT FORWARD* (1943), and *Thousands Cheer* (1943) before playing leads or second leads in *Swing Fever* (1943), *Lost in a Harem* (1944), *SUMMER HOLIDAY* (1948), *The Lemon Drop Kid* (1951), *Rock-a-Bye Baby* (1958), and *The Lively Set* (1964). The voluptuous Maxwell entertained troops overseas and, in her late forties, headed a burlesque show on tour across the country.

MAYO, ARCHIE (1891–1968), a reliable film director who helmed everything from action yarns to screwball comedies, directed eight musicals during his busy career, most memorably *MY MAN* (1928), *Is Everybody Happy?* (1929), *GO INTO YOUR DANCE* (1935), *ORCHESTRA WIVES* (1942), and *Sweet and Low-Down* (1944).

MAYO, VIRGINIA (1920–   ), a glamourous leading lady of the 1940s who was partnered with DANNY KAYE in four musicals, was more popular in lighter fare even though her dramatic efforts were commendable. The blonde singer-dancer was in *UP IN ARMS* (1944) only briefly, but she made such an impression that she was soon featured in *Seven Days Ashore* (1944), *Wonder Man* (1945), *The Kid From Brooklyn* (1946), *The Secret Life of Walter Mitty*

(1947), *A Song Is Born* (1948), *The West Point Story* (1950), *She's Working Her Way Through College* (1952), and others.

MAYTIME (MGM 1937) was one of the best looking and sung of the Hollywood OPERETTAS of the 1930s even though only one song was retained from SIGMUND ROMBERG's 1917 stage score. The number was "Will You Remember?" (with lyrics by Rida Johnson Young), and it was heard no less than six times, so the musical still seemed like a Romberg piece. The rest of the score consisted of traditional songs and opera selections ranging from "Summer Is a Cummin In" to Donizetti's "Chi Me Frena." When producer HUNT STROMBERG tossed out the Broadway score, he also jettisoned the plot and Noel Langley devised a new one about an aging American singer (JEANETTE MacDONALD) who warns the young Lynne Carver against marrying for position over love by telling her of her own tragic past. As a promising opera singer in Paris years ago, she was helped by the machinations of impresario John Barrymore, who also loved her. MacDonald fell for the tenor NELSON EDDY but decided to override her emotions and marry Barrymore. But years later, when MacDonald and Eddy were both engaged to sing at the Met in New York, their romance was rekindled and the jealous Barrymore killed Eddy in a fit of passion. It may have been a bit thick for light opera, but ROBERT Z. LEONARD directed the tale gently, getting strong performances from the principals, with even Barrymore avoiding the indulgence that the part must have tempted. Of the musical sequences, the most interesting was a fictitious opera called *Czaritza* that ROBERT WRIGHT and GEORGE FORREST concocted from Tchaikovsky's Fifth Symphony.

McCAREY, LEO (1898–1969), one of Hollywood's most successful directors and screenwriters, began his career in silents writing scripts for and directing LAUREL and HARDY shorts. When McCarey moved into features, he excelled at comedies but had his fair share of musical and melodrama hits as well. McCarey's early musicals include *Red Hot Rhythm* (1929), *Indiscreet* (1931), and *The Kid From Spain* (1932), but he hit his stride with *DUCK SOUP* (1933), *Belle of the Nineties* (1934), and *Love Affair* (1939). He wrote, directed, and produced the popular *GOING MY WAY* (1944), *THE BELLS OF ST. MARY'S* (1945), and *An Affair to Remember* (1957).

McDANIEL, HATTIE (1895–1952), the African American character actress forever remembered as Mammy in *Gone With the Wind* (1939), broke barriers for her race in all three major media. McDaniel was the first black woman to sing on network radio, the first black actress to win an ACADEMY AWARD, and the first African American to star in her own television series (*Beulah*). Although she often played maids and housekeepers and became a stereotypic image to many African Americans, McDaniel was an accomplished singer and actress who paved the way for others to follow. Among her musical credits were *I'm No Angel* (1933), *SHOW BOAT* (1936), *CAREFREE* (1938), *THANK YOUR LUCKY STARS* (1946), and *SONG OF THE SOUTH* (1946).

McDONALD, GRACE (1918–1999), a perky singer-dancer who came from vaudeville, where she performed with her brother RAY McDONALD, appeared in seventeen musicals in the 1940s, though rarely in leading roles and usually in grade B features. McDonald's credits include *Dancing on a Dime* (1941), *Behind the Eight Ball* (1941), *Give Out, Sisters* (1942), *Strictly in the Groove* (1943), *Crazy House* (1943), *Follow the Boys* (1944), and *Honeymoon Ahead* (1945).

McDONALD, RAY (1920–1959) was a boyish-looking song-and-dance man who lit up a half dozen MGM musicals in the 1940s in supporting roles. His most notable musicals were *BABES ON BROADWAY* (1941), *Born to Sing* (1942), *Presenting Lily Mars* (1943), *TILL THE CLOUDS ROLL BY* (1946), and *GOOD NEWS* (1947). His sister was GRACE McDONALD.

McGUIRE, MARCY (1925–   ), an energetic bobbysoxer type who was featured in a handful of 1940s musicals, is best remembered as the redheaded teen who pursued FRANK SINATRA in *Higher and Higher* (1943). McGuire's other film musicals include *Seven Days' Leave* (1942), *Follies Girl* (1943), and *Sing Your Way Home* (1945).

McHUGH, FRANK (1899–1981) was a favorite character actor in Hollywood, playing best friends and other congenial characters in over 150 feature films between 1930 and 1968. Known for his silly, high-pitched laugh, McHugh gave able support in such musicals as *Top Speed* (1930), *FOOTLIGHT PARADE* (1933), *Happiness Ahead* (1934), *GOLD DIGGERS OF 1935*, *Stars Over Broadway* (1935), *Mr. Dodd Takes the Air* (1937), *GOING MY WAY* (1944), *Bowery to Broadway* (1944), *STATE FAIR* (1945), *Carnegie Hall* (1947), *THERE'S NO BUSINESS LIKE SHOW BUSINESS* (1954), *Easy Come, Easy Go* (1967), and many others.

McHUGH, JIMMY (1892–1969), one of the most successful composers on Broadway, Tin Pan Alley, and in Hollywood, began his career scoring Cotton Club shows and stage revues with lyricist DOROTHY FIELDS before going West. He and Fields wrote the songs for the early film musicals *Love in the Rough* (1930), *Hooray for Love* (1935), and *EVERY NIGHT AT EIGHT* (1935). With TED KOEHLER he scored *KING OF BURLESQUE* (1935) and *Dimples* (1936), but his most frequent collaborator was HAROLD ADAMSON, with whom he worked on nineteen films. The most notable Adamson-McHugh musicals were *Banjo on My Knee* (1936), *You're a Sweetheart* (1937), *Mad About Music* (1938), *Higher and Higher* (1943), *Four Jills in a*

Jeep (1943), *Doll Face* (1945), and *If You Knew Susie* (1948). With FRANK LOESSER, McHugh scored *Buck Benny Rides Again* (1940), *HAPPY GO LUCKY* (1943), and others, and with JOHNNY MERCER he contributed songs to *You'll Find Out* (1940) and *You're the One* (1941). McHugh wrote dozens of hit songs, including "I'm in the Mood for Love," "I Can't Give You Anything but Love," "I Feel a Song Comin' On," and "On the Sunny Side of the Street," several of which were used in the musical bio *The Helen Morgan Story* (1957), where he made a brief screen appearance.

McLEOD, NORMAN (1898–1964) was a Hollywood director who helmed his first features at the end of the silent era. McLeod worked with the greatest comics of his day, from the MARX BROTHERS to HOPE and CROSBY to DANNY KAYE. Among his fifteen musicals were *HORSE FEATHERS* (1932), *Many Happy Returns* (1934), *Coronado* (1935), *PENNIES FROM HEAVEN* (1936), *Lady, Be Good* (1941), *The Kid From Brooklyn* (1946), *The Secret Life of Walter Mitty* (1947), *ROAD TO RIO* (1947), and *THE PALEFACE* (1948).

McPHAIL, DOUGLAS (1910–1944) was a beefy, baby-faced tenor who was featured in five musicals: *SWEETHEARTS* (1938), *BABES IN ARMS* (1939), *Little Nellie Kelly* (1940), *BROADWAY MELODY OF 1940*, and *Born to Sing* (1942).

MEEK, DONALD (1880–1946) was a favorite character actor on Broadway and in films, often playing people as reticent as his name. Meek can be seen in the film musicals *MURDER AT THE VANITIES* (1934), *THE MERRY WIDOW* (1934), *TOP HAT* (1935), *ARTISTS AND MODELS* (1937), *Little Miss Broadway* (1938), *BABES ON BROADWAY* (1941), and *STATE FAIR* (1945).

MEET ME IN ST. LOUIS (MGM 1944) remains a favorite with audiences over the decades because the nostalgic piece is sentimental but never maudlin and the nearly plotless film celebrates values that were more precious than ever during the wartime when it was released. Taken from a series of stories by Sally Benson, the screenplay by IRVING BRECHER and Fred Finklehoffe follows the doings of the upper-middle-class Smith family of St. Louis during the course of twelve months in 1903 and 1904. As the seasons pass, teenage daughters JUDY GARLAND and LUCILLE BREMER fall in love, little sister MARGARET O'BRIEN has a thrilling Halloween adventure, much excitement and many tears are shed over the Christmas dance, father Leon Ames informs his wife Mary Astor and the rest of the family that they will not be moving to New York as planned, and everyone sets out in the spring for the opening of the St. Louis World's Fair. Director VINCENTE MINNELLI turned each section into a visual and emotional postcard, and choreographer CHARLES WALTERS staged the songs with simple but thrilling joy, as in the famous

"The Trolley Song." HUGH MARTIN and RALPH BLANE wrote their best score ever, introducing the yearning ballad "The Boy Next Door" and a new holiday standard "Have Yourself a Merry Little Christmas." Old songs from the period, such as the title number, were also used, none more amusingly than "Under the Bamboo Tree," which Garland and O'Brien sang to entertain guests at a party. The supporting cast was first class, with MARJORIE MAIN, Tom Drake, HARRY DAVENPORT, Hugh Marlowe, CHILL WILLS, Henry Daniels, Jr., June Lockhart, Darryl Hickman, and Joan Carroll each adding a charming touch to the whole. *Meet Me in St. Louis* was turned into a Broadway musical in 1989 but failed to run very long.

MELCHIOR, LAURITZ (1890–1973), the renowned Danish tenor who was considered one of the greatest interpreters of Wagner's operas, was featured in five Hollywood musicals to add a touch of class. The giant singer played jovial characters in *Thrill of a Romance* (1945), *Two Sisters From Boston* (1946), *This Time for Keeps* (1947), *Luxury Liner* (1948), and *The Stars Are Singing* (1953). He is the father of Danish filmmaker Ib Melchior.

MELTON, JAMES (1904–1961) was an operatic tenor who reversed the usual pattern by finding acceptance in three Hollywood musicals and then was made a member of the Metropolitan Opera company. Melton was featured in *Stars Over Broadway* (1935), *Sing Me a Love Song* (1936), and *Melody for Two* (1937); he later returned to Hollywood to do a specialty in *ZIEGFELD FOLLIES* (1946).

MENJOU, ADOLPHE (1890–1963) had one of the longest Hollywood careers on record, playing dapper military men and figures of authority in a multitude of films between 1916 and 1960. Menjou and his precise mustache can be seen in two dozen musicals, including *Morocco* (1930), *New Moon* (1930), *Little Miss Marker* (1934), *GOLD DIGGERS OF 1935, Broadway Gondolier* (1935), *ONE IN A MILLION* (1936), *ONE HUNDRED MEN AND A GIRL* (1937), *THE GOLDWYN FOLLIES* (1938), *Syncopation* (1942), *YOU WERE NEVER LOVELIER* (1942), *Sweet Rosie O'Grady* (1943), *Step Lively* (1944), *My Dream Is Yours* (1949), *Dancing in the Dark* (1949), and *Bundle of Joy* (1956).

MENKEN, ALAN (1950–   ), one of the most successful movie composers in film history, scored more hits and won more awards in the 1990s than most other recognized artists did in a lifetime. Menken and his lyricist partner HOWARD ASHMAN scored a handful of Off-Broadway musicals before moving into film. Their stage hit *LITTLE SHOP OF HORRORS* (1986) was their film debut, but it was their screen score for *THE LITTLE MERMAID* (1989) that earned them wide recognition and ushered in a golden age for DISNEY-animated musicals. The team scored *BEAUTY AND THE BEAST*

(1991) and half of the songs for *ALADDIN* (1992) before Ashman died of AIDS. TIM RICE completed the lyrics for the film and collaborated with Menken on additional songs when *Beauty and the Beast* was made into a Broadway musical in 1994. Menken scored the live-action musical *Newsies* (1992) with Jack Feldman and the animated *POCAHONTAS* (1995) and *THE HUNCHBACK OF NOTRE DAME* (1996) with STEPHEN SCHWARTZ. Lyricist David Zippel wrote the songs with Menken for *HERCULES* (1997). Menken also composed the musical soundtracks for his movies, winning Oscars for them as well as for songs. Menken's music is very tuneful, rich in harmony, and captures the flavor of the period and location in which his films are set.

MERCER, JOHNNY (1909–1976) was a favorite lyricist in Hollywood, where he scored some thirty musicals and wrote some of America's most popular songs. Mercer on occasion wrote his own music with success ("Something's Gotta Give" is a good example), but it was his collaboration with various composers that produced such hits as "Jeepers Creepers," "Blues in the Night," "In the Cool Cool Cool of the Evening," "On the Atchison, Topeka and the Santa Fe," and many more. He started out as a band vocalist but by 1935 was contributing songs for the movies. With RICHARD A. WHITING, he scored *Ready, Willing and Able* (1937), *VARSITY SHOW* (1937), *HOLLYWOOD HOTEL* (1937), and *Cowboy From Brooklyn* (1938). With HARRY WARREN he wrote for *Garden of the Moon* (1938), *Going Places* (1938), *Naughty but Nice* (1939), and *THE HARVEY GIRLS* (1946). HAROLD ARLEN was his partner on *Blues in the Night* (1941), *STAR SPANGLED RHYTHM* (1942), *The Sky's the Limit* (1943), and *HERE COME THE WAVES* (1944). With others he contributed to *Navy Blues* (1941), *THE FLEET'S IN* (1942), *YOU WERE NEVER LOVELIER* (1942), *Dangerous When Wet* (1953), *SEVEN BRIDES FOR SEVEN BROTHERS* (1954), *You Can't Run Away From It* (1956), *Merry Andrew* (1958), and others. Two of Mercer's Broadway shows were filmed: *Top Banana* (1954), in which he wrote both music and lyrics, and *LI'L ABNER* (1959) with composer GENE DE PAUL. His last film score was *DARLING LILI* (1969) with HENRY MANCINI. Mercer also wrote theme or title songs for nonmusicals, such as the Oscar-winning "Moon River" and "The Days of Wine and Roses." His lyrics can be characterized by their slangy expressions and folksy imagery. Mercer's work was celebrated in the Broadway revue *Dream* (1997).

MERKEL, UNA (1903–1986) played supporting roles (usually the wise-cracking friend of the heroine) in dozens of films, including twenty-one musicals. Although Merkel had played leading roles in silent movies and early talkies, it was her character roles that made her a familiar favorite with audiences. Among her musical credits were *42ND STREET* (1933), *THE MERRY WIDOW* (1934 and 1952), *BROADWAY MELODY OF 1936* (1935), *BORN TO DANCE* (1936), *Destry Rides Again* (1939), *ROAD TO ZANZI-*

BAR (1941), *THIS IS THE ARMY* (1943), *My Blue Heaven* (1950), *WITH A SONG IN MY HEART* (1952), *I Love Melvin* (1953), *The Girl Most Likely* (1957), *Summer Magic* (1963), and *Spinout* (1966).

MERMAN, ETHEL (1909–1984) may not have enjoyed the same kind of popularity in films as she received on Broadway, but the funny, full-voiced belter gave some delectable screen performances in her dozen movie musicals. Merman got to repeat only two of her stage roles in Hollywood: the swinging evangelist Reno Sweeney in *ANYTHING GOES* (1936) and the ambassadress Sally Adams in *CALL ME MADAM* (1953). Her first film appearance was in *Follow the Leader* (1930), followed by *WE'RE NOT DRESSING* (1934), *KID MILLIONS* (1934), *BIG BROADCAST OF 1936* (1935), *Strike Me Pink* (1936), *Straight, Place and Show* (1938), and *Happy Landing* (1938). Merman also gave memorable performances in *ALEXANDER'S RAGTIME BAND* (1938) and *THERE'S NO BUSINESS LIKE SHOW BUSINESS* (1954), as well as a specialty in *STAGE DOOR CANTEEN* (1943). Her last musical credit was the voice of the Wicked Witch in *Journey Back to Oz* (1972).

MERRILL, BOB (1920–1998) wrote lyrics and/or music for a handful of Broadway musicals (such as *Carnival* and *Take Me Along*) and penned some popular ditties (such as "How Much Is That Doggie in the Window?") for Tin Pan Alley. His only stage show to be filmed was *FUNNY GIRL* (1968), which he wrote with composer JULE STYNE, but Merrill wrote the score solo for the movie musical *The Wonderful World of the Brothers Grimm* (1962).

MERRY WIDOW, THE, Franz Lehar's masterpiece and probably the finest of all Viennese OPERETTAS, was filmed twice as a silent movie before MGM's Irving Thalberg put together a 1934 sound version with LORENZ HART providing a fresh lyric translation and Ernest Vajda and SAMSON RAPHAELSON writing a screenplay that gracefully transferred the famous story to the screen. JEANETTE MacDONALD was the wealthy widow Sonia, MAURICE CHEVALIER was the dashing Captain Danilo, who woos her to keep her from marrying a foreigner, EDWARD EVERETT HORTON was Ambassador Popoff, UNA MERKEL Queen Dolores, and GEORGE BARBIER her husband the king, with STERLING HOLLOWAY, DONALD MEEK, Henry Armetta, AKIM TAMIROFF, HERMAN BING, Ruth Channing, and BILLY GILBERT filling out the cast of characters. ERNST LUBITSCH directed, his famous "touch" well in evidence, and ALBERTINA RASCH choreographed the musical numbers, the waltz at the embassy ball remaining one of Hollywood's most sumptuous dance sequences. The whole venture was as near to perfection as could be asked for, but MGM offered a new version in 1952 with LANA TURNER (vocals by Trudy Erwin) playing an American widow, FERNANDO LAMAS handling most of the singing as Count Danilo, and Richard Haydn as Popoff. PAUL FRANCIS WEBSTER wrote yet another set of English lyrics, and director Curtis Bernhardt staged the piece like a turgid melodrama. JACK COLE's choreography is vivaciously inappropriate though it is fun to spot GWEN VERDON doing the can-can in one number.

METRO-GOLDWYN-MAYER (MGM), the biggest and most prestigious studio in Hollywood for much of the 1930s and 1940s, was formed in 1924 by a merger of the Metro Picture Corporation, SAMUEL GOLDWYN's company, and Loew's subsidiary run by Louis B. Mayer. The three-way combination, plus Loew's vast chain of movie theatres, made MGM a powerful company from the start, and under Mayer's leadership and the expert management by Irving Thalberg as head of production, it quickly became the king of Hollywood studios. By the time sound came in, MGM had the staff, facilities, and stars to grow rapidly and turn out more and better pictures than its competitors. It quickly established its reputation for movie musicals with such early successes as *THE BROADWAY MELODY* (1929), *THE HOLLYWOOD REVUE OF 1929*, and *RIO RITA* (1929). Highlights of the 1930s included OPERETTAS such as *THE MERRY WIDOW* (1934) and the JEANETTE MacDONALD-NELSON EDDY musicals, the SERIES of *BROADWAY MELODY* films, the first BIOGRAPHICAL MUSICAL hit *THE GREAT ZIEGFELD* (1936), MARX BROTHERS vehicles such as *A NIGHT AT THE OPERA* (1935), spectacle features such as *SAN FRANCISCO* (1936) and *BORN TO DANCE* (1936), and the landmark fantasy musical *THE WIZARD OF OZ* (1939). MGM remained strong during the 1940s with the MICKEY ROONEY–JUDY GARLAND backstagers, unusual entries such as *CABIN IN THE SKY* (1943) and *ZIEGFELD FOLLIES* (1946), period musicals like *MEET ME IN ST. LOUIS* (1944) and *THE HARVEY GIRLS* (1946), GENE KELLY and FRANK SINATRA vehicles such as *ANCHORS AWEIGH* (1945) and *ON THE TOWN* (1949), BIOGRAPHICAL MUSICALS like *TILL THE CLOUDS ROLL BY* (1946) and *WORDS AND MUSIC* (1948), and FRED ASTAIRE showcases such as *EASTER PARADE* (1948) and *THE BARKLEYS OF BROADWAY* (1949). Many of these musicals were products of the famous Freed unit consisting of producer ARTHUR FREED with directors VINCENTE MINNELLI, CHARLES WALTERS, and STANLEY DONEN. MGM was hit with corporate problems as well as a decline in movie attendance in the 1950s, but several superior musicals were still made, including *ANNIE GET YOUR GUN* (1950), *SHOW BOAT* (1951), *AN AMERICAN IN PARIS* (1951), *SINGIN' IN THE RAIN* (1952), *THE BAND WAGON* (1953), *SEVEN BRIDES FOR SEVEN BROTHERS* (1954), *HIGH SOCIETY* (1956), *SILK STOCKINGS* (1957), and *GIGI* (1958). By the 1960s the giant was severely wounded and the studio even auctioned off memorabilia in its property and costume warehouses to raise the much-needed cash, and in the 1970s the studio stopped releasing its own films. A merger with UNITED ARTISTS in 1981 formed the short-lived

MGM/UA Entertainment, and by 1986 the studio was bought by Turner Broadcasting, which virtually turned the company into a library of classics from the past. What made the MGM musicals so special was the high level of artistry in every department, from the star talent to the art directors to the orchestraters. The resulting products were lavish but rarely gaudy, boldly presented but attention paid to details, innovative but always entertaining.

MGM. See Metro-Goldwyn-Mayer

MILESTONE, LEWIS (1895–1980), the Russian-born director who learned about filmmaking while serving in the U.S. Army during World War One, helmed many famous dramatic features and four musicals: *HALLELU-JAH, I'M A BUM* (1933), *Paris in Spring* (1935), *ANYTHING GOES* (1936), and *Melba* (1953).

MILLAND, RAY (1907–1986), the suave, gentlemanly leading man who made nearly a 100 films during his long career, showed up in nonsinging roles in a handful of movie musicals, including *Many Happy Returns* (1934), *WE'RE NOT DRESSING* (1934), *BIG BROADCAST OF 1937* (1936), *Three Smart Girls* (1936), *Tropic Holiday* (1938), *Irene* (1940), *STAR SPAN-GLED RHYTHM* (1942), and *Variety Girl* (1947).

MILLER, ANN (1919–   ), one of Hollywood's most accomplished tap dancers, rarely played leading ladies but was so memorable in second leads or as the "other woman" that she became a star. When she first went to Hollywood in the mid-1930s, Miller spent a decade in mostly grade B musicals, such as *Life of the Party* (1937), *Having Wonderful Time* (1938), *TOO MANY GIRLS* (1940), *True to the Army* (1942), *Reveille With Beverly* (1943), *The Thrill of Brazil* (1946), and others. But after her breakout role of dancing star Nadine Hale in *EASTER PARADE* (1948), she got juicier parts in such MGM classics as *ON THE TOWN* (1949) and *KISS ME, KATE* (1953). Miller's other musicals include *The Kissing Bandit* (1948), *Texas Carnival* (1951), *LOVELY TO LOOK AT* (1952), *Small Town Girl* (1953), *DEEP IN MY HEART* (1954), *HIT THE DECK* (1955), and *The Opposite Sex* (1956). She returned to the stage in the 1960s, was on Broadway in the 1970s, and was still performing in the 1990s.

MILLER, GLENN (1904–1944), the trombone-playing orchestra leader and a giant in the Big Band era, appeared in two Hollywood musicals, *SUN VALLEY SERENADE* (1941) and *ORCHESTRA WIVES* (1942), both times playing a bandleader with his famous players. JAMES STEWART portrayed Goodman in the musical bio *THE GLENN MILLER STORY* (1954), with Joe Yukl doing the trombone playing on the soundtrack. Miller died when the plane taking him to Europe to entertain American troops disappeared over the Atlantic.

MILLER, MARILYN (1898–1936), one of Broadway's most adored musical comedy stars of the 1920s, got to recreate two of her stage roles on film: the title waitress-turned-star in *Sally* (1929) and the title circus performer in *Sunny* (1930). Miller made one more film musical, as barmaid Lia Toerreck in *Her Majesty Love* (1931), before her untimely death at the age of thirty-seven. JUDY GARLAND played Miller in *TILL THE CLOUDS ROLL BY* (1946), and JUNE HAVER played her in the musical bio *Look for the Silver Lining* (1949), named after the famous song Miller introduced on Broadway.

MILLS BROTHERS, THE, a harmonizing trio made up of siblings Herbert (1912–1989), Harry (1913–1982), and Donald (1915–1999), were popular in concerts, in nightclubs, and on records for their low-key, smooth sound. The group was featured in specialty spots in a dozen films, including *THE BIG BROADCAST* (1932), *Twenty Million Sweethearts* (1934), *Strictly Dynamite* (1934), *Broadway Gondolier* (1935), *Rhythm Parade* (1942), *Reveille With Beverly* (1943), *When You're Smiling* (1950), and *The Big Beat* (1957). For a time the eldest brother John, Jr., was in the group; after his death in 1936, the father John, Sr., joined them for twenty years.

MINNELLI, LIZA (1946–   ), the energetic and emotional star of stage, concerts, and film, has had a see-saw career (and personal life) but maintains a strong following despite (or because) of it. The daughter of JUDY GARLAND and director VINCENTE MINNELLI, she made her film debut as a child in the finale of *IN THE GOOD OLD SUMMERTIME* (1949). Her first professional jobs were Off-Broadway and then on Broadway, winning acclaim (and a Tony Award) at the age of seventeen. Although she began making films in 1967, Minnelli's first musical was *CABARET* (1972), in which she gave her most celebrated performance as hedonist nightclub singer Sally Bowles. She did the voice of Dorothy in the animated *Journey Back to Oz* (1972), played the chambermaid Nina in *A Matter of Time* (1976), directed by her father, and shone as Big Band singer Francine Evans in *NEW YORK, NEW YORK* (1977). Minnelli has made several television specials, dramatic features, and comedies, such as the semimusical *Stepping Out* (1991), and remains active on the concert stage.

MINNELLI, VINCENTE (1903–1986), one of the musical film's top directors, studied art and worked as a scenic and costume designer in theatre before staging musicals on Broadway. He was brought to Hollywood by producer ARTHUR FREED, who had Minnelli learn about the different aspects of film from MGM masters. After staging some sequences in *STRIKE UP THE BAND* (1940) and *BABES ON BROADWAY* (1942), he directed

CABIN IN THE SKY (1943), which secured his new career. Minnelli's films, both musicals and nonmusicals, are known for their strong visuals and bold use of color and camera movement. His greatest achievements were *MEET ME IN ST. LOUIS* (1944), *AN AMERICAN IN PARIS* (1951), *THE BAND WAGON* (1953), and *GIGI* (1958), but there is much to recommend in some of his other dozen musicals as well, including *I Dood It* (1943), *Yolanda and the Thief* (1945), *ZIEGFELD FOLLIES* (1946), *THE PIRATE* (1948), *BRIGADOON* (1954), *KISMET* (1955), *BELLS ARE RINGING* (1960), and *ON A CLEAR DAY YOU CAN SEE FOREVER* (1970). He also directed sections of *TILL THE CLOUDS ROLL BY* (1946) and *LOVELY TO LOOK AT* (1951). Minnelli's last film was the musical *A Matter of Time* (1976) featuring his daughter LIZA MINNELLI. He was married for a time to JUDY GARLAND.

MIRANDA, CARMEN (1909–1955) was billed as the "Brazilian Bombshell" for her flamboyant personality, colorful costumes, and tongue-twisting English. A star of films in Brazil, Miranda was brought to New York as a featured guest star in a Broadway revue. Hollywood quickly grabbed her up and put her in supporting but flashy roles in mostly south-of-the-border musicals. Her film debut was in a specialty bit in *DOWN ARGENTINE WAY* (1940), followed by comic roles in *THAT NIGHT IN RIO* (1941), *WEEK-END IN HAVANA* (1941), *SPRINGTIME IN THE ROCKIES* (1942), *THE GANG'S ALL HERE* (1943), *Greenwich Village* (1944), *Something for the Boys* (1944), *Doll Face* (1945), *If I'm Lucky* (1946), *Copacabana* (1947), *A Date With Judy* (1948), *Nancy Goes to Rio* (1950), and *Scared Stiff* (1953), as well as a specialty spot in *Four Jills in a Jeep* (1944). Miranda remains one of the most imitated of all Hollywood stars because she was such a unique and satirical performer.

MISSISSIPPI (Paramount 1935) was one of BING CROSBY's few period musicals, but he inherited the role by replacing LANNY ROSS, who looked so dull in the rushes that producer ARTHUR HORNBLOW, JR., took him off the film. The plot, based on Booth Tarkington's novel and play *Magnolia*, concerned a nineteenth-century pacifist (Crosby) from Philadelphia who failed to fight and defend the honor of his southern fiancée Gail Patrick and so was shunned by her family and labeled a coward. But Crosby gets a job as a singer on a riverboat captained by W.C. FIELDS, regains his honor by outwitting a murderous villain, and falls in love with his ex-fiancée's sister JOAN BEN- NETT. RICHARD RODGERS and LORENZ HART provided the songs, three of which were hits: "Down by the River," "Soon," and "Easy to Remember." As pleasing as Crosby and the musical numbers were, the film's highpoints were Fields' poker game and his exaggerated yarn about fighting savages in the wilderness.

MITCHELL, SIDNEY (1888–1942) was a Hollywood lyricist who, working with a variety of composers, scored eighteen musicals in the late 1920s and 1930s. Mitchell wrote songs for the early talkies *Fox Movietone Follies* (1929), *Broadway* (1929), *Let's Go Places* (1930), *Dancing Feet* (1936), *Laughing Irish Eyes* (1936), and others before teaming with composer LEW POLLACK on eight films, including *CAPTAIN JANUARY* (1936), *Pigskin Parade* (1936), *ONE IN A MILLION* (1936), *Thin Ice* (1937), *IN OLD CHICAGO* (1938), and *REBECCA OF SUNNYBROOK FARM* (1938).

MONACO, JAMES V. (1885–1945) was a Hollywood and Tin Pan Alley composer who, working with three different lyricists, wrote songs for film musicals in the late 1930s and 1940s, including seven BING CROSBY vehicles. With JOHNNY BURKE, Monaco scored *Doctor Rhythm* (1938), *Sing You Sinners* (1938), *East Side of Heaven* (1939), *The Star Maker* (1939), *ROAD TO SINGAPORE* (1940), *If I Had My Way* (1940), and *RHYTHM ON THE RIVER* (1940). AL DUBIN was his lyricist for *STAGE DOOR CANTEEN* (1943), and with MACK GORDON he contributed songs to *Pin-Up Girl* (1944), *Sweet and Low-Down* (1944), and *Irish Eyes Are Smiling* (1944).

MONROE, MARILYN (1926–1962), the Hollywood legend and icon of sexuality, made her film debut as a chorus girl in the low-budget musical *Ladies of the Chorus* (1949), then returned to the film musical three times after she had become a star. Monroe played the gold digger Lorelei Lee in *GENTLEMEN PREFER BLONDES* (1953), nightclub singer Vicky in *THERE'S NO BUSINESS LIKE SHOW BUSINESS* (1954), and Off-Broadway performer Amanda Dell in *Let's Make Love* (1960). She also sang some songs in the nonmusicals *River of No Return* (1954), *Bus Stop* (1956), and *Some Like It Hot* (1959). Monroe's kittenish purr in delivering a song equaled her sensuous way with dialogue, yet there was often the flavor of self-parody in her musical performances. She was married to baseballer Joe DiMaggio and then to playwright Arthur Miller.

MONTALBAN, RICARDO (1920–   ), a dashing leading man in musicals and dramas, made movies in his native Mexico before Hollywood beckoned and put him in a series of musicals where he played Latin lovers: *Fiesta* (1947), *On an Island With You* (1948), *The Kissing Bandit* (1948), *NEPTUNE'S DAUGHTER* (1949), *Two Weeks With Love* (1950), *Sombrero* (1953), and *Latin Lovers* (1953). As much as he wished to shake off these cliché roles, Montalban was not able to do it until he moved into television in the 1970s. He returned to the film musical to play a priest in *The Singing Nun* (1966) and an Italian movie star in *SWEET CHARITY* (1968).

MONTE CARLO (Paramount 1930) was another one of director ERNST LUBITSCH's featherweight musical comedies of the 1930s that seemed to float magically by rather than unspool on the screen. Impoverished countess JEANETTE MacDONALD leaves her wealthy fiancé at the altar and flees to Monte Carlo, where she falls in love with aristocrat JACK BUCHANAN, who is disguised as a barber. Lubitsch told the story with charm, a wry satirical subtext, and delicate cinemagraphic skill. MacDonald and Buchanan sang the duet "Give Me a Moment Please" on the phone and attended the fictitious opera *Monsieur Beaucaire*, where the plot paralleled their own situation. The most famous scene in the movie is the countess's train ride on the *Blue Express* to Monte Carlo with MacDonald singing "Beyond the Blue Horizon," waving to the peasants working in the field, and the peasants joining her in song, all perfectly set to the rhythm of the train and the clinking on the rails, all climaxing together. LEO ROBIN, RICHARD A. WHITING, and W. FRANKE HARLING wrote the superior score, which also included the up-tempo ballad "Always in All Ways." Buchanan and MacDonald made a charming couple, but he left Hollywood after this film and didn't return for twenty-three years.

MOON OVER MIAMI (Fox 1941) was a colorful diversion that found enough south-of-the-border romance without going any farther than Florida. Waitress BETTY GRABLE pulls together her money and heads to Miami to snag a millionaire, her sister CAROLE LANDIS posing as her secretary and her aunt CHARLOTTE GREENWOOD pretending to be her maid. She almost gets wealthy playboy ROBERT CUMMINGS but falls in love with not-wealthy playboy DON AMECHE. The opportunity for musical numbers was easy to come by, and the dances staged by HERMES PAN and (uncredited) JACK COLE sparkled. So did much of the score by LEO ROBIN and RALPH RAINGER, the best songs being the freewheeling "Kindergarten Conga," the spirited ballad "You Started Something," and the daffy character song "Is That Good?," which Greenwood sang with hotel waiter JACK HALEY. The movie was recycled as **THREE LITTLE GIRLS IN BLUE** (Fox 1946), which placed the tale in 1902 and had New Jersey farm girl JUNE HAVER set out for Atlantic City with friends VIVIAN BLAINE and VERA-ELLEN (dubbed by Carol Stewart) posing as the secretary and the maid. They ended up with fortune hunter George Montgomery (dubbed by Ben Gage), waiter Charles Smith (dubbed by Del Porter), and titled aristocrat Frank Latimore. MACK GORDON and JOSEPH MYROW supplied the songs this time, and some of them ("Somewhere in the Night," "This Is Always," and "On the Boardwalk in Atlantic City") captured the period nicely. Yet the big hit song was the swinging "You Make Me Feel So Young," which was used for a dream ballet featuring Vera-Ellen and Smith. CELESTE HOLM took Greenwood's place in delivering the comedy, especially with the number "Always a Lady."

MOORE, CONSTANCE (1919–   ), a blonde singer who had started out performing with bands in nightclubs and on the radio, was featured in seventeen Hollywood musicals, but most of them were grade B pictures and she never achieved wide popularity. Moore can be seen in *Swing That Cheer* (1938), *Hawaiian Nights* (1939), *Argentine Nights* (1940), *Las Vegas Nights* (1941), *Earl Carroll Vanities* (1945), *Hit Parade of 1947*, and others.

MOORE, GRACE (1901–1947), a stately blonde singer who conquered Broadway and the Metropolitan Opera before turning to films, helped popularize opera in America because of her recordings. Moore's biggest success was as the struggling soprano Mary Barrett in *One Night of Love* (1934), but she gave fine performances also in *A Lady's Morals* (1930), *New Moon* (1930), *Love Me Forever* (1935), *The King Steps Out* (1936), *When You're in Love* (1937), and *I'll Take Romance* (1937). She died in a plane crash during a European concert tour. KATHRYN GRAYSON played Moore in the musical bio *So This Is Love* (1953).

MOORE, IDA (1883–1964), the perennial mother or sweet old lady in many 1940s and 1950s films, had featured roles in such musicals as *Easy to Look At* (1945), *Easy Come, Easy Go* (1947), *Mr. Music* (1950), *Fancy Pants* (1950), *The Lemon Drop Kid* (1951), *SHOW BOAT* (1951), *THE COUNTRY GIRL* (1954), and *Rock-a-Bye Baby* (1958).

MOORE, VICTOR (1876–1962) was one of Broadway's favorite character actors, a short and pudgy clown who specialized in befuddled and bumbling roles in musicals and comedies. Moore recreated two of his stage roles for the movies, bootlegger Skippy Dugan in *Heads Up* (1930) and the easily seduced Senator Oliver P. Loganberry in *Louisiana Purchase* (1941), and played delightful fools in another fifteen film musicals, including *The Gift of Gab* (1934), *SWING TIME* (1936), *Life of the Party* (1937), *STAR SPANGLED RHYTHM* (1942), *Riding High* (1943), *Carolina Blues* (1944), *Duffy's Tavern* (1945), and *ZIEGFELD FOLLIES* (1946).

MOOREHEAD, AGNES (1906–1974), the stage actress who made her film debut as part of the Mercury Players in *Citizen Kane* (1941), rarely sang on screen but later in her career was featured in memorable roles in a handful of musicals. Moorehead can be seen in *SUMMER HOLIDAY* (1948), *SHOW BOAT* (1951), *Those Redheads From Seattle* (1953), *Meet Me in Las Vegas* (1956), *The Opposite Sex* (1956), *Pardners* (1956), *The Singing Nun* (1966), and a voiceover for the animated *CHARLOTTE'S WEB* (1973).

MORENO, RITA (1931–   ), the vibrant Puerto Rican singer-dancer most remembered for playing the fiery Anita in *WEST SIDE STORY* (1961), was on Broadway at the age of thirteen and in movies the next year. Moreno can be spotted in ethnic roles in the films *The Toast of New Orleans* (1950), *Pagan Love Song* (1950), *SINGIN' IN THE RAIN* (1952), and *Latin Lovers* (1953);

she graduated to more substantial parts, playing the concubine Tuptim in *THE KING AND I* (1956) and the saucy Huguette in *The Vagabond King* (1956). Much of her work after *West Side Story* was on stage and in television. In fact, Moreno is the only performer to have won a Tony, Oscar, Emmy, and Grammy Award.

MOREY, LARRY (1905–1971), a movie lyricist, is best known for the scores he wrote with composer FRANK CHURCHILL for two DISNEY musicals: the animated classic *SNOW WHITE AND THE SEVEN DWARFS* (1937) and the live-action *So Dear to My Heart* (1948).

MORGAN, DENNIS (1910–1994), an operatic tenor who played romantic leads in a dozen movie musicals in the 1940s, made an odd musical film debut in *THE GREAT ZIEGFELD* (1936): He was hired to sing IRVING BERLIN's "A Pretty Girl Is Like a Melody" but his voice was dubbed by ALLAN JONES. Morgan's other musical credits include *THE DESERT SONG* (1943), *THANK YOUR LUCKY STARS* (1943), *Shine On Harvest Moon* (1944), *Two Guys From Milwaukee* (1946), *The Time, the Place and the Girl* (1946), *My Wild Irish Rose* (1947), *Two Guys From Texas* (1948), and *Painting the Clouds With Sunshine* (1951). He played himself in specialty spots in *HOLLYWOOD CANTEEN* (1944) and *It's a Great Feeling* (1949). Morgan portrayed heroic types in comedies and action features as well, often with JACK CARSON as his sidekick.

MORGAN, FRANK (1890–1949), one of filmdom's greatest character actors, played absent-minded fools, congenial rogues, dapper governors, hapless producers, sputtering professors, and many other types. His most famous of his seventy film roles was Professor Marvel and the Wizard in *THE WIZARD OF OZ* (1939) and his two dozen musicals include *Queen High* (1930), *HALLELUJAH, I'M A BUM* (1933), *THE CAT AND THE FIDDLE* (1934), *NAUGHTY MARIETTA* (1935), *THE GREAT ZIEGFELD* (1936), *Dimples* (1936), *ROSALIE* (1937), *SWEETHEARTS* (1938), *BALALAIKA* (1939), *BROADWAY MELODY OF 1940, Thousands Cheer* (1943), *Yolanda and the Thief* (1945), and *SUMMER HOLIDAY* (1948). Morgan was preparing to play Buffalo Bill in *ANNIE GET YOUR GUN* (1950) when he died unexpectedly. His brother Ralph Morgan was also a prolific character actor in films.

MORGAN, HELEN (1900–1941), the quintessential torch singer, worked her way from seedy Chicago nightclubs to Broadway, where she played tragic heroines with a tiny but heartfelt singing voice. Morgan got to recreate her most famous stage role, the riverboat actress Julie, in *SHOW BOAT* (1936) and made a guest appearance in the 1929 part-talkie version of the tale. Her greatest film role was the abused torch singer Kitty Darling in *APPLAUSE* (1929), but she gave memorable performances also in *Glorifying the American*

Girl (1929), *Roadhouse Nights* (1930), *You Belong to Me* (1934), *Marie Galante* (1934), *Sweet Music* (1935), *GO INTO YOUR DANCE* (1935), and *Frankie and Johnny* (1935). Like that of the characters she played, Morgan's life was a sad one. After battling alcoholism and financial ruin, she died at the age of forty-one. ANN BLYTH played her in the musical bio *The Helen Morgan Story* (1957).

MOTHER WORE TIGHTS (Fox 1947) was one of BETTY GRABLE's many period musicals and her most lucrative, grossing over $4 million and spurring three more films with her co-star DAN DAILEY. The nostalgic plot began in 1900 with a vaudeville couple (Grable and Dailey) on the road and trying to raise a family. As their daughters Mona Freeman and Connie Marshall grow up, they rebel against their parents' barnstorming lifestyle, especially when Freeman gets out of finishing school and is embarrassed by her family. But time passes and everything is cured by a tear, a song, and a dance. Vaudeville song favorites were used in the score, and MACK GORDON and JOSEF MYROW's new additions included the pastiche soft-shoe number "Kokomo, Indiana," the jaunty "On a Little Two-Seat Tandem," and the ballad "You Do" that was used effectively as a leitmotif throughout the film. The supporting cast of characters was as lively as the stars: Robert Arthur, Sara Allgood, WILLIAM FRAWLEY, Vanessa Brown, SIG RUMANN, CHICK CHANDLER, Ruth Nelson, Señor Wences, Lee Patrick, and the voice of Ann Baxter, who narrated the story as the grownup Marshall.

MOVIE MOVIE (Warner 1978) was a tongue-in-cheek double bill that pastiched the movies of the 1930s with two mini-features, a boxing melodrama and a parody of BUSBY BERKELEY musicals that was called *Baxter's Beauties*. Broadway producer George C. Scott has only a few months to live, but he insists on putting on his big show even when his star Trish Van Devere gets drunk and chorus girl Rachel York has to go on in her place. Barry Bostwick was the songwriter who fell for York and wrote the show's tunes on a tenement rooftop. The affectionate spoof was written by Larry Gelbart, directed with style by STANLEY DONEN, and choreographed with Berkeley-like nonsense by MICHAEL KIDD. Gelbart and RALPH BURNS penned a few pastiche songs, one of which, "Just Shows to Go Ya," was as infectiously silly as the real thing.

MOWBRAY, ALAN (1893–1969), a London-born actor who settled in America in 1923, played British character types on stage and in over 150 movies. Mowbray could be seen as everything from a butler to a general in such musicals as *ROMAN SCANDALS* (1933), *ROSE MARIE* (1936), *ON THE AVENUE* (1937), *HOLLYWOOD HOTEL* (1938), *The Boys From Syracuse* (1940), *Where Do We Go From Here?* (1945), and *THE KING AND I* (1956).

MUNSHIN, JULES (1916–1970) was a comic character actor from Broadway whose fussy persona lit up a handful of movie musicals, including *EASTER PARADE* (1948), *TAKE ME OUT TO THE BALL GAME* (1949), *ON THE TOWN* (1949), *SILK STOCKINGS* (1957), and *Ten Thousand Bedrooms* (1957).

MUPPET MOVIE, THE (ITC 1979) brought the famous cloth characters from television to the big screen with box office success, though the film was rarely as inspired as the Muppets were on the tube. Kermit the Frog (operated and voiced by producer Jim Henson) leaves the swamp and heads for Hollywood with his friends Miss Piggy, Fozzie Bear, Rowlf the Dog, and so on; all the while he is being chased by entreprenuer Charles Durning, who wants Kermit to be the spokesperson for his fast-food chain of fried frogs' legs. Along the way the Muppets meet up with guest stars in cameo roles, from veterans BOB HOPE, MILTON BERLE, and EDGAR BERGEN to more recent celebrities such as STEVE MARTIN, Richard Pryor, and Madeline Kahn. PAUL WILLIAMS and Kenny Ascher wrote an agreeable set of songs ("The Rainbow Connection" was a hit and became Kermit's signature song), but they were rarely staged with the panache that characterized the television show's numbers. In many ways the Muppet sequels handled the musical numbers better. *The Great Muppet Caper* (1981) was set in London and gave Miss Piggy a chance to parody ESTHER WILLIAMS, *The Muppets Take Manhattan* (1984) had lively show tunes as Kermit and friends try to open a revue on Broadway, and *The Muppet Christmas Carol* (1992) musicalized the familiar story with some pleasing songs. Other musicals in the series were *Muppet Treasure Island* (1996), and *Muppets From Space* (1999).

MURDER AT THE VANITIES (Paramount 1934), an odd but pleasing mixture of musical and murder mystery, was set backstage of an Earl Carroll Broadway revue where a murderer is afoot. The thriller was not quite thrilling enough, but the songs by SAM COSLOW and ARTHUR JOHNSTON were top drawer, including the giant hit "Cocktails for Two," the melting ballad "Live and Love Tonight," and "Ebony Rhapsody," a swinging variation of Liszt's "Second Hungarian Rhapsody" by DUKE ELLINGTON and his orchestra. CARL BRISSON was the revue's leading man, KITTY CARLISLE his leading lady, JACK OAKIE a suspicious press agent, Victor McLauglen as the police lieutenant who came to investigate, and Dorothy Stickney, DONALD MEEK, Gertrude Michael, Gail Patrick, and ANN SHERIDAN on hand as well.

MURPHY, GEORGE (1902–1992) was a song-and-dance man from vaudeville, nightclubs, and later Broadway who in 1934 went to Hollywood, where he was cast as hoofers and light comic leads in twenty musicals before going on to play dramatic roles. Murphy made his film debut with *KID MIL-*

LIONS (1934), followed mostly by likable second leads in *After the Dance* (1935), *Top of the Town* (1937), *BROADWAY MELODY OF 1938* (1937), *You're a Sweetheart* (1937), *Little Miss Broadway* (1938), *BROADWAY MELODY OF 1940, TWO GIRLS ON BROADWAY* (1940), *Little Nellie Kelly* (1940), *FOR ME AND MY GAL* (1942), *The Powers Girl* (1942), *THIS IS THE ARMY* (1943), *Broadway Rhythm* (1944), *Step Lively* (1944), and others. Long interested in politics, Murphy was later a U.S. Senator from California.

MUSIC IN THE AIR (Fox 1934) was based on a 1932 modern OPERETTA scored by OSCAR HAMMERSTEIN and JEROME KERN, but the film version, scripted by Howard Young and BILLY WILDER, cut some of the songs and a lot of the operetta clichés and came up with an engaging musical comedy. June Lang (vocals dubbed by Betty Hiestand), as a meek little maid from the Bavarian mountains, goes to Munich to be a singer and is caught up in the intrigues of show business. Opera diva Gloria Swanson has had a fight with her lover, librettist JOHN BOLES, so she seduces the young schoolteacher Douglass Montgomery (dubbed by James O'Brien). When Swanson walks out on the show, Boles gets even by putting the inexperienced Lang in her place. But Lang must not have seen the previous year's *42ND STREET* because she is hopelessly inadequate on stage and fails miserably. Lund and Montgomery return to their Bavarian village, and Swanson is eagerly welcomed back into the cast. MARJORIE MAIN, Al Shean (both of whom were in the Broadway production), REGINALD OWEN, Joseph Cawthorn, and FUZZY KNIGHT rounded out the enjoyable cast, under the direction of Joe May. The score was still operetta and first-rate operetta at that: "I Told Ev'ry Little Star," "We Belong Together," "There's a Hill Beyond a Hill," "I'm Alone," "One More Dance," and others.

MUSIC MAN, THE (Warner 1962), a big brass band of a Broadway hit, lost none of its luster when it transferred to the screen with ROBERT PRESTON recreating his legendary performance as con-man Professor Harold Hill, who brings life to a small Iowa town by promising a boys band. SHIRLEY JONES was also luminous as the piano teacher and librarian who sees right through Hill's game but falls in love with him all the same. The rest of the cast, directed by Morton DaCosta, were equally delightful: BUDDY HACKETT as Hill's sidekick, Paul Ford as the bumbling mayor, HERMIONE GINGOLD as his gorgon of a wife, Ronnie Howard as Jones' lisping little brother, Pert Kelton as their Irish mother, and the harmonizing Buffalo Bills as the town councilmen. MEREDITH WILLSON's score was left pretty much untampered with and the screen overflowed with music, from the brilliant patter song "Rock Island" aboard a train to the rousing finale of "Seventy-Six Trombones," in which cinema and imagination took over where the 1957 Broadway musical left off. Other memorable songs in the score included "Goodnight, My Someone,"

"Lida Rose," "Gary, Indiana," "Marian the Librarian," and the hit ballad "Till There Was You."

MY FAIR LADY (Warner 1964) had to try to live up to the reputation of the 1956 Broadway hit, arguably the greatest of all American musicals, so some disappointment was inevitable. And when producer Jack L. Warner opted not to use the stage Eliza Doolittle JULIE ANDREWS and wanted CARY GRANT to play Henry Higgins, omens were not good. But Grant refused to play it, REX HARRISON got to put his renowned performance on film, AUDREY HEPBURN (vocals dubbed by MARNI NIXON) was surprisingly effective as Eliza, and much of *My Fair Lady* was quite enjoyable. ALAN JAY LERNER adapted his own stage libretto for the screen, and the songs, by Lerner and FREDERICK LOEWE, were faithfully intact. GEORGE CUKOR directed with a romanticized studio look that seemed appropriate, and CECIL BEATON designed both sets and costumes, making sure to dazzle on both counts. STANLEY HOLLOWAY repeated his jolly dustman Alfred P. Doolittle, Wilfred Hyde-White was the gentlemanly Col. Pickering, Jeremy Brett (dubbed by Bill Shirley) a handsome Freddie, and Gladys Cooper added a touch of class as Mrs. Higgins. The whole venture came off a little dull but intelligently done and not the embarrassment many feared. "The Rain in Spain," "I Could Have Danced All Night," "An Ordinary Man," "On the Street Where You Live," " Wouldn't It Be Loverly?," and other numbers lacked the spark they had on stage, but "Get Me to the Church on Time" was quite vibrantly done, "Just You Wait" was able to visualize Eliza's imagination, and Harrison was quite moving in his ruminating ballad "I've Grown Accustomed to Her Face." The movie was popular enough to justify all the expenses (Warner paid over $5 million just for the screen rights to the musical), and it won a flowerbasketful of Oscars.

MY GAL SAL (Fox 1942) told the story of nineteenth-century songwriter Paul Dresser without letting the facts get in the way of making it a vehicle for RITA HAYWORTH as Sal, a fictitious musical-comedy star whom the tunesmith supposedly loved. The unlikely VICTOR MATURE played Dresser from his humble beginnings as a medicine show performer to a Broadway composer (though the real Dresser never quite made it there and died in poverty). Ironically, only six Dresser songs were used (including "On the Banks of the Wabash" and the title number) and new ones were added by LEO ROBIN and RALPH RAINGER, the best one being "Here You Are," which actually sounded like a Dresser tune. Hayworth's singing was dubbed by Nan Wynn and lacked her sultry, deep register, but the star did not disappoint in other ways, giving a vibrant performance and looking sensational in the Gay Nineties attire. Also in the cast were John Sutton, PHIL SILVERS, James Gleason, CAROLE LANDIS, WALTER CATLETT, Curt Bois, Andrew Tombes, and HERMES PAN, who also choreographed the numbers with Val Raset.

MY MAN (Warner-Vitaphone 1928) was the studio's first feature after *THE JAZZ SINGER* (1927) and was also only partially a talkie and also featured a great Broadway star, FANNY BRICE. The melodramatic story told of a struggling singer (Brice) who falls for Guinn Williams, who models exercise equipment in a store window. They are about to get married, but Brice's jealous sister Edna Murphy steals Williams away from her and Brice is rescued from despair by producer Andre De Segurola, who gets her on the stage. The movie only came to life (and into sound) when Brice sang her recognized favorites such as "I'd Rather Be Blue," "Second Hand Rose," "If You Want a Rainbow (You Must Have the Rain)," "I'm an Indian Too," and the title song.

MYROW, JOSEPH (1910–   ), usually working with lyricist MACK GORDON, wrote the music for eight movie musicals, mostly at 20TH CENTURY–FOX. Myrow contributed songs to *If I'm Lucky* (1946), *THREE LITTLE GIRLS IN BLUE* (1946), *MOTHER WORE TIGHTS* (1947), *WABASH AVENUE* (1950), *I Love Melvin* (1953), *The Girl Next Door* (1953), *The French Line* (1954), and *Bundle of Joy* (1956). His most famous song is "You Make Me Feel So Young."

N

NAISH, J. CARROLL (1897–1973) was an Irish American character actor who specialized in foreign dialects, playing Italians, Latins, Asians, Native Americans, Jews, and even Arabs but, because of his dark complexion, rarely Irishmen. After some stage experience, Naish starting acting in films in 1926 and went on to do some 200 features over the next four decades. Among Naish's musicals were *The Kid From Spain* (1932), *DOWN ARGENTINE WAY* (1940), *THAT NIGHT IN RIO* (1941), *BIRTH OF THE BLUES* (1941), *The Kissing Bandit* (1948), *ANNIE GET YOUR GUN* (1950), *The Toast of New Orleans* (1950), and *HIT THE DECK* (1955).

NASHVILLE (Paramount/ABC 1975) was an intriguing, one-of-a-kind musical that followed twenty-four characters in the Tennessee music capital during a couple of weeks while a presidential campaign is going on. Part documentary and part satire, the intricate movie was a collage of characters and themes taking place on stage, backstage, and everywhere else in the city. Joan Tewkesbury wrote the complex script with help from the cast (sections of dialogue are clearly improvised), who also penned some of the many songs in the piece. Keith Carradine, Ronee Blakely, Lily Tomlin, Gwen Welles, Henry Gibson, Barbara Harris, Shelley Duvall, Karen Black, Ned Beatty, Michael Murphy, KEENAN WYNN, and Geraldine Chaplin were standouts in a large cast that was never less than outstanding. But the real star of the show was Robert Altman, who directed the sprawling giant of a movie with cockeyed affection for the country-music business and the American character itself. The songs, ranging from hillbilly parodies to folk to light rock-and-roll, gave the film its tempo and verve. Carradine wrote and sang the Oscar-winning "I'm Easy" and the lazy "It Don't Worry Me," but just as accomplished were "Dues," "200 Years," "My Idaho Home," "Tapedeck in His Tractor," "Memphis," and others.

NAUGHTY MARIETTA (MGM 1935) introduced the singing team of JEANETTE MacDONALD and NELSON EDDY to screen audiences and not only inspired seven more films for the pair but paved the way for the popularity of film OPERETTAS for the next decade. Considered VICTOR HERBERT's finest score, the 1910 Broadway hit saw its plot greatly altered, but it was always the songs that counted and they survived beautifully: "Tramp, Tramp, Tramp," " 'Neath the Southern Moon," "Italian Street Song," "I'm Falling in Love With Someone," and the much-parodied duet "Ah, Sweet Mystery of Life." The story, scripted by John Lee Mahin, FRANCES GOODRICH, and ALBERT HACKETT, centered on French princess MacDonald, who flees 1790s Paris and a wedding to a Spanish count and takes passage on a cargo ship sailing to Louisiana. On the way they are attacked by pirates, but mercenary Eddy rescues her, and after complications involving her hidden identity, they end up harmonizing together. Also in the cast were FRANK MORGAN, Elsa Lanchester, Douglass Dumbrille, Joseph Cawthorn, MARJORIE MAIN, Cecilia Parker, and AKIM TAMIROFF, all under the no-nonsense direction of W.S. VAN DYKE.

NEAGLE, DAME ANNA (1904–1986), a musical comedy star of the London stage and British films, is mostly known for her dramatic roles in Hollywood features, usually playing historical characters such as Queen Victoria and Florence Nightingale. But she made several musical films in her home country and three Hollywood musicals: *Irene* (1940), *No No Nanette* (1941), and *Sunny* (1941), playing the title role in each.

NELSON, GENE (1920–1996) was one of Hollywood's most agile dancers and personable leading men even though he was often the second romantic man in his dozen musicals. Formerly a skater with SONJA HENIE's ice shows, Nelson made his film debut with *I Wonder Who's Kissing Her Now* (1947). His other musical credits include *Tea for Two* (1950), *The West Point Story* (1950), *Lullaby of Broadway* (1951), *She's Working Her Way Through College* (1952), *Three Sailors and a Girl* (1953), and *So This Is Paris* (1954). His most memorable role was that of naive cowboy Will Parker in *OKLAHOMA!* (1955). Nelson turned to directing in the 1950s and helmed several television shows and the movie musicals *Hootenanny Hot* (1963), *Kissin' Cousins* (1964), *Harum Scarum* (1965), and *Your Cheatin' Heart* (1965).

NELSON, OZZIE (1906–1975) was a bandleader who found minimal success in films but stardom through his long-running radio and television show (*The Adventures of Ozzie and Harriet*) with wife HARRIET HILLIARD. Starting his band in college, Nelson was soon on some popular radio shows with Hilliard as his vocalist. He made a half dozen grade B films, mostly with his wife and usually playing himself in a specialty bit. Nelson's musical credits include *Strictly in the Groove* (1942), *Hi, Good Lookin'* (1944), and *People Are*

Funny (1946). He was the father of singer Ricky Nelson and TV director-producer David Nelson, both of whom appeared in the Nelsons' popular television series.

NEPTUNE'S DAUGHTER (MGM 1949) was the most profitable of the ESTHER WILLIAMS vehicles, a breezy and melodic romp that featured splendid songs by FRANK LOESSER: "I Love Those Men," "My Heart Beats Faster," and the ACADEMY AWARD–winning duet "Baby, It's Cold Outside," which Loesser had written years earlier for him and his wife to sing at parties. Ex–swimming champ Williams runs a swimsuit manufacturing company and is throwing a big fashion show when Latin American polo star RICARDO MONTALBAN comes to town. Williams' oversexed sister BETTY GARRETT mistakes clubhouse masseur RED SKELTON for the famous sportsman, and harmless merriment results. KEENAN WYNN, Ted De Corsia, Mel Blanc, and XAVIER CUGAT and his orchestra were thrown into the mix while JACK DONOHUE staged some spectacular water ballets for Williams.

NEW YORK, NEW YORK (United Artists 1977) was director Martin Scorcese's attempt to capture the stylized look and feel of a 1940s studio musical while the characters had a gritty 1970s sensibility. Although it was not entirely successful, the film had moments that soared like few others in the decade. Free-wheeling saxophone player Robert De Niro and struggling band singer LIZA MINNELLI meet during the frenzied celebration of VJ day in New York's Rainbow Room, embark on a bumpy courtship and marriage, and then split after their child is born. The story was a downer in the expected Scorcese vein, but the music made it all worthwhile. The sounds of the Big Band era flowed throughout with Georgie Auld dubbing De Niro's sax playing. Minnelli sang some old favorites ("You Are My Lucky Star," "Honeysuckle Rose," "The Man I Love," "Blue Moon," and others), and FRED EBB and JOHN KANDER provided a handful of new songs that were expert, including "There Goes the Ball Game," "But the World Goes Round," and the runaway hit "Theme From *New York, New York*" which joined the list of song standards about Manhattan. The movie initially ran over four hours, so the studio cut ninety minutes before releasing it. Lost was a lengthy musical montage called "Happy Endings," featuring Minnelli and Larry Kert, which recalled the extended "Born in a Truck" section that Minnelli's mother JUDY GARLAND had performed in *A STAR IS BORN* (1954). When *New York, New York* was reissued in 1981, the number was reinstated.

NEWLEY, ANTHONY (1931–), the versatile British entertainer who writes and sings songs, was a child actor on stage and in films—he was the Artful Dodger in the nonmusical *Oliver Twist* (1948)—and appeared in only a few screen musicals as an adult, all of them English and only *DOCTOR*

DOLITTLE (1967) familiar to Americans. His West End and Broadway hit *Stop the World—I Want to Get Off*, written with LESLIE BRICUSSE, was filmed in 1966 and 1978 (as *Sammy Stops the World*). Also with Bricusse he wrote the songs for the movie fantasy *WILLY WONKA AND THE CHOCO-LATE FACTORY* (1971). Newley scored and starred in the musicals *Can Heironymus Merkin Ever Forget Mercy Humppe and Find True Happiness?* (1969) and *Mr. Quilp* (1975), which was later re-released as *The Old Curiosity Shop*. He has also had a long and lucrative career in nightclubs and in concert singing his own hits such as "What Kind of Fool Am I?," "Who Can I Turn To?," and "Candy Man."

NEWMAN, ALFRED (1901–1970) was one of Hollywood's busiest and best conductors, composers, and musical arrangers, though he wrote the songs for only one movie musical, *The Blue Bird* (1940), with lyricist WALTER BULLOCK. Newman conducted several symphonies and Broadway shows before starting in films in 1930. He worked on some 200 movies, both musicals and dramatic features, and won many awards in the process. Among the musicals Newman arranged and/or conducted were *WHOOPEE* (1930), *ROMAN SCANDALS* (1933), *BROADWAY MELODY OF 1936* (1935), *ALEXANDER'S RAGTIME BAND* (1938), *TIN PAN ALLEY* (1940), *LILLIAN RUSSELL* (1940), *MOTHER WORE TIGHTS* (1947), *WITH A SONG IN MY HEART* (1952), *CALL ME MADAM* (1953), *THE KING AND I* (1956), *STATE FAIR* (1962), and *CAMELOT* (1967). His brother LIONEL NEWMAN was also a successful film composer and arranger, his son David Newman wrote soundtrack scores for many features, and his nephew is the pop songwriter Randy Newman.

NEWMAN, LIONEL (1916–1989) was the musical director at 20TH CENTURY–FOX for many years and during his long career conducted and/or arranged the scores for over 200 feature films. Among Newman's credits were the musicals *You Were Meant for Me* (1948), *WABASH AVENUE* (1950), *Bloodhounds of Broadway* (1952), *GENTLEMEN PREFER BLONDES* (1953), *THERE'S NO BUSINESS LIKE SHOW BUSINESS* (1954), *Love Me Tender* (1956), *DOCTOR DOLITTLE* (1967), and *HELLO, DOLLY!* (1969). He is the younger brother of ALFRED NEWMAN.

NEWMAR, JULIE (1935–   ), the leggy, voluptuous television actress, is known to film audiences for recreating her Broadway role of Stupefyin' Jones in the film version of *LI'L ABNER* (1959). Earlier she was seen in the musicals *THE BAND WAGON* (1953) and *SEVEN BRIDES FOR SEVEN BROTHERS* (1954). Newmar has the rare and odd distinction of having her name in a movie title, *To Wong Foo, Thanks for Everything! Julie Newmar* (1995), a nonmusical in which she made a cameo appearance.

NEWTON-JOHN, OLIVIA (1948–), the English-born Australian pop singer who had many top singles in the 1970s, has made a few films, none as popular as *GREASE* (1978), in which she played the Sandra Dee–like high schooler Sandy. The blonde singer made the musical *Tomorrow* (1970) in Britain and the Hollywood curiosity *Xanadu* (1980), in which she got to sing and dance with GENE KELLY.

NICHOLAS BROTHERS, THE, two of the greatest tap dancers and athletic hoofers in the history of show business, were featured in nine movie musicals together and never failed to stop the show. Fayard (1917–) and Harold Nicholas (1924–2000) came from a performing family and found success at the Cotton Club in Harlem and on Broadway before going to Hollywood in 1932 as youngsters. Their amazing flips, leaps, and splits were seen in *KID MILLIONS* (1934), *BIG BROADCAST OF 1936* (1935), *DOWN ARGENTINE WAY* (1940), *TIN PAN ALLEY* (1940), *The Great American Broadcast* (1941), *SUN VALLEY SERENADE* (1941), *ORCHESTRA WIVES* (1942), *STORMY WEATHER* (1943), and *THE PIRATE* (1948). Harold also appeared in *The Reckless Age* (1944) and *Carolina Blues* (1944). The African American brothers rarely got to play characters in their films (even though they played roles on Broadway) but were featured as specialty acts that could be edited out when the film was shown in the South. The duo remained active in nightclubs and television and later appeared in or choreographed Broadway musicals. Harold was married to DOROTHY DANDRIDGE.

NIESEN, GERTRUDE (1910–1975) was a small and sensuous blonde singer who found success in vaudeville and nightclubs, on Broadway, and on the radio, but in Hollywood she usually found herself in forgettable B pictures. Niesen's seven musical credits include *Top of the Town* (1937), *Rookies on Parade* (1941), *Thumbs Up* (1943), and *THIS IS THE ARMY* (1943).

NIGHT AND DAY (Warner 1946), the BIOGRAPHICAL MUSICAL about songwriter COLE PORTER, may get the award for being the most inaccurate of the many fictionalized musical bios that Hollywood has presented over the years. Even though it dealt with events and shows of recent memory and many of the people involved were still alive and working (including Porter himself), the movie was a travesty all around. Porter's homosexuality and snobbery were understandably omitted, but his zest for life and ability to charm and entertain were lost in CARY GRANT's proper and detached performance. Songs and stars were attributed to the wrong shows, and the context of the celebrated numbers was changed to satisfy the production numbers staged by director MICHAEL CURTIZ and choreographer LeROY PRINZ. On the plus side, Alexis Smith was elegant as Porter's stately wife Linda, MARY MARTIN recreated her stage triumph "My Heart Belongs to Daddy," and Porter's close friend Monty Woolley was played by Woolley himself.

GINNY SIMMS sang several of the songs that had been introduced by ETHEL MERMAN while JANE WYMAN, EVE ARDEN, ALAN HALE, Dorothy Malone, Victor Francen, Selena Royale, HERMAN BING, Carlos Ramirez, Donald Woods, MEL TORMÉ, and others wandered in and out of the unexciting story. Despite all its shortcomings, the film was very popular and Porter himself professed to have loved it, his real life not at all touched on by the movie.

NIGHT AT THE OPERA, A (MGM 1935) revealed the MARX BROTHERS at the peak of their careers as they stow away on an ocean liner to New York, disguise themselves as Russian aviators to get ashore, and wreck havoc on a performance of *Il Trovatore*. George S. Kaufman and Morrie Ryskind, who had written for the brothers on Broadway, concocted the script, which was supposedly about the siblings helping tenor ALLAN JONES get together with his sweetheart KITTY CARLISLE and sing at the opera house. But the plot left room for the famous stateroom scene, for Groucho to woo and insult opera patroness MARGARET DUMONT, for Chico to play "All I Do Is Dream of You" on the piano, and for Harpo to pluck out "Alone" on the harp. The last was written for the film by ARTHUR FREED and NACIO HERB BROWN and also sung beautifully by Jones and Carlisle. Another laudable number, by NED WASHINGTON, BRONISLAW KAPER, and Walter Jurmann, was the sing-along ditty "Cosi Cosa."

NIXON, MARNI (1931–   ), the most famous of the many singers who dubbed the singing voices of others in musicals, was a classical and pop vocalist as a child and made many recordings. Her trilling soprano voice was heard coming out of MARGARET O'BRIEN in *Big City* (1948), DEBORAH KERR in *THE KING AND I* (1956), Natalie Wood in *WEST SIDE STORY* (1961), and AUDREY HEPBURN in *MY FAIR LADY* (1964). Nixon was seen as well as heard as Sister Sophia in *THE SOUND OF MUSIC* (1965). She was married to film composer Ernest Gold.

NOBLE, RAY (1903–1978), an Englishman who came to America and became a celebrated bandleader and purveyor of jazz, played piano and conducted his jazzmen in the Hollywood musicals *Here We Go Again* (1942), *Lake Placid Serenade* (1945), and *Out of This World* (1945). Noble also got to play the silly Brit Reggie in *A DAMSEL IN DISTRESS* (1937).

NORTH, SHEREE (1933–   ), a vibrant blonde singer-dancer who was groomed to be a MARILYN MONROE–like sex symbol by 20TH CENTURY–FOX, appeared in dancing roles in *Excuse My Dust* (1951), *Here Come the Girls* (1953), and *Living It Up* (1954) before getting major roles in *The Best Things in Life Are Free* (1956) and *Mardi Gras* (1958). As film musicals declined and she was upstaged by newcomers like Jayne Mansfield, North went on the road with plays and concerts. She returned to films in the 1960s as a character actress in dramatic roles and in the ELVIS PRESLEY musical *The Trouble With Girls* (1969).

NORTON, JACK (1889–1958), a veteran character actor of over 100 feature films, specialized in lovable drunks even though off camera he was a teetotaler. Norton's many musical credits include *A DAY AT THE RACES* (1937), *Thanks for the Memory* (1938), *Louisiana Purchase* (1941), *THE FLEET'S IN* (1942), *Wonder Man* (1945), *BLUE SKIES* (1946), and *The Kid From Brooklyn* (1946).

NOVAK, KIM (1933–   ), the icy blonde sexpot of the 1950s whose private life was more interesting than most of her film roles, was groomed by COLUMBIA to be the next RITA HAYWORTH. She later co-starred with Hayworth in *PAL JOEY* (1957) and gave the elder star no reason for worry. Novak's film debut was a bit part in *The French Line* (1954) and her other musicals included *The Eddy Duchin Story* (1956), *Pepe* (1960), and *Kiss Me, Stupid* (1964).

NOVARRO, RAMON (1899–1968), a romantic figure of the silents in the manner of Rudolph Valentino, was a singer before he went into the movies and returned to music when talkies came in. Never as popular as in the silent era, Novarro gave personable performances in the early musicals *Devil May Care* (1929), *In Gay Madrid* (1930), *Call of the Flesh* (1930), *THE CAT AND THE FIDDLE* (1934), and *The Night Is Young* (1935).

NUGENT, ELLIOTT (1896–1980) was a vaudeville performer, a Broadway playwright, and later a film director. Nugent appeared in the early movie musical *So This Is College* (1929) before going on to direct *She Loves Me Not* (1934), *Strictly Dynamite* (1934), *Love in Bloom* (1935), *Give Me a Sailor* (1938), *UP IN ARMS* (1944), *Welcome, Stranger* (1947), and *Just for You* (1952).

OAKIE, JACK (1903–1978), a portly and usually jolly character actor, left the stage for Hollywood in 1929 and acted in over eighty films, often playing good-natured buffoons or sidekicks of the hero. Known for his double (and even triple) takes, Oakie was often featured as a college student in 1930s musicals and comedies, though he hardly looked the age or type. He appeared in some forty musicals, sometimes in lead roles but usually in support. Among Oakie's notable musicals were *Close Harmony* (1929), *Sweetie* (1929), *PARAMOUNT ON PARADE* (1930), *HIT THE DECK* (1930), *College Humor* (1933), *Too Much Harmony* (1933), *MURDER AT THE VANITIES* (1934), *COLLEGE RHYTHM* (1934), *BIG BROADCAST OF 1936* (1935), *KING OF BURLESQUE* (1935), *Collegiate* (1936), *Thanks for Everything* (1938), *TIN PAN ALLEY* (1940), *Navy Blues* (1941), *ICELAND* (1942), *Song of the Islands* (1942), *HELLO, FRISCO, HELLO* (1943), *Sweet and Low-Down* (1944), *Bowery to Broadway* (1944), and *When My Baby Smiles at Me* (1948).

OAKLAND, BEN (1907–1979), a Tin Pan Alley composer who worked with a variety of lyricists during his career, contributed songs to four Hollywood musicals: *Hats Off* (1936), *All American Sweetheart* (1938), *The Lady Objects* (1938), and *Laugh It Off* (1939). Among Oakland's popular songs were "I'll Dance at Your Wedding," "The Champagne Waltz," and "I'll Take Romance."

O'BRIEN, MARGARET (1937–), one of Hollywood's most-polished child actors, made her film debut as a three-year-old auditioning for a show in *BABES ON BROADWAY* (1941) and went on to featured kid roles in musicals and dramas. O'Brien's most-remembered performance was as JUDY GARLAND's little sister Tootie in *MEET ME IN ST. LOUIS* (1944), and she can also be seen in the musicals *Thousands Cheer* (1943), *Music for Millions* (1944), *The Unfinished Dance* (1947), and *Big City* (1948). Although her popularity faded when she grew up, O'Brien continued acting on stage and occasionally in films into the 1980s.

O'BRIEN, PAT (1899–1983), filmdom's favorite Irish cop, priest, detective, or coach, started acting in silent films but his career took off with the advent of sound. O'Brien was cast as a lightweight leading man in several 1930s musicals before going on to dramatic roles. His musical credits include *Flying High* (19431), *College Coach* (1933), *Twenty Million Sweethearts* (1934), *Flirtation Walk* (1934), *In Caliente* (1935), *Stars Over Broadway* (1935), *Cowboy From Brooklyn* (1938), and *Garden of the Moon* (1938). He returned to the genre with *Broadway* (1942) and *His Butler's Sister* (1943).

O'BRIEN, VIRGINIA (1921–   ) had such a wry, droll, and sexy way of delivering her lines and songs that the fan magazines called her "Miss Red Hot Frozen Face." The seemingly expressionless comedienne was featured in supporting roles in a dozen film musicals in the 1940s and managed to steal the show in a very subtle way. O'Brien can be seen in *The Big Store* (1941), *Lady, Be Good* (1941), *Panama Hattie* (1942), *DuBarry Was a Lady* (1943), *Thousands Cheer* (1943), *TWO GIRLS AND A SAILOR* (1944), *THE HARVEY GIRLS* (1945), *TILL THE CLOUDS ROLL BY* (1946), *ZIEGFELD FOLLIES* (1946), and others.

O'CONNOR, DONALD (1925–   ), the nimble song-and-dance man who seemed to defy gravity in his sprightly performances, lit up many a musical during his long career. O'Connor was in vaudeville as a child and did preteen roles in the film musicals *Melody for Two* (1937), *Sing You Sinners* (1938), and *On Your Toes* (1939). He matured into adult roles in the 1940s and appeared in many low-budget musicals, including *Private Buckaroo* (1942), *Get Hep to Love* (1942), *Top Man* (1943), *Follow the Boys* (1944), *The Merry Monahans* (1944), *Bowery to Broadway* (1944), *Something in the Wind* (1947), and *Yes, Sir, That's My Baby* (1949). His luck changed in the 1950s with a series of comedies with "Francis the Talking Mule" that finally brought him wide recognition. O'Connor then got a shot at grade A musicals and gave memorable performances as funnyman Cosmo Brown *SINGIN' IN THE RAIN* (1952), photographer's assistant Melvin Hoover in *I Love Melvin* (1952), ambassador's aide Kenneth Gibson in *CALL ME MADAM* (1953), ex-GI Jigger Millard in *Walking My Baby Back Home* (1953), troubled performer Tim Donahue in *THERE'S NO BUSINESS LIKE SHOW BUSINESS* (1954), and Broadway star Ted Adams in *ANYTHING GOES* (1956). O'Connor also had two popular television shows, appeared frequently on stage, and even conducted symphonies in pieces that he composed.

O'KEEFE, DENNIS (1908–1968), a dependable leading man in action dramas, started as a vaudeville performer and was cast in a handful of movie musicals in the 1930s. Among O'Keefe's musical credits were *GOLD DIGGERS OF 1933, I'm No Angel* (1933), *DUCK SOUP* (1933), *WONDER BAR* (1934), *MISSISSIPPI* (1935), *SAN FRANCISCO* (1936), *ANYTHING GOES* (1936), *BORN TO DANCE* (1936), and *THE FIREFLY* (1937).

OKLAHOMA! (Magna 1955) was a faithful screen adaptation of the 1943 landmark Broadway hit, perhaps too faithful, for the long movie seems more reverent than fun at times. All the right elements were in place: The RODGERS and HAMMERSTEIN score (minus two songs) still sounded glorious, Agnes De Mille recreated her stunning Broadway choreography, director Fred Zinnemann filmed it both in the studio and on location (in Arizona) so the film looked right, and the cast was excellent: GORDON MacRAE as the cowboy Curly, SHIRLEY JONES (in her film debut) as his sweetheart Laurey, Rod Steiger as the villainous Jud who comes between them, Gloria Grahame as the flirtatious Ado Annie, GENE NELSON as the cowboy Will who loves her, Eddie Albert as the Persian peddler Ali Hakim who nearly gets stuck with her, and CHARLOTTE GREENWOOD as Aunt Eller who tries to make everything work out for the lovers. It was an admirable film record of a great Broadway musical, but as a movie musical it lacked the excitement and joyous spirit that the title song suggested. Other numbers included "People Will Say We're in Love," "I Cain't Say No," "Kansas City," "Oh, What a Beautiful Mornin'," "Out of My Dreams," "The Surrey With the Fringe on Top," and "Many a New Day."

OLIVER! (Columbia 1968), based on Charles Dickens' novel *Oliver Twist*, which had been filmed seven times before, had also been a stage hit in London's West End and on Broadway, so it was given the prestige treatment by the studio. Renowned British film director Carol Reed helmed his only musical but gave it an atmospheric edge that cut through some of the musical's sentimentality. ONNA WHITE's choreography was more Hollywood than the rest of the picture but certainly was lively (as in "Consider Yourself") and big (as in the quiet song "Who Will Buy?" turning into a parade). The other Lionel Bart songs included "As Long as He Needs Me," "Where Is Love?," "You've Got to Pick a Pocket or Two," and the derisive title song. After a wide search, young Mark Lester was given the role of young Oliver and what he lacked in sparkle was made up for by radiant performances by Ron Moody as the thief Fagin, Jack Wild as his head pickpocket Artful Dodger, Oliver Reed as the murderous Bill Sikes, and Shani Wallis as the barmaid who loves him. Also memorable was designer John Box's evocative depiction of Victorian London. The movie was showered with an armful of Oscars including one for Best Picture, the last time a musical won that award.

OLIVER AND COMPANY (Disney 1988) was made right before the studio's animation renaissance began with *THE LITTLE MERMAID* (1989), but it has the artistry, confidence, and entertainment value of the later hits. Loosely adapted from Charles Dickens' *Oliver Twist*, the story follows an orphaned kitten named Oliver (voice of Joey Lawrence) who falls in with a gang of street-smart dogs led by Dodger (Billy Joel) and overseen by the human Fagin (DOM DeLUISE). When Oliver is rescued by a wealthy little girl, the pampered canine Georgette (Bette Midler) sees the stray as a threat and works with the gang to get rid of her. All the characters were vivid and funny, with skillful voice work also from Cheech Marin, Richard Mulligan, Sheryl Lee Ralph, Roscoe Lee Browne, and Robert Loggia. The songs, by a variety of pop songwriters, were equally vibrant, especially the rhythmic "Why Should I Worry?," the satirical "Perfect Isn't Easy," the pulsating "Streets of Gold," and the bluesy "Once Upon a Time in New York City." The animation was superb, with Manhattan presented in a sharp, stylized manner that was neither gritty nor glorified. The success of the movie, helped by the popularity of the stars heard on the soundtrack, encouraged the DISNEY studio to invest more money and talent in its neglected animation department.

OLIVIER, SIR LAURENCE (1907–1989), the preeminent British classical actor of his era, made many films throughout his long career but only three musicals: as the cutthroat MacHeath in *The Beggar's Opera* (1952), imperialistic Sir John French in *Oh! What a Lovely War* (1969), and Cantor Rabinovitch in the third version of *THE JAZZ SINGER* (1980). Olivier also sang a handful of music hall ditties in the "kitchen sink" drama *The Entertainer* (1960).

OLSEN AND JOHNSON, a vaudeville comedy team that slew Broadway with their madcap revue *Hellzapoppin*, consisted of Ole Olsen (1892–1963) and Chic Johnson (1891–1962). Known for their broad, physical, and juvenile comedy and running gags, the duo filmed their stage hit in 1941 and were featured in the movie musicals *Oh, Sailor Behave* (1931), *Crazy House* (1943), *The Ghost Catchers* (1944), and *See My Lawyer* (1945).

ON A CLEAR DAY YOU CAN SEE FOREVER (Paramount 1970) was a complicated mess of a musical about ESP that was saved at various points by the sheer energy and talent of BARBRA STREISAND as chain-smoking Daisy Gamble from Brooklyn. When she is treated by psychiatrist Yves Montand to curtail her tobacco addiction through hypnosis, the doctor discovers Daisy's previous life as Melinda, a notorious *femme fatale* in Regency England, and proceeds to fall in love with her past persona. Daisy's dull fiancé Larry Blyden and her stepbrother Jack Nicholson also showed up, but it was never clear why. ALAN JAY LERNER radically rewrote his 1961 stage libretto for the screen, but different wasn't necessarily better. Composer BURTON LANE joined Lerner on two new songs to add to their Broadway score, and the musical numbers, at least, made sense. "Hurry, It's Lovely Up Here," "Melinda," "What Did I Have That I Don't Have?," "Go to Sleep," "Come Back to Me," and the entrancing title song were expert, and Streisand, who sang most of them, was funny and endearing. VINCENTE MINNELLI, in his waning days, directed rather woodenly, his best work having been in a past life of its own.

ON THE AVENUE (Fox 1937) was a routine backstager that rose above the others because of its effervescent IRVING BERLIN score and the appealing cast. DICK POWELL, as the star, author, and producer of a Broadway revue called *On the Avenue*, gets in trouble with wealthy socialite Madeleine Carroll when she objects to the way her famous family is satirized in one of the show's sketches. Powell and Carroll lock horns and then lips, much to the disappointment of the revue's leading lady ALICE FAYE. Most of the songs in the film were presented as part of the revue and never tied in with the proceedings, but they were so wonderful that few complained. "This Year's Kisses," "Slumming on Park Avenue," "He Ain't Got Rhythm," "The Girl on the Police Gazette," "You're Laughing at Me," and "I've Got My Love to Keep Me Warm" were performed (mostly by Faye) and staged (by director ROY DEL RUTH and choreographer SEYMOUR FELIX) with zest. Also in the musical were the RITZ BROTHERS, ALAN MOWBRAY, GEORGE BARBIER, JOAN DAVIS, WALTER CATLETT, Stepin Fetchit, SIG RUMANN, Cora Witherspoon, BILLY GILBERT, and LYNN BARI.

ON THE RIVIERA. See *Folies Bergère de Paris*

ON THE TOWN (MGM 1949) was arguably the best of the many "sailors on leave" musicals that came before and after it, and although the plot was stale, the movie was fresh and inventive. GENE KELLY, co-directing for the first time with STANLEY DONEN, filled the film with so much dance that it almost resembled a modern ballet. (Actually, the 1944 Broadway show was taken from the ballet piece *Fancy Free* by JEROME ROBBINS.) When the cast was not dancing, the camera was, crosscutting to different places in Manhattan (it was the first major musical shot on location in New York) or zooming in and out to capture the frenzy of the city. Kelly was the lovesick sailor who pursued the poster girl VERA-ELLEN during his twenty-four hours' leave, FRANK SINATRA was the shy sailor who wanted to see the sights but ended up seeing a lot of the man-hungry cab driver BETTY GARRETT, and JULES MUNSHIN was the curious sailor who meets anthropologist ANN MILLER in a museum and the two tear the place apart with enthusiasm. Half of the stage score by BETTY COMDEN, ADOLPH GREEN, and LEONARD BERNSTEIN was dropped, but Bernstein's instrumental music was used for some stunning dance sections, most memorably the "Miss Turnstiles Ballet" and "A Day in New York Ballet." Also saved from Broadway was the rousing paean to "New York, New York" and the comic seduction song "Come Up to My Place." Comden and Green, who also penned the screenplay, collaborated with ROGER EDENS on some new numbers, the best being the vigorous "Prehistoric Man." Alice Pearce was Garrett's sniffling roommate, Florence Bates was a soused ballet instructor, and George Meader, HANS CONREID, CAROL HANEY, Bern Hoffman, and Bea Benaderet made appearances as well.

ON WITH THE SHOW (Warner 1929) is an early and rather primitive backstager that revealed the goings-on behind the scenes of a Broadway show in out-of-town tryouts. Scenes from the musical on stage were shown in such a way that audiences could follow both on and offstage plots. Backstage, temperamental star Betty Compson quarrels with the producers and walks out during the performance, so newcomer Sally O'Neil has to go on in her place. It was one of the first times this ruse had been used in a talkie and seemed unique enough at the time. Also unique was the way time was used: The movie started with the theatre audience assembling in the house, all the action occurred during the performance, and it ended with the company's curtain call. The whole concept remains interesting yet much of the film falls flat. The studio decided to shoot the entire movie in color, and the technical problems, both visual and aural, make it a difficult picture to watch. Also, Compson and O'Neil do poorly, both of them having their singing dubbed by Josephine Houston, and Compson's dancing is so inadequate that she needed a double for some of the numbers. But the saving grace of the film is the presence of young ETHEL WATERS as a plantation worker in the show-within-the-show. GRANT CLARKE and HARRY AKST wrote her two songs, "Birmingham Bertha" and "Am I Blue?," the latter the first hit song introduced by an African American in a film.

ONE HOUR WITH YOU (Paramount 1932) may not compare favorably with the best MAURICE CHEVALIER–JEANETTE MacDONALD vehicles, but it still sparkles with wit, playful performances, and a fine score by LEO ROBIN, OSCAR STRAUS, and RICHARD A. WHITING. In SAMSON RAPHAELSON's screenplay, Chevalier is a doctor happily married to MacDonald but is tempted by his wife's flirtatious friend Genevieve Tobin. MacDonald pushes the two together to test her husband and then merry revelations follow. Some parts of the movie were directed by ERNST LUBITSCH and some of it by GEORGE CUKOR (there were fights about the final billing), but a frothy and suggestive tone remains throughout the musical. Although only the title song became a hit, all the numbers are superb and smoothly integrated into the story. Chevalier praises the charms of "Oh, That Mitzi!" and recommends that she take a tonic "Three Times a Day" while she seductively suggests she come see him thrice daily. The married couple slyly note "What a Little Thing Like a Wedding Ring Can Do" and affectionately confirm that "We Will Always Be Sweethearts." Most nimble of all, Chevalier sings to the camera, asking the men in the audience "What Would You Do?" if in his situation; he concludes the song with a wink and explains, "That's what I did too!"

ONE HUNDRED MEN AND A GIRL (Universal 1937) was a modern but charming fairy tale featuring teenager DEANNA DURBIN, who, with her energetic smile and heavenly soprano voice, seemed to have come out of a storybook herself. As the daughter of an unemployed trombonist (ADOLPHE MENJOU), Durbin struggles to form an orchestra for her father's out-of-work fellow musicians. She not only gets a patron and a hall but even convinces world-famous maestro LEOPOLD STOKOWSKI (playing himself) to come and conduct them. At the opening night concert the ambitious teen is called to the stage for acknowledgment and, when asked to sing, launches into an air from *La Traviata*. Durbin got to sing some other numbers as well, and movements by Tchaikovsky, Liszt, Mozart, and Berlioz were performed by the orchestra. The strong supporting cast included ALICE BRADY, EUGENE PALLETTE, MISCHA AUER, BILLY GILBERT, Alma Kruger, and Jack Smart. It was Dubin's second feature film and it secured her career.

ONE IN A MILLION (Fox 1936) is the musical that introduced SONJA HENIE to film audiences, though the Norwegian skating champion had been in newsreels for a while. Producer DARRYL F. ZANUCK signed the blonde athlete to a nine-picture contract without ever auditioning her for singing or acting abilities. But the gamble paid off the moment Henie hit the ice and audiences were enthralled. As the daughter of Swiss innkeeper Jean Hersholt, Henie prepares for the Olympics while she is urged by ADOLPHE MENJOU to join him and skate to the music of his all-girl orchestra. She is also wooed by American reporter DON AMECHE, whom she falls for despite his brashness. By the final reel Henie has done her bit with Menjou and ends up skating in a lavish ice show at Madison Square Garden. Along the way the RITZ BROTHERS, LEAH RAY, DIXIE DUNBAR, Arline Judge, NED SPARKS, and Borrah Minnevitch and his Harmonica Rascals were on hand to provide comedy and/or music. The songs by LEW POLLACK and SIDNEY MITCHELL were not particularly memorable, although the title number, used several times throughout the movie, started to sound catchy.

ONE NIGHT IN THE TROPICS (Universal 1940) had a silly and improbable excuse of a plot but offered some masterful songs by DOROTHY FIELDS, OSCAR HAMMERSTEIN, OTTO HARBACH, and JEROME KERN, all of which were written four years earlier for an unproduced musical called *Riviera*. Set on the fictitious Caribbean island of San Marcos, insurance salesman ALLAN JONES makes his playboy friend ROBERT CUMMINGS buy a policy promising to settle down and marry his fiancée Nancy Kelly. But Jones falls for Kelly and on the wedding day she runs off with him. MARY BOLAND, Peggy Moran, WILLIAM FRAWLEY, and Leo Carillo were somehow involved in the plot but seemed to get lost in it, just as the fine songs were. The scintillating rhumba "Remind Me," the heartfelt "Your Dream (Is the Same as My Dream)," and the lovely "You and Your Kiss" were top-flight numbers by three brilliant songwriters at their peak, but the film bombed at the box office and it took a while for the three songs to catch on. UNIVERSAL lost a bundle on the lavish film but eventually had the last laugh: producer Leonard Spigelgass hired two radio comics, BUD ABBOTT and LOU COSTELLO, to play undercover men in the movie and the team immediately clicked. They would go on to make twenty-eight more movies for Universal and save the company from bankruptcy.

ONE NIGHT OF LOVE (Columbia 1934), GRACE MOORE's most satisfying film, was the first movie musical to feature a *bone fide* opera star in a leading role and was such a hit that studios started besieging famous divas to come to Hollywood. Moore played an American soprano studying in Italy with her devoted teacher TULLIO CARMINATI. Her dream of becoming an opera star is somewhat sidetracked by her romance with visiting American LYLE TALBOT, but eventually Moore realizes that music is her true love and she ends up starring at the Metropolitan Opera in New York. Moore sang selections from *Lucia di Lammermoor, Madama Butterfly, Carmen*, and other standard repertoire pieces, and audiences found that they liked the highbrow music in limited dosages. With lyricist GUS KAHN, director VICTOR SCHERTZINGER composed a flowing title song, which also became a hit (though Schertzinger was the first to point out that the main melody came from Puccini).

O'NEILL, HENRY (1891–1961), a reliable character actor in some 200 feature films, could play just about anything but was best at gentle and understanding men in high positions. O'Neill's many musical appearances include *WONDER BAR* (1934), *Flirtation Walk* (1934), *Girl Crazy* (1943), *BEST FOOT FORWARD* (1943), *TWO GIRLS AND A SAILOR* (1944), and *ANCHORS AWEIGH* (1945).

OPERA SINGERS started appearing on film in silent shorts and features even though their singing talents could hardly be enjoyed under the circumstances. Opera diva Mary Garden actually had a considerable following from her performances in silents. Met soprano GRACE MOORE was the first opera singer to find success in the talkies. After appearing in two film musicals in 1930, she found acclaim for her performance as a struggling American opera singer in *ONE NIGHT OF LOVE* (1934). Aside from radio broadcasts, it was the first mainstream exposure Americans had to opera and the movie was such a hit that all the studios started courting singers from the Metropolitan Opera and European troupes. Moore made four more films and was soon joined by LILY PONS, the French coloratura who starred in such vehicles as *I DREAM*

TOO MUCH (1935) and *That Girl From Paris* (1936). Mezzosoprano GLADYS SWARTHOUT was the opera diva in residence at PARAMOUNT, where she was featured in *Rose of the Rancho* (1935) and *Give Us This Night* (1936), mezzo RISE STEVENS can be found in a handful of the same studio's films, and ILONA MASSEY appeared in five musicals in the 1930s and 1940s. Male opera singers were not forgotten, Richard Tauber performing in a handful of British musical films in the 1930s, Italian tenor NINO MARTINI singing in four films in the same decade, and basso EZIO PINZA appearing in *Carnegie Hall* (1947) and some 1950s musicals. Danish-born heldertenor LAURITZ MELCHIOR, one of the world's greatest interpreters of Wagner, found himself in such Hollywood musicals as *Thrill of a Romance* (1945), *Two Sisters From Boston* (1946), and *Luxury Liner* (1948). In a reversal of the usual pattern, tenor JAMES MELTON made such an impression in his 1930s musicals that he later moved on to the Met. The most beloved of all the screen opera singers was the dashing tenor MARIO LANZA, who probably prompted more interest in opera than any other singer. Lanza made seven musicals and provided the vocals for an eighth film, the most promising of all the classical singers. But his temperamental lifestyle and addiction to drugs and alcohol ended his career at the age of thirty eight. Few of these opera singers enjoyed lengthy movie careers because their novelty quickly wore out or they maintained a busy concert and stage schedule. More recently tenor Luciano Pavarotti made his bid for movie stardom with *Yes, Giorgio* (1982) but failed miserably. Since films of operas have become more common, many of the great opera singers are now preserved on film, but their ability to cross over to musicals remains rare.

OPERETTA FILMS have existed since before the advent of talkies when a handful of stage operettas were filmed as silent features or shorts. (The 1923 version of *The Student Prince* was quite popular.) By definition, operetta refers to a light form of opera that utilizes dialogue and tends toward the amusing rather than the thought provoking or melodramatic. Viennese, French, British, and American operettas had been popular on Broadway since the 1880s, and the 1920s were a highwater mark for the genre when American composers RUDOLF FRIML and SIGMUND ROMBERG were at their peak. The first filmed operetta with sound was *THE DESERT SONG* (1929), which was remade in 1943 and 1953. Other stage operettas that transferred to the screen during the early days of the talkies included *RIO RITA* (1929), *The Vagabond King* (1930), *Song of the Flame* (1930), *Golden Dawn* (1930), *New Moon* (1930), and *Kiss Me Again* (1931), based on VICTOR HERBERT's *Mlle. Modiste*. The Depression pretty much killed off the old-style operetta on Broadway, but ironically, Hollywood had great success in the 1930s with such favorites as *THE MERRY WIDOW* (1934), *NAUGHTY MARIETTA* (1935), *ROSE MARIE* (1936), *MAYTIME* (1937), *THE FIREFLY* (1937), and *SWEETHEARTS* (1938) largely because of the popularity of JEANETTE

MacDONALD and NELSON EDDY. The movie studios came up with their own form of operetta with the original musicals *THE LOVE PARADE* (1929), *THE SMILING LIEUTENANT* (1931), *ONE HOUR WITH YOU* (1932), and *LOVE ME TONIGHT* (1932), all starring MAURICE CHEVA-LIER and set in a romanticized European setting with princesses, dukes, counts, countesses, and a touch of boudoir comedy on hand. VICTOR SCHERTZ-INGER, OSCAR STRAUS, JEROME KERN, OSCAR HAMMERSTEIN, RICHARD RODGERS, LORENZ HART, Friml, and Romberg would write most of the best film operettas over the years. Although the genre would wane somewhat in the 1940s, popular screen operettas would emerge on occasion in the 1950s. In addition to those already mentioned, the finest film operettas include *Bitter Sweet* (1933 and 1940), *BABES IN TOYLAND* (1934), *THE CAT AND THE FIDDLE* (1934), *MUSIC IN THE AIR* (1934), *SWEET ADELINE* (1935), *ROBERTA* (1935), *SHOW BOAT* (1936 and 1951), *ROSALIE* (1937), *THE GREAT WALTZ* (1938), *The Mikado* (1939), *THE STUDENT PRINCE* (1954), *KISMET* (1955), *CAROUSEL* (1956), and *The Pirates of Penzance* (1983).

ORCHESTRA WIVES (Fox 1942) is perhaps the quintessential Big Band musical, being about a touring band and featuring GLENN MILLER with his orchestra and his mainstay vocalists. The plot was rather a dark one, about the bitchy and vindicative behavior of the musicians' wives toward ANN RUTHER-FORD when she marries into the group. The film pulled no punches about the sometimes dreary life of touring from city to city in a band bus, and even the happy ending (Rutherford gets the group together again after their petty differences have led them to disband) hinted that a musician's life was far from glamourous. But it was the music that counted, and the movie was filled with the best: "People Like You and Me," "Serenade in Blue," "At Last," and "I've Got a Gal in Kalamazoo," all written by MACK GORDON and HARRY WARREN. The vocalists were Tex Beneke, Billy May, Ray Eberle, Hal McIntyre, MARION HUTTON, and the Modernaires, with the dancing NICHOLAS BROTHERS setting the stage on fire. George Montgomery, JACKIE GLEASON, Harry Morgan, and CESAR ROMERO were among the musicians (all dubbed by the real Miller boys), and CAROLE LANDIS, LYNN BARI, Mary Beth Hughes, Tamara Geva, and Virginia Gilmore were among the wives.

ORRY-KELLY (1897–1964) designed more fashionable gowns for movie stars on screen than perhaps any other Hollywood costume designer. The Australian-born designer started as an actor on stage but was soon fashioning costumes and supplied the dazzling wardrobe for several editions of *George White's Scandals* on Broadway. He went to Hollywood in 1930 and costumed hundreds of films and won several Oscars along the way. Orry-Kelly's work can be seen in the musicals *42ND STREET* (1933), *GOLD DIGGERS OF 1933*,

WONDER BAR (1934), *DAMES* (1934), *FLIRTATION WALK* (1934), *On Your Toes* (1939), *THE DOLLY SISTERS* (1945), *MOTHER WORE TIGHTS* (1947), *AN AMERICAN IN PARIS* (1951), *OKLAHOMA!* (1955), *LES GIRLS* (1957), *GYPSY* (1963), and many others.

OSCARS. See Academy Awards

OWEN, REGINALD (1887–1972), a British actor working in America after 1924, moved from a successful career on the stage to the movies in the late 1920s and appeared in dozens of films over the next forty years, usually in supporting roles and more often than not as foreigners. Among Owen's musical credits were *MUSIC IN THE AIR* (1934), *ROSE MARIE* (1936), *THE GREAT ZIEGFELD* (1936), *ROSALIE* (1937), *Lady, Be Good* (1941), *THE PIRATE* (1948), *Red Garters* (1954), and *MARY POPPINS* (1964).

P

PAIGE, JANIS (1922–) played the comic second leads in nine 1940s musicals, often paired with JACK CARSON, whom she later appeared with in nightclubs and on television. Paige made her film debut in a bit part in *Bathing Beauty* (1944), then was featured in *HOLLYWOOD CANTEEN* (1944), *The Time, the Place and the Girl* (1946), *Love and Learn* (1947), *ROMANCE ON THE HIGH SEAS* (1948), *Two Gals and a Guy* (1951), *SILK STOCKINGS* (1956), and *Follow the Boys* (1963). The leggy singer, who was married to composer Ray Gilbert, also performed on Broadway and was a regular on a few television shows.

PAIGE, ROBERT (1910–1987) moved from bit parts in movie musicals to leads, but it was usually in forgettable B pictures. His most frequent screen partner was JANE FRAZEE, but he is best remembered singing "Californ-i-ay" with DEANNA DURBIN in *CAN'T HELP SINGING* (1944). Among Paige's two dozen other musicals were *Cain and Mabel* (1936), *The Lady Objects* (1938), *Dancing on a Dime* (1941), *Hellzapoppin* (1941), *What's Cookin'?* (1942), *Get Hep to Love* (1942), *Cowboy in Manhattan* (1943), *Crazy House* (1943), *Follow the Boys* (1944), and *BYE BYE BIRDIE* (1963). In the 1950s Paige was frequently seen on television as both an actor and a quiz show host.

PAINT YOUR WAGON (Paramount 1969) was one of the era's overproduced and overspent ($17 million) behemoths that helped make the big-budget Hollywood musical extinct. Shot on location in Oregon, where director JOSHUA LOGAN built a complete gold mining town (and then destroyed it in the movie's climax) with a cast of expensive nonsingers like Lee Marvin and Clint Eastwood, the musical seemed doomed to financial failure. It was far from a critical hit as well. ALAN JAY LERNER wrote the screenplay that tossed out much of the plot and half the songs from his 1951 Broadway show and substituted a new story (with writer Paddy Chayevsky) and some new numbers with composer ANDRÉ PREVIN. Still set in the prospecting days of the 1840s in California, the tale now came down to a *ménage à trois* with old-timer Marvin and greenhorn Eastwood both in love with Jean Seberg (vocals dubbed by Anita Gordon). Having been one of two wives of a Mormon husband, Seberg is more than happy to share both men until respectability forces her to choose Eastwood. Then the boom town goes bust (literally) and Marvin sets out looking for new and unspoiled wilderness. Eastwood revealed a pleasant, untrained singing voice, Marvin growled his songs (sometimes rather effectively), and reliable HARVE PRESNELL gave "They Call the Wind Maria" a full-voiced rendering that was thrilling. Also saved from the Lerner and FREDERICK LOEWE stage score was the lovely ballad "I Talk to the Trees," the rousing numbers "There's a Coach Comin' In" and "I'm On My Way," and the simple folk song "I Still See Elisa."

PAJAMA GAME, THE (Warner 1957) came to the screen with just about the entire cast and creative staff of the 1954 Broadway show, yet the light-hearted and bouncy musical looked far from stagebound. When new plant superintendent John Raitt arrives at a pajama factory in Cedar Rapids, Iowa, he is smitten by union organizer DORIS DAY (the only major cast change from the play) and she with him, but the workers are about to strike for a seven-and-a-half-cent raise, so pleasant complications arise. Director GEORGE ABBOTT (now co-directing with STANLEY DONAN), choreographer BOB FOSSE, and most of the RICHARD ADLER and JERRY ROSS score came along with the Broadway cast, and all were in top form. "Once-a- Year Day" became a raucous picnic frolic, dance numbers "Hernando's Hideaway" and "Steam Heat" were stylized and funny, "Seven and a Half Cents" was turned into a fashion show, and the big ballad "Hey, There" was still a showstopper. The supporting cast was exceptionally enjoyable, especially EDDIE FOY, JR., as a time management expert jealous of his flirtatious girlfriend CAROL HANEY, as well as Reta Shaw, Barbara Nichols, Thelma Pelish, and dancers Buzz Miller, Kenneth LeRoy, and Peter Gennaro.

PAL JOEY (Columbia 1957) may not have been the tough and adult 1940 stage musical it was based on, but parts of it were terrific, and FRANK SINATRA, in a role originated by GENE KELLY on stage and intended for the film, had the right persona and hard edge that the part of nightclub singer Joey Evans called for. In the sanitized screen version, Joey has a fling with a wealthy San Francisco widow (RITA HAYWORTH, dubbed by Jo Ann Greer) who was once a stripper before she became a Nob Hill snob. She sets Joey up with his own club, where he falls for innocent chorine KIM NOVAK (dubbed by Trudy Erwin), and instead of both women dumping the heel, as in the play, in the end Sinatra and Novak walk off into the sunset together. Director GEORGE SIDNEY did what he could with the tampered piece and got electric performances out of Hayworth and Sinatra; Novak seemed hopelessly lost. Half of the LORENZ HART–RICHARD RODGERS score was dumped, keeping "Zip," "Bewitched, (Bothered and Bewildered)," "I Could Write a Book," and a few others and tossing in some other Rodgers and Hart standards like "My Funny Valentine," "The Lady Is a Tramp," and "There's a Small Hotel," which were welcomed even if they seemed out of place.

PALEFACE, THE (Paramount 1948) barely qualifies as a musical with its mere three songs but they were all gems, as was the slaphappy script by Frank Tashlin and its two stars, BOB HOPE and JANE RUSSELL. In one of the best roles of his long career, Hope played Painless Potter, a quack dentist from the East who travels the Wild West looking for a quick buck but finding sexy, gun-slinging Calamity Jane (Russell) instead. She talks the timid Potter into marrying her so that she has a front for her activities as a government agent, and the resulting complications gave Hope a chance to play his fumbling, wise-cracking persona to the hilt. Saloon gal Iris Adrian sang Joseph J. Lilley's "Get a Man" with a sardonic grin, she tried to seduce the hapless Hope with "Meetcha 'Round the Corner (At Half Past Eight)," and Hope sang the Oscar-winning "Buttons and Bows" to Russell as he longed for the creature comforts back East, both songs by RAY EVANS and JAY LIVINGSTON. Russell got to sing "Buttons and Bows" with ROY ROGERS in the sequel *SON OF PALEFACE* (Paramount 1952), in which Hope played the son of Painless Potter, now dead and memorialized by a statue in the town square. Painless, Jr., recently graduated from Harvard and now out West to claim his inheritance, is as cowardly as his dad and no match for Russell as a bandit disguised as a saloon singer. Rogers played a government agent who is on to Russell but is starting to fall for her. He eventually captured her (and her heart), but Hope got a hysterical scene trying to sleep in a bed with a horse and so everyone in the audience was happy. Evans and Livingston wrote a congenial ballad "California Rose" for Rogers to sing, and JACK BROOKS penned the waggish duet "Am I in Love?" for Hope and Russell, sung while she gave Hope a shave. Tashlin wrote and directed the film, and it was that rare case when a sequel was as enjoyable (if not more so) as the original.

PALLETTE, EUGENE (1889–1954), one of Hollywood's most easily identified character actors with his round girth and frog voice, started in the silent era and played leading roles, but by the time sound came in he was being cast in supporting roles. Pallette can be seen in over 200 features, including the musicals *THE LOVE PARADE* (1929), *Pointed Heels* (1929), *PARAMOUNT ON PARADE* (1930), *Let's Go Native* (1930), *Playboy of Paris* (1930), *All the King's Horses* (1935), *Stowaway* (12936), *ONE HUNDRED MEN AND A GIRL* (1937), *A Little Bit of Heaven* (1940), *THE GANG'S ALL HERE* (1943), *Lake Placid Serenade* (1944), *Pin Up Girl* (1944), *Step Lively* (1944), and others.

PAN, HERMES (1905–1990) was perhaps the most sought-after choreographer in Hollywood in its golden age, staging the musical numbers in over fifty musicals and occasionally doing a dancing role as well. Pan physically resembled FRED ASTAIRE and was called the star's alter ego, the two working together on seventeen films as well as television specials. Pan also choreographed BETTY GRABLE in ten films. His career extended from a sensational debut choreographing *FLYING DOWN TO RIO* (1933) to the lackluster dances in *Lost Horizon* (1973). In between were such memorable classics as *THE GAY DIVORCEE* (1934), *TOP HAT* (1935), *FOLLOW THE FLEET* (1936), *SWING TIME* (1936), *SHALL WE DANCE* (1937), *A DAMSEL IN DISTRESS* (1937), *CAREFREE* (1938), *THAT NIGHT IN RIO* (1941), *MOON OVER MIAMI* (1941), *SUN VALLEY SERENADE* (1941), *WEEK-END IN HAVANA* (1941), *SPRINGTIME IN THE ROCKIES* (1942), *CONEY ISLAND* (1943), *BLUE SKIES* (1946), *THE BARKLEYS OF BROADWAY* (1949), *THREE LITTLE WORDS* (1950), *LOVELY TO LOOK AT* (1952), *KISS ME, KATE* (1953), *SILK STOCKINGS* (1956), *PAL JOEY* (1957), *PORGY AND BESS* (1959), *CAN-CAN* (1959), *FLOWER DRUM SONG* (1961), and *MY FAIR LADY* (1964).

PANGBORN, FRANKLIN (1893–1958) fussed and fumed as a harassed maitre d', hotel manager, or store clerk in dozens of films in the 1930s and 1940s. He started as a dramatic performer on the stage but went to Hollywood in 1926 and became one of its most easily recognized character actors. Pangborn's musical credits include *FLYING DOWN TO RIO* (1933), *INTERNATIONAL HOUSE* (1933), *COLLEGE RHYTHM* (1934), *REBECCA OF SUNNYBROOK FARM* (1938), *JOY OF LIVING* (1938), *CAREFREE* (1938), *Crazy House* (1943), and *Two Guys From Milwaukee* (1946).

PARAMOUNT ON PARADE (Paramount 1929) was the studio's chance to flaunt the many stars it had under contract, and unlike MGM's *HOLLYWOOD REVUE OF 1929* and WARNER BROTHERS' *THE SHOW OF SHOWS* (1929), this REVUE depended less on spectacle and more on star turns by everyone from MISCHA AUER to Fay Wray. JACK OAKIE, RICHARD "SKEETS" GALLAGHER, LEON ERROL, VIRGINIA BRUCE, and Mitzi Mayfair, and the Paramount Publix Ushers acted as hosts and emcees introducing so many songs, comedy sketches, and dramatic scenes that eleven directors were used in the filming. Musical highlights included MAURICE CHEVALIER as a gendarme strolling through a Paris park filled with loving couples and crooning LEO ROBIN and RICHARD A. WHITING's "All I Want Is Just One Girl"; Clara Bow, Oakie, and a chorus of Marines singing and dancing to the self-mocking Elsie Janis–Jack King ditty "I'm True to the Navy Now"; LILLIAN ROTH and CHARLES "BUDDY" ROGERS claiming "Any Time's the Time to Fall in Love" by the same songwriters; Ruth Chatterton as a Montmartre prostitute lamenting "My Marine" by Whiting and Ray

Egan; HELEN KANE as a flapper-teacher asking the Janis-King musical question "What Did Cleopatra Say?"; and a marvelous finale with chimney sweep Chevalier and a chorus of comely sweepettes singing SAM COSLOW's "Sweeping the Clouds Away" as they formed kaleidoscopic patterns while Chevalier climbed a ladder up into the clouds.

PARAMOUNT PICTURES was formed in 1916 when Adolph Zukor's Famous Players Film Company merged with H.H. Hodkinson's Paramount Pictures Corporation to become one of the "big five" studios in Hollywood. Actress Mary Pickford, producer SAMUEL GOLDWYN, and director Cecil B. DeMille helped ensure both the quality and the box office popularity of the new company which specialized in family entertainment. All the same, the studio barely avoided bankruptcy in 1933 and didn't reach financial security until the 1940s, thanks to the *BIG BROADCAST* series, the "Road" pictures, and other musicals featuring BING CROSBY such as *HOLIDAY INN* (1942), *GOING MY WAY* (1944), and *BLUE SKIES* (1946). Notable Paramount musicals of the 1930s and 1940s included the MAURICE CHEVALIER operettas such as *LOVE ME TONIGHT* (1932) and MAE WEST's *SHE DONE HIM WRONG* (1933), *HIGH, WIDE AND HANDSOME* (1937), *BIRTH OF THE BLUES* (1941), *STAR SPANGLED RHYTHM* (1942), and *THE FLEET'S IN* (1942). The comedy team of MARTIN and LEWIS helped Paramount ride through the 1950s, as did such hits as *WHITE CHRISTMAS* (1954), *THE COUNTRY GIRL* (1954), and *FUNNY FACE* (1957). The 1960s included some costly flops, such as *PAINT YOUR WAGON* (1969), but the 1970s brought marginal hits like *ON A CLEAR DAY YOU CAN SEE FOREVER* (1970) and *LADY SINGS THE BLUES* (1972) as well as giant blockbusters such as *SATURDAY NIGHT FEVER* (1977) and *GREASE* (1978). Aside from the occasional hit like *FLASHDANCE* (1983), musicals at the studio dwindled into obscurity. The conglomerate Gulf & Western bought Paramount in 1983, and in 1989 the studio adopted its current title Paramount Communications. Today the studio is owned by Viacom, which also controls Nickelodeon, MTV, and Showtime television.

PARKER, ALAN (1944–   ), an English-born director who works on both sides of the Atlantic, has directed everything from documentaries to musicals to socially relevant dramas. Parker helmed the musicals *BUGSY MALONE* (1976), *FAME* (1980), *Pink Floyd—The Wall* (1082), *The Commitments* (1991), and *EVITA* (1996).

PARKS, LARRY (1914–1975) was a routine contract player at COLUMBIA until he suddenly became a star playing the title role in *THE JOLSON STORY* (1946) and *JOLSON SINGS AGAIN* (1949). Although AL JOLSON provided the singing voice for him in the two BIOGRAPHICAL MUSICALS, Parks did his own vocals in *Sing for Your Supper* (1941), *YOU WERE NEVER*

LOVELIER (1942), *Is Everybody Happy?* (1943), *Reveille With Beverly* (1943), *She's a Sweetheart* (1944), *Down to Earth* (1947), and others. Parks' popularity immediately ceased in the 1950s when he admitted to being a member of the Communist party and the studios quickly dropped him. He occasionally appeared on the stage and later on television and in some nonmusical films, sometimes with his wife BETTY GARRETT.

PARKYAKARKUS (1904–1958) was the stage name for comic Harry Einstein, who became well known on EDDIE CANTOR's radio program and appeared in a handful of grade B musical films, including *Strike Me Pink* (1936), *New Faces of 1937*, *The Life of the Party* (1937), *Sweethearts of the USA* (1944), *Earl Carroll Vanities* (1945), and *Out of This World* (1945). Parkyakarkus, who sometimes went under the name Harry Parke, was the father of film director–actor Albert Brooks.

PASTERNAK, JOE (1901–1991) was the Hungarian-born Hollywood producer who, working at different studios, presented some sixty movie musicals between 1937 and 1966. After supervising feature films in Europe, Pasternak secured his Hollywood career by discovering DEANNA DURBIN and producing ten of her vehicles. He was also responsible for making or reviving the careers of JANE POWELL, ESTHER WILLIAMS, MARIO LANZA, and MARLENE DIETRICH. Pasternak was known mainly for his wholesome family films, though he also produced the provocative *Destry Rides Again* (1939) and the gutsy *LOVE ME OR LEAVE ME* (1955). Among his other musical credits were *Three Smart Girls* (1937), *ONE HUNDRED MEN AND A GIRL* (1937), *Mad About Music* (1938), *First Love* (1939), *Presenting Lily Mars* (1943), *TWO GIRLS AND A SAILOR* (1944), *ANCHORS AWEIGH* (1945), *No Leave, No Love* (1946), *A Date With Judy* (1948), *IN THE GOOD OLD SUMMERTIME* (949), *SUMMER STOCK* (1950), *The Toast of New Orleans* (1950), *THE GREAT CARUSO* (1951), *THE MERRY WIDOW* (1952), *THE STUDENT PRINCE* (1954), *HIT THE DECK* (1955), *Meet Me in Las Vegas* (1956), *Where the Boys Are* (1960), *JUMBO* (1962), and *Spinout* (1966).

PATINKIN, MANDY (1947–   ), the energetic star of Broadway musicals and dramas as well as a favorite on television and in concert, has made only a handful of films and rarely gets to show off his musical talents. Patinkin played the Hebrew student Avigdor in *YENTL* (1983), the pianist Eighty-Eight Keys in *DICK TRACY* (1990), and the greedy villain Huxley in *THE ADVENTURES OF ELMO IN GROUCHLAND* (1999).

PATTERSON, ELIZABETH (1874–1966), a familiar character actress in films from the silent era to 1960, usually played maternal types or grumpy senior citizens. She can be seen in the musicals *THE SMILING LIEUTENANT*

(1931), *LOVE ME TONIGHT* (1932), *HIGH, WIDE AND HANDSOME* (1937), *Sing You Sinners* (1938), *The Sky's the Limit* (1943), *THE SHOCKING MISS PILGRIM* (1947), *PAL JOEY* (1957), and others.

PAYNE, JOHN (1912–1989) was a personable leading man who played opposite most of 20TH CENTURY–FOX's musical ladies in the 1940s, including ALICE FAYE, JUNE HAVER, SONJA HENIE, and BETTY GRABLE. The masculine singer-actor appeared in *Hats Off* (1936), *Love on Toast* (1938), *College Swing* (1938), *Garden of the Moon* (1938), and *Star Dust* (1940) before reaching stardom with *TIN PAN ALLEY* (1940), followed by *The Great American Broadcast* (1941), *WEEK-END IN HAVANA* (1941), *SUN VALLEY SERENADE* (1941), *Footlight Serenade* (1942), *ICELAND* (1942), *SPRINGTIME IN THE ROCKIES* (1942), *HELLO, FRISCO, HELLO* (1943), *THE DOLLY SISTERS* (1945), and *Wake Up and Dream* (1946). When Payne outgrew his musical leading roles, he concentrated on dramatic features, television, and the stage.

PEARCE, ALICE (1913–1966), a farcical character actress in films and television, made her screen debut as the sniffling Lucy Schmeeler in *ON THE TOWN* (1949), a role she had created in the Broadway version. The often-befuddled Pearce was also seen in the musicals *THE BELLE OF NEW YORK* (1952), *The Opposite Sex* (1956), and *Kiss Me, Stupid* (1964) before her untimely death.

PENNER, JOE (1905–1941) was a vaudeville and radio comic who used a form of baby talk for laughs and coined the phrases "Oh, you nasty man!" and "Wanna buy a duck?" He was featured in the film musicals *COLLEGE RHYTHM* (1934), *Collegiate* (1936), *New Faces of 1937, Life of the Party* (1937), *Go Chase Yourself* (1938), and played the Dromio twins in *The Boys From Syracuse* (1940).

PENNIES FROM HEAVEN (Columbia 1936) was one of the many examples of a mediocre film made memorable by BING CROSBY playing a likable fellow who sings his way into the audience's (and other character's) favor. Depression drifter and street singer Crosby lands in jail for smuggling, and a convicted murderer gives him the address of his victim's family. When Crosby is released, he goes to their home and befriends them, especially ten-year-old Edith Fellows and grandfather DONALD MEEK. It was pretty treacly stuff, but JOHNNY BURKE and ARTHUR JOHNSTON wrote a handful of superb songs and Crosby made the most of them: the heartfelt ballads "Let's Call a Heart a Heart" and "So Do I," the simple, prayer-like "One, Two, Button Your Shoe," the rousing "Skeleton in the Closet," which he sang with LOUIS ARMSTRONG, and the wistful, optimistic title tune. ***PENNIES FROM HEAVEN*** (MGM 1981) was not a remake but an inventive, dark, and uneven musical that used old standards in its fantasy sequences. Chicago sheet-music salesman STEVE MARTIN trudges through the Depression and escapes from his dreary wife Jessica Harper and pathetic mistress BERNADETTE PETERS by imagining his life situations turned into glamourous, BUSBY BERKELEY–like musical production numbers. Dennis Potter wrote the odd piece, HERBERT ROSS directed it on Ken Adams' stylized Edward Hoppereque settings, and Danny Daniels choreographed the songs with panache. Martin and the others in his fantasies usually lip-synced to celebrated old recordings of the songs, so the effect was almost Brechtian rather than entertaining, but some sequences were intriguing, such as Martin and Peters in a movie theatre watching FRED ASTAIRE and GINGER ROGERS dance to "Let's Face the Music and Dance" and suddenly the real-life couple appear in the movie couple's place on the screen, or the title number heard on the Arthur Tracy recording but with a tramp (Vernel Bagneris) prancing in a shower of golden pennies.

PEREIRA, HAL (1905–1983), one of Hollywood's top production designers, supervised the art direction at PARAMOUNT and personally designed over 100 films, from westerns to modern dramas to epic period pieces. Pereira's musical credits include *THE COUNTRY GIRL* (1954), *Red Garters* (1954), *WHITE CHRISTMAS* (1954), *ARTISTS AND MODELS* (1955), *FUNNY FACE* (1957), *KING CREOLE* (1958), *Rock-a-Bye Baby* (1958), *St. Louis Blues* (1958), *THE FIVE PENNIES* (1959), *LI'L ABNER* (1959), and *BLUE HAWAII* (1961).

PERELMAN, S.J. (1904–1979), the celebrated American humorist with a score of comic essays and poetry to his credit, was brought out to Hollywood to write gags for the MARX BROTHERS' comedy *Monkey Business* (1931) and musical *HORSE FEATHERS* (1932). He also contributed to the scripts for the musicals *Sitting Pretty* (1933), *THE BIG BROADCAST OF 1936* (1935), and *One Touch of Venus* (1948), based on his 1943 Broadway musical.

PERLBERG, WILLIAM (1896–1968), a Hollywood producer who often worked with director GEORGE SEATON, produced fourteen musicals, including *The King Steps Out* (1936), *The Lady Objects* (1938), *HELLO, FRISCO, HELLO* (1943), *CONEY ISLAND* (1943), *Where Do We Go From Here?* (1945), *THE SHOCKING MISS PILGRIM* (1947), *WABASH AVENUE* (1950), *Somebody Loves Me* (1952), and *THE COUNTRY GIRL* (1954).

PETE KELLY'S BLUES (Mark VII/Warner 1955) was a gritty gangster melodrama and a backstage musical trying to coexist, and the result was sometimes fascinating, other times tedious. Richard L. Breen's screenplay was about the conflict between trumpet player Jack Webb (who also produced and directed the film), who plays in a Kansas City speakeasy in 1927, and the bootlegger-owner Edmond O'Brien, who is trying to edge into the talent agency business. At the club is singer PEGGY LEE, who has taken to drink as her career declines, and various lowlifes and patrons played by Andy Devine, Lee Marvin, Martin Milnar, Mort Marshall, Jayne Mansfield, Matty Matlock, and ELLA FITZGERALD. Webb's trumpet playing was dubbed by Dick Cathcart, and Lee sang most of the movie's twelve songs, all old standards ("Bye Bye Blackbird," "Somebody Loves Me," "Sugar," "Hard-Hearted Hannah," and others) except for a new title song by SAMMY CAHN and RAY HEINDORF. Lee's acting and singing were outstanding, the highpoint for her movie career, and there was a *film noir* atmosphere about the whole picture that was unique.

PETERS, BERNADETTE (1944–   ), one of Broadway's favorite leading ladies, was singing and dancing on the stage since childhood. By the 1970s she was one of the theatre's few *bona fide* musical stars. Peters has made a handful films, none of them box office hits, and was memorable in the movie musicals *PENNIES FROM HEAVEN* (1981) and *ANNIE* (1982) and on the soundtrack of the animated *ANASTASIA* (1997).

PETERS, BROCK (1927–   ), a rugged-looking African American actor whose powerful presence made him ideal in dramas and virile action movies, was also effective in the movie musicals *CARMEN JONES* (1954), *PORGY AND BESS* (1959), and *Lost in the Stars* (1974).

PHANTOM OF THE PARADISE (Fox 1974) was a disco-rock version of Leroux's classic tale *The Phantom of the Opera*, in which a crazed composer (William Finley), his face deformed by an accident with a record press, takes revenge on music publisher PAUL WILLIAMS for stealing one of his songs by haunting Williams' popular "Paradise Discothèque." Jessica Harper was the young singer that both men craved, and Gerrit Graham was the eccentric rock singer "Beef" who brought in the crowds. Brian De Palma wrote and directed the unusual piece, with Williams providing the songs, the most satisfying being the rock ballad "Old Souls," the Beach Boys spoof "Upholstery," and the moody "Phantom's Theme." The movie did marginal business when released but later developed a cult following.

PHANTOM PRESIDENT, THE (Paramount 1932) was showman GEORGE M. COHAN's first film musical, and because it was a box office failure, he never attempted another. But his performance in a dual role is magnetic, and watching the film one can understand his hypnotic appeal on stage. Cohan, a performer in a medicine show, just happens to look just like a prominent banker who is running for president of the United States. Party cronies substitute the performer for the real candidate because of his showmanship, and the entertainer is soon wooing the public and the banker's fiancée Claudette Colbert. In the end the party (and Colbert) goes with the phony candidate and they win the election. JIMMY DURANTE was outstanding as the medicine performer's partner, but the whole cast, which included GEORGE BARBIER, Sidney Toler, ALAN MOWBRAY, and Louise Mackintosh, gave strong and satirical performances under NORMAN TAUROG's direction. LORENZ HART and RICHARD RODGERS wrote the score, which included the warm ballad "Give Her a Kiss" (only heard on a car radio in the film!) and the inventive "The Convention," in which lyrics, dialogue, and actions at the political convention were precisely set to music.

PIDGEON, WALTER (1897–1984) was a durable leading man in Hollywood from the last days of the silent era to the end of the 1970s. He played compassionate leading men until he grew into mature parts, usually compassionate fathers, husbands, doctors, and producers. Pidgeon sometimes sang on the stage and in his early musical films such as *Melody of Love* (1928), *Viennese Nights* (1930), *Kiss Me Again* (1931), *The Hot Heiress* (1931), and others, but later he was usually a nonsinging presence in the story. His later musicals include *The Girl of the Golden West* (1938), *It's a Date* (1940), *Holiday in Mexico* (1946), *Million Dollar Mermaid* (1952), *DEEP IN MY HEART* (1954), *HIT THE DECK* (1955), and *FUNNY GIRL* (1968).

PINOCCHIO (Disney/RKO 1940), the second animated feature from WALT DISNEY and for many the greatest of all the studio's works, combined a gripping story (based on an 1880 story by Carlo Collodi), memorable characters, tuneful songs, and remarkable animation that has rarely been equaled. Jiminy Cricket (voice of CLIFF EDWARDS), a Disney creation, acts as the tale's narrator and the "conscience" for puppet Pinocchio (Dickie Jones) as they brave the conniving J. Worthington Foulfellow (WALTER CATLETT), the greedy puppeteer Stromboli (Charles Judels), the horrors of Pleasure Island, and captivity inside Monstro the whale. All the villains were balanced by the kindly Gepetto (Christian Rub), the wily cat Figaro, the goldfish Cleo, and the understanding Blue Fairy (Evelyn Venable), who turns Pinocchio into a real boy once he has proven himself to be brave and unselfish. The songs by NED WASHINGTON and LEIGH HARLINE were enjoyable in themselves but also fit nicely into the narrative: "Hi-Diddle-Dee-Dee (An Actor's Life for Me)," "I've Got No Strings," "Give a Little Whistle," and the Oscar-winning "When You Wish Upon a Star." The movie has dated perhaps less than any other animated film; what was frightening then still is, and what was once joyous still soars.

PINZA, EZIO (1892–1957), a renowned opera basso who took time off from singing at the Metropolitan to star in the Broadway musicals *South Pacific* (1949) and *Fanny* (1954), did not fare as well in his four movie musicals: *Carnegie Hall* (1947), *Mr. Imperium* (1950), *Strictly Dishonorable* (1951), and *Tonight We Sing* (1953).

PIRATE, THE (MGM 1948) may be the most cartoonish live-action musical ever made, with its artificial sets, garishly colored costumes, and larger-than-life characters performing with wild abandon that strikes some as inspired, others as wearing. Set on a fictional Caribbean island (though obviously filmed in a studio), the story concerns dreamy lass JUDY GARLAND, who, bored with her fiancé Walter Slezak, imagines being carried off by the dashing pirate Macoco, also known as Mack the Black. When strolling actor GENE KELLY comes to town, he woos Garland by telling her he is the pirate but suffers her anger when she learns the truth. It turns out that Slezak is the real Macoco, and Garland, her illusions dashed, joins Kelly in the end. It was an adult fairy tale played with grand passions, silly athletics, and not a touch of subtlety. COLE PORTER penned the score and tried to match all the derring-do on the set: the sly "Niña," the overromantic "Love of My Life," the rousing "Mack the Black," the wistful "You Can Do No Wrong," and the celebratory "Be a Clown," which the NICHOLAS BROTHERS performed defying gravity and Garland and Kelly reprised at the end. Also in the cast were Gladys Cooper, REGINALD OWEN, George Zucco, and Lola Albright, all under VINCENTE MINNELLI's painterly direction and choreographed by Kelly and ROBERT ALTON. The movie did poorly at the box office but has found its advocates over the years.

PLUNKETT, WALTER (1902–1982), one of Hollywood's most prestigious costume designers, moved from theatre design to the movies at the advent of sound. His many musical credits include *FLYING DOWN TO RIO* (1933), *THE GAY DIVORCEE* (1934), *THE STORY OF VERNON AND IRENE CASTLE* (1939), *SUMMER HOLIDAY* (1948), *SHOW BOAT* (1951), *AN AMERICAN IN PARIS* (1951), *SINGIN' IN THE RAIN* (1952), *KISS ME, KATE* (1953), *SEVEN BRIDES FOR SEVEN BROTHERS* (1954), and *BELLS ARE RINGING* (1960).

POCAHONTAS (Disney 1995) is the only DISNEY animated featured based on history, though no one claimed it was very accurate history. But as a love story it was beautifully told and rather low key for a kids' movie. In fact, many children were bored. None of the animals talked, there was no fantasy or magic save a little conjuring by Grandmother Willow, the issues were mature ones (ecological awareness, racial tolerance, the evils of imperialism), and at the end the lovers were separated. No wonder adults found more to savor. Pocahontas (voice of Irene Bedard, singing by Judy Kuhn) was portrayed as a full-grown woman rather than the young girl she really was, and Captain John Smith (Mel Gibson) looked more like a movie star than an explorer, but their scenes together were honest, funny, and very moving. The Englishmen were portrayed as simply greedy, but the Native Americans were handled sympathetically without being patronizing. The melodic songs by STEPHEN SCHWARTZ and ALAN MENKEN sometimes took an inspirational tone, especially with the ACADEMY AWARD–winning "Colors of the Wind."

POLLACK, LEW (1895–1946) was a Hollywood composer who worked with a variety of lyricists, mostly at 20TH CENTURY–FOX. With SIDNEY MITCHELL, he scored *Pigskin Parade* (1936), *CAPTAIN JANUARY* (1936), *ONE IN A MILLION* (1936), *Thin Ice* (1937), *IN OLD CHICAGO* (1938), *REBECCA OF SUNNYBROOK FARM* (1938), and others. Pollack also contributed songs to *Song and Dance Man* (1936), *The Yanks Are Coming* (1942), *Jitterbugs* (1943), *Sweethearts of the USA* (1944), *Music in Manhattan* (1944), *The Girl Rush* (1944), and others.

PONS, LILY (1904–1976), one of the Metropolitan Opera's greatest and favorite coloraturas, was courted by Hollywood after the success of opera singer GRACE MOORE on the screen. The petite, dark-haired singer scored a hit with her first film, *I DREAM TOO MUCH* (1936), but was less popular in *That Girl From Paris* (1936), *Hitting a New High* (1937), and *Carnegie Hall* (1947). The French-born Pons was married to conductor André Kostelanetz.

POOR LITTLE RICH GIRL (Fox 1936) was a typical SHIRLEY TEMPLE vehicle in that it combined contemporary, toe-tapping razzle-dazzle with good old-fashioned sentimentality. Yet the story (based on an old Mary Pickford silent film) held together better than some, and Temple got to display her many talents within the context of the plot. The neglected, motherless daughter of soap manufacturer Michael Whalen, eight-year-old Temple runs away from home and is befriended by married vaudeville partners ALICE FAYE and JACK HALEY, who, spotting talent, put her in the act. Soon the singing-dancing moppet has the three of them in the big time, but when they appear on a radio show sponsored by a rival soap company, dad comes back and promises to change his ways. MACK GORDON and HARRY REVEL wrote some tailor-made tunes for Temple, including "You Gotta Eat Your Spinach, Baby," "When I'm With You," "Oh, My Goodness," "But Definitely," and the tapping production number "Military Man." IRVING CUMMINGS directed the cast, which also included GLORIA STUART, Sara Haden, JANE DARWELL, and (briefly) TONY MARTIN.

PORGY AND BESS (Columbia 1959), GEORGE GERSHWIN's 1935 folk opera masterpiece, took quite a while to reach the screen, and despite the first-class production that producer SAMUEL GOLDWYN (it was his last picture) gave it, the film suffered from the problems that plagued all opera movies. OTTO PREMINGER's heavy-handed direction did not help bridge the gag between a gritty, realistic story and its jazzy, stylized music. Sidney Poitier (vocals dubbed by Robert McFerrin) was the cripple Porgy who loves the sultry Bess (DOROTHY DANDRIDGE, dubbed by Adele Addison), but she belongs to the murderous Crown (BROCK PETERS). The whole cast was exceptional with SAMMY DAVIS, JR., as the sleazy Sportin' Life and PEARL BAILEY, Diahann Carroll, Ruth Attaway, and Leslie Scott among the residents of Catfish Row in Charleston, South Carolina. Much of Gershwin's intricate score was retained, though not enough for those wishing to see the full expanse of this mighty opera. The lyrics were by IRA GERSHWIN and DuBose Heyward, with N. Richard Nash providing the screenplay and HERMES PAN handling the choreography. Among the celebrated songs used in the movie were "Summertime," "A Woman Is a Sometime Thing," "There's a Boat Dat's Leavin' Soon for New York," "Bess, You Is My Woman Now," "My Man's Gone Now," "I Got Plenty o' Nuthin,'" and "It Ain't Necessarily So."

PORTER, COLE (1891–1964), the celebrated American composer-lyricist whose songs and lifestyle represented the sophisticated high life for over forty years, saw many of his Broadway hits transferred to the screen, though rarely with their scores intact. Porter's stage-to-screen musicals were *ANYTHING GOES* (1936 and 1956), *Panama Hattie* (1942), *DuBarry Was a Lady* (1943), *Let's Face It* (1943), *KISS ME, KATE* (1953), *SILK STOCKINGS* (1957), and *CAN-CAN* (1960). He wrote songs directly for the screen for *BORN TO DANCE* (1936), *ROSALIE* (1937), *BROADWAY MELODY OF 1940*, *YOU'LL NEVER GET RICH* (1941), *Something to Shout About* (1943), *THE PIRATE* (1948), *HIGH SOCIETY* (1956), and *LES GIRLS* (1957). Porter's songs were used in the highly fictitious BIOGRAPHICAL MUSICAL of his life, *NIGHT AND DAY* (1946), with CARY GRANT as the songwriter, and in the misconceived musical *At Long Last Love* (1975). Few lyricists captured the breezy elegance and romantic yearning that Porter put in his lyrics, and his music, which tended toward the exotic and Latin sound, continues to entrance.

POTTER, H.C. (1904–1977), a versatile director of plays and films, was best known for his comedies, but he did direct the movie musicals *Romance in the Dark* (1938), *THE STORY OF VERNON AND IRENE CASTLE* (1939), *Second Chorus* (1940), *Hellzapoppin* (1941), and *Three for the Show* (1955).

POWELL, DICK (1904–1963) had three successful careers in Hollywood: as the leading man who crooned his way through several WARNER BROTHERS' musicals (often with RUBY KEELER as his partner) in the 1930s; as a dramatic actor specializing in private eye roles in the 1940s; and as a director-producer in films and television in the 1950s. Powell was the ideal juvenile lead in early musicals, his youthful looks and clear singing voice making him a favorite in thirty-two films. After a bit part in *Blessed Event* (1932), he made a splash with *42ND STREET* (1933), followed by *GOLD DIGGERS OF 1933*, *FOOTLIGHT PARADE* (1933), *DAMES* (1934), *Flirtation Walk* (1934), *Shipmates Forever* (1935), and *Colleen* (1936), all with Keeler. Powell had various leading ladies for *WONDER BAR* (1934), *Twenty Million Sweet-*

hearts (1934), *Happiness Ahead* (1934), *GOLD DIGGERS OF 1935*, *Broadway Gondolier* (1935), *THANKS A MILLION* (1935), *GOLD DIGGERS OF 1937* (1936), *ON THE AVENUE* (1937), *HOLLYWOOD HOTEL* (1937), *Cowboy From Brooklyn* (1938), *Going Places* (1938), *STAR SPANGLED RHYTHM* (1942), *HAPPY GO LUCKY* (1943), *Riding High* (1943), and others. He was married to JOAN BLONDELL and then to JUNE ALLYSON.

POWELL, ELEANOR (1910–1982), the tall, leggy beauty who was arguably filmdom's best female tap dancer, starred in a dozen movie musicals in which she demonstrated her almost machine-like rhythm and precision. On the stage since she was a child, Powell was featured on Broadway before going to Hollywood in 1935. Although mostly remembered for her solo spots, she also danced with some of Hollywood's best hoofers. Her musical film debut was a supporting role in *George White's Scandals* (1935), followed by playing dancer Irene Foster disguised as a foreigner in *BROADWAY MELODY OF 1936* (1935), understudy Nora Paige in *BORN TO DANCE* (1936), race horse owner Sally Lee in *BROADWAY MELODY OF 1938* (1937), the title princess in *ROSALIE* (1937), dancing star Dorothy March in *Honolulu* (1939), another dancing star Clare Bennett in *BROADWAY MELODY OF 1940*, yet another dancing star Marilyn Marsh in *Lady, Be Good* (1941), cruise line passenger Tallulah Winters in *Ship Ahoy* (1942), melodrama actress Constance Shaw in *I Dood It* (1943), and publicity-hungry Ginny Walker in *Sensations* (1944), as well as a specialty spot in *Thousands Cheer* (1943). As America's fascination with tap waned, so did her popularity, so Powell left films to perform in nightclubs and on stage, returning to Hollywood to do a guest spot in *The Duchess of Idaho* (1950). She was married to actor Glenn Ford.

POWELL, JANE (1929–   ) managed to become one of MGM's most popular musical stars in the 1940s and 1950s even though few of her films were grade A pictures. The diminutive blonde with the piercingly clear soprano voice made her screen debut as herself in *Song of the Open Road* (1944) and appeared as a singing teenager in *Delightfully Dangerous* (1945), *Holiday in Mexico* (1946), *Three Darling Daughters* (1948), *A Date for Judy* (1948), *Nancy Goes to Rio* (1950), and others. She was seen in more mature roles in *ROYAL WEDDING* (1951), *Rich, Young and Pretty* (1951), *Small Town Girl* (1953), *Three Sailors and a Girl* (1953), *Athena* (1954), *SEVEN BRIDES FOR SEVEN BROTHERS* (1954), *HIT THE DECK* (1955), *The Girl Most Likely* (1957), and others, as well as a specialty spot in *DEEP IN MY HEART* (1954). When she outgrew her musical ingenue roles, Powell concentrated on the stage, nightclubs, and television.

POWELL, WILLIAM (1892–1984), one of Hollywood's most debonair and pliable stars, played producer Florenz Ziegfeld in *THE GREAT ZIEGFELD* (1936) and *ZIEGFELD FOLLIES* (1946). The nonsinging actor was also in the movie musicals *Pointed Heels* (1929), *PARAMOUNT ON PA-RADE* (1930), *Fashions of 1934, Reckless* (1935), and *Dancing in the Dark* (1949).

POWER, TYRONE (1913–1958), a popular matinee idol in various genres of film, came from a long line of actors in his family. Although he never sang on screen, Power played major roles in a half dozen musicals. He can be seen as a cadet in *Flirtation Walk* (1934), then as the romantic lead in *Thin Ice* (1937), *IN OLD CHICAGO* (1938), *ALEXANDER'S RAGTIME BAND* (1938), *ROSE OF WASHINGTON SQUARE* (1939), *Second Fiddle* (1939), and *The Eddy Duchin Story* (1956).

PREISSER, JUNE (1921–1984), a vaudeville dancer known for her oddly athletic footwork and perennially youthful looks, played teenagers in such movie musicals as *BABES IN ARMS* (1939), *Dancing Coed* (1939), *STRIKE UP THE BAND* (1940), *Sweater Girl* (1940), and others. Her later musicals were mostly B movies, such as *Let's Go Steady* (1945), *Junior Prom* (1946), *High School Hero* (1946), *Vacation Days* (1947), and others.

PREMINGER, OTTO (1906–1986), the prolific Hollywood director who began his career playing heavies in European and American films, directed (and sometimes produced) all genres of film, including the musicals *Under Your Spell* (1936), *CENTENNIAL SUMMER* (1946), *That Lady in Ermine* (1948), *CARMEN JONES* (1954), and *PORGY AND BESS* (1959).

PRESLEY, ELVIS (1935–1977), the legendary rock-and-roll icon who remains as popular today, if not more so, than when he was alive, made thirty-three films tailored to his image and audience. Presley was a limited actor, but even a more accomplished thespian would have looked foolish performing the scripts the "King" was often handed. Since each movie made money and produced hit songs for record sales, the studios were pleased and rarely provided Presley with top directors or production values. Presley's better films were at the beginning of his career. He debuted with *Love Me Tender* (1956), followed by *Loving You* (1957), *JAILHOUSE ROCK* (1957), and *KING CREOLE* (1958). Other notable musicals include *BLUE HAWAII* (1961), *Kid Galahad* (1962), *It Happened at the World's Fair* (1963), *Fun in Acapulco* (1963), *Kissin' Cousins* (1964), *VIVA LAS VEGAS* (1964), *Girl Happy* (1965), *Frankie and Johnny* (1966), *Double Trouble* (1967), *Live a Little, Love a Little* (1968), and *The Trouble With Girls* (1970). Whereas over sixty biographies have been written about him and thousands impersonate him on stages all over the world, Presley has been the subject of only a few film documentaries or musical bios, most notably *Elvis—That's the Way It Is* (1970), *Elvis on Tour* (1972), and *Elvis* (1979), in which the superstar was portrayed by Kurt Russell.

PRESNELL, HARVE (1933–   ), a virile baritone who recreated his stage role of lucky Johnny Brown in *THE UNSINKABLE MOLLY BROWN* (1964), arrived on the scene too late to find the kinds of musical parts (and musical movies) that were ideal for him. He appeared as dude ranch owner Danny Churchill in *When the Boys Meet the Girls* (1965) and gold prospector Rotten Luck Willie in *PAINT YOUR WAGON* (1969) and then concentrated on the stage and nightclubs.

PRESTON, ROBERT (1918–1987) was a routine contract player whose many dramatic roles in westerns and B movies were getting him nowhere. Then he created the role of Professor Harold Hill in *THE MUSIC MAN* on Broadway in 1957, and his career opened up musical and comedy parts in film and on stage. Before Preston filmed *The Music Man* in 1962, he had appeared in thankless roles in the movie musicals *Moon Over Burma* (1940), *Variety Girl* (1947), and *Big City* (1948). Later he was featured as southerner Beauregard Burnside in *Mame* (1974) and gay nightclub entertainer "Toddy" in *VICTOR/ VICTORIA* (1982), as well as in a variety of nonmusicals.

PREVIN, ANDRÉ (1929–   ), one of the few American composers and conductors to find success in both classical and popular music, began his career as an arranger for Hollywood films while he was still in high school. Soon he was orchestrating, conducting, and occasionally composing for musicals and nonmusicals. With lyricists BETTY COMDEN and ADOLPH GREEN, Previn wrote the songs for *IT'S ALWAYS FAIR WEATHER* (1955) and contributed to the scores for *Pepe* (1960) and *PAINT YOUR WAGON* (1969). He also did the musical direction and/or conducted *THREE LITTLE WORDS* (1951), *GIGI* (1958), *PORGY AND BESS* (1959), *MY FAIR LADY* (1964), *Kiss Me, Stupid* (1964), and *THOROUGHLY MODERN MILLIE* (1967). Previn's career as a conductor of world-famous symphony orchestras blossomed in the late 1960s, and he infrequently found time to return to films. He was married for a time to actress Mia Farrow.

PRINZ, LeROY (1895–1983) choreographed more movie musicals than any other person, arriving in Hollywood in 1929 and staging the production numbers for some sixty movies before retiring in 1958 to produce and direct industrial and educational films. Although he was born in Missouri, LeRoy choreographed films for Max Reinhardt in Europe and dances for the Folies Bergère in Paris before assisting on the choreography for *INNOCENTS OF PARIS* (1929). Among the notable musicals that followed were *Too Much Harmony* (1933), *BIG BROADCAST OF 1936* (1935), *SHOW BOAT* (1936), *Waikiki Wedding* (1937), *HIGH, WIDE AND HANDSOME* (1937), *BIG BROADCAST OF 1938*, *ROAD TO SINGAPORE* (1940), *TOO MANY GIRLS* (1940), *YANKEE DOODLE DANDY* (1942), *THIS IS THE ARMY* (1943), *THANK YOUR LUCKY STARS* (1943), *THE*

DESERT SONG (1943 and 1953), *HOLLYWOOD CANTEEN* (1944), *RHAPSODY IN BLUE* (1945), *The Time, the Place and the Girl* (1946), *Tea for Two* (1950), *On Moonlight Bay* (1951), *April in Paris* (1952), *THE JAZZ SINGER* (1953), *The Helen Morgan Story* (1957), and *SOUTH PACIFIC* (1958).

PRYOR, ROGER (1901–1974) was a personable actor-singer who played featured roles in nine 1930s movie musicals, but they were mostly B pictures and his career never took off, although he fared better on the radio in the 1940s. Pryor's musical credits include *Moonlight and Pretzels* (1933), *Belle of the Nineties* (1934), *Romance in the Rain* (1934), *Wake Up and Dream* (1934), *To Beat the Band* (1935), and *Sitting on the Moon* (1936).

PUTTIN' ON THE RITZ (United Artists 1930) marked the film debut of Broadway song-and-dance favorite HARRY RICHMAN, though the camera didn't manage to capture the performer's talents and he made only one other Hollywood musical. The backstager told the already too familiar tale of a vaudvillian who makes it big on Broadway, lets success goes to his head, falls from popularity, and then is saved by the love of faithful JOAN BENNETT. But it was worth sitting through to enjoy the songs, especially two new IRVING BERLIN gems: the flowing ballad "With You" and the dapper title number, one of the songwriter's most sophisticated and breezy works. Richman himself contributed to the score, collaborating with various tunesmiths on the fatalistic "There's Danger in Your Eyes, Cherie" and the crooning serenade "Singing a Vagabond Song," which became Richman's theme song on radio and in nightclubs for years.

QUINE, RICHARD (1920–1989) was a child performer in vaudeville and on Broadway who made his screen debut at the age of twelve and played juvenile roles in such musicals as *BABES ON BROADWAY* (1941), *FOR ME AND MY GAL* (1942), and *WORDS AND MUSIC* (1948). When Quine outgrew such youthful roles, he retired from acting and directed a handful of musicals for COLUMBIA. His directing credits include *On the Sunny Side of the Street* (1951), *Rainbow 'Round My Shoulder* (1952), *Cruisin' Down the River* (1953), *So This Is Paris* (1954), *My Sister Eileen* (1955), and many nonmusicals.

R

RADIO MUSICALS flourished as long as the airwaves medium did, which is interesting since radio was Hollywood's biggest competition for audiences in the 1930s and 1940s. Since several stars, such as RUDY VALLEE, BOB HOPE, FRANCES LANGFORD, JACK BENNY, JANE FRAZEE, BING CROSBY, EDGAR BERGMAN, FANNY BRICE, KATE SMITH, RUSS COLUMBO, GEORGE BURNS and GRACIE ALLEN, KENNY BAKER, DINAH SHORE, and the Big Band conductors all came from radio, it was thought prudent to keep them in their familiar milieu so audiences could more easily accept them on the screen. Not all made the transition successfully. The plots of PARAMOUNT's *THE BIG BROADCAST* (1932) and others in its SERIES all revolved around a radio show, as did many of the SHIRLEY TEMPLE vehicles at 20TH CENTURY–FOX. Other films over the years dealing with broadcast entertainment include *Say It With Songs* (1929), *Hello Everybody* (1933), *Torch Singer* (1933), *Myrt and Marge* (1934), *Twenty Million Sweethearts* (1934), *Strictly Dynamite* (1934), *Gift of Gab* (1934), *Millions in the Air* (1935), *Sing, Baby, Sing* (1936), *With Love and Kisses* (1937), *WAKE UP AND LIVE* (1937), *Mr. Dodd Takes the Air* (1937), *Love and Hisses* (1937), *The Hit Parade* (1937), *Melody and Moonlight* (1940), *A Little Bit of Heaven* (1940), *LOVE THY NEIGHBOR* (1940), *The Great American Broadcast* (1941), *Reveille With Beverly* (1943), *Hi, Good Lookin'* (1944), *Hot Rhythm* (1944), *I'll Tell the World* (1945), *Ladies' Man* (1947), and *My Dream Is Yours* (1949). Perhaps the fondest and most nostalgic tribute to the medium was Woody Allen's *Radio Days* (1987).

RAFT, GEORGE (1895–1980), a brooding actor who specialized in gangster roles, began his career as a champion Charleston dancer and showed his fancy footwork in a dozen movie musicals. Among Raft's musical credits were *Queen of the Night Clubs* (1929), *Palmy Days* (1931), *Dancers in the Dark*

(1932), *Bolero* (1934), *Rhumba* (1935), *EVERY NIGHT AT EIGHT* (1935), *Follow the Boys* (1944), *Nob Hill* (1945), and *The Ladies' Man* (1961), as well as guest spots in *Broadway* (1942) and *STAGE DOOR CANTEEN* (1943). Ray Danton played the actor in the highly fictionalized movie bio *The George Raft Story* (1961).

RAINER, LUISE (1914–   ) had a brief but spectacular career in Hollywood, winning an Oscar two years in a row and then suddenly disappearing. Rainer appeared in some European films before going to Hollywood in the mid-1930s. The dramatic actress made a memorable impression in two musicals: as the *Follies* star Anna Held in *THE GREAT ZIEGFELD* (1936) and as the neglected wife of Johann Strauss II in *The Great Waltz* (1938).

RAINGER, RALPH (1901–1942) was one of Hollywood's busiest composers, writing scores for some thirty musicals within an eleven-year period. The former Broadway composer and pianist usually teamed up with lyricist LEO ROBIN, as with their Oscar-winning song "Thanks for the Memory." Rainger's musicals include *This Is the Night* (1932), *Blonde Venus* (1932), *THE BIG BROADCAST* (1932), *SHE DONE HIM WRONG* (1933), *INTERNATIONAL HOUSE* (1933), *Little Miss Marker* (1934), *BIG BROADCAST OF 1936* (1935), *MILLIONS IN THE AIR* (1935), *Rose of the Rancho* (1936), *BIG BROADCAST OF 1937* (1936), *Paris Honeymoon* (1939), *GULLIVER'S TRAVELS* (1939), *MOON OVER MIAMI* (1941), *MY GAL SAL* (1942), *Footlight Serenade* (1942), *CONEY ISLAND* (1943), and *Riding High* (1943). Among Rainger's hit songs were "I Have Eyes," "Love in Bloom," "What Have You Got That Gets Me?," and "Blue Hawaii."

RALL, TOMMY (1929–   ), a nimble Broadway singer-dancer who could also handle dramatic roles, made only a half dozen movie musicals but was exceptional each time. He played the gambling hoofer Bill Calhoun in *KISS ME, KATE* (1953), the Pontipee brother Frank in *SEVEN BRIDES FOR SEVEN BROTHERS* (1954), newsman Chick Clark in *My Sister Eileen* (1955), circus performer Giacomo Gallini in *Merry Andrew* (1958), and a featured dancer in *INVITATION TO THE DANCE* (1954), *FUNNY GIRL* (1968), and *PENNIES FROM HEAVEN* (1981).

RAPHAELSON, SAMSON (1896–1983) was a Broadway playwright who penned scripts in Hollywood, including some classic ERNST LUBITSCH comedies. Raphaelson's stage play *THE JAZZ SINGER* was filmed in 1927, 1953, and 1980. He also wrote *THE SMILING LIEUTENANT* (1931), *ONE HOUR WITH YOU* (1932), *THE MERRY WIDOW* (1934), *THE HARVEY GIRLS* (1946), *That Lady in Ermine* (1948), *IN THE GOOD OLD SUMMERTIME* (1949), and other musicals directly for the screen.

RASCH, ALBERTINA (1896–1967) was a classically trained choreographer who brought a touch of traditional ballet to a dozen Hollywood musicals in the 1930s. Rasch's handiwork was glimpsed in the early talkies *HOLLY-WOOD REVUE OF 1929, Devil May Care* (1929), and *Lord Byron of Broadway* (1933), followed by extended musical numbers in *GOING HOLLYWOOD* (1933), *THE CAT AND THE FIDDLE* (1934), *BROAD-WAY MELODY OF 1936* (1935), *The King Steps Out* (1936), *ROSALIE* (1936), *THE FIREFLY* (1937), *SWEETHEARTS* (1938), and others. She was married to film composer Dimitri Tiomkin.

RATOFF, GREGORY (1897–1960), a Russian-born actor who performed with the Moscow Art Theatre before coming to America, played characters with thick European accents in 1930s films. Ratoff portrayed eccentric directors, colorful working-class folk, and aristocratic foreigners equally well. He can be seen in the musicals *I'm No Angel* (1933), *Broadway Through a Keyhole* (1933), *Sitting Pretty* (1933), *George White's Scandals* (1934), *KING OF BURLESQUE* (1935), *Sing, Baby, Sing* (1936), *Top of the Town* (1937), *Sally, Irene and Mary* (1938), and others. By the late 1930s Ratoff became a director and helmed such musicals as *ROSE OF WASHINGTON SQUARE* (1939), *Footlight Serenade* (1942), *Something to Shout About* (1943), *Irish Eyes Are Smiling* (1944), *Where Do We Go From Here?* (1945), *Carnival in Costa Rica* (1947), and others.

RAY, LEAH (1915–   ), a band vocalist who often played just such a singer in 1930s musicals, appeared in eight films, including *A Bedtime Story* (1933), *ONE IN A MILLION* (1936), *WAKE UP AND LIVE* (1937), *Sing and Be Happy* (1937), *Thin Ice* (1937), and *Happy Landing* (1938).

RAYE, DON (1909–1985), a Hollywood lyricist in the 1940s, collaborated with composers Hughie Prince and GENE DE PAUL on such musicals as *BUCK PRIVATES* (1941), *In the Navy* (1941), *Keep 'Em Flying* (1941), *Behind the Eight Ball* (1941), *Hellzapoppin* (1941), *Ride 'Em Cowboy* (1942), *Pardon My Sarong* (1942), *Broadway Rhythm* (1944), and *A Song Is Born* (1948). His most remembered song is probably "Boogie Woogie Bugle Boy."

RAYE, MARTHA (1908–1994), the elastic-mouth comedienne of night-clubs, films, television, stage, and tours to the front lines in three wars, lit up twenty movie musicals with her robust singing style and physical comedy. A veteran of vaudeville and clubs before her film debut in 1936, Raye rarely played leading roles but generally stole the show when she was on screen. Among her musical credits were *Rhythm on the Range* (1936), *BIG BROAD-CAST OF 1937* (1936), *College Holiday* (1936), *Waikiki Wedding* (1937), *Mountain Music* (1937), *ARTISTS AND MODELS* (1937), *DOUBLE OR NOTHING* (1937), *BIG BROADCAST OF 1938, College Swing* (1938), *Give*

Me a Sailor (1938), *Tropic Holiday* (1938), *The Boys From Syracuse* (1940), *Keep 'Em Flying* (1941), *Hellzapoppin* (1941), *Four Jills in a Jeep* (1944), *Pin-Up Girl* (1944), and *JUMBO* (1962). She also did the voice of the witch in the animated *Pufnstuf* (1970). Dancer Nick Condos, composer David Rose, and makeup expert Bud Westmore were among her six husbands.

RAYMOND, GENE (1908–1998), a blonde leading man who was the romantic (if unexciting) interest in eleven musicals, was on the stage as a child and in films from the early 1930s. He can be seen in *FLYING DOWN TO RIO* (1933), *Sadie McKee* (1934), *Transatlantic Merry-Go-Round* (1934), *Hooray for Love* (1935), *Life of the Party* (1937), *Smilin' Through* (1941), *HIT THE DECK* (1955), *I'd Rather Be Rich* (1964), and others. He was married to JEANETTE MacDONALD.

REAGAN, RONALD (1911–   ), the personable leading man in Hollywood and government, did not sing on screen but played featured roles in the musicals *Going Places* (1938), *Naughty But Nice* (1939), *Juke Girl* (1942), *THIS IS THE ARMY* (1943), and *She's Working Her Way Through College* (1952), as well as guest bits in *HOLLYWOOD HOTEL* (1937) and *It's a Great Feeling* (1949). He married actresses JANE WYMAN and Nancy Davis. Reagan's greatest role was as the the fortieth President of the United States.

REBECCA OF SUNNYBROOK FARM (Fox 1938) was an oft-told story, having been filmed twice already, but this SHIRLEY TEMPLE musical version strayed further from the Kate Douglas Wiggin story than had its two nonmusical predecessors. All the same, it was one of Temple's best vehicles and musically one of the strongest. City girl Rebecca joins her Aunt Miranda (HELEN WESTLEY) on Sunnybrook farm to get away from show business, but radio producer RANDOLPH SCOTT puts her on the air and she becomes a hit, attracting her greedy stepfather WILLIAM DEMAREST. Six different tunesmiths contributed to the score, and Temple got to do two numbers with farm hand BILL ROBINSON, the freewheeling "An Old Straw Hat" and the march tune "Parade of the Wooden Soldiers," as well as the optimistic "Come Get Your Happiness." At one point in the film, the ten-year-old veteran sat down at the piano and sang a medley of her past hits: "Animal Crackers in My Soup," "On the Good Ship Lollipop," "When I'm With You," and others. Rounding out the cast were JACK HALEY, Phyllis Brooks, Slim Summerville, GLORIA STUART, and the Raymond Scott Quintet.

REGAN, PHIL (1906–1996), an Irish tenor who was usually featured as a singer in the plot, never became a star because too few of his musicals were grade A or very memorable. Regan's best films were his earliest efforts: *DAMES* (1934), *SWEET ADELINE* (1934), *GO INTO YOUR DANCE*

(1935), and *In Caliente* (1935). His other musicals include *Laughing Irish Eyes* (1936), *Hit Parade of 1937, Manhattan Merry-Go-Round* (1937), *Las Vegas Nights* (1941), *Sweet Rosie O'Grady* (1943), *Sweetheart of Sigma Chi* (1946), *THREE LITTLE WORDS* (1950), and others.

REINKING, ANN (1949–   ), one of Broadway's favorite dancing stars, best represented the BOB FOSSE style in the 1980s and 1990s, working with him and, after his death, recreating his choreography on Broadway. She can be seen on film as the Fosse-like director's mistress in *ALL THAT JAZZ* (1979) and billionaire Daddy Warbucks' assistant in *ANNIE* (1982).

REVEL, HARRY (1905–1958) wrote music for Broadway and West End musicals but found more success in Hollywood, where, working with various lyricists, he scored thirty musicals. His most frequent collaborator was MACK GORDON, with whom he wrote the songs for *Broadway Through a Keyhole* (1933), *Sitting Pretty* (1933), *WE'RE NOT DRESSING* (1934), *COLLEGE RHYTHM* (1934), *Love in Bloom* (1935), *Collegiate* (1935), *POOR LITTLE RICH GIRL* (1936), *Stowaway* (1936), *WAKE UP AND LIVE* (1937), *Love Finds Andy Hardy* (1938), *Thanks for Everything* (1938), and others. With Mort Greene, Revel scored *Four Jacks and a Jill* (1941), *Call Out the Marines* (1942), *The Mayor of 44th Street* (1942), and others. Lyricist PAUL FRANCIS WEBSTER was Revel's collaborator on *It Ain't Hay* (1943), *Hit the Ice* (1943), *The Ghost Catchers* (1944), and *Minstrel Man* (1944). "There's a Lull in My Life," "Take a Number From One to Ten," "Did You Ever See a Dream Walking?," and "You Say the Sweetest Things, Baby" are among Revel's many hit songs.

REVUE MUSICALS, long popular on Broadway, enjoyed a brief but potent life during the early days of sound. Each studio gathered the talent available on the lot and, tying the music, dance, and comedy acts together with one or more masters of ceremonies, had an all-star line up to dazzle audiences still reveling in the novelty of the new medium. MGM was the first to jump on the idea, presenting its roster of stars in *THE HOLLYWOOD REVUE OF 1929*, followed later that same year with WARNER BROTHERS' *ON WITH THE SHOW* and *THE SHOW OF SHOWS*. UNIVERSAL's *KING OF JAZZ* (1930) emphasized PAUL WHITEMAN and his orchestra and other musical talent, but *PARAMOUNT ON PARADE* (1930) boasted dozens of stars, from MAURICE CHEVALIER to Clara Bow. But soon the studios felt compelled to add some sort of plot to tie their specialties together, and the true musical revue on screen faded away. Instead, movie SERIES that began with *THE BIG BROADCAST* (1932) and *THE BROADWAY MELODY OF 1936* (1935) used a revue format only for the big show in the film's last reel. Many other 1930s musicals were similarly disguised revues. In the 1940s, when BIOGRAPHICAL MUSICALS proliferated, producers saw another chance to feature various artists and songs within the framework of a composer's or performer's life story. Take away the feeble plots and *RHAPSODY IN BLUE* (1944), *NIGHT AND DAY* (1946), *TILL THE CLOUDS ROLL BY* (1946), and *WORDS AND MUSIC* (1948) are really musical revues. Every once in a while a true revue would be made, such as *ZIEGFELD FOLLIES* (1946) or the DISNEY anthology musicals like *Make Mine Music* (1946) and *Melody Time* (1948), but the genre would not resurface until the popular documentary *THAT'S ENTERTAINMENT* (1974) and its spinoffs.

REYNOLDS, DEBBIE (1932–   ), the ever-youthful singer-dancer who managed to find a career in movie musicals just before the genre started to decline, was one of Hollywood's most popular stars in the 1950s. A beauty contest winner, she began in films in 1948 and early in her career had featured parts in the musicals *The Daughter of Rosie O'Grady* (1950), *THREE LITTLE WORDS* (1950), *Two Weeks With Love* (1950), and *Mr. Imperium* (1951). Her reputation for a bubbly, effervescent performer was made with *SINGIN' IN THE RAIN* (1952), followed by *Skirts Ahoy* (1952), *The Affairs of Dobbie Gillis* (1952), *GIVE A GIRL A BREAK* (1952), *I Love Melvin* (1952), *Athena* (1953), *HIT THE DECK* (1955), *Bundle of Joy* (1956), *Say One for Me* (1959), *THE UNSINKABLE MOLLY BROWN* (1964), and *The Singing Nun* (1966). She also did specialty spots in *Meet Me in Las Vegas* (1956) and *Pepe* (1960), as well as the voice of Charlotte the spider in the animated *CHARLOTTE'S WEB* (1972). Reynolds made many nonmusical films and performed in nightclubs, on Broadway, and on television. She was once married to singer-actor Eddie Fisher, and her children are actress Carrie Fisher and television director Todd Fisher.

REYNOLDS, MARJORIE (1921–1997) was a child actress in silents under the name Marjorie Moore; she then changed her name for adult roles, appearing in melodramas and musicals such as *Wine, Women and Song* (1933) and *Collegiate* (1935). Her most remembered movie role was in *HOLIDAY INN* (1942), followed by *STAR SPANGLED RHYTHM* (1942), *Dixie* (1943), *Bring on the Girls* (1945), *Duffy's Tavern* (1945), and others. When her film career declined, she moved on to television (*The Life of Riley*) where she found new success.

RHAPSODY IN BLUE (Warner 1945) may have had little to say about composer GEORGE GERSHWIN (and what was said wasn't very accurate), but this BIOGRAPHICAL MUSICAL had an agreeable cast and twenty-four Gershwin selections, so it was highly entertaining and very popular at the box office. Mickey Roth and Darryl Hickman played young George and IRA GERSHWIN, later growing up to be Robert Alda and Herbert Rudley, and their parents were portrayed by ROSEMARY DeCAMP and Morris Carnov- sky. The routine rags-to-riches plot was given a touch of authenticity by performers who actually knew Gershwin, such as AL JOLSON, Hazel Scott, Anne Brown, George White, PAUL WHITEMAN (who conducted "Rhapsody in Blue"), and OSCAR LEVANT (who played the "Piano Concerto in F"). Also on hand to perform the songs or fill out the cast were JOAN LESLIE, ALEXIS SMITH, Charles Coburn, Albert Basserman, Julie Bishop, and Andrew Tombes. Among the twenty-four Gershwin songs performed were "Somebody Loves Me," "Someone to Watch Over Me," "I Got Rhythm," "The Man I Love," "Summertime," "Fascinating Rhythm," and "I'll Build a Stairway to Paradise."

RHODES, BETTY JANE (1921–   ) was popular on radio and in night-clubs when she was still a teenager; she then played youthful roles in such musi-cal films as *Life of the Party* (1937), *THE FLEET'S IN* (1942), *Priorities on Parade* (1942), *Sweater Girl* (1942), *STAR SPANGLED RHYTHM* (1942), and others.

RHODES, ERIK (1906–1990) was a comic character actor on stage and in the early days of television, but he will always be remembered for the effete and meticulous Italians he played in 1930s films. Rhodes can be seen in the musi-cals *THE GAY DIVORCEE* (1934), *TOP HAT* (1935), *Old Man Rhythm* (1935), *Music for Madame* (1937), and *On Your Toes* (1939).

RHYTHM ON THE RIVER (Paramount 1940) was a low-budget, unpre-tentious BING CROSBY vehicle and one of his best, with a sparkling score by JOHNNY BURKE and JAMES V. MONACO and engaging performances by a first-class cast. Crosby is a laid-back songwriter who'd rather live the lazy life on his modest houseboat on the river than deal with the hectic world of Tin Pan Alley, so he ghost-writes music for dried-out songwriter Basil Rathbone. But when Crosby meets Rathbone's ghost-writing lyricist MARY MARTIN, the two fall in love and start making music together under their own names. VICTOR SCHERTZINGER directed the musical, which included OSCAR LEVANT as Rathbone's wry assistant, as well as Charlie Grapewin, WILLIAM FRAWLEY, and Lillian Cornell. In addition to the lyrical title song, the score included the romantic ballads "That's for Me" and "Only Forever," the sly narrative number "Ain't It a Shame About Mame?," and the teary torch song "I Don't Want to Cry Anymore," which Schertzinger wrote himself and inter-polated into the Burke-Monaco score.

RICE, TIM (1944–   ), the British lyricist who began his career writing a se-ries of London and Broadway musicals with Andrew Lloyd-Webber, saw his stage hits *JESUS CHRIST SUPERSTAR* (1973) and *EVITA* (1997) filmed. When lyricist HOWARD ASHMAN died prematurely, Rice completed the score for the animated *ALADDIN* (1992) with composer ALAN MENKEN and won an Oscar for the song "A Whole New World." With composer-singer Elton John, Rice also scored the animated musicals *THE LION KING* (1994) and *The Road to El Dorado* (2000).

RICHMAN, HARRY (1895–1972) was a highly stylized song-and-dance man in nightclubs and Broadway revues whom FRED ASTAIRE and other hoofers wished to emulate early in their careers. Richman's unique brand of performing can be seen in two Hollywood films, *PUTTIN' ON THE RITZ* (1930) and *The Music Goes Round* (1936). Richman's style did not appeal to moviegoers, so he returned to the stage.

RIO RITA (RKO 1929) was the first successful screen version of a Broadway musical, receiving both critical and popular approval. Producer WILLIAM LeBARON brought the 1927 stage hit to the screen with all but two of its songs, its comedians BERT WHEELER and ROBERT WOOLSEY making their film debut as the comic relief, and even divided the movie into two acts with the second half in color. The story also remained the same, with Texas Ranger JOHN BOLES pursuing the mysterious bandit Kinkajou across the American Southwest and falling for Rita (BEBE DANIELS), who is the sister of the man he suspects. But the villainous General Ravenoff (George Renavent) turns out to be Kinkajou, so Boles and Daniels can wed without complication. Joseph McCarthy and Harry Tierney's near-operatic score included "The Rangers' Song," "If You're in Love You'll Waltz," "The Kinkajou," the adoring title number, as well as "You're Always in My Arms (But Only in My Dreams)," which the team wrote for the film and which became a hit. MGM made a version of *Rio Rita* in 1942 as a vehicle for BUD ABBOTT and LOU COSTELLO in the Wheeler and Woolsey roles, with JOHN CARROLL and KATHRYN GRAYSON as the lovers. The plot was greatly altered to add World War Two–era intrigue (a sabotage plan by spies became important to the story), and just about all of the score was cut to make room for Abbott and Costello's comic shenanigans. As a comedy vehicle it was entertaining, but as a musical it was a travesty.

RITZ BROTHERS, THE, Al (1901–1965), Jimmy (1903–1985), and Harry (1906–1986), may not have been the MARX BROTHERS, but their crazy antics and juvenile clowning made them top attractions in vaudeville, in nightclubs, on television, and even on Broadway. The trio were featured in thirteen movie musicals, usually playing themselves and adding a touch of nonsense to the proceedings. Their most notable films were *Sing, Baby, Sing* (1936), *ONE IN A MILLION* (1936), *ON THE AVENUE* (1937), *You Can't Have Everything* (1937), *THE GOLDWYN FOLLIES* (1938), *The Three Musketeers* (1939), *Argentine Nights* (1940), *Behind the Eight Ball* (1942), and *Never a Dull Moment* (1943).

RKO was always one of Hollywood's minor studios but an influential one all the same. With its roots in vaudeville at the turn of the century, Radio-Keith-Orpheum was founded in 1928 by merging a variety circuit with a Minneapolis nickelodeon chain. The company hit its peak in the 1930s with its horror films and star-studded romantic comedies but was most famous for its series of FRED ASTAIRE–GINGER ROGERS musicals. Except for distributing WALT DISNEY's animated films, the studio generated few musicals after 1940. HOWARD HUGHES purchased the company in 1948, and its financial troubles in the 1950s caused RKO to switch to television. The RKO studios were sold to Desilu in 1953, and the library of old films was purchased by Ted Turner in the 1980s.

ROAD TO BALI. See *Road to Singapore*

ROAD TO HONG KONG, THE. See *Road to Singapore*

ROAD TO MOROCCO. See *Road to Singapore*

ROAD TO RIO. See *Road to Singapore*

ROAD TO SINGAPORE (Paramount 1940) was the first of the seven phenomenally popular "Road" pictures starring BING CROSBY and BOB HOPE. In all the plots of the series, Crosby was straightman, sang the ballads, and got DOROTHY LAMOUR in the end. HOPE was the put-upon chump, always got into difficult straits because of Crosby, and invariably lost Lamour or any other beautiful woman who came along. The movies were known for their unpretentious gags, ridiculous plots, and breaking of character. The two comics often spoke directly into the camera and made fun of PARAMOUNT, Hollywood, and their own careers. In the first outing, Crosby is shipping millionaire Charles Coburn's son who doesn't want to marry Judith Barrett, and he runs off with his penniless pal Hope to the South Seas, where they rescue Lamour from Anthony Quinn, who makes his living whipping cigarette ends out of her mouth. JOHNNY BURKE, VICTOR SCHERTZINGER, and JAMES V. MONACO wrote the songs, which included the enticing ballads "Too Romantic" and "The Moon and the Willow Tree" and rhythmic ditty "Sweet Potato Piper." The picture was such a hit that the trio of stars was quickly reassembled for ***ROAD TO ZANZIBAR*** (Paramount 1941), which was a better comedy all around. Con-men Crosby and Hope have to skip town when they sell a phony diamond mine to an unhappy customer, so they go to Africa, where they meet con-women Lamour and UNA MERKEL on safari. In addition to spoofing every jungle picture ever made, the film offered two pleasing ballads by Burke and JAMES VAN HEUSEN (who would score the rest of the "Road" movies): "You're Dangerous" and "It's Always You." ***ROAD TO MOROCCO*** (Paramount 1942) had fun ribbing Arabian Nights movies as the twosome set off across the desert and found themselves rescuing Princess Lamour from murderous chieftain Quinn. One of the funniest of the entries, the film also boasted a superb score headed by "Moonlight Becomes You," the best-selling song to come out of the whole series and one of Crosby's biggest hits. There was also the easygoing "Ain't Got a Dime to My Name," the fervent ballad "Constantly," and the playful title song. ***ROAD TO***

UTOPIA (Paramount 1945) is generally considered the classic of the seven movies. Hope and Crosby were two vaudevillians on their way to the Klondike with a map showing the location of a lost gold mine. They team up with saloon singer Lamour and, pursued by a set of villains, set off on dog sleds on a merry misadventure. Years later Hope and Lamour are an old married couple, but their baby looks suspiciously like Crosby. Once again, the songs were superior: the slap-happy "Good-Time Charley," the warm ballad "Welcome to My Dreams (and How Are You?)," the buddy duet "Put It There, Pal," the optimistic "It's Anybody's Spring," and the sassy and suggestive "Personality." *ROAD TO RIO* (Paramount 1947) was more conventional, a little less inspired, but just as popular as the others. When they accidentally burn down the carnival they work for, musicians Crosby and Hope board a boat for Rio de Janeiro and on the way meet heiress Lamour, who is being hypnotized by her evil aunt (Gale Sondergaard) into marrying a Brazilian she does not love. The ANDREWS SISTERS joined in on the singing this time, the best numbers being the sly "You Don't Have to Know the Language" and the romantic standard "But Beautiful." Audiences had to wait five years for *ROAD TO BALI* (Paramount 1952), and although some of the jokes were aging along with the stars, it was still an enjoyable romp. As vaudevillians once again on the run, the duo headed to the South Seas searching for hidden treasure but found Lamour instead. The movie was enlivened by brief guest appearances by Humphrey Bogart, BOB CROSBY, JANE RUSSELL, and the newest comedy team, MARTIN and LEWIS. The Burke–Van Heusen songs were not as expert, though "Chicago Style" was a lively narrative number, "The Merry-Go-Runaround" a frolicsome trio, and Crosby and Hope got to do a wicked Scottish parody with "Hoot Mon." The twosome returned once again with *THE ROAD TO HONG KONG* (Melnor/United Artists 1962)but though the plot was as outrageous as ever, the spirit of the series was gone. As two conmen selling rocket ships in Tibet, Hope and Crosby set off for Hong Kong, chased by spies for the secret rocket fuel formula the two carry. Although they briefly meet Lamour when they visit a nightclub where she performs, the woman they fight over this time is Dorothy Collins. By the end of the story, the two comics are shot off into space, where they come across fellow spacemen FRANK SINATRA and DEAN MARTIN. Van Heusen wrote the songs with SAMMY CAHN this time, and three were delightful: the buddy trio "Teamwork," the soothing ballad "Warmer Than a Whisper," and the romantic duet "Let's Not Be Sensible." The "Road" pictures were products of their time yet still are enjoyable. Various studios have tried to copy the formula but never successfully, although the animated musical take-off *The Road to El Dorado* (2000) was popular.

ROAD TO UTOPIA. See *Road to Singapore*

ROAD TO ZANZIBAR. See *Road to Singapore*

ROBBINS, JEROME (1918–1998), one of the giants in Broadway history, directed and/or choreographed many innovative stage shows but rarely worked in film. He did recreate his Broadway choreography for the screen versions of *THE KING AND I* (1956) and *WEST SIDE STORY* (1961), which he co-directed as well, and others reproduced much of his staging for the films of *ON THE TOWN* (1949), *GYPSY* (1963), and *FIDDLER ON THE ROOF* (1971).

ROBERTA (RKO 1935) lost much of its JEROME KERN score from the 1933 Broadway production, but because it gained FRED ASTAIRE and GINGER ROGERS in a new subplot, the film was actually an improvement on the stage original. The plot was never *Roberta*'s strong point, having to do with an American football star (RANDOLPH SCOTT) who inherits a Paris dress salon called Roberta from his Aunt Minnie (HELEN WESTLEY) and falls in love with the shop assistant IRENE DUNNE. Astaire played Scott's bandleader friend from America who comes to Paris to perform and is reunited with hometown girl, Rogers, who is singing in a nightclub as the Countess Tanka Scharwenka. The OTTO HARBACH–Kern songs retained from the stage score were "Let's Begin," "Yesterdays," and "Smoke Gets in Your Eyes," whereas Kern collaborated with DOROTHY FIELDS on "Lovely to Look At" and "I Won't Dance" (based on an OSCAR HAMMERSTEIN lyric). Although the secondary couple was more interesting than the Scott-Dunne romance, the whole film sparkled whenever the musical numbers took over, especially as choreographed by Astaire and HERMES PAN. In "I'll Be Hard to Handle" (by Bernard Dougall and Kern), Astaire and Rogers got to perform the first of their memorable competitive dance routines. The movie ended with a fashion show while the cast sang "Lovely to Look At," and the song became so popular that eighteen years later the movie was remade as *LOVELY TO LOOK AT* (MGM 1952) with a greatly altered plot that was no better than the original. American stage comedian RED SKELTON inherits a share in the shop this time and goes to Paris with his buddies HOWARD KEEL and GOWER CHAMPION and nightclub dancer ANN MILLER, only to find sisters KATHRYN GRAYSON and MARGE CHAMPION as the co-owners and fighting off bankruptcy. A big fashion show is produced to save the shop, and there are three happy couples by the final reel. This version actually included more of the stage score than the 1935 film and added the merry romp "Lafayette." The finale once again was the fashion show, directed by VINCENTE MINNELLI, choreographed by Pan, and featuring forty-two gowns by ADRIAN. MERVYN LEROY directed the rest of the film, which was indeed lovely to look at and, even better, quite thrilling to hear as the strong cast gave full voice to the Kern songs.

ROBERTI, LYDA (1909–1938) was a Polish-born blonde whose thick accent made her singing seem exotic and sensual. She starred in vaudeville and on Broadway before making her screen debut in 1932. The funny, lively

Roberti was featured in the movie musicals *Dancers in the Dark* (1932), *The Kid From Spain* (1932), *Torch Singer* (1933), *COLLEGE RHYTHM* (1934), *George White's Scandals* (1935), *BIG BROADCAST OF 1936* (1935), and *Nobody's Baby* (1937) before her premature death.

ROBERTS, ALAN (1905–1966) was a film composer and lyricist who, collaborating with DORIS FISHER or Lester Lee, scored nine B musicals in the 1940s, including *The Thrill of Brazil* (1946), *Talk About a Lady* (1946), *Cigarette Girl* (1947), *Ladies of the Chorus* (1949), and *Slightly French* (1949). Roberts' most remembered song is "Put the Blame on Mame."

ROBIN AND THE SEVEN HOODS (PC/Warner 1964) was a modern parody of the Robin Hood legend and, unintentionally, a parody of a movie musical as a handful of stars kidded and smirked their way through the film as if on a television special. All the same, there was much to enjoy, such as BING CROSBY's pleasing performance and FRANK SINATRA's throw-away performance (it was the final movie musical for both of them), and the songs by SAMMY CAHN and JAMES VAN HEUSEN were enjoyable, especially the soft-shoe "Style," the revival-like "Mr. Booze," the sing-along "Don't Be a Do-Badder," and the popular anthem "My Kind of Town (Chicago)." The plot read like a television sketch but a funny one. Chicago gangster Robbo (Sinatra) is pitted against rival mobster Guy Gisborn (Peter Falk) over the gang headed by Edward G. Robinson until he is gunned down. Robinson's daughter Marian (Barbara Rush) hopes to get revenge for her dad's murder and insinuates herself into both warring factions. Robbo's merry men included Little John (DEAN MARTIN), Will (SAMMY DAVIS, JR.), and Allen A. Dale (Crosby), with Victor Buono, Hank Henry, Allen Jenkins, Jack LaRue, HANS CONREID, SIG RUMANN, and Philip Crosby filling out the cast. As a "Rat Pack" vehicle, it was one of the Sinatra-Davis-Martin team's better efforts; as a musical, it made one long for the days when these performers still cared.

ROBIN, LEO (1900—1984), though never a household name, was one of Hollywood's most prolific and reliable lyricists who penned such song favorites as "Love in Bloom," "Beyond the Blue Horizon," "June in January," "Hooray for Love," "Blue Hawaii," and the Oscar-winning "Thanks for the Memory." Often writing with composer RALPH RAINGER, Robin penned the lyrics for over fifty movie musicals between 1929 and 1955, as well as a handful of stage musicals and Tin Pan Alley hits. His first assignment was *INNOCENTS OF PARIS* (1929), with composer RICHARD WHITING, which introduced MAURICE CHEVALIER to American audiences with "Louise." In the 1930s Robin contributed to *HIT THE DECK* (1930), *MONTE CARLO* (1930), *ONE HOUR WITH YOU* (1932), *Little Miss Marker* (1934), *BIG BROADCAST OF 1938*, *Waikiki Wedding* (1937), and *GULLIVER'S TRAVELS* (1939). During the war years he wrote lyrics for such BETTY GRABLE vehicles as *MOON OVER MIAMI* (1941), *Footlight Sere-*

nade (1942), and *CONEY ISLAND* (1943). His most popular film in the 1950s was *GENTLEMEN PREFER BLONDES* (1953), based on his 1949 Broadway musical with JULE STYNE. Robin's lyric style is eclectic, providing gushing love songs, sophisticated character songs, and comic ditties as needed.

ROBINSON, BILL "BOJANGLES" (1878–1949), the renowned African American tap dancer who developed the famous stair tap routine, was a headliner in vaudeville and on Broadway before making too-brief appearances in such movie musicals as *Dixiana* (1930), *Hooray for Love* (1935), and *BIG BROADCAST OF 1936* (1935). Robinson is most remembered dancing with SHIRLEY TEMPLE in *The Little Colonel* (1935), *The Littlest Rebel* (1935), *REBECCA OF SUNNYBROOK FARM* (1938), and *Just Around the Corner* (1938). He choreographed Temple's routines in *Dimples* (136) and played nightclub entertainer Bill Williamson in *STORMY WEATHER* (1943), his only leading role in Hollywood.

ROCK MUSICALS not only appeared on screen from the beginning of rock-and-roll but actually helped popularize the new sound. Nonmusical *Rock Around the Clock* (1956), featuring Bill Haley and the Comets, the Platters, and others, launched the new genre, and follow-up films such as *Rock Rock Rock* (1956), *Don't Knock the Rock* (1957), *Carnival Rock* (1957), *Mr. Rock 'n' Roll* (1957) and other early efforts also promoted the music even though most of the films were cheaply made and failed to attract audiences beyond the youth market. It was the series of ELVIS PRESLEY musicals that made rock-and-roll a money-making source for Hollywood. His thirty films, made between 1956 and 1970, were rarely given the first-class producers, scripts, directors, or production values, yet they all made money and led to dozens of hit records. The theatre, in contrast, was slow to pick up on the rock craze, and no rock musical was seen on Broadway until *HAIR* in 1968. After a rush of stage musicals with rock scores in the early 1970s, the genre would return infrequently, with only two of them—*GODSPELL* (1973) and *JESUS CHRIST SUPERSTAR* (1973)—made into movies. Also filmed were three stage musicals that spoofed or pastiched rock-and-roll: *BYE BYE BIRDIE* (1963), *GREASE* (1978), and *LITTLE SHOP OF HORRORS* (1986). Other notable rock musicals over the years have included *A HARD DAY'S NIGHT* (1964), *HELP!* (1965), *Head* (1968), *YELLOW SUBMARINE* (1968), *PHANTOM OF THE PARADISE* (1974), *TOMMY* (1975), *THE ROCKY HORROR PICTURE SHOW* (1975), *A STAR IS BORN* (1976), *I Wanna Hold Your Hand* (1978), *FM* (1978), *American Hot Wax* (1978), *THE BUDDY HOLLY STORY* (1978), *Thank God It's Friday* (1978), *Rock 'n' Roll High School* (1979), *Quadrophenia* (1979), *Elvis* (1979), *THE ROSE* (1979), *HAIR* (1979), *FAME* (1980), *The Blues Brothers* (1980), *THE JAZZ SINGER* (1980), *Pink Floyd—The Wall* (1982), *FLASHDANCE* (1983), *FOOTLOOSE* (1984), *Labyrinth* (1986), *DIRTY DANCING* (1987), *LA*

BAMBA (1987), and *Spice World* (1998). There have also been several filmed rock concerts and ROCKUMENTARIES over the years.

ROCKUMENTARIES, film documentaries covering a rock concert, festival, tour, or recording session, go back to 1956 when *Rockin' the Blues* chronicled performances by several African American artists (the Hurricanes, the Miller Sisters, Flournoy Miller, the Harptones) who were just starting to popularize the rock-and-roll sound. Films featuring rock groups were common by the late 1950s, but a major documentary about them would not come until *The T.A.M.I. Show* (1964), which covered the Teenage Awards Music International in California and featured the Rolling Stones, Lesley Gore, Marvin Gaye, the Beach Boys, the Supremes, Gerry and the Pacemakers, and others. Similar films included *The Big T.N.T. Show* (1966), *You Are What You Eat* (1968), and *Monterey Pop* (1969). The rockumentary that would prove the most effective (and influential on subsequent films of the genre) was *WOODSTOCK* (1970), Michael Wadleigh's coverage of the legendary 1969 festival at Bethel, New York. Other notable rockumentaries over the years have included *Gimme Shelter* (1970), about a Rolling Stones tour; *Mad Dogs and Englishmen* (1970, with Joe Cocker and entourage touring America; *Let It Be* (1970, covering the BEATLES' last recording session; *The Concert for Bangladesh* (1972), featuring George Harrison and various performers at a Madison Square Garden benefit concert; *Let the Good Times Roll* (1973), with a nostalgic look at rock artists in the 1950s; and *The Last Waltz* (1978), Martin Scorcese's vivid coverage of a farewell concert by The Band. There have also been a handful of movie spoofs of rockumentaries, most notably *THIS IS SPINAL TAP* (1984).

ROCKY HORROR PICTURE SHOW, THE (Fox 1975) became the ultimate cult film in the decade following its release as patrons dressed up, brought props, and participated in midnight showings of the spoof in cities all across the country. As a cross between a sci-fi parody and a rock sex comedy, the movie succeeds in being entertaining and weird enough to satisfy most audiences. Based on the long-running London musical *The Rocky Horror Show*, the plot follows a straight, engaged couple, Barry Bostwick and Susan Sarandon, whose car breaks down on a dark and stormy night and they find refuge in the creepy mansion of Dr. Frank N Furter (TIM CURRY), a transvestite from Transylvania. The house is full of bizarre types, including a butler played by Richard O'Brien (who wrote the script and the score) and a body-builder monster (Peter Hinwood) whom the cross-dressing doctor lusts after. The songs are as disjointed as the logic, but some are delicious spoofs, such as "Time Warp," "Wild and Untamed Thing," and "Dammit Janet." Much of the same creative staff reteamed for the spinoff *Shock Treatment* (1981), which spoofed television game shows, but the movie never caught on.

RODGERS, RICHARD (1902–1979), the dean of Broadway composers with a career of sixty years in the theatre, films, and television, had two brilliant (and very different) lyricist collaborators: LORENZ HART and OSCAR HAMMERSTEIN. Rodgers scored twenty-six Broadway musicals, several of which were filmed: *Spring Is Here* (1930), *Heads Up* (1930), *BABES IN ARMS* (1939), *On Your Toes* (1939), *The Boys From Syracuse* (1940), *TOO MANY GIRLS* (1940), *I Married an Angel* (1942), *PAL JOEY* (1957), and *JUMBO* (1962), all written with Hart. The Rodgers and Hammerstein shows that were filmed were *OKLAHOMA!* (1955), *CAROUSEL* (1956), *THE KING AND I* (1956), *SOUTH PACIFIC* (1958), *FLOWER DRUM SONG* (1961), and *THE SOUND OF MUSIC* (1965). Although Rodgers was unhappy with the way Hollywood altered most of the Rodgers and Hart shows, the team wrote some superb scores for original movie musicals, such as the innovative features *LOVE ME TONIGHT* (1932), *THE PHANTOM PRESIDENT* (1932), and *HALLELUJAH, I'M A BUM* (1933), as well as the British classic *EVERGREEN* (1934). Other films with Hart include *Leathernecking* (1930), *The Hot Heiress* (1931), *Hollywood Party* (1934), *MISSISSIPPI* (1935), *Dancing Pirate* (1936), *Fools for Scandal* (1938), and *They Met in Argentina* (1941). Later Rodgers collaborated with Hammerstein on one original movie musical, *STATE FAIR* (1945), which was remade in 1962. Tom Drake played Rodgers in the musical bio *WORDS AND MUSIC* (1948), which was made up of Rodgers and Hart songs. Rodgers' music is highly melodic, widely versatile, and always theatrically charged.

ROGERS, CHARLES "BUDDY" (1904–   ), an affable leading man in silents and early talkies, had a wholesome and endearing quality that made him so charming in his nine movie musicals, several of them co-starring NANCY CARROLL. Rogers can be seen in *Close Harmony* (1929), *PARAMOUNT ON PARADE* (1930), *Safety in Numbers* (1930), *Follow Thru* (1930), *Heads Up* (1930), *Best of Enemies* (1933), *Take a Chance* (1933), *Old Man Rhythm* (1935), and *This Way Please* (1937). He was married to silent screen star Mary Pickford.

ROGERS, GINGER (1911–1995) was perhaps the quintessential Hollywood musical star: a glamourous, funny blonde whose dancing and singing could be romantic or silly. Rogers learned her craft in dance contests, in vaudeville, and then on Broadway before making her first film, *Young Man of Manhattan* (1930), followed by the musicals *Queen High* (1930), *The Sap From Syracuse* (1930), and *Follow the Leader* (1930). After she appeared as wisecracking chorines in *42ND STREET* (1933), *GOLD DIGGERS OF 1933*, and *Sitting Pretty* (1933), Rogers' career took a momentous turn when she was cast in the supporting role of Honey Hale in *FLYING DOWN TO RIO* (1933) with FRED ASTAIRE, and the two immediately caught the fancy of the studio and the public. She and Astaire would co-star in nine more films together: *THE GAY DIVORCEE* (1934), *ROBERTA* (1935), *TOP HAT*

(1935), *FOLLOW THE FLEET* (1936), *SWING TIME* (1936), *SHALL WE DANCE* (1937), *CAREFREE* (1938), *THE STORY OF VERNON AND IRENE CASTLE* (1939), and *THE BARKLEYS OF BROADWAY* (1949). Her musicals without Astaire include *Twenty Million Sweethearts* (1934), *In Person* (1935), *Having Wonderful Time* (1938), and *Lady in the Dark* (1944). Rogers also made several nonmusicals, both comedies and dramas, in the 1950s and returned to nightclubs and Broadway in the 1960s. Movie actor Lew Ayres was one of her five husbands.

ROGERS, ROY. See Evans, Dale

ROMAN SCANDALS (Goldwyn/United Artists 1933) was EDDIE CANTOR's most lavish, ridiculous, and farcical vehicle. As a delivery boy in West Rome, Oklahoma, Cantor is upset by the political corruption in the small burg and dreams that he is back in ancient Rome, where corruption is on an even larger scale. He is the food-tasting slave of the Emperor Valerius (Edward Arnold), whose wife Agrippa (Verree Teasdale) is always trying to poison him; Cantor, after helping out the lovers GLORIA STUART and David Manners, proves the emperor a cheat and wins the day. The film had everything from RUTH ETTING singing the torch song "No More Love" to a chariot race. AL DUBIN and HARRY WARREN wrote the score, and BUSBY BERKELEY staged the musical numbers, two of them outstanding for opulence and questionable taste. While Etting sang her torch song, the camera drooled over dozens of slave girls, naked except for their long blonde hair, chained to the walls, and writhing as a grotesque jailer went about lashing his whip. (It is believed that this scene did more to bring on the censorship-based Production Code in Hollywood than any other.) Another unforgettable scene took place in a Roman bath house with Cantor (in blackface) urging hundreds of black and white beauties to "Keep Young and Beautiful" while they exercised and applied makeup, surrounded by revolving mirrors, to make themselves attractive for men.

ROMANCE ON THE HIGH SEAS (Warner 1948) was DORIS DAY's first film and instantly made her a star, helped no doubt by the fact that she got to introduce two SAMMY CAHN–JULE STYNE hits, "It's Magic" and "Put 'Em in a Box, Tie 'Em With a Ribbon, and Throw 'Em in the Deep Blue Sea." Wealthy New Yorker JANIS PAIGE suspects her husband Don DeFore of infidelity and so she hires singer Day to impersonate her and sail to Rio on a luxury liner while she stays behind to spy on him. But DeFore thinks his wife is meeting another man on board, and so he hires detective JACK CARSON to keep an eye on her. What happened then was no surprise, but Day made quite an impression with audiences, the newcomer coming across as an experienced pro. Also on board were OSCAR LEVANT, S.Z. SAKALL, Fortunio Bonanova, ERIC BLORE, FRANKLIN PANGBORN, and specialty numbers by The Samba Kings, Avon Long, and the Page Cavanaugh Trio, all directed by MI-

CHAEL CURTIZ and choreographed by BUSBY BERKELEY in one of his more-restrained moods.

ROMBERG, SIGMUND (1887–1951), one of Broadway's master composers of OPERETTA, had a long career on stage and screen and scored many nonoperatic shows as well. Romberg's Broadway hits, most written with lyricists OSCAR HAMMERSTEIN and OTTO HARBACH, that were filmed include *THE DESERT SONG* (1929, 1943, and 1953), *New Moon* (1930 and 1940), *Up in Central Park* (1948), and *THE STUDENT PRINCE* (1954). For the screen he contributed songs to *Viennese Nights* (1930), *Children of Dreams* (1931), *The Night Is Young* (1935), all with Hammerstein, and *The Girl of the Golden West* (1938) with lyricist GUS KAHN. Romberg's songs were used throughout the bio musical *DEEP IN MY HEART* (1954), in which José Ferrer played the Hungarian-born composer.

ROMERO, CESAR (1907–1994), one of Hollywood's favorite "Latin lovers," began his career in nightclubs and ballrooms before getting a few parts on Broadway and then making his screen debut in 1933. Romero was equally effective in light musicals and action movies, but he usually was cast as Hispanic characters, either villains or dashing heroes. He appeared in the musicals *Metropolitan* (1935), *Happy Landing* (1938), *My Lucky Star* (1938), *Tall, Dark and Handsome* (1941), and *The Great American Broadcast* (1941) before finding his niche in *WEEK-END IN HAVANA* (1941). His best roles were in *ORCHESTRA WIVES* (1942), *SPRINGTIME IN THE ROCKIES* (1942), and *CONEY ISLAND* (1943), followed by *Wintertime* (1943), *Carnival in Costa Rica* (1947), *That Lady in Ermine* (1948), *The Beautiful Blonde From Bashful Bend* (1949), *Happy Go Lovely* (1951), and *Pepe* (1960).

ROONEY, MICKEY (1920–   ) has had a longer and more varied career than any other Hollywood child star, conquering film, records, nightclubs, television, and Broadway. On the screen since the age of six, Rooney made a series of comedy shorts as comic-strip character Mickey McGuire. In 1935 he played Puck in the star-studded film version of *A Midsummer Night's Dream*, and by 1937 he started a series of fifteen "Andy Hardy" comedies. Although he had played bit parts in the musicals *Broadway to Hollywood* (1933), *I Like It That Way* (1934), and *Reckless* (1935), Rooney began his singing-dancing career on film with *Love Finds Andy Hardy* (1938). He starred in a handful of youth-oriented classics such as *BABES IN ARMS* (1939), *Andy Hardy Meets Debutante* (1940), *STRIKE UP THE BAND* (1940), and *BABES ON BROADWAY* (1941). Since he never grew taller than five feet three inches and retained his boyish looks, even Rooney's adult roles had the energetic and pugnacious flavor of a juvenile about them. While continuing to make nonmusical features, he also starred in *Girl Crazy* (1943), *SUMMER HOLIDAY* (1948), *WORDS AND MUSIC* (1948), *The Strip* (1951), *Sound Off* (1952), and *All Ashore* (1958), as well as a specialty spot in *Thousands Cheer*

(1943). While his film career faded somewhat in the 1950s and 1960s, he was still very active on television, in nightclubs, and later on Broadway. Rooney returned to the film musical with *Pete's Dragon* (1977) and did a guest spot in *The Magic of Lassie* (1978), as well as nonmusicals in which he played older but still energetic character parts into the 1990s. Actresses AVA GARDNER and Martha Vickers were among his eight wives.

ROSALIE (MGM 1937) was a blend of European OPERETTA and campus musical comedy that was never short of ridiculous and nothing less than a huge box office hit. Princess ELEANOR POWELL from Romanza comes to America to attend college and falls for footballer NELSON EDDY even though she is engaged to a prince (Tom Rutherford) back home. But Eddy manages to put down a political coup and ends up as both king and spouse. The 1928 Broadway hit had boasted songs by SIGMUND ROMBERG and GEORGE GERSHWIN, all of which were thrown out for the movie version, which COLE PORTER scored with success, both "In the Still of the Night" and the adoring title song becoming major hits. FRANK MORGAN, as the King of Romanza, sang "Why Should I Care?," Lois Clements (dubbed by Camille Sorey) and Eddy each had a chance to sing the affectionate ballad "Who Knows?," and Powell got to tap away to the robust "I've a Strange New Rhythm in My Heart" and to the title song, a finale staged by W.S. VAN DYKE with literally thousands of extras. Also thrown into the silly concoction were RAY BOLGER, Virginia Grey, ILONA MASSEY, Edna May Oliver, REGINALD OWEN, WILLIAM DEMAREST, BILLY GILBERT, GEORGE ZUCCO, and JERRY COLONNA.

ROSE, HELEN (1904–1985) was a busy and much-awarded costume designer in Hollywood from the early 1940s through the end of the 1960s, when she left to start her own fashion business. Rose designed costumes for the musicals *HELLO, FRISCO, HELLO* (1943), *STORMY WEATHER* (1943), *ZIEGFELD FOLLIES* (1945), *THE HARVEY GIRLS* (1946), *TILL THE CLOUDS ROLL BY* (1947), *GOOD NEWS* (1947), *ON THE TOWN* (1949), *TAKE ME OUT TO THE BALL GAME* (1949), *ANNIE GET YOUR GUN* (1950), *THREE LITTLE WORDS* (1950), *SUMMER STOCK* (1950), *The Toast of New Orleans* (1950), *THE GREAT CARUSO* (1951), *THE BELLE OF NEW YORK* (1952), *THE MERRY WIDOW* (1952), *ROSE MARIE* (1954), *The Glass Slipper* (1955), *I'LL CRY TOMORROW* (1955), *Interrupted Melody* (1955), *LOVE ME OR LEAVE ME* (1955), *HIGH SOCIETY* (1956), *The Opposite Sex* (1956), *SILK STOCKINGS* (1957), and others.

ROSE MARIE (MGM 1936) can be considered the quintessential JEANETTE MacDONALD-NELSON EDDY musical, filled with such familiar clichés as the two of them crooning "Indian Love Call" together. It was one of the four OTTO HARBACH–OSCAR HAMMERSTEIN–RUDOLF

FRIML songs that producer HUNT STROMBERG kept from the 1924 Broadway blockbuster. The original plot was also jettisoned, the story now concerning opera star MacDonald heading for the Canadian Rockies to find her brother (young JAMES STEWART), a man falsely convicted of murder who has escaped from prison. Also looking for Stewart is the Mountie sergeant Eddy who falls in love with MacDonald and is torn between passion and duty. Shot on location near Lake Tahoe, Nevada, by director W.S. VAN DYKE, the movie was as lovely to look at as to listen to. The score also featured the rhythmic "Totem Tom Tom," the rousing march "The Mounties," the gushing title song, and two popular standards of the past: "Some of These Days" and "Dinah." ALLAN JONES was the opera singer with whom MacDonald sang selections from Puccini's *Tosca* and Gounod's *Romeo and Juliet*, and REGINALD OWEN, Una O'Connor, ALAN MOWBRAY, George Regas, HERMAN BING, Lucien Littlefield, and newcomer David Niven rounded out the cast. The musical was even more popular than MacDonald and Eddy's recent operetta triumph *NAUGHTY MARIETTA* (1935) and made them unquestionably the nation's favorite singing team. MGM's 1954 remake of *Rose Marie* was actually closer to the plot of the stage operetta, though again only four of the Broadway songs were heard in the movie. Aged Friml came up with a few new numbers with lyricist PAUL FRANCIS WEBSTER that director MERVYN LeROY used to fill out his lush Cinemascope production filmed on location in the Canadian Rockies. ANN BLYTH was fur trapper's daughter Rose Marie, who is in love with prospector FERNANDO LAMAS, falsely accused of murder and being hunted by Mountie HOWARD KEEL. In a new subplot, Wanda (Joan Taylor), the daughter of an Indian chief, loves Keel and gets him in the end. MARJORIE MAIN ran the local saloon, and stealing the show as always, BERT LAHR was on hand for the comedy and sang "I'm a Mountie Who Never Got His Man." BUSBY BERKELEY handled the choreography, the high point being "Totem Tom Tom" with Taylor dancing with 100 foot-stomping braves. Although it was neither commercially nor artistically as successful as the earlier version, the remake had much to recommend.

ROSE OF WASHINGTON SQUARE (Fox 1939) did not advertise itself as a BIOGRAPHICAL MUSICAL about entertainer FANNY BRICE, but the plot was so similar to her life that the comedienne sued 20TH CENTURY–FOX and got a hefty out-of-court settlement. Singer Rose Sargent (ALICE FAYE) is climbing to the top of her profession, but her love for disreputable TYRONE POWER keeps dragging her down. Eventually he goes to prison, she sings Brice's signature number "My Man," and everybody knew this was not fiction. The score consisted of several old standards (such as "I'm Just Wild About Harry" and the title song), AL JOLSON sang an armful of his old hits (including "California, Here I Come" and "My Mammy"), and MACK GORDON and HARRY REVEL provided a new ballad, "I Never Knew That

Heaven Could Speak." The whole story would be told without disguises in *FUNNY GIRL* (1968).

ROSE, THE (TCF 1979) marked the film debut of Bette Midler, who gave a no-holds-barred performance that turned her from a light rock and camp figure into a movie star. Loosely based on the tragic life of the late Janis Joplin, the story followed the final months in the life of "The Rose" (Midler), a popular rock-and-roll star who is pushed by her manager Alan Bates to keep up a demanding concert tour schedule that leads her deeper into alcohol and drugs. She finds some fleeting happiness in the arms of an ex-soldier (Frederic Forrest), but life is just too much and so, back in her Florida hometown for a concert performance, she overdoses on heroin and dies on stage. It was all pretty melodramatic, but Midler was so magnetic that the film never flagged. A variety of pop composers provided the songs, all sung by Midler, including "Midnight in Memphis," "Stay With Me," "Whose Side Are You On?," "Sold My Soul to Rock and Roll," and the tender title song heard only over the final credits, but it became the biggest hit of the lot. Midler's movie career would be prodigious but uneven, and rarely did she return to the movie musical genre.

ROSS, DIANA (1944–   ), the classy African American pop singer who found fame as a member of the singing group The Supremes, has appeared in two movie musicals: as blues singer Billie Holiday in *LADY SINGS THE BLUES* (1972) and as a grown-up Dorothy in the ill-fated *The Wiz* (1978).

ROSS, HERBERT (1927–   ) moved from Broadway dancer to choreographer to film director and producer, as well as serving as resident choreographer for the American Ballet Theatre. Ross staged the musical numbers for the films *CARMEN JONES* (1954), *DOCTOR DOLITTLE* (1967), and *FUNNY GIRL* (1968); he then directed *GOODBYE, MR. CHIPS* (1969), *FUNNY LADY* (1975), *PENNIES FROM HEAVEN* (1981), and *FOOTLOOSE* (1984). He also directed the dance films *The Turning Point* (1977), *Nijinsky* (1980), and *Dancers* (1987).

ROSS, JERRY. See Adler, Richard

ROSS, LANNY (1906–1988) was a wholesome blond tenor whose operatic voice made him a favorite on the radio. He appeared in featured roles in the musicals *Melody in Spring* (1934), *COLLEGE RHYTHM* (1934), and *The Lady Objects* (1938), provided the voice for Prince David in the animated *GULLIVER'S TRAVELS* (1939), and did a specialty bit in *STAGE DOOR CANTEEN* (1943).

ROSS, SHIRLEY (1909–1975) was a redheaded band vocalist who never quite became a movie star, but she did get to introduce such hit songs as "Thanks for the Memory," "The Lady's in Love With You," and an early version of "Blue Moon." Ross appeared in thirteen musicals, a handful of them with BOB HOPE, including *Hollywood Party* (1934), *THE MERRY WIDOW* (1934), *SAN FRANCISCO* (1936), *BIG BROADCAST OF 1937* (1936), *Hideaway Girl* (1937), *Waikiki Wedding* (1937), *BIG BROADCAST OF 1938*, *Thanks for the Memory* (1938), *Paris Honeymoon* (1939), *Café Society* (1939), and others.

ROTH, LILLIAN (1910–1980) was on the stage as a child and had experience in vaudeville and on Broadway before making her first film in 1918. Looking like the quintessential flapper, the dark-haired, round-faced actress possessed a belting singing voice, which she showed off in the early movie musicals *Illusion* (1929), *THE LOVE PARADE* (1929), *The Vagabond King* (1930), *Honey* (1930), *PARAMOUNT ON PARADE* (1930), *ANIMAL CRACKERS* (1930), *Madam Satan* (1930), and *Take a Chance* (1933). Roth disappeared from view in the mid-1930s, and it was not until she published her autobiography in 1954 that the public learned of her battle with alcoholism and her eight unsuccessful marriages. SUSAN HAYWARD played Roth in the musical bio *I'LL CRY TOMORROW* (1955) based on her memoirs.

ROYAL WEDDING (MGM 1951) was the first musical STANLEY DONAN directed alone, the first major lead for JANE POWELL, and the first Hollywood assignment for screenwriter-lyricist ALAN JAY LERNER. They all did themselves proud and came up with an entertaining musical that falls short of being a classic because of some weak performances in the personage of PETER LAWFORD and SARAH CHURCHILL (Winston Churchill's daughter). Broadway performers FRED ASTAIRE and Powell, who are brother and sister, bring their musical hit to London as England prepares for the wedding of Princess Elizabeth to Philip Mountbatten. Powell falls for an English lord (Lawford) while Astaire is entranced by a publican's daughter (Churchill). Since neither romance was particularly engrossing, it fell to the musical numbers to carry the show and they did more than that. Lerner wrote the songs with composer BURTON LANE, and every one was a gem, including the entrancing ballads "Open Your Eyes" and "Too Late Now," the sexy comedy number "Every Night at Seven," the raucous vaudeville turn "How Could You Believe Me When I Said I Loved You When You Know I've Been a Liar All My Life?," the stomping "Sunday Jumps," and the ecstatic "You're All the World to Me," which Astaire sang and, in the film's most famous scene, danced on the walls and ceiling of his hotel room. NICK CASTLE and Astaire did the choreography, which also included a clever *pas de deux* for Astaire and a hat stand.

RUBY, HARRY (1895–1974) and his lyricist partner BERT KALMAR were popular Broadway songwriters who saw three of their stage hits filmed: *The Cuckoos* (1930) which had been called *The Ramblers* on Broadway, *ANIMAL CRACKERS* (1930), and *Top Speed* (1930). They also wrote the songs and script for two other MARX BROTHERS films, *HORSE FEATHERS* (1932) and *DUCK SOUP* (1933). Ruby and Kalmar contributed songs to *Check and Double Check* (1930), *The Kid From Spain* (1932), *Hips Hips Hooray* (1934), *Walking on Air* (1936), and *Everybody Sing* (1938). With other lyricists, Rudy composed the songs for *Wake Up and Dream* (1946) and *Carnival in Costa Rica* (1947). RED SKELTON played Ruby in the musical bio *THREE LIT-TLE WORDS* (1950) about the team.

RUGGLES, CHARLIE (1886–1970), one of filmdom's favorite character actors, specialized in well-dressed but nervous types who were gullible and/or henpecked. A frequent actor on Broadway, Ruggles managed to appear in over ninety films as well. Among his two dozen musicals were *The Battle of Paris* (1929), *Roadhouse Nights* (1930), *Queen High* (1930), *THE SMILING LIEUTENANT* (1931), *ONE HOUR WITH YOU* (1932), *This Is the Night* (1932), *LOVE ME TONIGHT* (1932), *Girl Without a Room* (1933), *BIG BROADCAST OF 1936* (1935), *ANYTHING GOES* (1936), *Turn Off the Moon* (1937), *BALALAIKA* (1939), *Incendiary Blonde* (1945), *Give My Regards to Broadway* (1948), *Look for the Silver Lining* (1949), and *I'd Rather Be Rich* (1964). His brother was director WESLEY RUGGLES.

RUGGLES, WESLEY (1889–1972) appeared in silent films before turning to directing, helming features between 1918 and 1946. His musical credits were *Street Girl* (1929), *Honey* (1930), *College Humor* (1933), *I'm No Angel* (1933), *Bolero* (1934), *Shoot the Works* (1934), and *SING YOU SINNERS* (1938). Character actor CHARLIE RUGGLES was his brother.

RUMANN, SIG (1884–1967) was an actor in German films before coming to America and making a career playing Teutonic fools, blustering Prussian authorities, and other foreign types. Rumann appeared in over 100 movies, including the musicals *A NIGHT AT THE OPERA* (1935), *ON THE AVENUE* (1937), *MAYTIME* (1937), *A DAY AT THE RACES* (1937), *Thin Ice* (1937), *The Great Waltz* (1938), *Honolulu* (1939), *Bitter Sweet* (1940), *THE DOLLY SISTERS* (1945), *NIGHT AND DAY* (1946), *MOTHER WORE TIGHTS* (1947), *The Emperor Waltz* (1948), *ON THE RIVIERA* (1951), *THE GLENN MILLER STORY* (1954), *WHITE CHRISTMAS* (1954), *ROBIN AND THE SEVEN HOODS* (1964), and others.

RUSSELL, JANE (1921–   ), the buxom protégé of billionaire Howard Hughes, made a sensational film debut in the western *The Outlaw* (1943), which was promoted with a publicity campaign that was notorious in its day for its vulgarity. But Russell soon revealed talents for comedy, singing, and dancing and was starred in seven musicals: *THE PALEFACE* (1948), *Double Dynamite* (1951), *The Las Vegas Story* (1952), *SON OF PALE-FACE* (1952), *GENTLEMEN PREFER BLONDES* (1953), *The French*

Line (1953), and *Gentlemen Prefer Brunettes* (1955), as well as a cameo in *ROAD TO BALI* (1952). Russell made few films after 1960 but was active on stage, in nightclubs, and on television.

RUSSELL, KEN (1927–   ), the eccentric British film director whose movies are known for their excess in all elements, started in television and documentary filmmaking before directing his first feature in 1963. *THE BOY FRIEND* (1971) and *TOMMY* (1975) are his traditional movie musicals (though both are far from conventional), and he also made some highly stylized and highly fictitious film biographies that utilized lots of music and/or dance: *The Music Lovers* (1971) about Tchaikovsky, *Mahler* (1974) about Gustav Mahler, *Lisztomania* (1975) about Liszt, and *Valentino* (1977) about Rudolph Valentino.

RUSSELL, ROSALIND (1912–1976), a tall, overbearing comedienne in many films and plays, could not sing very well but pulled off her musical roles with confidence and hilarity. She appeared in movie musicals as the Countess Rafay in *The Night Is Young* (1934), showgirl Jo in *Reckless* (1935), casino owner Kay Holliday in *The Girl Rush* (1955), and domineering stage mother Rose in *GYPSY* (1962).

RYAN, PEGGY (1924–   ), a chipper child performer who became a teenage dancer featured in several musicals in the 1940s, was usually partnered with DONALD O'CONNOR. Ryan usually did specialty spots or played a youngster named Peggy in her films, many of which were low-budget musicals. She can be seen in *Top of the Town* (1937), *Private Buckaroo* (1942), *Give Out, Sisters* (1942), *Get Hep to Love* (1942), *Top Man* (1943), *The Merry Monahans* (1944), *Bowery to Broadway* (1944), *Here Come the Coeds* (1945), *On Stage Everybody* (1945), *There's a Girl in My Heart* (1949), *All Ashore* (1952), and others. Ryan later found a second career on television (*Hawaii Five-O*).

S

SAKALL, S.Z. (1884–1955), a short, rotund character actor who was so endeared to audiences that he was nicknamed Cuddles, appeared in many German movies until the rise of Nazism sent him to America in 1940. The Hungarian-born Sakall excelled in nervous managers, frustrated impresarios, and kindly uncles, fracturing the language with his East European accent and slapping his cheeks in frustration. After bit parts in *It's a Date* (1940) and *Spring Parade* (1940), he started to get juicier roles in *THAT NIGHT IN RIO* (1941), *Broadway* (1942), *YANKEE DOODLE DANDY* (1942), and others. Among his twenty-eight movie musicals were *THANK YOUR LUCKY STARS* (1943), *Shine On Harvest Moon* (1944), *Wonder Man* (1945), *THE DOLLY SISTERS* (1945), *The Time, the Place and the Girl* (1946), *ROMANCE ON THE HIGH SEAS* (1948), *IN THE GOOD OLD SUMMERTIME* (1949), *Look for the Silver Lining* (1949), *The Daughter of Rosie O'Grady* (1950), *Tea for Two* (1950), *Painting the Clouds With Sunshine* (1951), *Small Town Girl* (1953), and *THE STUDENT PRINCE* (1954).

SAN FRANCISCO (MGM 1936) was a rarity on two fronts: It was a musical disaster movie, and even rarer, it was a disaster film where the people and the story were as intriguing as the special effects. Anita Loos and Robert Hopkins penned the script, in which opera singer JEANETTE MacDONALD goes to San Francisco's notorious Barbary Coast in 1906 to sing in a saloon run by Blackie Norton (CLARK GABLE). She begins a romance with the tough but charming proprietor, but soon high society calls and MacDonald is singing at the Tivoli Opera House to the delight of all the swells on Nob Hill. Blackie refuses to turn genteel to keep MacDonald, and their relationship is at an impasse when the earthquake strikes and the two lovers, surviving the disaster and looking at life differently now, are reunited. Spencer Tracy (in a career-boosting performance) led the supporting cast as a priest who runs a Barbary Coast mission, with Jack Holt, Ted Healy, Jessie Ralph, SHIRLEY ROSS, Margaret Irving, EDGAR KENNEDY, and Al Shean filling out the ensemble. W.S. VAN DYKE directed, and James Basevi did the spectacular earthquake sequence that has rarely been topped. The songs, heard in the saloon and the music hall, were a mixed bag by various songwriters. GUS KAHN and BRONISLAW KAPER wrote the title number, which was played as both a rousing anthem and a tender hymn, and ARTHUR FREED and NACIO HERB BROWN provided the waltzing "Would You?" The rest of the score was either old standards ("At the Georgia Camp Meeting," "Battle Hymn of the Republic") or selections from classical opera (*La Traviata, Faust*).

SANDRICH, MARK (1900–1945), a top Hollywood director and producer, worked his way up from prop boy to directing silent films to musicals, most memorably five of the FRED ASTAIRE–GINGER ROGERS vehicles. From 1940 until his premature death at the age of forty-three, Sandrich produced most of his films as well. The most notable of his thirteen musicals were *THE GAY DIVORCEE* (1934), *TOP HAT* (1935), *FOLLOW THE FLEET* (1936), *SHALL WE DANCE* (1937), *CAREFREE* (1938), *Buck Benny Rides Again* (1940), *LOVE THY NEIGHBOR* (1940), *HOLIDAY INN* (1942), *HERE COME THE WAVES* (1944), and *BLUE SKIES* (1946), which he did not live to complete.

SANDS, TOMMY (1937–   ), a teenage singing star of the late 1950s, was a clean-cut rock-and-roll guitarist and vocalist who made four movie musicals during his brief era of fame: *Sing, Boy, Sing* (1958), *Mardi Gras* (1958), *Love in a Goldfish Bowl* (1961), and *BABES IN TOYLAND* (1961). After a sharp decline Sands reappeared on television in the 1970s.

SANTLEY, JOSEPH (1889–1971) managed to anticipate important trends in show business and switch careers at the most opportune moments. A child actor on the stage and in silent films, Santley became one of Broadway's favorite leading men in light comedies and musicals in the 1920s. But he went back to Hollywood just as sound was introduced and directed the early MARX BROTHERS musical *THE COCOANUTS* (1929). For the next two decades he directed twenty-some musicals, though mostly low-budget B pictures. Among his notable films were *Swing High* (1930), *Laughing Irish Eyes* (1936), *Music in My Heart* (1940), *Dancing on a Dime* (1941), *Sis Hopkins* (1941), *Yokel Boy* (1942), *Thumbs Up* (1943), *Here Comes Elmer* (1943), *Rosie the Riveter* (1944), *Earl Carroll Vanities* (1945), and *When You're Smiling* (1950). Sensing the decline of his assignments and of movie musicals, Santley was one one of the first film directors to move into television, where he produced and directed for many years.

SATURDAY NIGHT FEVER (Paramount 1977) made a star out of JOHN TRAVOLTA and gave disco dancing a much-needed lift as it proved that the lowest of society's discontents can achieve ecstasy on the dance floor. Travolta played an aimless Brooklyn youth who has a dead-end job working at a paint store by day and getting into trouble with gangs and girls at night. But on Saturday night he transforms into a dance sensation at the local disco club and finds some fleeting meaning to his life. The story followed Travolta's ambiguous relationship with ambitious Karen Lynn Gorney, who degrades his lifestyle but serves as his dancing partner so that they can win a couples contest at the disco. They win, but Travolta, having watched his equally dissatisfied pal Barry Miller jump off a bridge in frustration, realizes that his Saturday nights' glory is not the answer. The plot may have resembled a 1950s urban melodrama, but Travolta's magnetic performance and the Bee Gees' pounding music on the soundtrack made it all seem new and exciting. Lester Wilson staged the vibrant disco dancing, and John Badham's direction went right to the nerve. None of the characters sang, but such popular numbers as "Staying Alive," "More Than a Woman," and "How Deep Is Your Love?" by Barry, Robin, and Maurice Gibb made it one of the most musical films of the 1970s. It was also one of the most popular, though the sequel *Staying Alive* (1983), also with Travolta, was a critical and box office dud. *Saturday Night Fever* became a Broadway musical in 1999.

SAVILLE, VICTOR (1896–1979) was an English film director who helmed several British movies in the 1930s, including the musical classic *EVERGREEN* (1934). In 1940 Saville came to America, where he became better known as a film producer, presenting such musicals as *Bitter Sweet* (1940), *Smilin' Through* (1941), *The Chocolate Soldier* (1941), and *Tonight and Every Night* (1945).

SCHERTZINGER, VICTOR (1880–1941) had an unusual combination of talents; he was a recognized film director and a talented composer, finding success in both fields. Schertzinger was trained as a concert violinist and started writing background music for silent films (as well as directing two dozen features) before scoring the early musical classic *THE LOVE PARADE* (1929) with lyricist CLIFFORD GREY. He both directed and scored *Fashions in Love* (1929), a feat he would repeat with *PARAMOUNT ON PARADE* (1930), *Heads Up* (1930), *ONE NIGHT OF LOVE* (1934), *Let's Live Tonight* (1935), *Love Me Forever* (1935), *The Music Goes Round* (1936), *Follow Your Heart* (1936), *Something to Sing About* (1937), *ROAD TO SINGAPORE* (1940), *RHYTHM ON THE RIVER* (1940), *Kiss the Boys Goodbye* (1941), and *THE FLEET'S IN* (1942). Among the musicals he only directed were *Safety in Numbers* (1930), *The Mikado* (1939), *ROAD TO ZANZIBAR* (1941), and *BIRTH OF THE BLUES* (1941). Schertzinger's lyricist partners included GUS KAHN, JOHNNY BURKE, JOHNNY MERCER, and FRANK LOESSER.

SCHWARTZ, ARTHUR (1900–1984) and lyricist HOWARD DIETZ were the masters of the Broadway revue, scoring several shows in the 1930s and writing some of the biggest hits of their day. Unfortunately, none of Schwartz's eighteen Broadway and West End musicals were ever filmed, but the Dietz-Schwartz stage songs provided the scores for *Dancing in the Dark* (1949) and *THE BAND WAGON* (1953). Working with Dietz, SAMMY CAHN, JOHNNY MERCER, DOROTHY FIELDS, and others, he composed the music for ten movie musicals, including *That Girl From Paris* (1936), *Navy Blues* (1941), *Cairo* (1942), *THANK YOUR LUCKY STARS* (1943), *The Time, the Place and the Girl* (1946), *Excuse My Dust* (1951), *Dangerous When Wet* (1953), and *You're Never Too Young* (1955). Schwartz sometimes produced films as well, as he did with the musicals *COVER GIRL* (1944) and *NIGHT AND DAY* (1946).

SCHWARTZ, STEPHEN (1948–   ), a composer-lyricist who had three giant Broadway hits before he was twenty-five years old, saw only one of his half dozen stage musicals filmed, *GODSPELL* (1973). He has written lyrics for the screen and found success with the animated musicals *POCAHONTAS* (1995), *THE HUNCHBACK OF NOTRE DAME* (1996), and *The Prince of Egypt* (1998), winning Oscars for the songs "Colors of the Wind" and "When You Believe." Schwartz is also a notable stage director and record producer.

SCOTT, HAZEL (1920–1981) played piano in nightclubs and created such a following that Hollywood beckoned and put her in specialty spots in five movie musicals. Scott was known for the way she could turn classical pieces into jazz or swing numbers, as witnessed in *Something to Shout About* (1943), *I Dood It* (1943), *The Heat's On* (1943), *Broadway Rhythm* (1943), and *RHAPSODY IN BLUE* (1945).

SCOTT, RANDOLPH (1898–1987) was one of Hollywood's favorite cowboy stars, but he started on the stage and appeared in several light comedies and musicals early in his film career. Scott can be seen in such musicals as *ROBERTA* (1935), *FOLLOW THE FLEET* (1936), *HIGH, WIDE AND HANDSOME* (1937), and *REBECCA OF SUNNYBROOK FARM* (1938).

SCROOGE (Cinema Center/Waterbury 1970) was an attempt to create another *OLIVER!* (1968) by taking a Dickens tale set in Victorian London, this time *A Christmas Carol*, and adding song and dance. Since there had been many film versions of the story since 1901, there were few surprises in the plot, and the songs seemed to slow up the action rather than add much to the famous ghost story. But there were certainly rewards along the way: Albert

Finney was a lively Scrooge, the decor by Terry Marsh was exquisite, and the titles sequence by Ronald Searle was very inventive. Ronald Neame directed efficiently, coming up with some unusual casting for the three spirits; Dame Edith Evans as the spirit of the past, Kenneth More as Christmas Present, and the future darkly portrayed by Paddy Stone, who also provided the music hall–like choreography. LESLIE BRICUSSE's songs were not top drawer, although the catchy "Thank You Very Much" was pleasing enough to stick around for a while.

SEATON, GEORGE (1911–1979) moved from actor to screenwriter to director to producer during his career. Seaton started as a radio actor (he was the original Lone Ranger on the airwaves) and then got into films by writing several screenplays, including the musicals *A DAY AT THE RACES* (1937), *THAT NIGHT IN RIO* (1941), and *CONEY ISLAND* (1943). He wrote and directed *Diamond Horseshoe* (1945), *THE SHOCKING MISS PILGRIM* (1947), *Little Boy Lost* (1953), and *THE COUNTRY GIRL* (1954). By the end of his film career, Seaton was producing movies, such as the musicals *Aaron Slick From Punkin Creek* (1951) and *Somebody Loves Me* (1952).

SECOND FIDDLE (Fox 1939) was a timely spoof of a topic very much on the minds of moviegoers in 1939: the casting of Scarlett O'Hara in *Gone With the Wind* (1939). Consolidated Pictures brings in candidate number 436 to test for the role of Violet Jansen in the period epic *Girl of the North*, and she turns out to be SONJA HENIE, a school teacher and skating instructor from Minnesota. Although he is smitten by her, publicity executive TYRONE POWER sets up a phony romance between Henie and movie star RUDY VALLEE in order to get publicity. But Henie flees Hollywood, and Power follows her all the way back to Minnesota, where he finds happiness with the teacher. Edna May Oliver was quite droll as Henie's aunt, with LYLE TALBOT, MARY HEALY, Alan Dinehart, Minna Gombell, and the Brian Sisters also lending support. IRVING BERLIN wrote the score, and though no classics came from the film, there was much to enjoy in the sincere ballads "I Poured Myself Into a Song" and "When Winter Comes," the torchy "I'm Sorry for Myself," the nostalgic "An Old Fashioned Tune Is Always New," and the swinging "Back to Back," which poked fun at Berlin's own "Cheek to Cheek."

SEGAL, VIVIENNE (1897–1992), one of Broadway's brightest stars of OPERETTAS and musical comedies, made only five movie musicals, leaving an incomplete record of her considerable talents. She can be seen in *Song of the West* (1930), *Bride of the Regiment* (1930), *Golden Dawn* (1930), *Viennese Nights* (1930), and *THE CAT AND THE FIDDLE* (1934).

SEITER, WILLIAM (1891–1964), one of the movies' most prolific directors, staged dozens of feature films between 1920 and 1954. Known as a quality craftsman rather than an inspired artist, Seiter's handiwork can be seen in the musicals *Footlights and Fools* (1929), *Smiling Irish Eyes* (1929), *Sunny* (1930), *Girl Crazy* (1932), *ROBERTA* (1935), *In Person* (1935), *Dimples* (1936), *Stowaway* (1926), *Life of the Party* (1937), *Sally, Irene and Mary* (1938), *Broadway* (1942), *YOU WERE NEVER LOVELIER* (1942), *Four Jills in a Jeep* (1944), *Belle of the Yukon* (1944), *I'll Be Yours* (1947), *Up in Central Park* (1948), *One Touch of Venus* (1948), and others.

SEQUELS for musicals are more common than one would suppose, although many times the link between the original and the follow-up was in title only. For example, *ARTISTS AND MODELS* (1937) had practically nothing to do with *ARTISTS AND MODELS ABROAD* (1938) save the presence of JACK BENNY. Of the true sequels (that is, a continuation of the story or character rather than a remake or rehash of previous material), the most successful have included: *THE JOLSON STORY* (1946) and *JOLSON SINGS AGAIN* (1949), where the last scene of the original film is the first of the sequel; *THE PALEFACE* (1948) and *SON OF PALEFACE* (1952), in which BOB HOPE played the son of the dentist whom he had portrayed in the first outing; *FUNNY GIRL* (1968) and *FUNNY LADY* (1975); *FANTASIA* (1940) and *FANTASIA 2000* (2000); and the *THE MUPPET MOVIE* (1979) and its various sequels. Examples of less lucrative sequels would have to include *Staying Alive* (1983), trying to capture the success of *SATURDAY NIGHT FEVER* (1977), the ill-fated *Journey Back to Oz* (1974) and *Return to Oz* (1985), and *Grease 2* (1982).

SERIES OF MUSICALS have never run as long as western serials or domestic series like the "Andy Hardy" movies (some of which were musicals), but when a studio thought it had a good thing, it would repeat the formula for as long as the box office warranted. The longest-running musical series was the BING CROSBY–BOB HOPE "Road" pictures, seven films made between 1940 and 1962. WARNER BROTHERS made five *Gold Diggers* musicals between 1929 and 1936 with various casts and plots that usually centered around chorus girls and producers. Less cohesive in plot but just as enjoyable was MGM's *Broadway Melody* series of four musicals between 1929 and 1940. Radio was the recurring premise in PARAMOUNT's *BIG BROADCAST* series of four films in the 1930s. Decades later the documentary *THAT'S ENTERTAINMENT* (1974) gave birth to three SEQUELS and spinoffs, the closest Hollywood has come to a new series since the 1940s. Although not a series in name, the collection of films featuring the same star or pairs of stars acted as a series in that the audiences expected certain elements to be repeated in each successive film. The RKO musicals featuring FRED ASTAIRE and GINGER ROGERS, the PARAMOUNT musicals teaming MAURICE CHEVALIER and JEANETTE MacDONALD, MGM's MacDONALD–NELSON EDDY operettas, and the same studio's "lets put on a show" vehicles for

MICKEY ROONEY and JUDY GARLAND are the most obvious examples of this kind of series, just as the SHIRLEY TEMPLE, EDDIE CANTOR, or DANNY KAYE vehicles had a predictability about them.

SEVEN BRIDES FOR SEVEN BROTHERS (MGM 1954) is perhaps the most exciting and enjoyable of all the FRONTIER MUSICALS to come out of Hollywood. With a smart and funny script by ALBERT HACKETT, FRANCES GOODRICH, and DOROTHY KINGSLEY (based on a Stephen Vincent Benet story), a soaring score by JOHNNY MERCER and GENE DE PAUL, STANLEY DONEN's no-nonsense direction, and MICHAEL KIDD's exuberant choreography, the musical manages to be both wholesome and sexy at the same time. Set in the 1850s in the mountains of Oregon, the plot centers on the seven Pontipee brothers: crude, brawling, ignorant, restless, and lonely for women. When eldest brother HOWARD KEEL goes into town and gets himself a wife by wooing the just-as-restless JANE POWELL, the other siblings start hankering for wives too. Powell tries to teach the boys genteel manners, but when they go into town to socialize everyone breaks out into fist fights. Out of frustration (and a little encouragement from Keel), the six brothers sneak into town one night, steal six young women, and bring them back home. They soon realize the error of their ways, but an avalanche blocks the pass back to civilization until spring and the boys have time to learn how to woo the ladies successfully. No musical had yet found such exciting ways to use dance in a wilderness setting. The bravado barn-raising sequence and the moody "Lonesome Polecat" number are justly famous as dance becomes a new layer of the characters and plot. Kidd and Donen cast dancers for the brothers, but they all gave expert acting performances as well: Jeff Richards, RUSS TAMBLYN, TOMMY RALL, Marc Platt, Jacques D'Amboise, and Matt Mattox. Their brides were played by Nancy Kilgras, JULIE NEWMAR (then billed as Newmeyer), Betty Carr, VIRGINIA GIBSON, Norma Goggett, and Ruta Kilmonis. All the songs were rustically poetic and fit snugly into the plot: "Bless Your Beautiful Hide," "Wonderful, Wonderful Day," "When You're in Love," "Goin Co'tin'," "Spring, Spring, Spring," and others. A Broadway version of the musical in 1982 was short-lived.

1776 (Columbia 1972) was so faithful to its 1969 Broadway original (the entire creative staff and most of the stage cast were in the film) that one kept looking for the curtain. Director Peter Hunt failed to find anything cinematic in his directing approach, and rarely has a movie musical seemed so static. However, it did preserve Sherman Edwards' score that ranged from the tender "Momma Look Sharp" to the silly "The Egg" to the inspirational "Is Anybody There?" The screenplay was virtually a copy of Peter Stone's intelligent and gripping libretto about the debates and compromises made by the Continental Congress in the weeks before they finally agreed to sign the Declaration of Independence. As with the play, what sounded like dull history was vivid storytelling.

The cast included William Daniels as a pompous John Adams, Howard Da Silva as a wry Benjamin Franklin, Ken Howard as a reluctant Thomas Jefferson, with Blythe Danner, Donald Madden, Virginia Vestoff, John Cullum, Roy Poole, Ron Holgate, Ray Middleton, and Rex Robbins adding to the historic proceedings.

SHALL WE DANCE (RKO 1937) had the finest score GEORGE and IRA GERSHWIN wrote for the movies and gave FRED ASTAIRE and GINGER ROGERS plenty of opportunities to beguile, amuse, and even bring a tear to their audience's eyes. The plot is improbably contrived and keeps searching for complications to justify itself: American dancer Astaire, in London to do a ballet but really more interested in jazz, is so taken with American performer Rogers that he puts on a phony act as a Russian to win her and then drops it when everyone (including the audience) is tired of listening to him. The two sail back to New York on the same boat, rumors get out that the two are married, and so to refute the press, the couple do marry when they land just so they can get a divorce. Director MARK SANDRICH did his best to help it all make sense, and HERMES PAN, Harry Losee, and Astaire came up with such inventive dances that all was forgiven. The musical's highlights included Astaire's tapping out "Slap That Bass" in a white art deco engine room of an ocean liner, roller skating in Central Park with Rogers after singing "Let's Call the Whole Thing Off," the two of them "Walking the Dog," and the indelible "They Can't Take That Away From Me" sung on a ferryboat in a dense romantic fog. The score also contained "They All Laughed," "Beginner's Luck," and the scintillating title song.

SHARAFF, IRENE (1910–1993), one of Broadway's top costume designers, worked on Hollywood films intermittently between 1943 and 1981. The oft-awarded Sharaff designed for the movie musicals *Girl Crazy* (1943), *MEET ME IN ST. LOUIS* (1944), *Yolanda and the Thief* (1945), *The Secret Life of Walter Mitty* (1947), *A Song Is Born* (1948), *AN AMERICAN IN PARIS* (1951), *CALL ME MADAM* (1953), *A STAR IS BORN* (1954), *BRIGADOON* (1954), *GUYS AND DOLLS* (1955), *THE KING AND I* (1956), *LES GIRLS* (1957), *PORGY AND BESS* (1959), *CAN-CAN* (1960), *WEST SIDE STORY* (1961), *THE FLOWER DRUM SONG* (1961), *FUNNY GIRL* (1968), *HELLO, DOLLY!* (1969), and others.

SHAW, WINIFRED (1899–1982) appeared in nine Hollywood musicals in the 1930s, sometimes in character roles but just as often as a featured singer in a production number. The serious-looking, torchy singer is best remembered for singing "Lullaby of Broadway" in *GOLD DIGGERS OF 1935* but can also be seen in *Million Dollar Ransom* (1934), *Wake Up and Dream* (1934), *SWEET ADELINE* (1935), *In Caliente* (1935), *The Singing Kid* (1936), *Ready, Willing and Able* (1937), and others.

SHE DONE HIM WRONG (Paramount 1933) was MAE WEST's first starring role in Hollywood and a resounding success in all departments. Based on
West's 1928 Broadway play *Diamond Lil*, it told the shady tale of a saloon
singer on the New York Bowery in the 1890s who deals in the white slave trade
and keeps various men on a string. But the tough broad's downfall comes
about when she falls for CARY GRANT, a policeman disguised as a Salvation
Army officer. Audiences were immediately taken with West's nasal double en-
tendres (this is the film in which she asked Grant, "Why don't you come up and
see me sometime?") and moan-like singing voice that made her unlike any
other movie star. The songs were just as sultry as the singer, including Shelton
Brooks' "I Wonder Where My Easy Rider's Gone," LEO ROBIN and RALPH
RAINGER's "A Guy What Takes His Time," and the old standbys "Pretty
Baby" and "Frankie and Johnny."

SHERIDAN, ANN (1915–1967), publicized by the studios as the "Oomph
Girl" for her no-nonsense sex appeal and down-to-earth persona, entered
movies by winning a beauty contest, but her career didn't take off until she
moved into dramatic roles in the 1940s. In the meantime she did bit parts in
such musicals as *Bolero* (1934), *MURDER AT THE VANITIES* (1934), *COL-
LEGE RHYTHM* (1934), and *MISSISSIPPI* (1935). Sheridan had more substantial parts in *Sing Me a Love Song* (1936), *Cowboy From Brooklyn* (1938),
Navy Blues (1941), *THANK YOUR LUCKY STARS* (1943), *Shine On Harvest Moon* (1944), and *The Opposite Sex* (1956).

SHERMAN, RICHARD M. (1928–   ) and **ROBERT B. SHERMAN**
(1925–   ), one of show business's few brother songwriting teams, wrote pop
ditties in the 1950s before WALT DISNEY hired them to provide songs for
the nonmusicals *The Parent Trap* (1961) and *In Search of the Castaways*
(1962). They soon became the studio's unofficial tunesmiths-in-residence
and penned the scores for *Summer Magic* (1963), *MARY POPPINS* (1964),
The Happiest Millionaire (1967), *The One and Only Genuine Original Family
Band* (1968), *BEDKNOBS AND BROOMSTICKS* (1968), as well as the animated features *The Sword in the Stone* (1963), *THE JUNGLE BOOK* (1967),
THE ARISTOCATS (1970), and years later *The Tigger Movie* (2000). For
other studios the brothers worked on the animated *CHARLOTTE'S WEB*
(1972), as well as writing the screenplays and scores for *Tom Sawyer* (1973),
Huckleberry Finn (1974), *The Slipper and the Rose* (1976), and *The Magic of
Lassie* (1978).

SHOCKING MISS PILGRIM, THE (Fox 1947) was a curiosity of a musical
that featured BETTY GRABLE as a progressive woman in stuffy Boston of
1874. She gets an office job as a "typewriter" in a shipping factory and joins
the suffragette movement, but to the audience's disappointment, she couldn't
come up with any reason to show her famous legs. DICK HAYMES was her

boss, who disagreed with Grable's political agenda but found himself in love
with her anyway. The supporting cast was unusual also, including various oddball artistic types living at Grable's boarding house: ELIZABETH
PATTERSON, Anne Revere, Allyn Joslyn, Gene Lockhart, Arthur Shields,
Lillian Bronson, and Charles Kemper. The score was also unique, being fashioned out of the late GEORGE GERSHWIN's unfinished songs to which IRA
GERSHWIN put completed lyrics. "For You, For Me, For Evermore" was the
only number to enjoy any popularity, but there was much to recommend in the
satirical "Back Bay Polka," the reflective "Changing My Tune," and the sly
"Aren't You Kind of Glad We Did?," which, despite its suggestive title, was
about an innocent ride in a carriage without a chaperone.

SHORE, DINAH (1917–1994), one of America's top recording artists for
three decades, found popularity on the radio but failed to catch on at the movie
box office. The smooth-voiced blonde played herself in the musical *THANK
YOUR LUCKY STARS* (1943), specialty spots in *Follow the Boys* (1944) and
TILL THE CLOUDS ROLL BY (1946), actual characters in *Belle of the Yukon*
(1944), *UP IN ARMS* (1944), and *Aaron Slick From Punkin Crick* (1951),
and voice-overs for the animated *Make Mine Music* (1946) and *Fun and Fancy
Free* (1946). Shore later found a new and stronger following on television.

SHOW BOAT, arguably the greatest of all Broadway musicals, has been
filmed three times with variable success, but each version has its strengths and
all manage to touch on the greatness of the stage original. UNIVERSAL was
completing a silent version of Edna Ferber's book when the Broadway musical
adaptation by OSCAR HAMMERSTEIN and JEROME KERN opened in
1927. The studio put the picture back into production, adding sound and music for selected sequences. Laura La Plante (singing dubbed by Eva Olivetti)
played Magnolia, a girl raised on the river boat owned by her parents Cap'n
Andy (Otis Harlan) and Parthenia Hawks (Emily Fitzroy) and who falls in love
with gambler Gaylord Ravenal (Joseph Schildkraut). Stepin Fetchit played the
black dock hand Joe, and Alma Rubens, in the film's most moving performance, portrayed the tragic mulatto Julie LaVerne. Producer Carl Laemmle
had an eighteen-minute prologue made with members of the Broadway cast
singing five of the numbers, introduced by the stage version's producer
Florenz Ziegfeld, in order to capitalize on the play's success. But audiences
were not thrilled with the choppy melodrama and the disjointed songs (mostly
Negro spirituals and vaudeville numbers) that were added in postproduction.
It was Laemmle's son, Carl Laemmle, Jr., who produced the acclaimed 1936
film version for Universal. Hammerstein adapted his stage libretto this time,
nine of the original score's sixteen songs were used, and James Whale directed
a superior cast: IRENE DUNNE and ALLAN JONES as Magnolia and Gaylord,
CHARLES WINNINGER and HELEN WESTLEY as the parents, HELEN
MORGAN as Julie, PAUL ROBESON as Joe, HATTIE McDANIEL as his

wife Queenie, and Sammy White and Queenie Smith as the song-and-dance couple Frank and Ellie May Schultz. The songs were delivered beautifully, giving full power and emotion to such classics as "Ol' Man River," "Make Believe," "Can't Help Lovin' Dat Man," "You Are Love," and "Bill" (lyric by P. G. Wodehouse). Hammerstein and Kern also wrote three new songs for the film: the lively "Gallivantin' Around," the warm character duet "Ah Still Suits Me," and the romantic "I Have the Room Above Her." MGM remade *Show Boat* in 1951 with a lavish Technicolor production directed by GEORGE SIDNEY and a stellar cast that included KATHRYN GRAYSON and HOWARD KEEL as the central lovers, AVA GARDNER (vocals by Annette Warren) as Julie, JOE E. BROWN and AGNES MOOREHEAD as the parents, William Warfield and Frances Williams as Joe and Queenie, and GOWER and MARGE CHAMPION as the Schultzes. The script followed Hammerstein's plot for the first half but then abridged years of story into a tidy ending that simplified but weakened the plotline. For all of its color and spectacle, the remake didn't capture the spirit of the 1936 version, though it was a solid piece of filmmaking. The lovely "Why Do I Love You?" was finally heard on screen, and most of the score was marvelously intact. The Champions practically stole the show with their energetic renditions of "Life Upon the Wicked Stage" and "I Might Fall Back on You." Another film version of *Show Boat* can be found in the Kern musical bio *TILL THE CLOUDS ROLL BY* (1946), in which a fifteen-minute condensation of the musical is shown as part of its landmark opening night on Broadway. It included Grayson and TONY MARTIN singing "Make Believe," VIRGINIA O'BRIEN doing a wry "Life Upon the Wicked Stage," Caleb Peterson delivering a brief section of "Ol' Man River," and (best of all) LENA HORNE turning "Can't Help Lovin' Dat Man" into a thrilling showstopper. (MGM later considered her for Julie in the 1951 film but couldn't quite find the courage to go through with it.)

SHOW OF SHOWS, THE (Warner 1929) was even more a hodgepodge of acts than most of the early musical showcases in which a studio cast all its stars in a Broadway-like REVUE. This one more resembled a vaudeville lineup with just about every performer at WARNER BROTHERS somehow getting into the act. In addition to the usual songs and dances, the revue featured a spoof of a melodrama, Rin Tin Tin barking out an introduction, John Barrymore doing a scene from Shakespeare's *Henry VI, Part Three*, a sketch performed by the incomparable BEATRICE LILLIE, MYRNA LOY as a Chinese princess being serenaded by Nick Lucas, and guest spots for LUPINO LANE, IDA LUPINO, Douglas Fairbanks, Jr., Richard Barthelmess, Dolores Costello, Irene Bordoni, Noah Berry, WINNIE LIGHTNER, ANN SOTHERN, SID SILVERS, Loretta Young, Ben Turpin, and on and on, hosted by Frank Fay. Two musical numbers stood out: "Meet My Sister," performed by eight sets of sisters from around the world, and the lengthy finale in which Betty Compson and Alexander Gray sang "Lady Luck" while fifteen acts broke in and reprised parts of the song as well.

SIDNEY, GEORGE (1916–   ), a director of lavish musicals at MGM, received his training directing short subjects for several years, winning awards and recognition for his work. He moved into features in 1941 and went on to direct the musicals *Thousands Cheer* (1943), *Bathing Beauty* (1944), *ANCHORS AWEIGH* (1945), *THE HARVEY GIRLS* (1946), *Holiday in Mexico* (1946), *ANNIE GET YOUR GUN* (1950), *SHOW BOAT* (1951), *KISS ME, KATE* (1953), *Jupiter's Darling* (1955), *The Eddy Duchin Story* (1956), *PAL JOEY* (1957), and *BYE BYE BIRDIE* (1963). Sidney produced as well as directed *Pepe* (1960), *VIVA LAS VEGAS* (1964), *The Swinger* (1966), and *Half a Sixpence* (1967).

SIEGEL, SOL C. (1903–1982), a producer at Republic Pictures, PARAMOUNT, 20TH CENTURY–FOX, and MGM before going independent, made his reputation on GENE AUTRY and John Wayne westerns but later branched out and presented all genres including musicals. Siegel's musicals include *Glamour Boy* (1941), *BLUE SKIES* (1946), *The Perils of Pauline* (1947), *My Blue Heaven* (1950), *ON THE RIVIERA* (1951), *CALL ME MADAM* (1953), *GENTLEMEN PREFER BLONDES* (1953), *THERE'S NO BUSINESS LIKE SHOW BUSINESS* (1954), *HIGH SOCIETY* (1956), *LES GIRLS* (1957), and *Merry Andrew* (1959).

SILK STOCKINGS (MGM 1957) was COLE PORTER's musical version of the film classic *Ninotchka* (1939) and a long-running Broadway musical. The familiar plot changed slightly from the nonmusical: the Soviet agent Nina "Ninotchka" Yoshenka (CYD CHARISSE, vocals dubbed by Carole Richards) comes to Paris to chastise three Russian emissaries (Peter Lorre, Joseph Buloff, and JULES MUNSHIN) who are being seduced by decadent Western ways and to bring back the composer Wim Sonneveld, who is thinking of going to Hollywood with AMERICAN producer FRED ASTAIRE to score movies. Nina succumbs to the charms of Paris and Astaire, helped by romantic Porter songs such as "Paris Loves Lovers." Much of the story was told in dance, and Astaire and Charisse's *pas de deux* during "Fated to Be Mated," "The Ritz Rock and Roll," and "All of You" were expert. Also in the nimble score were the character songs "Siberia," "It's a Chemical Reaction, That's All," and "Stereophonic Sound." The last was sung by JANIS PAIGE as a Hollywood swimming star, outstanding in a cast that also included GEORGE TOBIAS, Barrie Chase, Betty Uitti, and Tybee Afra. ROUBEN MAMOULIAN directed in a studio soundstage, but it felt like Paris all the same.

SILVERS, PHIL (1911–1985), one of the great clowns of early television, started in burlesque and began making feature films in 1940, usually playing comics, bubbling friends to the hero, or emcees. The bespectacled comedian can be seen in *Hit Parade of 1941* (1940), *Lady, Be Good* (1941), *Ice Capades* (1941), *MY GAL SAL* (1942), *Footlight Serenade* (1942), *CONEY ISLAND* (1943), *COVER GIRL* (1944), *Four Jills in a Jeep* (1944), *Something for the Boys* (1944), *Diamond Horseshoe* (1945), *If I'm Lucky* (1946), *SUMMER STOCK* (1950), *Top Banana* (1954), *Lucky Me* (1954), and *A Funny Thing Happened on the Way to the Forum* (1967).

SILVERS, SID (1901–1976) had two concurrent careers: as a comic in featured parts in movies and as a screenwriter. The small, very physical comedian appeared in *THE SHOW OF SHOWS* (1929), *Dancing Sweeties* (1930), *My Weakness* (1933), *Transatlantic Merry-Go-Round* (1934), and *52nd Street* (1937). He contributed to the screenplays for the musicals *Follow the Leader* (1930), *BROADWAY MELODY OF 1938* (1937), *THE FLEET'S IN* (1942), and *FOR ME AND MY GAL* (1942). Silvers both wrote and performed in *Bottoms Up* (1934), *BROADWAY MELODY OF 1936* (1935), and *BORN TO DANCE* (1936).

SIMMS, GINNY (1916–1994), a vocalist with KAY KYSER's band, appeared as herself with the orchestra in the movie musicals *That's Right, You're Wrong* (1939), *You'll Find Out* (1940), and *Playmates* (1942). Simms then went solo and was seen in *Here We Go Again* (1942), *Seven Days' Leave* (1942), *Hit the Ice* (1943), *Broadway Rhythm* (1944), *Shady Lady* (1945), *NIGHT AND DAY* (1946), and *Disc Jockey* (1951).

SINATRA, FRANK (1915–1998), the durable superstar who managed to maintain a huge following for five decades, was one of the first band vocalists to go off on his own and find celebrity in all the media, from concerts and records to films and television. Sinatra was just starting to become a teenage idol when he appeared on film as himself or as a vocalist in *Las Vegas Nights* (1941), *Ship Ahoy* (1942), *Reveille With Beverly* (1943), and *Higher and Higher* (1943). He got to play characters, usually naive and wholesome juveniles, in *Step Lively* (1944), *ANCHORS AWEIGH* (1945), *IT HAPPENED IN BROOKLYN* (1947), *The Kissing Bandit* (1948), *TAKE ME OUT TO THE BALL GAME* (1949), *ON THE TOWN* (1949), *Double Dynamite* (1951), and *Meet Danny Wilson* (1952). Sinatra's more adult roles came in *GUYS AND DOLLS* (1955), *HIGH SOCIETY* (1956), *CAN-CAN* (1960), and *ROBIN AND THE SEVEN HOODS* (1964). When he started to get juicy dramatic roles in films in the 1950s, Sinatra also got to play more complex characters in musicals, most memorably *Young at Heart* (1954), *THE JOKER IS WILD* (1957), and *PAL JOEY* (1957). He also made guest appearances or did specialty spots in *TILL THE CLOUDS ROLL BY* (1946), *Meet Me in Las Vegas* (1955), *Pepe* (1960), and *THE ROAD TO HONG KONG* (1962). Sinatra's special way with a song and relaxed singing style made him a longtime favorite, but he also possessed a strong film presence and managed to be intriguing even when his vehicles were second rate. He was married to actresses AVA GARDNER and Mia Farrow, and his children are singers Nancy Sinatra and Frank Sinatra, Jr.

SING YOU SINNERS (Paramount 1938) was a musical about the domestic squabbling of three siblings—hard-working FRED MacMURRAY, horse race gambler BING CROSBY, and pint-size kid brother DONALD O'CON-NOR—and what happens when Crosby is attracted to MacMurray's fiancée Ellen Drew. Winning a pile at the track, Crosby buys a junk shop and a race horse that O'Connor rides to victory. It was an unusual plotline for a musical but one that worked, especially when Crosby sang two JAMES V. MONACO–JOHNNY BURKE hits, "I've Got a Pocket Full of Dreams" and "Don't Let That Moon Get Away." Yet the highlight of the film was the three brothers cutting loose with FRANK LOESSER and HOAGY CARMICHAEL's cautionary ditty "Small Fry," which also became a hit.

SINGIN' IN THE RAIN (MGM 1952) may or may not be the greatest of all Hollywood musicals, but it is probably more fun than any other. BETTY COMDEN and ADOLPH GREEN wrote the satirical script about the early days of the talkies, using the ARTHUR FREED–NACIO HERB BROWN song catalog as their inspiration. Silent screen idol GENE KELLY falls for struggling chorus girl DEBBIE REYNOLDS, who gets a job dubbing the speaking and singing vocals for twangy-voiced silent star Jean Hagen. The difficulties in making the early musical films are presented hilariously and accurately, and a good-natured spoof of Hollywood in general is achieved. By the end Reynolds is revealed as the real voice behind Hagen, and she becomes a star in her own right. The plot found room for sidekick DONALD O'CONNOR to give his most nimble performance ever and for naughty flapper CYD CHARISSE to make quite an impact wearing a Louise Brooks–like wig in a sultry *pas de deux* with Kelly. Except for the silly ditty "Moses (Supposes)" written by Comden, Green, and ROGER EDENS for the film and a new Freed-Brown number "Make 'Em Laugh," the score was filled with old favorites that were so marvelously staged by director-choreographers Kelly and STANLEY DONEN that they are usually remembered for this film rather than their initial screen appearances. "All I Do Is Dream of You," "The Wedding of the Painted Doll," "Would You?," "You Were Meant for Me," "Should I?," "You Are My Lucky Star," and "Good Morning" were sparklingly fresh, and Kelly's solo performance of the title number as he joyously splashed down the street is movie musical perfection. The big "Broadway Rhythm" ballet at the end was more playful than Kelly's usual extended dance pieces and retained the satirical tone of the whole movie. Although it was only moderately successful in its first release, *Singin' in the Rain* has achieved cult status over the years and represented the finest hour of its stars and the whole Freed unit at MGM.

SINGING FOOL, THE (Warner 1928) may be little seen (or remembered) today, but this part-talkie was the top-grossing movie in Hollywood history until *SNOW WHITE AND THE SEVEN DWARFS* (1937) came along. The highly sentimental tale told of the rise of singing waiter AL JOLSON, whose success goes to his head and whose wife Josephine Dunn walks out on him. Left to raise his little boy Davey Lee, Jolson sings "Sonny Boy" to him before the child dies, and then Jolson is rescued from total despair by the love of cigarette girl Betty Bronson. Jolson's unabashed, maudlin performance was rescued by his mighty delivery of the songs (by various tunesmiths) such as "It All Depends on You," "I'm Sittin' on Top of the World," "There's a Rainbow 'Round My Shoulder," and "Keep Smilin' at Trouble." LLOYD BACON directed the C. Graham Baker script with all the emotional stops pulled out, and audiences flocked to the theatre in droves. "Sonny Boy," which legend has it that B.G. DE SYLVA, LEW BROWN, and RAY HENDERSON wrote with every saccharine cliché they could think of as a joke, was also a major hit, selling over three million copies of sheet music and Jolson's recording going over a million disks.

SKELTON, RED (1910–1997), a beloved clown on film and television, was involved in just about every form of show business, starting in circuses, medicine shows, and vaudeville, then working his way to radio and, by 1938, movies. Skelton rarely played the leading role in his fifteen film musicals but added sparkle as the sidekick or child-like buffoon. He made his screen debut as the camp clown Itchy in *Having Wonderful Time* (1938), followed by musicals such as *Lady, Be Good* (1941), *Panama Hattie* (1942), *Ship Ahoy* (1942), *DuBarry Was a Lady* (1943), *I Dood It* (1943), *Bathing Beauty* (1944), *NEPTUNE'S DAUGHTER* (1949), *THREE LITTLE WORDS* (1950), *Excuse My Dust* (1951), *Texas Carnival* (1951), and *LOVELY TO LOOK AT* (1952). He also did specialty spots in *Thousands Cheer* (1943), *ZIEGFELD FOLLIES* (1946), and *The Duchess of Idaho* (1950). Skelton's real fame came with television, where he entertained America for years with his pantomime and daffy collection of characters.

SMILING LIEUTENANT, THE (Paramount 1931) was a scintillating fairy tale for adults that boosted MAURICE CHEVALIER's ever-growing popularity and provided some continental sophistication to contrast the more vulgar musicals that were flooding the market. SAMSON RAPHAELSON, Ernest Vajda, and ERNST LUBITSCH adapted OSCAR STRAUS' 1907 Viennese operetta for the screen, CLIFFORD GREY wrote English lyrics to the songs, and Lubitsch directed with the lightness of a soufflé. Officer Chevalier has an eye for the ladies, but for reasons not worth explaining, he weds the rather plain Princess Anna (Miriam Hopkins) even though he is more attracted to the flirtatious CLAUDETTE COLBERT, who leads an all-woman orchestra. Realizing she cannot compete with a princess, Colbert gives up Chevalier and even provides Hopkins with tips on how to make herself look more beautiful and act more vivacious. CHARLES RUGGLES, GEORGE BARBIER, Hugh O'Connell, and Robert Strange rounded out the cast, and the waltzing score included "Breakfast Table Love," "One More Hour of Love," and "While Hearts Are Singing (Live for Today)."

SMITH, ALEXIS (1921–1993), the elegant and statuesque actress of many films in the 1940s and 1950s, appeared in nonsinging roles in such musicals as *THANK YOUR LUCKY STARS* (1943), *HOLLYWOOD CANTEEN* (1944), *RHAPSODY IN BLUE* (1945), *NIGHT AND DAY* (1946), *HERE COMES THE GROOM* (1951), and *Beau James* (1957). Smith left the movies in the late 1950s, and not until the 1970s did she reveal considerable singing and dancing talents when she starred on Broadway in *Follies* (1971). She continued to do musicals on stage but only appeared in nonmusicals when she returned to the screen in 1975. Smith was married to actor Craig Stevens.

SNOW WHITE AND THE SEVEN DWARFS (Disney/RKO 1937) was a landmark collection of firsts: the first full-length animated film, the first cartoon to use life models to simulate human movement, the first animated feature to use a multiplane camera to achieve depth, the first movie musical to produce (in 1944) a best-selling soundtrack album, and the first Hollywood film to earn over $6 million on its initial release. But the movie's greatness lies in the fact that it doesn't look like the primitive first of anything. Producer WALT DISNEY and hundreds of artists labored four years on the project, which the film community saw as a grand folly. The very idea of a cartoon lasting eighty-three minutes, of animated characters singing love songs to each other, and of artists creating a complex and detailed art decor for a kids' movie was laughable. Yet *Snow White and the Seven Dwarfs* changed the way audiences thought about cartoons, children's movies, and Disney. The script took liberties with the original Grimm Brothers' tale and created names and individual characters for the dwarfs. Although softening some of the original's more gruesome aspects, the film was still frightening and powerful at times, yet warm-hearted and farcical in other spots. Adriana Caselotti provided Snow White's speaking and singing voice, Lucille LaVerne did the wicked Queen, Harry Stockwell the Prince, and Scotty Mattraw, BILLY GILBERT, Otis Harlan, Pinto Colvig, and Roy Atwell voiced the various dwarfs. LARRY MOREY and FRANK CHURCHILL wrote the songs, several of which became hits, and just about all of them are now part of musical folklore: "Heigh-Ho," "Some Day My Prince Will Come," "I'm Wishing," "With a Smile and a Song," "One Song," "Whistle While You Work." and others. To celebrate the fiftieth anniversary of the film, the studio re-released it in 1987 with 4,000 prints seen in fifty-eight countries on the same day, the largest opening day in the history of the movies.

SON OF PALEFACE. See *Paleface, The*

SONDHEIM, STEPHEN (1930–   ), the most experimental and innovative composer-lyricist on Broadway since the late 1950s, has seen only four of his many musicals filmed: *WEST SIDE STORY* (1961) and *GYPSY* (1962), for which he wrote lyrics, and *A Funny Thing Happened on the Way to the Forum* (1967) and *A Little Night Music* (1978), for which he provided both music and lyrics. Although he has contributed songs to nonmusical films, Sondheim's only score written directly for the screen was *DICK TRACY* (1990). He is one of the few artists to have won a Tony, Grammy, and ACADEMY AWARD, as well as a Pulitzer Prize.

SONG OF THE SOUTH (Disney/RKO 1946) was not the DISNEY studio's first blending of animation and live action, but the process had never been perfected and used as effectively as it was in this folklore musical that drew from Joel Chander Harris' *Tales of Uncle Remus* for its inspiration. The live-action portion of the film concerned young BOBBY DRISCOLL, whose parents separate and he goes to live in the South, where he befriends Uncle Remus (James Baskett) and the local farm girl Luana Patten. The boy's dealings with his overprotective mother (Ruth Warrick), his grandmother (Lucile Watson), and some bullies in the neighborhood are interrupted by the animated stories that Remus tells him about Brer Rabbit (voice of Johnny Lee), Brer Fox (Baskett), and Brer Bear (Nicodemus Stewart). The animated sequences are much more satisfying than the melodrama involving the humans, but the whole film has a lazy charm about it that is still winning. Various tunesmiths wrote the songs, most of them excellent: "Everybody's Got a Laughing Place," "How Do You Do?," "Sooner or Later," and the Oscar-winning "Zip-a-Dee-Doo-Dah" by Ray Gilbert and ALLIE WRUBEL. Although the movie was very popular in both the South and across the country in its first release, some African American groups complained about the antiquated view of southern blacks, and rumblings got so loud during the civil rights movement in the 1960s that the studio withdrew the film from circulation. It was not made available again until 1972.

SOTHERN, ANN (1909–   ) has enjoyed a long and varied career in several media, beginning with a bit part in the early musical film *THE SHOW OF SHOWS* (1929). After securing a reputation as a smart and funny comedienne on stage, the short, blonde actress returned to Hollywood and appeared in many comedies and musicals, including *Let's Fall in Love* (1934), *KID MILLIONS* (1934), *Hooray for Love* (1935), *Walking on Air* (1936), *Lady, Be Good* (1941), *Panama Hattie* (1942), *Thousands Cheer* (1943), *April Showers* (1948), *WORDS AND MUSIC* (1948), and *Nancy Goes to Rio* (1950). Sothern had two very successful television shows in the 1950s, toured in theatre productions, and made occasional films up into the 1980s.

SOUND OF MUSIC, THE (Argyle/Fox 1965), the movie musical some love to hate and others hate to love, was a first-class product with all the artistic elements in place. Its sentimentality could be considered the film's greatest strength or weakness, but its craftsmanship is superb. ERNEST LEHMAN adapted the 1959 Broadway musical for the wide screen, opening up the story to include the breathtaking Austrian mountains and the atmospheric city of Salzburg. The political aspects of the stage work were soft-peddled for the screen (the Captain leaves his fiancée because he loves the governess Maria rather than over a disagreement about the Nazis), but mostly it was a tight and efficient screenplay. The RICHARD RODGERS and OSCAR HAMMER-STEIN score lost three stage numbers, gained two new ones (with Rodgers providing the lyrics, since his partner had died in 1960), and shifted the songs around a bit. But the spirit of the score was there and every song became an audience favorite: "Climb Ev'ry Mountain," "Do Re Mi," "My Favorite Things," "The Lonely Goatherd," "(How Do You Solve a Problem Like) Maria?," "Something Good," "I Have Confidence," "Edelweiss," and the title number filmed on a mountain top in such a way as to remind everybody that movies can do things the stage cannot begin to attempt. Christopher Plummer's Captain (singing dubbed by Bill Lee) may have been a little too subtle for the rest of the film, but JULIE ANDREWS managed to be sweet, funny, appealing, and firmly in control. Peggy Wood (dubbed by Margery McKay) was the Mother Abbess, Eleanor Parker the fiancée, Richard Hayden the impresario Max, and Charmian Carr and Daniel Truhite the eldest Von Trapp girl and the budding Nazi she loves. ROBERT WISE produced and directed the musical, which grossed more than any previous film and still remains on the list of BOX OFFICE CHAMPS.

SOUTH PACIFIC (Fox 1958) had the right cast but the wrong director and missed becoming a movie classic because of its wooden staging and distracting use of filters in trying to capture the mystery of the Pacific islands. JOSHUA LOGAN had co-written and directed the 1949 Broadway production, so he was retained for the film along with the whole score (including "My Girl Back Home," which had been dropped out of town) and JUANITA HALL as the conniving Bloody Mary (though her singing was dubbed by Muriel Smith). MITZI GAYNOR had the role of her career as the American nurse Nellie Forbush in World War Two who has a love affair with an older French planter (Rossano Brazzi, dubbed by Giorgio Tozzi) but whose prejudices keep her from marrying him when she learns he has two Polynesian children. John Kerr (dubbed by Bill Lee) and France Nuyen played the secondary couple, a lieutenant and a native girl, whose romance is cut short by his death in a special mission. RAY WALSTON, as the scheming GI Luther Billis, matched Hall in bringing a sharp cynicism to all the romantic proceedings. Paul Osborn's script was faithful to OSCAR HAMMERSTEIN's adult stage libretto, but what was rough, lusty, and masculine on stage too often looked like a genteel travelogue on the screen, aided by the dreamy Hawaiian Islands used for filming. RICH-ARD RODGERS and Hammerstein's score was one of their best, and the songs still packed a wallop: "There Is Nuthin' Like a Dame," "Bloody Mary," "I'm Gonna Wash That Man Right Outa My Hair," "Some Enchanted Evening," "Honey Bun," "Younger Than Springtime," "Bali Hai," "A Wonderful Guy," "Happy Talk," "This Nearly Was Mine," and others.

SPARKS, NED (1883–1957) was a gravel-voiced character actor who, after many years on the stage, went to Hollywood in 1922 and became a familiar face in silents and then talkies, including the musicals *42ND STREET* (1933), *GOLD DIGGERS OF 1933, Too Much Harmony* (1933), *GOING HOLLY-WOOD* (1933), *SWEET ADELINE* (1935), *Collegiate* (1936), *ONE IN A MILLION* (1937), *WAKE UP AND LIVE* (1937), *The Star Maker* (1939), *STAGE DOOR CANTEEN* (1943), and others.

SPRINGTIME IN THE ROCKIES (Fox 1942) was a facile BETTY GRABLE vehicle that was all about nothing but so enjoyable that it seemed like gold. Broadway performers Grable and JOHN PAYNE love each other but are always fighting (he has a roving eye for the ladies), so when she runs off to Lake Louise in the Canadian Rockies with her former dancing partner CESAR ROMERO, Payne follows and tries to make her jealous by having a fling with CARMEN MIRANDA. It was a plot that ached for interruption and the interruptions were delicious. Grable and Payne performed the zesty duet "Run Little Raindrop," Miranda sang "Chattanooga Choo-Choo" in Portuguese, vocalist Helen Forrest introduced "I Had the Craziest Dream" with HARRY JAMES and his band, and the whole cast (including high-kicking CHARLOTTE GREENWOOD, fidgety EDWARD EVERETT HORTON, and roly-poly JACKIE GLEASON) cut loose with HERMES PAN's choreography for the "Pan American Jubilee" finale. MACK GORDON and HARRY WARREN penned the catchy songs, and IRVING CUMMINGS directed with gusto.

STAGE DOOR CANTEEN (Lesser/United Artists 1943) was a musical tribute to the American Theatre Wing, the organization that sponsored the title's famous New York hot spot for servicemen during the war. Although there was a thread of a plot, about a GI (William Terry) and a canteen hostess (Cheryl Walker) and their wartime romance, the movie was more a parade of theatre stars who were making appearances at the canteen. Theatrical *grande dames* like Katharine Hepburn, Helen Hayes, Katharine Cornell, Ina Claire, and Judith Anderson showed up to wash dishes and pass out food while music was provided by Big Band favorites such as BENNY GOODMAN, XAVIER CUGAT, KAY KYSER, Freddie Martin, and GUY LOMBARDO, and vocals by LANNY ROSS, RAY BOLGER, PEGGY LEE, and others. A variety of songwriters contributed to the scattershot score, the best numbers being RODGERS and HART's comic "The Girl I Love to Leave Behind" and AL

DUBIN and JAMES V. MONACO's teary ballad "We Mustn't Say Good-bye." The unusual REVUE was popular, and because 90 percent of the box office went to the Theatre Wing, it was a great morale booster. The West Coast jumped on the band wagon and offered **HOLLYWOOD CANTEEN** (Warner 1944), the Los Angeles version of Manhattan's Stage Door Canteen. There being more stars in the neighborhood, the movie was stuffed with nearly thirty name-above-the-title stars, from the swinging ANDREWS SISTERS to the violin virtuoso Efrem Zimbalist. Again there was a slim plot, this time about two sailors (Robert Hutton and Dane Clark) on sick leave from the Pacific campaign and Hutton's winning a contest that gives him a dream date with JOAN LESLIE. JIMMY DORSEY, Carmen Cavallaro, and their bands provided the music, and several songs by Hollywood songwriters were introduced. Among the many memorable moments: ROY ROGERS and the Sons of the Pioneers pleading "Don't Fence Me In" by COLE PORTER, EDDIE CANTOR and Nora Martin proclaiming "We're Having a Baby (My Baby and Me)," Leslie and KITTY CARLISLE bidding "Sweet Dreams, Sweetheart," and the Andrews Sisters singing how they got "Corns for My Country" by waiting on all the servicemen.

STAR! (Fox 1968) was intended to celebrate the life and career of Gertrude Lawrence, the musical star who had conquered the West End and Broadway in the 1920s and remained popular for decades. But the film seemed to shed little light on Lawrence and a lot on the very different star JULIE ANDREWS who played her. At the peak of her popularity, Andrews valiantly held the long (175 minutes), overextended, and overproduced BIOGRAPHICAL MUSICAL together, helped by terrific old tunes by NOEL COWARD, COLE PORTER, KURT WEILL, and the GERSHWINS. The rags-to-riches tale followed Lawrence from her humble beginnings in the Clapham section of London to her music hall days and then her celebrity on both sides of the Atlantic. Her friend Coward, played with a diffident charm by Daniel Massey, and supportive second husband (Richard Crenna) were the anchors in Lawrence's stormy life, yet audiences got weary of her tale long before the picture concluded. But MICHAEL KIDD choreographed some lively numbers, such as "The Physician" and "Jenny," and director ROBERT WISE made the whole thing look and feel right. Other songs, most of them performed by Andrews, included "Parisian Pierrot," "Burlington Bertie From Bow," "My Ship," "Someday I'll Find You," "Someone to Watch Over Me," "Limehouse Blues," and a new title song by SAMMY CAHN and JAMES VAN HEUSEN. When the movie bombed at the box office, the studio cut nearly an hour out of the original and re-released it as *Those Were the Happy Days*, but it bombed again. Yet over the years the long version has found its admirers.

STAR IS BORN, A (Transcona/Warner 1954) was JUDY GARLAND's last major movie musical and, in the opinion of many, featured her finest performance. The story was already familiar to movie audiences, based on the 1937 melodrama of the same title, which was loosely based on *What Price Holly-wood?* (1932), but the musical version was never less than enthralling thanks to MOSS HART's unsentimental screenplay, GEORGE CUKOR's rich direction, IRA GERSHWIN and HAROLD ARLEN's dynamic score, and the performances by Garland and James Mason. Band singer Esther Blodgett (Garland) meets alcoholic movie star Mason at a Hollywood benefit, and after he hears her sing "The Man That Got Away" in a quiet night spot, he is determined to help her climb to stardom. He marries her, but as Vicky Lester (as she is renamed by the studio) climbs, Mason descends until he ends up drowning himself in despair. It was perhaps the most sobering musical backstager yet, and even the comic numbers had a painful subtext to them. Yet there was something glorious about so much talent in full bloom. When Garland sang "Someone at Last" to Mason in their living room and enacted the entire plot of the simple-minded movie she is making, the power of a star was celebrated. Her rendition of the ballad "It's a New World," the swinging "Gotta Have a Go With You," and the intricate montage "Born in a Trunk" (by Leonard Gershe and ROGER EDENS) proved that Garland, whose personal life was descending even faster than Mason's character, was better than anyone imagined. Because the picture ran over three hours, the studio cut scenes and two numbers ("Lose That Long Face" and "Here's What I'm Here For") before releasing it in a 154-minute version. Some of the missing footage was restored for the 1983 re-release, and many felt a great movie musical was made even better. The remake *A STAR IS BORN* (Warner/Barwood-First Artists 1976) featured its era's superstar BARBRA STREISAND with Kris Kristofferson in the world of rock concerts rather than Hollywood. Although the milieu and songs were completely different, the plot was surprisingly similar: ambitious pop singer rising to the top as her mentor and husband descends into drugs and suicide by crashing his Ferrari. Just as the earlier films sought to expose the hypocrisy of the show business of their day, the remake provided a very unglamourous view of rock singers and their world. PAUL WILLIAMS and Streisand's Oscar-winning "Evergreen" (aka "Love Theme From *A Star Is Born*") was the best song in the score, though there was much to like in Rupert Holmes' "Queen Bee," "Woman in the Moon" by Williams and Kenny Ascher, and "I Believe in Love" by ALAN and MARILYN BERGMAN and Kenny Loggins. The critics carped but the movie was a resounding hit at the box office.

STAR SPANGLED RHYTHM (Paramount 1942) was the first of a handful of wartime musicals that used a slender plot as an excuse to feature plenty of stars on the studio lot in a patriotic bonanza. Others to follow included *STAGE DOOR CANTEEN* (1943), *THANK YOUR LUCKY STARS* (1943), *Thousands Cheer* (1943), *HOLLYWOOD CANTEEN* (1944), and *Follow the Boys* (1944). This original entry concerned GI EDDIE BRACKEN, who, wanting to impress his shipmates, schemes with switchboard operator BETTY HUTTON to pass off Bracken's father VICTOR MOORE, a gatekeeper at PARAMOUNT, as a studio executive. The plan starts off successfully, but soon Moore finds himself in charge of a huge stage show for servicemen. JOHNNY MERCER and HAROLD ARLEN wrote the score and struck gold twice: "That Old Black Magic," sung by JOHNNY JOHNSTON and danced by VERA ZORINA, and "Hit the Road to Dreamland," introduced by MARY MARTIN, DICK POWELL, and the Golden Gate Quartet. Also enjoyable were Paulette Goddard, DOROTHY LAMOUR, and VERONICA LAKE spoofing their Hollywood image with "A Sweater, a Sarong and a Peek-a-Boo Bang," CASS DALEY lamenting "He Loved Me Till the All-Clear Came," and Hutton riding along in a jeep full of sailors and slyly singing "I'm Doing It for Defense." Other stars stopping by the set were BING CROSBY, BOB HOPE, FRED MacMURRAY, FRANCHOT TONE, SUSAN HAYWARD, EDDIE "ROCHESTER" ANDERSON, Alan Ladd, Macdonald Carey, MARJORIE REYNOLDS, and many others.

STATE FAIR (Fox 1945) was RICHARD RODGERS and OSCAR HAMMERSTEIN's only movie score together, and it was full of gems like "A Grand Night for Singing," "That's For Me," "Isn't It Kinda Fun?," and the Oscar-winning "It Might as Well Be Spring." Hammerstein adapted the 1933 nonmusical film and Phil Strong's novel into a bucolic musical piece that moved along leisurely and melodically. The Iowa farmer CHARLES WINNINGER, his wife FAY BAINTER, their restless daughter JEANNE CRAIN (vocals by Luanne Hogan), and naive son DICK HAYMES set off for the state fair, where Crain finds romance with newspaper reporter Dana Andrews, Haymes gets wise to the world when he falls for band singer VIVIAN BLAINE, Winninger's pet hog wins a prize, and Bainter's pickles win a blue ribbon. Under WALTER LANG's homespun direction it was as charming as it was unexciting and, in many ways, was Hollywood's answer to Rodgers and Hammerstein's recent Broadway hit *Oklahoma!* (1943). After Hammerstein's death in 1960, Rodgers wrote music and lyrics for five new songs for the 1962 remake, which set the tale in Texas and eliminated any rustic or folksy aspects of the story or characters. Tom Ewell and ALICE FAYE (returning to the screen after seventeen years) were the parents, Pamela Tiffin (dubbed by Anita Gordon) was the daughter who linked up with BOBBY DARIN, and PAT BOONE was the son who found more than a touch of fire in ANN-MARGARET. José Ferrer directed in such a way that the whole venture resembled a Las Vegas floor show more than a state fair, but Faye was warm and engaging in her first maternal role, and Ann-Margaret sparkled more than the requisite fireworks at the fair. Some of the old songs were retained but jazzed up with a 1960s mentality, and Rodgers' new numbers offered a pleasing "Never Say No to a Man" for Faye and "This Isn't Heaven" which Darin sang and turned into a modest hit record.

STEELE, TOMMY (1936–   ), a blonde, youthful pop singer in England in the 1950s, appeared in a handful of movie musicals on both sides of the Atlantic in the 1960s, usually playing energetic cockney types. Steele can be seen as the chipper butler John Lawless in *The Happiest Millionaire* (1967), the unlikely heir Arthur Kipps in *Half a Sixpence* (1967), and Og the leprechaun in *FINIAN'S RAINBOW* (1968), as well as in some British musicals.

STEPT, SAM H. (1897–1964) was a bandleader-turned-composer who, working with various Hollywood lyricists, provided songs for a dozen movie musicals, including *Lucky in Love* (1929), *Playing Around* (1930), *Shady Lady* (1933), *This Is the Life* (1935), *Dancing Feet* (1936), *Laughing Irish Eyes* (1936), *Having Wonderful Time* (1938), and *Yokel Boy* (1942). Stept's most famous song is "Don't Sit Under the Apple Tree (With Anyone Else but Me)."

STEVENS, GEORGE (1904–1975), one of Hollywood's most distinguished directors, made only three musicals: *Nitwits* (1935), *SWING TIME* (1936), and *A DAMSEL IN DISTRESS* (1937). His son is film executive George Stevens, Jr.

STEVENS, RISE (1913–   ), an acclaimed mezzosoprano from the Metropolitan Opera who made many recordings of classical and Broadway music, appeared in three Hollywood musicals: *The Chocolate Soldier* (1941), *GOING MY WAY* (1944), and *Carnegie Hall* (1949), as well as providing the voice of the Good Witch in the animated *Journey Back to Oz* (1972).

STEWART, JAMES (1908–1997), arguably Hollywood's most versatile and personable of all stars, could barely sing or dance but was featured in nine movie musicals during his long and amazing career (1935 to 1991). Stewart appeared as murder suspect John Fowler in *ROSE MARIE* (1936), Manhattanite Ted Barker in *BORN TO DANCE* (1936), skater-turned-producer Larry Hall in *Ice Follies of 1939*, gentle sheriff Tom Destry in *Destry Rides Again* (1939), radio performer Jimmy in *Pot o' Gold* (1941), truck driver Gilbert Young in *ZIEGFELD GIRL* (1941), the clown Buttons in *The Greatest Show on Earth* (1952), the famous bandleader in *THE GLENN MILLER STORY* (1954), and kindly grandfather Clovis Mitchell in *The Magic of Lassie* (1978).

STIGWOOD, ROBERT (1934–   ), the international producer of films, Broadway and West End shows, concerts, and records, presented several of the few movie musicals made in the 1970s, most of them hits. The Australian-born impresario produced *JESUS CHRIST SUPERSTAR* (1973), *TOMMY* (1975), *BUGSY MALONE* (1976), *SATURDAY NIGHT FEVER* (1977), *GREASE* (1978), *Sgt. Pepper's Lonely Hearts Club Band* (1978), and *Times Square* (1980).

STOKOWSKI, LEOPOLD (1882–1977), the renowned and eccentric conductor of the Philadelphia Orchestra for many years, was one of the few international maestros recognized by the general public because of his shock of long hair, flamboyant conducting techniques, and appearances in the movie musicals *BIG BROADCAST OF 1937* (1936), *ONE HUNDRED MEN AND A GIRL* (1937), *FANTASIA* (1940), and *Carnegie Hall* (1949).

STOLL, GEORGE (1905–1985), one of Hollywood's most requested and respected musical conductors for thirty years, supervised the music for many MGM films, including such classics as *BROADWAY MELODY OF 1938* (1937), *BABES IN ARMS* (1939), *STRIKE UP THE BAND* (1940), *FOR ME AND MY GAL* (1942), *CABIN IN THE SKY* (1943), *MEET ME IN ST. LOUIS* (1945), and *ANCHORS AWEIGH* (1945), as well as *The Kissing Bandit* (1949), *THE STUDENT PRINCE* (1954), *Meet Me in Las Vegas* (1956), *JUMBO* (1962), *VIVA LAS VEGAS* (1964), and many others.

STOLLER, MIKE. See Leiber, Jerry

STORMY WEATHER (Fox 1942) offered the grandest collection of African American talent ever assembled in a major Hollywood musical, and the movie itself is an archival treasure trove. LENA HORNE, BILL "BOJANGLES" ROBINSON, THOMAS "FATS" WALLER, CAB CALLOWAY and his band, DOOLEY WILSON, the NICHOLAS BROTHERS, Flournoy Miller, Ada Brown, Babe Wallace, Mae E. Johnson, Benny Carter, and Katherine Dunham and her dancers all were captured on film doing what they did best. Although it seemed like a REVUE, the movie had a storyline that showed tap-dancer Robinson pursuing singer Horne from 1911 to 1936 and then winning her during World War Two. Aside from the fact that it gave Robinson the only leading role of his film career, the plot was dispensable. But the songs and dances (choreographed by Clarence Robinson and Nick Castle) told a story all their own. Waller played the piano and warbled "Ain't Misbehavin,'" Horne crooned the torchy "There's No Two Ways About Love," the Nicholas Brothers exploded with "Jumpin' Jive," Horne and Robinson sang "I Can't Give You Anything But Love," Calloway joined Robinson for "Rhythm Cocktail," Johnson lamented "I Lost My Sugar in Salt Lake City," and Horne delivered the 1933 TED KOEHLER–HAROLD ARLEN title number for the first time in her screen career and it immediately became her signature song.

STORY OF VERNON AND IRENE CASTLE, THE (RKO 1939) was more intriguing as a FRED ASTAIRE–GINGER ROGERS film than as a biography of the famous dance team of pre–World War One. Because they were playing real people and Irene Castle was on the set as an advisor, Rogers and Astaire seemed rather constricted in their dialogue scenes together. But when they took to the dance floor all was forgiven. The plot followed the couple from their first meeting in 1910, their marriage and struggles for recognition, their introduction of the Castle Walk in Paris, their subsequent fame and tour of America, to Vernon's death in a plane crash while preparing to go overseas to fight in the Great War. It was one of the team's least popular films, probably because it didn't have the glitzy, art deco look of their previous movies and somewhat because Astaire died in the end, which audiences did not like. The supporting cast was exceptionally strong: Edna May Oliver, WALTER BRENNAN, Lew Fields, LEONID KINSKEY, Janet Beecher, MARGE CHAMPION, Clarence Derwent, and others. H.C. POTTER directed, HERMES PAN and Astaire choreographed, and the score was made up of period standards and a new romantic ballad "Only When You're in My Arms" by BERT KALMAR, CON CONRAD, and HARRY RUBY.

STOTHART, HERBERT (1885–1949) was a Broadway and film composer and arranger who worked with some of the giants in music but was little known outside the music business. Stothart contributed songs to many Broadway shows in the 1920s and 1930s, three of which were filmed: *Golden Dawn* (1930), *Song of the Flame* (1930), and *ROSE MARIE* (1936). In Hollywood he wrote music for the scores of *Devil May Care* (1929), *The Rogue Song* (1930), *BALALAIKA* (1939), and *I Married an Angel* (1942). But Stothart made his greatest contribution as a music arranger and composer of background scores for such MGM musicals as *New Moon* (1931 and 1940), *THE MERRY WIDOW* (1934), *NAUGHTY MARIETTA* (1935), *A NIGHT AT THE OPERA* (1935), *SAN FRANCISCO* (1936), *THE FIREFLY* (1937), *SWEETHEARTS* (1938), *THE WIZARD OF OZ* (1939), *Bitter Sweet* (1940), *ZIEGFELD GIRL* (1941), *RIO RITA* (1942), *Thousands Cheer* (1943), and many others.

STRAUS, OSCAR (1870–1954) was a composer of over forty operas and operettas in Vienna who saw three of his stage works filmed: *Married in Hollywood* (1929), *THE SMILING LIEUTENANT* (1931), and *The Chocolate Soldier* (1941). Working with various lyricists, he also wrote directly for the screen and scored the musicals *A Lady's Morals* (1930), *ONE HOUR WITH YOU* (1932), and *Make a Wish* (1937).

STREISAND, BARBRA (1942–   ), the only female movie star to be top-ranked in popularity for much of the 1970s, has made only a handful of movie musicals in her astonishing career, but each one was memorable. For her film debut she recreated her stage performance as FANNY BRICE in *FUNNY GIRL* (1968), then managed to override miscasting and triumph as matchmaker Dolly Levi in *HELLO, DOLLY!* (1969). Although Streisand would go on to star in (and sometimes direct and produce) many films, she only rarely returned to the musical genre. She played the kookie Daisy Gamble in *ON A*

CLEAR DAY YOU CAN SEE FOREVER (1969), Fanny Brice again in FUNNY LADY (1975), rising pop singer Esther Hoffman in A STAR IS BORN (1976), for which she also composed the music for the Oscar-winning song "Evergreen," and a village girl questing for education in YENTL (1983), also contributing to the score. Streisand's remarkable singing range, her knack for comedy as well as pathos, and her powerful screen presence have made her one of the era's superstars. It is interesting to consider what she might have accomplished if she had lived during the golden age of movie musicals. She was married to actor Elliott Gould and is presently married to actor James Brolin.

STRIKE UP THE BAND (MGM 1940), the second MICKEY ROONEY–JUDY GARLAND "let's put on a show" musical produced by ARTHUR FREED, kept neither story nor score from the 1930 GERSHWINS' Broadway hit except the title song. High schooler Rooney has a jazz band with Garland as his vocalist, and he wants to take the whole group to Chicago to audition for PAUL WHITEMAN. But the complications include lack of money for bus fare, his mother (Ann Shoemaker) wanting him to become a doctor, and the arrival of rich and pretty JUNE PREISSER as a threat for Garland. After the money is raised by producing a hysterical musical melodrama that showed off Rooney's superb farceur talents, Whiteman arrives in town to play for Preisser's birthday party and puts the school band in a national contest, which they win. There were some slow and maudlin stretches, but for the most part BUSBY BERKELEY's direction and choreography bounced along. The highlights included Garland's wistful rendition of ROGER EDENS' "Nobody" in the local library, Freed and Edens' "Our Love Affair," which the young couple sang and then was played by animated fruits as musicians conducted by Rooney, and the finale in which the title number was performed by multiple bands and chorale groups with creative camera work and editing.

STROMBERG, HUNT (1894–1968) was a Hollywood producer who presented several films at MGM, including eight JEANETTE MacDONALD–NELSON EDDY musicals; he then became a successful independent producer. His musical credits include NAUGHTY MARIETTA (1935), ROSE MARIE (1936), THE GREAT ZIEGFELD (1936), MAYTIME (1937), THE FIREFLY (1937), SWEETHEARTS (1938), I Married an Angel (1942), and Lady of Burlesque (1943).

STROUSE, CHARLES. See Adams, Lee

STUART, GLORIA (1910–), a striking blonde ingenue on screen in the 1930s and 1940s, appeared in sympathetic roles in a handful of musicals, though rarely singing or dancing. She can be seen in ROMAN SCANDALS (1933), GOLD DIGGERS OF 1935, POOR LITTLE RICH GIRL (1936), REBECCA OF SUNNYBROOK FARM (1938), and others. Stuart retired from the screen in 1946 and became a reputable artist. She made quite a stir when she returned to movies five decades later to play the aged Rose in the nonmusical *Titanic* (1997).

STUDENT PRINCE, THE (MGM 1954) was one of the American theatre's most durable of OPERETTAS, so it was surprising that a sound version of the 1924 Broadway hit did not come until the 1950s. But MARIO LANZA's popularity encouaged producer JOE PASTERNAK to go ahead with the project. Lanza recorded the songs, but either because he had put on too much weight to play the young prince or because he broke his contract and walked off the set (or both), the movie was made with slim and handsome Edward Purdom playing the prince and Lanza's voice coming incongruously out of his mouth. The story told of the heir to the throne going off to college in 1894 Heidelberg and falling in love with the zesty beer garden waitress Kathie (ANN BLYTH), only for the lovers to be forced to part when the king dies and the prince must return home to marry the princess the government has picked out for him. Their story was augmented by the presence of some of Hollywood's favorite character actors, including S.Z. SAKALL, LOUIS CALHERN, Edmund Gwenn, and John Williams. The rhapsodic stage score by Dorothy Donnelly and SIGMUND ROMBERG was one of the best in operetta history, and four of the finest numbers were used in the film: "Deep in My Heart," "The Drinking Song," "Golden Days," and "Serenade." PAUL FRANCIS WEBSTER and NICHOLAS BRODSZKY wrote a few news songs as well, the best being the serenading "Beloved" and the hymn "I'll Walk With God."

STYNE, JULE (1905–1994) composed songs for Hollywood, Broadway, Tin Pan Alley, the ballet, and television during his long and fruitful career. A child prodigy at the piano, the London-born Styne got his first job as a vocal coach in movies, soon working his way up to arranger and then composer. Collaborating with various lyricists, Styne wrote the scores for many B pictures in the 1940s, including *Hit Parade of 1941* (1940), *Melody Ranch* (1940), *Puddin' Head* (1941), *Sleepy Time Gal* (1942), *Priorities on Parade* (1942), *The Powers Girl* (1942), and *Hit Parade of 1943*. Two low-budget efforts written with FRANK LOESSER boasted notable scores: *Sis Hopkins* (1941) and *Sweater Girl* (1942). Styne got better assignments with lyricist SAMMY CAHN, and they worked together on nineteen musicals beginning with *Youth on Parade* (1942), followed by *Thumbs Up* (1943), *Step Lively* (1944), *Tonight and Every Night* (1945), *ANCHORS AWEIGH* (1945), *The Kid From Brooklyn* (1946), *Ladies' Man* (1947), *IT HAPPENED IN BROOKLYN* (1947), *ROMANCE ON THE HIGH SEAS* (1948), *It's a Great Feeling* (1949), *The West Point Story* (1950), and others. With lyricist LEO ROBIN he scored *Meet Me After the Show* (1951), *Two Tickets to Broadway* (1951), *My Sister Eileen* (1955), and others. Unlike many of his colleagues, Styne found success in films first and then went on to Broadway in 1948. His stage shows to reach the screen were *GENTLEMEN PREFER BLONDES* (1953) with Robin, *BELLS ARE RINGING* (1960) with BETTY COMDEN and ADOLPH GREEN, *GYPSY* (1962) with STEPHEN SONDHEIM, and *FUNNY GIRL* (1968) with BOB MERRILL. Styne's last original film musical was *What a Way to Go* (1964), but he remained active on Broadway until 1993. His music can be characterized as tuneful, bold, and in the brash Broadway style.

SUMMER HOLIDAY (MGM 1947) was an atmospheric piece of Americana in the vein of *MEET ME IN ST. LOUIS* (1944), but it never caught on even if it was an exceptional musical in all departments. Based on Eugene O'Neill's only comedy, *Ah, Wilderness!* (1933), the story centered on the Miller family of Connecticut around the turn of the century, particularly the teenage son Richard (MICKEY ROONEY) and his coming of age. Walter Huston and Selena Royle played his parents, AGNES MOOREHEAD his spinster aunt, FRANK MORGAN the alcoholic who loves her, and GLORIA DeHAVEN the innocent girl Richard pines for. When the youthful sweethearts are separated by DeHaven's father, Richard goes to the local bar, where he gets drunk and has a run-in with saloon singer MARILYN MAXWELL before sobering up in time to be reunited with his true love. ROUBEN MAMOULIAN directed the period piece with precision and warmth, and WALTER PLUNKETT's costumes and CEDRIC GIBBONS and Jack Martin Smith's decor were wonderfully evocative. RALPH BLANE and HARRY WARREN's unappreciated score is filled with rich melody and sincere sentiments: the amiable "Our Home Town," which introduced the members of the Miller household, the innocent "Afraid to Fall in Love," the mature reflection "Spring Isn't Everything," the yearning "Wish I Had a Braver Heart," and the merry travel song "The Stanley Steamer."

SUMMER STOCK (MGM 1950) differed little from the MICKEY ROONEY–JUDY GARLAND youthful backstagers of a decade earlier except that GENE KELLY was Garland's co-star and the troupers putting on a show were all adults. When some Manhattan actors are desperate for a place to perform, GLORIA DeHAVEN suggests the barn on her family farm in New England. They all descend on the homestead, but DeHaven's sister (Garland) is not thrilled and insists that the actors help with chores to pay for food and lodging. But to no one's surprise, she changes her tune when she slips into a romance with the company's author-performer (Kelly) and even takes over the leading role in the show when DeHaven can't go on. What was barely palatable with kids looked even more ridiculous with adults, but the spirited musical numbers relieved the tedium of the plot. MACK GORDON and HARRY WARREN wrote most of the songs and, as choreographed by NICK CASTLE and Kelly, they all deserved a better vehicle. Garland sang the yearning ballad "Friendly Star " and the carefree "If You Feel Like Singing, Sing" while Kelly wooed her with "You, Wonderful You" (by JACK BROOKS, SAUL CHAP-

LIN, and Warren) and then performed a remarkable dance solo in which he tapped and ripped apart a floor full of newspapers. But the musical highlight of the film was Garland's jazzy version of the 1930 standard "Get Happy" by TED KOEHLER and HAROLD ARLEN. The number was filmed months after the rest of the movie and a slimmer, more vital Garland is unmistakable. CHARLES WALTERS directed the frail script as best he could and got a lot of help from supporting cast members EDDIE BRACKEN, PHIL SILVERS, MARJORIE MAIN, Ray Collins, HANS CONREID, CAROL HANEY, CARLETON CARPENTER, and Nita Bieber.

SUN VALLEY SERENADE (Fox 1941) was SONJA HENIE's best film, a vibrant Big Band musical featuring GLENN MILLER and a crackerjack score by MACK GORDON and HARRY WARREN. When Miller's band sponsors a Norwegian child refugee but find themselves saddled with grown-up Henie, pianist JOHN PAYNE is put in charge of her and they all head to a gig at a resort in Sun Valley, Idaho. The complications arising from Henie's falling for Payne while he tries to juggle the affections of other women in his life made up the plot, which seemed harmless enough when set on the snow-covered slopes. The cast also featured MILTON BERLE, LYNN BARI (dubbed by Pat Friday), JOAN DAVIS, and Martha Tilton, as well as Miller regulars Ray Anthony, Bill May, Tex Beneke, Paula Kelly, Hal McIntye, and the Modernaires. The biggest hit song to come from the film was "Chattanooga Choo-Choo," played and vocalized by Miller and his group, then sung by teenage DORO-THY DANDRIDGE and danced by the flying NICHOLAS BROTHERS. Also in the score were "It Happened in Sun Valley," "I Know Why (And So Do You)," and "The Kiss Polka." Miller's band played its signature number "In the Mood" (by Andy Razaf and Joe Garland), and for the finale there was a stunning ice skating sequence choreographed by HERMES PAN that had Henie gliding across black ice.

SUNDBERG, CLINTON (1906–1987) was a Broadway and West End actor who turned to the movies in the 1940s and played character roles in many comedies and musicals. Often cast as a subservient butler or sympathetic clerk, Sundberg can be seen in the musicals *GOOD NEWS* (1947), *EASTER PARADE* (1948), *A Date With Judy* (1948), *The Kissing Bandit* (1948), *WORDS AND MUSIC* (1948), *THE BARKLEYS OF BROADWAY* (1949), *IN THE GOOD OLD SUMMERTIME* (1949), *ANNIE GET YOUR GUN* (1950), *The Toast of New Orleans* (1950), *ON THE RIVIERA* (1951), *THE BELLE OF NEW YORK* (1952), *The Caddy* (1953), *The Wonderful World of the Brothers Grimm* (1962), and many others.

SUNNY SIDE UP (Fox 1929) was an important step in the new musical talkie genre as it experimented with ways to present song and dance outside the confines of a stage show. The illustrious team of DE SYLVA, (LEW) BROWN, and

HENDERSON wrote the songs and script about a poor Yorkville girl, JANET GAYNOR, whose singing of the cheery title song so dazzles millionaire CHARLES FARRELL that he puts on a charity show at his Long Island estate featuring her. The story resembled a half dozen Cinderella musicals seen on Broadway in the 1920s, but director DAVID BUTLER and choreographer SEYMOUR FELIX placed the musical numbers on the street and in other nontheatrical locales, so it seemed rather cinematic. The songs were tuneful and memorable, especially the enchanting "I'm a Dreamer, Aren't We All?," the cozy "If I Had a Talking Picture of You," and the buoyant title number. There was also a clever production number for "Turn On the Heat," in which fur-clad chorines in the frozen North shed their coats to reveal bathing suits, palm trees came up out of the ice, fire rose from everywhere, and the girls escaped the heat by diving into a cool lagoon.

SUTHERLAND, A. EDWARD (1895–1974) was a performer in the Keystone Kops silents before becoming a director of features in 1925. His specialty was comedies (including several with W.C. FIELDS) and musicals, which Sutherland directed until the late 1940s, when he moved on to television. Among his musical credits were *Close Harmony* (1929), *Pointed Heels* (1929), *The Sap From Syracuse* (1930), *Palmy Days* (1931), *INTERNATIONAL HOUSE* (1933), *Too Much Harmony* (1933), *MISSISSIPPI* (1935), *Poppy* (1936), *Every Day's a Holiday* (1937), *The Boys From Syracuse* (1940), *ONE NIGHT IN THE TROPICS* (1942), *Dixie* (1943), and *Follow the Boys* (1944).

SUTTON, GRADY (1908–1995), a durable character actor who played paunchy hicks and other types in dozens of films and television shows, popped up in the movie musicals *College Humor* (1933), *Pigskin Parade* (1936), *Waikiki Wedding* (1937), *ALEXANDER'S RAGTIME BAND* (1938), *ANCHORS AWEIGH* (1945), *A STAR IS BORN* (1954), *WHITE CHRISTMAS* (1954), *JUMBO* (1962), *MY FAIR LADY* (1964), *Paradise Hawaiian Style* (1966), and many more.

SWARTHOUT, GLADYS (1904–1969) was a beautiful mezzosoprano from the Metropolitan Opera who joined the parade of opera singers brought to Hollywood to compete with GRACE MOORE and others. Swarthout was very photogenic and displayed acting talent in her four movie musicals, but she never caught on and left films for concerts, radio, and later television. Her musical credits were *Rose of the Rancho* (1935), *Give Us This Night* (1936), *Champagne Waltz* (1937), and *Romance in the Dark* (1938).

SWEET ADELINE (Warner 1935) was a surprisingly faithful screen version of the 1929 Broadway hit which starred HELEN MORGAN and featured an overwhelming score by OSCAR HAMMERSTEIN and JEROME KERN. Eight of the stage songs were kept, but IRENE DUNNE played the central character on film, a beer hall singer at the turn of the century who is admired by many men as she climbs the ladder to Broadway stardom but loves only songwriter Donald Woods. Also in the cast were HUGH HERBERT, NED SPARKS, Joseph Cawthorn, WINIFRED SHAW, LOUIS CALHERN, PHIL REGAN, Dorothy Dare, and Noah Berry, all under the competent direction of MERVYN LEROY. "Why Was I Born?" was the most famous number from the stage score, but just as thrilling were "Here Am I," " 'Twas Not So Long Ago," and "Don't Ever Leave Me."

SWEET CHARITY (Universal 1969) was BOB FOSSE's directorial film debut, and he filled it with jazzy crosscutting, stark camera angles, and big garish performances that thrilled some spectators and annoyed others. But his choreography was unquestionably dynamic and a major talent was clearly at work here. The 1966 Broadway hit (which Fosse had also staged) was little more than a vehicle for GWEN VERDON, so the story's weaknesses were revealed when a competent but less dynamic SHIRLEY MacLAINE took on the role of Charity, a taxi dancer with a heart of gold and no luck in love. John McMartin repeated his stage performance as the weak-kneed man who almost marries her, RICARDO MONTALBAN was the Italian movie star she almost has an affair with, and STUBBY KAYE was the scene-stealing Herman who sings "I Love to Cry at Weddings" when she almost gets married. Strong support also came from Chita Rivera and Paula Kelly as Charity's chums and SAMMY DAVIS, JR., as a swinging evangelist who promotes the "Rhythm of Life." Other songs in the vibrant DOROTHY FIELDS–Cy Coleman score included the cool and cynical "Big Spender," the jubilant "If My Friends Could See Me Now," the determined "There's Got to Be Something Better Than This," and the merry march "I'm a Brass Band" that used various New York City locations effectively.

SWEETHEARTS (MGM 1938) was a screen rarity: an OPERETTA set in contemporary times and one that downplayed sentiment and romance for three-dimensional characters and sassy dialogue. Much of the credit was due to Dorothy Parker and Alan Campbell, who wrote the script, tossing out the book (about a prince and princess in disguise) and lyrics of VICTOR HERBERT's 1913 stage work and coming up with a modern tale about a married couple, JEANETTE MacDONALD and NELSON EDDY, who have been performing in a Broadway show called *Sweethearts* for six years. Bored with the theatre (and a little with each other too), the twosome are encouraged by the crafty agent REGINALD GARDINER to head for Hollywood, much to the dismay of the show's producer FRANK MORGAN, author MISCHA AUER, and composer HERMAN BING. Once in Tinsel Town, the couple break up over a misunderstanding and are treated crassly by the movies, so they are reunited and back on Broadway by the big finale. ROBERT WRIGHT and GEORGE FORREST provided the new lyrics, so the modern tone of the screenplay was continued when the characters broke into the old songs: "Wooden Shoes," "Every Lover Must Meet His Fate," "Pretty as a Picture," and the sweeping title number. W.S. VAN DYKE directed the cast, which also included Florence Rice, DOUGLAS McPHAIL, Allyn Joslyn, Gene Lockhart, RAY BOLGER, GEORGE BARBIER, and Raymond Walburn. ALBERTINA RASCH choreographed the production numbers, the most impressive being the show-within-a-show rendition of the title song. It was MGM's first film in the three-color Technicolor process and, with its glittering costumes and lush settings, was a delight for the eye as well as the ear.

SWING TIME (RKO 1936) has some pretty convoluted plot twists and turns, but it still ranks as a strong candidate for the best of the FRED ASTAIRE and GINGER ROGERS musicals. Irresponsible Astaire takes a break from gambling (and continually leaving his fiancee Betty Furness at the altar) to slip into a dance school, where he falls for instructor Rogers even though she cares more for bandleader Georges Metaxa. But the twosome dance so well together that they are soon auditioning at a swank supper club and find success just about the time they find love. The thin story allowed for plenty of dance, and all of it was superb: the couple's effervescent "Waltz in Swing Time," Astaire's rhythmic "Bojangles of Harlem," the seductive *pas de deux* "Never Gonna Dance," and the clever "Pick Yourself Up," in which Astaire pretends he cannot dance very well in order to keep getting lessons from Rogers. HERMES PAN and Astaire did the choreography, and DOROTHY FIELDS and JEROME KERN wrote what is arguably the finest movie score by either of them. "A Fine Romance" was a wry musical conversation with the lovers quarreling in a snow-covered wood, and Astaire sang the Oscar-winning "The Way You Look Tonight" to Ginger as she lathered her head with shampoo. GEORGE STEVENS directed with a sharp eye, and the supporting cast shone as brightly as the stars, particularly HELEN BRODERICK as Rogers' acid chum, VICTOR MOORE as Astaire's bumbling sidekick, and ERIC BLORE as the frustrated dance school owner.

T

TAKE ME OUT TO THE BALL GAME (MGM 1949) was one of the few movie musicals dealing with sports, but the main characters, turn-of-the-century shortstop GENE KELLY and second baseman FRANK SINATRA, worked as vaudevillians during the off season in order to ensure enough opportunities for song and dance. Scriptwriters Harry Tugend and GEORGE WELLS also had their work cut out for them when swimming star ESTHER WILLIAMS was cast as the lady who buys the team and they had to work in some aquatic opportunities. (She ended up taking a balletic dip in a pool in one scene.) The story was a traditional triangle with bashful Sinatra infatuated with Williams, but she has her eye on the brash Kelly while oversexed BETTY GARRETT is chasing after Sinatra. The predictability of it all was relieved by several playful production numbers staged by Kelly and STANLEY DONEN while BUSBY BERKELEY directed (for the last time) the tale breezily. BETTY COMDEN, ADOLPH GREEN, and ROGER EDENS penned most of the sprightly songs: Garrett trying to seduce Sinatra with "It's Fate, Baby, It's Fate," Sinatra dreaming of "The Right Girl for Me," Kelly, Sinatra, and team member JULES MUNCHIN's daffy trios "Yes, Indeedy" and "O'Brien to Ryan to Goldberg," and the ensemble's patriotic paean "Strictly U.S.A." Kelly's most impressive choreographic feat was a barrel dance set to "The Hat My Father Wore on St. Patrick's Day" (by William Jerome and Jean Schwartz), and he joined Sinatra for a soft-shoe version of the 1908 title song.

TALBOT, LYLE (1902–1996) managed to play both heavies in melodramas and leading men in light comedies and musicals for three decades before finding a whole new career in situation comedies on television. Talbot had considerable stage experience before he made his film debut in 1932. He can be seen in the movie musicals *ONE NIGHT OF LOVE* (1934), *The Singing Kid* (1936), *SECOND FIDDLE* (1939), *UP IN ARMS* (1944), *WITH A SONG*

IN MY HEART (1952), *THERE'S NO BUSINESS LIKE SHOW BUSINESS* (1954), and others.

TAMBLYN, RUSS (1934–   ), one of Hollywood's most athletic and nimble dancers, began as a child performer on stage and radio and then started playing juvenile roles on film in 1948. Tamblyn is most remembered as the youngest Pontipee brother Gideon in *SEVEN BRIDES FOR SEVEN BROTHERS* (1954) and as Riff, the leader of the Jets gang, in *WEST SIDE STORY* (1961). The boyish actor's other movie musicals were *HIT THE DECK* (1955), *Tom Thumb* (1958), *The Wonderful World of the Brothers Grimm* (1962), and *Follow the Boys* (1963). He continued to act on screen and on television into the 1990s.

TAMIROFF, AKIM (1899–1972) was a Russian-born and -trained actor who came to America in 1923 with the Moscow Art Theatre and stayed to have a long and notable career first on the stage and then in Hollywood. Tamiroff usually played villains, foreigners, authority figures, or eccentrics and was known for using his thick Eastern European accent for chills or laughs. He can be seen in the musicals *THE MERRY WIDOW* (1934), *NAUGHTY MARIETTA* (1935), *GO INTO YOUR DANCE* (1935), *BIG BROADCAST OF 1936* (1935), *HIGH, WIDE AND HANDSOME* (1937), *CAN'T HELP SINGING* (1944), and others.

TAUROG, NORMAN (1899–1981) was a favorite director of the studios, since his pictures always had high box office appeal on a low budget. Acting as a child in silents before becoming a director making shorts in 1919, Taurog tackled all genres of film and managed to turn many of them into well-crafted hits. He was particularly successful in directing a string of JERRY LEWIS–DEAN MARTIN and ELVIS PRESLEY films. Among his nearly forty musicals were *Lucky Boy* (1929), *Follow the Leader* (1930), *THE PHANTOM PRESIDENT* (1932), *WE'RE NOT DRESSING* (1934), *COLLEGE RHYTHM* (1934), *BIG BROADCAST OF 1936* (1935), *Strike Me Pink* (1936), *Mad About Music* (1938), *BROADWAY MELODY OF 1940*, *Little Nellie Kelly* (1940), *Presenting Lily Mars* (1943), *Girl Crazy* (1943), *WORDS AND MUSIC* (1948), *The Toast of New Orleans* (1950), *Rich, Young and Pretty* (1951), *Living It Up* (1954), *Pardners* (1956), *GI Blues* (1960), *BLUE HAWAII* (1962), *It Happened at the World's Fair* (1963), *Live a Little, Love a Little* (1968), and many more.

TAYLOR, DAME ELIZABETH (1932–   ) represented what a movie star was for several decades and still commanded attention even after she stopped making movies on a regular basis. On the screen since she was a ten-year-old, the dark-haired beauty was placed in the musicals *A Date With Judy* (1948) and *Rhapsody* (1954) even though she was hardly known for her singing or dancing talents. Years later Taylor returned to the screen musical with two ill-fated ventures: *The Blue Bird* (1976) and *A Little Night Music* (1978). Among her many husbands were producer Mike Todd, actors Michael Wilding and Richard Burton, hotelier Nick Hilton, and senator John Warner.

TAYLOR, ROBERT (1911–1969) was a dashing leading man who rivaled CLARK GABLE in his appeal to women in the 1930s and 1940s. The romantic actor was featured in three Hollywood musicals, *BROADWAY MELODY OF 1936* (1935), *BROADWAY MELODY OF 1938* (1937), and *This Is My Affair* (1937), as well as a bit part in *I Love Melvin* (1952).

TEMPLE, SHIRLEY (1928–   ), the most popular CHILD STAR in the history of the movies, was making bit appearances in short films and features by the age of four, but it was her "Baby Take a Bow" number in *Stand Up and Cheer* (1934), which caught the attention of audiences and sent the curly-haired moppet on her way. While much of her appeal had to do with Depression-weary audiences seeing Temple as a symbol of innocence and optimism, there was no question she was one of the most talented kids ever put on film. Not only could Temple sing and dance but she had the acting know-how to make sentimentality warm and funny. Her movie musicals were *Little Miss Marker* (1934), *Baby Take a Bow* (1934), *Bright Eyes* (1934), *The Little Colonel* (1935), *CURLY TOP* (1935), *The Littlest Rebel* (1935), *CAPTAIN JANUARY* (1936), *POOR LITTLE RICH GIRL* (1936), *Dimples* (1936), *Stowaway* (1936), *REBECCA OF SUNNYBROOK FARM* (1938), *Little Miss Broadway* (1938), *Just Around the Corner* (1938), *The Little Princess* (1939), *The Blue Bird* (1940), *Young People* (1940), and *Honeymoon* (1947). She mostly played variations of the same character, the optimistic orphan who could make the most jaded of adults behave with humanity, and when she outgrew that persona her popularity waned. After attempting television in the late 1950s, Temple took up politics and charitable causes and even served as ambassador to Ghana and Czechoslovakia for a while. She has been married to actor John Agar and television executive Charles Black.

TERRY, RUTH (1920–   ), a band singer who was featured in *ALEXANDER'S RAGTIME BAND* (1938), was often starred in 1940s musicals but rarely in grade A pictures. Terry's musical credits include *Love and Hisses* (1937), *Hold That Coed* (1938), *Blondie Goes Latin* (1941), *Heart of the Golden West* (1942), *Hands Across the Border* (1943), *The Man From Music Mountain* (1943), *Lake Placid Serenade* (1944), *Jamboree* (1944), and others.

THANK YOUR LUCKY STARS (Warner 1943) was probably the best of the all-star REVUES the studios put out during World War Two to entertain the troops abroad and their families back home. Like the others, the songs were thinly strung together by the most negligible of plots: songwriter JOAN

LESLIE, crooner DENNIS MORGAN, and fledgling song-and-dance hopeful EDDIE CANTOR try to break into the movie business while producers EDWARD EVERETT HORTON and S.Z. SAKALL try to put together a big benefit show, everybody and everything converging together for said show at the climax of the movie. More intriguing than the story were the oddities to be found in the film, such as Cantor also playing himself as an egotistical, talentless star who steps on everybody beneath him. FRANK LOESSER and ARTHUR SCHWARTZ wrote the sparkling songs, and WARNER BROTHERS pulled in everyone on contract to sing them, even those not known for their musical talents. This led to some delightful surprises, such as Errol Flynn spoofing his masculinity with "That's What You Jolly Well Get" and ANN SHERIDAN arguing "Love Isn't Born, It's Made"; and also to some embarrassments, such as John Garfield trying to croon the classic JOHNNY MERCER–HAROLD ARLEN standard "Blues in the Night." Other memorable moments: DINAH SHORE singing the pastiche number "How Sweet You Are" to a group of Civil War soldiers, Willie Best and a chorus of Harlem residents encouraging "Ice Cold Katie" (HATTIE McDANIEL) to marry her GI sweetheart before he goes off to war, Leslie and Morgan's jaunty duet "I'm Ridin' for a Fall," Shore and company's cheery delivery of the title song, and, best of all, Bette Davis lamenting "They're Either Too Young or Too Old."

THANKS A MILLION (Fox 1935) benefited from a sharp and knowing script by Nunnally Johnson about vaudevillian DICK POWELL, who runs for governor on the strength of his singing rather than his political ability. FRED ALLEN (in his screen debut) was his manager, an entertainment agent who knows best what the public wants. ANN DVORAK was the woman who loved Powell but walked out on him when he was elected unfairly; so he resigned and got her back. But the voters wouldn't accept his resignation, so he returned to office with Dvorak's approval. It was sassy stuff, and ROY DEL RUTH pulled no punches in directing the musical satire. GUS KAHN and ARTHUR JOHNSTON provided the songs, the best two being the cocky "I'm Sitting High on a Hilltop" and the heartfelt title number. DARRYL F. ZANUCK produced the musical, and it was the first box office hit for the newly formed 20TH CENTURY–FOX studio. The story was remade as *If I'm Lucky* (1946) with PERRY COMO as the candidate.

THAT NIGHT IN RIO. See *Folies Bergère de Paris*

THAT'S ENTERTAINMENT (MGM 1974) was a documentary about the variety and genius of MGM musicals compiled by Jack Haley, Jr., and it did more to revitalize interest in the golden age of film musicals than a hundred nights on the late late show. The familiar classic moments from *THE WIZARD OF OZ* (1939), *THE HARVEY GIRLS* (1946), *SINGIN' IN THE RAIN* (1952), and others were nicely balanced with selections from oft-forgotten films like *THE GREAT ZIEGFELD* (1936) and the ESTHER WIL-LIAMS aquatic vehicles. The narration by FRANK SINATRA, DEBBIE REYNOLDS, FRED ASTAIRE, ELIZABETH TAYLOR, GENE KELLY, and others struck some as gratuitous, but the clips were everything. For some in the audience it was the first time they had seen much of the footage, and for most it was the first time on a movie screen. The popularity of the documentary prompted *That's Entertainment, Part Two* (MGM 1976), which suffered in comparison. Not only were the clips less thrilling but they were badly truncated and haphazardly presented. Aging Kelly and Astaire sang new lyrics to the HOWARD DIETZ–ARTHUR SCHWARTZ title tune, and the result was more embarrassing than nostalgic. Still, there were some pleasing moments and even an inept documentary about gold still shone on occasion. *That's Dancing* (1985) sought out dance footage not already covered in the previous films, and *That's Entertainment! III* (1994) used "never before seen" footage to fill out its running time.

THERE'S NO BUSINESS LIKE SHOW BUSINESS (Fox 1954) was the last musical IRVING BERLIN worked on, writing two new numbers to go with the twelve pulled out of the proverbial trunk. As a showcase for his song catalog and the mostly talented cast, the movie was quite satisfying. As a story it was lengthy and maudlin as it followed the ups and downs of a show biz family: ETHEL MERMAN and DAN DAILEY as the parents and DONALD O'CONNOR, MITZI GAYNOR, and Johnnie Ray as their three performing offspring. O'Connor has a drinking problem, especially when he loses his heart to showgirl MARILYN MONROE and can't win her, and Ray throws the family a curve by deciding to become a priest. But it all worked out in the end, and the musical numbers helped one forget the plot by the big finale. Some of the highlights along the way included the foursome in the vaudeville spot "When the Midnight Choo-Choo Leaves for Alabam'," Merman and Dailey in the duets "Play a Simple Melody" and "A Pretty Girl Is Like a Melody," Monroe's sensual renditions of "Heat Wave" and "After You Get What You Want You Don't Want It," O'Connor singing "A Man Chases a Girl (Until She Catches Him)" and then dancing with some statues come to life, and the ensemble claiming the title song and having fun with "Alexander's Ragtime Band" by performing it as a French, Scottish, and Swiss number. WALTER LANG directed, ROBERT ALTON and JACK COLE choreographed, and the studio had a hit.

THIS IS SPINAL TAP (Embassy 1984) was a mock ROCKUMENTARY that spoofed the tell-all films about rock groups on tour. Director Rob Reiner played a documentary director joining a has-been British rock band called Spinal Tap as they tour the States and find a less than enthusiastic reception. Interviews, cameo appearances, and footage of the rehearsals and concerts were devastatingly accurate and very funny, if a bit uncomfortable at times. Christopher Guest, Harry Shearer, R.J. Parnell, and David Kaff were the members of the band and, with Reiner and Michael McKean, collaborated on the bogus heavy-metal songs like "Big Bottom" and "Hell Hole." The comic documentary became a cult favorite and garnered such a following that the cast reassembled a decade later and made some music videos and went on tour for real.

THIS IS THE ARMY (Warner 1943) was a fund-raising movie based on the 1942 Broadway fund-raising revue, the proceeds for both going to the Army Emergency Relief Fund. Because the days of the Hollywood REVUE were long gone, a plot was devised to justify the parade of numbers performed by stars, enlisted men, or both. Starting in 1918, the story has GEORGE MURPHY putting on a benefit show to raise money for the Armed Forces. A generation later, his son RONALD REAGAN is putting on a similar show and its preparation and presentation framed the IRVING BERLIN songs. Even with the spirit of the moment passed, much of the movie is still quite effective, with director MICHAEL CURTIZ moving things along well and choreographers LEROY PRINZ and Robert Sidney finding a nice balance between military maneuvers and dance. The most intriguing piece of footage is Berlin himself, dressed in a World War One private's uniform, singing "Oh, How I Hate to Get Up in the Morning" in his thin, sincere voice just as he had on Broadway in 1918. Other musical highlights included KATE SMITH singing "God Bless America," James Burell explaining "I'm Getting Tired So I Can Sleep" and dream of his girl, Earl Oxford lamenting "I Left My Heart at the Stage Door Canteen," and the full company of 350 soldiers proclaiming "This Is the Army, Mr. Jones."

THOMAS, DANNY (1914–1991) was a comic-singer who appeared in vaudeville, nightclubs, and films but reached fame as an actor and producer in television (*Make Room for Daddy*). The hawk-nosed performer had his best movie role as Jerry Golding in the first remake of *THE JAZZ SINGER* (1953), but he can also be seen in the musicals *The Unfinished Dance* (1947), *Big City* (1948), *Call Me Mister* (1951), *I'll See You in My Dreams* (1952), and *Looking for Love* (1964). Thomas was usually cast as Jewish or other ethnic types, although he was a Catholic from Michigan. He was the father of actress Marlo Thomas.

THOMPSON, KAY (1902–1998), a multitalented woman who acted, sang, composed music, wrote lyrics, and did vocal arrangements, made only three movie appearances but worked behind the scenes of many other films. Thompson is most remembered as the flamboyant editor Maggie Prescott in *FUNNY FACE* (1957), but she can be seen briefly in *Manhattan Merry-Go-Round* (1937) and *The Kid From Brooklyn* (1946).

THOROUGHLY MODERN MILLIE (Universal 1967) was a nostalgic yet satirical spoof of the Jazz Age, silent films, and movie musicals themselves.

Flapper JULIE ANDREWS comes to New York to work as a secretary and find a dream husband. She lives with her best friend Mary Tyler Moore in a rooming house run by BEATRICE LILLIE, who traffics in white slavery as a sideline. Paper clip millionaire James Fox loves Andrews, and pipe-smoking gent John Gavin is after Moore, but it took some time and a repertoire of period tunes to get them together. A special treat was the appearance of Carol Channing as a wealthy widow who loves daredevil stunts. Richard Morris wrote the featherheaded script, and ROSS HUNTER directed with old-fashioned title cards, iris-openings and closings, and actors winking at the camera. In addition to 1920s standards such as "Baby Face," "Do It Again," and "I'm Sittin' on Top of the World," SAMMY CAHN and JAMES VAN HEUSEN wrote the zesty title song and a dance-song spoof called "The Tapioca."

THORPE, RICHARD (1896–1991) was a Hollywood director from 1923 until 1967, known for his proficiency and handling of stars as varied as ESTHER WILLIAMS to ELVIS PRESLEY. Among his sixteen musicals were *Rainbow Over Broadway* (1933), *TWO GIRLS AND A SAILOR* (1944), *Thrill of a Romance* (1945), *Fiesta* (1947), *A Date With Judy* (1948), *THREE LITTLE WORDS* (1950), *THE GREAT CARUSO* (1951), *THE STUDENT PRINCE* (1954), *Athena* (1954), *Ten Thousand Bedrooms* (1957), *JAILHOUSE ROCK* (1957), *Follow the Boys* (1963), and *Fun in Acapulco* (1963).

THREE CABALLEROS, THE (Disney/RKO 1945) was a Donald Duck cartoon, an anthology program, a musical celebration of Latin America, and a travelogue, all wrapped up with dizzying visuals and expert animation. It was a one-of-a-kind film that still pleases audiences. The movie is structured around a series of gifts that Donald (voice of Clarence Nash) receives in the mail for his birthday. Each package contains either a story, pop-up book, or film that transports him to Mexico and Brazil, where, with his pal the parrot Joe Carioca (José Olivera), they attend a bull fight, see some local folk tales animated for them, and ogle the lovely ladies south of the border. The songs, sung in Portuguese, Spanish, and English, ranged from the romantic "You Belong to My Heart" to the dreamy "Baia" to the raucous title number performed by Donald, Carioca and the feathered Panchito (Joaquin Garay) in a surrealistic frenzy of animation. The finished print sat on the shelves for a year while WALT DISNEY waited for Technicolor film to become available during the wartime shortage. But when the movie finally opened it was a box office hit, and it found a new audience when re-released on video four decades later.

THREE LITTLE GIRLS IN BLUE. See *Moon Over Miami*

THREE LITTLE WORDS (MGM 1950) differed from most BIOGRAPHICAL MUSICALS in that the central characters, lyricist BERT KALMAR and composer HARRY RUBY, were not household names and GEORGE

WELLS' screenplay was more interested in the two men than in a series of lavish production numbers. FRED ASTAIRE played Kalmar, a hoofer who turned to lyric writing after a knee injury ended his dancing days. RED SKELTON was Ruby, who was more interested in baseball and girls than in songwriting and needed continual prodding by his partner. VERA-ELLEN (vocals dubbed by Anita Ellis) was Mrs. Kalmar, and Arlene Dahl played Mrs. Ruby, the two women who bring the team back together after a falling out. Although some of the Kalmar-Rudy songs were instantly recognizable, there were many forgotten gems in the film, and as staged by HERMES PAN, they made for some delectable surprises. Astaire and Vera-Ellen sang the duet "Where Did You Get That Girl?" and danced to "Mr. and Mrs. Hoofer at Home," GLORIA DeHAVEN played her own mother, Mrs. Carter DeHaven, and sang "Who's Sorry Now," and DEBBIE REYNOLDS impersonated the "Boop-Boop-a-Doop" girl HELEN KANE and sang "I Wanna Be Loved By You" with the real Kane providing the vocals. Also in the cast were KEENAN WYNN, Gale Robbins, Harry Shannon, CARLETON CARPENTER, PHIL REGAN as himself, and the actual Harry Ruby in a cameo as a baseball player.

TIBBETT, LAWRENCE (1896–1960), perhaps the world's greatest operatic baritone of the 1920s, was featured in six movie musicals in the 1930s, one of the first opera singers to attempt talkies. Tibbett's film credits were *The Rogue Song* (1930), *New Moon* (1930), *The Prodigal* (1931), *Cuban Love Song* (1931), *Metropolitan* (1935), and *Under Your Spell* (1936).

TILL THE CLOUDS ROLL BY (MGM 1946) probably packed more stars in than any of the other BIOGRAPHICAL MUSICALS Hollywood had manufactured over the years, and it was a good thing too because the storyline for the life of composer genius JEROME KERN was as dull as it was inaccurate. The picture starts in 1927 with the opening night of *SHOW BOAT*, and the fifteen-minute version of that landmark musical, featuring KATHRYN GRAYSON, TONY MARTIN, LENA HORNE, and others, was beautifully done. Then the plot jumps back to the young and struggling Kern (Robert Walker) as he gets advice from teacher Van Heflin, goes to England and meets his future bride Dorothy Patrick, and eventually becomes famous. Three different directors contributed to the film, and none of them could breathe life into it anytime the music stopped. Luckily it didn't stop often, and over two dozen Kern songs were paraded by with professional panache. JUDY GARLAND, as 1920s Broadway star MARILYN MILLER, got to sing "Who?" and "Look for the Silver Lining," a young ANGELA LANSBURY got to do her own vocals with the coy "How'd You Like to Spoon With Me?," DINAH SHORE recalled "The Last Time I Saw Paris," Grayson performed the dreamy "Long Ago and Far Away," Martin did justice to the entrancing "All the Things You Are," and JUNE ALLYSON showed a wry sense of humor with "Cleopatterer." ROBERT ALTON did the spirited choreography, the dance highlight being Allyson and RAY McDONALD's vivacious version of the title song. Some numbers were oddly out of sync, such as a tuxedoed FRANK SINATRA crooning "Ol' Man River" like a lounge singer, but for the most part producer ARTHUR FREED knew how to use the talent available on the studio lot and he used them well.

TIN PAN ALLEY (Fox 1940) was the only musical to feature both of the 1940s' favorite blondes, ALICE FAYE and BETTY GRABLE, though Faye's was clearly the leading role. They played performing sisters between the years 1915 to 1939 (though neither aged a day) who become involved with two songwriters, JOHN PAYNE and JACK OAKIE, as they struggle to make their music publishing company succeed in Tin Pan Alley. MACK GORDON and HARRY WARREN wrote one new number for the film, the hit "You Say the Sweetest Things, Baby," and the rest of the score was comprised of old standards, some of which were not correct for the period. All four stars, joined by the NICHOLAS BROTHERS, Allen Jenkins, BILLY GILBERT, Esther Ralston, and others, were in fine form as they delivered such favorites as "The Sheik of Araby," "K-K-K-Katy," "Honeysuckle Rose," and "Moonlight Bay." 20TH CENTURY–FOX retold the story in *I'll Get By* (1950).

TOBIAS, GEORGE (1901–1980), a character actor with many movie and television credits, played everything from gangsters to buffoons beginning with his film debut in 1939. Among Tobias' screen musicals were *BALA-LAIKA* (1939), *YANKEE DOODLE DANDY* (1942), *THIS IS THE ARMY* (1943), *THANK YOUR LUCKY STARS* (1943) *My Wild Irish Rose* (1947), *THE GLENN MILLER STORY* (1954), *The Seven Little Foys* (1955), *SILK STOCKINGS* (1957), and others.

TOMMY (Hemdale 1975) was director KEN RUSSELL's spaced-out movie version of the trail-blazing rock opera by The Who that he filled with bizarre images, over-the-top performances, and pretentious symbolism. The storyline of the opera is strange enough (about a boy struck deaf, dumb, and blind when he witnesses his father's murder and how he survives sexual abuse by his uncle to become a pinball-machine guru and the leader of a cult of pinball worshipers), but Russell heaped on his own incongruities such as a temple honoring MARILYN MONROE, Tommy's mother experiencing an orgasm as colored liquids flood her apartment, and a crucified Tommy with a crown of flowers rather than thorns. Rock singer Roger Daltry captured the innocence of Tommy, ANN-MARGARET was stunning as his oddball mother, Tina Turner was the Acid Queen, Elton John the Pinball Wizard, and others, such as Eric Clapton, Keith Moon, Oliver Reed, and Jack Nicholson, did their bit. The film was a moderate success at its release but has gathered a cult following of sorts over the years.

TONE, FRANCHOT (1905–1968), the dashing leading man who excelled at playing rich playboys and men of privilege, appeared in a dozen movie musicals, although he rarely sang or danced in them. Tone can be seen in *DANCING LADY* (1933), *Moulin Rouge* (1934), *Reckless* (1935), *The King Steps Out* (1936), *True to Life* (1943), *Because of Him* (1946), *HERE COMES THE GROOM* (1951), and others.

TOO MANY GIRLS (RKO 1940) was one of the few times LUCILLE BALL played the romantic lead instead of the sarcastic sidekick, and she handled it well, even if her singing had to be dubbed by Trudy Erwin. GEORGE AB-BOTT, who directed the 1939 Broadway hit, produced and directed the film version, bringing most of the RODGERS and HART score and four cast members with him to Hollywood: EDDIE BRACKEN, VAN JOHNSON, DESI ARNAZ (all in their screen debuts), and Hal LeRoy. Better plotted than most college musicals, John Twist's screenplay told of heiress Ball, who is sent by her father to Pottawatomie College in Stop Gap, New Mexico, to keep her from fortune hunters. He also sends four football players, Bracken, Johnson, Arnaz, and Richard Carlson, to Pottawatomie disguised as students but assigned to keep an eye on Ball. But she and Carlson fall in love as the other three men get involved in their own female complications. Like most of Abbott's films, it was a bit stagy at times but bounced along with the help of ANN MILLER, FRANCES LANGFORD, and GRADY SUTTON in the cast. Rodgers and Hart wrote one new song, the tender "You're Nearer," to join others from the Broadway score, most memorably "I Didn't Know What Time It Was," "Love Never Went to College," and "Spic and Spanish," which Arnaz led in a rousing production number staged by LeROY PRINZ. The ELVIS PRESLEY vehicle *Girl Happy* (1965) used the same plot premise.

TOP HAT (RKO 1935) may be the quintessential FRED ASTAIRE movie if for no other reason than the fact that he wears white tie, tails, and titular hat for most of the film. It also has classic moments, such as singing and dancing "Cheek to Cheek" with GINGER ROGERS, that define Astaire. The plot stretched mistaken identity to its limits, but the players were so adept at this sort of thing that the story almost seemed to make logical sense. American hoofer Astaire falls in love with Rogers at first sight when in London with his new show. But Rogers mistakenly thinks he is married to her chum HELEN BRODERICK, so Astaire's romantic advances puzzle and then infuriate her. Broderick's real husband is EDWARD EVERETT HORTON, Astaire's fussy producer, so she finds Rogers' tales of his wooing her surprisingly refreshing. In her confusion, Rogers marries the Italian dress designer ERIK RHODES, but it turns out the preacher was Horton's valet ERIC BLORE, so the wedding is invalid and everything is straightened out to the festive strains of "The Piccolino." The delectable score by IRVING BERLIN also boasted the slaphappy "No Strings," the intoxicating "Isn't This a Lovely Day (To Be

Caught in the Rain)?," and the debonair "Top Hat, White Tie and Tails." Not only was each number radiant, but the songs actually had something to do with the plot. MARK SANDRICH directed with a light touch, and HERMES PAN and Astaire did the dances, which ranged from precision tapping to gliding fox-trot to BUSBY BERKELEY–like formations by the dancing couples on the Lido.

TORMÉ, MEL (1925–1999), the velvet-voiced singer and songwriter known for his distinctive jazz interpretations of songs, appeared in eight movie musicals, usually as a nightclub singer or as himself. Tormé can be seen in *Higher and Higher* (1943), *GOOD NEWS* (1947), *WORDS AND MUSIC* (1948), *The Duchess of Idaho* (1950), and *A Man Called Adam* (1960), as well as heard in *So Dear to My Heart* (1949).

TRAVOLTA, JOHN (1954–   ), the screen heart throb of the 1970s, first found celebrity on television (*Welcome Back, Kotter*) and then movie stardom as disco dancer Tony Manero in *SATURDAY NIGHT FEVER* (1977). An even bigger hit was *GREASE* (1978), in which he played high schooler Danny Zuko. Travolta has since appeared in several nonmusicals of varying quality and one musical, the unfortunate sequel *Staying Alive* (1983), in which Tony Manero goes to Broadway.

TREACHER, ARTHUR (1894–1975) was the quintessential British character actor, usually playing dour-faced butlers or stuffy figures of authority. He can be seen in the musicals *CURLY TOP* (1935), *GO INTO YOUR DANCE* (1935), *ANYTHING GOES* (1936), *Stowaway* (1936), *Mad About Music* (1938), *My Lucky Star* (1938), *The Little Princess* (1939), *Irene* (1940), *STAR SPANGLED RHYTHM* (1942), *MARY POPPINS* (1964), and others.

TRUEX, ERNEST (1890–1973) played meek and henpecked characters on stage and in films (silent and talkies) with great success; he later portrayed older versions of the same type on television. The diminutive actor appeared in the movie musicals *Start Cheering* (1938), *Freshman Year* (1938), *Swing, Sister, Swing* (1938), *LILLIAN RUSSELL* (1940), *Dance, Girl, Dance* (1940), *STAR SPANGLED RHYTHM* (1942), *Don't Get Personal* (1942), *THIS IS THE ARMY* (1943), *Pan-American* (1945), and others.

TUCKER, SOPHIE (1884–1966), self-proclaimed as the "Last of the Red-Hot Mamas," was a buxom and ribald belt singer in nightclubs, on Broadway, and in five Hollywood films. Tucker was featured in *Honky Tonk* (1929) and *BROADWAY MELODY OF 1938* (1937), and she did specialty bits in *Follow the Boys* (1944), *Sensations of 1945* (1944), and *THE JOKER IS WILD* (1957).

TUFTS, SONNY (1911–1970) was a tall, athletic leading man who played in light comedy and musicals on Broadway and in Hollywood. Although Tufts had trained as an opera singer as a youth, he appeared only in five film musicals: *Bring on the Girls* (1944), *HERE COME THE WAVES* (1944), *Duffy's Tavern* (1945), *Cross My Heart* (1946), and *Variety Girl* (1947).

TUNE, TOMMY (1939–   ), the leggy, perennially youthful singer, dancer, choreographer, and director of Broadway musicals, has appeared only in supporting roles in two film musicals, as artist Ambrose in *HELLO, DOLLY!* (1969) and as hoofer Bobby in *THE BOY FRIEND* (1971), but each one gave him a chance to show off his agile dancing talents.

TURNER, LANA (1920–1995), the curvaceous glamour girl who excelled in torrid Hollywood melodramas, was placed in several musicals by the studios until they figured out her true niche. Usually in nonsinging roles or dubbed, Turner can be seen in the musicals *Love Finds Andy Hardy* (1938), *Dancing Coed* (1939), *TWO GIRLS ON BROADWAY* (1940), *ZIEGFELD GIRL* (1941), *DuBarry Was a Lady* (1943), *Mr. Imperium* (1951), *THE MERRY WIDOW* (1952), and *Latin Lovers* (1953).

TUTTLE, FRANK (1892–1963) started as a scriptwriter but was directing feature films by 1922. He helmed pictures in all genres, usually bringing a high level of craftsmanship to his work. Among his fifteen Hollywood musicals were *Sweetie* (1929), *PARAMOUNT ON PARADE* (1930), *True to the Navy* (1930), *THE BIG BROADCAST* (1932), *ROMAN SCANDALS* (1933), *Two for Tonight* (1935), *College Holiday* (1936), *Waikiki Wedding* (1937), *Doctor Rhythm* (1938), and *Paris Honeymoon* (1939).

20TH CENTURY–FOX was formed in 1935 with a merger between the established Fox Film Corporation, going back to the nickelodeon days and incorporated in 1915, and the newly formed 20th Century, a production company founded in 1933 by DARRYL F. ZANUCK and Joseph M. Schenck. Even before the merger, SHIRLEY TEMPLE rose as the predominant star at Fox and continued to remain box office gold for the rest of the decade. Other musical stars that shone at 20th Century–Fox were ALICE FAYE, SONJA HENIE, DON AMECHE, BETTY GRABLE, and MARILYN MONROE. Although the Fox musicals of the 1930s and 1940s were never as lavish or spectacular as at MGM and other studios, they had a glossy, polished look and high entertainment value, as seen in such films as *FOLIES BERGÈRE DE PARIS* (1935), *ON THE AVENUE* (1937), *ALEXANDER'S RAGTIME BAND* (1938), *DOWN ARGENTINE WAY* (1940), *SUN VALLEY SERENADE* (1941), *THE GANG'S ALL HERE* (1943), *STATE FAIR* (1945), and *MOTHER WORE TIGHTS* (1947). In the 1950s the studio countered the threat of television with Cinemascope wide-screen spectaculars, including the musicals *THERE'S NO BUSINESS LIKE SHOW BUSINESS* (1954), *THE KING AND I* (1956), and *SOUTH PACIFIC* (1958). In the 1960s they hit the jackpot with *THE SOUND OF MUSIC* (1965) but found themselves deep in the red with *STAR!* (1968) and *HELLO, DOLLY!* (1969). 20th Century– Fox had little success with musicals after 1970, their most interesting offerings being *ALL THAT JAZZ* (1979) and *THE ROSE* (1979). The company remains strong today because of low-budget comedies such as *Home Alone* (1990) and big-budget spectaculars such as *Titanic* (1997), with musicals long ago discarded as profitable possibilities.

TWO GIRLS AND A SAILOR (MGM 1944) was a thinly disguised REVUE that solved the problem of rationalizing all its songs and guest appearances by setting itself in an old warehouse that was turned into a servicemen's canteen. JUNE ALLYSON and GLORIA DeHAVEN played the performing sisters who opened the canteen, JIMMY DURANTE was the ex-vaudevillian who managed it, and sailor VAN JOHNSON turned out to be the millionaire-in-disguise who financed the whole operation. Among the stars who stopped by were LENA HORNE singing "Paper Doll," GRACIE ALLEN knocking them silly with "Concerto for Index Finger," ELLA FITZGERALD smoothly delivering "A-Tisket-a-Tasket," Amparo and JOSÉ ITURBI playing Falla's "Ritual Fire Dance," Durante doing his signature song "Inka Dinka Doo," VIRGINIA O'BRIEN singing "Take It Easy," and Allyson and the HARRY JAMES orchestra performing "Young Man With a Horn," the last two numbers written for the film. As a wartime musical diversion, the movie was right on target.

TWO GIRLS ON BROADWAY. See *The Broadway Melody*

U

UNITED ARTISTS was founded in 1919 by four screen artists, actors Charles Chaplin, Mary Pickford, Douglas Fairbanks, and director D.W. Griffith, in order to have more control over their films. Producing and releasing movies featuring themselves and others, such as Buster Keaton, Rudolph Valentino, and Gloria Swanson, the new company flourished in the 1920s. But because United Artists never had the extensive production facilities and roster of contract stars that the other major studios had, it experienced a shaky history after the advent of sound. Most of the company's notable musicals were made by independents such as SAMUEL GOLDWYN and released through United Artists, such as the early *WHOOPEE* (1930), *ROMAN SCANDALS* (1933), and *FOLIES BERGÈRE DE PARIS* (1935). Some of the studio's most memorable musicals of the 1930s were *HALLELUJAH, I'M A BUM* (1933), *KID MILLIONS* (1934), and *THE GOLDWYN FOLLIES* (1938). By the war years United Artists infrequently presented musicals until the 1960s, when the studio found success with *WEST SIDE STORY* (1961), *A HARD DAY'S NIGHT* (1964), and *HELP!* (1965), followed by such 1970s hits as *FIDDLER ON THE ROOF* (1971) and *HAIR* (1978). The company was bought by Trans-America Corporation in 1967, and after some profitable dramas and comedies, such as *Rocky* (1976) and *Annie Hall* (1977), and some monumental flops, such as *Heaven's Gate* (1980), it merged with MGM and formed the new MGM/UA in 1981. When that company was bought out by a French bank, the name was changed to Metro-Goldwyn-Mayer Inc. and the old United Artists identity was gone forever.

UNIVERSAL PICTURES never made it near the top position in studio power, but the company usually managed to survive by arranging shrewd tie-ins with record companies, television, and tourism. Film exhibitor Carl Laemmle founded the studio in 1912 by merging several small moviemaking concerns.

The company built its 230-acre studio lot Universal City in 1915, the most complete and up-to-date movie facility with the capability of filming both interiors and exterior locations. Universal thrived through the silent picture era and the early 1930s (mostly because of its horror films and melodramas), but struggled soon after and only presented notable musicals on occasion, such as the innovative *KING OF JAZZ* (1930) and *SHOW BOAT* (1936). The studio was saved from bankruptcy in the late 1930s by the introduction of DEANNA DURBIN, whose musicals between 1936 and 1948 were the company's greatest asset. W.C. FIELDS, DONALD O'CONNOR, and MARLENE DIETRICH vehicles, as well as more horror pictures and some distinguished dramas, helped Universal pull though the decades, but only rarely did a musical hit arrive, such as *THE GLENN MILLER STORY* (1954). The 1960s and 1970s were a boom time for the studio with DORIS DAY–Rock Hudson comedies, disaster spectaculars, and other nonmusicals leading the way. Again musicals were scarce with only a handful worth recalling, such as *THOROUGHLY MODERN MILLIE* (1967), *SWEET CHARITY* (1969), *JESUS CHRIST SUPERSTAR* (1973), and *COAL MINER'S DAUGHTER* (1980). Universal merged with Decca Records in 1962, and in the late 1960s the vast studio lot became one of television's busiest production factories. Today the company draws considerable income from tours of its California facility and its Florida theme park.

UNSINKABLE MOLLY BROWN, THE (MGM 1964) was a robust outdoor musical starring DEBBIE REYNOLDS and the Colorado Rockies, based on the 1960 musical scored by MEREDITH WILLSON. Half the songs were left behind, but HARVE PRESNELL made his film debut recreating his "Leadville Johnny," who always seems to strike it rich. Reynolds was backwoods hillbilly Molly, who tried to drop her tomboyish ways when she marries Johnny, but despite all their wealth, Denver high society turns their noses up at the *nouveau riche* couple. So Molly and Johnny head for Europe, where the higher she climbs the social ladder, the more she loses her husband's affection. Returning to America on the *Titanic*, Molly becomes a hero when she mans a lifeboat and both Johnny and Denver welcome her with open arms. CHARLES WALTERS directed competently, but it was Peter Gennaro's choreography that brought the film to life, particularly in the raucous "Belly Up to the Bar, Boys" and spirited "He's My Friend," the second written for the film. Other numbers included "I'll Never Say No," "Colorado, My Home," and "I Ain't Down Yet."

UP IN ARMS (Avalon/RKO 1944) introduced DANNY KAYE to film audiences, and when they saw the hyperactive clown scat-sing, produce different accents, and race through tongue-twisting lyrics, it was love at first sight. Producer SAMUEL GOLDWYN brought Kaye from Broadway and had the movie built around his special talents. Kaye plays a hypochondriac who works as an elevator boy in a building full of doctors, so he's always near a physician. When Kaye and his roommate Dana Andrews are drafted, their girlfriends DINAH SHORE and Constance Dowling sign up and follow them to the South Pacific, where Kaye bumbles his way into capturing twenty Japanese soldiers. Sylvia Fine and Max Liebman wrote two specialty numbers for Kaye: "Theatre Lobby Number" (aka "Manic Depressive Pictures Presents"), in which he acted out an entire film while waiting in line to get into a movie house, and "Melody in 4-F" (which he had performed on stage in 1941), a rapid-fire scat song about the plight of a draftee. TED KOEHLER and HAR-OLD ARLEN penned the rest of the score, the best numbers being the swinging lament "Tess's Torch Song" and the gentle ballad "Now I Know," both sung by Shore.

V

VALLEE, RUDY (1901–1986), an extremely popular crooner even though he had a small, nasal voice, started as a bandleader of the Connecticut Yankees, singing numbers through his trademark megaphone when he wasn't playing saxophone. After becoming known from radio, nightclubs, and Broadway, Vallee made his film debut in *The Vagabond Lover* (1929), named after his signature song that he had popularized. He played romantic leads in such films as *Glorifying the American Girl* (1929), *George White's Scandals* (1934), *Sweet Music* (1935), *GOLD DIGGERS IN PARIS* (1938), *SECOND FIDDLE* (1939), and others. But Vallee was more believable in characters roles, usually playing finicky millionaires and stuffy upper-class types. He can be seen with this persona in *Time Out for Rhythm* (1941), *Too Many Blondes* (1941), *HAPPY GO LUCKY* (1942), *People Are Funny* (1946), *The Beautiful Blonde From Bashful Bend* (1949), and *Gentlemen Marry Brunettes* (1955). Vallee did specialty bits in *INTERNATIONAL HOUSE* (1933), *The Helen Morgan Story* (1957), and *Live a Little, Love a Little* (1968), as well as narrating *The Night They Raided Minsky's* (1968). He scored a triumphant return to Broadway in 1961 playing corporate boss J.B. Biggley in *HOW TO SUCCEED IN BUSINESS WITHOUT REALLY TRYING*, which he got to film in 1966.

VAN, BOBBY (1930–1980) lit up a handful of 1950s movie musicals with his athletic dancing and youthful energy in second leads. After a bit part in *Skirts Ahoy* (1952), Van was featured in *Because You're Mine* (1952), *Small Town Girl* (1953), *The Affairs of Dobbie Gillis* (1953), and *KISS ME, KATE* (1953). In the 1960s he concentrated on stage work, nightclubs, and television (sometimes serving as a choreographer), but did make dancing appearances in the movies *The Ladies' Man* (1961), *It's Only Money* (1962), and *Lost Horizon* (1973).

VAN DYKE, DICK (1925–   ), a tall and physical comic actor who starred in three popular television series, went to Hollywood when he recreated his Broadway role of music agent Albert Peterson for the movie version of *BYE BYE BIRDIE* (1963). His film career would be off and on during the next four decades, but he was featured in two other musicals, as chimney sweep Bert in *MARY POPPINS* (1964) and inventor Caractacus Potts in *CHITTY CHITTY BANG BANG* (1968), and he had supporting roles in two others, *What a Way to Go!* (1964) and *DICK TRACY* (1990). His brother is television actor Jerry Van Dyke.

VAN DYKE, W.S. (1889–1943), a very busy Hollywood director known as "One Shot Woody" for his efficiency on the set and refusal to overshoot film footage, started as an assistant to D.W. Griffith and was directing features by 1917. Van Dyke helmed all genres of movies, including musicals such as five of the JEANETTE MacDONALD–NELSON EDDY vehicles: *NAUGHTY MARIETTA* (1935), *ROSE MARIE* (1935), *SWEETHEARTS* (1938), *Bitter Sweet* (1940), and *I Married an Angel* (1942). His other movie musicals included *Cuban Love Song* (1931), *SAN FRANCISCO* (1936), *ROSALIE* (1937), and *Cairo* (1942).

VAN HEUSEN, JAMES (1913–1990) wrote hit songs for the movies with two lyricist partners, JOHNNY BURKE and SAMMY CAHN, in two separate but successful careers. In 1940 he went to Hollywood, where he teamed up with Burke to score musicals for BING CROSBY, providing the singer with plenty of hits in such films as *ROAD TO ZANZIBAR* (1941), *ROAD TO MOROCCO* (1942), *Dixie* (1943), *GOING MY WAY* (1944), *ROAD TO UTOPIA* (1945), *Welcome Stranger* (1947), *ROAD TO RIO* (1947), *A CONNECTICUT YANKEE IN KING ARTHUR'S COURT* (1949), *Top o' the Morning* (1949), *Riding High* (1950), *Mr. Music* (1950), *ROAD TO BALI* (1952), and others. His other films with Burke include *LOVE THY NEIGHBOR* (1940), *Playmates* (1941), *And the Angels Sing* (1944), *Belle of the Yukon* (1944), and *Cross My Heart* (1946). When Burke retired from films in the 1950s, Van Heusen formed a proficient partnership with Cahn and produced scores for such musicals as *ANYTHING GOES* (1956), *Pardners* (1956), *Say One for Me* (1959), *Let's Make Love* (1960), *High Time* (1960), *THE ROAD TO HONG KONG* (1962), *ROBIN AND THE SEVEN HOODS* (1964), and *The Pleasure Seekers* (1964). He also provided theme songs for several nonmusical films. The Burke–Van Heusen song catalog was celebrated in the Broadway revue *Swinging on a Star* (1995).

VARSITY SHOW (Warner 1937) was the biggest, if far from the best, college musical, with BUSBY BERKELEY staging the finale with hundreds of students spelling out the names of various colleges in an overhead shot. The plot dealt with Broadway producer DICK POWELL, who returns to his alma mater Winfield College to organize the annual musical show. But the stuffy administration gives him trouble, so he heads back to New York, only to have the students follow him and put their show on Broadway. PRISCILLA and ROSEMARY LANE (in their debut) were the featured coeds with Ted Healy, WALTER CATLETT, JOHNNY DAVIS, Mabel Todd, STERLING HOLLOWAY, Buck and Bubbles, and Fred Waring and his Pennsylvanians on hand to fill out the large cast. JOHNNY MERCER and RICHARD A. WHITING contributed the songs, including the romantic "You've Got Something There," the swaggering "Have You Any Castles, Baby?," the rousing "Love Is on the Air Tonight," and the pie-eyed musical claim "We're Working Our Way Through College." The silly musical was remade as *Fine and Dandy* (1950).

VELEZ, LUPE (1908–1944), the sultry Mexican dancer-actress who seduced many a male on the silent screen, performed in a series of "Mexican Spitfire" comedies with LEON ERROL in the 1940s. Earlier she was featured as a fiery lady of sensuality in ten Hollywood musicals, but most of them were B pictures. Velez can be seen in *Lady of the Pavements* (1929), *Cuban Love Song* (1931), *Hollywood Party* (1934), *Strictly Dynamite* (1934), *The Girl From Mexico* (1939), *The Redhead From Manhattan* (1941), *Playmates* (1941), and others. As tempestuous off screen as on, Velez was married to actor-athlete Johnny Weissmuller for a time and committed suicide over one of her many failed love affairs.

VERA-ELLEN (1921–1981), the petite blonde dancer who partnered with the greatest hoofers in Hollywood, worked as a Rockette at Radio City and was featured on Broadway before starting her film career in 1945. Her singing was usually dubbed, but her accomplished dancing and acting skills allowed her to shine in such classics as *ON THE TOWN* (1949) and *WHITE CHRISTMAS* (1954). Vera-Ellen made ten Hollywood musicals before she retired in the late 1950s: *Wonder Man* (1945), *The Kid From Brooklyn* (1946), *THREE LITTLE GIRLS IN BLUE* (1946), *Carnival in Costa Rica* (1947), *WORDS AND MUSIC* (1948), *THREE LITTLE WORDS* (1950), *THE BELLE OF NEW YORK* (1952), and *CALL ME MADAM* (1953).

VERDON, GWEN (1926–2000), Broadway's finest dancing star of the 1950s and 1960s, made only a handful of musicals and never got to recreate her stage roles on the screen except for her funny temptress Lola in *DAMN YANKEES* (1958). Verdon could be seen doing dance specialties in *ON THE RIVIERA* (1951), *Meet Me After the Show* (1951), *THE MERRY WIDOW* (1952), and *THE FARMER TAKES A WIFE* (1953). In the 1980s she returned to films in character roles in nonmusicals. Verdon was once married to BOB FOSSE, who choreographed most of her stage performances.

VICTOR/VICTORIA (MGM 1982) gave JULIE ANDREWS one of her better roles in years even though she had to dress like a man to play it. Starving singer Vicki is having so much trouble getting work in Paris during the 1930s that, encouraged by gay nightclub performer ROBERT PRESTON, she masquerades as Victor, a female impersonator who can hit the high notes when singing. She/he soon becomes the toast of Paris night life with American gangster James Garner falling for Victoria while his blonde mistress Lesley Ann Warren has the hots for Victor. BLAKE EDWARDS wrote, produced, and directed the movie, which some found a sophisticated romp, others a one-joke dud. LESLIE BRICUSSE and HENRY MANCINI wrote the score that included the facetious "Chicago, Illinois," the steamy "Le Jazz Hot," the soft-shoe "You and Me," and the flowing ballad "Crazy World." Andrews also starred in the 1995 Broadway version of the musical.

VIDOR, CHARLES (1900–1959), a Hungarian-born director who studied film in Germany before coming to America in 1924, started helming Hollywood features in 1932 and was known as a technically proficient artist in various genres. His five movie musicals were *COVER GIRL* (1944), *A Song to Remember* (1945), *HANS CHRISTIAN ANDERSEN* (1952), *LOVE ME OR LEAVE ME* (1955), and *THE JOKER IS WILD* (1957). Vidor died before completing *Song Without End* (1960).

VIVA LAS VEGAS (MGM 1964) is arguably ELVIS PRESLEY's best film, with top-notch director GEORGE SIDNEY at the helm, ANN-MARGARET as a costar who actually created a bit of chemistry with Presley, and a better-than-average set of songs by various pop songwriters. Race car driver Presley comes to Vegas to enter the Grand Prix, but engine trouble puts him out of the race. He gets a job at a Vegas resort, where he meets swimming instructor Ann-Margaret and the two set off sparks. Cesare Danova, WILLIAM DEMAREST, Jack Carter, and Nicky Blair were also in it, with David Winters choreographing the dances, which were more interesting than the hip swiveling usually found in the King's vehicles. "The Lady Loves Me," "I Need Somebody to Lean On," "My Rival," and the rocking country-western title number were the musical highlights. Love it or leave it, *Viva Las Vegas* was the most popular of the singer's thirty-one films.

W

WABASH AVENUE. See *Coney Island*

WAKE UP AND LIVE (Fox 1937) had more fun with RADIO than most of the movie musicals about the airwaves as it capitalized on the current radio feud between columnist Walter Winchell and orchestra leader BEN BERNIE. JACK HALEY played a crooner who froze up every time he got in front of a radio microphone, and ALICE FAYE, as an advice-giver with her own radio talk show "Wake Up and Live," was the girl who helped him overcome his airwaves fears. When Haley's singing is accidentally broadcast during Bernie's show, he becomes famous as the "Phantom Troubadour," and Winchell and Bernie fight over who discovered the new singer. It was mostly slaphappy nonsense with MACK GORDON and HARRY REVEL supplying such songs as the silly "I Love You Much Too Much, Muchacha," the doting ballads "It's Swell of You" and "Never in a Million Years," the spirited title number, and the popular torch song "There's a Lull in My Life," which was a bestseller for Faye. The cast also included LEAH RAY, PATSY KELLY, NED SPARKS, Grace Bradley, WALTER CATLETT, JOAN DAVIS, WILLIAM DEMAREST, EDDIE ANDERSON, the Condos Brothers, and the Brewster Twins. Ironically, Haley's singing voice was considered too weak for the crooner who was supposed to conquer the airwaves, so his songs were dubbed by Buddy Clark.

WALKER, HAL (1896–1972), a director who specialized in lightweight comedies and musicals, stayed in Hollywood for a decade before going on to television. Walker's musicals were *Out of This World* (1945), *Duffy's Tavern* (1945), *The Stork Club* (1945), *ROAD TO UTOPIA* (1945), *My Friend Irma Goes West* (1950), *At War With the Army* (1950), *That's My Boy* (1951), *Sailor Beware* (1951), and *ROAD TO BALI* (1951).

WALKER, NANCY (1922–1992), an inspired comedienne whose dour faced and wisecracking delivery made her a unique feature on Broadway and in television, made only a handful of movies, including four musicals. She recreated her hysterical stage performance as the blind date in *BEST FOOT FORWARD* (1943) and stole the laughs in *Girl Crazy* (1943), *Broadway Rhythm* (1944), and *Lucky Me* (1954), as well as directing the oddball movie musical *Can't Stop the Music* (1980).

WALLER, THOMAS "FATS" (1904–1943) was a renowned jazz pianist and singer whose distinct way with a song was preserved in many recordings. The round, genial African American performed mainly in nightclubs across the country but made memorable guest appearances in the films *Hooray for Love* (1935), *KING OF BURLESQUE* (1935), and *STORMY WEATHER* (1943). Waller was celebrated in the hit Broadway revue *Ain't Misbehavin'* (1978).

WALLIS, HAL (1899–1986) was one of Hollywood's most influential and prolific producers and studio executives, leading WARNER BROTHERS through its golden age in the 1930s and later having a distinguished career as an independent producer. Wallis oversaw some 400 films, including thirty-six musicals featuring everyone from JAMES CAGNEY to ELVIS PRESLEY. Among his notable musicals were *GOLD DIGGERS OF 1937* (1936), *The Singing Marine* (1937), *HOLLYWOOD HOTEL* (1937), *GOLD DIGGERS IN PARIS* (1938), *Cowboy From Brooklyn* (1938), *On Your Toes* (1939), *Blues in the Night* (1941), *YANKEE DOODLE DANDY* (1942), *THIS IS THE ARMY* (1943), *My Friend Irma* (1949), *Sailor Beware* (1951), *Scared Stiff* (1953), *ARTISTS AND MODELS* (1955), *Loving You* (1957), *KING CREOLE* (1958), *Rock-a-Bye Baby* (1958), *BLUE HAWAII* (1961), *Roustabout* (1964), *Easy Come, Easy Go* (1967), and others.

WALSH, RAOUL (1887–1980), the rugged he-man director who was acclaimed for his straightforward storytelling in male action pictures beginning in 1914, seems an unlikely candidate for directing musicals, but he helmed a dozen of them, including *GOING HOLLYWOOD* (1933), *EVERY NIGHT AT EIGHT* (1935), *Klondike Annie* (1936), *ARTISTS AND MODELS* (1937), *College Swing* (1938), *St. Louis Blues* (1939), *The Man I Love* (1946), and *A Private's Affair* (1959).

WALSTON, RAY (1918–   ), a popular character actor on Broadway, in films, and on television (*My Favorite Martian*), usually played quirky, eccentric parts with a devilish gleam in his eye. In fact, his most famous Broadway role was the devil Applegate, which he recreated for the film version of *DAMN YANKEES* (1958). Walston can also be seen in the movie musicals *SOUTH*

PACIFIC (1958), *Kiss Me, Stupid* (1964), *PAINT YOUR WAGON* (1969), and *Popeye* (1981).

WALT DISNEY COMPANY, THE, Hollywood's most successful and comprehensive entertainment corporation today with major activity in live-action and animated films, television, Broadway musicals, publishing, and theme parks, started with a single and rather simple focus: movie cartoons. Founder WALT DISNEY and his brother Roy Disney began the company in 1923 with Mickey Mouse as the figurehead of a series of cartoon shorts. The young studio produced its first sound short, *Steamboat Willie,* in 1928 and the mouse's popularity soared. Over the years no one used the development of sound, color, multiplane camera shooting, split screen, and other innovations better than Disney, who assembled the most talented artists in the business and dominated the animated field for decades. The company's gamble with the expensive *SNOW WHITE AND THE SEVEN DWARFS* (1937), the first full-length animated feature, paid off a hundredfold, so Disney moved on to even more ambitious projects. While continuing to provide shorts featuring Mickey, Donald Duck, and other favorites, the studio regularly turned out animated features, usually releasing them through RKO. Just as with the first effort, these movies utilized songs effectively in the plot and created dozens of popular song favorites over the years. Other musicals based on classic fairy tales included *PINOCCHIO* (1940), *SONG OF THE SOUTH* (1946), *CINDERELLA* (1950), *Peter Pan* (1953), *SLEEPING BEAUTY* (1959), *The Sword in the Stone* (1963), and *THE JUNGLE BOOK* (1967). Lesser-known stories soon became classics after the Disney touch, as with *DUMBO* (1941), *Bambi* (1942), *LADY AND THE TRAMP* (1955), and *101 Dalmations* (1961). The studio experimented with anthology features, sometimes mixing live action and animation in a series of stories or musical specialties: *Saludos Amigos* (1943), *Make Mine Music* (1946), *Fun and Fancy Free* (1947), *Melody Time* (1948), and others. And some entries were so unique they defied simple description, as with *FANTASIA* (1940) and *THE THREE CABALLEROS* (1945). By the 1950s Disney had moved into television, built its first theme park, and produced live-action features including comedies, adventure tales, and even nature documentary. The studio's first foray into a major live-action musical was the moderate hit *BABES IN TOYLAND* (1961), followed by the charming but unexceptional *Summer Magic* (1963). But with *MARY POPPINS* (1964) the company came up with a movie musical that rivaled those of Hollywood's golden age. However, subsequent efforts, such as *The Happiest Millionaire* (1967) and *The One and Only, Genuine Original Family Band* (1968), failed to capture the magic (and the audiences) of *Mary Poppins,* and over the next three decades only occasionally would the studio produce a live-action musical of interest, such as *BEDKNOBS AND BROOMSTICKS* (1971). Walt Disney, who had involved himself in every aspect of the huge company, died in 1966, and the whole operation declined. Some memorable animated musicals were made over the next two decades, such as *THE ARISTOCATS* (1970) and *OLIVER & COMPANY* (1988), but mostly the studio turned out inferior comedies and some ambitious but unsatisfying efforts, such as *Return to Oz* (1985) and *The Black Cauldron* (1985). The corporation's fortunes improved with new management in the mid-1980s and the establishment of Touchstone Pictures that made features not necessarily directed to the usual family audience. After a power struggle that left Michael Eisner in control and had Roy E. Disney revitalizing the animation division, the company experienced a renaissance with a return to television, growth in the theme park sector, and a series of superb animated features that compared favorably with the classics of the past: *THE LITTLE MERMAID* (1989), *BEAUTY AND THE BEAST* (1991), *ALADDIN* (1992), *THE LION KING* (1994), *POCAHONTAS* (1995), *THE HUNCHBACK OF NOTRE DAME* (1996), *Mulan* (1998), *Tarzan* (1999), and others. Disney developed stop-action musicals such as *The Nightmare Before Christmas* (1993) and *James and the Giant Peach* (1996), was the first studio to present a fully computerized feature, *Toy Story* (1995), and participated in producing Broadway musicals, such as with *Beauty and the Beast*, *The Lion King*, *Aida*, and *The Hunchback of Notre Dame*. All these ventures proved to be popular and (sometimes) critical hits. As Disney acquired a television network, expanded its cable programming and theme park attractions, and led the way in merchandising techniques, the giant corporation seemed to grow too powerful and disturbing to some. The conglomerate has suffered some financial setbacks of late as this growth became overwhelming and a little unwieldy at times, yet the quality of the Disney animated films has rarely suffered and the exacting and innovative spirit of Walt Disney's days seems to survive.

WALTERS, CHARLES (1911–1982), a talented director and part of the famous FREED unit at MGM, began as a dancer on Broadway and was later a choreographer. He went to Hollywood in the early 1940s and staged the production numbers for such musicals as *Presenting Lily Mars* (1942), *Seven Days' Leave* (1942), *DuBarry Was a Lady* (1943), *Girl Crazy* (1943), *BEST FOOT FORWARD* (1943), *Meet the People* (1943), *Broadway Rhythm* (1943), *MEET ME IN ST. LOUIS* (1944), *THE HARVEY GIRLS* (1945), *SUMMER HOLIDAY* (1948), and others. Walters started directing in the late 1940s, beginning with *GOOD NEWS* (1947), followed by *THE BARKLEYS OF BROADWAY* (1949), *Texas Carnival* (1951), *THE BELLE OF NEW YORK* (1952), *Easy to Love* (1953), *HIGH SOCIETY* (1956), *JUMBO* (1962), and *THE UNSINKABLE MOLLY BROWN* (1964). He both directed and choreographed *EASTER PARADE* (1948), *SUMMER STOCK* (1950), *Torch Song* (1953), *LILI* (1953), *Dangerous When Wet* (1953), and *The Glass Slipper* (1955).

WARNER BROTHERS virtually invented the movie musical and would dominate the market for the new genre during its early years. Founded by Jack

L. Warner and his three brothers in 1923, the fledging company bought up some small studios like Vitagraph and First National Pictures but by 1927 found themselves on the verge of bankruptcy. The brothers decided to sink their remaining assets into an experiment called Vitaphone, which provided sounds that coordinated with the images on the screen. After testing Vitaphone with a music soundtrack and sound effects for the swashbuckler *Don Juan* (1926), the studio opened up a world of sound with the partial-talkies *THE JAZZ SINGER* (1927) and *THE SINGING FOOL* (1928). Other companies scrambled to incorporate sound, but Warner Brothers had the lead and maintained it with such early musicals as *ON WITH THE SHOW* (1929), the *GOLD DIGGERS* movies, *42ND STREET* (1933), *FOOTLIGHT PARADE* (1933), *WONDER BAR* (1934), *DAMES* (1934), and others. AL JOLSON, DICK POWELL, RUBY KEELER, JAMES CAGNEY, and JOAN BLONDELL were among the stars who made the Warner musicals sparkle, and with its popular series of gangster pictures, the studio flourished. Although the products of Warner Brothers never had the glossiness of some of the other major studios, there was a clean, dramatic look to its films and even the musicals had a toughness and crude attractiveness about them. The 1940s and 1950s saw a decline in musicals at the studio, though there were the occasional hits like *YANKEE DOODLE DANDY* (1942), *THANK YOUR LUCKY STARS* (1943), *RHAPSODY IN BLUE* (1944), *NIGHT AND DAY* (1946), *A STAR IS BORN* (1954), and *DAMN YANKEES* (1958). The 1960s saw some big-budget musicals that paid off, such as *THE MUSIC MAN* (1962), *GYPSY* (1962), *ROBIN AND THE SEVEN HOODS* (1964), and *MY FAIR LADY* (1964). The studio was bought up by Seven Arts Productions in 1967 and was known for a time as Warner Bros.–Seven Arts. Soon after it became Warner Communications, and then in 1989 a merger created Time Warner, an empire controlling music, television, and films. Like most studios, musicals were mostly abandoned in the 1970s, and the company remains one of the industry's most potent at the box office without them.

WARREN, HARRY (1893–1981) was the quintessential Hollywood composer, spending most of his long career writing songs for the movies and scoring everything from BUSBY BERKELEY backstagers in the 1930s to Big Band musicals in the 1940s to JERRY LEWIS vehicles in the 1950s. No one in Hollywood was more prolific (nearly sixty musical films) and more adaptable to the changing styles in popular music. Warren started writing songs for the stage in the 1920s but arrived in Hollywood just as sound came in and the studios needed original material to fill the demand for musical talkies. His first score was for *Spring Is Here* (1930), written with lyricists Sam Lewis and Joe Young; then he was teamed up with AL DUBIN for a remarkable collaboration that included such classics as *42ND STREET* (1933), *GOLD DIGGERS OF 1933*, *FOOTLIGHT PARADE* (1933), *DAMES* (1934), and *GO INTO YOUR DANCE* (1935). The partnership lasted for twenty-three films, including *ROMAN SCANDALS* (1933), *Moulin Rouge* (1934), *WONDER BAR* (1934), *Twenty Million Sweethearts* (1934), *GOLD DIGGERS OF 1935*, *Broadway Gondolier* (1935), *Shipmates Forever* (1935), *Stars Over Broadway* (1935), *Colleen* (1936), *GOLD DIGGERS OF 1937* (1936), *Mr. Dodd Takes the Air* (1937), *The Singing Marine* (1937), *GOLD DIGGERS IN PARIS* (1938), *Garden of the Moon* (1938), and others. On the last picture, Warren worked with lyricist JOHNNY MERCER on some of the songs because Dubin's chronic drinking problem was breaking up the team. Warren and Mercer also scored *Going Places* (1938), *Naughty but Nice* (1939), *THE HARVEY GIRLS* (1946), and *THE BELLE OF NEW YORK* (1952). Warren's most frequent collaborator in the 1940s was MACK GORDON, and together they contributed to a dozen films, including *Young People* (1940), *DOWN ARGENTINE WAY* (1940), *THAT NIGHT IN RIO* (1941), *The Great American Broadcast* (1941), *SUN VALLEY SERENADE* (1941), *WEEK-END IN HAVANA* (1941), *ORCHESTRA WIVES* (1942), *ICELAND* (1942), *SPRINGTIME IN THE ROCKIES* (1942), *SUMMER STOCK* (1950), and others. With various lyricists, Warren also wrote songs for *Honolulu* (1939), *THE GANG'S ALL HERE* (1943), *Yolanda and the Thief* (1945), *ZIEGFELD FOLLIES* (1946), *THE BARKLEYS OF BROADWAY* (1949), *Pagan Love Song* (1950), *The Caddy* (1953), *ARTISTS AND MODELS* (1955), *An Affair to Remember* (1955), *Cinderfella* (1960), *The Ladies' Man* (1961), and others. Warren's gift for melody, intoxicating harmony, and strong musical line helped him write dozens of song standards over the years, from "Shuffle Off to Buffalo" to "That's Amore."

WASHINGTON, NED (1901–1976) was a lyricist who wrote with various composers in Hollywood on thirteen musicals, most memorably the animated *PINOCCHIO* (1940) and *DUMBO* (1941). Among Washington's other musical credits were *The Forward Pass* (1929), *Little Johnny Jones* (1930), *Bright Lights* (1931), *Tropic Holiday* (1938), *Sleepy Lagoon* (1943), *Mexicana* (1945), and *Let's Do It Again* (1953).

WATERS, ETHEL (1896–1977), the multitalented African American singer and actress, was renowned for singing the blues in nightclubs, on Broadway, and on records, but she managed, in her few screen appearances, to conquer musicals and dramas as well. Waters was the first black female to get star billing in a Broadway play and in a Hollywood musical. Film audiences saw her do specialty spots in *ON WITH THE SHOW* (1929), *Gift of Gab* (1934), and *STAGE DOOR CANTEEN* (1943), as well as the character parts of the maid Cleona Jones in *Cairo* (1942) and faithful wife Petunia Jackson in *CABIN IN THE SKY* (1943).

WAYNE, DAVID (1914–1995), an all-purpose character actor on Broadway, in films, and on television, could play any kind of role, from leprechaun to heavy, in comedies, dramas, and musicals. Wayne's movie musicals include *My Blue Heaven* (1950), *WITH A SONG IN MY HEART* (1952), *Wait 'Til the Sun Shines, Nellie* (1952), *The I-Don't-Care Girl* (1953), *Tonight We Sing* (1953), and *Huckleberry Finn* (1974).

WEBSTER, PAUL FRANCIS (1907–1984) wrote lyrics with many different movie composers during an award-winning career that started with *Under the Pampas Moon* (1936). With HARRY REVEL, SAMMY FAIN, and others, he contributed lyrics to *Rainbow on the River* (1936), *Make a Wish* (1937), *Hit the Ice* (1943), *Ghost Catchers* (1944), *The Stork Club* (1945), *THE MERRY WIDOW* (1952), *CALAMITY JANE* (1953), *ROSE MARIE* (1954), *Lucky Me* (1954), *THE STUDENT PRINCE* (1954), *April Love* (1957), *Mardi Gras* (1958), and others.

WEEK-END IN HAVANA (Fox 1941) may be hard to distinguish from the other 20TH CENTURY–FOX south-of-the-border musicals with ALICE FAYE and CARMEN MIRANDA in them, but it doesn't make it any less enjoyable. This time Faye is a Macy's Department Store salesgirl who takes a cruise to Cuba but threatens to sue the steamship company when her ship runs aground. Executive JOHN PAYNE takes Faye on an all-paid trip to Havana to get her to sign a release form but ends up head over heels in love with her. CESAR ROMERO was a Brooklyn-born Cuban who was after the fortune he thinks Faye has, and Miranda was his jealous sweetheart. Corbina Wright, Jr., LEONID KINSKEY, GEORGE BARBIER, Sheldon Leonard, and BILLY GILBERT were added to the merriment, and MACK GORDON and HARRY WARREN wrote such first-class songs as "Tropical Magic," "When I Love I Love," "Romance and Rumba" (music by JAMES MONACO), the Latin-flavored title number, and "The Nango," a swinging tango that HERMES PAN staged with Miranda and the chorus girls, tearing down the house.

WEIDLER, VIRGINIA (1927–1968), a CHILD STAR of 1930s and 1940 films, specialized in outgoing brats and lovable preteens. She can be seen in the musicals *THE BIG BROADCAST OF 1937* (1936), *BABES ON BROADWAY* (1942), *Born to Sing* (1942), *BEST FOOT FORWARD* (1943), and others.

WEILL, KURT (1900–1950), the German-born composer who created landmark musical theatre in his homeland and later on Broadway, saw some of his stage works filmed: *Lady in the Dark* (1944), *Knickerbocker Holiday* (1944), *One Touch of Venus* (1948), and *Lost in the Stars* (1974). Weill's masterwork, *The Threepenny Opera* written with Bertolt Brecht, was filmed in German in 1931 and 1964, and in English as *Mack the Knife* (1989). For Hollywood he wrote songs for the musicals *You and Me* (1938) and *Where Do We Go From Here?* (1945). Weill was married to actress-singer Lotte Lenya.

WELLS, GEORGE (1909–   ), a Hollywood screenwriter and sometime producer, started writing scripts in radio but by the mid-1940s was penning light comedies and musicals. Among Wells' musical scripts were *TILL THE CLOUDS ROLL BY* (1946), *TAKE ME OUT TO THE BALL GAME* (1949), *THREE LITTLE WORDS* (1950), *SUMMER STOCK* (1950), *The Toast of New Orleans* (1950), *Where the Boys Are* (1960), and others. He produced *Dangerous When Wet* (1953) and *Jupiter's Darling* (1955), and both wrote and produced *Everything I Have Is Yours* (1952) and *I Love Melvin* (1953).

WE'RE NOT DRESSING (Paramount 1934) allowed BING CROSBY to start coming into his own as a light comic actor instead of just a crooner, and he was charmingly offbeat as the carefree outsider, a persona he would perfect over the years. The plot, borrowed from James M. Barrie's Edwardian comedy *The Admirable Crichton,* put spoiled heiress CAROLE LOMBARD on her yacht in the South Seas with some friends, but when they are shipwrecked on a desert island it is the lowly sailor Crosby who has the wherewithal to take charge. Lombard resents him at first, but after a few songs and walks along a moonlit beach, she succumbs to his charms. Also on board were ETHEL MERMAN, LEON ERROL, and RAY MILLAND, with naturalists GRACIE ALLEN and GEORGE BURNS studying flora and fauna on the island and providing most of the jokes. It was a daffy adventure and one, under NORMAN TAUROG's direction, that worked effortlessly. MACK GORDON and HARRY REVEL penned the songs, and they were equally expert: the touching ballads "She Reminds Me of You" and "Once in a Blue Moon," the sly "May I?," the merry "Love Thy Neighbor," and the lullaby "Goodnight, Lovely Little Lady," which Crosby sang to his pet bear.

WEST, MAE (1892–1980), filmdom's funniest and most self-mocking sex symbol, started as a child performer in burlesque who perfected her sly and suggestive persona later in vaudeville and on Broadway, usually having a hand in the writing of her vehicles. West went to Hollywood in 1933 and made a smash debut in *SHE DONE HIM WRONG* (1933), followed by the musicals *I'm No Angel* (1933), *Belle of the Nineties* (1934), *Goin' to Town* (1935), *Klondike Annie* (1936), *Go West, Young Man* (1936), *Every Day's a Holiday* (1937), and *The Heat's On* (1943). She retired from films in the 1940s but kept in the public eye by personal appearances and the reruns of her movies on television. When in her eighties, West made two nonmusical films that revealed she hadn't changed her act one bit. One of the most imitated performers in show business, West sang in a nasal, tight-mouthed manner, delivered her lines in a consistently flirty way, and walked with a sashaying style that once seen was never forgotten.

WEST SIDE STORY (Mirisch/United Artists 1961) was mockingly called "the *Ben-Hur* of movie musicals," and there is a bigness and majesty about the film that clamors for greatness. But it took just such confidence to pull off a screen version of the 1957 Broadway hit that relied on dance (even ballet) and operatic singing to tell its gritty, modern *Romeo and Juliet* story. Co-director ROBERT WISE and co-director-choreographer JEROME ROBBINS (who had staged the original on Broadway) managed to mix the realism of the streets (parts were filmed on location in New York) with the poetic world of song and dance right from the dynamic opening shot, and audiences were immediately swept up with it all. ERNEST LEHMAN's screenplay sticks close to Arthur Laurents' stage libretto as Puerto Rican immigrant NATALIE WOOD (dubbed by MARNI NIXON) betrays her family and Latino community by loving white gang leader Richard Beymer (dubbed by Jim Bryant), and the tragedy that results sobers up the rival factions. RUSS TAMBLYN led the American-born Jets and GEORGE CHAKIRIS headed the Puerto Rican Sharks. RITA MORENO shone as Chakiris' hot-blooded girlfriend and Wood's confidant and the cast also featured Tucker Smith, Simon Oakland, Tony Mordente, Eliot Feld, Carole D'Andrea, David Winters, Sue Oakes, Burt Michaels, José de Vega, and John Astin. Robbins recreated his dynamic stage choreography but opened it up cinematically, especially in the opening scenes and in the vibrantly frustrating "Cool." Just about all of the STEPHEN SONDHEIM–LEONARD BERNSTEIN score was transferred to the screen and, more surprisingly, most of the dance music as well. Among the memorable numbers were "Tonight," "Something's Coming," "Somewhere," "Maria," "Gee, Officer Krupke!," "I Feel Pretty," "America," and "A Boy Like That/I Have a Love." The film won a whopping ten ACADEMY AWARDS and turned the Broadway musical version from a critical hit to a popular favorite.

WESTLEY, HELEN (1875–1942), a familiar character actress who excelled at playing domineering aunts, matrons, and spinsters, had a long and distinguished career on the stage before turning to the movies in the 1930s. She can be seen in the movie musicals *Moulin Rouge* (1934), *ROBERTA* (1935), *SHOW BOAT* (1936), *Dimples* (1936), *Stowaway* (1936), *REBECCA OF SUNNYBROOK FARM* (1938), *ALEXANDER'S RAGTIME BAND* (1938), *LILLIAN RUSSELL* (1940), *Sunny* (1941), and others.

WHEELER AND WOOLSEY was a popular comedy team on Broadway and in films, made up of Bert Wheeler (1895–1968), a roly-poly innocent with a forlorn expression, and Robert Woolsey (1889–1938), a fast-talking con-man with owl-like glasses. The team was formed when producer Florenz Ziegfeld cast them as comics in his 1927 Broadway hit *RIO RITA*; they repeated the roles on screen in 1929. The singing-clowning twosome also appeared in the movie musicals *The Cuckoos* (1930), *Dixiana* (1930), *Girl Crazy* (1932), *Cockeyed Cavaliers* (1934), *Hips Hips Hooray* (1934), and *Nitwits* (1935). After Woolsey's premature death, Wheeler continued on alone, appearing on stage, on television, and in a few movies, including the musical *Las Vegas Nights* (1941).

WHITE CHRISTMAS (Paramount 1954) capitalized on the consistent popularity of the 1942 title song and used sections of a few other IRVING BERLIN standards, but most of the numbers were original, making it Berlin's last full movie score. Army buddies BING CROSBY and DANNY KAYE go into show business after World War Two and find themselves performing in a Florida nightclub, where they meet the sister act of ROSEMARY CLOONEY and VERA-ELLEN. The four travel up to Vermont to spend a white Christmas at a lodge, but the lack of snow has turned the inn into a ghost town. When the ex-GIs find out that their old general (Dean Jagger) is the proprietor and going bankrupt, Crosby decides to try out his Broadway-bound show at the inn to attract business and even goes on television to encourage former servicemen who served under the general to come to New England for the bash. They do, the snow finally arrives, and everyone joyously sings the title song in the final reel. MARY WICKES led the supporting cast that also included GRADY SUTTON, SIG RUMANN, John Brascia, and Anne Whitfield, all directed by MICHAEL CURTIZ and choreographed by ROBERT ALTON. The new Berlin numbers included the vaudeville turns "Sisters" and "Gee, I Wish I Was Back in the Army," the entrancing "The Best Things Happen While You're Dancing," the torchy "Love, You Didn't Do Right by Me," and the lullaby "Count Your Blessings." The movie was the top-grossing picture of the year and remains a holiday-time favorite.

WHITE, ONNA choreographed hit musicals on Broadway and in London's West End, sometimes recreating her dances for the film versions, as with *THE MUSIC MAN* (1962), *1776* (1972), and *Mame* (1974). She also choreographed the movie musicals *BYE BYE BIRDIE* (1963), *OLIVER!* (1968), and *Pete's Dragon* (1977). The Canadian-born choreographer has managed to keep her birth date a secret for many years.

WHITEMAN, PAUL (1891–1967) was the first and most durable of the popular bandleaders, he and his orchestra gaining fame in the 1920s and introducing jazz and dance music to concert halls. The rotund, mustached Whiteman played himself in seven movie musicals, usually with his renowned band. He can be seen in *KING OF JAZZ* (1930), *THANKS A MILLION* (1935), *STRIKE UP THE BAND* (1940), *Lady, Let's Dance* (1944), *Atlantic City* (1944), *RHAPSODY IN BLUE* (1945), and *The Fabulous Dorseys* (1947).

WHITING, RICHARD A. (1891–1938), a film composer who worked with such lyricists as LEO ROBIN and JOHNNY MERCER, scored eighteen movie musicals in which the songs were usually better than the films. Whiting's first movie score was *INNOCENTS OF PARIS* (1929) with Robin, followed by Whiting-Robin songs in *The Dance of Life* (1929), *MONTE CARLO* (1930), *Playboy of Paris* (1930), *ONE HOUR WITH YOU* (1932), and *BIG BROADCAST OF 1936* (1935). With Mercer, Whiting scored *Ready, Willing and Able* (1937), *VARSITY SHOW* (1937), *HOLLYWOOD HOTEL* (1937), and *Cowboy From Brooklyn* (1938). He collaborated with other lyricists on such films as *Sweetie* (1929), *Safety in Numbers* (1930), *Adorable* (1933), *My Weakness* (1933), *Take a Chance* (1933), *Transatlantic Merry-Go-Round* (1934), and *Coronado* (1935). Among Whiting's most-remembered songs were "My Blue Heaven," "Hooray for Hollywood," "My Ideal," "On the Good Ship Lollipop," and "Too Marvelous for Words." His work was celebrated in the Broadway revues *A Day in Hollywood—A Night in the Ukraine* (1980) and *Dream* (1997). Singer Margaret Whiting is his daughter.

WHITNEY, ELEANORE (1917–   ), a petite tap-dancing starlet in PARAMOUNT musicals in the 1930s, was featured in seven films before retiring from the screen at the age of twenty-one. Whitney's credits include *Millions in the Air* (1935), *BIG BROADCAST OF 1937* (1936), *College Holiday* (1936), *Turn Off the Moon* (1937), and *Thrill of a Lifetime* (1937).

WHOOPEE! (Goldwyn/United Artists 1930), an important film in the developing movie musical genre, seems primitive and stagy at times and wonderfully cinematic in other moments. It almost looks like the creators (choreographer BUSBY BERKELEY, in particular) were learning things along the way and the whole film is a bubbly experiment. Producer SAMUEL GOLDWYN made a deal with Broadway impresario Florenz Ziegfeld to close his 1928 hit and bring the show intact to Hollywood. Its star EDDIE CANTOR was included in the deal, but most of the songs and much of the cast were left in New York, though George Olsen's orchestra was retained. THORNTON FREELAND directed perfunctorily, but Berkeley promised Goldwyn he would break away from the static way production numbers were usually filmed. He made good on his claim, getting rid of multiple cameras so that each number had one specific point of view, filming the chorus girls in close up for the first time and putting his camera overhead and creating the first of his famous kaleidoscope shots of women making geometric patterns. It was Cantor's first starring role in a talkie and the movie made him a screen star. He played a nervous hypochondriac who flees to the West for his health but is mixed up with cowboys, Indians, and a convenient chorus line of girls. Cantor also runs afoul of the law when he helps Eleanor Hunt run away from sheriff Jack Rutherford, to whom she is fianced, in order to be with her true love, half-breed Paul Gregory. It was all nonsense but delightfully so with Spencer Charters, Chief Caupolican, ALBERT HACKETT, Marilyn Morgan, and, best of all, Ethel Shutta stealing the show at times from Cantor. (Also, BETTY GRABLE and VIRGINIA BRUCE can easily be spotted in the chorus.) The popular "Makin' Whoopee" was one of the three GUS KAHN–WALTER

DONALDSON songs left from the stage score; the best of the new ones were "My Baby Just Cares for Me" and "Stetson," the last ingeniously filmed by Berkeley with the chorines popping up in front of the camera sporting hats.

WICKES, MARY (1916–1995) was one of the most familiar faces in films and television though she was rarely in a leading role. The tall, gawky character actress, who played wisecracking spinsters, aunts, housekeepers, and secretaries, can be seen adding her wry comic touch in such musicals as *Private Buckaroo* (1942), *Higher and Higher* (1943), *On Moonlight Bay* (1951), *I'll See You in My Dreams* (1951), *WHITE CHRISTMAS* (1954), *THE MUSIC MAN* (1962), and others. Her last film credit was the voice of one of the gargoyles in the animated *THE HUNCHBACK OF NOTRE DAME* (1996).

WILCOX, HERBERT (1892–1977) was an Irish-born director and producer who made a name for himself in Europe by directing his wife ANNA NEAGLE in some successful films. He came to Hollywood in 1939 and made a handful of movies, including the musicals *Irene* (1940), *No No Nanette* (1941), and *Sunny* (1941). Among his most well known British musicals (all starring Neagle) were *Bitter Sweet* (1933), *The Courtneys of Curzon Street* (1947), and *King's Rhapsody* (1954).

WILDER, BILLY (1906–   ), the legendary scriptwriter-turned-director, worked on many films in Germany and France before arriving in Hollywood in 1934 and gradually became one of filmdom's most distinct directors of both comedies and dramas. Wilder was involved in only a handful of movie musicals, writing scripts for *Music in the Air* (1934), *RHYTHM ON THE RIVER* (1940), and *A Song Is Born* (1948), and writing and directing *The Emperor Waltz* (1947), *A Foreign Affair* (1948), and *Kiss Me, Stupid* (1964). One of his most beloved films is the semi-musical *Some Like It Hot* (1959).

WILLIAMS, ESTHER (1923–   ), Hollywood's favorite (and only) swimming musical star, was featured in a series of lavish movies that showcased her appealing water skills and attractiveness in bathing suits. Discovered in a Billy Rose Aquacade, Williams was introduced to film audiences with a specialty spot in the nonmusical *Andy Hardy's Double Life* (1942). After being featured in *Bathing Beauty* (1944) her popularity soared and she appeared in eighteen more musicals, including *Thrill of a Romance* (1945), *ZIEGFELD FOLLIES* (1946), *On an Island With You* (1948), *TAKE ME OUT TO THE BALL GAME* (1949), *NEPTUNE'S DAUGHTER* (1949), *Pagan Love Song* (1950), *Texas Carnival* (1951), *Million Dollar Mermaid* (1952), *Easy to Love* (1953), *Jupiter's Darling* (1955), and *The Big Show* (1960). Williams' landlocked vehicles did not fare as well so she retired from the movies and went into business. Her husband was FERNANDO LAMAS.

WILLIAMS, PAUL (1940–   ) is a pint-sized actor and singer with a full-sized talent for writing songs. The five-foot two-inch performer did some bit parts in 1960s films but became more notable in the 1970s for his pop songs, sung by himself and others. Williams scored the movie musical *PHANTOM OF THE PARADISE* (1974) and played the villain Swan as well. He was heard on the soundtrack of *BUGSY MALONE* (1976), which he also scored, and contributed songs to *A STAR IS BORN* (1976), *THE MUPPET MOVIE* (1979), and *A Muppet Christmas Carol* (1992).

WILLS, CHILL (1903–1978), the crusty character actor known for his many roles in westerns and for providing the voice of Francis the Talking Mule in a series of comedies, started in vaudeville as a singer and toured with his own singing group before finding success in the movies. Although rarely called on to sing, Wills can be seen in the film musicals *ANYTHING GOES* (1936), *Honky Tonk* (1941), *BEST FOOT FORWARD* (1943), *MEET ME IN ST. LOUIS* (1944), *THE HARVEY GIRLS* (1946), and others.

WILLSON, MEREDITH (1902–1984), a longtime orchestra conductor and arranger on radio and television, began a successful career as a Broadway songwriter late in life. Two of his stage musicals were filmed: *THE MUSIC MAN* (1962) and *THE UNSINKABLE MOLLY BROWN* (1964).

WILLY WONKA AND THE CHOCOLATE FACTORY (Wolper/Paramount 1971) was an odd but engaging musical version of a Roald Dahl story that was supposed to be for kids but had a dark subtext (as all of Dahl's books had) that made it more nightmarish than pure fantasy. English lad Charlie (Peter Ostrum) is one of the lucky winners of a candy manufacturer's contest and is invited, with four obnoxious kids from around the world, to tour the candy factory run by the eccentric Willy Wonka (Gene Wilder). The tour turns out to be a test of character, which the other children fail miserably and are punished for. But Charlie and his grandpa Jack Albertson pass the test, inherit the factory, and go flying into the air in one of Wonka's many strange and wondrous contraptions. ANTHONY NEWLEY and LESLIE BRICUSSE collaborated on the songs, "The Candy Man" being the big hit. But more accomplished was the enchanting "Pure Imagination." Sometimes maudlin, other times cruel, the movie took a while to gain the following it enjoys today on video.

WILSON, DOOLEY (1894–1953), the African American singer-actor immortalized in film history when he sang "As Time Goes By" in the nonmusical *Casablanca* (1943), started in vaudeville and worked his way up to a major role in the Broadway musical *Cabin in the Sky* (1940). Wilson made his film debut in 1942 but rarely got more than supporting parts on the screen. His musical credits include *Cairo* (1942), *STORMY WEATHER* (1943), *Higher and Higher* (1943), and *Seven Days Ashore* (1944).

WING, TOBY (1915–   ), the perennial platinum-blonde cutie of the 1930s, played coeds or chorus girls in such musicals as *The Kid From Spain* (1932), *42ND STREET* (1933), *College Humor* (1933), *Too Much Harmony* (1933), *MURDER AT THE VANITIES* (1934), *With Love and Kisses* (1936), and *Sing While You Are Able* (1937).

WINNINGER, CHARLES (1884–1969), a veteran comic actor of vaudeville, Broadway, and silent and talking films, played crusty oldsters, bumbling fathers, and blustering bureaucrats in several movies between 1924 and 1963. Among his two dozen film musicals were *Children of Dreams* (1931), *Flying High* (1931), *SHOW BOAT* (1936), *Three Smart Girls* (1937), *Every Day's a Holiday* (1937), *BABES IN ARMS* (1939), *Destry Rides Again* (1939), *Little Nellie Kelly* (1940), *ZIEGFELD GIRL* (1941), *CONEY ISLAND* (1943), *Broadway Rhythm* (1944), *Belle of the Yukon* (1944), *STATE FAIR* (1945), *Something in the Wind* (1947), *Give My Regards to Broadway* (1948), and others.

WISE, ROBERT (1914–   ), the distinguished Hollywood director of epics, dramas, and sci-fi movies, directed two B musicals earlier in his career, *Mystery in Mexico* (1948) and *This Could Be the Night* (1957), and then returned to helm the big-budget musicals *WEST SIDE STORY* (1961), co-directed with JEROME ROBBINS, *THE SOUND OF MUSIC* (1965), and *STAR!* (1968).

WITH A SONG IN MY HEART (Fox 1952) was a BIOGRAPHICAL MUSICAL about singer Jane Froman whose plot, as they used to say, was torn right from the headlines. It was a two-handkerchief weeper so well acted by SUSAN HAYWARD and produced so smartly that it transcended its genre and still packs a wallop. Radio singer Froman from Cincinnati works her way to Broadway and is on the brink of stardom when World War Two breaks out and she goes off to entertain the troops. But her plane crashes in Portugal, and Froman, left badly injured and partially paralyzed, undergoes years of treatments and operations before she makes a professional comeback. DAVID WAYNE was her husband, who shaped her career, Rory Calhoun was the pilot who rescued and then fell in love with her, and THELMA RITTER was the nurse and friend who helped Froman survive her ordeal. Also in the cast were Robert Walker, UNA MERKEL, LYLE TALBOT, Leif Erickson, Richard Allan, and Max Showalter, directed by WALTER LANG with plenty of pathos. Froman herself did the vocals for Hayward, and the twenty numbers (all familiar hits from "Blue Moon" to the title song) were beautifully presented. Most moving of all was "I'll Walk Alone" by SAMMY CAHN and JULE STYNE, which Froman recorded and became her biggest hit.

WITHERS, JANE (1926–   ), a CHILD STAR of the 1930s who, with her dark hair and bratty persona, contrasted nicely with SHIRLEY TEMPLE, was featured as a tot and later as a teenager in such B musicals as *Bright Eyes* (1934), *This Is the Life* (1935), *Paddy O'Day* (1935), *Can This Be Dixie?* (1936), *The Holy Terror* (1937), *Rascals* (1938), *Shooting High* (1940), *Johnny Doughboy* (1942), and *My Best Gal* (1944). Withers found little film work as an adult but was seen often on television.

WIZARD OF OZ, THE (MGM 1939), arguably the most beloved and continually popular musical Hollywood ever produced, has become such a part of American pop culture that it seems to have been created by magic. Yet the troublesome movie went through a dozen scriptwriters, four directors, several cast changes, and one of the most complicated and difficult production histories on record. It is amazing that none of the strain shows in the final cut, and the movie can be enjoyed over and over again without losing its luster. Producer ARTHUR FREED and MERVYN LeROY both claimed credit for pitching the idea of a musical version of the L. Frank Baum classic children's tale to MGM studio head Louis B. Mayer. (A Broadway musical treatment in 1903 had been very popular, but no one thought it filmable.) Luckily, the movie Mayer envisioned, with SHIRLEY TEMPLE as Dorothy and W.C. FIELDS as the Wizard, never materialized, and JUDY GARLAND shot to stardom for her innocent, sincere performance as the young girl whisked by a tornado to the land of Oz. FRANK MORGAN played the Wizard and various other characters Dorothy encounters, RAY BOLGER the scarecrow, JACK HALEY the tin man, BERT LAHR the cowardly lion, MARGARET HAMILTON the Wicked Witch of the West and Miss Gulch, BILLIE BURKE (vocals by Lorraine Bridges) Glinda the good witch, with Clara Blandick as Auntie Em, and Charley Grapewin as Uncle Henry. Victor Fleming, KING VIDOR, GEORGE CUKOR, and RICHARD THORPE each directed different sections of the film, with BOBBY CONNOLLY doing the choreography, CEDRIC GIBBONS and William Horning the sets, and ADRIAN the costumes. E.Y. HARBURG and HAROLD ARLEN penned one of filmdom's greatest scores, led by the Oscar-winning "Over the Rainbow," which was nearly left on the cutting room floor until wiser minds prevailed. "Ding Dong! The Witch Is Dead," "We're Off to See the Wizard," "If I Only Had a Brain," and others are part of American folklore rather than just popular songs from Hollywood. Yet even acknowledging the high quality of all the movie's elements doesn't quite explain why *The Wizard of Oz* is so special. Billed as a treat for "children of all ages," it goes beyond anyone's idea of a children's movie. It is very adult in many ways, from its expressionistic look (the change from black and white in Kansas to color for Oz was a bold and original idea) to its firm and difficult themes of friendship and home. Perhaps the movie is the great American fantasy, one that refuses to outdate or fade with each new generation that experiences it.

WONDER BAR (Warner 1934) was a soft-boiled melodrama (with songs) that told of the racy doings going on one night at the Paris nightclub of the title. The proprietor Al Wonder (AL JOLSON) has got his heart set on cabaret singer DOLORES DEL RIO, but so has club crooner and songwriter DICK POWELL. Del Rio cares for neither of them, her affections going to her dancing partner Ricardo Cortez, who has a roving eye for the ladies. Meanwhile GUY KIBBEE and HUGH HERBERT are trying to lose their wives Louise Fazenda and Ruth Donnelly in order to chase two of the Wonder Bar's hostesses, Fifi D'Orsay and Merna Kennedy. The evening's complications climax when socialite Kay Francis sinks her hooks into Cortez, he likes it, and Del Rio stabs him to death in a fit of jealousy. Based on one of Jolson's few Broadway flops, the story was directed by LLOYD BACON in the tough WARNER BROTHERS' style of the 1930s, and BUSBY BERKELEY staged the dances in his usual fantasy vein. One sequence, "Goin' to Heaven on a Mule," in which heaven was depicted with hundreds of Negroes eating watermelon while they sang and danced, was considered in bad taste even in its day. But Berkeley was in better form with "Don't Say Goodnight," which was staged with chorus girls dancing in front of revolving mirrors, the handful of chorines turning into thousands in the many reflections. AL DUBIN and HARRY WARREN wrote the score, which also included the enthralling ballad "Why Do I Dream Those Dreams?" and the snappy title tune.

WOOD, DEEDEE. See Breaux, Marc

WOOD, NATALIE (1938–1981), a favorite leading lady of the 1950s and 1960s, began her film career as a child performer but retained her popularity as an adult. She appeared in musicals as BING CROSBY's teenage daughter Barbara in *Just for You* (1952), as Puerto Rican immigrant Maria in *WEST SIDE STORY* (1961), and stripper GYPSY ROSE LEE in *GYPSY* (1962), her singing in the last two dubbed by MARNI NIXON. Wood was married to actor Robert Wagner.

WOOD, SAM (1883–1949), the pioneering film director who started directing features in 1919 and brought a skillful artistry to many dramas and comedies, helmed the early musicals *It's a Great Life* (1929), *So This Is College* (1929), and *They Learned About Women* (1930), as well as the MARX BROTHERS vehicles *A NIGHT AT THE OPERA* (1935) and *A DAY AT THE RACES* (1937).

WOODSTOCK (Warner 1970), the grandaddy of all ROCKUMENTARIES about the grandaddy of all rock festivals, captured the "three days of peace and music" with split screen, dizzying montage, multipaneled images, and vibrant use of color. Michael Wadleigh was the director who filmed interviews with patrons, performers, police, even local farmers, put it together with exciting footage of the acts themselves, then spliced in fascinating scenes backstage and in the crowd. Not all the artists who performed at the 1969 festival got on film, but a "director's cut" version released in 1994 added forty more minutes of performance. Most memorable of the performers and/or groups were Jimi Hendrix, Joe Cocker, Sly and the Family Stone, Ten Years After, The Who, Arlo Guthrie, Joan Baez, Jefferson Airplane, Richie Havens, and Crosby, Stills and Nash. Most rockumentaries that came after *Woodstock* were affected by its techniques and could not help copying it, though rarely did they measure up to the original.

WOOLSEY, ROBERT. See Wheeler and Woolsey

WORDS AND MUSIC (MGM 1948) was supposedly about the lives and works of songwriters RICHARD RODGERS and LORENZ HART, and as Hollywood fabrications went, it was one of the most fictitious. Rodgers' real life was simply dull, and Hart's story, that of a tormented homosexual who died of alcoholism, was unfilmable at the time, so it was turned into the tale of a songster who loved a nightclub singer but she didn't love him because he was short and so he drank himself to death. Tom Drake was fitfully unexciting as Rodgers, MICKEY ROONEY was a petulant but energetic Hart, and BETTY GARRET was the fictional love of his life. Producer ARTHUR FREED had the good sense to fill the BIOGRAPHICAL MUSICAL with seventeen Rodgers and Hart tunes and gathered a crackerjack cast to perform them. Among the highlights were Rooney and JUDY GARLAND (together on screen for the last time) recapturing the old magic with "I Wish I Were in Love Again," LENA HORNE's distinctive renditions of "The Lady Is a Tramp" and "Where or When," JUNE ALLYSON and the Blackburn Twins in a zesty version of "Thou Swell," Garland's exciting "Johnny One Note," and the modern ballet "Slaughter on Tenth Avenue" choreographed by GENE KELLY and featuring Kelly and VERA-ELLEN. Among the other performers who strutted their stuff were CYD CHARISSE, MEL TORMÉ, PERRY COMO, ANN SOTHERN, JANET LEIGH, RICHARD QUINE, and Marshall Thompson. ROBERT ALTON choreographed the rest of the numbers, and NORMAN TAUROG directed the movie like a piece of backstage fiction, which it was.

WRIGHT, ROBERT. See Forrest, George

WRUBEL, ALLIE (1905–1973) was a Tin Pan Alley composer who, working with various lyricists, scored eight Hollywood musicals. With MORT DIXON he wrote the songs for *Flirtation Walk* (1934), *Happiness Ahead* (1934), *Broadway Hostess* (1935), and *I Live for Love* (1935). HERB MAGIDSON was his collaborator on *Life of the Party* (1937), *Radio City Revels* (1938), and *Sing Your Way Home* (1945). Wrubel's most famous song,

"Zip-a-Dee-Doo-Dah" with Ray Gilbert, was from his score for *SONG OF THE SOUTH* (1946). He returned to the movies to score *Never Steal Anything Small* (1959) with lyricist-playwright MAXWELL ANDERSON.

WYMAN, JANE (1914–   ), a film actress known more for her award-winning dramatic roles, started in the chorus of movie musicals such as *KING OF BURLESQUE* (1935), *Cain and Mabel* (1936), *GOLD DIGGERS OF 1937* (1936), and *Stage Struck* (1936) before getting featured in *The King and the Chorus Girl* (1937), *Ready, Willing and Able* (1937), *Mr. Dodd Takes the Air* (1937), *The Singing Marine* (1937), *Footlight Serenade* (1942), and others. Wyman returned to musicals in between her dramatic features, doing guest spots or supporting roles in *HOLLYWOOD CANTEEN* (1944), *NIGHT AND DAY* (1945), *It's a Great Feeling* (1949), *HERE COMES THE GROOM* (1951), *Starlift* (1951), *Just for You* (1952), and *Let's Do It Again* (1953). She was married to RONALD REAGAN and then to composer Fred Karger.

WYMORE, PATRICE (1926–   ) played beautiful but deadly females in a handful of movies in the 1950s. The tall and alluring dancer can be seen in the musicals *Tea for Two* (1950), *Starlift* (1951), *I'll See You in My Dreams* (1951), *She's Working Her Way Through College* (1952), and *She's Back on Broadway* (1953). Wymore was married to Errol Flynn.

WYNN, ED (1886–1966), one of vaudeville, radio, Broadway, and television's favorite clowns, brought his giggling laugh and bird-like hand gestures to only a handful of movies, though he made quite an impression each time. Wynn's film musical credits include the waiter-turned-mobster Cricket in *Follow the Leader* (1930), a guest bit in *STAGE DOOR CANTEEN* (1943), the Fairy Godfather in *Cinderfella* (1960), the Toymaker in *BABES IN TOYLAND* (1961), and laughing Uncle Albert in *MARY POPPINS* (1965), as well as providing the voice of the Mad Hatter in the animated *ALICE IN WONDERLAND* (1951). He was the father of actor KEENAN WYNN.

WYNN, KEENAN (1916–1986) was a versatile film actor who played everything from congenial con-men to brash villains in nearly fifty movies between 1942 and 1986. In musicals he was usually the irascible agent or lovable side-kick, bringing a precise sense of sarcastic comedy to such films as *FOR ME AND MY GAL* (1942), *ZIEGFELD FOLLIES* (1946), *No Leave, No Love* (1946), *NEPTUNE'S DAUGHTER* (1949), *ANNIE GET YOUR GUN* (1950), *THREE LITTLE WORDS* (1950), *ROYAL WEDDING* (1951), *Texas Carnival* (1951), *THE BELLE OF NEW YORK* (1952), *KISS ME, KATE* (1953), *The Glass Slipper* (1955), *Bikini Beach* (1964), *FINIAN'S RAINBOW* (1968), and others. Wynn's last musical was as the aged Mr. Green in *NASHVILLE* (1975). He was the son of comic ED WYNN.

Y

YANKEE DOODLE DANDY (Warner 1942) may have got many of the facts about the life of show business giant GEORGE M. COHAN wrong, but it got everything else right, from a dynamic performance by JAMES CAGNEY to the superb production numbers using the songwriter's trunkful of tuneful songs. Told in flashback by Cohan to Franklin Roosevelt during a visit to the White House in 1937, the plot followed "little Georgie" from his birth on the Fourth of July, his early days as a hoofer with the family's vaudeville act, his bold move to write, compose, direct, produce, and star in his own Broadway shows, his meeting the singer Mary and marrying her, his string of hits and then eventual decline, and his comeback in RODGERS and HART's Broadway hit *I'd Rather Be Right*, in which he played FDR. Having told his story, Cohan is then presented with the Congressional Medal of Honor by the president for his patriotic songs, and he goes tap dancing off joyously. It was a tight and entertaining fiction that MICHAEL CURTIZ directed with flair and plenty of brash humor. Walter Huston and ROSEMARY DeCAMP played Cohan's performing parents, Jeanne Cagney his sister, and JOAN LESLIE was Mary, with Richard Whorf, FRANCES LANGFORD, GEORGE TOBIAS, S.Z. SAKALL, GEORGE BARBIER, Irene Manning, WALTER CATLETT, and EDDIE FOY, JR. (as Eddie Foy, Sr.) lending support in either the story or the musical numbers. But the movie was really Cagney's, making Cohan brash, funny, stubborn, and invigorating. His dancing was contagious, and his showmanship in the stage sequences illustrated how one man could dazzle Broadway for years. The most effective numbers in the movie were the two scenes from *Little Johnny Jones* in which Cagney got to sing "Yankee Doodle Boy" and "Give My Regards to Broadway." Other notable songs included "Mary's a Grand Old Name," "Over There," "You're a Grand Old Flag," "Oh, You Wonderful Girl," "So Long, Mary," and "Harrigan." *Yankee Doodle Dandy* was the first major Hollywood picture about an American songwriter, and its success would launch many others, few coming even close to the original in quality.

YELLEN, JACK (1892–1991) was a Tin Pan Alley lyricist who wrote for Broadway as well, working with many different composers during his career. He also contributed songs to nine Hollywood musicals, including *Honky Tonk* (1929), *Chasing Rainbows* (1930), *KING OF JAZZ* (1930), and *They Learned About Women* (1930) with MILTON AGER. Among Yellen's other film credits were *George White's Scandals* (1934, 1935, and 1945), *Under Pressure* (1935), and *Happy Landing* (1938). His most famous song, written with Ager, was "Happy Days Are Here Again."

YELLOW SUBMARINE. See *A Hard Day's Night*

YENTL (United Artists/Barwood 1983) was a powerhouse directorial debut for BARBRA STREISAND, who also co-wrote, produced, and starred in the musical tale of young Yentl in an eastern European village in 1904, who disguises herself as a boy in order to study the Torah at a yeshiva. She finds herself attracted to fellow student MANDY PATINKIN but instead ends up marrying Patinkin's sweetheart Amy Irving before the truth is revealed. In the end, Yentl sets off for America, where a woman has more freedom. The far-fetched fable was told with care and warmth, and the songs, by ALAN and MARILYN BERGMAN and MICHEL LEGRAND, were used mostly as interior soliloquies for the main character. "Papa, Can You Hear Me?," "No Wonder," "The Way He Makes Me Feel," "A Piece of Sky," and others were all expertly written and performed even though the score lacked variety and one longed to hear Patinkin get a chance to sing as well. *Yentl* was one of the most visually beautiful films of the decade, much of it filmed on location in Czechoslovakia, and there was no question Streisand had learned a great deal about directing after appearing before the camera for fourteen years. But the film comes up short in some ways, and it takes a true Streisand fan to totally embrace it.

YOU WERE NEVER LOVELIER (Columbia 1942) was another musical set in Latin America (Buenos Aires this time), yet the characters, music, and plot seemed to have nothing to do with its location. Manhattan nightclub hoofer FRED ASTAIRE goes to Argentina to gamble on the horses, loses all his money, and seeks a job at a ritzy hotel, only to have the owner (ADOLPHE MENJOU) hire him because he thinks the young man a good match for his daughter RITA HAYWORTH (vocals dubbed by Nan Wynn). Menjou even goes so far as to write love letters to his daughter signing Astaire's name. JOHNNY MERCER and JEROME KERN wrote a set of memorable songs to entertain audiences until the plot came to its inevitable conclusion, and Astaire and Hayworth had some sensational dance duets to fill in the dull stretches. "I'm Old Fashioned" was sung and danced in a moonlit garden by the two stars in one of the era's most romantic sequences. Also in the score were the snappy wedding number "Dearly Beloved" and the delectable title song. XA-VIER CUGAT and his orchestra provided the only Hispanic touch unless you count fifteen-year-old Fidel Castro, who was one of the extras in the movie.

YOU'LL NEVER GET RICH (Columbia 1941) revealed that RITA HAY-WORTH was a musical star to reckon with as she proved to be a dancer able to match co-star FRED ASTAIRE step by step. COLUMBIA bet the bankroll on the production, spending more than they ever had before on a film. Yet the highlights of the movie are not the spectacle scenes but the duets by the stars and the songs by COLE PORTER. Astaire first is smitten with Hayworth when he directs her in the Broadway show he is staging. But before you know it, Astaire is drafted and spends a good portion of the film tap dancing in the guard house. The two lovers are reunited for the big military show, the finale of which was the "Wedding Cake Walk" (choreographed by ROBERT ALTON) with a chorus of eighty dancing on a giant wedding cake that had an Army tank sitting on top. Other songs included the too-neglected ballad "Dream Dancing," the swinging torch song "Since I Kissed My Baby Goodbye," the rhythmic "So Near and Yet So Far," and the patriotic "Shootin' the Works for Uncle Sam." ROBERT BENCHLEY, John Hubbard, Osa Massen, Frieda Inescort, Ann Shoemaker, and the Delta Rhythm Boys were also featured, but the movie belonged to Hayworth, who single-handedly kept the studio solvent for several years.

YOUMANS, VINCENT (1898–1946), the innovative Broadway composer whose output during his short life was limited in quantity but not quality, saw four of his dozen stage works filmed: *HIT THE DECK* (1930 and 1955), *No No Nanette* (1930 and 1940), *Song of the West* (1930), which was called *Rainbow* on Broadway, and *Take a Chance* (1933). Few of these survived the transition from stage to screen with the score untampered with, but Youmans wrote directly for Hollywood as well, as with *What a Widow!* (1930) and *FLYING DOWN TO RIO* (1933). His songs were also used in the movie musical *Tea for Two* (1950). Youmans, who wrote with many different lyricists, was a master at creative use of rhythm and was responsible for bringing a Latin-flavored sensibility to popular American music.

YOUNG MAN WITH A HORN (Warner 1950) was a dark melodrama with music based (not too accurately) on the career of jazz trumpet musician Bix Beiderbecke, played by Kirk Douglas with HARRY JAMES providing the horn playing on the soundtrack. Douglas/Beiderbecke plays in a big band but longs to make his own kind of music and has trouble being just a subservient side man. His society wife Lauren Bacall is not much help, driving him to drink so that he eventually gets fired. Only band singer DORIS DAY believes in him and helps him find his way to jazz recognition. MICHAEL CURTIZ directed with a somber tone, and HOAGY CARMICHAEL brought a sense of be-hind-the-scenes familiarity as the film's narrator and one of Douglas' fellow musicians. The selections heard were from the standard band repertoire with such offerings as "I Only Have Eyes for You," "Too Marvelous for Words," and "With a Song in My Heart" sounding terrific in James' smooth renditions.

YOUNG, ROBERT (1907–1998), a personable leading man of over 100 films and two popular television series (*Father Knows Best* and *Marcus Welby, M.D.*), played youthful romantics and then grew into loving husbands and eventually understanding fathers. Young rarely sang on screen but was fea-tured in eight Hollywood musicals, including *The Kid From Spain* (1932), *Stowaway* (1936), *Honolulu* (1939), *Lady, Be Good* (1941), *Cairo* (1942), and *Sweet Rosie O'Grady* (1943).

YOUNG, VICTOR (1900–1956) was a prolific music arranger and conduc-tor who worked on hundreds of movies from the early 1930s until his untimely death. A child prodigy on the violin, Young gave up the concert hall for popu-lar music. Among his many Hollywood musicals were *ANYTHING GOES* (1936), *Klondike Annie* (1936), *BIG BROADCAST OF 1937* (1936), *ART-ISTS AND MODELS* (1937), *THE PALEFACE* (1948), *The Emperor Waltz* (1948), *My Favorite Spy* (1951), *THE COUNTRY GIRL* (1954), and many more.

Z

ZANUCK, DARRYL F. (1902–1979), the legendary movie mogul who was instrumental in the development of talkies, produced *THE JAZZ SINGER* (1927) for WARNER BROTHERS and supervised thirty-five subsequent musicals for various studios and as an independent producer. Zanuck started as a scriptwriter in silents and later wrote some of the films he presented. He both penned and produced the musicals *MY MAN* (1928), *Life of the Party* (1930), and *THANKS A MILLION* (1935). Other musicals Zanuck produced include *ON WITH THE SHOW* (1929), *42ND STREET* (1933), *GOLD DIGGERS OF 1933*, *FOOTLIGHT PARADE* (1933), *Moulin Rouge* (1934), *FOLIES BERGÈRE DE PARIS* (1935), *KING OF BURLESQUE* (1936), *CAPTAIN JANUARY* (1936), *Pigskin Parade* (1936), *ONE IN A MILLION* (1937), *ON THE AVENUE* (1937), *WAKE UP AND LIVE* (1937), *IN OLD CHICAGO* (1938), *Little Miss Broadway* (1938), *ALEXANDER'S RAGTIME BAND* (1938), *Thanks for Everything* (1938), *SECOND FIDDLE* (1939), *Swanee River* (1939), *The Little Princess* (1939), *LILLIAN RUSSELL* (1940), *DOWN ARGENTINE WAY* (1940), and others. His son is film producer Richard Darryl Zanuck.

ZIEGFELD FOLLIES (MGM 1946) was the first time a major studio attempted a musical REVUE on film since the early days of the talkies, and as entertaining as sections of it were, the audience did not fall in love with the concept and another revue would not come along until the documentary *THAT'S ENTERTAINMENT* (1974). In the prologue WILLIAM POWELL played producer Florenz Ziegfeld up in heaven dreaming about the sort of *Follies* he could create using the talent at MGM. What followed was a series of singing, dancing, and comedy acts as put together by producer ARTHUR FREED and directed by VINCENTE MINNELLI and others. FANNY BRICE, KEENAN WYNN, RED SKELTON, WILLIAM FRAWLEY, VIC-

TOR MOORE, and Edward Arnold were featured in the skits, most of which were genuine in spirit to those in the *Follies* if not all that funny today. LENA HORNE'S sultry rendition of "Love" (by RALPH BLANE and HUGH MARTIN) and JUDY GARLAND impersonating Greer Garson in the satirical "The Great Lady Gives an Interview" (by ROGER EDENS and KAY THOMPSON) were the best of the singing entries. But like a true *Follies*, the highlights were the dance pieces and opulent production numbers. The opening featured FRED ASTAIRE, LUCILLE BALL, and CYD CHARISSE in the lavish "Bring on the Beautiful Girls" (by Earl Brent and Edens) complemented by VIRGINIA O'BRIEN'S noticing the lack of males on stage and wryly suggesting "Bring on Those Wonderful Men." Freed and HARRY WARREN's "This Heart of Mine " was a partially sung ballet with Astaire as a jewel thief and LUCILLE BREMER as his victim, with whom he falls in love while stealing her diamond bracelet. Astaire and Bremer were also featured in a lush, oriental production number for the old standard "Limehouse Blues." The most-remembered number from the movie was the GERSHWINS' droll duet "The Babbitt and the Bromide" sung and danced by GENE KELLY and Astaire, the only time the two sang and danced together on film until a guest spot together in *That's Entertainment, Part Two* (1976).

ZIEGFELD GIRL (MGM 1940) followed the struggles of three girls who aim to star in the *Follies*, and each story was as tiresome as the next in this soapy musical directed by ROBERT Z. LEONARD and produced by PANDRO S. BERMAN with all his attention apparently going to the production numbers staged by BUSBY BERKELEY. Elevator girl LANA TURNER dumps her boyfriend JAMES STEWART in order to be a kept woman and reach the top; but her plan fails and she is punished with Hollywood justice. Hedy Lamarr, in contrast, leaves her penniless violinist husband Philip Dorn but sees the error of her ways and gives up show business to rejoin him by the final reel. Only eager vaudevillian JUDY GARLAND gets to become a Ziegfeld girl and is propped up on the top of a wedding cake setting (footage reused from the superior *THE GREAT ZIEGFELD*) for the big finale. The musical numbers manage to make the film watchable, especially Garland's frivolous rendition of "Minnie From Trinidad" (by ROGER EDENS), an exciting Spanish dance by Antonio and Rosario, and TONY MARTIN's warm delivery of "You Stepped Out of a Dream" by GUS KAHN and NACIO HERB BROWN. More interesting than the main characters were the expert supporting players such as Jackie Cooper, Ian Hunter, CHARLES WINNINGER, Al Shean (as himself), Paul Kelly, EDWARD EVERETT HORTON, DAN DAILEY, EVE ARDEN, and FELIX BRESSART.

ZORINA, VERA (1917–   ), a classical ballet dancer who later starred in musicals on Broadway and in London's West End, made only a few screen appearances, but her dancing was memorable in each one: *THE GOLDWYN*

FOLLIES (1938), *On Your Toes* (1939), *Louisiana Purchase* (1941), *STAR SPANGLED RHYTHM* (1942), and *Follow the Boys* (1944). Zorina, who later became an opera manager, was married to choreographer George Balanchine and then record producer Goddard Lieberson.

ZUCCO, GEORGE (1886–1960), a British-born performer in American vaudeville and on Broadway, made many films in Hollywood in the 1930s and 1940s, usually playing villains, madmen, and eccentric scientists. Zucco also played heavies in such movie musicals as *THE FIREFLY* (1937), *ROSALIE* (1937), *New Moon* (1940), *THE PIRATE* (1948), and *THE BARKLEYS OF BROADWAY* (1949).

Chronological
List of Musicals

The following films have individual entries in the encyclopedia.

1927	*The Jazz Singer*
1928	*My Man*
	The Singing Fool
1929	*The Broadway Melody*
	Syncopation
	The Desert Song
	Innocents of Paris
	The Cocoanuts
	Show Boat
	Hollywood Revue of 1929
	Gold Diggers of Broadway
	Hallelujah
	Sunny Side Up
	The Love Parade
	Applause
	Rio Rita
	On With the Show
	The Show of Shows
1930	*Puttin' on the Ritz*
	Paramount on Parade
	King of Jazz

Monte Carlo

Animal Crackers

Hit the Deck

Good News

Whoopee

1931   *The Smiling Lieutenant*

Delicious

1932   *The Phantom President*

One Hour With You

The Big Broadcast

Love Me Tonight

1933   *She Done Him Wrong*

Hallelujah, I'm a Bum

International House

42nd Street

Footlight Parade

Gold Diggers of 1933

Flying Down to Rio

Going Hollywood

Duck Soup

Dancing Lady

Roman Scandals

1934   *The Cat and the Fiddle*

Wonder Bar

We're Not Dressing

Murder at the Vanities

Dames

The Merry Widow

One Night of Love

The Gay Divorcee

Music in the Air

Kid Millions

Babes in Toyland

College Rhythm

Evergreen

1935   *Sweet Adeline*

Roberta

Folies Bergère de Paris

Mississippi

Gold Diggers of 1935

Naughty Marietta

Go Into Your Dance

Every Night at Eight

Top Hat

Big Broadcast of 1936

Broadway Melody of 1936

Thanks a Million

I Dream Too Much

Curly Top

A Night at the Opera

1936   *King of Burlesque*

Anything Goes

Rose Marie

Follow the Fleet

Captain January

Poor Little Rich Girl

Let's Sing Again

The Great Ziegfeld

Show Boat

San Francisco

Swing Time

The Big Broadcast of 1937

Born to Dance

Pennies From Heaven

1937   *On the Avenue*

One in a Million

Maytime

Wake Up and Live

High, Wide and Handsome

A Day at the Races

Shall We Dance

Artists and Models

Double or Nothing

Broadway Melody of 1938

The Firefly

One Hundred Men and a Girl

Varsity Show

A Damsel in Distress

Rosalie

Gold Diggers of 1937

1938   *In Old Chicago*

The Goldwyn Follies

Snow White and the Seven Dwarfs

The Big Broadcast of 1938

Hollywood Hotel

Rebecca of Sunnybrook Farm

Joy of Living

Sing You Sinners

Alexander's Ragtime Band

Carefree

Artists and Models Abroad

Sweethearts

1939   *Second Fiddle*

The Story of Vernon and Irene Castle

Rose of Washington Square

The Wizard of Oz

Gulliver's Travels

Balalaika

At the Circus

Babes in Arms

1940   *Pinocchio*

Road to Singapore

Two Girls on Broadway

Broadway Melody of 1940

Lillian Russell

Rhythm on the River

Strike Up the Band

Down Argentine Way

Tin Pan Alley

Fantasia

Too Many Girls

One Night in the Tropics

Love Thy Neighbor

1941 *Buck Privates*

That Night in Rio

Road to Zanzibar

Ziegfeld Girl

Moon Over Miami

Dumbo

Sun Valley Serenade

You'll Never Get Rich

Birth of the Blues

Week-End in Havana

1942 *Babes on Broadway*

Springtime in the Rockies

The Fleet's In

Yankee Doodle Dandy

My Gal Sal

Rio Rita

Holiday Inn

Orchestra Wives

For Me and My Gal

Iceland

Road to Morocco

Star Spangled Rhythm

You Were Never Lovelier

1943 *Hello, Frisco, Hello*

Happy Go Lucky

Cabin in the Sky

Stage Door Canteen

Stormy Weather

Coney Island

Best Foot Forward

This Is the Army

Thank Your Lucky Stars

The Gang's All Here

The Desert Song

1944   *Cover Girl*

Two Girls and a Sailor

Going My Way

Up in Arms

Meet Me in St. Louis

Here Come the Waves

Hollywood Canteen

Can't Help Singing

1945   *The Three Caballeros*

Rhapsody in Blue

Anchors Aweigh

Bells of St. Mary's

State Fair

The Dolly Sisters

1946   *The Harvey Girls*

Road to Utopia

Ziegfeld Follies

Night and Day

Centennial Summer

The Jolson Story

Three Little Girls in Blue

Song of the South

Blue Skies

Till the Clouds Roll By

1947   *The Shocking Miss Pilgrim*

It Happened in Brooklyn

Mother Wore Tights

Good News

1948   *Road to Rio*

Casbah

The Pirate

Romance on the High Seas

Easter Parade

	The Paleface
	Summer Holiday
	Words and Music
1949	*Take Me Out to the Ball Game*
	A Connecticut Yankee in King Arthur's Court
	The Barkleys of Broadway
	Neptune's Daughter
	In the Good Old Summertime
	Jolson Sings Again
	On the Town
1950	*Cinderella*
	Annie Get Your Gun
	Three Little Words
	Young Man With a Horn
	Summer Stock
	Wabash Avenue
1951	*Royal Wedding*
	The Great Caruso
	Show Boat
	Here Comes the Groom
	Alice in Wonderland
	An American in Paris
1952	*The Belle of New York*
	Singin' in the Rain
	With a Song in My Heart
	The Merry Widow
	Lovely to Look At
	Son of Paleface
	Hans Christian Andersen
1953	*Road to Bali*
	The Jazz Singer
	Lili
	Call Me Madam
	The Desert Song
	The Farmer Takes a Wife
	The 5,000 Fingers of Dr. T

The Band Wagon
Gentlemen Prefer Blondes
Calamity Jane
Kiss Me, Kate
Give a Girl a Break
1954 *The Glenn Miller Story*
Seven Brides for Seven Brothers
Rose Marie
The Country Girl
Carmen Jones
A Star Is Born
Brigadoon
Deep in My Heart
The Student Prince
White Christmas
There's No Business Like Show Business
Hit the Deck
1955 *Lady and the Tramp*
Pete Kelly's Blues
Daddy Long Legs
It's Always Fair Weather
Artists and Models
Guys and Dolls
I'll Cry Tomorrow
Kismet
Love Me or Leave Me
Oklahoma!
1956 *Carousel*
The Court Jester
High Society
Invitation to the Dance
The King and I
Anything Goes
1957 *Funny Face*
Silk Stockings
Pal Joey

	The Joker Is Wild
	Les Girls
	The Pajama Game
	Jailhouse Rock
1958	*Gigi*
	King Creole
	South Pacific
	Damn Yankees
1959	*Porgy and Bess*
	The Five Pennies
1960	*Can-Can*
	Bells Are Ringing
1961	*West Side Story*
	Babes in Toyland
	Flower Drum Song
1962	*State Fair*
	Blue Hawaii
	The Road to Hong Kong
	The Music Man
	Gypsy
	Jumbo
1963	*Bye Bye Birdie*
1964	*Mary Poppins*
	Viva Las Vegas
	My Fair Lady
	The Unsinkable Molly Brown
	Robin and the Seven Hoods
	A Hard Day's Night
1965	*The Sound of Music*
	Help!
1967	*Thoroughly Modern Millie*
	How to Succeed in Business Without Really Trying
	Camelot
	The Jungle Book
	Doctor Dolittle
1968	*Funny Girl*

Star!

Finian's Rainbow

Chitty Chitty Bang Bang

Oliver!

Yellow Submarine

1969   *Goodbye, Mr. Chips*

Sweet Charity

Paint Your Wagon

Hello, Dolly!

1970   *The Aristocats*

Darling Lili

Scrooge

Woodstock

On a Clear Day You Can See Forever

1971   *Willy Wonka and the Chocolate Factory*

Fiddler on the Roof

Bedknobs and Broomsticks

The Boy Friend

1972   *1776*

Lady Sings the Blues

Cabaret

1973   *Charlotte's Web*

Jesus Christ Superstar

Godspell

1974   *That's Entertainment*

Phantom of the Paradise

1975   *Funny Lady*

Nashville

Tommy

The Rocky Horror Picture Show

A Chorus Line

1976   *A Star Is Born*

That's Entertainment, Part Two

Bugsy Malone

1977   *New York, New York*

Saturday Night Fever

1978	*Grease*
	The Buddy Holly Story
	Movie Movie
1979	*Hair*
	The Muppet Movie
	The Rose
	All That Jazz
1980	*Fame*
	Coal Miner's Daughter
	The Jazz Singer
1981	*The Great Muppet Caper*
	Pennies From Heaven
1982	*Victor/Victoria*
	Annie
	Grease 2
1983	*Flashdance*
	Yentl
	Footloose
1984	*The Cotton Club*
	This Is Spinal Tap
1985	*Follow That Bird*
1986	*Little Shop of Horrors*
1987	*Dirty Dancing*
	La Bamba
1988	*Bird*
	Oliver and Company
1989	*The Little Mermaid*
1991	*Beauty and the Beast*
1992	*Aladdin*
1994	*The Lion King*
1995	*Pocahontas*
1996	*The Hunchback of Notre Dame*
1997	*Anastasia*
	Everyone Says I Love You
	Evita
	Hercules

Academy Award–Winning Musicals

BEST PICTURE

Only nine movie musicals have won the Best Picture Oscar, a small number when one considers the hundreds of entries over the decades. Below are the forty-five film musicals that were nominated, with the nine winners in bold.

1929 **The Broadway Melody**

       Hollywood Revue of 1929

1930 *The Love Parade*

1931 *One Hour With You*

       The Smiling Lieutenant

1933 *42nd Street*

       She Done Him Wrong

1934 *Flirtation Walk*

       The Gay Divorcee

       One Night of Love

1935 *Broadway Melody of 1936*

       Naughty Marietta

       Top Hat

1936 **The Great Ziegfeld**

       San Francisco

       Three Smart Girls

1937 *In Old Chicago*

       One Hundred Men and a Girl

1938	*Alexander's Ragtime Band*
1939	*The Wizard of Oz*
1942	*Yankee Doodle Dandy*
1944	***Going My Way***
1945	*Anchors Aweigh*
1948	*The Red Shoes*
1951	***An American in Paris***
1954	*Seven Brides for Seven Brothers*
	The Country Girl
1956	*The King and I*
1958	***Gigi***
1961	***West Side Story***
1962	*The Music Man*
1964	***My Fair Lady***
	Mary Poppins
1965	***The Sound of Music***
1967	*Doctor Dolittle*
1968	***Oliver!***
	Funny Girl
1969	*Hello, Dolly!*
1971	*Fiddler on the Roof*
1972	*Cabaret*
1975	*Nashville*
1976	*Bound for Glory*
1979	*All That Jazz*
1980	*Coal Miner's Daughter*
1991	*Beauty and the Beast*
1997	*Evita*

BEST SONG

The Academy has given an award for Best Song since 1934, though several winners over the years came from non-musicals. The award is given to a song written specifically for the screen, though in 1941 "The Last Time I Saw Paris" won even though the number had been interpolated into *Lady Be Good* after it had become popular as a Tin Pan Alley hit.

1934   "The Continental" from *The Gay Divorcee*

1935	"Lullaby of Broadway" from *Gold Diggers of 1935*
1936	"The Way You Look Tonight" from *Swing Time*
1937	"Sweet Leilani" from *Waikiki Wedding*
1938	"Thanks for the Memory" from *The Big Broadcast of 1938*
1939	"Over the Rainbow" from *The Wizard of Oz*
1940	"When You Wish Upon a Star" from *Pinocchio*
1941	"The Last Time I Saw Paris" from *Lady, Be Good*
1942	"White Christmas" from *Holiday Inn*
1943	"You'll Never Know" from *Hello, Frisco, Hello*
1944	"Swinging on a Star" from *Going My Way*
1945	"It Might as Well Be Spring" from *State Fair*
1946	"On the Atchison, Topeka and the Santa Fe" from *The Harvey Girls*
1947	"Zip-a-Dee-Doo-Dah" from *Song of the South*
1948	"Buttons and Bows" from *The Paleface*
1949	"Baby, It's Cold Outside" from *Neptune's Daughter*
1950	"Mona Lisa" from *Captain Carey, USA*
1951	"In the Cool, Cool, Cool of the Evening" from *Here Comes the Groom*
1952	"High Noon" from *High Noon*
1953	"Secret Love" from *Calamity Jane*
1954	"Three Coins in the Fountain" from *Three Coins in the Fountain*
1955	"Love Is a Many-Splendored Thing" from *Love Is a Many-Splendored Thing*
1956	"Whatever Will Be, Will Be" from *The Man Who Knew Too Much*
1957	"All the Way" from *The Joker Is Wild*
1958	"Gigi" from *Gigi*
1959	"High Hopes" from *A Hole in the Head*
1960	"Never on Sunday" from *Never on Sunday*
1961	"Moon River" from *Breakfast at Tiffany's*
1962	"Days of Wine and Roses" from *Days of Wine and Roses*
1963	"Call Me Irresponsible" from *Papa's Delicate Condition*
1964	"Chim-Chim-Cheree" from *Mary Poppins*
1965	"The Shadow of Your Smile" from *The Sandpiper*
1966	"Born Free" from *Born Free*
1967	"Talk to the Animals" from *Doctor Dolittle*
1968	"The Windmills of Your Mind" from *The Thomas Crown Affair*
1969	"Raindrops Keep Fallin' on My Head" from *Butch Cassidy and the Sundance Kid*

1970   "For All We Know" from *Lovers and Other Strangers*

1971   "Theme from *Shaft*" from *Shaft*

1972   "The Morning After" from *The Poseidon Adventure*

1973   "The Way We Were" from *The Way We Were*

1974   "We May Never Love Like This Again" from *The Towering Inferno*

1975   "I'm Easy" from *Nashville*

1976   "Evergreen" from *A Star Is Born*

1977   "You Light Up My Life" from *You Light Up My Life*

1978   "Last Dance" from *Thank God It's Friday*

1979   "It Goes Like It Goes" from *Norma Rae*

1980   "Fame" from *Fame*

1981   "Arthur's Theme" from *Arthur*

1982   "Up Where We Belong" from *An Officer and a Gentleman*

1983   "Flashdance . . . What a Feeling" from *Flashdance*

1984   "I Just Called to Say I Love You" from *The Woman in Red*

1985   "Say You, Say Me" from *White Nights*

1986   "Take My Breath Away" from *Top Gun*

1987   "(I've Had) The Time of My Life" from *Dirty Dancing*

1988   "Let the River Run" from *Working Girl*

1989   "Under the Sea" from *The Little Mermaid*

1990   "Sooner or Later" from *Dick Tracy*

1991   "Beauty and the Beast" from *Beauty and the Beast*

1992   "A Whole New World" from *Aladdin*

1993   "Streets of Philadelphia" from *Philadelphia*

1994   "Can You Feel the Love Tonight?" from *The Lion King*

1995   "Colors of the Wind" from *Pocahontas*

1996   "You Must Love Me" from *Evita*

1997   "My Heart Will Go On" from *Titanic*

1998   "When You Believe" from *Prince of Egypt*

1999   "You'll Be in My Heart" from *Tarzan*

BEST ACTRESS

Only six actresses have won Oscars for leading roles in a movie musical. Grace Kelly did not even sing in her award-winning performance. Both Julie Andrews and Barbra Streisand won for their screen debuts, and Rainer won for her first English-language film.

1936   Luise Rainer in *The Great Ziegfeld*

1954   Grace Kelly in *The Country Girl*

1964   Julie Andrews in *Mary Poppins*

1968   Barbra Streisand in *Funny Girl*

1972   Liza Minnelli in *Cabaret*

1980   Sissy Spacek in *Coal Miner's Daughter*

BEST ACTOR

Of the four actors to win for a leading role in a musical, Yul Brynner and Rex Harrison had also won Tony Awards for their stage portrayals of the same characters.

1942   James Cagney in *Yankee Doodle Dandy*

1944   Bing Crosby in *Going My Way*

1956   Yul Brynner in *The King and I*

1964   Rex Harrison in *My Fair Lady*

BEST SUPPORTING ACTRESS

Despite the dozens of memorable performances by actresses in supporting roles who stole movie musicals, only two have won Oscars.

1937   Alice Brady in *In Old Chicago*

1961   Rita Moreno in *West Side Story*

BEST SUPPORTING ACTOR

The winners in this category are deceptive. Barry Fitzgerald didn't sing a note in his film, George Chakiris's role was primarily a dancing one, and Joel Grey's was obviously a leading role in his musical.

1944   Barry Fitzgerald in *Going My Way*

1961   George Chakiris in *West Side Story*

1972   Joel Grey in *Cabaret*

BEST DIRECTOR

Ironically, of the winners for Best Director, only Vincente Minnelli, Jerome Robbins, and Bob Fosse had careers associated with musicals. The other directors were mostly known for helming dramatic projects.

1944   Leo McCarey for *Going My Way*

1958   Vincente Minnelli for *Gigi*

1961   Robert Wise, Jerome Robbins for *West Side Story*

1964   George Cukor for *My Fair Lady*

1965   Robert Wise for *The Sound of Music*

1968   Carol Reed for *Oliver!*

1972   Bob Fosse for *Cabaret*

BEST ORIGINAL SCORE

This is a tricky category and an award given to both musicals and non-musicals. It recognizes the background music in a film, not the songs, though sometimes the same composer did both.

1939   Herbert Stothart for *The Wizard of Oz*

1940   Leigh Harline, Paul J. Smith, Ned Washington for *Pinocchio*

1964   Richard M. and Robert B. Sherman for *Mary Poppins*

1967   Elmer Bernstein for *Thoroughly Modern Millie*

1980   Michael Gore for *Fame*

1982   Leslie Bricusse, Henry Mancini for *Victor/Victoria*

1983   Michel Legrand, Alan and Marilyn Bergman for *Yentl*

1984   Prince for *Purple Rain*

1988   Alan Menken for *The Little Mermaid*

1991   Alan Menken for *Beauty and the Beast*

1992   Alan Menken for *Aladdin*

1994   Hans Zimmer for *The Lion King*

BEST SCORE

This award acknowledged the musical arrangements and orchestrations of the songs and dances in a musical. It was discontinued in 1980.

1934   Louis Silvers, Victor Schertzinger, Gus Kahn for *One Night of Love*

1937   Charles Previn for *One Hundred Men and a Girl*

1938   Alfred Newman for *Alexander's Ragtime Band*

1940   Alfred Newman for *Tin Pan Alley*

1941   Frank Churchill, Oliver Wallace for *Dumbo*

1942   Ray Heindorf, Heinz Roemheld for *Yankee Doodle Dandy*

1943   Ray Heindorf for *This Is the Army*

1944   Carmen Dragon, Morris Stoloff for *Cover Girl*

1945   George Stoll for *Anchors Aweigh*

1946   Morris Stoloff for *The Jolson Story*

1947   Alfred Newman for *Mother Wore Tights*

1948   Johnny Green, Roger Edens for *Easter Parade*

1949   Roger Edens, Lennie Hayton for *On the Town*

1950	Adolph Deutsch, Roger Edens for *Annie Get Your Gun*
1951	Johnny Green, Saul Chaplin for *An American in Paris*
1952	Alfred Newman for *With a Song in My Heart*
1953	Bronislau Kaper for *Lili*
1953	Alfred Newman for *Call Me Madam*
1954	Adolph Deutsch, Saul Chaplin for *Seven Brides for Seven Brothers*
1955	Robert Russell Bennett, Jay Blackton, Adolph Deutsch for *Oklahoma!*
1956	George Stoll, Johnny Green for *The King and I*
1958	André Previn for *Gigi*
1959	André Previn, Ken Darby for *Porgy and Bess*
1960	Morris Stoloff, Harry Sukman for *Song Without End*
1961	Saul Chaplin, Johnny Green, Sid Ramin, Irwin Kostal for *West Side Story*
1962	Ray Heindorf for *The Music Man*
1964	André Previn for *My Fair Lady*
1965	Irwin Kostal for *The Sound of Music*
1966	Ken Thorne for *A Funny Thing Happened on the Way to the Forum*
1967	Alfred Newman, Ken Darby for *Camelot*
1968	John Green for *Oliver!*
1969	Lennie Hayton, Lionel Newman for *Hello, Dolly!*
1970	The Beatles for *Let It Be*
1971	John Williams for *Fiddler on the Roof*
1972	Ralph Burns for *Cabaret*
1976	Leonard Rosenman for *Bound for Glory*
1977	Jonathan Tunick for *A Little Night Music*
1978	Joe Renzetti for *The Buddy Holly Story*
1979	Ralph Burns for *All That Jazz*

BEST ORIGINAL STORY

No longer given today, this award was for the basic story rather than the actual screenplay of the movie.

1944	Leo McCarey for *Going My Way*
1955	Daniel Fuchs for *Love Me or Leave Me*

BEST ORIGINAL SCREENPLAY

Given for an original script (as opposed to an adaptation of a play or book), this award was rarely given to musicals. Curiously, *The Country Girl* closely followed the non-musical play it was based on yet won for original screenplay anyway.

1944	Frank Butler, Frank Cavett for *Going My Way*

1951   Alan Jay Lerner for *An American in Paris*

1954   George Seaton for *The Country Girl*

1955   William Ludwig, Sonya Levien for *Interrupted Melody*

BEST DANCE DIRECTION

Discontinued long before the decline of the movie musical, this award was given too few times to even begin to acknowledge the dozens of superb choreographers in Hollywood.

1935   David Gould for *Broadway Melody of 1936, Folies Bergère de Paris*

1936   Seymour Felix for *The Great Ziegfeld*

1937   Hermes Pan for *Damsel in Distress*

BEST INTERIOR DECORATION/ART DIRECTION

Movie musicals would seem to be likely candidates for scenic design, yet the award was more often given to non-musicals.

1930   Herman Rosse for *King of Jazz*

1934   Cedric Gibbons, Frederic Hope for *The Merry Widow*

1942   Richard Day, Joseph Wright, Thomas Little for *My Gal Sal*

1948   Hein Heckroth, Arthur Lawson for *The Red Shoes*

1951   Cedric Gibbons, Preston Ames, Edwin B. Willis, Keogh Gleason for *An American in Paris*

1956   Lyle R. Wheeler, John DeCuir, Walter M. Scott, Paul S. Fox for *The King and I*

1958   William A. Horning, Preston Ames, Henry Grace, Keogh Gleason for *Gigi*

1961   Boris Leven, Victor A. Gangelin for *West Side Story*

1964   Gene Allen, Cecil Beaton, George James Hopkins for *My Fair Lady*

1967   John Truscott, Edward Carrere, John W. Brown for *Camelot*

1968   John Box, Terence Marsh, Vernon Dixon, Ken Muggleston for *Oliver!*

1969   John DeCuir, Jack Martin Smith, Herman Blumenthal, Walter M. Scott, George Hopkins, Raphael Bretton for *Hello, Dolly!*

1972   Rolf Zehetbauer, Jurgen Kiebach, Herbert Strabel for *Cabaret*

1979   Philip Rosenberg, Tony Walton, Edward Stewart, Gary Brink for *All That Jazz*

1990   Richard Sylbert, Rick Simpson for *Dick Tracy*

BEST COSTUME DESIGN

Another seemingly obvious category for musicals, this award has only been given to nine musicals and six different designers.

1951   Orry-Kelly, Walter Plunkett, Irene Sharaff for *An American in Paris*

1956   Irene Sharaff for *The King and I*

1957   Orry-Kelly for *Les Girls*

1958   Cecil Beaton for *Gigi*

1961   Irene Sharaff for *West Side Story*

1962   Mary Willis for *The Wonderful World of the Brothers Grimm*

1964   Cecil Beaton for *My Fair Lady*

1967   John Truscott for *Camelot*

1979   Albert Wolsky for *All That Jazz*

BEST CINEMATOGRAPHY

This category was once divided into two awards: one for black and white and another for color cinematography. With the decline of black and white films, it was combined into one.

1938   Joseph Ruttenberg for *The Great Waltz*

1951   Alfred Gilks, John Alton for *An American in Paris*

1958   Joseph Ruttenberg for *Gigi*

1961   Daniel L. Fapp for *West Side Story*

1964   Harry Stradling for *My Fair Lady*

1971   Oswald Morris for *Fiddler on the Roof*

1972   Geoffrey Unsworth for *Cabaret*

1976   Haskell Wexler for *Bound for Glory*

BEST FILM EDITING

An award rarely understood by the general public, it has only been given to musicals for big-budget Hollywood projects.

1961   Thomas Stanford for *West Side Story*

1964   Cotton Warburton for *Mary Poppins*

1965   William Reynolds for *The Sound of Music*

1972   David Bretherton for *Cabaret*

1979   Alan Heim for *All That Jazz*

BEST SPECIAL VISUAL EFFECTS

Science fiction and disaster movies usually win in this category, but there have been three musicals whose movie magic was acknowledged.

1964   Peter Ellenshaw, Hamilton Luske, Eustace Lycett for *Mary Poppins*

1967   L.B. Abbott for *Doctor Dolittle*

1971   Alan Maley, Eustace Lycett, Danny Lee for *Bedknobs and Broomsticks*

SPECIAL AWARDS

Special awards have been given to creative artists, inventors and technicians, and organizations. Below are some given for achievements in a specific movie musical.

1928   Warner Brothers for pioneering the use of sound in *The Jazz Singer*

1938   Walt Disney for innovations in *Snow White and the Seven Dwarfs*

1938   Oliver Marsh and Allen Davey for color cinematography in *Sweethearts*

1941   Walt Disney, William Garity, John N.A. Hawkins for use of sound in *Fantasia*

1968   Onna White for her choreography for *Oliver!*

Selected Bibliography

Altman, Rick. *The American Film Musical.* Bloomington: Indiana University Press, 1987.

————. (ed.). *Genre: The Musical.* London: Routledge and Kegan Paul, 1981.

Aylesworth, Thomas G. *Broadway to Hollywood.* New York: Gallery Books, W.H. Smith Publishers, 1985.

Barrios, Richard. *A Song in the Dark: The Birth of the Musical Film.* New York: Oxford University Press, 1995.

Benjamin, Ruth, and Arthur Roseblatt. *Movie Song Catalog.* Jefferson, NC: McFarland, 1993.

Bergman, Andrew. *We're in the Money: Depression America and Its Films.* New York: Harper & Row, 1971.

Bradley, Edwin M. *The First Hollywood Musicals.* Jefferson, NC: McFarland, 1996.

Burton, Jack. *The Blue Book of Hollywood Musicals.* Watkins Glen, NY: Century House, 1975.

Craig, Warren. *Great Songwriters of Hollywood.* New York: A.S. Barnes, 1980.

————. *Sweet and Low Down: America's Popular Song Writers.* Metuchen, NJ: Scarecrow Press, 1978.

Croce, Arlene. *The Fred Astaire and Ginger Rogers Book.* New York: Dutton, 1987.

Crowther, Bosley. *The Lion's Share: The Story of an Entertainment Empire.* New York, E.P. Dutton & Co., 1957.

Deutsch, Didier C. *VideoHound's Soundtracks: Music from the Movies, Broadway and Television.* Detroit: Visible Ink Press, 1998.

Druxman, Michael B. *The Musical from Broadway to Hollywood.* New York: Barnes, 1980.

Eames, John Douglas. *The MGM Story.* New York: Crown Publishers, 1975.

————. *The Paramount Story.* New York: Crown Publishers, 1985.

Ewen, David. *American Songwriters.* New York: H.W. Wilson Co., 1987.

————. *Great Men of American Popular Song.* Englewood Cliffs, NJ: Prentice-Hall, 1972.

Fehr, Richard, and Frederick G. Vogel. *Lullabies of Hollywood: Movie Music and the Movie Musical, 1915–1992*. Jefferson, NC: McFarland, 1993.

Feuer, Jane. *The Hollywood Musical*. Bloomington: Indiana University Press, 1982.

Fitzgerald, Michael G. *Universal Pictures: A Panoramic History*. Westport, CT: Arlington House, 1977.

Fordin, Hugh. *The World of Entertainment: Hollywood's Greatest Musicals*. New York: Avon Books, 1975.

Furia, Philip. *The Poets of Tin Pan Alley: A History of America's Great Lyricists*. New York: Oxford University Press, 1990.

Geduld, Harry M. *The Birth of the Talkies*. Bloomington: Indiana University Press, 1975

Grattan, Virginia L. *American Women Songwriters: A Biographical Dictionary*. Westport, CT: Greenwood Press, 1993.

Green, Stanley. *Encyclopedia of Musical Film*. New York: Oxford University Press, 1981.

———. *Hollywood Musicals, Year by Year*. Milwaukee, WI: Hal Leonard Publishing Corp., 1990.

Halliwell, Leslie. *Halliwell's Film Guide*. New York: Harper & Row, 1989.

———. *Halliwell's Who's Who in the Movies*. 3rd ed. New York: HarperCollins, Publishers, 1999.

Hemming, Roy. *The Melody Lingers On: The Great Songwriters and Their Movie Musicals*. New York: Newmarket Press, 1986.

Hirschhorn, Clive. *The Hollywood Musical*. New York: Crown Publishers, 1981.

———. *The Universal Story*. New York: Crown Publishers, 1983.

———. *The Warner Bros. Story*. New York: Crown Publishers, 1979.

Hischak, Thomas S. *The American Musical Film Song Encyclopedia*. Westport, CT: Greenwood Press, 1999.

Hyland, William G. *The Song Is Ended: Songwriters and American Music, 1900–1950*. New York: Oxford University Press, 1995.

Jacobs, Dick, and Harriet Jacobs. *Who Wrote That Song?* Cincinnati: Writer's Digest Books, 1994.

Jewell, Richard B., and Vernon Harbin. *The RKO Story*. New York: Arlington House, 1982.

Kaplan, Phillip J. (ed.). *The Best, Worst & Most Unusual Hollywood Musicals*. New York: Beekman House, 1983.

Katz, Ephraim. *The Film Encyclopedia*. 3rd Ed. New York: HarperCollins Publishers, 1998.

Kobal, John. *Gotta Sing, Gotta Dance: A Pictorial History of Film Musicals*. London/New York: Hamlyn, 1971.

Kreuger, Miles (ed.). *The Movie Musical: From Vitaphone to 42nd Street*. New York: Dover, 1975.

Lasky, Betty. *RKO: The Biggest Little Major of Them All*. Englewood Cliffs, NJ: Prentice-Hall, 1984.

Lynch, Richard Chigley. *Movie Musicals on Record*. Westport, CT: Greenwood Press, 1989.

Maltin, Leonard. *The Disney Films*. New York: Hyperion, 1995.

Mast, Gerald. *Can't Help Singin': The American Musical on Stage and Screen*. Woodstock, NY: Overlook Press, 1987.

McVay, Douglas. *The Musical Film*. London: A. Zwemmer/New York: A.S. Barnes, 1967.

Mielke, Randall G. *The Road to Box Office: The Seven Comedies of Bing Crosby, Bob Hope and Dorothy Lamour, 1940—1962*. Jefferson, NC: McFarland, 1996.

Mordden, Ethan. *The Hollywood Musical*. New York: St. Martin's Press, 1981.

Parish, J.R., and Ronald L. Bowers. *The MGM Stock Company: The Golden Era*. New York: Bonanza Books, 1972.

Parish, J.R., and Michael R. Pitts. *The Great Hollywood Musicals*. Metuchen, NJ: Scarecrow Press, 1992.

———. *Hollywood Songsters: A Biographical Dictionary*. New York: Garland, 1991.

Reed, William. *Rock on Film*. New York: Delilah/Putnam, 1982.

Rubin, Martin. *Showstoppers: Busby Berkeley and the Tradition of Spectacle*. New York: Columbia University Press, 1993.

Sennett, Ted. *Hollywood Musicals*. New York: Harry Abrams, 1982.

———. *Warner Brothers Presents*. Secaucus, NJ: Castle Books, 1971.

Springer, John. *All Talking! All Singing! All Dancing!* New York: Citadel Press, 1966. Reissued as *They Sang, They Danced, They Romanced*, 1991.

Stern, Lee Edward. *The Movie Musical*. New York: Pyramid Books, 1974.

Taylor, John Russell, and Arthur Jackson. *The Hollywood Musical*. New York: McGraw-Hill, 1971.

Thomas, Lawrence B. *The MGM Years*. New York: Columbia House/Arlington House, 1971.

Thomas, Tony. *Music for the Movies*. New York: A.S. Barnes and Co., 1973.

Thomas, Tony, and Aubrey Solomon. *The Films of 20th Century Fox*. Secaucus, NJ: Citadel Press, 1979.

Vallance, Thomas. *The American Musical*. New York: A.S. Barnes & Co., 1970.

White, Mark. *"You Must Remember This . . .": Popular Songwriters, 1900–1980*. New York: Charles Scribner's Sons, 1985.

Wilder, Alec. *American Popular Song: The Great Innovators, 1900–1950*. New York: Oxford University Press, 1972.

Wiley, Mason, and Damien Bona. *Inside Oscar: The Unofficial History of the Academy Awards*. New York: Ballantine Books, 1996.

Wilk, Max. *They're Playing Our Song*. New York: Athenaeum, 1973.

Wlaschin, Ken. *Opera on Screen*. Los Angeles: Beachwood Press, 1997.

Woll, Allen L. *The Hollywood Musical Goes to War*. Chicago: Nelson-Hall, 1983.

———. *Songs from Hollywood Musical Comedies, 1927 to the Present: A Dictionary*. New York: Garland Press, 1976.

Index

Note: page numbers in **bold** refer to individual entries.

About the Author

THOMAS HISCHAK is a Professor of Theatre at the State University of New York College at Cortland and a playwright who is a member of the Dramatists Guild, Inc. His recent books include *American Theatre: A Chronicle of Comedy and Drama, 1969–2000, The American Musical Film Song Encyclopedia* (Greenwood, 1999), *The Theatregoer's Almanac* (Greenwood, 1997), and *The American Musical Theatre Song Encyclopedia* (Greenwood, 1995) which received the 1995 *Choice* Outstanding Academic Book award. He is also the author of twenty-three published plays.